THE
SOUTH

THE SOUTH

A COLLECTION FROM

HARPER'S MAGAZINE

GALLERY BOOKS

an imprint of W.H. Smith Publishers, Inc.
112 Madison Avenue
New York, New York 10016

This volume first published in 1990 by

The Octopus Group Limited
Michelin House, 81 Fulham Road, London SW3 6RB

This edition published in 1990 by Gallery Books
an imprint of W.H. Smith Publishers Inc.
112 Madison Avenue, New York 10016

ISBN 0 8317 4253 4

Printed in Great Britain by The Bath Press, Avon

CONTENTS

IMPRESSIONS OF THE SOUTHERN STATES.............1

COTTON AND ITS KINGDOM......................... 7

NEW ORLEANS.................................... 23

GEORGE WASHINGTON..............................45

THE INDUSTRIAL SOUTH...........................68

AMONG THE BLUE-GRASS TROTTERS..................87

MY LIFE AS A SLAVE............................ 104

MISSISSIPPI RIVER PROBLEM.....................113

CRACKER COWBOYS OF FLORIDA................... 120

THE ARCADIAN LAND............................ 126

SOME RICHMOND PORTRAITS...................... 143

KENTUCKY FARMS...............................155

SOUTHERN LITERATURE.......................... 160

PLANTATION LIFE.............................. 179

THE SOUTH REVISITED.......................... 195

SAVANNAH..................................... 202

CRUISING ON THE GULF COAST OF FLORIDA........ 216

THE SALZBURGER EXILES, IN GEORGIA............ 225

THE NEW ORLEANS BENCH AND BAR................ 233

A LUMP OF SUGAR. 245

MEMPHIS AND LITTLE ROCK. 268

THE SOUTH AND THE SCHOOL PROBLEM 278

ALONG THE BAYOU TECHE. 285

COUNTY COURT DAY IN KENTUCKY. 299

THE OLD WAY TO DIXIE 311

COLONIAL VIRGINIA. 331

THE SOUTHERN GATEWAY OF THE ALLEGHANIES 344

THE BLUE-GRASS REGION OF KENTUCKY 361

CHARLESTON, SOUTH CAROLINA. 377

DRAINAGE OF THE EVERGLADES 387

IN SUNNY MISSISSIPPI 395

A VISIT TO A COLONIAL ESTATE 412

AT HOME IN VIRGINIA 420

CHARLESTON AND THE CAROLINAS 443

INDUSTRIAL EDUCATION IN THE SOUTH. 466

GENERAL LEE AS I KNEW HIM 475

HERE AND THERE IN THE SOUTH 485

IMPRESSIONS OF THE SOUTHERN STATES

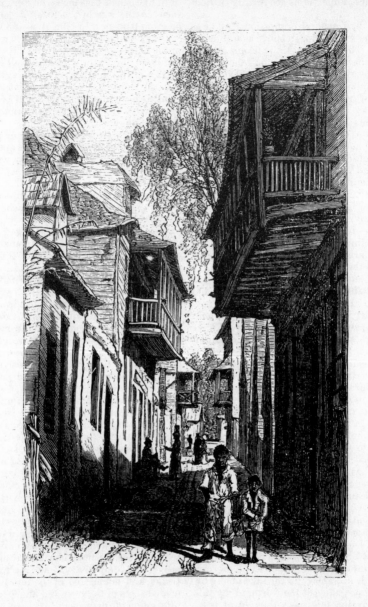

IT is borne in upon me, as the Friends would say, that I ought to bear my testimony of certain impressions made by a recent visit to the Gulf States. In doing this I am aware that I shall be under the suspicion of having received kindness and hospitality, and of forming opinions upon a brief sojourn. Both these facts must be confessed, and allowed their due weight in discrediting what I have to say. A month of my short visit was given to New Orleans in the spring, during the Exposition, and these impressions are mainly of Louisiana.

The first general impression made was that the war is over in spirit as well as in deed. The thoughts of the people are not upon the war, not much upon the past at all, except as their losses remind them of it, but upon the future, upon business, a revival of trade, upon education, and adjustment to the new state of things. The thoughts are not much upon politics either, or upon offices; certainly they are not turned more in this direction than the thoughts of people at the North are. When we read a dispatch which declares that there is immense dissatisfaction throughout Arkansas because offices are not dealt out more liberally to it, we may know that the case is exactly what it is in, say, Wisconsin—that a few political managers are grumbling, and that the great body of the people are indifferent, perhaps too indifferent, to the distribution of offices.

Undoubtedly immense satisfaction was felt at the election of Mr. Cleveland, and elation of triumph in the belief that now the party which had been largely a nonparticipant in Federal affairs would have a large share and weight in the administration. With this went, however, a new feeling of responsibility, of a stake in the country, that manifested itself at once in attachment to the Union as the common possession of all sections. I feel sure that Louisiana, for instance, was never in its whole history, from the day of the Jefferson purchase, so consciously loyal to the United States as it is to-day. I have believed that for the past ten years there has been growing in this country a stronger feeling of nationality—a distinct American historic consciousness—and nowhere else has it developed so rapidly of late as at the South. I am convinced that this is a genuine development of attachment to the Union and of pride in the nation, and not in any respect a political movement for unworthy purposes. I am sorry that it is necessary, for the sake of any lingering prejudice at the North, to say this. But it is time that sober, thoughtful, patriotic people at the North should quit representing the desire for office at the South as a desire to get into the government saddle and ride again with a "rebel" impulse. It would be, indeed, a discouraging fact if any considerable portion of the South held aloof in sullenness from Federal affairs. Nor is it any just cause either of reproach or of uneasiness that men who were prominent in the war of the rebellion should be prominent now in official positions, for with a few exceptions the worth and weight of the South went into the war. It would be idle to discuss the question whether the masses of the South were not dragooned into the war by the politicians; it is sufficient to recognize the fact that it became practically, by one means or another, a unanimous revolt.

One of the strongest impressions made upon a Northerner who visits the extreme South now, having been familiar with it only by report, is the extent to which it suffered in the war. Of course there was extravagance and there were impending bankruptcies before the war, debt, and methods of business inherently vicious, and no doubt the war is charged with many losses which would have come without it, just as in every crisis half the failures wrongfully accuse the crisis. Yet, with all allowance for these things, the fact remains that the war practically wiped out personal property and the means of livelihood. The completeness of this loss and disaster never came home to me before. In some cases the picture of the *ante bellum* civilization is more roseate in the minds of those who lost everything than cool observation of it would justify. But conceding this, the actual disaster needs no embellishment of the imagination. It seems to me, in the reverse, that the Southern people do not appreciate the sacrifices the North made for the Union. They do not, I think, realize the fact that the North put into the war its best blood, that every battle brought mourning into our households, and filled our churches day by day and year by year with the black garments of bereavement; nor did they ever understand the tearful enthusiasm for the Union and the flag, and the unselfish devotion that underlay all the self-sacrifice. Some time the Southern people will know that it was love for the Union, and not hatred of the South, that made heroes of the men and angels of renunciation of the women.

Yes, say our Southern friends, we can believe that you lost dear ones and were in mourning; but, after all, the North was prosperous; you grew rich; and when the war ended, life went on in the fullness of material prosperity. We lost not only our friends and relatives, fathers, sons, brothers, till there was scarcely a household that was not broken up, we lost not only the cause on which we had set our hearts, and for which we had suffered privation and hardship, were fugitives and wanderers, and endured the bitterness of defeat at the end, but our property was gone, we were stripped, with scarcely a home, and the whole of life had to be begun over again, under all the disadvantage of a sudden social revolution.

It is not necessary to dwell upon this or to heighten it, but it must be borne in mind when we observe the temper of the South, and especially when we are looking for remaining bitterness, and the wonder to me is that after so short a space of time there is remaining so little of resentment or of bitter feeling over loss and discomfiture. I believe there is not in history any parallel to it. Every American must take pride in the fact that Americans have so risen superior to circumstances, and come out of trials that thoroughly threshed and winnowed soul and body in a temper so gentle and a spirit so noble. It is good stuff that can endure a test of this kind.

A lady, whose family sustained all the losses that were possible in the war, said to me—and she said only what several others said in substance: "We are going to get more out of this war than you at the North, because we suffered more. We were drawn out of ourselves in sacrifices, and were drawn together in a tenderer feeling of humanity; I do believe we were chastened into a higher and purer spirit."

Let me not be misunderstood. The people who thus recognize the moral training of adversity and its effects upon character, and who are glad that slavery is gone, and believe that a new and better era for the South is at hand, would not for a moment put themselves in an attitude of apology for the part they took in the war, nor confess that they were wrong, nor join in any denunciation of the leaders they followed to their sorrow. They simply put the past behind them, so far as the conduct of the present life is concerned. They do not propose to stamp upon memories that are tender and sacred, and they cherish certain sentiments which are to them loyalty to their past and to the great passionate experiences of their lives. When a woman, who enlisted by the consent of Jeff Davis, whose name appeared for four years upon the rolls, and who endured all the perils and hardships of

the conflict as a field nurse, speaks of "President" Davis, what does it mean? It is only a sentiment. This heroine of the war on the wrong side had in the Exposition a tent, where the veterans of the Confederacy recorded their names. On one side, at the back of the tent, was a table piled with touching relics of the war, and above it a portrait of Robert E. Lee, wreathed in immortelles. It was surely a harmless shrine. On the other side was also a table, piled with fruit and cereals—not relics, but signs of prosperity and peace—and above it a portrait of Ulysses S. Grant. Here was the sentiment, cherished with an aching heart maybe, and here was the fact of the Union and the future.

Another strong impression made upon the visitor is, as I said, that the South has entirely put the past behind it, and is devoting itself to the work of rebuilding on new foundations. There is no reluctance to talk about the war, or to discuss its conduct and what might have been. But all this is historic. It engenders no heat. The mind of the South to-day is on the development of its resources, upon the rehabilitation of its affairs. I think it is rather more concerned about national prosperity than it is about the great problem of the negro—but I will refer to this further on. There goes with this interest in material development the same interest in the general prosperity of the country that exists at the North—the anxiety that the country should prosper, acquit itself well, and stand well with the other nations. There is, of course, a sectional feeling—as to tariff, as to internal improvements—but I do not think the Southern States are any more anxious to get things for themselves out of the Federal government than the Northern States are. That the most extreme of Southern politicians have any sinister purpose (any more than any of the Northern "rings" on either side have) in wanting to "rule" the country, is, in my humble opinion, only a chimera evoked to make political capital.

Illustrations in point as to the absolute subsidence of hostile intention (this phrase I know will sound queer in the South), and the laying aside of bitterness for the past, are not necessary in the presence of a strong general impression, but they might be given in great number. I note one that was significant from its origin, re-

membering, what is well known, that women and clergymen are always the last to
experience subsidence of hostile feeling
after a civil war. On the Confederate
Decoration Day in New Orleans I was
standing near the Confederate monument
in one of the cemeteries when the veterans marched in to decorate it. First came
the veterans of the Army of Virginia, last
those of the Army of Tennessee, and between them the veterans of the Grand
Army of the Republic, Union soldiers now
living in Louisiana. I stood beside a lady
whose name, if I mentioned it, would be
recognized as representative of a family
which was as conspicuous, and did as
much and lost as much, as any other in
the war—a family that would be popular-
ly supposed to cherish unrelenting feelings. As the veterans, some of them on
crutches, many of them with empty sleeves,
grouped themselves about the monument,
we remarked upon the sight as a touching
one, and I said, "I see you have no address on Decoration Day; at the North we
still keep up the custom." "No," she replied; "we have given it up. So many
imprudent things were said that we
thought best to discontinue the address."
And then, after a pause, she added,
thoughtfully, "Each side did the best it
could; it is all over and done with, and
let's have an end of it." In the mouth of
the lady who uttered it, the remark was
very significant, but it expresses, I am
firmly convinced, the feeling of the South.
Of course the South will build monuments to its heroes, and weep over their
graves, and live upon the memory of their
devotion and genius. In Heaven's name,
why shouldn't it? Is human nature itself
to be changed in twenty years?

A long chapter might be written upon
the dis-likeness of North and South, the
difference in education, in training, in
mental inheritances, the misapprehen-
sions, radical and very singular to us, of
the civilization of the North. We must
recognize certain historic facts, not only
the effect of the institution of slavery, but
other facts in Southern development.
Suppose we say that an unreasonable prejudice exists, or did exist, about the people of the North. That prejudice is a
historic fact, of which the statesman must
take account. It enters into the question
of the time needed to effect the revolution
now in progress. There are prejudices in
the North about the South as well. We

admit their existence. But what impress-
es me is the rapidity with which they are
disappearing in the South. Knowing
what human nature is, it seems incredible
that they could have subsided so rapidly.
Enough remain for national variety, and
enough will remain for purposes of social
badinage, but common interests in the
country and in making money are melting them away very fast. So far as loyalty to the government is concerned, I am
not authorized to say that it is as deeply
rooted in the South as in the North, but
it is expressed as vividly, and felt with
a good deal of fresh enthusiasm. The
"American" sentiment, pride in this as
the most glorious of all lands, is genuine,
and amounts to enthusiasm with many
who would in an argument glory in their
rebellion. "We had more loyalty to our
States than you had," said one lady, "and
we have transferred it to the whole country."

But the negro? Granting that the
South is loyal enough, wishes never another rebellion, and is satisfied to be rid of
slavery, do not the people intend to keep the
negroes practically a servile class, slaves
in all but the name, and to defeat by chicanery or by force the legitimate results
of the war and of enfranchisement? This
is a very large question, and can not be
discussed in my limits. If I were to say
what my impression is, it would be about
this: the South is quite as much perplexed by the negro problem as the North is,
and is very much disposed to await devel-
opments, and to let time solve it. One
thing, however, must be admitted in all
this discussion. The Southerners will
not permit such Legislatures as those
assembled once in Louisiana and South
Carolina to rule them again. "Will you
disfranchise the blacks by management or
by force?" "Well, what would you do
in Ohio or in Connecticut? Would you
be ruled by a lot of ignorant field hands
allied with a gang of plunderers?"

In looking at this question from a
Northern point of view we have to keep
in mind two things: first, the Federal government imposed colored suffrage without
any educational qualification—a hazardous experiment; in the second place, it has
handed over the control of the colored people in each State to the State, under the
Constitution, as completely in Louisiana
as in New York. The responsibility is on
Louisiana. The North can not relieve her

of it, and it can not interfere, except by ways provided in the Constitution. In the South, where fear of a legislative domination has gone, the feeling between the two races is that of amity and mutual help. This is, I think, especially true in Louisiana. The Southerners never have forgotten the loyalty of the slaves during the war, the security with which the white families dwelt in the midst of a black population while all the white men were absent in the field; they often refer to this. It touches with tenderness the new relation of the races. I think there is generally in the South a feeling of good-will toward the negroes, a desire that they should develop into true manhood and womanhood. Undeniably there is indifference and neglect and some remaining suspicion about the schools that Northern charity has organized for the negroes. As to this neglect of the negro, two things are to be said: the whole subject of education (as we have understood it in the North) is comparatively new in the South; and the necessity of earning a living since the war has distracted attention from it. But the general development of education is quite as advanced as could be expected. The thoughtful and the leaders of opinion are fully awake to the fact that the mass of the people must be educated, and that the only settlement of the negro problem is in the education of the negro, intellectually and morally. They go further than this. They say that for the South to hold its own—since the negro is there and will stay there, and is the majority of the laboring class—it is necessary that the great agricultural mass of unskilled labor should be transformed, to a great extent, into a class of skilled labor, skilled on the farm, in shops, in factories, and that the South must have a highly diversified industry. To this end they want industrial as well as ordinary schools for the colored people.

It is believed that, with this education and with diversified industry, the social question will settle itself, as it does the world over. Society can not be made or unmade by legislation. In New Orleans the street cars are free to all colors; at the Exposition white and colored people mingled freely, talking and looking at what was of common interest.

We who live in States where hotel-keepers exclude Hebrews can not say much about the exclusion of negroes from Southern hotels. There are prejudices remaining. There are cases of hardship on the railways, where for the same charge perfectly respectable and nearly white women are shut out of cars while there is no discrimination against dirty and disagreeable white people. In time all this will doubtless rest upon the basis it rests on at the North, and social life will take care of itself. It is my impression that the negroes are no more desirous to mingle socially with the whites than the whites are with the negroes. Among the negroes there are social grades as distinctly marked as in white society. What will be the final outcome of the juxtaposition nobody can tell; meantime it must be recorded that good-will exists between the races.

I had one day at the Exposition an interesting talk with the colored woman in charge of the Alabama section of the exhibit of the colored people. This exhibit, made by States, was suggested and promoted by Major Burke in order to show the whites what the colored people could do, and as a stimulus to the latter. There was not much time—only two or three months—in which to prepare the exhibit, and it was hardly a fair showing of the capacity of the colored people. The work was mainly women's work—embroidery, sewing, household stuffs, with a little of the handiwork of artisans, and an exhibit of the progress in education; but small as it was, it was wonderful as the result of only a few years of freedom. The Alabama exhibit was largely from Mobile, and was due to the energy, executive ability, and taste of the commissioner in charge. She was a quadroon, a widow, a woman of character and uncommon mental and moral quality. She talked exceedingly well, and with a practical good sense which would be notable in anybody. In the course of our conversation the whole social and political question was gone over. Herself a person of light color, and with a confirmed social prejudice against black people, she thoroughly identified herself with the colored race, and it was evident that her sympathies were with them. She confirmed what I had heard of the social grades among colored people, but her whole soul was in the elevation of her race as a race, inclining always to their side, but with no trace of hostility to the whites. Many of her best friends were whites, and perhaps the most valuable part of her education was acquired in families of social distinction. "I can illustrate," she said, "the state of feeling between the two races in Mobile by an incident last summer. There was an election coming off in the city government, and I knew that the reformers wanted and needed the colored vote. I went, therefore, to some of the chief men, who knew me and had confidence in me, for I had had business relations with many of them [she had kept a fashionable boarding-house], and told them that I wanted the Opera-house for the colored people to give an entertainment and exhibition in. The request was extraordinary. Nobody but white people had ever been admitted to the Opera-house. But, after some hesitation and consultation, the request was granted. We gave the exhibition, and the white people all attended. It was really a beautiful affair, lovely tableaux, with gorgeous dresses, recitations, etc., and everybody was astonished that the colored people had so much taste and talent, and had got on so far in education. They said they were delighted and surprised, and they liked it so well that they wanted the entertainment repeated—it was given for one of our charities—but I was too wise for that. I didn't want to run the chance of destroying the impression by repeating, and I said we would wait awhile, and then show them something better. Well, the election came off in August, and everything went all right, and now the colored people in Mobile can have anything they want. There is the best feeling between the races. I tell you we should get on beautifully if the politicians would let us alone. It is politics that has made all the trouble in Alabama and in Mobile." And I learned that in Mobile, as in many other places, the negroes were put in minor official positions, the duties of which they were capable of discharging, and had places in the police.

On "Louisiana Day" in the Exposition the colored citizens took their full share of the parade and the honors. Their societies marched with the others, and the races mingled on the grounds in unconscious equality of privileges. Speeches were made, glorifying the State and its history, by able speakers, the Governor among them, but it was the testimony of Democrats of undoubted Southern orthodoxy that the honors of the day were carried off by a colored clergyman, an educated man, who united eloquence with excellent good sense, and who spoke as a citizen of Louisiana, proud of his native State, dwelling with richness of allusion upon its history. It was a perfectly manly speech in the assertion of the rights and the position of his race, and it breathed throughout the same spirit of good-will and amity in a common hope of progress that characterized the talk of the colored woman commissioner of Mobile. It was warmly applauded, and accepted, so far as I heard, as a matter of course.

No one, however, can see the mass of colored people in the cities and on the plantations, the ignorant mass, slowly coming to moral consciousness, without a recognition of the magnitude of the negro problem. I am glad that my State has not the practical settlement of it, and I can not do less than express profound sympathy with the people who have. They inherit the most difficult task now anywhere visible in human progress. They will make mistakes, and they will do injustice now and then; but one feels like turning away from these, and thanking God for what they do well.

There are many encouraging things in the condition of the negro. Good-will, generally, among the people where he lives is one thing; their tolerance of his weaknesses and failings is another. He is himself, here and there, making heroic sacrifices to obtain an education. There are negro mothers earning money at the wash-tub to keep their boys at school and in college. In the Southwest there is such a call for colored teachers that the Straight University in New Orleans, which has about five hundred pupils, can not begin to supply the demand, although the teachers, male and female, are paid from thirty-five to fifty dollars a month. A colored graduate of this school a year ago is now superintendent of the colored schools in Memphis, at a salary of $1200 a year. Are these exceptional cases? Well, I suppose it is also exceptional to see a colored clergyman in his surplice seated in the chancel of the most important white Episcopal church in New Orleans, assisting in the service; but it is significant. There are many good auguries to be drawn from the improved condition of the negroes on the plantations, the more rational and less emotional character of their religious services, and the hold of the temperance movement on all classes in the country places.

COTTON AND ITS KINGDOM

IT has long been the fortune of the South to deal with special problems—slavery, secession, reconstruction. For fifty years has the settlement of these questions engaged her people, and challenged the attention of the world. As these issues are set aside finally, after stubborn and bloody conflict, during which she maintained her position with courage, and abided results with fortitude, she finds herself confronted with a new problem quite as important as either of those that have been disposed of. In the cultivation and handling, under the new order of things, of the world's great staple, cotton, she is grappling with a matter that involves essentially her own welfare, and is of the greatest interest to the general public. To the slave-holder the growing of cotton was straight and easy, as the product of his land was supplemented by the increase of his slaves, and he prospered in spite of himself. To the Southern farmer of *post bellum* days, impoverished, unsettled, and thrown upon free labor, working feverishly with untried conditions, poorly informed as to the result of experiments made by his neighbors, and too impatient to wait upon his own experience, it is quite a different affair. After sixteen years of trial, everything is yet indeterminate. And whether this staple is cultivated in the South as a profit or a passion, and whether it shall bring the South to independence or to beggary, are matters yet to be settled. Whether its culture shall result in a host of croppers without money or credit, appealing to the granaries of the West against famine, paying toll to usurers at home, and mortgaging their crops to speculators abroad even before it is planted— a planting oligarchy of money-lenders, who have usurped the land through foreclosure, and hold by the ever-growing margin between a grasping lender and an enforced borrower—or a prosperous self-respecting race of small farmers, cultivating their own lands, living upon their own resources, controlling their crops until they are sold, and independent alike of usurers and provision brokers—which of these shall be the outcome of cotton culture the future must determine. It is certain only in the present that the vigor of the cotton producers and the pace at which they are moving are rapidly forcing a settlement of these questions, and that the result of the experiments now swiftly working out in the South will especially concern a large part of the human race, from the farmer who plods down the cotton row, cutting through his doubts with a hoe, to the spinner in Manchester who anxiously balances the totals of the world's crop.

It may be well to remark at the outset that the production of cotton in the South is practically without limit. It was 1830 before the American crop reached 1,000,000 bales, and the highest point ever reached in the days of slavery was a trifle above 4,500,000 bales. The crop of 1880–81 is about 2,000,000 in excess of this, and there are those who believe that a crop of 8,000,000 bales is among the certainties of the next few years. The heavy increase in the cotton crop is due entirely to the increase of cotton acreage brought about by the use of fertilizers. Millions of acres of land, formerly thought to be beyond the possible limit of the cotton belt, have been made the best of cotton lands by being artificially enriched. In North Carolina alone the limit of cotton production has been moved twenty miles northward and twenty miles westward, and the half of Georgia on which no cotton was grown twenty years ago now produces fully half the crop of the State. The "area of low production" as the Atlantic States are brought to the front by artificial stimulation is moving westward, and is now central in Alabama and Florida. But the increase in acreage, as large as it is, will be but a small factor in the increase of production, compared to the intensifying the cultivation of the land now in use. Under the present loose system of planting, the average yield is hardly better than one bale to three acres. This could be easily increased to a bale an acre. In Georgia five bales have been raised on one acre, and a yield of three bales to the acre is credited to several localities. President Morehead, of the Mississippi Valley Cotton Planters' Association, says that the entire cotton crop of the present year might have been easily raised in fourteen counties along the Mississippi River. It will be seen, therefore, that the capacity of the South to produce cotton is practical-

ly limitless, and when we consider the enormous demand for cotton goods now opening up from new climes and peoples, we may conclude that the near future will see crops compared to which the crop of the past year, worth $300,000,000, will seem small.

Who will be the producers of these vast crops of the future ? Will they be landowners or tenants—planters or farmers ? The answer to this inquiry will be made by the average Southerner without hesitation. "Small farms," he will say, "well tended by actual owners, will be the rule in the South. The day of a landholding oligarchy has passed forever." Let us see about this.

The history of agriculture—slow and stubborn industry that it is—will hardly show stronger changes than have taken place in the rural communities of the South in the past fifteen years. Immediately after the war between the States there was a period of unprecedented disaster. The surrender of the Confederate armies found the plantations of the South stripped of houses, fences, stock, and implements. The planters were without means or prospects, and uncertain as to what should be done. The belief that extensive cotton culture had perished with slavery had put the price of the staple up to thirty cents. Lured by the dazzling price, which gave them credit as well as hope, the owners of the plantations prepared for vast operations. They refitted their quarters, repaired their fences, summoned hundreds of negro croppers at high prices, and invested lavishly their borrowed capital in what they felt sure was a veritable bonanza. The few years that followed are full of sickening failure. Planters who had been princes in wealth and possessions suddenly found themselves irretrievably in debt and reduced to beggary. Under the stimulation of high prices the crops grew, until there was a tumble from thirty to ten cents per pound. Unable to meet their engagements with their factors, who, suddenly awakening to the peril of the situation, refused to make further advances or grant extensions, the planters had no recourse but to throw their lands on the market. But so terrible had been their experience—many losing $100,000 in a single season—that no buyers were found for the plantations on which they had been wrecked. The result of this panic

IN THE FIELD AND THE FACTORY.

to sell and disinclination to buy was a toppling of land values. Plantations that had brought from $100,000 to $150,000 before the war, and even since, were sold at $6000 to $10,000, or hung on the hands of the planter and his factor at any price whatever. The ruin seemed to be universal and complete, and the old plantation system, it then seemed, had perished utterly and forever. While no definite reason was given for the failure—free labor and the credit system being the causes usually and loosely assigned—it went without contradiction that the system of planting under which the South had amassed its riches and lived in luxury was inexorably doomed.

Following this lavish and disastrous period came the era of small farms. Led into the market by the low prices to which the best lands had fallen, came a host of small buyers, to accommodate whom the plantations were subdivided, and offered in lots to suit purchasers. Never perhaps was there a rural movement, accomplished without revolution or exodus, that equalled in extent and swiftness the partition of the plantations of the ex-slave-holders into small farms. As remarkable as was the eagerness of the negroes—who bought in Georgia alone 6850 farms in three years—

the earth-hunger of the poorer class of the whites, who had been unable under the slave-holding oligarchy to own land, was even more striking. In Mississippi there were in 1867 but 412 farms of less than ten acres, and in 1870, 11,003; only 2314 of over ten and less than twenty acres, and in 1870, 8981; only 16,024 between twenty and one hundred acres, and in 1870, 38,015. There was thus in this one State a gain of nearly forty thousand small farms of less than one hundred acres in about three years. In Georgia the number of small farms sliced off of the big plantations from 1868 to 1873 was 32,824. In Liberty County there were in 1866 only three farms of less than ten acres; in 1870 there were 616, and 749 farms between ten and twenty acres. This splitting of the old plantations into farms went on with equal rapidity all over the South, and was hailed with lively expressions of satisfaction. A population pinned down to the soil on which it lived, made conservative and prudent by land-ownership, forced to abandon the lavish method of the old time as it had nothing to spare, and to cultivate closely and intelligently as it had no acres to waste, living on cost as it had no credit, and raising its own supplies as it could not afford to buy—this the South boasted it had in 1873, and this many believe it has to-day. The small farmer — who was to retrieve the disasters of the South, and wipe out the last vestige of the planting aristocracy, between which and the people there was always a lack of sympathy, by keeping his own acres under his own supervision, and using hired labor only as a supplement to his own—is still held to be the typical cotton-raiser.

But the observer who cares to look beneath the surface will detect signs of a reverse current. He will discover that there is beyond question a sure though gradual rebunching of the small farms into large estates, and a tendency toward the re-establishment of a land-holding oligarchy. Here and there through all the Cotton States, and almost in every county, are reappearing the planter princes of the old time, still lords of acres, though not of slaves. There is in Mississippi one planter who raises annually 12,000 bales of cotton on twelve consolidated plantations, aggregating perhaps 50,000 acres. The Capeheart estate on Albemarle Sound, originally of several thousand acres, had $52,000 worth of land added last year. In the Mississippi Valley, where, more than anywhere else, is preserved the distinctive cotton plantation, this re-absorbing of separate farms into one ownership is going on rapidly. Mr. F. C. Morehead, an authority on these lands, says that not one-third of them are owned by the men who held them at the close of the war, and that they are passing, one after the other, into the hands of the commission merchants. It is doubtful if there is a neighborhood in all the South in which casual inquiry will not bring to the front from ten to a dozen men who have added farm after farm to their possessions for the past several years, and now own from six to twenty places. It must not be supposed that these farms are bunched together and run after the old plantation style. On the contrary, they are cut into even smaller farms, and rented to small croppers. The question involved is not whether or not the old plantation methods shall be revived. It is the much more serious problem as to whether the lands divided forever into small farms shall be owned by the many or by the few, whether we shall have in the South a peasantry like that of France, or a tenantry like that of Ireland,

By getting at the cause of this threatened re-absorption of the small farmer into the system from which he so eagerly and bravely sought release, we shall best understand the movement. It is primarily credit—a false credit based on usury and oppression, strained to a point where it breeds distrust and provokes a percentage to compensate for risk, and strained, not for the purchase of land, which is a security as long as the debt is unpaid, but for provisions and fertilizers, which are valueless to either secure the lender or assist the borrower to pay. With the failure of the large planters and their withdrawal from business, banks, trust companies, and capitalists withdraw their money from agricultural loans. The new breed of farmers held too little land and were too small dealers to command credit or justify investigation. And yet they were obliged to have money with which to start their work. Commission merchants therefore borrowed the money from the banks, and loaned it to village brokers or store-keepers, who in turn loaned it to farmers in their neighborhood, usually in the form of advancing supplies. It thus came to the farmer after it had been through three principals, each of whom demanded a heavy percentage for the risk he assumed. In every case the farmer gave a lien or mortgage upon his crop or land. In this lien he waived exemptions and defense, and it amounted in effect to a deed. Having once given such a paper to his merchant, his credit was of course gone, and he had to depend upon the man who held the mortgage for his supplies. To that man he must carry his crop when it was gathered, pay him commission for handling it, and accept the settlement that he offered. To give an idea of the oppressiveness of this system it is only necessary to quote the Commissioner of Agriculture of Georgia, who by patient investigation discovered that the Georgia farmers paid prices for supplies that averaged fifty-four per cent. interest on all they bought. For instance, corn that sold for eighty-nine cents a bushel cash was sold on time secured by lien at a dollar and twelve cents. In Mississippi the percentage is even more terrible, as the crop lien laws are in force there, and the crop goes into the hands of the merchant, who charges commission on the estimated number of bales, whether a half crop or a full one is raised. Even this maladjustment of credits would not impoverish the farmer if he did not yield to the infatuation for cotton-planting, and fail to plant anything but cotton.

Those who have the nerve to give up part of their land and labor to the raising of their own supplies and stock have but little need of credit, and consequently seldom get into the hands of the usurers. But cotton is the money crop, and offers such flattering inducements that everything yields to that. It is not unusual to see farmers come to the cities to buy butter, melons, meal, and vegetables. They rely almost entirely upon their merchants for meat and bread, hay, forage, and stock. In one county in Georgia last year, from the small dépôts, $80,000 worth of meat and bread was shipped to farmers. The official estimate of the National Cotton Planters' Association, at its session of 1881, was that the Cotton States lacked 42,252,244 bushels of wheat, 166,684,279 bushels of corn, 77,762,108 bushels of oats, or 286,698,632 bushels of grain, of raising what it consumed. When to this is added 4,011,150 tons of hay at thirty dollars a ton, and $32,000,000 paid for fertilizers, we find that the value of the cotton crop is very largely consumed in paying for the material with which it was made.

On this enormous amount the cotton farmer has to pay the usurious percentage charged by his merchant broker, which is never less than thirty per cent., and frequently runs up to seventy per cent. We can appreciate, when we consider this, the statement of the man who said, "The commission merchants of the South are gradually becoming farmers, and the farmers, having learned the trick, will become merchants."

The remedy for this deplorable tendency is first the establishment of a proper system of credit. The great West was in much worse condition than the South some years ago. The farms were mortgaged, and were being sold under mortgages, under a system not half so oppressive as that under which the Southern farmer labors. Boston capital, seeking lucrative investment, soon began to pour toward the West, in charge of loan companies, and was put out at eight per cent., and the redemption of that section was speedily worked out. A similar movement is now started in the South. An English company, with head-quarters at New Orleans, loaned over $600,000 its first year at eight per cent., with perfect security. The farmers who borrowed this money were of course immensely relieved, and the testimony is that they are rapidly working out. In Atlanta, Georgia, a company is established with $2,000,000 of Boston and New York capital, which it is loaning on farm lands at seven per cent. In the first three months of its work it loaned $120,000, and it has now appointed local agents in thirty counties in the State, and advertises that it wishes to lend $50,000 in each county. The managers say that they can command practically unlimited capital for safe risks at seven per cent. Companies working on the same plan have been established elsewhere in the South, and it is said that there will be no lack of capital for safe risks on rural lands in a few years.

The first reform, however, that must be made is in the system of farming. The South must prepare to raise her own provisions, compost her fertilizers, cure her own hay, and breed her own stock. Leaving credit and usury out of the question, no man can pay seventy-five cents a bushel for corn, thirty dollars a ton for hay, twenty dollars a barrel for pork, sixty cents for oats, and raise cotton for eight cents a pound. The farmers who prosper

CUFFEE'S ONE BALE.

at the South are the "corn-raisers," *i. e.*, the men who raise their own supplies, and make cotton their surplus crop. A gentleman who recorded 320 mortgages last year testified that not one was placed on the farm of a man who raised his own bread and meat. The shrewd farmers who always have a bit of money on hand with which to buy any good place that is to be sold under mortgage are the "corn-raisers," and the moment they get possession they rule out the all-cotton plan, and plant corn and the grasses. That the plan of farming only needs revision to make the South rich beyond measure is proven by constant example. A corn-raiser bought a place of 370 acres for $1700. He at once put six tenants on it, and limited their cotton acreage to one-third of what they had under cultivation. Each one of the six made more clear money than the former owner had made, and the rents for the first year were $1126. The man who bought this farm lives in Oglethorpe, Georgia, and has fifteen farms all run on the same plan.

The details of the management of what may be the typical planting neighborhood of the South in the future are furnished me by the manager of the Capeheart estate in North Carolina. This estate is divided into farms of fifty acres each, and rented to tenants. These tenants are bound to plant fifteen acres in cotton, twelve in corn, eight in small crops, and let fifteen lie in grass. They pay one-third of the crop as rent, or one-half if the proprietor furnishes horses and mules. They have comfortable quarters, and are entitled to the use of surplus herring and the dressings of the herring caught in the fisheries annexed to the place. In the centre of the estate is a general store managed by the proprietor, at which the tenants have such a line of credit as they are entitled to, of course paying a pretty percentage of profit on the goods they buy. They are universally prosperous, and in some cases, where by skill and industry they have secured 100 acres, are laying up money. The profits to Dr. Capeheart are large, and show the margin there is in buying land that is loosely farmed, and putting it under intelligent supervision. Of the $52,000 worth of land added to his estates last year, at a valuation of twenty-five dollars per acre, he will realize in rental nine dollars per acre for every acre cultivated, and calculates that in five years at the most the rentals of the land will have paid back what he gave for it.

Amid all this transition from landowner to tenant there is, besides the corn-raiser, one other steadfast figure, undisturbed by change of relation or condition, holding tenaciously to what it has, though little inclined to push for more. This is Cuffee, the darky farmer. There is no more interesting study in our agriculture than this same dusky, good-natured fellow—humble, patient, shrewd—as he drives into town with his mixed team and his one bag of cotton, on which, drawn by a sympathetic sense of ownership, his whole family is clustered. Living simply and frugally, supplementing his humble meal with a 'possum caught in the night hunt, or a rabbit shot with the old army musket that he captured from some deserted battle-field, and allowing no idlers in the family save the youngsters who "'tend de free school," he defies alike the usurer and the land-shark. In the State of Georgia he owns 680,000 acres of land, cut up into farms that barely average ten acres each, and in the Cotton States he owns 2,680,800 acres, similarly divided. From this pos-

peculiar. Although he spends the most of his life in the cotton field, and this staple is the main crop with which he is concerned, it does not enter into his social life, catch his sentiment, or furnish the occasion for any of his pleasures. None of his homely festivals hinge upon the

HALLIE.

session it is impossible to drive him, and to this possession he adds gradually as the seasons go by. He is not ambitious, however, to own large tracts of land, preferring the few acres that he has constantly under his eye, and to every foot of which he feels a rude attachment.

The relations of the negro to cotton are

culture or handling of the great staple. He has his corn-shuckings, his log-rollings, his quilting bees, his threshing jousts, and indeed every special work about the farm is made to yield its element of frolic, except the making of cotton. None of those tuneful melodies with which he beguiles his work or gladdens his play-time acknowledge cotton as a subject or an incident. None of the folklore with which the moonlight nights are whiled away or the fire-lit cabins sanctified, and which finds its home in the corn patch or the meadows, has aught to do with the cotton field. I have never heard a negro song in which the cotton field is made the incidental theme or the subject of allusion, except in a broken perversion of that incomparable ballad, "The Mocking-Bird," in which the name of the heroine, the tender sentiment, and the tune, which is a favorite one with the negroes, are preserved. This song, with the flower of Southern girlhood that points the regretful tenderness changed into a dusky maiden idealized by early death, with the "mocking-bird singing o'er her grave," and sung in snatches almost without words or coherence, is popular with the field hands in many parts of the South.

But when we have discussed the questions involved in the planting and culture of the cotton crop, as serious as they are, we have had to do with the least important phase of our subject. The crop of 7,000,000 bales, when ready for the market, is worth in round numbers $300,000,000. The same crop when manufactured is worth over $900,000,000. Will the South be content to see the whole of this added value realized by outsiders? If not, how much of the work necessary to create this value will she do within her own borders? She has abundant water-powers, that are never locked a day by ice or lowered by drought, that may be had for a mere song; cheap labor, cheap lands, an unequalled climate, cheap fuel, and the conditions of cheap living. Can these be utilized to any general extent?

It may be premised that there are questions of the utmost importance to the South outside of the manufacture of the lint, which is usually held to cover the whole question of cotton manufacture. There is no particle of the cotton plant that may not be handled to advantage. Mr. Edward Atkinson is authority for the statement that if a plant similar to cotton, but having no lint, could be grown in the North, it would be one of the most profitable of crops. And yet it is true that up to a late date the seed of the cotton has been wholly wasted, and even now the stalk is thrown away as useless. A crop of 7,000,000 bales will yield 3,500,000 tons of cotton seed. Every ounce of this seed is valuable, and in the past few years it has been so handled as to add very heavily to the value of the crop. The first value of the seed is as a fertilizer. It has been

discovered of late that the seed that had been formerly allowed to accumulate about the gin-houses in vast piles and rot as waste material, when put upon the fields would add twenty-five to thirty-three per cent. to the crop, and was equal to many of the fertilizers that sell in the market for $25 per ton. In 1869 a mill was established in New Orleans for the purpose of pressing the oil from the cotton seed, and manufacturing the bulk into stock food. Its success was so pronounced that there are now fifty-nine seed-oil mills in the South, costing over $6,000,000, and working up $5,500,000 worth of seed annually. The product of the seed used sells for $9,600,000, so that the mills create a value of $4,500,000 annually. They use only one-seventh of the seed produced in the South. A ton of seed which can be worked for $5 50 a ton, and costs originally $8 to $10, making an average cost when worked of $15, is estimated to produce thirty-five gallons of oil worth $11 50, seed-cake worth $5 50, and lint worth $1 50—a total of $18 50, or profit of $3 50, per ton. The oil is of excellent quality, and is used in the making of soaps, stearine, white oils, and when highly refined is a table oil of such flavor and appearance as will deceive the best judges. A quality has been lately discovered in it that makes it valuable as a dye-stuff. It is shipped largely to Europe, 130,000 barrels having been exported last year, chiefly to Antwerp. It is put up carefully, and reshipped to this country as olive-oil to such an extent that prohibitory duties have been put on it by the Italian government, and it is ruled out of that country. Before it is placed in the oil mill the cotton seed is hulled. The hulls are valuable, and may be used for tanning, made into pulp for paper stock, or used as fuel, and the ashes sold to the soap-makers for the potash they contain. The mass of kernels left after the hulls have been removed and the oil pressed out is made into seed-cake, a most desirable food for stock, which is exported largely to Europe. It is also worked into a fertilizer that yields under analysis $37 50 in value per ton, and can be sold for $22 a ton. It is a notable fact that the ton of seed-cake is even more valuable as a stock food after the $11 50 worth of oil has been taken from it than before, and quite as valuable as a fertilizer. In the four hundred pounds of lint in a bale of cotton there are but four pounds of chemical elements taken from the soil; in the oil there is little more; but in the seed-cake and hulls there are forty pounds of potash and phosphate of lime. But admirable as is the disposition of the cotton seed for manufacture, ample as is the margin of profit, and rapid as has been the growth in the industry, there exists can not be gathered promptly or cheaply enough for the oil mills. Of the 3,500,000 tons of seed, 500,000 tons only are worked up, and perhaps as much more used for seed. This leaves 2,500,000 tons not worked, and in which is lost nearly $30,000,000 worth of oil. For whether this two and a half million tons is used as a fertilizer or

EDGE OF THE COTTON FIELD.

the same disorganization that is noticeable in the handling of the whole cotton question. Although less than one-seventh of the seed raised is needed by the mills, they are unable to get enough to keep them running. The cotton is ginned in such awkward distribution, and in such small quantity at any one locality, that it fed to stock, it would lose none of its value for either purpose if the thirty-five gallons of oil, worth $11 50, were extracted from each ton of it.

Even when the South has passed beyond the proper handling of cotton seed, she has very important ground to cover before she arrives at what is generally known as cotton manufacturing. "The manufacture of this staple," says a very eminent authority, "is a unit, beginning at the field when the cotton is picked, and ending at the factory from which the cloth is sent to the merchant." How little this essential truth has been appreciated is apparent from the fact that, until the last census, ginning, pressing, and baling have been classed with the "production" of cotton, and its manufacture held to consist solely of spinning and weaving. Yet there is not a process to which the lint is submitted after it is thrown from the negro's "pocket" that does not act directly on the quality of the cloth that is finally produced, and on the cheapness and efficiency with which the cloth is made. The separation of the fibre from the seed, the disposition made of the fluffy lint before it is compressed, the compression itself, and the baling of the compressed cotton— these are all delicate operations, involving the integrity of the fibre, the cost of getting it ready for the spindle, and the ease with which it may be spun. Indeed, Mr. Hammond, of South Carolina, a most accomplished writer, contends that the gin-house is the pivotal point around which the whole manufacture of cotton revolves. There is no question that with one-tenth of the money invested in improved gins, cleaners, and presses that would be required for factories, and with incomparably less risk, the South could make one-half the profit, pound for pound, that is

A POCKET OF COTTON.

NOON AT THE COTTON-GIN.

made in the mills of New England. Mr. F. C. Morehead, already alluded to in this article, says: "A farmer who produces 500 bales of cotton—200,000 pounds—can, by the expenditure of $1500 on improved gins and cleaners, add one cent per pound to the value of his crop, or $2000. If he added only one-half of one cent, he would get in the first year over fifty per cent. return of his outlay." Mr. Edward Atkinson—to close this list of authorities—says that the cotton crop is deteriorated ten per cent. at least by being improperly handled from the field to the factory. It is, of course, equally true that a reform in this department of the manufacture of cotton would add ten per cent. to the value of the crop—say $30,000,000—and that, too, without cost to the consumer. Much of the work now done in the mills of New England is occasioned by the errors committed in ginning and packing. Not only would the great part of the dust, sand, and grit that get into cotton from careless handling about the gin-house be kept out if it were properly protected, but that which is in the fibre naturally could be cleaned out more efficiently and with one-third the labor and cost, if it were taken

before it has been compressed and baled. Beyond this, the excessive beating and tearing of the fibre necessary to clean it after the sand has been packed in weaken and impair it, and the sand injures the costly and delicate machinery of the mills.

The capital available to the farmers of any neighborhood in the South is entirely adequate to make thorough reform in this most important, safest, and most profitable department of the manufacture of cotton. A gin-house constructed on the best plan, supplied with the new roller gins lately invented in England, that guarantee to surpass in quantity of cotton ginned as well as quality of lint our rude and imperfect saw gins, having automatic feeders to pass the picking to the gin, and an apron to receive the lint as it comes from the gin and carry it to the beater, or cleaner, where all the motes and dust can be taken from the freshly ginned fibre, and then, instead of rolling this fleecy mass on a dirty floor, where it would catch every particle of dust and grit, to carry it direct to a Dedrick press that would compress forty pounds within a cubic foot, and reduce the little bale of one hundred and twenty pounds to the consistency of elm-wood, and as little liable to soak water or catch dirt—an establishment of this sort would add one cent per pound to every pound of cotton put through it, and would be worth more as an example than a dozen cotton factories. Annexed to this gin-house should be a huller to take the hulls from the seed, and to this huller the seed should be taken as it comes from the gins. Once hulled, the hulls should be fed to the stock, restored to the soil, or sold, and the kernels sent to the nearest oil mill, the oil sold, and the meal fed to sheep or stock, or used as a fertilizer. These improvements, costing little, and within the skill of ordinary laborers, would bring as good a profit as could be realized by a factory involving enormous outlay, great risk, and the utmost skill of management. The importance of reform here will be seen when we state that there is half as much capital—say $70,000,000—invested in machinery for baling, pressing, and ginning cotton as there is invested in the United States in machinery for weaving and spinning it. So great has been the progress in invention, and so sluggish the cotton farmer to reform either his methods or his machinery, that experts agree that the ginning, pressing, and baling of the crop could be done with one-half or possibly one-third of the labor and cost of the present, and done so much better that the product would be worth ten per cent. more than it now commands, if the best machinery were bought, and the best methods employed.

The urgency and the magnitude of the reforms needed in the field and about the gin-house have not deterred the South from aspiring to spin and weave at least the bulk of the cotton crop. Indeed, there is nothing that so appeals to Southern pride as to urge the possibility that in time the manufacture of this crop as well as the crop itself shall be a monopoly of the cotton belt. As the South grows richer and the conditions of competition are nearer equal, there will be a tendency to place new machinery intended for the manufacture of cotton near the field in which the staple is growing; but the extent to which this tendency will control, or the time in which it will become controlling, is beyond the scope of this article. We shall rather deal with things as they are, or are likely to be in the very near future. We note, then, that in the

past ten years the South has more than doubled the amount of cotton manufactured within her borders. In 1870, there were used 45,032,866 pounds of cotton; in 1880, 101,937,256 pounds. In 1870, there were 11,602 looms and 416,983 spindles running; in 1880, 15,222 looms and 714,078 spindles. This array of figures hardly indicates fairly the progress that the South will make in the next ten years, for the reason that the factories in which these spindles are turned are experiments in most of the localities in which they are placed. It is the invariable rule that when a factory is built in any city or country it is easier to raise the capital for a subsequent enterprise than for the first one. At Augusta, Georgia, for instance, where the manufacture of cloth has been demonstrated a success, the progress is remarkable. In the past two years two new mills, the Enterprise and Sibley, with 30,000 spindles each, have been established; and a third, the King, has been organized, with a capital of $1,000,000 and 30,000 spindles. The capital for these mills was furnished about one-fourth in Augusta, and the balance in the North. With these mills running, Augusta will have 170,000 spindles, and will have added about 70,000 spindles to the last census returns. In South Carolina the same rapid growth is resulting from the establishment of one or two successful mills; and in Columbus, Georgia, the influence of one successful mill, the Eagle and Phœnix, has raised the local consumption of cotton from 1927 bales in 1870 to 19,000 bales in 1880. In Atlanta, Georgia, the first mill had hardly been finished before the second was started; a third is projected; and two companies have secured charters for the building of a forty-mile canal to furnish water-power and factory fronts to capital in and about the city. These things are mentioned simply to show that the growth of cotton manufacture in the South is sympathetic, and that each factory established is an argument for others. There is no investment that has proved so uniformly successful in the South as that put into cotton factories. An Augusta factory just advertises eight per cent. semi-annual dividend; the Eagle and Phœnix, of Columbus, earned twenty-five per cent. last year; the Augusta factory for eleven years made an average of eighteen per cent. per annum. The net earnings of the Langley Mills was $480,000 for its

THE OLD SPINNING-WHEEL.

first eight years on a capital of $400,000, or an average of fifteen per cent. a year. The earnings of sixty Southern mills, large and small, selected at random, for three years, averaged fourteen per cent. per annum.

Indeed, an experience varied and extended enough to give it authority teaches that there is absolutely no reason why the South should not profitably quadruple its capacity for the manufacture of cotton every year in the next five years except the lack of capital. The lack of skilled labor has proved to be a chimerical fear, as the mills bring enough skilled labor to any community in which they are established to speedily educate up a native force. It may be true that for the most delicate work the South will for a while lack the efficient labor of New England that has been trained for generations, but it is equally true that no factory in the South has ever been stopped a week for the lack of suitable labor. The operatives can live cheaper than at the North, and can be had for lower wages. As sensible a man as Mr. Edward Atkinson claimed lately that in the cotton country proper a person could not keep at continuous in-door labor during the summer. The answer to this is that during the present summer, the hottest ever known, not a Southern mill has stopped for one day or hour on account of the heat, and this, too, when scores of establishments through the Western and Northern cities were closed. One of the strongest points of advantage the South has is that for no extreme of climate, acting on the machinery, the operatives, or the water-supply, is any of her mills forced to suspend work at any season. Beyond this, Southern water-powers can be purchased low, and the land adjacent at a song; there are no commissions to pay on the purchase of cotton, no freight on its transportation, and it is submitted to the picker before it has undergone serious compression. Mr. W. H. Young, of Columbus, perhaps the best Southern authority, estimates that the Columbus mills have an advantage of $\frac{9}{10}$ of a cent per pound over their Northern competitors, and this in a mill of 1600 looms will amount to nine per cent. on the entire capital, or $120,099. The Southern mills, without exception, pulled through the years of depression that followed the panic of 1873, paying regular dividends of from six per cent. to fifteen, and, it may be said, have thoroughly won the confidence of investors North and South. The one thing that has retarded the growth of manufacturing in the Cotton States, the lack of capital, is being overcome with astonishing rapidity. Within the past two years considerably over $100,000,000 of Northern capital has been subscribed, in lots of $1,000,000 and upward, for the purchase and development of Southern railroads and mining properties; the total will probably run to $120,000,000. There is now being expended in the building of new railroads from Atlanta, Georgia, as head-quarters, $17,800,000, not one dollar of which was subscribed by Georgians or by the State of Georgia. The men who invest these vast amounts in the South are interested in the general development of the section into which they have gone with their enterprise, and they readily double any local subscription for any legitimate local improvement. By the sale of these railroad properties to Northern syndicates at advanced prices the local stockholders have realized heavily in cash, and this surplus is seeking manufacturing investment. The prospect is that the next ten years will witness a growth in this direction beyond what even the most sanguine predict.

The International Cotton Exposition, opening October 5 of the present year, in Atlanta, must have a tremendous influence in improving the culture, handling, and manufacture of the great staple of the South. The Southern people do not lack the desire to keep abreast with improvement and invention, but on the contrary have shown precipitate eagerness in reaching out for the best and newest. Before the war, when the Southern planter had a little surplus money he bought a slave. Since the war, he buys a piece of machinery. The trouble has been that he was forced to buy without any guide as to the value of what he bought, or its adaptability to the purposes for which he intended it. The consequence is that the farms are littered with ill-adapted and inferior implements and machines, representing twice the investment that, intelligently placed, would provide an equipment that with half the labor would do better work. It is the purpose of the exposition to bring the farmers face to face with the very best machinery that invention and experience have produced. The buildings themselves will be models each of its kind, and will represent the judgment of experts as to cheapness, durability, safety, and general excellence. The past and present will be contrasted in the exhibition. The old loom on which the rude fabrics of our forefathers were woven by hands gentle and loving will be put against the more elaborate looms of to-day. The spinning-wheel of the past, that filled all the country-side with its drowsy music, as the dusky spinner advanced and retreated, with not ungraceful courtesy and a swinging sidewise shuffle, will find its sweet voice lost in the hum of modern spindles. The cycle of gins and ginning will be there completed, invention coming back, after a half-century of trial with the brutal saw, to a perfected varia-

COTTON PORT, GALVESTON, TEXAS.

tion of the patient and gentle roller with which the precious fleece was pulled from the seed years upon years ago. There are the most wonderful machines promised, including a half-dozen that claim to have solved the problem—supposed to be past finding out—of picking cotton by machinery. Large fields flank the buildings, and on these are tested the various kinds of cotton seed, fed by the various kinds of fertilizers, each put in fair competition with the others.

One of the most important special inventions at the exposition will be the Clement attachment—a contrivance for spinning the cotton as it comes from the gin. The invention is simply the marriage of the gin to the spindle. These are joined by two large cards that take the fibre from the gin, straighten it out, and pass it directly to the spinning boards, where it is made into the best of yarns. The announcement of this invention two years ago created very great excitement. If it proved a success, the whole system of cotton manufacture was changed. If the cotton could be spun directly from the gin, all the expense of baling would be eliminated, and four or five expensive steps in the process of cotton from field to cloth would be rendered unnecessary. Better than all, the South argued, the Clement attachment brought the heaviest part of manufacturing to the cotton field, from which it could never be divorced. By the simple joining of the spindles to the gin, the cotton worth only eight or nine cents as baled lint, in which shape

it had been shipped North, became worth sixteen to eighteen cents as yarns. The home value of the crop was thus to be doubled, and by such process as New England could never capture. Several of the attachments were put to work, and were visited by thousands. They produced an excellent quality of yarns, and made a clear profit of two cents per pound on the cotton treated. The investment required was small, and it was held that $5000 would certainly bring a net annual profit of $2200. Many of these little mills are still running, and profitably ; but difficulties between the owner and his agents, and a general suspicion raised by his declining to put the machine on its merits before certain agricultural associations, prevented its general adoption. That this attachment, or some machine of similar character for spinning the cotton into yarns near the field where it is grown, will be generally adopted through the South in the near future, I have not a particle of doubt; that the exposition with its particular exhibits on this point will hasten the day, there is every reason to hope. There are many yarn mills already scattered through the South, but none of them promise the results that will be achieved when the spindles are wedded to the gin, and the same motive power drives both, carrying the cotton without delay or compression from seed to thread.

Such, then, in brief and casual review, is King Cotton, his subjects, and his realm. Vast as his concerns and possessions may appear at present, they are but the hint of what the future will develop. The best authority puts the amount of cotton goods manufactured in America at about fourteen pounds per head of population, of which twelve pounds per capita are retained for home consumption, leaving only a small margin for export. On the Continent there is but one country, probably — Switzerland — that manufactures more cotton goods than it consumes; and the Continent demands from Great Britain an amount of cotton cloth that, added to its own supply, exhausts nearly one-half the product of the English mills. It is hardly probable that, under the sharp competition of American mills, the capacity of either England or the Continent for producing ordinary cotton cloths will be greatly increased. But, with the yield of the English and Continental mills at least measurably defined and now rapidly absorbed, there is an enormous demand for machine-made cotton fabrics springing from new and virtually exhaustless sources. The continents of Asia, Africa, South America, Australia, and the countries lying between the two American continents, contain more than 800,000,000 people, according to general authority. This immense population is clothed in cotton almost exclusively, and almost as exclusively in hand-made fabrics. That the cheap and superior products of the modern factory will displace these hand-made goods as rapidly as they can be delivered upon competing terms can not be doubted. To supply China alone with cotton fabrics made by machine, deducting the 35,000,000 people or thereabout already supplied, and estimating the demand of the remainder at five pounds per capita, would require 3,000,000 additional bales of cotton and 30,000,000 additional spindles. The goods needed for this demand will be the lower grades of cottons, for the manufacture of which the South is especially adapted, and in which there is serious reason to believe she has demonstrated she has advantages over New England. The demand from Mexico, Central and South America, will grow into immense proportions as cotton and its products cheapen under increased supply, and improved methods of culture and manufacture. The South will be called upon to furnish the cotton to meet the calls of the peoples enumerated. That she can easily do so has been made plain by previous estimate, but it may be added that hardly three per cent. of the cotton area is now devoted to cotton, and that on one-tenth of a single Cotton State—Texas—double the present crop might be raised. Whether or not she will do this profitably, and without destroying the happiness and prosperity of her former population, and building up a land-holding oligarchy, depends on a reform in her system of credit and her system of planting. The first is being effected by the introduction of capital that recognizes farming lands as a safe risk worthy of a low percentage of interest; the latter must depend on the intelligence of her people, the force of a few bright examples, and the wisdom of her leaders. She will be called upon to supply a large proportion of the manufactured goods for this new and limitless demand. It has already been shown that she has felicitous conditions for this work.

"TAKE OFF DAT CROWN."

NEW ORLEANS

"THE biggest little city in the country," is what an adopted citizen of New Orleans calls that town. With but little more than a quarter of a million of inhabitants, the Crescent City has most of the features of a true capital and metropolis. It is among the few towns in our country that can be compared with New York in respect of their metropolitan qualifications, but New Orleans leads all the rest, though in population it is small beside any of the others. It has an old and exclusive society, whose claims would be acknowledged in any of our cities. It supports grand opera; its clubs are fully what the term implies, and not mere empty club-houses. It has fine theatres and public and church buildings. The joys of the table, which Chesterfield ranked first among the dissipations of intellectual men, are provided not only in many fine restaurants and in the clubs, but in a multitude of homes. No city has finer markets. Its commerce is with all the world, and its population is cosmopolitan, with all which a long continuance of those conditions implies. Like the greater cities, it has distinct divisions or quarters, which offer the visiting sightseer novelty and change. Its "sights" are the accumulation of nearly two centuries, and of Spanish, French, and American origin.

It is of value to study the qualities which make the Southern capital what it is, because it is evident that it is to become the chief winter resort of those who journey southward to escape the winters in the North. The *mardi gras* carnival is advertising its attractions to such an extent that the last occurrence of this festival found 100,000 strangers there, representing every State and large city in the Union. It is on the southern or winter route to California, it is on the way from the West and Northwest to Florida and the Georgia resorts, and it stands in the path to Texas and Mexico. It is the best of all the American winter resorts, because it has what the others possess (which is to say, warm weather and sunshine), and, in addition, it offers the theatres, shops, restaurants, crowds, clubs, and multiform entertainments of a city of the first class. It is *par excellence* a city of fun, fair women, rich food, and flowers. Its open-air surface-drainage system is about to be replaced by a different one that may not be more wholesome, but will have the advantage of being out of sight. Only one other reform must be instituted, and the carpers will be silent perforce. The local idea that a hotel which was the best in the country in 1837 will remain first class forever is an untenable proposition. A new management, fixed rates that do not bound into the realm of extortion when a crowd comes along, and a modern, million-dollar establishment would fetch more persons there, keep them longer, and send them away happier than most of the citizens have any idea of. Those other cities that are at the end of a long route of travel, out on the Pacific coast, exemplify the value of first-class hotels in all their histories. The consequence is that in a tiny city called Fairhaven, at the upper end of Puget Sound, there is a better hotel than can be found along the whole coast of the Gulf of Mexico west of Florida. The Pacific coast people have found out that tourists will pass an otherwise important place to stop in one that boasts a fine hotel. We Americans will exchange a Wyoming stage-coach for a log-cabin inn, but we will not leave a Pullman train for a bad hotel if we can help it. It is a pity that strangers arriving in New Orleans cannot all be expected to know how remarkably fine are the better class of boarding and lodging places, or how charming a mode of living it is to secure good rooms and coffee of a morning, and dine about in the restaurants, which are among the leading attractions of the hospitable city.

On *mardi gras*, the day before the beginning of Lent, is the time to be in New Orleans, particularly for a stranger, because in the scenes of the carnival is found the key to the character of the people. They are not like the rest of us. Our so-called carnivals, wherever and whenever we have tried to hold them, have been mere commercial ventures, illustrated with advertisements, carried out by hired men, and paid for by self-seeking persons, who had not the backing of any populace. But in New Orleans the carnival displays are wholly designed to amuse and entertain the pleasure-loving, light-hearted, largely Latin people who originally took part in them, but who have surrendered active participation to the leading and wealthy men of the town. The secret carnival societies are six in number, and are named the Argonauts, Atlanteans, Krewe of Proteus, Mistick Krewe of Comus, Momus, and Rex. Business men, and those who have earned the additional title of "society men," make up the membership of the societies. If any one or two of these coteries fancy themselves of "higher social tone" than the others, the fact would be natural, but the distinction will not be pointed out here. The oldest of the societies is the Comus, which was organized in 1857 to give a night parade and ball. These it has given ever since. In 1879 the Momus Society came into being; in 1880, the Rex Society; in 1881, the Krewe of Proteus; and in 1891, the Atlanteans and Argonauts. The members pay into the treasuries of these organizations a fixed sum per annum, and this, added together and drawn upon by a treasurer, who supervises all the accounts, is used to defray the expense of the whole carnival.

The keeping of this especial festival is a very old custom of Latin and Catholic origin, like the establishment of the city itself. For many years it was entirely popular and promiscuous in the sense that it was unordered and without either head or programme. The Mistick Krewe of Comus brought order and form into the first night parade in 1857, and in 1880 the Rex Society, by taking the lead in the open-air pageantry on the day before *mardi gras*, made it possible and advantageous to do away with the promiscuous masking and merrymaking, attendant upon which had been the throwing of lime and flour, the drunkenness, and the usual disorder which must everywhere characterize a loosely managed festival of the sort. Since then the only spontaneous masking among the people has been by children; there has never been a serious affray; there are no more tipsy persons in the streets than on any other day; and there has seldom been an occasion to make an arrest for a cause traceable to the carnival spirit.

All our cities are distinguished for the orderliness of their holiday crowds, but such absolute self-control as is shown by the people of New Orleans at *mardi gras* is a thing above and beyond what is known anywhere else in the country. To me it was inexplicable. I could understand the patient good-nature of a people trained for an occasion, but in the crowds were 100,000 strangers, many of them of the sort that would naturally be attracted to a festival that was to be followed by a prize-fight between noted pugilists. It must have been that all caught the spirit of the occasion. It is chiefly on Canal Street that the bulk of the holiday crowd assembles when there is a parade, but only ten policemen were detailed to keep order during the day parade of Rex in 1892; only seven for the greater night pageant of the Comus Society.

The actual *mardi gras* celebration is only the climax of a series of festivities lasting ten days or more. First is held the Bal des Roses, in the week before the week which precedes the public carnival. This ball is purely a "society affair," like our Patriarchs' Ball in New York.

The week which follows is one of almost daily sensations. First, on Monday, the Argonauts begin the prolonged festival with a tourney and chariot-racing. A ball at night follows. On Tuesday the Atlanteans give their ball. On Thursday Momus gives a ball, with tableaux, in costume. On Friday of this gala week is held the Carnival german. The Carnival German Club is composed of twenty-five society men, who give the german by subscription. Only seventy-five couples participate in it.

The carnival proper is celebrated with pageantry and dancing that occupy the afternoons and nights of Monday and "Fat Tuesday." Rex, the king of the carnival, comes to town on Monday afternoon. Who he is a few persons know at the time; who he was is sometimes published, as in 1891, and more often is not.

What is called a royal yacht is chosen to bring him from some mysterious realm over which he rules in the Orient, to visit his winter capital in the Crescent City. Last time the royal yacht was the revenue-cutter *Galveston*, but ordinarily the societies hire one of the big river steamboats. The yacht is always accompanied by ten or fifteen other steamers, gayly decorated, crowded with men and women, and appointed with bands of music and all that makes good cheer. It is supposed that the yacht has taken the king aboard at the jetties. The fleet returns, and the royal landing is made upon the levee at the foot of Canal Street, amid a fanfaronade of the whistles of boats, locomotives, and factories, and the firing of guns. The king is met by many city officers and leading citizens, who are called the dukes of the realm, and constitute his royal court. These temporary nobles wear civilian attire, with a badge of gold, and bogus jewels as a decoration. Many persons in carriages accompany them. A procession is formed, and the principal features of the display are a gorgeous litter for the king, a litter carrying the royal keys, and a number of splendid litters in which ride gayly costumed women, representing the favorites of the harem. This the public sees and enjoys.

The king goes to the City Hall accompanied as I have described. The way is lined with tens of thousands of spectators; flags wave from every building; music is playing, the sun is shining; the whole scene, with the gorgeous pageant threading it, is magnificent. At the City Hall, the Duke of Crescent City, who is the Mayor, welcomes Rex, and gives him the keys and the freedom of the city. The king mysteriously disappears after that, presumably to his palace.

That night, the night before *mardi gras*, the Krewe of Proteus holds its parade and ball, and in extent and cost and splendor this is a truly representative pair of undertakings. "A Dream of the Vegetable Kingdom" was what the last Proteus parade was entitled. It consisted of a series of elaborate and splendid floats forming a line many blocks long, and representing whatever is most picturesque, or can be made so, among vegetable growths. The float that struck me as the most peculiar and noteworthy bore a huge watermelon, peopled, as all the devices were, with gayly costumed men and

women, and decked with nodding blossoms, waving leaves, dancing tendrils, and
the glitter and sheen of metal, lustrous
stones, and silk.   Butterflies, caterpillars,
birds, a great squirrel on the acorn float,
snails, and nameless grotesque animal
forms were seen upon the vegetables and
their leaves, while men dressed as fairies,
of both sexes, were grouped picturesquely
on every one.   These devices were not in-
artistic or tawdry.   They
were made by skilled
workmen trained for this
particular work, and were
not only superior to any
of the show pieces we see
in other pageants else-
where—they were equal
to the best that are ex-
hibited in theatres.   They
were displayed to the ut-
most advantage in the
glare of the torches and
flambeaux carried by the
men who led the horses
and marched beside the
hidden wheels.   The figures in Paris-made cos-
tumes, theatrical paint,
and masks were 150 to 200
members of the Krewe—
serious and earnest men
of affairs during the other days of each year.

On Tuesday, *mardi gras*, Rex really
made his appearance, leading a pageant
called "the symbolism of colors," just
such another display of the blending
of strong and soft colors, but a thousand-
fold more difficult to render satisfactorily
by daylight.   The twenty enormous floats
in line represented boats, castles, towers,
arches, kiosks, clouds. and thrones, and
one, that I thought the best of all, a
great painter's palette, lying against two
vases, and having living female figures
recumbent here and there to represent
such heaps of color as might be looked
for on a palette in use.   Canal Street,
one of the broadest avenues in the world,
was newly paved with human forms, and
thousands of others were on the review-
ing-stands built before the faces of the
houses, over the pavements.   The sight
of such a vast concourse of people was as
grand as the chromatic, serpentlike line
of floats that wound across and across
the street.   That night all the people
turned out once again and witnessed the

parade of the Mistick Krewe of Comus, a
Japanesque series of floats called "Nip-
pon, the Land of the Rising Sun."   The
display was, to say the least, as fine as
any of the season.

But the splendid function, one that I
never saw excelled in this country, was
the ball of the same society, that night,
in the old French Opera-house.   All the
kings and their queens, representing all

ON CANAL STREET.

the carnival societies, were in the opening quadrille, all crowned and robed and
with their splendid suites.   Looking down
upon that brilliant mass of dancers were
seven rows of the belles of the city—rows
unbroken by the jarring presence of a
man.   These ladies were all simply at-
tired in white, pink, pale blue, and all
the soft faint colors which distinguish the
dress of New Orleans women.   Here and
there a young girl wore upon her head a
narrow fillet of gold, but jewels were few
and far apart—a striking omission which
greatly dignified the gathering and enhanced the beauty of the spectacle.   If
the reader has seen the beauteous women
of Spanish descent and the petite and
sweet-faced French creoles of that city,
let him fancy these, and the loveliest
American belles, forming seven rows in a
theatre of grand size—and then let him
try his best to picture to himself the
wondrous garden of personified flowers
that was thus presented.

I have said that "society" controls the

opera. This institution, regularly maintained only in New Orleans, of all the cities of our country, is almost self-supporting. It is grand opera, and it is always French, and given in the old French inherent in all our Southerners who have an excuse for it, meets an equal pride of family and name among the poorer creoles. The two combine to create a large exclusive set, among whose members the

CREOLE TYPES.

ways French, and given in the old French Opera-house, which reminds New-Yorkers of the "Academy," in Fourteenth Street. The troupe that I saw was a complete one, with a double set of leading voices, with a *corps de ballet*, and a force of *bouffe* artists for the presentation of comic opera, which is given at regular intervals, and always on Sunday nights. Many of the chief performers were from the Grand Opéra of Paris.

The fashionable society of New Orleans is not in any sense a plutocracy. The wealth of those who have it is shared by or hidden from those who have it not. This is because the pride of birth and family,

exclusive set, among whose members the terrible ravages of the war spread a disaster that is privately understood and publicly ignored. Among the fashionables, the rich and the impoverished meet on a footing which the rich are at such pains to make equal that they are often plain in their entertainments in order that they may not hurt the sensitiveness or strain the resources of the others when it is their turn to open their houses. The men and women of this society maintain among themselves the purest, most wholesome, and honest conditions, unblemished by any hint of scandal, latitude of speech, or debatable behavior.

Again, while "society" here loves pleasure keenly, and, as we have seen, makes a business of some sorts of it, there is, nevertheless, an intellectual wing to it, with a liking for and an inclination to pursue art and literature. Several ladies, led, perhaps, by Mrs. Mollie Moore Davis, who has a marvellous gift for gathering bright folks about her in her quaint house in the French quarter, find it a pleasure to entertain and introduce such visitors as have interested them by their work. In the intervals between these gracious ministrations these ladies—with not a blue-stocking, but a host of beauties among them—entertain one another with well-written papers, wise debates, and music and recitations at meetings that only end with the fracture of a circle that has formed around a tempting display of refreshments.

Though a winter resort, New Orleans is pre-eminently a summer town—a city of galleried houses, of gardens, of flowers, and of shops which open wide upon

IN THE OLD FRENCH QUARTER.

the streets. It is hot there from June to November, and during those months the Americans who can afford to do so exchange it for the mountains and the forests. The wealthy among the creoles are apt to go to France, and there are many who divide the year thus, wintering in New Orleans and summering in Paris. Those who are obliged to stay insist that it is not dreadfully hot, and that there is almost always a breeze. They have no patent on that; we say the same thing in New York and Philadelphia and Boston and St. Louis. But I suspect New Orleans has a very debilitating air in summer. The most unobservant visitor can see one general proof of its heat in its architecture, whether it be of the new or the old, the creole or the American houses. I refer to the ubiquitous balconies — "galleries" they call them there. And for every gallery you see from the streets there is at least one in the back, on the courts and gardens. Thus the creoles, having the warm weather solely in view, are like the Italians at home, who stoop over their charcoal hand - stoves during the few days when it is very chilly, suffering a little time in order to enjoy the greater part

AN OLD COURT IN THE FRENCH QUARTER.

THE CLAIBORNE COTTAGES—A SUMMER RESORT OF NEW ORLEANS IN THE PINY WOODS.

of the year. I did not hear how they dress in summer, but when I rode through the Garden District — the new part of the town — my lady friends pointed to the galleries and said: "You should see them in the summer, before the people leave or after they come back. The entire population is out-of-doors in the air, and the galleries are loaded with women in soft colors, mainly white. They have white dresses by the dozen. They go about without their hats, in carriages and the street cars, visiting up and down the streets. In-doors one must spend one's whole time and energy in vibrating a fan." They have mosquitoes there, but they have also electric fans which mosquitoes eschew.

A WINDOW IN THE OLD FRENCH QUARTER.

The water supply of the city is from the Mississippi, which has had millions expended upon the improvement of its banks, but not a cent upon its water. It is not offered in the clubs or the general run of dwellings, but they do not hesitate to serve it in the two principal hotels.

In the clubs mineral water is freely set about on the dining-tables. This is attractive to the eye, but those who have not already made the discovery will find that effervescent waters are too thin and gaseous to satisfy thirst; in fact, nothing but honest water will do that. Therefore I drank a great deal of Mississippi water, and followed the local custom of dashing a pitcher of filtered fluid over me after each bath. The residents of the American quarter use it filtered. One of the strangest and most distinctive features of New Orleans is the presence of the collecting-tanks for rain-water in almost every door-yard. Rising above the palms, the rose-trellises, and the stately magnolias are these huge, hooped, green cylinders of wood. They suggest enormous watermelons on end and with the tops cut off. The creoles keep the rain-water cool in enormous jars of pottery sitting about in their pretty courts—such jars as Ali Baba had an adventure with, in which oil was once stored, and probably is now, in the Orient. They are from half to two-thirds the size of flour-barrels, symmetrical in shape, and come from the south of France. They are painted with some light fresh color, and prettily ornament the cool, paved, jalousied courts. Nine-tenths of the water used for cooking and drinking is this cistern water, and when the cisterns get low, as they do two or three times a year, there is actual suffering in the poor districts, back from the river. The river water was not filtered when I was there, but large filters were contracted for, and are by this time supplying an abundance of clear water.

I should think that the coolest place in New Orleans in summer must be the Boston Club. It suggests some club-houses that I have seen in the Cuban cities, but it is little like any other in this country.

the full title being "The Chess, Checkers, and Whist Club." The Harmony is the Jewish club, in essence, though it is not sectarian. The most modern house and most youthful club in membership and spirit is the Pickwick. Social activity centres there in quarters in which any Northern man would feel at home. Down

THE NEW ORLEANS YACHT CLUB.

It is white without and light and open within. An open porch on one side, hidden from the street, serves to cool the entire house in summer, and as a pleasant retreat for card-players and smokers all through the year. There are four notable clubs in New Orleans, and they stand near one another in a row upon Canal Street. The Boston is the oldest and choicest. It was organized in 1845, and was not named in honor of the Athens of America, but after a game at cards which was popular at the time. Another game furnished the Chess Club its title, though that is but a nickname,

on the ground-floor, in fact, before the men's quarters on the upper floors are reached, is a dining and reception room for ladies. This dining-room is the subject of by far the finest decorative work in the city, and is in what we in New York would call Stanford White's happiest mode. Here, after the opera or a country ride, or rout of any sort, the most brilliant beauties of the old and the new town may be seen in the softened light of electricity lunching with their cavaliers, while the usual club routine above goes on as if there were no women within a mile thereof.

READING A DEATH-NOTICE.

The best place to see the famed belles of New Orleans is in the French Opera-house on a fashionable night at the opera. Then there are scores there—blondes with limpid blue eyes, and complexions of roses and cream; brunettes of the purest types with rounding forms, great black orbs, hair of Japanese black, and skins of softest brown; Spanish creoles with true oval faces, long narrow eyes, the same soft sun-kissed complexions, with proud bearing, and mouths like Cupid's bow. With them are our American girls from all over the country, boasting the eclectic beauty of many blended nationalities. The place is like a great bouquet. They dress almost like Parisians, and that is one great secret of the splendid fame they have won.

To a great extent the creoles even now remain apart from the Americans, in pursuance of the spirit that led their ancestors never to cross Canal Street beyond their own old quarter, and even to riot when the shipping began to collect in front of the American half of the town. But there is more and more mixing of the races, and marriages between the two grow more and more frequent, so that it is

felt that another generation may break down all the false barricades between the peoples. As to the marriages, it is said to require a bold and indomitable man to court a creole, because when he calls upon her he finds the court and the parlor dark, and he waits while the servants light up the place for him. Then the parents come in, European fashion, and sit in the room while he "sparks" the ravisher of his heart. But all agree that when the end is come, and she is his bride, he is going to be envied among men, for there are no better wives or lovelier mothers than those dark-tressed, brown-skinned, graceful, soft-voiced creole women.

It gives a peculiar sensation to hear Cable abused by the creoles—and you never can hear anything but abuse of him. "George W. Cable and Benjamin Butler? Bah! Let them show themselves in New Orleans; that's all." This astonished me, though I had heard I was to expect it. It had seemed to me that they must in their hearts recognize the tenderness with which he deals with many of his heroes and heroines, the grace with which he clothes them, the soft light he turns upon most of them; and to-day I

believe that in their hearts they know
that he has done for them something of
what Longfellow did for the Acadians
in "Evangeline." Surely he it was who
lifted them to a sentimental and romantic
realm, out from their walled-in courts of
the French quarter. I still believe that
it is only a sense of mistaken self-respect
that causes them to fancy that they must
assail him, because they showed me many
of the places he described, and told me
with poorly hidden pride that much, ay,
most of what he describes is true. But
he was a New Orleans man, and should
not have betrayed his neighbors. Some
said "he was of the South, yet he writes
like an old-time abolitionist." And yet
these are not the true reasons for their
animosity, not the whole truth. I believe
I am right when I say that what really
wounds them most deeply is his
mocking their broken English.
As a writer, I have never been
so certain of hurting the feelings of others as when I imi-
tated their dialects, or mistakes
in grammar, or awkward efforts
to pronounce our words. It an-
gers every race, and the more
intelligent the race, the deeper
the sting and the anger. I am
the more sure this diagnosis of
the case in point is correct, because the manner in which he
makes his characters talk was
always bitterly alluded to, if at
all. "He puts negro words
into our mouths; he copies the
servants' talk, and puts it in
the mouths of the ladies and gentlemen."

The funeral notices tacked upon the
telegraph poles and awning posts interest
strangers. I have heard Northern men in
business in New Orleans speak in praise
of this method of publishing the deaths,
because, they say, these cards are read
when the newspaper funeral notices might
not be. I copied one or two, and will
reproduce them here, with the names
changed, of course:

JEANNE,

Fille de James Coudert et de Adèle Palm.

Les amis et connaissance des familles Coudert,
Palm, Rochefort, et Bellecamp sont priés d'assister à

ses funérailles, qui auront lieu Samedi, après-midi,
à 4 heures.
Le convoi partira de la résidence des parents, No.
2091 rue Plaisant, entre St. Jacque et Couronne.

And here is one in English:

BIRMINGHAM.

DIED,

Wednesday evening, March 2, 1892, at half past
six o'clock, R. L. BIRMINGHAM, aged forty-seven years.

The friends and acquaintances of the Birmingham, Smith, Robinson, and Decatur families are respectfully invited to attend the funeral, which will
take place this (Thursday) evening at half past four
o'clock from Trinity Church.

An eccentric gentleman, exercising the
inalienable privileges of freedom, makes

THE QUEER OLD CHURCH OF ST. ROCHE.

it his business to read all these placards,
and to tear down those that have served
their purpose, else no one can say what
would become of the poles and posts as
they accumulated. Another custom in
mortuary matters there is the publication
in the *Picayune* and *Times-Democrat* of
eulogistic references to the dead by way
of notifying the public of the sad occurrence. These obituary cards are quite as
peculiar in their own way as the rhyming
notices of Baltimore and Philadelphia.

Without turning far from the subject,
it may be said that (though I do not in any
degree favor the custom which leads our
citizens everywhere to insist upon driving
visitors to the cemeteries as first among the
"sights" of our cities) it is certain that
the cemeteries of New Orleans are worth
a visit. They are not only unlike any

ALONG THE SHELL ROAD.

white and gray from mounds of green, beside white shell roads, beneath orange-trees laden with golden fruit, magnolias, cedars, and oaks, some of the trees being draped or bearded with pendant moss.

Of course it is understood that the burials are aboveground because of the moisture in the soil. Yet I saw earthy graves in a shabby little cemetery in the city, where also weeping-willows lent a familiar aspect to the scene. This was at the yard of the chapel of St. Roche (pronounced "Roke"), by far the strangest place of worship I have seen—even in Canada or California. Standing up tall and shallow, like a little brick chapel whose front is all but hidden behind ivy. It has kneeling-benches but no pews, and under its altar is a recumbent life-size figure of the Saviour, unclad as He was lifted from the cross. But it is what is on the altar that is most novel. All about upon its shelves are lozenges of marble shaped like great visiting-cards. On them are carved such legends as "Thanks"; "Thanks, J. W.;" "Merci;" "Thanks, granted June 30, 1891." Hanging by ribbons on the same altar are wax casts of little baby hands, or hands and forearms, or tiny feet. One large pair of hands stands there in a glass case. All these are offerings of those for whose prayers such members have been rescued from disease or uselessness. A double score of candles burn on the altar, and as many men and women pray before it. The fourteen stations of the cross, seen in all Catholic churches, are here placed out-of-doors in little shelters of open-work wood, upon which vines creep and illuminate their foliage with blossoms. It would be difficult to find in

burial-yards known to the rest of the country, they are beautiful as well. The grounds are laid out much as are our own in the North, but the white shell roads and paths enhance the neat and tidy effect such places usually boast. They are truly "cities of the dead," for the tombs are houses built upon the ground, and provided with cubby-hole or drawerlike compartments, to be sealed with a marble slab as each coffin is put in place. The term "oven tombs" describes them well. I can easily believe that in no other cemeteries is seen such evidence of a great outlay of money, for these mausoleums are built of marble and granite, or, at the worst, of brick stuccoed to look like stone. Some are round-topped, but more are of the form of miniature Grecian temples. They exhibit statues, crowns, crosses, and even most elaborate panelling and carving. These buildings rise

New Orleans anything more picturesque than is seen when hopeful women are passing from one to another of these holy emblems, to kneel at each in prayer.

to be funny, but he is exceedingly so. He goes about hammering the virgins and saints on the figured tablets of the stations of the cross, and saying, " You see dot.

AT THE OLD FRENCH OPERA-HOUSE.

A very remarkable German is in charge of this sanctuary, and unconsciously relieves the tension upon those who are awed by the funereal and religious character of the premises. He does not mean

Dot vos pronze from Munich; chenuwine pronze." He bustles into the chapel, past all the kneeling supplicants, and talks about the things there—even the most sacred ones—like an auctioneer. He

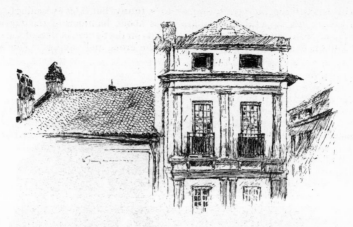

A BIT OF OLD ARCHITECTURE IN THE FRENCH QUARTER.

must not be harmed by my saying this, or offended, for he is certainly a zealous and dutiful man.

"Ach," he exclaimed to me, "I do vish dey vouldn't bury all der time. Efen on Sundays dey bury; all der whole vhile it goes on, und I can't get avay by myneself for a rest. In Chermany, vhere I used to been, ve took Sundays off, und tied from a bell alretty some strings to der big toe of each corpse. Sure, then, if der corpse gets alive und moves, der bell rings—eh? But here it is efery day de same—bury, bury, all der whiles. Vell, it don't matter, pecause vhen I do go avay to haf a gwiet glass of beer I get no beace. Everybody knows me, und everybody points me out und says, 'See! dot's der olt man from St. Roche's.'"

He wondered if he would ever be where

STREET RAILWAY OF NEW ORLEANS.

people would not point him out and tell one another who he was. Alas! it will not be in heaven, good old soul. Even those whose tongues are silent in the yard you watch will find voices there to tell the others who you are.

I have neither the space nor the inclination to describe the French market, the cathedral, the French quarter, and those other really charming bits of the city which have been the subjects of descriptive articles and letters since our grandfathers' days. I like them none the less, and they remain powerful magnets to draw future battalions of tourists there. These are parts of the thing we call the "foreign air" of the city, and I hope that with the manifest new energy of New Orleans they will not be "improved." I suppose it cannot be expected that people will ever understand the full value of the relics of their past. The bric-à-brac we treasure is always what some one else has parted with. Here in New Orleans, as up in Montreal, the people insist upon taking visitors to see the new part of each city, among the modern residences; and the visitors persist in hastening back to the old French quarters, always and every time.

St. Charles Avenue and the Garden District are almost semi-rural, like the best parts of "the Hill" in Brooklyn, or the outlying parts of our finer cities. The large galleried houses stand back in broad gardens, with the most beautiful surroundings of lawn, banana-plants, orange-trees, clouds of roses—especially of Cherokee roses, which bloom in clouds—magnolias, China berries, and hedges of many sorts. Trees of pretty shapes and lordly shade-giving quality stand in ranks along the streets, and the views down the cross-streets are bowery; often they are vistas under meeting branches. There are some rambling old Southern mansions with halls through the centres, some modern stately mansions, and some little boxes of the universal sort that coquet with the tiresome memory of good Queen Anne.

Those bashful men whose courage grows weak on the door-steps where they are about to make a call would never, I am sure, get into the average house in the Garden District if they did not know any more about New Orleans customs than I did when I paid my first visit there. They would find before them a door with a handle, and no other protuberance—button, knocker, pull, handle, or anything else. Much to the delight of several very young ladies on an opposite veranda (the thought of how much pleasure I was able to give them will long console me), I fell at last to knocking with my knuckles, like a mendicant at a window. By-and-by a maid let me in.

"Oh, was that you making that funny noise?" the mistress of the house inquired. "I've been listening to it for a long while, and could not imagine what it could be."

With what pride remained to me I modestly suggested that I could not ring a bell when there was none to ring, as spirits do in table-rappers' closets. I added that I would give five dollars to the local blind asylum if any one could show me a bell anywhere on or around the front door.

"Of course there isn't any," remarked the lady; "in New Orleans we put the bell on the post of the front gate."

How on earth—who could blame—but, as she remarked, that is where they hide the front-door bells in New Orleans.

Certainly a typical Chicago man would throw up his hands in horror at the lamentable backwardness of the city, at the absence of most of the newfangled means for making modern lives automatic and mechanical. We who seek change in travel, and who are rested where others rest, love New Orleans all the better for its so-called faults. The chief beast of burden is the mule, and they have the finest mules and the sorriest horses imaginable. The horse-cars—all of which

STREET IN THE OLD FRENCH QUARTER, FROM THE HÔTEL ROYAL.

start from and fetch up at the neighborhood of Canal and St. Charles streets—are little untidy boxes that creak and jolt and wabble along, with a pair of mule's ears flapping ahead like a yacht's jibs when she sails too close to the wind. The electric lights are mounted on tall towers of iron lattice-work, just as they were in Detroit the last time I was there, and as if the object of the people was to light the clouds rather than the city.

A NEW ORLEANS
POLICEMAN.

The milk-carts are worth going to see. They are little two-wheelers like our New York butcher carts, and each one has in front two gorgeous great cans bound with brass hoops that are as lustrous as jewelry. Women drive many of these carts, but when they are managed by men they dart madly about, and accidents to them are frequent. A lady friend of mine who once failed to receive the day's milk went to the door next day to dismiss the offender. She came back almost in tears, for he appeared to her with his face peeled and one arm in a sling. "Par-r-r-don me," he said; "ze 'ole business h'all tip ovaire on de street."

The hod-carriers tote the bricks on their heads, balancing heavy loads on cushions that fit upon their crowns. The dog-catchers go about snaring vagrant curs with slipnooses at the end of short sticks. Then they pitch the dogs into strange barrel-like wagons. Such a row as a New Orleans cur sets up when he feels himself jerked up by a hind leg ought to soften the hearts of the stones under their feet. It does bring the women out from the doors and windows of several blocks of houses. Men stand about selling alligators that they keep in baskets and cages, many of the beasts being too young to know that the proper thing for an alligator is to be sluggish and slow. In their ignorance they slap about and climb and snap with their jaws with the activity and malice of so many hornets. Women sell pralines and pecan candy, of which we know nothing until we go there, and "oyster loaves" (advertised as "family peace-makers: take one with you when you go home late") are among the queer edibles of the place. I desired to taste one for the peace of my curiosity, but I never found out where I could take or what I could do with a loaf of bread stuffed with cooked oysters. Men make jewelry in the streets by curling gold wire into the forms of the written names of women, and these are worn as breastpins. Such artificers know more than wiser men, for who would dream that women would care to display their given names and pet names to the public in shining letters? But the men were kept busy as long as I was there, and I saw a two-hundred-and-twenty-pound woman fasten the word "Birdie" to the throat of her dress and walk proudly away.

The law courts are in the ancient Spanish government building, and, in keeping with that still impressive pile, the officials barricade the street in front with a chain drawn across it, to preserve quiet during the proceedings. The police, who are few in number, for there is no hoodlum or "gang" element of ruffians in the city, are dressed, like our New York firemen, in caps and coats with silver buttons. The lottery being legalized, tickets are openly displayed in the shop windows, and are sold on the sidewalks by men, women, and children. One store for the sale of these tickets bears such a legend as this on its sign: "This is lucky Number Eleven. More winning tickets sold here than anywhere else in town."

There was a drawing while I was in the city, and knowing that the lottery company was not to ask for a renewal

BAKER'S CART.

of its privileges, and that its power and the scenes and customs growing out of it were soon to become mere memories, I availed myself of the opportunity to witness its chief public operation and the historic characters who have been induced by large salaries to figure for it. The drawing took place in a theatre called "the Academy of Music," at eleven o'clock in the morning. The yellow gas-jets battled feebly with the daylight in the lobby into which the people were pressing without let or qualification. The theatre was two-thirds full at last. On the stage, set with a parlor scene, was a knot of men between two wheels. The wheel on the right was a band of silver, with sides of glass and with a door in the metal rim. A bushel of little black gutta-percha envelopes the size of dominoes had been poured into this wheel, and a white boy, blindfolded with a handkerchief, stood at the handle of the crank by which the wheel was turned. He had one arm in the door of the wheel, and with the hand of the other arm was offering a tiny envelope to General Beauregard—the last surviving general who served on either side in our late war. A fine, most gentlemanly-looking man he is, with the features of a French courtier, with snowy hair, a white mustache, a little goatee, and the pinkest skin a baby ever knew. He was faultlessly dressed. Across the stage, beside a very much larger wheel of parti-colored boards, sat Major-General Jubal A. Early—a perfect type of the conventional figure of Father Time; tall, portly, stoop-shouldered, partly bald, and with a long, heavy white beard. He was dressed all in the color of the uniform he distinguished by his valor as a soldier. Alas, for human frailty! These two heroes are said to receive $30,000 apiece each year for their duties performed at the monthly public drawings of the lottery.

By each general stood a blindfolded boy, taking numbers out of the wheels and handing them to the generals. From the big wheel to Major-General Early came the numbers of the tickets; from the little wheel to General Beauregard came the numbers of dollars that formed the prize each ticket had won. By each general stood a crier. Early read out, "Twenty-one thousand one hundred and fifty-two"; and Beauregard, having shelled the gutta-percha case off a billet, read out,

"Two hundred dollars." Then the criers took the billets and cried the numbers, "Twenty-one thousand one hundred and fifty-two" from one; "Tew hundred dollars" from the other, who, by-the-way, called out tew hundred dollars at least tew hundred times. But all the prizes were not of that amount. I chanced to hear the capital prize read out.

VENDER OF LOTTERY TICKETS.

"Twenty-eight thousand four hundred and thirty-nine," said Early. "Three hundred thousand dollars," said Beauregard.

The effect was startling; indeed the startled senses refused to grasp the meaning of the words. The criers repeated the figures. The people in the theatre craned forward, a hundred pencils shot over pads or bits of paper in men's and women's laps. Then a murmur of voices sounded all over the house. The routine on the stage was halted, for the criers took the two bits of paper to some clerks, who sat at tables in the farther part of the stage, to allow them to verify the important figures. Then the routine began anew. The wheels were revolved every few min-

TYPES OF THE DAGO.

utes, and the rubber shells rattled around like coffee beans in a roasting-cylinder. The boys took off their bandages, and other boys were blindfolded and put in their places. The criers were relieved by others, and General Beauregard at last grew tired, and went out for half an hour. Among others came two criers who kept their hats on. Think of it! Their hats on, covered, in the presence of the God of

Chance! It was an offence against the unities; it was making light of the solemn mystery of luck. Every man who drew a blank that month owes those rowdies a kick. I wondered whether such a thing could have happened before the passage of the postal bill which took the cream off the business and the nerve out of the misguided men who had been pressing for a renewal of the lottery charter.

They have a stranger thing than the lottery in New Orleans, and that is the word "lagniappe." "Take that for a lagniappe" (pronounced lan-yap), says a storekeeper as he folds a pretty calendar into the bundle of stationery you have purchased. "What are you going to give me for a lagniappe?" a child asks after ordering five cents' worth of candy. A lagniappe means something thrown in, something extra, something more than is paid for; and lagniappes are looked for in New Orleans by servants and children especially. The merchants give something, if it is only a stick of candy or a shining trinket, and he who chooses such things wisely profits in an increased business. It is the thirteen of "a baker's dozen," the "this for good measure," which we are all more or less accustomed to. I read an unlikely story to account for it in one of the New Orleans

DAGOS AND THEIR BOATS.

papers, telling how a grocer kept a long ape that annoyed him by pilfering, and how, when a child came to complain that he had not given good measure to her mother when she had bought butter that day, he threw the ape at the child, saying, "Here, take lagniappe [long ape], and be off with you." I asked many of the more intelligent men of the town, but not one who could give me the derivation of the word, the custom itself being familiar as humanity, though seldom practised so generally in a large city.

The second-hand shops in New Orleans, taken together, equal a great museum. Strangers hang around them like moths near candle-lights, for in the city are many old families that are obliged to part with heirlooms one by one, or that cease to value them, and prefer newer things. Here, then, one may buy whole sets of solid Empire and Directoire furniture and furnishings—clocks, candle-glasses, china, cut glass, andirons, tongs, snuffers, four-post canopied bedsteads, and no one knows what all.

I find that in such a paper as this there is not room to do justice to half of what is noteworthy in New Orleans. I had hoped to tell of the picturesque Italians, their occupations, their fleet of luggers, and their standing in the community since "the Mafia affair." I meant to describe the charming resorts and the beauties of the piny-woods regions, the Bayou Teche country, and the shores of Lake Pontchartrain. The delicious cooking and notable dishes peculiar to the place were in my mind when I laid out this article, and—though I had meant to confine myself to what others had not dwelt strongly upon—the educational institutions, the promise of a strong art atmosphere, and even the notable athletic, gymnastic, and yachting clubs deserved description. The excellent sport with rod and gun afforded in the neighborhood of the city also interested me, but I must leave the field to others and turn to a study of the commercial interests of the enterprising city.

Over fifty per cent. of the active business men of the city are from the North and West, and the work of so-called reconstruction is partly in the hands of nature by means of intermarriage and partly left to business in the forming of commercial partnerships. I did not happen to meet a single "hostile" there. I met only one in the course of my entire journey

THE OLD AND THE NEW. SOUTH.

from St. Louis to Florida and home again. I sympathized with that one because she was an aristocratic old lady of nearly eighty years, who had been locked up in a jail for ten days for refusing to salute the soldiers who had seized her mansion for their headquarters. I was told in New Orleans that there are a few unreconstructed men there, but no one heeds them, and they are such only because in no other way than by startling and loud talking would they be able to attract attention to themselves. On the contrary, the warmest patriotism prevails, even among the wrecks and ruins of fortunes and of futures which have turned thousands of lives into the next thing to tragedies. Northern men are made welcome there, and so heartily that in one of the leading clubs heretofore sustained by the native leaders of the people two of the three members elected as the executive committee are men from the North.

It must be remembered that, in a great measure, the original business men of the city were Northerners and foreigners, the natives in ante-war days having been land-owners, planters, and clerks. Now, as I say, the Northern men are in the majority in trade. They tell me, what I heard everywhere in the South, that the prosperity of that most attractive section of our land will be permanently assured when cotton is grown only as a surplus crop or by-product. The planter will then be able to sell cotton for two cents a pound, but will be in a position to demand twelve cents.

New Orleans, from a commercial point of view, is new-born, or, at least, she is

ALONG THE LEVEE.

but newly recovering the relation to our great country of the present time which she bore to the smaller one of *ante-bellum* days. The constant dread of fever retarded her progress, or she might now have been one of the very great cities of the world. Now fourteen years have passed without a visit from yellow fever, and it has become evident not only that this dread disease is an exotic, but that the city is in other respects a safe and pleasant place of residence.

It has a fresh-water harbor, with a permanent twenty-six-foot channel, and solid, unchanging banks for buildings. Its inland waterways lead to the iron region of Pennsylvania, the lead mines of Missouri, and the copper region of Michigan. It is the seaport terminus of several great trunk railway lines and the supply depot for Texas, the Southwest, Mexico, and Central America. It commands 1500 miles of seaboard, and its

merchants assert that the internal waterways behind it, which are navigable or can be made so, reach 18,000 miles.

The building up of populations in Texas and the Southwest, a region that is growing like a bed of weeds, is helping New Orleans as its natural depot of supplies. Mexico, the Central American states, and the country along the Southern Pacific system to California, are but slightly less tributary to it. The inland water system terminating at New Orleans affects a region extending beyond Kansas City. Chicago, St. Paul, St. Louis, and other Western cities now import through New Orleans, which is thus put in direct competition with New York for the foreign business with our West. The actual traffic on the Mississippi River and its tributaries is relatively small, yet it establishes low freight rates by land and water, and the more the river is improved the cheaper will be the transportation of all bulky and non-perishable freights.

Business in New Orleans is on a very solid and conservative basis. With cotton grown at a loss there have been practically no failures, that is to say, there has been no increase of failures. The main trouble has been that the capital at hand has been insufficient for the development of industries. The capital, surplus, and deposits of the New Orleans banks is about $33,000,000, and this is relied upon for the handling of from two hundred to three hundred millions of dollars' worth of crops every year.

The importation of fruit through New Orleans is a very heavy interest. Only a few years ago the city was behind New York in the volume of its banana imports, and the receipts of other tropical fruits were small, but during the year ending in the spring of 1892 that city led all the rest in the banana business, beating New York by nearly 170,000 bunches. The trade is only ten years old, but now employs several lines of steamers, bringing from three to five cargoes a week.

During 1891, in addition to an enormous mass of cocoanuts and other fruits, 3,735,481 bunches of bananas were unladen there. The reasons for this development are obvious. The run from the fruit lands to New Orleans is a short one, and is made in vessels especially fitted for the trade. The climate of the city insures the fruit against cold that would be injurious to it during its transshipment to the cars, and these cars, built especially for the trade and run on express time, quickly distribute it among all the centres of population in the West. The direct importation of fruits from the Mediterranean shores is also growing into a considerable business, which owes its increase to the constantly multiplying number of vessels that come to New Orleans to get wheat, cotton, and other return cargoes. The swift steamers in the Central American fruit trade carry back American products, and this business is seen to be growing under our reciprocity treaties, which thus operate to give New Orleans a share of this trade, that, but for the fruit business, she never would have had.

The transshipment of wheat from cars and Mississippi barges to steamers for abroad is a tremendous industry that had grown up within a year of the time when I was there (March, 1892). It is a consequence of the immense crops, of the inability of the Atlantic coast ports to handle them, and of the fact that a large number of European vessels come to New Orleans, either with cargoes or in ballast, from other ports to which they have taken cargoes. The wheat reaches this port by way of the Illinois Central, Mississippi Valley, and Texas Pacific railroads, and by the Mississippi Barge Company. The Mississippi Valley Railroad Company has an elevator that is small, but handled three millions of bushels of wheat and corn between September, 1891, and April, 1892. Another and larger elevator and a line of transatlantic steamers were contracted for by this company at that time. The Texas Pacific road was, at the same period, building an elevator with 350,000 bushels capacity. The elevator capacity of the port has alone set a limit upon the volume of this business that can be got, and it is evident that the railroads do not mean to stand in their own way in this respect. The exportation of flour had also been very considerable within

the year which closed while I was there. This trade is due to our reciprocal tariff arrangements with Cuba and the South and Central American nations. As it is, the city does not yet include a flouring-mill, and that staple comes from Missouri and Kansas, always in bags, to meet the demand of the Latin countries. Flour, agricultural implements, beeves, mules, and horses are now articles of large export to those lands.

The manufacture of fertilizers is an important industry. Pebble phosphates from Florida are manufactured into marketable phosphate, but there are other fertilizer companies using potash, cotton-seed meal, and phosphate to make a product that is used on the cotton and sugar plantations. It is interesting to find that one staple of the South thus depends upon the other, for cotton-seed meal is extensively used to enrich the sugar lands. About 10,000 tons of this one product are taken off the land in one set of places to be put upon it in another. In all, 15,000 tons of fertilizers for the cotton, sugar, and

A RELIC OF THE "OLD" SOUTH.

rice plantations are annually made and sold in New Orleans. But at the same time that cotton thus helps sugar, it is in another way benefited, in turn, by sugar. The sugar is put up in sacks and bags made of cotton cloth. A very large business in cotton and burlap sacks has grown out of the sugar-refining in New Orleans. The Western people, among whom this sugar finds its consumers, prefer 100-pound sacks to barrels. The sacks are easier to handle, since they must be carried on the backs of mules and men, and then, again, the sacks are more useful after the sugar is used than barrels would be.

The refining of sugar is a notable industry in New Orleans. There are four refineries in and out of the great sugar combination, and all are kept running by night and by day. This product is made of Louisiana and West Indian crude sugar, and is marketed at home and in the West and Northwest. The business is increasing so rapidly as to lead serious men to predict that in time New Orleans will supply the entire country between the Rockies and the Mississippi.

A side industry of the Southern (cotton-seed) Oil Company is the fattening of two and three year old cattle from Texas on cotton-seed hulls and meal. This results in considerable shipments of cattle to Liverpool and to the stock-yards of the West, and is so simple and profitable an industry that in view of the quantity of such food which is obtainable, it would seem bound to grow. Cotton-seed oil-cake is a large item of the export busi-

CORNER OF BANK BUILDING.

ness. It goes to England, Scotland, and Germany, to be used in the feeding of cattle. New Orleans is the birthplace of the now great cotton-seed oil industry. It has five or six mills, some that are in the trust and some that are independent, and the seed is brought from Texas, Alabama, Mississippi, Arkansas, and the Mississippi Valley.

The cotton-pressing industry is extensive enough to have tempted English capital, which was offered for the control of it while I was there. It is one of the largest businesses and fields for labor in the city. The cotton is brought to town by rail and boat. It is then classed, graded, and stored, and when sold is reclassed, weighed, and compressed for shipment. The proportion of the cost of a bale of cotton which is paid for the New Orleans labor is so large as to amount to the lion's share, I was told. The unique position of the city as the point of export for the cotton crop is well understood, and I need not enlarge upon the subject. In 1891 there was handled at that port more cotton than was handled there in any year except 1860, the net receipts being 2,270,190 bales, exclusive of receipts from or *via* other seaboard cities.

New Orleans has two large cotton-mills, making brown goods, sheetings, shirtings, unbleached and colored goods, and hosiery and other yarns. One mill runs 45,000 spindles, and the other 16,000. The city also has a very large brewing interest, maintaining fourteen large breweries, and supplying not only the city and surrounding country, but a heavy demand from Central and South America.

Four large cigar and cigarette factories employ 2500 hands. The tobacco in use is obtained from Cuba, Mexico, and Sumatra, and from Connecticut, Florida, and Wisconsin. The cigars and cigarettes are sold largely in Texas and California, but find a strong market in Chicago, and, to a less extent, in New York and Philadelphia. One house turns out 36,000,000 of cigars a year, and the total output of all the factories is 54,000,000 cigars a year. One hundred and fifty millions of cigarettes are made there annually. The output of manufactured tobaccos is small.

No foreign ice now goes to New Orleans. The eight or ten large factories, run with the ammonia process, supply a great section of country around the Louisiana metropolis, going to the cities and small towns far out on the railroads. Mississippi River water, filtered, is that which is used. This making of artificial ice was begun ten or twelve years ago, but has greatly increased in the last half-dozen years. The people there used to pay $14 and $15 a ton for ice, but it is now sold for $5 or $6 a ton.

Another industry that has grown amazingly in the last three to five years is the manufacture of ready-made clothing. The city has an advantage over its competitors in being able to draw upon an extra-intelligent class of workers on these goods—the creoles and the more intelligent and industrious negroes. Many of these, especially the creoles, will not work in factories, but perform the labor at home, and do much better work for less money than can be obtained in the North. New Orleans supplies the South and Southwest, and is even beginning to ship clothing to the North.

All the rough rice raised in Louisiana is milled in New Orleans in twelve or fifteen mills. A trust has been organized there, and has taken in most of these establishments. The rice is of a high grade, and is sold all over the country. There is a small but swelling business in the making of boots and shoes. The fisheries employ 2000 men, the oyster business 3000 men, and the catching and canning of shrimps almost 1000 men. There are more than sixty firms handling Spanish moss, which is used in mattresses and upholstering work.

Olive oil is being made in New Orleans from the fruit of an olive orchard in Mississippi, eighty-four miles from the city. This is thought to be the beginning of a future industry of great extent. It is ten years since olives were first planted by the present experimenter, and he has found that the trees will bear all over southern Louisiana, and that frosts which will destroy oranges will not harm this fruit. This gentleman, one of the shrewdest business men in the city, now has 1500 trees, whose fruit he last season pressed into oil. The trees will bear in five years after they are planted. The fruit ripens in August and September, and the crop is thus ready for picking three to five months before olives are gathered in southern Europe. The fresh American oil will have that advantage over the European oil, besides the saving of freight and the customs tax. The American trees are seen to be prolific bearers, and the fruit is of a large size, and of a quality to compete with any in the world. This gentleman says that the soil of the entire Gulf coast from Florida to Texas is suitable for the cultivation of olives.

Louisiana exempts from license and taxation all establishments employing not less than five hands in the manufacture of textile fabrics, leather, shoes, harness, saddlery, hats, flour, machinery, fertilizers, and chemicals, furniture and all articles of wood, marble and stone, soap, stationery, ink and paper, boats, and chocolate.

They say in New Orleans that the mortality among the colored residents is so much greater than among the same proportion of whites that the published death-tables do not fairly represent the character of the city as a place of residence for the last-named race. I cut from the *Picayune* the death-table for the second week in March, 1892, and found that the deaths among the whites numbered 79, or 22.33 per 1000 per annum, while of negroes 66 died, or 49.55 per 1000 per annum. Of the causes, phthisis pulmonalis and pneumonia led the list.

The signal-service records yield this account of the temperature of the seasons:

Season.	Temperature—deg. Fahr.			Normal rainfall—inches.	Per cent. of sunshine.	Mean relative humidity—per cent.
	Normal mean.	Mean maximum.	Mean minimum.			
Winter	56	63	49	13.09	47	71
Spring	69	77	62	13.67	53	70
Summer	81	88	76	17.97	54	73
Autumn	70	76	62	11.94	58	72

GEORGE WASHINGTON

GEORGE WASHINGTON was cast for his career by a very scant and homely training. Augustine Washington, his father, lacked neither the will nor the means to set him handsomely afoot, with as good a schooling, both in books and in affairs, as was to be had; he would have done all that a liberal and provident man should do to advance his boy in the world had he lived to go with him through his youth. He owned land in four counties, more than five thousand acres all told, and lying upon both the rivers that refresh the fruitful Northern Neck, besides several plots of ground in the promising village of Fredericksburg, which lay opposite his lands upon the Rappahannock; and one-twelfth part of the stock of the Principio Iron Company, whose mines and furnaces in Maryland and Virginia yielded a better profit than any others in the two colonies. He had commanded a ship in his time, as so many of his neighbors had in that maritime province, carrying iron from the mines to England, and no doubt bringing convict laborers back upon his voyage home again. He himself raised the ore from the mines that lay upon his own land, close to the Potomac, and had it carried the easy six miles to the river. Matters were very well managed there, Colonel Byrd said, and no pains were spared to make the business profitable. Captain Washington had represented his home parish of Truro, too, in the House of Burgesses, where his athletic figure, his ruddy skin, and frank gray eyes must have made him as conspicuous as his constituents could have wished. He was a man of the world, every inch, generous, hardy, independent. He lived long enough, too, to see how stalwart and capable and of how noble a spirit his young son was to be, with how manly a bearing he was to carry himself in the world; and had loved him and made him his companion accordingly. But the end came for him before he could see the lad out of boyhood. He died April 12, 1743, when he was but forty-nine years of age, and before George was twelve; and in his will there was, of course, for George only a younger son's portion. The active gentleman had been twice married, and there were seven children to be provided for. Two sons of the first marriage survived. The bulk of the estate went, as Virginian custom dictated, to Lawrence, the eldest son. To Augustine, the second son, fell most of the rich lands in Westmoreland. George, the eldest born of the second marriage, left to the guardianship of his young mother, shared with the four younger children the residue of the estate. He was to inherit his father's farm upon the Rappahannock, to possess, and to cultivate if he would, when he should come of age; but for the rest his fortunes were to make. He must get such serviceable training as he could for a life of independent endeavor. The two older brothers had been sent to England to get their schooling and preparation for life, as their father before them had been to get his— Lawrence to make ready to take his father's place when the time should come; Augustine, it was at first planned, to fit himself for the law. George could now look for nothing of the kind. He must continue, as he had begun, to get such elementary and practical instruction as was to be had of schoolmasters in Virginia, and the young mother's care must stand him in the stead of a father's pilotage and oversight.

Fortunately Mary Washington was a wise and provident mother, a woman of too firm a character and too steadfast a courage to be dismayed by responsibility. She had seemed only a fair and beautiful girl when Augustine Washington married her, and there was a romantic story told of how that gallant Virginian sailor and gentleman had literally been thrown at her feet out of a carriage in the London streets by way of introduction,— where she, too, was a visiting stranger out of Virginia. But she had shown a singular capacity for business when the romantic days of courtship were over. Lawrence Washington, too, though but five-and-twenty when his father died and left him head of the family, proved himself such an elder brother as it could but better and elevate a boy to have. For all he was so young, he had seen something of the world, and had already made notable friends. He had not returned home out of England until he was turned of twenty-one, and he had been back scarcely a

twelvemonth before he was off again, to seek service in the war against Spain. The colonies had responded with an unwonted willingness and spirit to the home government's call for troops to go against the Spaniard in the West Indies in 1740; and Lawrence Washington had sought and obtained a commission as captain in the Virginian regiment which had volunteered for the duty. He had seen those terrible days at Cartagena, with Vernon's fleet and Wentworth's army, when the deadly heat and blighting damps of the tropics wrought a work of death which drove the English forth as no fire from the Spanish cannon could. He had been one of that devoted force which threw itself twelve hundred strong upon Fort San Lazaro, and came away beaten with six hundred only. He had seen the raw provincials out of the colonies carry themselves as gallantly as any veterans through all the fiery trial; had seen the storm and the valor, the vacillation and the blundering, and the shame of all the rash affair; and had come away the friend and admirer of the gallant Vernon, despite his headstrong folly and sad miscarriage. He had reached home again, late in the year 1742, only to see his father presently snatched away by a sudden illness, and to find himself become head of the family in his stead. All thought of further service away from home was dismissed. He accepted a commission as Major in the colonial militia, and an appointment as Adjutant-General of the military district in which his lands lay; but he meant that for the future his duties should be civil rather than military in the life he set himself to live, and turned very quietly to the business and the social duty of a proprietor amongst his neighbors in Fairfax County, upon the broad estates to which he gave the name Mount Vernon, in compliment to the brave sailor whose friend he had become in the far, unhappy South.

Marriage was, of course, his first step towards domestication, and the woman he chose brought him into new connections which suited both his tastes and his training. Three months after his father's death he married Anne Fairfax, daughter to William Fairfax, his neighbor. 'Twas William Fairfax's granduncle Thomas, third Lord Fairfax, who had in that revolutionary year 1646 summoned Colonel Henry Washington to give into his hands

THOMAS, SIXTH LORD FAIRFAX.
Drawn by J. W. Alexander from the painting in the possession of the Alexandria Washington Lodge, No. 22, F. A. M.

the city of Worcester, and who had got so sharp an answer from the King's stout soldier. But the Fairfaxes had soon enough turned royalists again when they saw whither the Parliament men would carry them. A hundred healing years had gone by since those unhappy days when the nation was arrayed against the King. Anne Fairfax brought no alien tradition to the household of her young husband. Her father had served the King, as her lover had—with more hard-

ship than reward, as behooved a soldier— in Spain and in the Bahamas; and was now, when turned of fifty, agent here in Virginia to his cousin Thomas, sixth Baron Fairfax, in the management of his great estates, lying upon the Northern Neck and in the fruitful valleys beyond. William Fairfax had been but nine years in the colony, but he was already a Virginian like his neighbors, and, as collector of his Majesty's customs for the South Potomac and President of the King's

Council, no small figure in their affairs— a man who had seen the world and knew how to bear himself in this part of it.

In 1746 Thomas, Lord Fairfax, himself came to Virginia—a man strayed out of the world of fashion at fifty-five into the forests of a wild frontier. The better part of his ancestral estates in Yorkshire had been sold to satisfy the creditors of his spendthrift father. These untilled stretches of land in the Old Dominion were now become the chief part of his patrimony. 'Twas said, too, that he had suffered a cruel misadventure in love at the hands of a fair jilt in London, and so had become the austere, eccentric bachelor he showed himself to be in the free and quiet colony. A man of taste and culture, he had written with Addison and Steele for the *Spectator;* a man of the world, he had acquired, for all his reserve, that easy touch and intimate mastery in dealing with men which come with the long practice of such men of fashion as are also men of sense. He brought with him to Virginia, though past fifty, the fresh vigor of a young man, eager for the free pioneer life of such a province. He tarried but two years with his cousin, where the colony had settled to an ordered way of living. Then he built himself a roomy lodge, shadowed by spreading piazzas, and fitted with such simple appointments as sufficed for comfort at the depths of the forest, close upon seventy miles away, within the valley of the Shenandoah, where a hardy frontier people had but begun to gather. The great manor-house he had meant to build was never begun. The plain comforts of "Greenway Court" satisfied him more and more easily as the years passed, and the habits of a simple life grew increasingly pleasant and familiar, till thirty years and more had slipped away and he was dead, at ninety-one—broken-hearted, men said, because the King's government had fallen upon final defeat and was done with in America.

It was in the company of these men, and of those who naturally gathered about them in that hospitable country, that George Washington was bred. "A stranger had no more to do," says Beverley, "but to inquire upon the road where any gentleman or good housekeeper lived, and there he might depend upon being received with hospitality;" and 'twas certain many besides strangers would seek out the young Major at Mount Vernon, whom his neighbors had hastened to make their representative in the House of Burgesses, and the old soldier of the soldierly house of Fairfax, who was President of the King's Council, and so next to the Governor himself. A boy who was much at Mount Vernon and at Mr. Fairfax's seat, Belvoir, might expect to see not a little that was worth seeing of the life of the colony. George was kept at school until he was close upon sixteen; but there was ample vacation time for visiting. Mrs. Washington did not keep him at her apron strings. He even lived, when it was necessary, with his brother Augustine, at the old home on Bridges Creek, in order to be near the best school that was accessible, while the mother was far away on the farm that lay upon the Rappahannock. Mrs. Washington saw to it, nevertheless, that she should not lose sight of him altogether. When he was fourteen it was proposed that he should be sent to sea, as so many lads were, no doubt, from that maritime province; but the prudent mother preferred he should not leave Virginia, and the schooling went on as before—the schooling of books and manly sports. Every lad learned to ride—to ride colt or horse, regardless of training, gait, or temper—in that country, where no one went afoot except to catch his mount in the pasture. Every lad, black or white, bond or free, knew where to find and how to take the roving game in the forests. And young Washington, robust boy that he was, not to be daunted while that strong spirit sat in him which he got from his father and mother alike, took his apprenticeship on horseback and in the tangled woods with characteristic zest and ardor.

He was, above all things else, a capable executive boy. He loved mastery, and he relished acquiring the most effective means of mastery in all practical affairs. His very exercise books used at school gave proof of it. They were filled, not only with the rules, formulæ, diagrams, and exercises of surveying, which he was taking special pains to learn, at the advice of his friends, but also with careful copies of legal and mercantile papers, bills of exchange, bills of sale, bonds, indentures, land warrants, leases, deeds, and wills, as if he meant to be a lawyer's or a merchant's clerk. It would seem that, passionate and full of warm blood as he was, he conned these things as he studied the use and structure of his fowling-piece, the bridle he used for his colts, his saddle-girth, and the best ways of mounting. He copied these forms of business as he might have copied Bev-

not yet quite sixteen, George quit his formal schooling, and presently joined his brother Lawrence at Mount Vernon, to seek counsel and companionship. Lawrence had conceived a strong affection for his manly younger brother. Himself a man of spirit and honor, he had a high-

MOUNT VERNON AT THE PRESENT DAY.

erley's account of the way fox or 'possum or beaver was to be taken or the wild turkey trapped. The men he most admired, his elder brothers, Mr. Fairfax, and the gentlemen planters who were so much at their houses, were most of them sound men of business, who valued good surveying as much as they admired good horsemanship and skill in sport. They were their own merchants, and looked upon forms of business paper as quite as useful as ploughs and hogsheads. Careful exercise in such matters might well enough accompany practice in the equally formal minuet in Virginia. And so this boy learned to show in almost everything he did the careful precision of the perfect marksman.

In the autumn of 1747, when he was

hearted man's liking for all that he saw that was indomitable and well purposed in the lad, a generous man's tenderness in looking to the development of this thoroughbred boy, and he took him into his confidence as if he had been his own son. Not only upon his vacations now, but almost when he would, and as if he were already himself a man with the rest, he could live in the comradeship that obtained at Belvoir and Mount Vernon. Men of all sorts, it seemed, took pleasure in his company. Lads could be the companions of men in Virginia. Her outdoor life of journeyings, sport, adventure, put them as it were upon equal terms with their elders, where spirit, audacity, invention, prudence, manliness, resource, told for success and comradeship. Young men and old can be companions in arms, in sport, in woodcraft, and on the trail of the fox. 'Twas not an in-door life of conference, but an out-door life of affairs in this rural colony. One man, indeed, gave at least a touch of another quality to the life Washington saw. This was Lord Fairfax, who had been almost two years in Virginia when the boy quit school, and who was now determined, as soon as might be, to take up his residence at his forest lodge within the Blue Ridge. George greatly struck his lordship's fancy, as he did that of all capable men, as a daring lad in the hunt and a sober lad in counsel; and drawn into such companionship, he learned a great deal that no one else in Virginia could have taught him so well—the scrupulous deportment of a high-bred and honorable man of the world; the use of books by those who preferred affairs; the way in which strength may be rendered gracious, and independence made generous. A touch of Old World address was to be learned at Belvoir.

His association with Lord Fairfax, moreover, put him in the way of making his first earnings as a surveyor. Fairfax had not come to America merely to get away from the world of fashion in London and bury himself in the wilderness. His chief motive was one which did him much more credit, and bespoke him a man and a true colonist. It was his purpose, he declared, to open up, settle, and cultivate the vast tracts of beautiful and fertile land he had inherited in Virginia, and he proved his sincerity by immediately setting about the business. It was necessary as a first step that he should have surveys made, in order that he might know how his lands lay, how bounded and disposed through the glades and upon the streams of the untrodden forests; and in young Washington he had a surveyor ready to his hand. The lad was but sixteen, indeed; was largely self-taught in surveying; and had had no business yet that made test of his quality. But surveyors were scarce, and boys were not tender at sixteen in that robust, out-of-door colony. Fairfax had an eye for capacity. He knew the athletic boy to be a fearless woodsman, with that odd calm judgment looking forth at his steady gray eyes; perceived how seriously he took himself in all that he did, and how thorough he was at succeeding; and had

no doubt he could run his lines through the thicketed forests as well as any man. At any rate, he commissioned him to undertake the task, and was not disappointed in the way he performed it. Within a very few weeks Washington conclusively showed his capacity. In March, 1748, with George Fairfax, William Fairfax's son, for company, he rode forth with his little band of assistants through the mountains to the wild country where his work lay, and within the month almost he was back again, with maps and figures which showed his lordship very clearly what lands he had upon the sparkling Shenandoah and the swollen upper waters of the Potomac. 'Twas all he wanted before making his home where his estate lay in the wilderness. Before the year was out he had established himself at Greenway Court; huntsmen and tenants and guests had found their way thither, and life was fairly begun upon the rough rural barony.

It had been wild and even perilous work for the young surveyor, but just out of school, to go in the wet springtime into that wilderness, when the rivers were swollen and ugly with the rains and melting snows from off the mountains, where there was scarcely a lodging to be had except in the stray comfortless cabins of the scattered settlers, or on the ground about a fire in the open woods, and where a woodman's wits were needed to come even tolerably off. But there was a strong relish in such an experience for Washington, which did not wear off with the novelty of it. There is an unmistakable note of boyish satisfaction in the tone in which he speaks of it. "Since you received my letter in October last," he writes to a young comrade, "I have not sleep'd above three nights or four in a bed, but, after walking a good deal all the day, I lay down before the fire upon a little hay, straw, fodder, or bear-skin, whichever is to be had, with man, wife, and children, like a parcel of dogs and cats; and happy is he who gets the berth nearest the fire.... I have never had my clothes off, but lay and sleep in them, except the few nights I have lay'n in Frederick Town." For three years he kept steadily at the trying business, without loss either of health or courage, now deep in the forests laboriously laying off the rich bottom lands and swelling hillsides of that wild but goodly country be-

THE POTOMAC FROM MOUNT VERNON.

tween the mountains, now at Greenway Court with his lordship, intent upon the busy life there,—following the hounds, consorting with huntsmen and Indians and traders, waiting upon the ladies who now and again visited the lodge; when other occupations failed, reading up and down in his lordship's copy of the *Spectator*, or in the historians who told the great English story. His first success in surveying brought him abundant employment in the valley. Settlers were steadily making their way thither, who must needs have their holdings clearly bounded and defined. Upon his lordship's recommendation and his own showing of what he knew and could do, he obtained appointment at the hands of the President and Master of William and Mary, the colony's careful agent in that matter, as official surveyor for Culpeper County, "took the usual oaths to his Majesty's person and government," and so got for his work the privilege of authoritative public record.

Competent surveyors were much in demand, and, when once he had been officially accredited in his profession, Washington had as much to do both upon new lands and old as even a young man's energy and liking for an independent income could reasonably demand. His home he made with his brother at Mount Vernon, where he was always so welcome; and he was as often as possible with his mother at her place upon the Rappahannock, to lend the efficient lady such assistance as she needed in the business of the estate she held for herself and her children. At odd intervals he studied tactics, practised the manual of arms, or took a turn at the broadsword with the old soldiers who so easily found excuses for visiting Major Washington at Mount Vernon. But, except when winter weather forbade him the fields, he was abroad, far and near, busy with his surveying, and incidentally making trial of his neighbors up and down all the country-side round about, as his errands threw their open doors in his way. His pleasant bearing and his quiet satisfaction at being busy, his manly efficient ways, his evident self-respect, and his frank enjoyment of life, the engaging mixture in him of man and boy, must have become

LAWRENCE WASHINGTON.
From a portrait, by an unknown artist, in the possession of Lawrence Washington, Alexandria, Virginia.

familiar to everybody worth knowing throughout all the Northern Neck.

But three years put a term to his surveying. In 1751 he was called imperatively off, and had the whole course of his life changed, by the illness of his brother. Lawrence Washington had never been robust; those long months spent at the heart of the fiery South with Vernon's fever-stricken fleet had touched his sensitive constitution to the quick, and at last

a fatal consumption fastened upon him. Neither a trip to England nor the waters of the warm springs at home brought him recuperation, and in the autumn of 1751 his physician ordered him to the Bahamas for the winter. George, whom he so loved and trusted, went with him, to nurse and cheer him. But even the gentle sea air of the islands wrought no cure of the stubborn malady. The sterling, gifted, lovable gentleman, who had made his quiet seat at Mount Vernon the home of so much that was honorable and of good report, came back the next summer to die in his prime, at thirty-four. George found himself named executor in his brother's will, and looked to of a sudden to guard all the interests of the young widow and her little daughter in the management of a large estate. That trip to the Bahamas had been his last outing as a boy. He had enjoyed the novel journey with a very keen and natural relish while it promised his brother health. The radiant air of those summer isles had touched him with a new pleasure, and the cordial hospitality of the homesick colonists had added the satisfaction of a good welcome. He had braved the small-pox in one household with true Virginian punctilio rather than refuse an invitation to dinner, had taken the infection, and had come home at last bearing some permanent marks of a three weeks' sharp illness upon him. But he had had entertainment enough to strike the balance handsomely against such inconveniences, had borne whatever came in his way very cheerily, with that wholesome strength of mind which made older men like him, and would have come off remembering nothing but the pleasure of the trip had his noble brother only found his health again. As it was, Lawrence's death put a final term to his youth. Five other executors were named in the will; but George, as it turned out, was to be looked to to carry the burden of administration, and give full proof of the qualities that had made his brother trust him with so generous a confidence.

His brother's death, in truth, changed everything for him. He seemed of a sudden to stand as Lawrence's representative. Before they set out for the Bahamas Lawrence had transferred to him his place in the militia, obtaining for him, though he was but nineteen, a commission as Major and District Adjutant in his stead; and after his return, in 1752, Lieutenant-Governor Dinwiddie, the crown's new representative in Virginia, added still further to his responsibilities as a soldier by reducing the military districts of the colony to four, and assigning to him one of the four, under a renewed commission as Major and Adjutant-General. His brother's will not only named him an executor, but also made him residuary legatee of the estate of Mount Vernon in case his child should die. He had to look to the discipline and accoutrement of the militia of eleven counties, aid his mother in her business, administer his brother's estate, and assume on all hands the duties and responsibilities of a man of affairs when he was but just turned of twenty.

The action of the colonial government in compacting the organization and discipline of the militia by reducing the number of military districts was significant of a sinister change in the posture of affairs beyond the borders. The movements of the French in the West had of late become more ominous than ever; 'twas possible the Virginian militia might any day see an end of that "everlasting peace" which good Mr. Beverley had smiled to see them complacently enjoy, and that the young Major, who was now Adjutant-General of the northern division, might find duties abroad even more serious and responsible than his duties at home. Whoever should be commissioned to meet and deal with the French upon the western rivers would have to handle truly critical affairs, decisive of the fate of the continent, and it looked as if Virginia must undertake the fateful business. The northern borders, indeed, were sadly harried by the savage allies of the French; the brunt of the fighting hitherto had fallen upon the hardy militiamen of Massachusetts and Connecticut, in the slow contest for English mastery upon the continent. But there was really nothing to be decided in that quarter. The French were not likely to attempt the mad task of driving out the thickly set English population, already established, hundreds of thousands strong, upon the eastern coasts. Their true lines of conquest ran within. Their strength lay in their command of the great watercourses which flanked the English colonies both north and west. 'Twas a long frontier to hold, that mazy line of lake and river that ran all the way from the Gulf of St. Lawrence to the wide mouths of the sluggish Mississippi. Throughout all the posts and settlements that lay upon it from end to end there were scarcely eighty thousand Frenchmen, while the English teemed upon the coasts more than a million strong. But the forces of New France could be handled like an army, while the English swarmed slowly westward without discipline or direction, the headstrong subjects of a distant government they would not obey, the wayward constituents of a score of petty and jealous assemblies, tardy at planning, clumsy at executing plans. They were still far away, too, from the mid-waters of the lakes and from the royal stream of the Mississippi itself, where lonely boats floated slowly down, with their cargoes of grain, meat, tallow, tobacco, oil, hides, and lead, out of the country of the Illinois, past the long thin line of tiny isolated posts, to the growing village at New Orleans and the southern Gulf. But they were to be feared, none the less. If their tide once flowed in, the French well knew it could not be turned back again. It was not far away from the Ohio now; and if once settlers out of Pennsylvania and Virginia gained a foothold in any numbers on that river, they would control one of the great highways that led to the main basins of the continent. It was imperative they should be effectually forestalled, and that at once.

The Marquis Duquesne, with his quick soldier blood, at last took the decisive step for France. He had hardly come to his colony, to serve his royal master as Governor upon the St. Lawrence, when he determined to occupy the upper waters of the Ohio, and block the western passes against the English with a line of military posts. The matter did not seem urgent to the doubting ministers at Versailles. "Be on your guard against new undertakings," said official letters out of France; "private interests are generally at the bottom of them." But Duquesne knew that it was no mere private interest of fur-trader or speculator that was at stake now. The rivalry between the two nations had gone too far to make it possible to draw back. Military posts had already been established by the bold energy of the French at Niagara, the key to the western lakes, and at Crown Point upon Champlain, where lake and river struck straight towards the heart of the English trading settlements upon the Hudson. The English, accepting the challenge, had planted themselves at Oswego, upon the very lake route itself, and had made a port there to take the furs that came out of the West, and though very sluggish in the business, showed purpose of aggressive movement everywhere that advantage offered. English settlers by the hundred were pressing towards the western mountains in Penn-

sylvania, and down into that "Virginian Arcady," the sweet valley of the Shenandoah; thrifty Germans, a few; hardy Scots-Irish, a great many,—the blood most to be feared and checked. It was said that quite three hundred English traders passed the mountains every year into the region of the Ohio. Enterprising gentlemen in Virginia—Lawrence and Augustine Washington among the rest—had joined influential partners in London in the formation of an Ohio Company for the settlement of the western country and the absorption of the western trade; had sent out men who knew the region to make interest with the Indians and fix upon points of vantage for trading-posts and settlements; had already set out upon its business by erecting storehouses at Will's Creek, in the heart of the Alleghanies, and, further westward still, upon Redstone Creek, a branch of the Monongahela itself.

It was high time to act; and Duquesne, having no colonial assembly to hamper him, acted very promptly. When spring came, 1753, he sent fifteen hundred men into Lake Erie, to Presque Isle, where a fort of squared logs was built, and a road cut through the forests to a little river whose waters, when at the flood, would carry boats direct to the Alleghany and the great waterway of the Ohio itself. An English lieutenant at Oswego had descried the multitudinous fleet of canoes upon Ontario carrying this levy to its place of landing in the lake beyond, and a vagrant Frenchman had told him plainly what it was. It was an army of six thousand men, he boasted, going to the Ohio, "to cause all the English to quit those parts." It was plain to every English Governor in the colonies who had his eyes open that the French would not stop with planting a fort upon an obscure branch of the Alleghany, but that they would indeed press forward to take possession of the Ohio, drive every English trader forth, draw all the native tribes to their interest by force or favor, and close alike the western lands and the western trade in very earnest against all the King's subjects.

Governor Dinwiddie was among the first to see the danger and the need for action, as, in truth, was very natural. In office and out, his study had been the colonial trade, and he had been merchant and official now a long time. He was

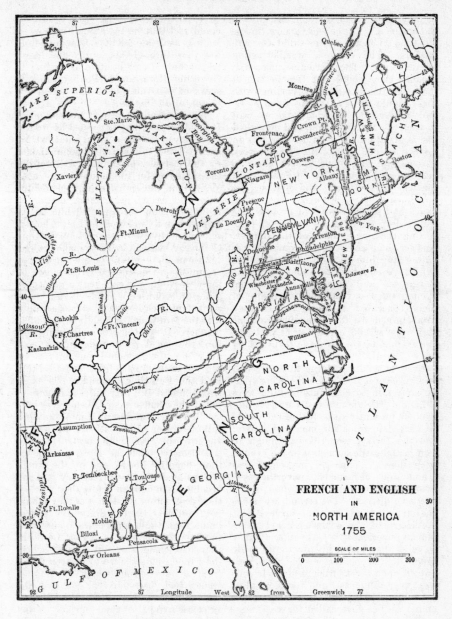

FRENCH AND ENGLISH
IN
NORTH AMERICA
1755

SCALE OF MILES
0   100   200   300

one of the twenty stockholders of the Ohio Company, and had come to his governorship in Virginia with his eye upon the western country. He had but to look about him to perceive that Virginia would very likely be obliged to meet the crisis unaided, if, indeed, he could induce even her to meet it. Governor Hamilton of Pennsylvania also saw how critically affairs stood, it is true, and what ought to be done. His agents had met and acted with the agents of the Ohio Company already in seeking Indian alliances and fixing upon points of vantage beyond the Alleghanies. But the Pennsylvania Assembly could by no argument or device be induced to vote money or measures in the business. The placid Quaker traders were as stubborn as the stolid German farmers. They opposed warlike action on principle. The Germans opposed it because they could not for the life of them see the necessity of parting with their money to send troops upon so remote an errand. Dinwiddie did not wait or parley. He acted first, and consulted his Legislature afterwards. In was in his Scots blood to take the business very strenuously, and in his trader's blood to take it very anxiously. He had kept himself advised from the first of the movements of the French. Their vanguard had scarcely reached Presque Isle ere he despatched letters to England apprising the government of the danger. Answer had come very promptly, too, authorizing him to build forts upon the Ohio, if he could get the money from the Burgesses; and meantime, should the French trespass further, "to require of them peaceably to depart." If they would not desist for a warning, said his Majesty, "we do hereby strictly charge and command you to drive them off by force of arms."

Even to send a warning to the French was no easy matter when the King's letter came, and the chill autumn rains were at hand. The mountain streams, already swollen, presently to be full of ice, would be very dangerous for men and horses, and the forests were likely enough to teem with hostile savages now the French were there. A proper messenger was found and despatched, nevertheless— young Major George Washington, of the northern district. The errand lay in his quarter; his three years of surveying at the heart of the wilderness had made him an experienced woodsman and hardy traveller, had tested his pluck and made proof of his character; he was well known upon the frontier, and his friends were very influential, and very cordial in recommending him for this or any other manly service that called for steadiness, hardihood, and resource. Dinwiddie had been a correspondent of Lawrence Washington's ever since the presidency of the Ohio Company had fallen to the young Virginian upon the death of his neighbor Thomas Lee, writing to him upon terms of intimacy. He knew the stock of which George, the younger brother, came, and the interests in which he might

be expected to embark with ardor; he could feel that he took small risk in selecting such an agent. Knowing him, too, thus through his family and like a friend, he did not hesitate in writing to Governor Hamilton of Pennsylvania to speak of this youth of twenty-one as "a person of distinction."

Washington performed his errand as Dinwiddie must have expected he would. He received his commission and the Governor's letter to the French commandant on the last day of October, and set out the same day for the mountains. Jacob Vanbraam, the Dutch soldier of fortune who had been his fencing-master at Mount Vernon, accompanied him as interpreter, and Christopher Gist, the hardy, self-reliant frontier trader, whom the Ohio Company had employed to make interest for them among the Indians of the far region upon the western rivers which he knew so well, was engaged to act as his guide and counsellor; and with a few servants and pack-horses he struck straight into the forests in the middle of bleak November. It was the 11th of December before the jaded party rode, in the cold dusk, into the drenched and miry clearing where the dreary little fort stood that held the French commander. Through two hundred and fifty miles and more of forest they had dragged themselves over swollen rivers, amidst an almost ceaseless fall of rain or snow, with not always an Indian trail, even, or the beaten track of the bison, to open the forest growth for their flagging horses, and on the watch always against savage treachery. It had become plain enough before they reached their destination what answer they should get from the French. Sixty miles nearer home than these lonely headquarters of the French commander at Fort Le Boeuf they had come upon an outpost where the French colors were to be seen flying from a house from which an English trader had been driven out, and the French officers there had uttered brutally frank avowal of their purpose in that wilderness as they sat at wine with the alert and temperate young Virginian. "It was their absolute design," they said, "to take possession of the Ohio, and, by G—, they would do it. . . . They were sensible the English could raise two men for their one, yet they knew their motions were too slow and dilatory to prevent any undertaking of theirs." The commandant at Fort Le Boeuf received the wayworn ambassador very courteously, and even graciously—a thoughtful elderly man, Washington noted him, "with much the air of a soldier"—but would make no profession even that he would consider the English summons to withdraw; and the little party of Englishmen presently turned back amidst the winter's storms to carry through the frozen wilderness a letter which boasted the French lawful masters of all the continent beyond the Alleghanies. When Washington reached Williamsburg, in the middle of January, 1754, untouched by even the fearful fatigues and anxieties of that daring journey, he had accomplished nothing but the establishment of his own character in the eyes of the men who were to meet the crisis now at hand. He had been at infinite pains at every stage of the dreary adventure to win and hold the confidence of the Indians who were accounted friends of the English, and had displayed an older man's patience, address, and fortitude in meeting all their subtile shifts; and he had borne hardships that tried even the doughty Gist. When the horses gave out, he had left them to come by easier stages, while he made his way afoot with only a single companion across the weary leagues that lay upon his homeward way. Gist, his comrade in the hazard, had been solicitously "unwilling he should undertake such a travel, who had never been used to walking before this time," but the imperative young commander would not be stayed, and the journey was made, spite of sore feet and frosts and exhausting weariness. He at least knew what the French were about, with what strongholds and forces, and could afford to await orders what to do next.

Dinwiddie had not been idle while Washington went his perilous errand. He had gotten the Burgesses together by the first of November, before Washington had left the back settlements to cross the wilderness, and would have gotten a liberal grant of money from them had they not fallen in their debates upon the question of the new fee charged since his coming for every grant out of the public lands of the colony, and insisted that it should be done away with. "Subjects," they said, very stubbornly, "cannot be deprived of the least part of their property without their consent;" and such a fee, they thought, was too like a tax to be endured. They would withhold the grant, they declared, unless the fee was abolished, notwithstanding they saw plainly enough in how critical a case things stood in the West; and the testy Governor very indignantly sent them home again. He ordered a draft of two hundred men from the militia, nevertheless, with the purpose of assigning the command to Washington, and seeing what might be done upon the Ohio without vote of assembly. A hard-headed Scotsman past sixty could not be expected to wait upon a body of wrangling and factious provincials for leave to perform his duty in a crisis, and inasmuch as the object was to save their own lands, and perhaps their own persons, from the French, could hardly be blamed for proposing in his anger that they be taxed for the purpose by act of Parliament. "A Governor," he exclaimed, "is really to be pitied in the discharge of his duty to his King and country in having to do with such obstinate, self-conceited people!" Some money he advanced out of his own pocket. When Washington came back from his fruitless mission, Dinwiddie ordered his journal printed and copies sent to all the colonial Governors. "As it was thought advisable by his Honour the Governor to have the following account of my proceedings to and from the French on Ohio committed to print," said the modest young Major, "I think I can do no less than apologize, in some measure, for the numberless imperfections of it." But it was a very manly recital of noteworthy things, and touched the imagination and fears of every thoughtful man who read it quite as near the quick as the urgent and repeated letters of the troubled Dinwiddie.

Virginia, it turned out, was, after all, more forward than her neighbors when it came to action. The Pennsylvania Assembly very coolly declared they doubted his Majesty's claim to the lands on the Ohio, and the Assembly in New York followed suit. "It appears," they said, in high judicial tone, "that the French have built a fort at a place called French Creek, at a considerable distance from the river Ohio, which may, but does not by any evidence or information appear to us to be an invasion of any of his Majesty's colonies." The Governors of the other colonies whose safety was most directly menaced by the movements of the French in the West were thus even less able to act than Dinwiddie. For the Virginian Burgesses, though they would not yield the point of the fee upon land grants, did not mean to leave Major Washington in the lurch, and before an expedition could be got afoot had come together again to vote a sum of money. It would be possible with the sum they appropriated to put three or four hundred men into the field; and as spring drew on, raw volunteers began to gather in some numbers at Alexandria,—a ragged regiment, made up for the most part of idle and shiftless men who did not always have shoes, or even shirts, of their own to wear; anxious to get their eightpence a day, but not anxious to work or submit to discipline. 'Twas astonishing how steady and how spirited they showed themselves when once they had shaken their lethargy off and were on the march or face to face with the enemy. A body of backwoodsmen had been hurried forward in February, ere spring had opened, to make a clearing and set to work upon a fort at the forks of the Ohio; but it was the 2d of April before men enough could be collected at Alexandria to begin the main movement towards the frontier, and by that time it was too late to checkmate the French. The little force sent forward to begin fortifications had set about their task very sluggishly and without skill, and their commander had turned back again with some of his men to rejoin the forces behind him before the petty works he should have staid to finish were well begun. When, therefore, on the 17th of April, the river suddenly filled with canoes bearing an army of more than five hundred Frenchmen, who put cannon ashore, and summoned the forty men who held the place to surrender or be blown into the water, there was no choice but to comply. The young ensign who commanded the little garrison urged a truce till he could communicate with his superiors, but the French commander would brook no delay. The boy might either take his men off free and unhurt, or else fight and face sheer destruction; and the nearest succor was a little force of one hundred and fifty men under Colonel Washington, who had not yet topped the Alleghanies in their painful work of cutting a way through the forests for their field-pieces and wagons.

The Governor's plans had been altered by the Assembly's vote of money and the additional levy of men which it made possible. Colonel Joshua Fry, whom Dinwiddie deemed "a man of good sense, and one of our best mathematicians," had been given the command in chief, and Washington had been named his second in command, with the rank of Lieutenant-Colonel. "Dear George," wrote Mr. Corbin, of the Governor's Council, "I enclose you your commission. God prosper you with it!" and the brunt of the work in fact fell upon the younger man. But three hundred volunteers could be gotten together; and, all too late, half of the raw levy was sent forward under Washington to find or make a way for wagons and ordnance to the Ohio. The last days of May were almost at hand before they had crossed the main ridge of the Alleghanies, so inexperienced were they in the rough labor of cutting a road through the close-set growth and over the sharp slopes of the mountains, and so ill equipped; and by that time it was already too late by a full month and more to forestall the French, who had only to follow the open highway of the Alleghany to bring what force they would to the key of the West at the forks of the Ohio. As the spring advanced, the French force upon the river grew from five to fourteen hundred men, and work was pushed rapidly forward upon fortifications such as the little band of Englishmen they had ousted had not thought of attempting —a veritable fort, albeit of a rude frontier pattern, which its builders called Duquesne, in honor of their Governor. Washington could hit upon no watercourse that would afford him quick transport; 'twould have been folly, besides, to take his handful of ragged provincials into the presence of an entrenched army. He was fain to go into camp at Great Meadows, just across the ridge of the mountains, and there await his Colonel with supplies and an additional handful of men.

It was "a charming field for an encounter," the young commander thought, but it was to be hoped the enemy would not find their way to it in too great numbers. An "Independent Company" of provincials in the King's pay joined him out of South Carolina, whence they had been sent forward by express orders from England; and the rest of the Virginia volunteers at last came up to join their comrades at the Meadows—without good Colonel Fry, the doughty mathematician, who had sickened and died on the way—so that there were presently more than three hundred men at the camp, and Washington was now their commander-in-chief. The officers of the Independent Company from South Carolina, holding their commissions from the King, would not, indeed, take their orders from Washington, with his colonial commission merely; and, what was worse, their men would not work; but there was no doubt they would fight with proper dignity and spirit for his Majesty, their royal master. The first blood had already been drawn, on the 28th of May, before re-enforcements had arrived, when Washington had but just come to camp. Upon the morning of that day, Washington, with forty men, guided by friendly Indians, had come upon a party of some thirty Frenchmen where they lurked deep within the thickets of the dripping forest, and with thrust of bayonet when the wet guns failed had brought them to a surrender within fifteen minutes of the first surprise. No one in the Virginian camp doubted that there was war already, or dreamed of awaiting the action of diplomats and cabinets over sea. The French had driven an English garrison from the forks of the Ohio with threats of force, which would certainly have been executed had there been need. These men hidden in the thickets at Great Meadows would have it, when the fight was over, that they had come as messengers merely to bear a peaceful summons; but did it need thirty-odd armed men to bear a message? Why had they lurked for five days so stealthily in the forest; and why had they sent runners back post-haste to Fort Duquesne to obtain support for their diplomacy? Washington might regret that young M. Jumonville, their commander, had lost his life in the encounter, but he had no doubt he had done right to order his men to fire when he saw the French spring for their arms at the first surprise.

Now, at any rate, war was unquestionably begun. That sudden volley fired in the wet woods at the heart of the lonely Alleghanies had set the final struggle ablaze. It was now either French or English in America: it could no longer be both. Jumonville with his thirty Frenchmen was followed ere many weeks were out by Coulon de Villiers with seven hundred—some of them come all the way from Montreal at news of what had happened to France's lurking ambassadors in the far-away mountains of Virginia. On the 3d of July they closed to an encounter at "Fort Necessity," Washington's rude intrenchments upon the Great Meadows. There were three hundred and fifty Englishmen with him able to fight, spite of sickness and short rations, and as the enemy began to show themselves at the edges of the neighboring woods through the damp mists of that dreary morning, Washington drew his little force up outside their works upon the open meadow. He "thought the French would come up to him in open field," laughed a wily Indian, who gave him counsel freely, but no aid in the fight; but Villiers had no mind to meet the gallant young Virginian in that manly fashion. Once, indeed, they rushed to his trenches, but finding hot reception there, kept their distance afterwards. Villiers brought them after that only "as near as possible without uselessly exposing the lives of the King's subjects," and poured his fire in from the cover of the woods. For nine hours the unequal fight dragged on, the French and their Indians hardly showing themselves outside the shelter of the forest, the English crouching knee-deep in water in their rude trenches, while the rain poured incessantly, reducing their breastworks to a mass of slimy mud, and filling all the air with a chill and pallid mist. Day insensibly darkened into night in such an air, and it was eight o'clock when the firing ceased and the French asked a parley. Their men were tired of the dreary fight, their Indian allies threatened to leave them when morning should come, and they were willing the English should withdraw, if they would, without further hurt or molestation. The terms they offered seemed very acceptable to Washington's officers as the interpreter read them out, standing there in the drenching downpour and the black night. "It rained so hard we could hardly keep the candle lighted to read them by," said an officer; but there was really no choice what to do. More than fifty men lay dead or wounded in the flooded camp; the ammunition was all but spent; the French strength had hardly been touched in the fight, and might at any moment be increased. Capitulation was inevitable, and Washington did not hesitate.

The next morning saw his wretched force making their way back again along the rude road they had cut through the forests. They had neither horses nor wagons to carry their baggage. What they could they burned; and then set out, sore stricken in heart and body, their wounded comrades and their scant store of food slung upon their backs, and dragged themselves very wearily all the fifty miles to the settlements at home. Two of the King's Independent Companies from New York ought to have joined them long ago, but had gotten no further than Alexandria when the fatal day came at the Great Meadows. North Carolina had despatched three hundred and fifty of her militiamen under an experienced officer to aid them, but they also came too late. It had been expected that Maryland would raise two hundred and fifty men, and Pennsylvania had at last voted money, to be spent instead of blood, for she would levy no men; but no succor had come from any quarter when it should. The English were driven in, and all their plans were worse than undone.

It was a bitter trial for the young Virginian commander to have his first campaign end so disastrously—to be worsted in a petty fight, and driven back hopelessly outdone. No one he cared for in Virginia blamed him. His ragged troops had borne themselves like men in the fight; his own gallantry no man could doubt. The House of Burgesses thanked him and voted money to his men. But it had been a rough apprenticeship, and Washington felt to the quick the lessons it had taught him. The discouraging work of recruiting at Alexandria, the ragged idlers to be governed there, the fruitless drilling of listless and insolent men, the two months' work with axe and spade cutting a way through the forests, the whole disheartening work of making ready for the fight, of seeking the enemy, and of choosing a field of encounter, he had borne as a stalwart young man can while his digestion holds good. He had at least himself done everything that was possible, and it had been no small relief to him to write plain-spoken letters to the men who were supposed to be helping him in Williamsburg, telling them

exactly how things were going and who was to blame—letters which showed both how efficient and how proud he was. He had even showed a sort of boyish zest in the affair when it came to actual fighting with Jumonville and his scouts hidden in the forest. He had pressed to the thick of that hot and sudden skirmish, and had taken the French volleys with a lad's relish of the danger. "I heard the bullets whistle," he wrote his brother, "and believe me there is something charming in the sound." But after he had stood a day in the flooded trenches of his wretched "fort" at Great Meadows, and fought till evening from the open with an enemy he could not see, he knew that he had been taught a lesson; that he was very young at this terrible business of fighting; and that something more must be learned than could be read in the books at Mount Vernon. He kept a cheerful front in the dreary retreat, heartening his men bravely by word and example of steadfastness; but it was a sore blow to his pride and his hopes, and he must only have winced without protest could he have heard how Horace Walpole called him a "brave braggart" for his rodomontade about the music of deadly missiles.

He had no thought, however, of quitting his duty because his first campaign had miscarried. When he had made his report at Williamsburg he rejoined his demoralized regiment at Alexandria, where it lay but an hour's ride from Mount Vernon, and set about executing his orders to recruit once more as if the business were only just begun. Captain Innes, who had brought three hundred and fifty men from North Carolina too late to be of assistance at the Meadows, and who had had the chagrin of seeing them take themselves off home again because there was no money forth-coming to pay them what had been promised, remained at Will's Creek, amid the back settlements, to command the King's provincials from South Carolina who had been with Washington at the Meadows, and the two Independent Companies from New York who had lingered so long on the way, in the building of a rough fortification, to be named Fort Cumberland, in honor of the far-away Duke who was commander-in-chief in England. Dinwiddie, having such hot Scots blood in him as could brook no delays, and hav-

GENERAL EDWARD BRADDOCK.

ing been bred no soldier or frontiersman, but a merchant and man of business, would have had Washington's recruiting despatched at once, like a bill of goods, and a new force sent hot-foot to the Ohio again to catch the French while they were at ease over their victory and slackly upon their guard at Duquesne. When he was flatly told it was impossible, he turned to other plans, equally ill-considered, though no doubt equally well meant. By October he had obtained of the Assembly twenty thousand pounds, and from the government at home ten thousand more in good specie, such as was scarce in the colony,—for the sharp stir of actual fighting had had its effect alike upon King and Burgesses,—and had ordered the formation and equipment of ten full companies for the frontier. But

the new orders contained a sad civilian blunder. The ten companies should all be Independent Companies; there should be no officer higher than a captain amongst them. This, the good Scotsman thought, would accommodate all disputes about rank and precedence, such as had come near to making trouble between Washington and Captain Mackay, of the Independent Company from South Carolina, while they waited for the French at Great Meadows.

Washington at once resigned, indignant to be so dealt with. Not only would he be reduced to a captaincy under such an arrangement, but every petty officer would outrank him who could show the King's commission. It was no tradition of his class to submit to degradation of rank thus by indirection and without fault committed, and his pride and sense of personal dignity, for all he was so young, were as high-strung as any man's in Virginia. He had shown his quality in such matters already six months ago, while he lay in camp in the wilderness on his way toward the Ohio. The Burgesses had appointed a committee of their own to spend the money they had voted to put his expedition afoot in the spring, lest Dinwiddie should think, were they to give him the spending of it, that they had relented in the matter of the fees; and these gentlemen, in their careful parsimony, had cut the officers of the already straitened little force down to such pay and food as Washington deemed unworthy a gentleman's acceptance. He would not resign his commission there at the head of his men upon the march, but he asked to be considered a volunteer without pay, that he might be quit of the humiliation of being stinted like a beggar. Now that it was autumn, however, and wars stood still, he could resign without reproach, and he did so very promptly, in spite of protests and earnest solicitations from many quarters. "I am concerned to find Colonel Washington's conduct so imprudent," wrote Thomas Penn. But the high-spirited young officer deemed it no imprudence to insist upon a just consideration of his rank and services, and quietly withdrew to Mount Vernon, to go thence to his mother at the "ferry farm" upon the Rappahannock, and see again all the fields and friends he loved so well.

It was a very brief respite. He had been scarcely five months out of harness when he found himself again in camp, his plans and hopes once more turned towards the far wilderness where the French lay. He had set a great war ablaze that day he led his forty men into the thicket and bade them fire upon M. Jumonville and his scouts lurking there; and he could not, loving the deep business as he did, keep himself aloof from it when he saw how it was to be finished. Horace Walpole might laugh lightly at the affair, but French and English statesmen alike — even Newcastle, England's Prime Minister, as busy about nothing as an old woman, and as thoroughly ignorant of affairs as a young man — knew that something must be done, politics hanging at so doubtful a balance between them, now that Frederick of Prussia had

driven France, Austria, and Russia into league against him. The French minister in London and the British minister in Paris vowed their governments still loved and trusted one another, and there was no declaration of war. But in the spring of 1755 eighteen French ships of war put to sea from Brest and Rochefort, carrying six battalions and a new Governor to Canada, and as many ships got away under press of sail from English ports to intercept and destroy them. Transports carrying two English regiments had sailed for Virginia in January, and by the 20th of February had reached the Chesapeake. The French ships got safely in at the St. Lawrence despite pursuit, losing but two of their fleet, which had the ill luck to be found by the English befogged and bewildered off the coast. The colonies were to see fighting on a new scale.

The English ministers, with whom just then all things went either by favor or by accident, had made a sorry blunder in the choice of a commander. Major-General Edward Braddock, whom they had commissioned to take the two regiments out and act as commander-in-chief in America, was a brave man, a veteran soldier, bred in a thorough school of action, a man quick with energy and indomitable in resolution, but every quality he had unfitted him to learn. Self-confident, brutal, headstrong, "a very Iroquois in disposition," he would take neither check nor suggestion. But energy, resolution, good soldiers, and a proper equipment might of themselves suffice to do much in the crisis that had come, whether wisdom held the reins or not; and it gave the Old Dominion a thrill of quickened hope and purpose to see Keppel's transports in the Potomac and Braddock's redcoats ashore at Alexandria.

The transports, as they made their way slowly up the river, passed beneath the very windows of Mount Vernon, to put the troops ashore only eight miles beyond. Washington had left off being soldier for Dinwiddie, but he had resigned only to avoid an intolerable indignity, not to shun service, and he made no pretence of indifference when he saw the redcoats come to camp at Alexandria. Again and again was he early in the saddle to see the stir and order of the troops, make the acquaintance of the officers, and learn, if he might, what it was that fitted his Majesty's regulars for their stern business. The self-confident gentlemen who wore his Majesty's uniform and carried his Majesty's commissions in their pockets had scant regard, most of them, for the raw folk of the colony, who had never been in London or seen the set array of battle. They were not a little impatient that they must recruit among such a people. The transports had brought but a thousand men—two half-regiments of five hundred each, whose colonels had instructions to add two hundred men apiece to their force in the colony. Six companies of "rangers," too, the colonists were to furnish, and one company of light horse, besides carpenters and teamsters. By all these General Braddock's officers set small store, deeming it likely they must depend, not upon the provincials, but upon themselves for success. They were at small pains to conceal their hearty contempt for the people they had come to help.

But with Washington it was a different matter. There was that in his proud eyes and gentleman's bearing that marked him a man to be made friends with and respected. A good comrade he proved, without pretence or bravado, but an ill man to scorn, as he went his way among them, lithe and alert, full six feet in his boots, with that strong gait as of a backwoodsman, and that haughty carriage as of a man born to have his will. He won their liking, and even their admiration, as a fellow of their own pride and purpose. General Braddock, knowing he desired to make the campaign if he might do so without sacrifice of self-respect, promptly invited him to go as a member of his staff, where there could be no question of rank, asking him, besides, to name any gentlemen of his acquaintance he chose for several vacant ensigncies in the two regiments. The letter of invitation, written by Captain Orme, aide-de-camp, was couched in terms of unaffected cordiality. Washington very gladly accepted, in a letter that had just a touch of the young provincial in it, so elaborate and over-long was its explanation of its writer's delicate position and self-respecting motives, but with so much more of the proud gentleman and resolute man that the smile with which Captain Orme must have read it could have nothing of disrelish in it. The young aide-de-camp and all the other members of the General's military "family" found its author, at any rate, a man after their own hearts

when it came to terms of intimacy amongst them.

By mid-April the commander-in-chief had brought five Governors together at Alexandria, in obedience to his call for an immediate conference—William Shirley, of Massachusetts, the stout-hearted old lawyer, every inch "a gentleman and politician," who had of a sudden turned soldier to face the French, for all he was past sixty; James De Lancey, of New York, astute man of the people; the brave and energetic Horatio Sharpe, of Maryland; Robert Hunter Morris, fresh from the latest wrangles with the headstrong Quakers and Germans of Pennsylvania; and Robert Dinwiddie, the busy merchant-Governor of the Old Dominion, whose urgent letters to the government at home had brought Braddock and his regiments to the Potomac. Plans were promptly agreed upon. New York and New England, seeing war come on apace, were astir no less than Virginia, and in active correspondence with the ministers in London. Two regiments had already been raised and taken into the King's pay; the militia of all the threatened colonies were afoot; in all quarters action was expected and instant war. Governor Shirley, the council agreed, should strike at once at Niagara with the King's new provincial regiments, in the hope to cut the enemy's connections with their western posts; Colonel William Johnson, the cool-headed trader and borderer, who had lived and thriven so long in the forests where the dreaded Mohawks had their strength, should lead a levy from New England, New York, and New Jersey to an attack upon Crown Point, where for twenty-four years the French had held Champlain; and Lieutenant-Colonel Monckton, of the King's regulars, must take a similar force against Beauséjour in Acadia, while General Braddock struck straight into the western wilderness to take Duquesne. 'Twere best to be prompt in every part of the hazardous business, and Braddock turned from the conference to push his own expedition forward at once. "After taking Fort Duquesne," he said to Franklin, "I am to proceed to Niagara; and after having taken that, to Frontenac, if the season will allow time; and I suppose it will, for Duquesne can hardly detain me above three or four days; and then I can see nothing that can obstruct my march to Niagara." "To be sure, sir;"

quietly replied the sagacious Franklin, "if you arrive well before Duquesne with these fine troops, so well provided with artillery, the fort....can probably make but a short resistance." But there was the trouble. 'Twould have been better, no doubt, had a route through Pennsylvania been chosen, where cultivated farms already stretched well into the West, with their own roads and grain and cattle and wagons to serve an army with, but the Virginia route had been selected (by intrigue of gentlemen interested in the Ohio Company, it was hinted), and must needs be made the best of. There was there, at the least, the rough track Washington's men had cut to the Great Meadows. This must now be widened and levelled for an army with its cumbrous train of artillery, and its endless procession of wagons laden with baggage and provisions. To take two thousand men through the dense forests with all the military trappings and supplies of a European army would be to put, it might be, four miles of its rough trail between van and rear of the struggling line, and it would be a clumsy enemy, as fighting went in the woods, who could not cut such a force into pieces—"like thread," as Franklin said.

The thing was to be attempted, nevertheless, with stubborn British resolution. It was the 19th of May before all the forces intended for the march were finally collected at Fort Cumberland, twenty-two hundred men in all—fourteen hundred regulars, now the recruits were in; nearly five hundred Virginians, horse and foot; two Independent Companies from New York; and a small force of sailors from the transports to rig tackle for the ordnance when there was need on the rough way. And it was the 10th of June when the advance began, straight into that "realm of forests ancient as the world" that lay without limit upon all the western ways. It was a thing of infinite difficulty to get that lumbering train through the tangled wilderness, and it kept the temper of the truculent Braddock very hot to see how it played havoc with every principle and practice of campaigning he had ever heard of. He charged the colonists with an utter want alike of honor and of honesty to have kept him so long awaiting the transportation and supplies they had promised, and to have done so little to end with, and so drew Washington into "frequent dis-

putes, maintained with warmth on both sides"; but the difficulties of the march presently wrought a certain forest change upon him, and disposed him to take counsel of his young Virginian aide—the only man in all his company who could speak out of knowledge in that wild country. On the 19th, at Washington's advice, he took twelve hundred men and pressed forward with a lightened train to a quicker advance, leaving Colonel Dunbar to bring up the rest of the troops with the baggage. Even this lightened force halted "to level every mole-hill, and to erect bridges over every brook," as Washington chafed to see, and "were four days in getting twelve miles"; but the pace was better than before, and brought them at last almost to their destination.

On the 9th of July, at mid-day, they waded the shallow Monongahela, but eight miles from Duquesne, making a brave show as the sun struck upon their serried ranks, their bright uniforms, their fluttering banners, and their glittering arms, and went straight into the rough and shadowed forest path that led to the French post. Upon a sudden there came a man bounding along the path to meet them, wearing the gorget of a French officer, and the forest behind him swarmed with a great host of but half-discovered men. Upon signal given, these spread themselves to right and left within the shelter of the forest, and from their covert poured a deadly fire upon Braddock's advancing lines. With good British pluck the steady regulars formed their accustomed ranks, crying, "God save the King!" to give grace to the volleys they sent back into the forest; the ordnance was brought up and swung to its work; all the force pressed forward to take what place it could in the fight; but where was the use? Washington besought General Braddock to scatter his men too, and meet the enemy under cover as they came, but he would not listen. They must stand in ranks, as they were bidden, and take the fire of their hidden foes like men, without breach of discipline. When they would have broken in spite of him, in their panic at being slaughtered there in the open glade without sight of the enemy, Braddock beat them back with his sword, and bitterly cursed them for cowards. He would have kept the Virginians, too, back from the covert if he could, when he saw them seek to close with the attacking party in true forest fashion. As it was, they were as often shot down by the terror-stricken regulars behind them as by their right foes in front. They alone made any head in the fight; but who could tell in such a place how the battle fared? No one could count the enemy where they sprang from covert to covert. They were, in fact, near a thousand strong at the first meeting in the way,—more than six hundred Indians, a motley host gathered from far and near at the summons of the French, sevenscore Canadian rangers, seventy-odd regulars from the fort, and thirty or forty French officers, come out of sheer eagerness to have a hand in the daring game. Contrecœur could not spare more Frenchmen from his little garrison, his connections at the lakes being threatened, and he sorely straitened for men and stores. He was staking everything, as it was, upon this encounter on the way. If the English should shake the savages off, as he deemed they would, he must no doubt withdraw as he could ere the lines of siege were closed about him. He never dreamed of such largess of good fortune as came pouring in upon him. The English were not only checked, but beaten. They had never seen business like this. 'Twas a pitiful, shameful slaughter,—men shot like beasts in a pen there where they cowered close in their scarlet ranks. Their first blazing volleys had sent the craven Canadians scampering back the way they had come; Beaujeu, who led the attack, was killed almost at the first onset; but the gallant youngsters who led the motley array wavered never an instant, and readily held the Indians to their easy work. Washington did all that furious energy and reckless courage could to keep the order of battle his commander had so madly chosen, to hold the regulars to their blind work and hearten the Virginians to stay the threatened rout, driving his horse everywhere into the thick of the murderous firing, and crying upon all alike to keep to it steadily like men. He had but yesterday rejoined the advance, having for almost two weeks lain stricken with a fever in Dunbar's camp. He could hardly sit his cushioned saddle for weakness when the fight began; but when the blaze of the battle burst, his eagerness was suddenly like that of one possessed, and his immunity from harm like that of one charmed. Thrice a horse was

shot under him, many bullets cut his clothing, but he went without a wound. A like mad energy drove Braddock storming up and down the breaking lines: but he was mortally stricken at last, and Washington alone remained to exercise such control as was possible when the inevitable rout came.

It was impossible to hold the ground in such fashion. The stubborn Braddock himself had ordered a retreat ere the fatal bullet found him. Sixty-three out of the eighty-six officers of his force were killed or disabled; less than five hundred men out of all the thirteen hundred who had but just now passed so gallantly through the ford remained unhurt: the deadly slaughter must have gone on to utter destruction. Retreat was inevitable—'twas blessed good fortune that it was still possible. When once it began it was headlong, reckless, frenzied. The men ran wildly, blindly, as if hunted by demons whom no man might hope to resist,— haunted by the frightful cries, maddened by the searching and secret fire of their foes, now coming hot upon their heels. Wounded comrades, military stores, baggage, their very arms, they left upon the ground, abandoned. Far into the night they ran madly on, in frantic search for the camp of the rear division, crying, as they ran, for help; they even passed the camp in their uncontrollable terror of pursuit, and went desperately on towards the settlements. Washington and the few officers and provincials who scorned the terror found the utmost difficulty in bringing off their stricken General, where he lay wishing to die. Upon the fourth day after the battle he died, loathing the sight of a redcoat, they said, and murmuring praises of "the blues," the once despised Virginians. They buried his body in the road, that the army wagons might pass over the place and obliterate every trace of a grave their savage enemies might rejoice to find and desecrate.

He had lived to reach Dunbar's camp, but not to see the end of the shameful rout. The terror mastered the rear-guard too. They destroyed their artillery, burned their wagons and stores, emptied their powder into the streams, and themselves broke into a disordered, feverish retreat which was a mere flight, their craven commander shamefully acquiescing. He would not even hold or rally them at Fort Cumberland, but went on, as if upon a hurried errand, all the way to Philadelphia, leaving the fort, and all the frontier with it, "to be defended by invalids and a few Virginians." "I acknowledge," cried Dinwiddie, "I was not brought up to arms; but I think common-sense would have prevailed not to leave the frontier exposed after having opened a road over the mountains to the Ohio, by which the enemy can the more easily invade us. The whole conduct of Colonel Dunbar seems to be monstrous." And so, indeed, it was. But the colonies at large had little time to think of it. Governor Shirley had gone against Niagara only to find the French ready for him at every point, now that they had read Braddock's papers, taken at Duquesne, and to come back again without doing anything. Beauséjour had been taken in Acadia, but it lay apart from the main field of struggle. Johnson beat the French off at Lake George when they attacked him, and took Dieskau, their commander; but he contented himself with that, and left Crown Point untouched. There were other frontiers besides those of Virginia and Pennsylvania to be looked to and guarded. For three long years did the fortunes of the English settlements go steadily from danger to desperation, as the French and their savage allies advanced from victory to victory. In 1756 Oswego was taken; in 1757, Fort William Henry. Commander succeeded commander among the English, only to add blunder to blunder, failure to failure. And all the while it fell to Washington, Virginia's only stay in her desperate trouble, to stand steadfastly to the hopeless work of keeping three hundred and fifty miles of frontier with a few hundred men against prowling bands of savages, masters of the craft of swift and secret attack, "dexterous at skulking," in a country "mountainous and full of swamps and hollow ways covered with woods."

For twenty years now settlers had been coming steadily into this wilderness that lay up and down upon the nearer slopes of the great mountains—Germans, Scots-Irish, a hardy breed. Their settlements lay scattered far and near among the foothills and valleys. Their men were valiant and stout-hearted, quick with the rifle, hard as flint when they were once afoot to revenge themselves for murdered wives and children and comrades. But how could they, scattered as they were,

meet these covert sallies in the dead of night—a sudden rush of men with torches, the keen knife, the quick rifle? The country filled with fugitives, for whom Washington's militiamen could find neither food nor shelter. "The supplicating tears of the women, and moving petitions of the men," cried the young commander, "melt me into such deadly sorrow that I solemnly declare, if I know my own mind, I could offer myself a willing sacrifice to the butchering enemy, provided that would contribute to the people's ease.... I would be a willing offering to savage fury, and die by inches to save a people." It was a comfort to know, at the least, that he was trusted and believed in. The Burgesses had thanked him under the very stroke of Braddock's defeat, in terms which could not be doubted sincere. In the very thick of his deep troubles, when he would have guarded the helpless people of the border but could not, Colonel Fairfax could send him word from Williamsburg, "Your good health and fortune are the toast at every table." "Our Colonel," wrote a young comrade in arms, "is an example of fortitude in either danger or hardships, and by his easy, polite behavior has gained not only the regard but affection of both officers and soldiers." But it took all the steadiness that had been born or bred in him to endure the strain of the disheartening task, from which he could not in honor break away. His plans, he complained, were "to-day approved, to-morrow condemned." He was bidden do what was impossible. It would require fewer men to go against Duquesne again and remove the cause of danger than to prevent the effects while the cause remained. Many of his officers were careless and inefficient, many of his men mutinous. "Your Honor will, I hope, excuse my hanging instead of shooting them," he wrote to the Governor; "it conveyed much more terror to others, and it was for example sake that we did it." It was a test as of fire for a young Colonel in his twenties.

But a single light lies upon the picture. Early in 1756, ere the summer's terror had come upon the border, and while he could be spared, he took horse and made his way to Boston to see Governor Shirley, now acting as commander-in-chief in the colonies, and from him at first hand obtain settlement of that teasing question of rank that had already driven this young officer once from the service. He went very bravely dight in proper uniform of buff and blue, a white and scarlet cloak upon his shoulders, the sword at his side knotted with red and gold, his horse's fittings engraved with the Washington arms, and trimmed in the best style of the London saddlers. With him rode two aides in their uniforms, and two servants in their white and scarlet livery. Curious folk who looked upon the celebrated young officer upon the road saw him fare upon his way with all the pride of a Virginian gentleman, a handsome man, and an admirable horseman,—a very gallant figure, no one could deny. Everywhere he was fêted as he went; everywhere he showed himself the earnest, high-strung, achieving youth he was. In New York he fell into a new ambush, from which he did not come off without a wound. His friend Beverly Robinson must needs have Miss Mary Philipse at his house there, a beauty and an heiress, and Washington came away from her with a sharp rigor at his heart. But he could not leave that desolate frontier at home unprotected to stay for a siege upon a lady's heart; he had recovered from such wounds before, had before that left pleasure for duty; and in proper season was back at his post, with papers from Shirley which left no doubt who should command in Virginia.

At last, in 1758, the end came, when William Pitt thrust smaller men aside and became Prime Minister in England. Amherst took Louisbourg, Wolf came to Quebec, and General Forbes, that stout and steady soldier, was sent to Virginia to go again against Duquesne. The advance was slow to exasperation in the view of every ardent man like Washington, and cautious almost to timidity; but the very delay redounded to its success at last. 'Twas November before Duquesne was reached. The Indians gathered there, seeing winter come on, had not waited to meet them; and the French by that time knew themselves in danger of being cut off by the English operations in the North. When Forbes's forces, therefore, at last entered those fatal woods again, where Brad-dock's slaughtered men had lain to rot, the French had withdrawn; nothing remained but to enter the smoking ruins of their abandoned fort, hoist the King's flag, and rename the post Fort Pitt, and Washington turned homeward again to seek the rest he so much needed. It had been almost a bloodless campaign, but such danger as it had brought, Washington had shared to the utmost. The French had not taken themselves off without at least one trial of the English strength. While yet Forbes lay within the mountains a large detachment had come from Duquesne to test and reconnoitre his force. Colonel Mercer, of the Virginian line, had been ordered forward with a party to meet them. He stayed so long, and the noise of the firing came back with so doubtful a meaning to the anxious ears at the camp, that Washington hastened with volunteers to his relief. In the dusk the two bodies of Englishmen met, mistook each other for enemies, exchanged a deadly fire, and were checked only because Washington, rushing between their lines, even while their pieces blazed, cried his hot commands to stop, and struck up the smoking muzzles with his sword. 'Twas through no prudence of his he was not shot.

For a long time his friends had felt a deep uneasiness about his health. They had very earnestly besought him not to attempt a new campaign. "You will in all probability bring on a relapse," George Mason had warned him, "and render yourself incapable of serving the public at a time when there may be the utmost occasion. There is nothing more certain than that a gentleman of your station owes the care of his health and his life not only to himself and his friends, but to his country." But he had deemed the nearest duty the most imperative; and it was only after that duty was disposed of that he had turned from the field to seek home and new pleasures along with new duties. The winter brought news from Quebec of the fall of the French power in America, which made rest and home and pleasure the more grateful and full of zest.

THE INDUSTRIAL SOUTH

ONE of the most remarkable curios in Uncle Sam's cabinet is Lookout Mountain, at Chattanooga, Tennessee. The traveller expects such occasional combinations of mountain and plain on the edges of the Rockies, the Selkirks, and other great mountain chains, and yet it is doubtful whether any other as beautiful is to be found. For it has seldom happened that a tall mountain rises abruptly to interrupt and dominate a view so majestic and of such varied features. Glistening water, smiling farm-land, forest, city, hill, and island, all lie upon the gorgeous and gigantic canvas of the Master Painter, who there invites mankind to his studio to enjoy such views as we had fancied only the stupid denizens of the air are privileged to dully scan.

To surfeit one's self with the wondrous changing, widening beauty of that splendid scene one does not have to consider the martial records that brave men wrote with their blood all over the foreground of the prospect. But when it happens that the spectator is an American whose soul has been stirred by the poor print-ed annals of Chickamauga and Mission Ridge, the feast spread before Lookout Mountain ministers to the understanding the while it ravishes the eye.

In nothing is this wonder-spot more wonderful than in its accessibility. It is even more convenient to the tourist than Niagara Falls—almost the solitary great natural curiosity in our country for which one does not have to travel far and labor hard. In this case the grand view is one of the sights of Chattanooga, "the Little Pittsburg" of the South. The city enjoys it as a householder does his garden, by merely travelling to a back window, as it were, for the historic mountain is at the end of a five-cent trolley line. During half the year the tourist is even better served, for the railroads haul the "sleepers" up the mountain-side in summer, and discharge the passengers on the very edge that divides *terra firma* and eagle's vision. Guided by Mr. Milton D. Ochs, of the Chattanooga *Times*, who could have offered a very wonderful view of his own from the towering pile in which that newspaper is housed, I took the trolley line during what the Southern folk are pleased to call winter-time. The way led to just such a looking railway as one finds at Niagara Falls going down to the water's edge, though this one darts up the two-thousand-foot-high mountain-side, and is famed among professional en-gineers as a remarkable creation. It was planned and built by Colonel W. R. King, U.S.A. It is 4500 feet in length, with an elevation of 1400 feet, and a grade of near-ly one foot in three at the steepest place.

The terminus is the Lookout Point

INN ON LOOKOUT MOUNTAIN.

Hotel, which appears to stand upon a bowlder suspended over the remainder of creation, as if a mountain rising out of a plain had thrust out a finger and men had put up a building on the finger-nail. The biblical word-picture which tells of our Saviour being taken up on a high mountain and shown the kingdoms of the earth conveys the idea that the view from this point suggests. One can but have an idea of it, and it can only be expressed or described with a figure of speech. To be told that it commands 500 miles of the earth's surface, and that the most distant objects are parts of seven different States, is too much for the mind to master. What the eye takes in is a checker-board made up of farms, roads, villages, woods, ridges, and mountain ranges, all in miniature. The Tennessee River gladdens the scene. Though it is 1400 feet wide, it looks like a ribbon, and, like a ribbon thrown carelessly from the mountain-top, it lies in many curves and convolutions, a dull green band everywhere fringed with a thin line of trees that wall in the farmers' fields. You may count ten of its curves, and three of them, immediately below the mountain, form the exact shape of an Indian moccasin, around the toe of which a toy freight-train crawls lazily with a muffled gasping out of all proportion to its size. A brown and white mound of smoke and steam beyond the nearest farms is pointed out as Chat-

tanooga, and a rolling wooded region on the right is spoken of as the bloodiest field of the rebellion—fearful Chickamauga. The low dark green mound in the immediate foreground is Mission Ridge, and between that and the curtain of smoke that hides the busy city a tiny bit of yellow road is seen to disappear at a microscopic white gate, which is the portal of a cemetery wherein thirteen full regiments of Northern heroes lie — the blue who have turned to gray in the long embrace of death—five thousand of them not remembered by name.

The rapid run by narrow-gauge road to Sunset Rock suggests a panorama in which the swiftly changing scene stands steady and the spectator whirls beside it. Coloradan views are strongly called to mind, but the memory of them is at a disadvantage, since here all nature is green and fertile instead of dead and burned. Here the land is peopled, and there it is deserted. And yet the mountain-side is precisely the same as if we were back in the Rockies, piled up with great gray rocks in mounds and giant fret-work. Sunset Rock itself is another finger or knuckle of the mountain, clinging to its side, yet seeming to hang in mid-air over the ravishing landscape far below. There are several minor battle-fields within the view from it, but at the first vantage-point the splendors of nature crowd the memories of the war out of the chief place in the mind. The charm that has made this rock the favorite rendezvous of the scores of thousands who journey to the mountain every year comes with the views at sunset when Phœbus's fires burn many-colored, and tint and tinge and illumine every distant object, from the lowly fields to the highest heavens, with slowly changing brilliant hues. I did not see it, and will not attempt a description of what I am assured is one of the most extravagant and splendid, almost daily, triumphs of nature. Let the reader imagine it, or go and be ravished by it. The stage-setting includes three ranges of hills, which even as I saw them in the early afternoon were rosy, green, and darkest blue, and behind the farthest of these the fire-god shifts his colored slides and throws his gorgeous lights from earth to sky.

Bridegrooms and beaux, and brides and *fiancées*—in a word, all lovers—make quite another use of Sunset Rock. There is a photographer there, and his exhibit of pictures shows him to be a modern Cupid, ever attendant upon Love. All around his show-room are photographs of the smitten, a pair at a time invariably, taken in the very act of being in love, seated side by side upon the gray insensate rock that juts above the diminished lands below. Each new couple that drifts along sees the portraits of all the others, and negotiations with the photographer follow close upon quick glances, hushed whispers, and coy giggling. Then out go the lovers to the rock, and out comes Cupid with his camera. He is a wag, this Cupid, for he says of his clients, "We git 'em in all stages of the disease." His collection easily divides the lovers into two classes—the self-conscious and the ecstatic. The self-conscious ones sit bolt-upright, a trifle apart, with glances fixed sternly upon nothing. The ecstatic lovers cling together, and look with sheep's eyes at one another or at Cupid. Sometimes the classes mix, and one sees an ecstatic bride leaning all her weight of love and charms upon a self-conscious groom, who frowns and pulls away. There are such pictures in the collection as would serve in a divorce court without a word of testimony on either side; but, thank Heaven, the ecstatics supply photographs that need

CHATTANOOGA AND MOCCASIN BEND, FROM LOOKOUT MOUNTAIN.

only to be kept framed at home in order to banish discord as long as the wedded pair have sight to see how happy they had planned to be and were. Mingled discordantly with these trophies of the court of love are reminders of that class of idiots who would manage to desecrate a junk-shop if they were admitted to it.

place earth on the inclined railway. The car is built in the form of an inclined plane, like the gallery in a playhouse, with one side open toward the nether wall of rocks, and the other side glazed to command the marvellous view which seems to rise as the car descends, just as fairy views come up out of the stage in

THE TENNESSEE RIVER AT CHATTANOOGA.

They have themselves pictured as flinging themselves off the dizzy rock; one has actually got his comrade to hold him by one too-servile trousers leg while he dangles head downwards over the precipice. That is a touch of nature that does not make the whole world kin.

There are too many other points of interest on the mountain for mention here —curious freaks of nature and charming spots in abundance. It is several days' work to see them, but there are plenty of hotels and villa settlements there for those who have the time to enjoy the place in its entirety. Lookout Inn, a hotel that will accommodate three hundred boarders, is on the tip-top of the mountain, and has the reputation of being one of the very best hotels in the South. It is owned and controlled by a land and improvement company, and the principal stockholders are New-Englanders. The railways carry cars to its doors, and it is to be kept open all the year round. At the end of such a visit as I made the visitor simply tumbles back to the common-

a transformation scene at the end of a Christmas pantomime. Then, suddenly, the car tumbles into a forest, and the only view is of the preposterous alley down which the vehicle is rolling like a ball sent back to the players in a bowling-alley.

My task here is to tell of something that lies under and in that mountain view of parts of seven Southern States, of something the eye cannot see except as a hint of it is thrown up in the clouds of smoke and steam that hang over Chattanooga. That something is the industrial awakening of the South, or more particularly of that part of that section where since the war the coal and iron buried in the rocks and soil now meet their resurrection in an activity that has connected Georgia with Pennsylvania.

A very sage writer upon the industrial history of the South has shown that early in the century it promised to lead the other sections of the country, but slavery exerted the effect of humbling the artisan beneath the planter and the professional man in the general estimation. A wonderful agricultural prosperity was developed, and mechanical pursuits languished. Up to the time of the late war the South did not enthrone cotton. The South then grew its own meat and meal and flour. But after the war, when the most frightful poverty oppressed the region, the people turned to the exclusive cultivation of cotton, because that was the only staple that could be mortgaged in advance of the crop to give the planters the means of living until it could be harvested. The poverty of the planters, their dependence on the negro, and the shiftlessness of the negro, which led him to favor cotton as the easiest crop to handle on shares and to borrow money upon, were the causes of cotton's enthronement. Carpet-bag rule and the demoralization of the peculiar labor of the South added ten years to the period of Southern prostration, and it was not until 1880 that the present great industrial development of that section began. It is therefore a growth of a dozen years—a wonderful growth for so short a time.

Before the war there were a few small furnaces in this now busy district overlooked by Chattanooga's mountain, and formed of parts of Tennessee, Alabama, and Georgia. These furnaces were mainly on the Tennessee River and in eastern Tennessee, and the smelting was done with charcoal. The first coke furnace was established at Rockwood in 1868 with Northern capital on Southern credit. The industry thus begun has continued to be

POINT LOOKOUT, LOOKOUT MOUNTAIN.

the enterprise of Southern men, for such are the majority of the persons engaged in the business—men of the wide-awake commercial class. The Chattanooga district, so called, is in the centre of a region of coking coals and iron ores, embracing a circle of 150 miles in diameter, and covering parts of Tennessee, northern Alabama, and northern Georgia. It takes in one medium-sized furnace in northern Georgia and some smaller ones, which number nineteen, where there were none

CHATTANOOGA, FROM THE RIVER.

COURT-HOUSE, CHATTANOOGA.

tanooga and in Bridgeport), both owned by one corporation, and there is also in the district a very large establishment for the manufacture of railway - brake shoes and other goods.

The region in which the Chattanooga district is situated is a reach of bituminous coal and red hematite iron ore of limitless abundance that extends from Roanoke, Virginia, to Birmingham, Alabama. The coal crops out in West Virginia, crosses eastern Kentucky, where it is worked as pure cannel, semi - anthracite, and bituminous; crosses Tennessee through the Tennessee Valley to northern Alabama.

at all before the war. Its Alabama section—where there was no iron industry when the war closed, except at a few little furnaces built by the Confederates to cast their cannon—now boasts fifty-three large plants. In a word, the development has grown from the smelting of 150,000 tons of charcoal and coke irons in 1870 to the making of no less than 1,800,000 tons of pig-iron in 1889, '90, and '91. The steel industry is prospective. The name of the town of Bessemer is misleading. Basic steel has been made in the district from the ordinary foundry ore, and has been tested by the government, and declared to be admirable. A mine of Bessemer ore has been worked at Johnson City, North Carolina, but the capital for a steel-works to compete with those of the North has not at this time been obtained.

Eighty per cent. of the Tennessee iron is sold in the East, North, and Northwest —in Cleveland, Chicago, St. Louis, New York, and Philadelphia. It competes with the best foundry iron for stove plates and all sorts of foundry-work. It ranks with the best Lehigh product, and is the favorite iron with the pipe, plough, and stove makers of the East and North. Considerable foundry-work is done in the Chattanooga district. There are several stove-works there and some machine-shops that turn out both heavy and light castings. There are two large pipe-works (in Chat-

It is a belt containing 26,000 square miles in three States, and everywhere the coal and iron accompany each other at pistol range. As an illustration, at Red Mountain, near Birmingham, the Tennessee Coal, Iron, and Railway Company gets coal on one side of a valley and iron on the other side. This great company has several plants, and made more than 400,000 tons of pig-iron in 1891. It has the largest coal plant in the Chattanooga district—one that has put out 600,000 tons of high - grade coking coal in a year. Its leading men are Southerners, and its capital is from the Northern States and England.

The labor in this great industrial section is mainly black, of course. The negroes dig all the iron ore and do all the rough work at the furnaces. The coal is mainly dug by white men. The very great quantities of limestone that are quarried for smelting-flux and for building-work are taken out by negroes. It is found that with what is called "thorough foremanizing" the negro is satisfactory at these occupations. He needs strict and even sharp "bossing" to keep him at his work, and it has been found that to invest one of his own race with the authority of an overseer is to produce the strictest, even the savagest, kind of a boss.

The whole coal and iron region has suffered severely since the Baring failure

in London. During three years the price of iron fell from $12 to $14 50 and $15 a ton down to $8 50 and $7 75, by reason of excessive overproduction. Only the few companies that relied upon convict labor were able to make both ends meet at those prices, and it became painfully apparent that there is no decent profit in iron-making at a lower price than $10 a ton.

factures are started. Such changes are brought about by one thing at a time, and already in addition to the works that have been mentioned there are large works in Chattanooga and in Atlanta for the making of ploughs and cane-mills, which contribute to a trade that already reaches into South America, the East Indies, and Australia.

MARKET STREET, CHATTANOOGA.

The Southern industry suffered more severely than it should have done because not enough of the iron product was utilized in home manufactures. The transition from an agricultural to an iron-making district had been brought about too suddenly, and was allowed to go to an extreme point. The time was one of money-making in the iron industry, and the people were led to "booming" their new industry, so that nearly every one went into the manufacture of pig-iron, and too few into the conversion of it into manufactured goods. This will be fully understood when it is known that not a pound of hardware and not a pound of steel boiler plate is made in the South. Where there is room for many large stove factories there are yet but a few small ones. But, as has been shown, the manu-

The *Tradesman*, of Chattanooga, Tennessee, the leading authority upon Southern industrial affairs, published for its chief article in its "Annual" for 1893 a paper by I. D. Imboden, of Damascus, Virginia, which makes very bold and confident prophecies for the iron and steel industries of the South, and fortifies them with expert and official government reports. This is interesting and valuable, at least as showing how the leaders of opinion in the South feel upon the subject. He says that from his knowledge he forms a conclusion as strong as if it were mathematical that "the period is near when, as a group, the States of Virginia, North Carolina, Tennessee, Georgia, Alabama, and Kentucky will become the largest and most successful iron and steel producing district of like area in the world." He adds that "contemporaneously or ultimately all the related industries will spring up and flourish at every exceptionally favorable locality in these States, such as Richmond, Lynchburg, and Roanoke; Chattanooga, Nashville, Knoxville, and Memphis; Atlanta; Greensboro, Wilmington, and Charlotte, North Carolina; Birmingham, Anniston, and Decatur, Alabama; Louisville and Covington, Kentucky; Wheeling, Charleston, and Huntington, West Virginia; and at many other points." He predicts an eventual overflow of material for iron and steel ship-building in the Atlantic and Gulf seaports, thus extending to the cotton, rice, and tobacco States an incidental participation in the inland mineral wealth, creating diversified industries and a larger home market for their crops. He answers "yes" to the important question whether the Southern mineral region can compete with the Northern mineral region in the supply of coal and iron. The mineral belt that underlies 25,000 square miles of the Virginias extends into and across North Carolina and Tennessee, carrying equally

rich and exhaustless stores of iron; "and even beyond the southern boundaries of these States, in Georgia and Alabama, there are supplies of these ores so great that exhaustion will not probably take place while the human race exists." Kentucky he includes as an ore-producing State of high rank. He asserts that in recent years the South has produced a richer and better coke than the famous Connellsville product, which is equalled nowhere else in the North. The New River, West Virginia, coke was six years ago proved to be better than the Connellsville article; but farther southwest, in Virginia and in the same coal-field, a still richer coal is found underlying Wise and Dickenson counties and extending far into Kentucky. "Taking the New River field in West Virginia, the Pocahontas and Big Stone Gap and intermediate basins in Virginia, and their unbroken extension into several counties in Kentucky (and in the Cahaba basin in Alabama), we have an aggregation of several thousand square miles of coking coals superior" (to that of Connellsville), "and so distributed as to make a comparatively short haul from some one or other of these districts to one of our ore districts." This writer believes that the average haul—an important consideration—will be shorter in the South than that by which the coal and iron of the North have been brought together. He says that six of the seven States he has named possess an abundance of bituminous coal, such as is largely used for a lower but useful grade of coke. Southern coal is much more easily and cheaply mined than that in the North, and of the Southern iron ores the greater part is mined, not at the bottom of deep shafts, but from the hill and mountain sides in the full light of the sun. He thinks that the continued presence of negro labor in such great force in the Southern States is "providential." The negro's brawn and muscle, his cheap labor, and his acquaintance and characteristic contentment with

ENTRANCE TO A COAL-MINE.

IN THE BLUE RIDGE RANGE.

his surroundings are considered as a large element in the early prospective growth of Southern coal and iron industries.

The last census bulletin upon the iron and steel industry of the South shows that in the ten years between 1880 and 1890 there has been a remarkable growth of these businesses, and that they have begun to follow a course of concentration, with the result that the capital invested in blast-furnaces has increased from sixteen millions to thirty-three millions of dollars, while the money put into rolling-mills and steel-works has grown from eleven millions to seventeen millions. The output has increased enormously, and the quality of the product has greatly improved. In the amount of capital invested, Alabama is now "far in the lead," Virginia is second, and West Virginia is third; but West Virginia is close to Alabama in the value of her iron products, because a larger proportion of her iron and steel is worked into valuable grades of finished products. In 1880 the South produced nine per cent. of the pig-iron yield of the whole country, but in 1890 she produced nineteen per cent. Alabama shows the greatest increase in the blast-furnace industry during the

decade, and Jefferson County—that in which Birmingham is situated—is now the most important iron-making district in the South. In 1880 there were but two establishments there, with a capital of one million; now there are ten such establishments, with a capital of almost nine millions of dollars. Steel-making has made but little progress, the government report says, because the Southern ores are generally unsuitable for use in the established processes of steel-manufacture. It is insisted, however, that good steel has been made in the South, though whether it can be made in competition with the North is certainly an open question yet.

Tennessee has more resources that can be utilized in manufactures than any other one of the Southern States, and already she leads in the possession of the greater number of manufacturing towns. She is the largest grain-producer among the Southern States, and the output of her flour and grist mills is so great as to amount to one-fifth of the total of her manufactured products. Cotton and woollen manufacturing grows there so rapidly that one mill now turns out more than the whole State produced ten years ago. Three millions of dollars are invested in twenty cotton-mills, and the woollen in-

FIRST BAPTIST CHURCH, CHATTANOOGA.

yet in greater or less degree I show the same facts about nearly all the Southern States. There are parts of our West of which it can truly be said that nearly the entire reliance of the people is upon silver ore or upon wheat; but the old indictment against the South will not stand anywhere, except it be in purely agricultural Mississippi; and there, as I shall show, the fruit-grower and truck-farmer are treading on the emaciated toes of old King Cotton.

Chattanooga (under its veil of steam and smoke, and backed against a towering hill suggestive of the wealth of which it is one capital) is a city in which a man of cosmopolitan training could live without shock or sacrifice. It and its close suburbs shelter nearly 50,000 persons. It is the third city in Tennessee, though it is more truly to be considered in its relation to the industrial district around it. It is an imposing, clean, tidy, modern, wide-awake town. The mixture that forms its population has prevented the formation of Southern types in architecture, dress, or any other detail, and left it what an artist would call commonplace, though it is in reality such a city as would be creditable to California, Minnesota, Ohio, or Pennsylvania. It is notable among all the smaller cities of the country for its well-paved and orderly streets. Its principal thoroughfare is floored with asphalt, but so many other streets are paved with fire-brick, made near by, that it may be said to be almost completely a brick city, brick below as well as above. All its improvements, like its industries and most of its people, have come since the war, and it is most peculiar in possessing a people so largely from the North and West that natives are very scarce indeed. It typifies the industrial region around it by its varied industries. Its manufactures embrace ploughs, wood-working factories, lead and slate pencil making, boiler-works, electrical apparatus manufacture, stove-building, the largest iron-pipe works in

dustry is sufficient to produce $1,250,000 worth of goods, or half as much as the manufactured cotton product of the State. Of tobacco and cotton-seed oil production there is a great deal, and the iron industry near Chattanooga has an importance that is dwelt upon elsewhere. The State is famous for its manufacture of wagons, which brought in $2,395,000 in 1892. Its cotton goods fetched a little more. No less than $4,617,000 was brought by its cotton-seed oil and other cotton-seed products. Its distilling and brewing, its furniture-making, and its slaughtering and packing, each was worth $2,000,000 in 1892. One million or more represents the value in that year of the following industries: tin-ware, manufactured tobacco and cigars, woollen goods, brick and tile, marble, clothing, saddlery and harness-making, printing and publishing, and blacksmithing and wheelwright work. The value of other leading industries was as follows: lumber, $10,000,000; flour and grist-mill products, $17,000,000; foundry and machine-shop work, $6,000,000; iron and steel, $5,000,000; and leather, $3,000,-000.

Is this dull reading? Stop a bit and consider whether such detailed accounts of the new industrial activity in the South do not show that times have changed since that section deserved to be ridiculed and pitied for a stupid and slavelike reliance upon one product of the soil. And the South, and a great malleable iron works that turns out car-couplings and railway-brake shoes. It has several flour-mills, a brewery, a clothing-manufactory, an engine and machine works, several foundries, an extensive cotton compress, a tobacco-warehouse, and the beginning of a cigar and tobacco manufacturing industry that must grow in unison with the new practice of tobacco-raising by the farmers of the neighboring country.

Chattanooga is a very pretty city, climbing two or three hills and abounding in view points that take in very beautiful land and water scenery, and city vistas that are parklike. Of course it has electric cars, and floods of electric light at night—for these new Southern towns are built by the same spirits that dominate the new West. It is typically American also in the fact that every family in it inhabits a separate house with a garden attached. It is distinguished, like Brooklyn, by its churches. All the considerable denominations have meeting-houses there, and even the Swedenborgians and Christian Scientists are in the list. Some of these edifices are very handsome. The Opera-house and the home of the Mountain City Club are deserving of equal praise, and all alike speak volumes for the taste and refinement of the dominant element of the population. Its people, its progressive government, and its proud educational system are deserving of extended mention, but the limits of each subject in a paper that aims to cover so busy and wide a territory are too narrow to make this possible.

Students of the progress of the State of Alabama show that it has made greater industrial advance in the twelve months of 1892-3 than in any preceding twenty years of its history. This is true alike of her manufactures, agriculture, commerce, and railroads. In the utilization of her mineral resources she has accomplished, relatively, greater progress than any State in the Union. Her iron productions constitute a third of her output, and have led

to the establishment of her rolling-mills, machine-shops, pipe-foundries, and the rest, though it is still true that the State sends out far too much of her iron for manufacture elsewhere into goods whose home manufacture would, and will yet, greatly swell her revenues. But, apart from her mineral resources, she has trebled her cotton-mill output, multiplied her cotton-seed produce by eight, and gone largely into the manufacture of lumber and wooden articles, agricultural implements, boots and shoes, wagons, furniture, flour and meal, and naval stores. The State stands fourth in the South in the manufacture of cotton goods. In two years previous to January 1, 1893, she added nearly 2000 looms and more than 100,000 spindles to her milling facilities. In 1880 she had invested $3,300,000 in her iron industries, but in 1890 this sum had been swelled to $19,000,000. In 1892 she furnished more than 5,000,000 tons of coal, or more than one-fifth of the entire Southern coal product, and led all her sister States except West Virginia. She is the fifth coal-producing State in the Union. Of coke her production in 1891 was about 1,300,000 short tons.

The census shows that the increase of population in the last decade was a little less than 20 per cent., but the assessed valuation of real estate in Alabama increased 60.40 per cent., and the enrolment of children in the public schools increased 61.53 per cent. Northern Alabama has felt the first tide of immigration to the South more

POST-OFFICE. BIRMINGHAM.

strongly than any other section of equal extent. Birmingham is said to have been a farm at the close of the rebellion, and busy Anniston was a group of timbered hills very much later than that. There is a truly Western flavor to the history of a land company in one of these cities. It divided more than $5,500,000 with its stockholders in a little more than five years, upon an investment of $100,000.

The new city of Birmingham in 1880 had 60 establishments and 27 industries, and in 1890 its establishments numbered 417 and its industries 48, while the capital invested had swelled from two millions to seven millions of dollars. Its leading workshops are carriage and wagon factories, foundries, and machine-shops, three iron and steel working plants, planing-mills, and printing and publishing works. In what is known as the Birmingham district there are 25 iron-furnaces, with a capacity for 2600 tons of pig-iron daily. All are within twenty miles of the town. Consolidations of large companies have recently strengthened this remarkable iron centre, adding to the economy with which its products are obtained, and fitting it to meet a dull market better than before. Experts have declared that several of the works at this place stand as models in judicious construction and economical results to the whole country and to Europe also. Some are so favorably located near ore and coal that it has been proved that nowhere in this country, and scarcely anywhere in Europe, can iron be made as cheaply as they can make it. These facts are of interest as showing the permanency and value of the industry which has revolutionized northern Alabama. It has not only come to stay, but it has come to grow. During the summer of 1892 the furnace men there were put to a severe test. They had to make iron at a minimum or shut up their works. They did make it, and only the smaller furnaces shut down for a time. The larger ones ran on steadily, and without losing money. Their owners assert that this experience proved that Alabama can make iron cheaper than it can be made in Pennsylvania.

Wherever coal, limestone, and iron are found close together the situation is favorable for the economical production of pig-iron, and as that condition distinguishes a large part of northern Alabama, the extension of the industrial activity of the Birmingham district is confidently looked for. On this account the capital of some shrewd Northern men has been invested in a promising new town—midway between Birmingham and Chattanooga—called Wyeth City. It is on the Tennessee River, which is 600 yards in width at that point, and offers uninterrupted navigation to the Ohio and Mississippi and their tributaries. The railroad from Brunswick, Georgia, makes Wyeth City the nearest to the Atlantic coast of any point upon the tremendous inland water system of the Mississippi and its connections. The railway facilities at Wyeth City are also excellent. The Nashville and Chattanooga Railroad, one of the best-equipped and most progressive roads in the South, has built into the new city, and work is being pushed upon two local railroads—all of which place the new city on the direct route from Brunswick, on the Atlantic coast, to Nashville, St. Louis, and the Northwest, and from New Orleans and Mobile to Cincinnati and the North and East. The Louisville and Nashville system is soon to meet the Nashville and Chattanooga at this point.

The Wyeth City lands are in and beside the old town of Guntersville, the county-seat of Marshall County. Large deposits of iron ore are close by, and extensive limestone quarries are even nearer, while in the mountains, only four miles away, coal seams have been exposed. The conditions there are, therefore, such as caused the marvellous development of Birmingham and Anniston. The present manufactures at this new point are such as utilize the abundant wood of the locality, and convert it into carved furniture, doors, sash and blinds, and wooden-ware. An interesting fact about the town is that as long ago as *ante bellum* times the geographical advantages of this point were appreciated. The States of Georgia and Alabama were at that time jointly interested in the construction of a railway that was to open up the northern parts of those States. The commissioners who were appointed to fix the route divided upon the question whether Chattanooga or what is now Wyeth City should be the terminus. Chattanooga was chosen by a majority of one. To-day it looks as though time is to work its revenge, since the capitalists interested in the new city are intent upon securing the establishment of iron-working and cotton and

THE LAKE, GRANT'S PARK, ATLANTA.

woollen factories there in the near future.

I never want to miss a chance to combat the idea that the waste lands of the South are sterile, and the worked lands are played out. This theory has taken a deep hold upon a large part of the popular mind, and is kept alive by able men who command influential avenues to the public ear, though why they do so I do not understand. I have found that the most prosperous farmers in the South, and perhaps in the United States, are operating on the tide-water lands of North Carolina, and that trucking and fruit-growing in the sandy soil of the Piney Woods land of Louisiana and Mississippi are accompanied by the very brightest prospects. I have no other master to serve than the truth, and the plain truth is that the reason I cannot declare the major part of that country gladdened by prosperous farming is that the South has not tried to attract poor immigrants, that her enemies and critics have kept them from going there unbidden, that the swarms of semi-idle and parasitic negroes stand in the way of better brawn and muscle, and that the total new or foreign-born part of the population of nineteen million souls in those States is less than three per cent.—is almost *nil* in some of the States.

And yet there are examples of what can be done there—strawlike in dimensions though they be. Let me condense the facts given by Mr. Thurston H. Allen in a recent issue of the *Manufacturers' Record* respecting an instance in Alabama. In 1878, he says, the Rev. Father Huser, a German Catholic priest, bought a tract of 2000 acres of worn-out land, known as the Wilson Plantation, in St. Florian, Lauderdale County, Alabama. It had grown cotton exclusively till at last it was abandoned to broom-sedge and briars, and pronounced worthless. The priest got it for four dollars an acre.

"Dr. Huser built a church and a school-house, and in 1878 divided the plantation into tracts of from ten to fifty acres each, and placed thereon some forty-five families, all German Catholics, from Pennsylvania, Ohio, Illinois, New York, and other States, to whom he sold these lands at from $8 to $15 per acre, according to location and improvements. These colonists had experienced the rigors of the Northern and Western climates with the certainty of cold and drought.

"They were all poor; their industry elsewhere had not hitherto availed them to any great extent. It had taken all the fruits of their labor to sustain them up to this time, so that most, if not all of them, were forced to go in debt for their land. Some of those who are now the most prosperous and independent commenced with mortgages upon their lands, and with but one mule or steer with which to break and cultivate the soil."

To add to their troubles, there was a defalcation which compelled them to pay twice for part of their holdings. They nursed the dead land back to life, and built houses, fences, and improvements; but wood was cheap, the winters were mild, they could work all the year round, and they needed to spend little for clothing. The long summers brought them two crops instead of one.

"Vineyards and orchards were planted, and it was not long before a general improvement began to be apparent not only in the lands, but in the condition of the colonists themselves. As they gradually became more independent they built better houses and larger barns, adopted improved machinery and raised better stock, until to-day I am informed that there is not a family among them that is in debt. They raise almost everything they need upon their own land, and always have something to sell. They pay cash for what they buy and ask credit of no man. Their houses are comfortable, their barns and barn-yards in good order, their fences substantial, their horses, mules, and cattle fat and sleek; their lands bring them every year abundant crops of wheat (at the rate of twenty bushels to the acre without the use of commercial fertilizers), corn, Irish potatoes, clover, millet, vegetables of all kinds, while their vineyards afford enormous yields of grapes, much of which is made into wine of a good quality, for which there is ready sale."

In 1878 the played-out land brought four dollars an acre, and many a laugh and shrug of the neighborhood shoulders. To-day it is rated at fifty dollars an acre. One may say that there was as much in the patience and industry and thrift of those settlers as there was in the soil, and, indeed, those are wonder-breeding qualities; but they will not enable a man to raise double crops in the summer even in the rich Red River Valley of Minnesota. They won't enable a man to work out-of-doors most of the year, not even in Ohio.

The palace-car in which I rode from Chattanooga to Atlanta represented something more than a mere vehicle to me, and so does every palace-car to every constant or frequent traveller. If there are forty-four States in the Union, the palace-car stands for a forty-fifth. True, it is all-pervasive and common to all, like the atmosphere or the national flag, the Derby hat and the revolver, but it is still a creation by itself, which, taken largely, constitutes a very great area of space and a distinctive condition and routine of daily life separate and apart from that in the other States. It has its own distinctive population, its own peculiar etiquette ; its conventions, its three classes of citizens (conductor, porter, and passengers),

even the food that its inhabitants live upon, all differ from those in the rest of the States of the republic. I have called the palace-car commonwealth all-pervasive, like an atmosphere, and yet it even has an atmosphere of its own — a hot African air that is seldom changed or freshened, and that is gotten ingeniously either out of the sun or out of a stove, according to the season of the year in the outer world, by a unanimous army of negroes, who insist, with a loyalty that pales enthusiasm, upon carrying the climate of the Congo wherever they may go.

Persons of microscopic intellect would remind the writer that there are two sorts of palace-cars—the Wagner and the Pullman ; but since they differ only in the buttons and cap plates of the servants, and in the presence of a fish-net stretched across the bunks that is found in one sort and not in the other, it is not worth while to make the mistake of dividing this new State of the Union into a North Palace and a South Palace, as was done with even less reason with the Territory of Dakota when that was taken into the Union. No; the Palace-car State is one commonwealth, indivisible and alike in all its parts. I will admit that it is viewed differently in different parts of the country. Even the constant traveller who has lived enough of his life in it to be able to vote there, if the right of suffrage were extended to its people, regards it with varying moods in differing localities. Between New York or Boston and Chicago he looks out of its windows at the splendid homes and hotels of New York, Ohio, and Illinois with regret that he is hurrying by them, and that, when the time comes, he must eat in the car, taking chicken à la Marengo or baked pork and beans this time, because he chose the mutton stew, the only other hot dish, for his last meal. But I know one resident of the Palace-car State who has deliberately left a mining town in Montana on Christmas to clamber joyously into a palace-car solely in order to breathe its familiar Congo air, to wag between the velvet cushions of his Lower Six and the similar cushions of the smoking compartment, to eat the chicken à la Marengo with an added pint of claret, solely because of a sentimental yearning for the same sort of a Christmas, poor fellow, that others were having at home in the East.

As the porter drew the customary pillows out of the walls of the car and scattered them about, and knelt and brushed the carpet around the passengers' feet, and as the conductor leaned over the settee that held the usual solitary woman passenger and grinned and chatted with her, the sentimental journeyer thought how strange it was that in every part of the land the palace-car held to its population, selecting it everywhere from the varying masses of the people. He need not have thought about it; he had only to look out of the windows and witness the process of selection at each station. The soft hats went into the other cars. The beavers and Derbys came into the palace-car. The hoods and shawls went elsewhere, but the French bonnets and seal-skins and modish gowns all swept into the palace-car. Not a pair of boots was there on any platform but was sure to lead its owner to the ordinary coaches; and so it was with the Indians, the negroes, the flat-faced Swedish laborers, and the poor toiling women with the tagging children. All went into the other coaches, and left the sentimental journeyer surrounded by a people that never

can be better described than when they are called the inhabitants of the Palace-car State; the same in looks, manners, dress, and tastes, whether they board the palace-car in Montana or New Jersey— the conventional folks — the men who smoke cigars and wear gloves, and the women who wear furs and read the magazines.

They are perfectly at home, as persons of one region are apt to be when they are where they belong. They greet the conductor with "Well, it's as usual here," and they say to the porter, "You need not bring the bill of fare; I know it by heart." At night they catch the white eye of the Afric-American, and remark, "Feet toward the engine, you know." When they converse with one another they tell how tired they used to become on the first day out, but that now they could ride a year without minding it. They add that at first they made it a rule to get out and walk at each divisional terminus where the engines were changed, but that they soon found that all depot sheds were disagreeable alike, and as for the exercise—well, a bottle of Apollinaris

PEACHTREE STREET, ATLANTA.

in the morning or a Seidlitz-powder answers instead. But the people of the forty-fifth State of the Union are not given to making one another's acquaintance. Their situation is not so novel and unfamiliar as to break the bonds of custom, like that of persons aboard an ocean liner. The one object of the inhabitants of the Palace-car State is to achieve a lethargic, semi-comatose condition, and loll the length of the railway, minding nobody's affairs, resenting all outside efforts to mind theirs, and capable of rousing to a normal activity and interest in life only when the train passes the débris of a collision-wreck, or rushes through a prairie fire, or a fire in an autumn forest.

In many respects the Palace-car State is the best feature of Southern travel; indeed, nothing else enables one to enjoy the beauties of that section and ignore its blemishes so well as does the palace-car. This is because the main blemishes of the South are its bad hotels. Until very lately the few "best hotels" in the South— such as the Charleston, the Ballard Exchange, the Royale, and the St. Charles— were all as old as the Astor House, and had the added and general defect of serving only fried food. There are new hotels just now at Savannah, Atlanta, St. Augustine, and one or two other places; otherwise the South still stands in need of a general reform.

In the Palace-car State of the Union there are perhaps twenty counties that

possess little smoking-car libraries, containing the earlier works of Messrs. Howells, Stockton, Harte, Clemens, and Hale, but the great majority of rolling villages, towns, and counties offer but one book for the distraction of the mind and the elevation thereof. That is the Hotel Directory. Having nothing half so good to do, after the lamps were lit and the shades were drawn down, during this journey from Chattanooga to Atlanta, I took this directory on my lap and counted the hotels at which I had stopped—one time or many—in the other forty-four States of the Union. I found that the inn to which I was going in Atlanta would become the two hundred and eighty-fourth hostelry on my list. What a volume of reminiscence that discovery suggested! A genius, an inspired instrument of kindly fate, whispered that there was a new hotel in Atlanta. To it I went, and entered a blaze of electric light that shone upon resplendent plate-glass and gilding and marble. Then to my room to find it better than I would have ordered it had I the fairy gift of making my way by wishing. It was a symphony of white lace curtains, creamy Wilton carpet, carved-oak furniture of the sort that proclaims Grand Rapids, Michigan, the mother of art and comfort, a great snow-white bed, and hovering about, with a touch of a feather duster here and a touch of it there, a *white* chambermaid in a mob-cap —the only white chambermaid I ever saw in the South. There were well-chosen etchings on the warmly tinted walls. There was a reading-lamp at the head of the immaculate bed. The battery of toilet ware upon the pretty wash-stand was pretty enough to stop all the women in the streets had it been exposed in a shop window. It did not seem possible. It was like a trick of the mind— a dream taken standing.

Then the dining-room! If I had been obliged to describe it while the full effect of its first burst of splendor was upon me, the

THE GRADY MONUMENT, ATLANTA.

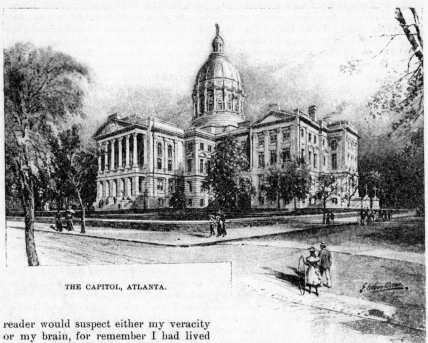

THE CAPITOL, ATLANTA.

reader would suspect either my veracity or my brain, for remember I had lived upon corn pone and bacon and bacon and corn pone, with occasional interruptions of fried chicken, for nearly a month. The ample, brilliant room, the swift, silent waiters, the white damask, the crystal, the plate, the broad hospitable chairs, the fashion-plate ladies with shining evening faces, each face between great shoulder-puffs of silk—these were the surprises that rushed upon my vision. And then the bill of fare! Blue Points led the elegant minuet, and consommé with marrow balls was the first fair partner. Then came smelts with tartare sauce, but without any final e on the name of the sauce, that having been lost in the long journey from France. Among the several sets that took their places in this gastronomic function were many such familiar cosmopolitans as young turkey and calf's head with brown sauce, and mushrooms and olives, banana ice-cream, six sorts of cheeses, every approved wine, nuts and raisins and candy with the pastry. Having eaten many times but never dined, I fear I misbehaved, and at the last I scattered silver like a Russian roué, giving a quarter to the waiter, another to the wine-boy, one to the head waiter, ten cents to the sable reminder of the court of Louis XV. who

handed round the hats, and barely succeeded in holding back a dime from the portly man who asked if I had dined well, and who lost the money by explaining that he was the manager of the hotel. In this age of introspective analysis and psychologic literature it is as well to put on record the sensations of an impressionable traveller upon encountering a good hotel.

The old soldier who, in revisiting each spot where he served under fire, fights his battles over again before his younger friends, will be puzzled how to play his rôle in Atlanta. What was a village when General Sherman destroyed it now spreads over a city's area. For Atlanta is truly a fine, substantial, genuine, bustling city. It is the busy, throbbing heart of a revolutionized region that includes the best parts of several States. It does not grow upon—it bursts upon the visitor. He alights from the cars in a noisy, crowded, smoke-grimed depot, and sees that his is but one of many trains—to New York, to New Orleans, to the West, and to smaller places nearer by. Leaving the depot, he finds himself in a solid, imposing, genuine city, built of brick, paved with stone, thick with towering buildings. It is Western, rather than Northern or Eastern, and the first impression is that it is Chicagoesque; but it is so only in the older parts. The newer districts are much more suggestive of Denver, clean and tasteful and artistic. However, that is not borne in upon the visitor's faculties until he has entered the newest office buildings and the newest hotels and theatres, and seen how rich and yet how chaste and well controlled is the use of costly material and the distribution of ornament. The Aragon, the Equitable

histories. I take it that the most interesting thing about Atlanta is that—even to a greater extent than this has been true of Chicago during many years—it is a city wherein every man works for his living. The bustle in the wholesale and the retail business streets, and the eternal whiz-ziz-ziz of the electric cars that run upon seventy-four miles of streets, typify and emphasize this feature that seems so peculiar to us of the older cities. Nine steam railway lines meet in the black, iron-mouthed railway depot, which is in the precise centre of a circular area of buildings and streets—a circle nearly four miles in diameter. Within this area is all

MARIETTA STREET, ATLANTA.

Building, the Opera-house, and more than one of the bank buildings might all have been built for Denver, the parlor or Pullman city of America.

Atlanta is the commercial distributing centre for the southeastern part of our country. It is both old and new. It was first settled in 1839, and presently was christened Terminus. Then it became Marthasville, and in 1847 it took the name Atlanta. It was destroyed in 1864—an occurrence that no more hinders the growth of American cities than heavy showers disturb so many ducks. New York and Boston have been all but burned up, and Chicago and Atlanta quite so, yet such trifles soon turn to memories, and then to mere sentences in the local

that should complete a city, and more besides, for the imposing State Capitol is one of the institutions it contains, and besides there is a notable collection of educational foundations, including several private medical colleges, a dental college, a law-school, several seminaries for girls, and two collegiate schools for boys, six institutions for the tuition of negroes, two libraries, and the State Technological School of Georgia. Of church buildings there are no less than ninety-eight. The piety of the masses of the Southern people is sufficiently remarkable to be worthy a paper by itself, and it is thus reflected in this work-a-day capital. Grant Park, the popular pleasure-ground, is, I suspect, the most ambitious city play-ground in

THE ZOOLOGICAL GARDEN AT GRANT'S PARK, ATLANTA.

the South, and will hold its rank if the people have their will with it.

But it is as a commercial and manufacturing city that Atlanta must get the most praise and excite the greatest wonder. According to the most reliable figures I could obtain the city contains 225 wholesale mercantile houses, which transact an annual business of $95,000,000. The city also operates six hundred and forty-odd manufactories that are capitalized at about $20,000,000. It is close to coal and iron, workable clays, and soft and hard wood forests, and these materials enter most largely into the local manufactures. All these are growing, and the annual investments in new buildings reach deep into the millions.

Very like so many Western folks—that is to say, very American—are the business men of the city. Nowhere else in the South do the methods of the merchants and manufacturers carry so many reminders of what, when we see it elsewhere, we call the "hustling" spirit. As an illustration, I have at hand an appeal to the Atlanta City Council for an appropriation of $10,000 for the Manufacturers' Association, which claims to represent about $10,000,000 in factories and other property. Its members say they want to spend the appropriation and twice as much of their own raising to "put Atlanta-made goods in every retail store in Georgia, and induce our people to patronize home industries and keep Georgia money in Georgia." They promised to keep at home millions of dollars a month that were then spent in purchasing elsewhere goods that are made and could be bought at home, and they add that they "can duplicate any order in the world" (the Western hustlers never stop short of "the world" in their similes) "for the same money. We can do it, we are doing it, and we want to teach that fact to the consumers."

In one respect Atlanta will disappoint the idle traveller; it is not Southern. The only proof it offers to the eye of being in the South is in the multitude of negroes in the streets, and, of course, in its mild winter climate. The climate reaches neither extreme of heat or cold, and although the city is upon a considerable elevation above the sea, it has had winters without snow, though a little which melts almost as it falls is expected there each year. Its negroes are fewer than one would expect to find, and though there may be other such cities, it is the only place where my attention has been called to the fact that white and black men work together—not merely in mixed gangs of unskilled men sweeping the streets and digging the cellars, but just such parti-colored bands of skilled workmen also, for Atlanta has both black and white masons, bricklayers, carpenters, and artisans of other sorts.

In the years between 1880 and 1890 the manufactures of Georgia were exactly doubled in value. The articles which return millions of revenue each are brick and tile, carpentering, road vehicles, cars, cotton goods, fertilizers, flour and meal, foundry and machine-shop work, iron and steel, liquors, lumber, cotton-seed products, rice-cleaning, tar, turpentine, and naval stores. Agricultural implements, leather, and printing and publishing, each brings nearly a million a year.

Improved methods of farming have greatly raised the yield of cotton, and the general agricultural prosperity is indicated by the fact that forty-two per cent. of the farmers own their farms, all but four per cent. of this number having them free and clear of encumbrance. The fifty-eight per cent. of non-owners are, of course, the negroes, who rent or farm on shares. There are less than 1,000,000 whites in Georgia and 858,000 negroes, but neither there nor anywhere else in the South are the negroes multiplying as rapidly as the whites. It was in Georgia that the movement to bring the cotton and the mill side by side had its first trial before the war. After the war the mills multiplied and grew, and considerable mill towns were developed. The State has been pushed down in the scale in this respect, rather in the number of its mills, however, than in the quality of its manufactures, which is still very high. Its iron industry is in what is part of the Chattanooga-Alabama district, but it has profited exceptionally from this minor resource by utilizing the iron in home manufactures to a greater extent than at least one of the neighboring States has done.

AMONG THE BLUE-GRASS TROTTERS

"WE Kentuckians are never in a hurry."

"But your horses are, for you, and they make ample amends," said I.

"Why, yes, they do not seem to waste a great deal of time, that is true."

These words were spoken, as the stories are fond of beginning, apropos of some slight delay, at the railway station at Lexington, in the heart of the blue-grass country, and my interlocutor was a courteous ex-Confederate general who was waiting to take me to see one of the great breeding-farms on which the American trotter has been brought to his highest grade of perfection.

The blue-grass country is reached by traversing central Virginia and Kentucky along the line of the picturesque Chesapeake and Ohio Railway, unless, indeed, one prefers the swift and solid Pennsylvania route to Cincinnati, and drops down to it from the north. On this particular journey, at any rate, it was reached past the battle-fields and springs of Virginia, and up and down the long slopes of the Blue Ridge and gorges of the Greenbrier and Kanawha, in the wilder Alleghanies.

It is found to be a little cluster of peculiarly favored counties in the centre of the State. Marked out on the map, it is like the kernel, of which Kentucky is the nut; or like one of those "pockets" of precious metals happened upon by miners in their researches. The soil is of a rich fertility, the surface charmingly undulating. Poverty seems abolished. On every hand are evidences of thrift corresponding with the genial bounty of nature. A leading crop in times past has been hemp, and land that will grow hemp will grow anything. This is being more and more withdrawn in favor of stock-raising exclusively, but the tall stacks of hemp, in shape like Zulu wigwams, still plentifully dot the landscape.

Lexington is its capital. It is a place of some eighteen thousand people, and has five important railroad connections. It is comfortably built of red brick. Its hotel, which has occasion to entertain not a few distinguished people, is on quite a large scale, and unexpectedly well kept. On a prominent knoll is the rusty-looking building of the Kentucky University, *alma mater* of Jefferson Davis. The old court-house, in the centre of the town, which is about to be pulled down—the more is the pity—has echoed to the eloquence of Clay, Marshall, Crittenden, and Breckinridge. On "court days," in the first of each month, the plaza about it, called Cheapside, is the scene of a bustling market sale of horses, cattle, mules, and sheep. A dozen mounted auctioneers are heard shouting at once. The whole area is a confusion of tossing horns, kicking legs, and blatant noises, among which the negro custodians keep such order as they can. These court days are held at other places in turn, and the stock is to be met with on the roads trooping from one to the other.

It must not be supposed that our blooded horses are thus disposed of. The very best must be sought on the stock-farms individually; at the same time, on court day, perhaps there may be found a choice of a hundred or more good saddle and harness horses on sale in a quieter way. Here is a long clean stable, for instance, almost as long as a rope-walk, next to the Phœnix Hotel, which is a typical establishment, and where they can be found. The owners gather them in from the breeders, and have themselves also a training and breeding establishment in the suburbs.

Ashland, once the home of Henry Clay, is to be seen, and again the cemetery, in which a tall column, somewhat resembling that in the Place Bastille at Paris, with his statue in a Senatorial attitude on the top of it, has been raised to his memory. Harry of the West, in earlier days the humble Mill Boy of the Slashes, came in time to have the prevailing taste for fast horses, and it is not likely that he was injured by this in the eyes of his peculiar class of constituents. He owned Yorkshire and a number of imported mares, which he left to his only surviving son, John M. Clay. The Ashland place is in the suburbs. It has a charming location and view, but the residence itself is disfigured, in a rebuilding of late years, by tawdry modern cast-iron work, "sanded" to represent stone. There are vestiges of a track behind it, where another son, James B. Clay, first brought out the capabilities of the great Mambrino Chief, a trotting stallion notable in the annals of horseflesh. It is gratifying to know that, after a long sequestration, the place has again passed into the hands of the family, in the

person of a granddaughter, the wife of Major Henry C. McDowell. This gentleman will remove there a fine stud of trotting stock, at the head of which is the beautiful Hambletonian stallion King René, and the name of the place will no doubt again be frequently heard through its connection with a leading industry of Kentucky.

At one side of the town is the track of the Lexington Jockey Club, the oldest active association of the kind in the United States, founded in 1795, only a year after Mad Anthony Wayne had broken the power of the Indian tribes on the Maumee. On the other are the track and much finer grounds and buildings of the quite modern Kentucky Trotting-horse Breeders' Association. The running track, formerly used for trotting as well, has naturally seen some notable achievements in its long existence. The immortal Lexington, bred by Dr. Elisha Warfield at The Meadows, within a stone's-throw of the town, Ten Broeck, Longfellow, King Alfonso, Kentucky, and Asteroid may be mentioned among the runners that have sped around its circuit. Lexington, whose influence is more potent than any other in the present American breed of runners, begot in his time no less than 236 winners of races, with aggregate winnings of $1,160,000. Of trotters it saw in early times of the movement such stallions as George Wilkes, Sentinel, Strathmore, Dictator, Banker, New York, Happy Medium, Administrator, Aberdeen, and Alexander's Abdallah, all sons of Rysdyk's Hambletonian, and brought out from the East to become progenitors of the stock which has since added millions of wealth to the State. It has historic memories from the late war. Ridden over by Morgan's men—Morgan himself having been a Lexingtonian, and originally commander of the Lexington Rifles—and bivouacked upon by both armies in turn, not a stick of value was left standing. Nowhere is there less trace of war or a more good-humored way of speaking about it than in this section, but its retarding effect upon the horse industry, through the scattering and loss of so many fine animals, was very great.

The Kentucky Trotting-horse Breeders' Association offer at their annual meeting in the fall only colt stakes and purses, the limit being at four years of age. They have also established of late a Trotting

Register of their own, to which the terms
of admission are much more severe than
to that of the National Association at New
York. The amphitheatre on their track
is a gay turreted edifice following the bend
of the course, and accommodating 10,000
people. Here Aldine, one of William H.
Vanderbilt's fast pair, made a great exhibition of staying power. She lost three
heats, "tied" the fourth, and finally won
the fifth, sixth, and seventh, "distancing,"
or leaving eighty yards behind, the horse
which was at first in the van. Monroe
Chief here made the best four-mile record,
in the fall of 1882, and what is the more
remarkable, each mile in exactly the same
time, 2 minutes 23 seconds.

There are some regulations in force
here which might well serve as a model
throughout the country. The association
has by its charter absolute control of its
grounds, and allows upon them neither
gambling, drinking, nor side-shows. Freed
thus from all obnoxious elements, the racing on this track is patronized without
fear by people of the best standing.

One or other of these tracks, up to two
years ago, had kept the highest one, two,
three, and four year old records. When
the two-year-old filly So-and-So made her
mile here in 2.31 in 1877, it was openly
scoffed at on the receipt of the telegrams
in New York, and deemed incredible.
Since then the prestige has momentarily
departed. The great Californian colts have
come up. As the record now stands, Governor Stanford heads the yearling list with
his Huida Rose in 2.36½, and the two-year-
olds with Wildflower in 2.21. Next comes
the three-year-old Phil Thompson, a Ken-
tucky-bred horse, however, in 2.21. The
four-year-olds are led by a Kentucky
horse also, Jay Eye See, in 2.19. It is said
by some, however, that the Californians,
raised in a climate which is favorable to
precocious development, can not hold out
to the maturer ages.

One drops into horse talk immediately
on alighting from the train at Lexington,
and does not emerge from it again till he
takes his departure. It is the one subject
always in order. Each successive proprietor, as he tucks you into his wagon, if
you will go with him—and if you will go
with him there is no limit to the courtesy
he will show you—declares that now, after having seen animals more or less well
in their way, he proposes to show you
a HORSE. Fortunately there are many

kinds of perfection. He may have the
best horse or colt of a certain age, the one
which has made the best single heat, or
fourth heat, or quarter of a mile, or average at all distances, or the best stallion, or
brood-mare, or the one which has done
some of these things at private if not public trials. Each one has, at any rate, the
colt which is *going to be* the great horse
of the world. This is an amiable vanity
easily pardoned, and the enthusiasm is
rather catching. A man's stock is greatly
to his credit and standing in this section
while he lives, and when he dies is printed prominently among the list of his virtues.

But meanwhile we keep waiting the
courteous host with whose words the chapter is opened, and to whom, in recognized
story fashion, we now return. He is a
Confederate general, who commanded the
artillery at Vicksburg. Before that he
was a soldier in the Mexican war, and
wounded at Buena Vista under Lieutenant-Colonel Clay, "Young Henry," who
lost his life there. He is a college graduate, lawyer by profession, was ruined by
the war, but recovered himself afterward,
considers it an easy matter to make fortunes, and has made the best of all of
them by his high-grade horse farm, conducted on enlightened principles. He has
one hundred and twenty brood-mares, and
two hundred and seventy-six blooded animals of all sorts and sizes set down in his
catalogue.

The possession of a fast horse curiously
gives a kind of vicarious merit to his proprietor. We are to esteem him too something of a high-stepper and flyer, and as
likely to run his factory, his newspaper or
railroad, or whatever it may be, a little
better than other people. It is the best advertising medium known. An audacious
patent-medicine firm is said to have offered
$25,000 for the bare privilege of changing
the name of Vanderbilt's Maud S., when it
would have made it, of course, that of the
nostrum in question. Maud S., it will be
remembered, is the fastest trotter in the
world, having made a mile in 2.10¼.
Again, we have the story of the impecun-
ious suitor who promised his prospective
father-in-law that within forty-eight hours
after getting control of his daughter and
her fortune he should secure a greater
reputation than Queen Victoria.

"How will you do it?" the affluent but
stern parent inquired.

"I shall buy Maud S."

The proposition of genius is said to have been interrupted at this point by the wails and discomfiture of speedy ejectment. If, however, such reverence is to be evoked by the owner of a single fast horse, what shall we say to one who has well nigh three hundred? But these questions pass away, and, hardened no doubt by familiarity, we soon find ourselves treating our entertainers quite on the terms of ordinary mortals.

General William T. Withers's "Fairlawn" is just at the edge of Lexington. It is a comfortable modern stone house in the midst of fine shade trees of the natural woods of Kentucky. It is approached up an avenue through a patent self-acting gate. Around it are scattered numerous barns, stables, and other out-buildings. The land is divided into various paddocks and pastures, in which the reddish spots of feeding colts are scattered about, by stretches of excellent white fence. A fence here, according to a saying of the section, must be "mule-high, bull-strong, and pig-tight." This place has but two hundred and forty acres, but the brood-mares are kept on another farm, of five hundred acres, elsewhere. At one side of the grounds is a commodious training track, laid out like one of those mythical fairy circles on which the spinning of rapid feet weaves spells of enchantment and prosperity. It is visible from the library window, and the general may stand there, even with the curtains closed, and see the performances of his horses, and act as a check on any negligent practices of his grooms.

The host seats us in this comfortable library, and explains to us his theories and shows us his books of record. Every birth, every pedigree, is accurately entered. It is a business, as thus conducted, which calls for a high order of intelligence. Horse-breeding as at one time conducted was but an innocent form of gambling. The processes were hap-hazard and the result of ignorance. Again, much money was lost through the choice of inferior stock. Of late the theory prevails that the very best is not too expensive; a great deal of valuable certainty has been deduced from the collective wisdom of the past, and, as a rule, money is made instead of lost.

The library cases are lined with books on the horse; the walls, with those of the house generally, and indeed of the blue-grass region throughout, are hung with his pictures. Over the door is the historic Rysdyk's Hambletonian, Roman-nosed, hollow-backed, and far from a model of good looks, upon a field of plain grass and sky. Opposite is a canvas showing Happy Medium in his stable. At the right is Cassius M. Clay, Jun., and at the left Almont, flying at the top of their speed, till their sulky wheels are but a ghostly blur. In the main hall are Almont and Clay again, standing; and in the hall above, on the way to my chamber—set apart also, it seems, in his time, for King Kalakaua, who has been a visitor and buyer of horseflesh here—are Almont and Hambletonian respectively in large landscapes of a purplish tinge and crude workmanship. Who are these horse artists? Well, they are specialists who have reduced the pose and rendering of the animal to a mechanical formula in obedience to the commands of their patrons, and though sometimes displaying not a little skill in color and modelling, would hardly be accepted in any recognized exhibition. More often they are irresponsible floaters, broken-down German noblemen, perhaps, according to their own story, who profess to ability in this direction, and produce daubs of the most hopeless kind. The pictures of an early artist, Edwin Troye, where extant among the blue-grass breeders, seem to be more esteemed than any others.

An amusing chapter might be devoted by itself to the caricatures on the subject, which have been profuse from the days of Cruikshank down. We might see the humors of the fancier with his sorry jade booted, blanketed, and weighted up to the nines, the shrewd bargainers endeavoring to overreach each other, the ambitious cockney setting out for a brush on Harlem Lane, beaten by an ash cart or beer wagon, and finally "hung up" in a tree with a buggy wheel around his neck; but these things are found mainly in the stables and hotel lobbies, and the breeders take quite a serious view of their case.

Now for out-of-doors to see the place in detail. In the first place, the blue-grass! Perhaps one has expected to see vegetation of such colors as it often displays on china plates or in young women's worsted-work; but it is not blue at all. The general pulls up a tuft of it in the pasture. It grows in bunches, is fine and wiry, and has no other stalk than the

Aberdeen.   Almont Lightning.
Ethan Allen, Jun.   Happy Medium.

AT THE STABLES.

seed-stalk. It remains fresh all winter, thrives under the snow, and is not cut, since it keeps itself better than it can be kept as hay. It is "blue limestone grass" properly, though there is a popular belief that it really takes a bluish color in June, and it is from the peculiar rock stratum of the country on which it grows that it takes its name.

The best stock is said to follow the limestone rather than clay and sandstone formations, the world over. It forms a perpetual fertilizer for the land, and gives out a pasturage upon which is knit fine bone and firm muscular tissue. The Kentucky blue limestone too is a quarry for the turnpike-roads, which are of phenomenal excellence, and the even stone walls, used for fencing, with a park-like effect, everywhere throughout the section. It crops up in picturesque ledges in the landscapes, and forms bold and striking palisades along the rivers. Curious caverns are sometimes formed in it, in which the streams disappear, to come up as mysteriously elsewhere. I have seen such a stream come out of the ground like a

spring, but strong enough to turn a mill wheel at the start.

General Withers's principal stable is a kind of horse cathedral. This is by no means common. Many a fine animal, almost as much the pride and pet of its owner's family as if they were of Arab stock, is led out from but shabby quarters. The stables of the region are clean and wholesome, but do not incline to fantastic elegances of adornment such as are growing in favor among ourselves in the Northern cities. Here the light strikes down upon us through colored glass windows; the whole interior is faced up with hard woods; and the floor of the principal aisle, or nave, strewn with soft straw for exhibiting the paces of the animals upon, could not be neater if it were that of a drawing-room. The main dimension is 155 feet, and this is crossed by a transept of 100. The stalls are toward sixteen feet square. They have outer as well as inner doors for egress in case of fire, and these are never kept locked. Little or no fancy iron-work in the way of stable fittings is used, wooden racks and mangers being preferred. Wide open spaces over the partitions and transom ventilators carry off all odors. The clean hay is piled in mows above, and the corn and oats slide down by traps into convenient bins. Then there is a place for sulkies and road-wagons, a harness room and harness-mending room, and a great collection of the mysterious-looking boots and weights used in breaking in the trotter.

These accommodations are for the benefit of the horses whose education is completed, so far as this is done at a breeding-farm, and which are for sale. There are, in fact, very few wholly mature horses of the best sort, except those reserved for stock purposes, to be found among the breeders. They are bought up at an early age, and taken away to professed trainers, or out of the State, to be prepared for their future triumphs. It is chiefly to a display of beautiful colts, with their sires and dams, that the visitor to the "horse-pasturing Argos" of Kentucky is invited.

An adjoining stable of an older fashion, though equally as neat, is devoted to the colts, taken up from those running at large in the fields, to be broken in. The stalls here are eight feet by ten for a single inmate, and ten by twelve for two. A narrow aisle runs through the centre, into which project from the stalls wooden troughs, by which food is expeditiously delivered. Next comes a long row of low brick buildings, containing the superintendent's house, and carpenter, paint, and blacksmith shops. The last is redolent of the peculiar smell of burning hoof, and merry with the clink of iron and gossip of the negro grooms, who will tell you wonderful stories all day long of the doings of their equine charges. Near by a little court-yard is reserved as a hospital, and in it stand a few animals awaiting dolefully the end of their woes.

"I am no great believer in veterinary doctors," says our host. "They kill more than they cure. I blanket my patients, protect them from sudden extremes of the weather, and give but little medicine. That is my system."

Visitors sit comfortably in chairs in the cathedral-like stable, and the horses are brought out before them. Representatives from this stable have gone to many climes. They have been sent to Canada and Prince Edward Island, to Oregon, to Australia and New Zealand, to Italy, and to the Russian province of Bessarabia, to mingle with the Orloff trotter, which is not greatly unlike our own.

Make way! make way! The spirited young stallion Almont Lightning, son of Almont, is led out into the straw-covered aisle. He is good nature itself, yet it would not be comfortable to be knocked by his heels into the middle of next week, even in play. What power and fire! He is sixteen hands high, dark bay, and has black points extending up to the knees and hocks. His groom, pressing one hand on the withers, and holding the halter in the other, runs with him up and down. It is like another representation of Alexander and Bucephalus.

In a house of his own, on another part of the place, is his sire, Almont, and near the latter the stallions Aberdeen, Happy Medium, and Ethan Allen, Jun., who all together constitute the strength of the estate. Almont, though a little rounder in the barrel and lower, and eighteen years of age, is full of exuberant life, and hardly to be distinguished from his son, who is six. He is spoken of as now the best in the State, Mr. A. J. Alexander's Harold, sire of Maud S., probably coming next. He is the best son of Alexander's Abdallah, as Abdallah was the best son of Rysdyk's Hambletonian. He is the sire of Aldine and Early Rose, who have trotted together in 2.16½, and of Piedmont, who made 2.17 in a fourth heat, and he has to his credit twenty sons and daughters with records of from 2.30 down, three of these being below 2.20. A great breeding sire may or may not be a flyer himself. It is said that the famous Hambletonian could not go inside of three minutes. It is his progeny that rise up and call him blessed. The prize most valued by the breeder of all that are offered at the exhibitions is for "the best stallion with the best three of his get."

If the pedigree of Almont, in the male line, were succinctly stated after Scriptural fashion, it would be somewhat as follows: The Darley Arabian, imported into England in the year 1709, begot Flying Childers, and Flying Childers begot Blaze, and Blaze begot Sampson, and Sampson begot Engineer, and Engineer begot English Mambrino, and English Mambrino begot Messenger (imported into the United States), and Messenger begot Abdallah, and Abdallah begot Rysdyk's Hambletonian, and Rysdyk's Hambletonian begot Alexander's Abdallah, and Alexander's

ALMONT.

Abdallah begot Almont. The pedigree in the breeder's catalogue, however, follows back his dam and granddam in the same way, the first tracing through the divergent stream of Mambrino Paymaster to the Darley Arabian also, and the second through Alexander's Pilot, Jun., and imported Diomed to the Godolphin Arabian. It traces also each male factor to his first, second, and third dam, and sets down his famous progeny and his time, so that the whole occupies two closely printed duodecimo pages.

The stallion Aberdeen is a son of Rysdyk's Hambletonian by the Star mare Widow Machree. The Widow was one of the gamest mares that ever lived. She would go in any condition of health, and in her greatest race had to be helped to her feet, and "could scarcely put one foot before the other" when she first came on the track. Happy Medium is another son of Rysdyk's Hambletonian, by Princess, the great rival of Flora Temple. Ethan Allen, Jun., represents the hardy Morgan family. Cassius M. Clay, Jun., lately dead, introduced into the Fairlawn stud the blood of the Clay family, descended

from imported Grand Bashaw, a barb presented by the Bey of Tunis to President Jefferson. It is a strain rather weak and faint-hearted by itself, apt to give out before the mile is over, but of great value in combination with others. The varieties mentioned sum up most of the favorite strains known to the breeder's art.

All these names, periods, families, and records, together with the other paraphernalia with which the professed horseman delights to surround himself, are something of a chaos at first to the beginner. By a little pains, however, the mystery may be dispelled, and at the same time the theory of breeding upon which the leading blue-grass residents are mainly agreed in their practice may be arrived at.

A horse must have made a mile in 2 minutes and 40 seconds to find admission to that Burke's Peerage of the race, the American Trotting Register. The Kentucky breeders have reduced this in their register to 2.30. Certain blood-relatives of these favored ones are also ennobled by their performances, and find a place.

There are no more than ninety-nine

horses in the world which have records of or below 2.20, though perhaps some fifteen hundred of or below 2.30. This simplifies the number of those important enough to be specially looked after, and it will be seen that all descend from a few leading sources. Where names are reduplicated the name of the owner of each is attached—as Rysdyk's Hambletonian, Bishop's Hambletonian, Vermont Hambletonian—to prevent confusion.

About all the trotting stock extant traces to some five families, based originally on the English thorough-bred, or running, stock. They are not at all of equal size; some are of a very minor sort; and by far the most prominent is that outlined in the descent of Almont, through imported Messenger. The Darley Arabian, the Godolphin Arabian—whom Eugène Sue has celebrated in his romance as "the King of the Winds"—and one or two others were brought over from Arabia in the early eighteenth century to improve the common stock of England. From them chiefly has been developed the whole English race of thorough-breds. The product is larger, stronger, swifter, and in most respects an improvement on his ancestry; but in the process he has lost the gentleness, the almost human intelligence, of the Arabian, and become overbearing and surly in temper. As original aristocracy derives from the Arabians, it would seem to be an easy matter to keep up the importations, and thus maintain the standard of form and temper at any pitch required. This has in fact been tried, and hundreds more of the horses of the East imported into the country since those times, but hardly ever with success. The belief went out, therefore, that the Arabians had degenerated, which was strengthened by the fact of English horses having beaten some of those of the Khedive in Egypt; but a Mr. Keene Richards, who imported Arabians into Kentucky, and whose story is an interesting one, maintained that the failure was due to not having secured horses of the best sort; and he adduced reasons to show the excessive difficulty of doing it, even with the best intentions.

However that may be, the English thorough-bred Messenger was brought to America before 1790. Though a runner by nature, he proved to be exceptionally strong in the trotting action, and to have the power to transmit it to his descendants as well. He was the progenitor of the most remarkable family of trotters the world has ever seen. To descend from Messenger, for a horse, is a good deal like having come over with the Conqueror, or landed with the Pilgrims at Plymouth Rock. But with animals as with men, great powers are transmitted only along certain lines and to a limited few. Although he left after him more than a thousand children, and these a myriad of others, but a very small number continued his dynasty and became centres of power themselves. His son Bush Messenger propagated his blood in Maine; his grandson Hambletonian, in Vermont; his son Mambrino, two best grandsons, Rysdyk's Hambletonian and Mambrino Chief, and some few others in New York and the Central States, and later in Kentucky and the South.

Trotting, it is well known, is of recent date as compared with the running gait. The thorough-bred running horse has almost innumerable crosses to his coat of arms, while the highest-bred trotter can not possibly at present show more than six. Some few enthusiasts all along, from the time of Messenger down, we may suppose, met together and celebrated this amusement. Hiram Woodruff, the veteran trainer, who was a large part of what he describes, has given us a book of memoirs, full of the rattle of hoofs and genial horse talk, which make it interesting reading. The period it covers, up to about 1860, may be called the last part of the dark age of the art. The trotters were ridden under saddle when he began. The participants in the sport were rather looked askance at, but perhaps enjoyed it only the more for their partial proscription. Now a vast interest has grown up, and while the runner still remains an exotic, the trotter is recognized as so essentially American a product that he might almost be engraved on the national shield. A national association has been formed, with head-quarters at Hartford, Connecticut, which holds congresses and courts of arbitration, and has supervision of some one hundred and eighty tracks throughout the country, and these represent property to the value of $200,000,000. The latest phase of the subject is the withdrawing of the best horses from the racing arena entirely by gentlemen of means, who reserve them for their own driving.

The general situation being as described,

THE STRANGER.—[SEE PAGE 725.]

John W. Hunt, toward forty years ago, brought out to Kentucky Commodore and Old Abdallah, grandsons of Messenger. They were not greatly appreciated just then, and were taken back. The list of horses mentioned in connection with the older Lexington track shortly followed, but it was not until Mambrino Chief was brought out in 1854, and Alexander's Abdallah in 1858, that the movement in the blue-grass region, which has had such notable results, really began. Mambrino Chief, sire, among others, of Lady Thorne, proved a prolific sire of mothers of trotters. He left after him in the direct male line seventy-four trotters with records of 2.30 or better. Alexander's Abdallah, though starting later and happening on the disastrous times of the war—in which he finally perished of ill usage at the hands of guerrillas—left thirty-nine trotters with records of 2.30 or better, one being Goldsmith Maid, whose record is 2.14. In these two names is epitomized a history of equine greatness. It is found in all breeding that the best results are realized from uniting again divergent streams of kindred blood which have been separated for a certain time; and this brings us to the theory of raising the fast trotters at present in favor in Kentucky.

"I take a list of all trotters which have ever made a record of 2.20 or better," says our host, the general, settling comfortably down to his demonstration, "and ascertain to what families they belong. This gives me at once the leading sources. I next trace the number of representatives in 2.30 or under belonging to each family, and find the test begun with the first experiment confirmed. Nearly all belong to a very few families, and as the speed test is increased, more and more belong to that of Rysdyk's Hambletonian. These are naturally the families to breed from, since if there is certainty anywhere, it is here, while outside, the domain of chance is too large."

Acting upon these principles, such a selection of stallions has been made, with Belmont at the head, as to include one from each of the main families. At the same time, in the large list of one hundred and twenty brood-mares an effort has been made to comprise some representative of every minor strain of blood as well which has ever accomplished anything of importance, in order to secure all the chances of happy combinations in crossing that are possible.

"But there seem to be now, as there always have been," I offer by way of argument, "soldiers of fortune who owe their position to their own good exertions solely. Flora Temple was taken from the tail of a drover's wagon, Dutchman from a brick cart, Justin Morgan had no ancestor that ever was known; and here in last year's list of winners are Joe Rhea, for instance, record 2.23, and Valley Boy, 2.24½, opposite whom is set the notice, 'pedigree unknown.'"

"That is true, but there are fewer every year, and it is more probable that the pedigrees have disappeared—gone down, like some of our Kentucky streams, to reappear elsewhere—than that they did not exist. If you will look at the head of last year's list you will see that the leaders are Clingstone, with a record of 2.14, and Jerome Eddy and Edwin Thorne, with 2.16½ each, and that these, with most of the rest of the long list, are out of the highest-bred trotting stock. It is but a short time, I know, since people have begun to be convinced that the trotter was not merely a happy accident, and could be bred at all; but look at the uniform improvement in the record since scientific breeding began:

Lady Suffolk,	one mile	......	1849	.....	2.28
Flora Temple,	"	......	1859	.....	2.19¾
Dexter,	"	......	1867	.....	2.17¼
Goldsmith Maid,	"	......	1874	.....	2.14
Rarus,	"	......	1878	.....	2.13¼
St. Julien,	"	......	1880	.....	2.11¼
Maud S.,	"	......	1881	.....	2.10¼

Failures are frequent, of course, but nothing is more certain now than that trotters are begotten by trotters. As any thorough-bred can beat any common horse at the run, so that it is not even necessary to have a trial to be sure of it, we expect to arrive at the same accuracy with the trotting horse."

"And what is the limit of time at which you will finally arrive?"

"Two minutes now is not more incredible than was two-twenty a quarter of a century ago," replies the general.

This is an interesting problem to speculate about, as it is always interesting to approach final facts. Will the trotter go on improving indefinitely till he reaches, with his less natural gait, the time of the running horse, which yet stands, as made by Ten Broeck in 1877, at 1.39¾, or will the very perfecting of the machine destroy it at a fixed point, causing it to flame out, perhaps, in some splendid effort like a costly fire-work? A practi-

tioner of high rank in the veterinary art testifies that of two thousand trotters examined by him fully one-half were unsound. He holds that training for trotting predisposes to diseases, and that there is more probability of finding some capital blemish in a trotter of great speed than in others.

But we have not yet inquired the cause of Kentucky's superiority—why it is that the same pains expended here produce better results than elsewhere. It is ascribed, first, to the character of the pasturage adverted to, and next to the existence in the State of an exceptionally good class of common stock for the new experiments in breeding to be based upon. Kentucky was settled up by Virginians who brought their Cavalier taste for fox-hunting and running horses into the State with them. We hear of Washington and Jefferson running horses at Alexandria in the year 1790. Colonel John Hoomes and Colonel John Tayloe, of Virginia, brought over, immediately after the Revolution, some of the best English thorough-breds, the latter bringing Diomed, the first winner of the Derby. The descendants of these constituted a stock of "warm blood," from which Richard Ten Broeck was enabled to derive horses to carry off the honors of the British turf between 1857 and 1867, and from which also have come Mr. Sanford's Preakness, winner of the Brighton cup in 1876, and later Mr. P. Lorillard's Iroquois, winner of the Derby and St. Leger, and Parole, winner at Newmarket and Epsom, and Mr. Keene's Foxhall, winner of the Ascot cup, the Grand Prize of Paris, and others.

The thorough-bred blood has always been a resource to draw upon to give the trotter "game" and "staying" power. It is a mooted question just how much of it can be used without overcoming the trotting tendency which it is desirable to cultivate. Some few trotting sires, and notably Alexander's Pilot, Jun., have had the power to transmit to their progeny the proper gait even when crossed directly with a thorough-bred, but as a general thing this is dangerous. Many consider two trotting crosses upon a thorough-bred foundation the nearest to perfection that has been reached, and as this process has produced Maud S., bred on the neighboring Alexander estate, it has no mean argument in its favor.

There are charming rural scenes on

such a place as this at which we find ourselves, quite irrespective of the merit of the animals. Goubie's pleasing picture "La Visite aux Mères" will often be recalled. We too drive over to the distant pasture, and make our visit to the drove of brood-mares. Few would take them, running abroad in comfortable plebeian fashion in their woodland, for the valuable beings they are. Who would suppose yonder unkempt bay, round-barrelled and lazy, to be the dam of the tireless Piedmont, with his record of 2.17¼ in a fourth heat? The group gather round in a staring meditative way, as if we should have had something more for them to eat. How naïvely they are governed by their appetites—the poor animals! Here is one with a wooden yoke about her neck—a jumper of fences, and a kicker of the rest at the feeding trough. Are you not ashamed to be seen in such insignia of disgrace, rogue? What! you take the pointed finger of scorn as an invitation, and come nosing too to see if there be not something for you in our pockets? Why, then, there is nothing for it but to go away ourselves.

A chief curiosity here is the Arab mares, offspring of stock brought over in person by a gentleman of romantic history, Keene Richards, Esq., and claimed by him to be of the purest blood extant. The pedigree of one of them, to quote a typical part of it, declared him to be "a Kobeylan, the son of a Kobeylan, and his mother is a Kobeylan purer than milk. He was born and brought up in the land of Nejd. This is the genealogy of the said horse, as God is omnipotent." They are small, these Arabians, none of them standing over 15¼ hands high, and exhibit grace and intelligence rather than power. This group of three, two grays and a chestnut, are children of Fysaul, of the choice Sacklowie race, and the mare Loulie, of the Kobeylan race, older yet. Are they reflecting still perhaps on the desert, the tents, the spears, the camels, and praying-carpets from the midst of which their fathers were brought here to consort with Yankee mates? The Arabs have but lately passed into the hands of General Withers from their owner, who died impoverished. The results of crossing them with native breeds have not yet proved remarkable in any way. Local peculiarities have hampered the experiment, which may be more successful under better conditions.

The groups of colts on the main place have a thousand poses and humors of graceful interest. Here is a delegation of the tender yearlings at a fence, looking over with shy boldness. The 1st of January is the common birthday of all of them, no matter when they were foaled— a convenient practice in reckoning. They are of many sorts and sizes, "dish-faced" and Roman-nosed, white stars, silver manes and tails sparkling among them, big-stepping clumsy colts, and glib low-going fillies as feminine as girls of thirteen. At a word they are off like the birds in a sudden panic, or create one for themselves for the pure delight in the exercise. Again they are snuggling up against the golden ground of a clean straw stack as if they meant to push through it, or they are munch, munch, munching all together in a row at the long crib of one of their shelter sheds, provided for them to run into and out of freely as a change from the pastures. As to securing their likenesses by photography, they know perfectly well that the camera is designed to shoot them, and they will never submit to so dreadful a fate while it can be avoided by motion.

They are distributed into separate paddocks, not more than a dozen or twenty in company. Those used to consort together in this way form a kind of close corporation to which a stranger is only admitted with difficulty. They let fly their light heels at the new-comer, and give him a casual nip or so as he approaches the feeding trough, so that he stands disconsolately about for several days, till by a gradual assimilation he is finally received on equal terms.

As the object in raising horses is to put bone and muscle upon them, and not, as with cattle, fat, they are encouraged to run about as much as possible, and made hardy by being kept out-of-doors all but a few days of the most exceptionally inclement weather. They are taken up from their mothers when weanlings, and put in a stall two together, supporting better in this way the novel experience. A man enters every day for a while, rubs and handles them gently, and familiarizes them with human society. Then they are halter-broke, and turned loose again, not to be taken up till they are well matured yearlings. By that time they have grown rather wild again, and the process is repeated. Harness-breaking is added immediately after, and once more they are turned out to wait till the age of two years, when, if forward, they are trained a little, and if not, a beginning is not made till a year later. The old days of battle and conquest by main force have passed away forever. With the best breeders all the processes are characterized by the utmost gentleness. It is impressed upon the colts from the first that they are to have nothing to fear, and that man is their friend and not an enemy.

Perhaps it would be no such great hardship, one is inclined to think, when looking on, were there some means of bringing up human beings to the perfection of their powers in the same way. Could the race be checked on the side of its vices and encouraged to the utmost on the side of its virtues, from generation to generation, by some arbitrary power, no doubt we should arrive at the dreamed-of millennium with considerable rapidity.

What is once learned by animals of this high grade of intelligence is rarely forgotten. To teach stopping at the word "whoa," as an example of the methods in use, a piece of soft webbing is attached first to one fore-foot, then the other, and the end held in the driver's hands with the reins. At the word he pulls the foot clear of the ground, and repeats this till the horse grasps the idea of an absolute connection between the sound and the act. In bringing out the speed of the younger animals on the training track the practice of leading them around with a running mate under saddle is growing in favor. If the pupil does not show a promising gait he is shod in various ingenious ways, or loaded with toe-weights of several ounces, that he may throw out his feet in a bold and open manner. If he "interferes," there is a multiplicity of boots and pads to protect every irritated point. His first race is an occasion for which he is prepared with as much pains as a young girl for her coming-out party.

Every morning in pleasant weather all the conveyances on the place are brought into use, and the animals taken out for a jog on the road. These processions of sulkies and road-wagons become a characteristic feature. The hands in charge are chiefly negroes, men and boys, who have a natural fondness for the horse. Over them is generally a white superintendent, like our friend Mr. Dillon, whose round-shouldered pose, from much sitting in sulkies, the fore and aft rake of his cap, and the worsted comforter about his neck, irresistibly stamp him as much a part of his horse as a centaur of old. The trainer, unlike the poet, is made, not born. He begins in the stables as a rubber at an early age, and works his way up.

Among the minor problems of the business that of finding names for all these new aspirants appearing every year is not always as easy as it may seem. Poetry and romance are ransacked by the more scholarly; others invent outright appellations which they think to have a musical flow. Many endeavor to carry regular systems, at least through particular lines of descent. Thus John M. Clay had a series of the principal battles of Napoleon, Arcole, Lodi, Borodino, and the like. At the Alexanders' place a series has been Nut-wood, Nut-shell, Nut-gall, etc. Dr. Herr, a veteran trainer and promoter of the trotting interest, owner of Mambrino King and Mambrino Patchen, the best survivors of the Mambrino Chief blood, makes his chiefly Boys and Girls and Kings and Queens. There is a series of dances, as War-dance, Reel, and Waltz, and affiliations of the precious metals, as Gold Fringe, Gold-dust, Goldbeater. Again, there are family names, names of politicians, and simple initials.

The high-bred American trotter, as thus far developed, is not so finely drawn out and whalebone-like as the thoroughbred, and does not "stand over so much ground." He has a more stocky build, more sloping pasterns, and a shorter and wider neck, through which plenty of air can be pumped to supply a deep full chest. It is a question whether there is not dead weight forward which will be bred off by successive stages. He has a fine intelligent face, wide between the eyes, rather low withers, powerful hind-quarters, and especially powerful hocks, the initial points from which his great bursts of speed proceed. If with such a structure he is low-going, and a wide-goer behind, that is to say, if he gets a long reach with his hind-legs by overlapping those in front, which should play between, then he is a good one, and more than likely a great one.

See him come down the track. I do not wish to disparage the free and spontaneous rush of the runner, but there is something in the gait of the trotter which

grows on one, and ends by having a strong
fascination.   Perhaps it is its very arti-
ficiality.   The trotter has been trained to
make the distance, not the most quickly—
for the runner surpasses him half a minute in time—but in a certain way.   He is
not to "break" under any circumstances,
and his self-control when forced is intelli-

some of his best achievements, like those
of Piedmont and Aldine referred to, have
been made at the middle and close of such
ordeals.   It appears from these that while
it is not so rapid, it is the best gait for endurance.

The growth into favor of the trotting
gait in the last thirty years may be some-

" WHOA !"

gence of a high order.   The difference in
the rhythm of the hoof beats tells the
story.   The runner passes like a whirl-
wind, the double stroke upon the ground
of his wild leaps almost merging into one.
But on comes the trotter with his tap, tap,
tap, tap, steady and accurate though making twenty feet to the stride.   He marks
off his paces like the ticking of an exquisite clock.

The tests demanded of him are much
more severe than those demanded of the
runner, now that the system of short dash-
es, after the English practice, for the latter, has succeeded the four-mile races formerly in vogue.   The trotter is often called upon to go eight and nine heats of a
mile each, and, what is most remarkable,

what connected with the improvement of
the roads of the country.   Whereas travelling in the saddle was formerly a necessity, wheeling is now everywhere easy.
Driving as a diversion is more easily
learned and carried on than riding; and
while a thorough-bred must be almost necessarily devoted to racing, so that if he is
not a good one, he is good for little or nothing at all, a trotter, though he may not
be among those who win laurels on the
track, can still be both serviceable and ornamental on the road.   We have a busi-
ness-like way, too, of concentrating on the
main point.   The trotter with his outfit is
like a piece of our light and elegant machinery.   The point at issue being the
motion of the horse, no side interest in the

WOODLAKE.

way of a rider with gallant and statuesque poses is brought in to interfere with it. It may be connected, too, with some slight deficiency in the artistic sense. The director of the trotter crouched behind him in the sulky has but slight relations with the sublime and beautiful. Even General Grant, driving out behind Dexter with Mr. Bonner, though he might be lithographed perfectly well for every horse-fancier's wall in the country, could never be utilized thus for his monument.

The nine or ten small counties belonging to the blue-grass region are liberally sprinkled over with places bearing titles of their own, such as "Blue-Grass Park," the former seat of Mr. Keene Richards, "Castleton," "Walnut Heights," "Woodland Hall." In riding through the country the life upon these is found to be a good deal after the English fashion. The proprietors live upon them all the year round, and are rather country gentlemen than ordinary farmers. The houses upon them are generally large and comfortable, with tall porticoes in the old-fashioned classic style. The only difference to be noted as compared with their aspect in slave times is that the negro cabins, which formerly clustered near them, have been

swept away, and the occupants have largely moved to town. The negro no longer submits with grace to be called "uncle" and "auntie" as of yore, nor wears the becoming bright-colored bandana and large golden ear-rings. The juniors tend to shiftlessness and vice, and often aspire to play the piano, and such like elegances, rather than the serious business of life. Still, after all that is necessary has been said about their idle habits, they are preferred to any other labor, and you hear from many mouths the opinion that "it is the whites and not the blacks who have been most emancipated." Not a few of them are seen making excellent progress. They are found living in very good brick houses. I was told of one who had raised a $1500 colt, and had others under way. They hold every year near Lexington a display on fair grounds of their own. The judges are barbers and hotel waiters, and are inclined to make the awards according to the neatness of the grooming, and the blue ribbons with which the aspirants for favor are tied up; and yet in this region everybody is more or less a judge of a horse.

"Woodlake," in Franklin County, near Frankfort, the State capital, may be called a fair example of residences of a more modern style. It is the home of the Major McDowell before mentioned as the late purchaser of Ashland, and within it are some of the best portraits of Henry Clay, together with one of "Young Henry," over which hangs the sword he carried to the field of Buena Vista. The Gothic house, of blue limestone, with rustic gates of approach and bridges, might easily pass for one of our villas up the Hudson. The ground hereabouts is boldly undulating. It is well scattered with groves of fine forest trees, and one of these on the place has a great oak which might rival the famous redwoods of California. We come to a point where the mansion, on its knoll, is reflected in a pond. The farther slope is spotted with grazing South-downs, the hither one with a herd of Alderney cattle, upon whose leader tinkles a bell which might have a place in a collection of bric-à-brac, while between them pasture the beautiful high-bred colts. The lines of life under such circumstances as these certainly seem cast in pleasant places. The flocks and herds are all of the most costly and gentle sorts, and might become such a dainty pastoral life as that shown in the canvases of Boucher and Watteau.

On another part of the estate, a centre for unstudied groupings of the colts, which wander thither from the vicinity of the stables and track near by, is an old house

ous would still prefer it, with the proper repairs, to those of the newer style.

But of all the old dwellings which yet survive to typify the ideal of an "old Kentucky home," such as may have been that of the Shelbys of *Uncle Tom's Cabin*, the most curious is probably that on the Alexander estate of "Woodburn," in Woodford County. This great estate is well known as the home, and one of the earliest breeding-places, of some of the very best American running stock. Of late it is becoming equally famous for trotting stock, into which, like others of the breeding establishments, it inclines to merge its activity in preference to the first. King Alfonso (sire of Foxhall), Glen Athol, Pat Molloy, Falsetto, Powhatan (brother of Parole), and Asteroid, and their progeny, of the one breed, are to be seen about the place, with Harold (sire of Maud S.), Miss Russell (her dam), Lord Russell (her brother), Belmont, and Annapolis, and their progeny, of the other. Lexington was very early purchased by the Alexanders for $15,000. The price was deemed exorbitant at the time, till one son of Kentucky was sold for $40,000, and $50,000 was refused for another, Asteroid.

The house is not now occupied by the family, who have taken the Buford house, in the neighborhood, instead. It was built originally by a younger brother of a Scotch baronet, whose wandering fancy

OLD ALEXANDER HOUSE, WOODBURN, KENTUCKY.

known as Llangollen. It has gone to decay now, and is occupied by a familiar figure in local horse circles, the trainer, "Old Buck"; but it has been in its time the residence of a family of ministers, the Lewises, who brought race-horses hither from Virginia, and later it was a boarding-school. Many amateurs of the curi

led him to settle and marry here in the Western wilderness. He refused to leave the spot even when his brother died and he became a baronet in his turn. He drew the revenues, however, and expended them in improving the large tract he had purchased till it had become, as it now is, quite a princely domain. He contem plated a new mansion, with the rest, but this was never carried out, and so he contented himself with additions to the old one. It is low and rambling, part brick, part wood, which is silvery gray with the weather, and has its chimneys outside, and a dilapidated modern veranda in front. It is like some quaint foreign grange, and makes an excellent subject for the water-color artist.

A son of the original Alexander, a brother of the present resident owner, was living in this house during the war, when guerrillas came down upon him twice, and carried off the most valuable of his animals. On the first of these raids the great trotting sire Abdallah, heretofore spoken of, and Bay Chief were taken. The superintendent endeavored to throw the robbers off the track by substituting inferior animals, till brought to a sense of the error of his ways with a rope around his neck. It is remarkable to say, as showing the completeness with which the issues of the civil war are over, that the only one of the guerrillas wounded in this foray, after having first been condemned to be hanged, then, as a commutation, to imprisonment for life, and finally set free altogether, was this last year employed as a harvest laborer on the Alexander place.

On the next occasion it was the thorough-bred Asteroid that was run off. The artist Troye was engaged in painting his portrait at the time, and his principal rage was at the interruption of his work. This portrait, in which the trainer, "Old Ansel," and the jockey, "Brown Dick," are introduced, though on a reduced scale, with a quaint idea of not detracting from the importance of the horse, was completed on the subsequent recovery of Asteroid, and hangs in the dining-room of Mr. L. Brodhead, the general manager of the estate; and Asteroid himself, long past his usefulness, now browses out a comfortable existence on the place, till he be overtaken by the usual lot of men and horses.

A radical difference is found in the education of the runner and the trotter, corresponding somewhat to the demands put upon them. The rule for the thoroughbred may be called "a short life and a merry one." He is brought on on the forcing system, expected to do his best on the turf at two and three years of age, and shortly after is good for little or nothing. The trotter, on the other hand, is developed much more slowly, and lasts for far

more than a corresponding time. Of some of the greatest that may be mentioned, for instance, Dexter did not begin a racing career till the age of six, Lady Thorne till eight, Goldsmith Maid till nine; and the last mentioned made her great time of a mile in 2.14 at the age of seventeen.

Each blue-grass breeder of prominence has his regularly printed catalogue of stock, revised yearly, generally with a wood-cut of his best stallion on the cover. Some, as General Withers, insert the selling prices, from which "no deviation" is advertised. In looking over such a catalogue, from $400 up to $2000 are found to be demanded for the younger animals, with proportionately more for older ones that could be at once made useful. But when a horse has really entered the ranks of the great "flyers," there is hardly any limit to his value. One with a record of 2.30 may be estimated in a general way worth $10,000. From 2.30 down to 2.20, $1000 may be added for each successive second. When we come into the teens, and near the head of the record, juggling with gold and diamonds is a coarse occupation in comparison. Mr. Bonner is said to have paid $33,000 for Dexter, and $36,000 for Rarus, and Mr. Vanderbilt $20,000 for Maud S. But this last was before she had made her great time; now that she has made it, you are told confidentially that a person stands ready to draw his check willingly for $75,000 whenever he can get a horse that will lead her, and give him the distinction of having the fastest trotter in the world. But how does it *pay?* Well, it pays first in stock-raising; it pays next in the opportunity to take purses and stakes afforded by the great system of racing circuits; and no doubt even those gentlemen who withdraw from racing, and do their driving in private life, find it pay in a pleasure and improved health from this kind of recreation, extravagant as it is, which they might not be able to procure so well from the expenditure of equal sums in any other direction.

The blue-grass proprietors are, on the whole, of a sober-minded, even religious cast. Whoever has expected to find them of the Swashbuckler, rioting sort will be much mistaken. There are exceptions, it is true, but as a rule there is little drinking, or even going to races, grace is said before meat, and the family conveyance is regularly got out on Sunday mornings for driving to church in the next town.

MY LIFE AS A SLAVE

THE following autobiographical narrative has been taken down almost verbatim from the lips of its hero, an old negro man, who has dictated or told the whole of it with absolutely no help but his own memory. He does not read at all, or, of course, write either, though he once knew his alphabet, and there are none of his contemporaries alive in this part of the country, all the older members of his last owner's family, with whom he still remains, being dead, and none of those among them, to whom old Charles has been a life-long servant and friend, I might almost say necessity, knowing anything about the names and dates of races and race-horses, which are given exactly as he remembers them. Nothing throughout has been altered in any way except to make the details as consecutive and the dialect as intelligible as possible, and perhaps it may be as well to add here the facts necessary to complete his story. He does not exaggerate in any way his life in Virginia; he was the favorite and trusted servant of Colonel Johnson during his whole career with him, was in charge of first one training stable, then another, and for several years was employed with the entire care of valuable race-horses and stud-horses, which he took from place to place and course to course in Kentucky, among others, as he mentions, Monsieur Tonson and Medley. At such a distance from his master, and unable even to read his letters of instruction himself, he yet discharged his duties excellently, keeping long accounts in his head, and handling the large sums of money which were constantly passing through his hands with scrupulous accuracy and care. All these facts about him are gathered from letters, family tradition, and the direct report of his masters to the writer's mother, all of which confirm his own perfectly literal and impartial statements. When purchased by Judge Porter, of Louisiana, he was at once placed in charge of a racing establishment where there were never less than twelve horses in training, and which kept forty or forty-five men and boys constantly employed. It was a position of much care and responsibility, for there was a race-course on the plantation which was a favorite centre for turfmen, and Charles was called upon to train horses for this or that gentleman so frequently that he was compelled to establish a system, and undertake so much and no more.

After Judge Porter's death, in 1843, Charles remained in his new home in the service of his late owner's brother, who left him where he found him, as head trainer; and in that position, travelling every spring and autumn to one course or another as the horses went to fulfill their engagements, he continued until his master's death, and the consequent breaking up of the racing establishment, reduced him to the less glorious level of family coachman, and general "boss" of everything in the way of horseflesh on the place. During the war he never left his mistress, who was alone on the plantation during the whole period, for a single day, and since its close he has been the constant, never-failing factotum, adherent, and, as he calls it, "'pendence" of the whole family.

About ten days ago the writer said to him: "Uncle Charles, I want you to come in this evening and tell me all you can remember that ever happened to you, from the very beginning, and let me see if I can not write it down so that people can read it. You have told me so many things about when you were young, I want to put it all down together in black and white." The old man was deeply interested at once, and when he fully understood the object in view, his pride and delight exceeded all bounds. He went off to his own house, which is quite near, and for the rest of the day refused to speak or be spoken to, on the plea that he was "studyin'." In the evening, at what he calls early candle-light, he appeared, arrayed in his Sunday clothes, and it being a warm night in June, the feeling of self-respect must have been genuine indeed which compelled him to put on a plush waistcoat reaching nearly to his knees, heavy white velveteen trousers ending in a pair of shooting gaiters, the whole surmounted by a long black frock-coat, a spotted silk cravat of vast size, and a small jockey's cap. It was a brilliant, clear evening, and his own cabin not two hundred yards off, yet he carried a blue cotton umbrella of the very largest size. In this costume he has presented himself every evening since for the *séances* whose results are given in this sketch, although during the day he works about the place in an airy suit of guinea blue much better adapted to the weather. In spite of his eighty-four or five years, Charles is an extremely active, hard-working man, always busy at carpentering, gardening, shoe-making, or "horse-doctoring," in which branch of medicine he is a great authority. His third wife, whom he married after he came to Louisiana, is still living, and has three grown children, who are of little assistance or profit to their father. But he has a nice little homestead of five or six acres, with a cabin on it, which he has almost entirely built himself within the past two years, and he has already planted the place, of which he only two years ago became owner, with fruit trees and vines and shrubs of every description.

De fust thing dat I remembers of is de little town of Pocahontas, 'crost de river from Petersburg, en Virginia, an' ef you sarched dat whole town troo from eend to eend you couldn't ha' lit down on no bigger little yaller rascal dan me when I fust begin to take good notice of myself. Dat I was! A rascal, hide an' hyar, sho's you born. My father—dat is, I hear folks say dat was my daddy, an' he 'lowed so his-self; but mammy she lived with Aunt Mary Stevens, an' 'cept fur her being his full sister she neber let on no more'n dat —he lived en a good, large house, an' he was a sea-farrin man, a mighty light mulatter; he looked like one o' dese yere Mexikin somebodies. His wife an' chil-len staid right dar all de time, an' I 'vid-ed my time 'twixt dar an' Aunt Mary Ste-vens's, whar mammy staid when she warn't out home at ole Marster Enoch Vaughan's, what she belonged to, an' I took a spell o' stayin' out dar sometimes. Mammy's name was Sally; father his name was Charles Stewart; he was free, an' so was all his folks. I lived amongst 'em all, jes' as limber an' mischievious as any little 'coon dat eber stole corn. Colonel Enoch Vaughan's place was two miles from town, on de heights near Ma-jor Butts's, ole Gin'ral Harrison's father-in-law. I neber knowed which I liked de best: to hear de white gen'lemen out dar tellin' 'bout de rebelspishonary wars, an' all de ely*ments* dat tuk place when dey was fightin' agin the British mens, or to set en de chimbley-corner en my daddy's house an' hear him a-tellin' an' narratin' all about dem whalin' vyages he went on, whar de fishes has got calves, an' gives milk same as cows, and cuts up *dat fat!* dar ain't no hog ever wallered in de mud dat could give a drap for a bucket, *even countin'*, wid one o' dem almighty fat critters. He was mighty good to me, an' I kin ricolleck now how it was share an' share alike wid his yother chillen, an' how his sister, Aunt Mary Stevens, was allers givin' me cake an' clo's an' candy.

You see, de ole Colonel Vaughan died when I was a baby-child, an' de 'state was sort of all sproshered [mixed] up, so dey jes' left me at my daddy's, an' he tried time an' agin to buy me; but dey wouldn't sell me, nor hear about it. Well, arter I was goin' on 'bout ten or 'leven year old, my young mistis, Miss Lizzie Pace, what used to be Miss Lizzie Vaughan, dat I done fell arr to when her pa done died, she got broke en conserkerwenz of her husband losin' money—something I neber could unnerstan', kase I allers heerd he neber had none, nohow—an 'so my daddy he was gone, an' dey jes' up an' sole me en my

tracks ter Colonel William R. Johnson. De Napoleon of de Turf was de name he went by from Dandy to Queen o' Sheba. Lord! he was a great man, sho enuff. Ef he didn't hab more stables an' more horses! De place where he lived was a mighty fine farm an' house named Oak-land, jes' eighteen mile fum Petersburg an' twenty-two fum Richmond; but I neber staid dar—no, sir. De Colonel he jes' dash-ed his eyes ober me—I was monst'ous lean an' peart fur twelve year ole—an' says to some of de quality dat was a-settin' 'long-side: "Here's a light weight for my New Market stables, an' Arthur Taylor's hand-ling. Do you know a horse when you see one, boy?" "Yas, sir," I says; "I knows a horse fum a mule jes' as far as I kin see 'em bofe walk." Dey all larfs at dat, an' de nex' thing dey gives me some new clo's all fixed up, an' I was sarnt down to de great big training stables my new marster owned at New Market, an' I was set to wuk—de fust wuk I eber done sence I was foaled—to rub down Reality, own sister to Vanity, what was owned by Colonel Allen. De head manager of de stable den was a Englishman named Ar-thur Taylor, an' dough he only had eight horses en trainin' at dat time, dar was a big force of boys an' men at wuk on 'em, two boys to each horse, an' another white man second in charge, named Peter. Jehu! how we did wuk on dem horses! Dey was John Stanley, sired by Sir Harry, imported by Harry Haxall, Esq., an' dar was a Sir Archy gray filly dat I can re-member well kase she warn't no 'count till she was four year ole, when she jumped ober creation. We had another dar be-longing to Collyer Minn, named Moses, half-brother to John Stanley by Sir Harry.

How I did love dem horses! It 'peared like dey loved me too, an' when dey turn-ed deir rainbow necks, all slick an' shinin', aroun' sarchin' fur me to come an' give 'em deir gallops, whew-e-e! how we did spin along dat old New Market course, right arter sunrise in de cool summer mornings! In dem times New Market was 'bout de head place in de Nu-ninted States fur horse-racin', an' all de gen'le-men fum far an' near used to come. No-body dat was anybody staid away, an' it was a fine sight when de spring an' au-tumn races come, I tell you. My marster was de picter of a fine ole gen'leman; he was a fa'r-lookin' man, with thick white hyar, an' eyes dat jes' snapped fire at you;

he was what you call a plain gen'leman, an' didn't b'lieve his coat an' pants was de makin' of him; he treated his servants like dey was de prime cut, an' dey all loved him. He was a yearthly gen'leman, an' ef dere is any good place anywhere, it 'pears to me like he ought to be in it. An' as fur horses, ef he jes' only walked by a horse to look at it, he could tell you jes' how far dat horse could run. Why, dere was a mar' named Clary Fisher, an' a nag called Bonnets of Blue, dat I raised myself, which was Reality's daughter. When dey was runnin', de ole man walked by Clary Fisher an' looked at her fore-legs, an' he seed a sign in one of her fore-legs dat she would lay down in runnin' a mile an' three-quarters; he tole Mr. Crowell to go back an' bet every dollar he had, an' Mr. Crowell went back an' bet his three plantations, an' won de wuth of 'em, jes' as Colonel Johnson tole him. Den dere was General Wynne an' Billy Wynne, Billy Badger and Sam Badger, John C. Stevens, Mr. Van Rance, an' plenty more what used to fotch deir stables down to New Market ebery spring an' autumn, jes' as reg'lar as clock-wuk, de second Tuesdays in May an' October. Dem was de grandest times dat eber lived. King of Heaven! it was a sight to see my ole marster, an' yothers like him, a-struttin' up an' down wid deir shirts all frilled an' ruffled down de front. Why, den you could build a ball-room as long as fum here to de stable, an' fill it wid folks, an' ebery one of 'em de real stuff. But nowadays what's it like? Name o' Heaven! blue trash, red trash, green trash, speckled trash, dar's plenty of ebery qualinfication, but nary one dat washes in lye soap an' dries on de grass widout fadin'. Why, dar was Otway Hare, Parker Hare, John C. Goode, Mr. Corbin, Mr. Taylor, Colonel Peter Mason (we used to walk our horses ebery evenin' pas' his house), John Drummond an' Allen Drummond, the two brothers dat raised Sir Charles, all belonged to the New Market Jockey Club. Lord! how proud dis nigger was when dey called me "Johnson's Charles," an' I used to come a-clippin' down de track en a two-mile heat! De fust real race eber I rid was in a sweepstake, a mile an' a repeat, on John Stanley, trained by Arthur Taylor, when I was 'bout thirteen year ole, an' weighed in at seventy pounds. I was one o' dese yer fever-an'-ague little fellers what ain't got no flesh to take off

nohow; an' ef I warn't de proudest nigger! One of de horses was Mr. Green's nag fum Norfolk. My king! it skeers me a'most to talk 'bout it all, it looks so fur back; it looks wicked to ricolleck all dese yere dead an' buried things. It seems kin' o' like shakin' up de speerits too hard.

It warn't long arter dis here fust race when I was sarnt down to Norf Kyallina to ride fur Mr. Peter Davis, an' dat was de fust journey eber I tuk. I went all alone, an' when I got up on de stage at Petersburg in my new suit o' store clo's, wid ten dollars in my pocket an' more to come; I was "high come up," I tell you. De stage was a high flyer, an' I was sorry enough when she stopped at Warrenton, whar I got out, right at Mars' William Faulkner's, Colonel Johnson's sister's son. A heap o' fine folks lived 'bout dar besides him in dem times—ole Major Dancy, Bob Ransom, Judge Jones, an' Heyward Johnson, an' John Johnson, besides ole Marmaduke Johnson, de daddy of 'em all, what was married three times, an' imported Diomed, de sire of Sir Archy, an' one of de finest horses—dough dey tell me he was twenty-one year old when dey fotched him fum England—dat eber knocked de wind in de face. De race I rid was on a nag called Aggy-up, agin a chestnut colt named Scott, by Timoleon. Dar was three o' dem Aggy nags. Dey was Aggy-up, Aggy-down, an' Oh-Aggy, an' dey was all three sarnt up to New Market to be trained even-tully. I staid down dar near Warrenton fur nigh on to six months, an' den I got a notion to go home, an' I done went. Den I staid pretty quiet at home, clost to marster, trainin' en de stables under Arthur Taylor, an' goin' back an' forth 'twixt de stables an' Oakland, or Petersburg, or maybe Richmond, wharsomeber me an' de Colonel mought be livin' en residence at de time. Ebery spring an' autumn I rid stakes for him, an' 'bout dese years we trained Bonnets o' Blue, Black Star, Jeannette Lafayette, Flyin' Childers, Betsey Richards, John Richards, an' Sir Henry. John Warlin an' me was de two best light weights. I kep' down to eighty pound. De day of de great race on Long Island 'twixt Eclipse an' Henry, me an' marster an' all on us was there en course. My king! what a crowd an' noise an' screechin' an' hallooin' dar was dat day! When de third heat come roun', Arthur Taylor rid Sir Henry, what John Warlin had rid de two fust, an' ole Purdy he jumped on

Eclipse, kase he 'lowed dat Sam Laird couldn't git de jump out of him dat he could. Dat same time I rid de stake fur John C. Stevens on his Young Sir Archy, an' los' it by jes' eighteen inches; but I made my three hundred dollars an' de fines' suit o' clo's you eber see. I tell you, I walked roun' like a ole gobbler wid a red flannel tail tied on to his hind-leg when we got back home agin. By de time I was twenty year ole, 'bout de time Van Buren was President, marster he calls to me one day, an' he says: "Charley, my boy, I has layed out fur you to hab a stable of your own separate 'pinting. You is ole enough, an' done seed de rights of things long enough, to be my depritty yourself, so I is goin' to send you ober to my stable one mile fum New Market, an' I specs you to take everything into your own keer, an' send home some o' dem lazy scoundrels dat is hidin' out dar, too thick to shake a stick at, an' jes' waiting fur me to go an' scrattle [scatter] 'em home."

So sho' enough I went to de stable outside o' New Market, an' dar I was de "boss" ober nine little niggers an' four big ones, 'sides two white trash dey called "helpers." Wa'al, I had a nice stable full of nags. Dar was Medley, an' Slender, an' Tariff, an' Arab, an' more too, but I disricollecks de oders now. Dat was de fust of my turnin' out, an' I tell you I felt so fine dat my own mudder wouldn't ha' knowed me fur her son. I had plenty o' money, an' nobody to say nothin' to me. I jes' had to train an' exercise my horses, an' send 'em up when dey was wanted. Wa'al, arter a couple of year pass away, I begin to think 'bout gittin' married. I says to myself dat I was lonesome en dat big harnsome cabin, dat I was well off fur eberything 'ceptin' a good nigger to cook an' wash fur me, an' as I neber had no notion o' wastin' victuals on a woman I didn't love, or pomperin' up one wid love an' victuals *bofe* what didn't belong to me, hide an' hyar, I jes' made up my mind to ax Colonel Burford to let me look ober a lot of mighty likely young gals he had on a place not very far fum whar I lived. It was a little slip of a farm, clost to Rock Spring meetin'-house, an' he had put a whole lot of South Kyallina nigger wenches dar till he could git 'em settled on his yother places. I had done looked all roun' Chesterfield County all ready to pick up de fust dat 'peared like she would suit; but de minute I drove

up to de quarters on Colonel Burford's place I see de gal fur me. She was standin' on de step of de corn-crib sharpenin' a hoe, an' I seed dat she was as strong as a mule an' as sharp as pepper seeds, befo' I lit down out of de buggy. I axed her her name, an' she 'lowed dat dey called her Betsey Dandridge; so I axed fur de honor of pursentment to her daddy, ole nigger Dandridge dey called him, an' by sundown de mahter was fixed dat I was to git Colonel Burford's say-so right off, an' we would hab de weddin' when de corn was bent, for Scripter says, "As de corn is bent, so is de wife inclined," an' also, "Feed me wid food convenient fur me," an' 'bout dat time de summer apples would be ripe, an' de peaches.

So I started off to Petersburg, but while I was huntin' all round fur Colonel Burford, lo an' git up! what does I hear but Sim Jackson a-tellin' somebody dat he heerd dat Colonel Burford was goin' to sell de whole kit an' bilin' of 'em, track o' land an' all, to Major Isham Puckett, Esq. So I jes' rid ober de nex' day to whar ole nigger Dandridge an' his folks was a-waitin' fur me to come an' be 'fianced—what dey allers does up in Virginny befo' de marriage—an' de ole gen'leman he steps out, wid his ole black head a-shinin' like a Kentucky walnut, an' says to me, "Why, Colonel Stewart," says he (kase I had done tuk my marster's title), "we espected to see you here dis mornin' sooner dan dis; you is not so peryactical en yo' courtin' as we had espected." So wid dat I jes' steps up an' makes him a low bow, an' says I, "Mr. Dandridge, sir, you will allow me de privily of obsarvin' dat I intends to be 'fianced to yo' darter, Miss Betsey, when I gits ready, an' not befo'; an' let me tell you, sir, dar is a heap o' difference 'twixt axin' a lady fur to be your spouse, an' buyin' a gal dat you don't know de price of." Kase, you see, dat was what was troublin' me. I knowed Colonel Burford like a book, an' could calkilate on his sayin', "Wa'al, Stewart, you can hab Betsey a year or so fust to see ef she will suit you, an' den we kin talk 'bout de price," but Major Puckett an' me was on diff'unt sort o' tums. He was an old-school Whig, I was one of de newschool ones, an' we had to git acquainted better befo' I could tell what kind o' bargain he would make. But, hi! I needn't ha' bothered none 'bout dat. Jes' as soon as I steps up to him en Richmond, whar I found him en front o' de Court-house, an' interjuces myself as being "Colonel Johnson's Charles," he was jes' as affable as a settin' hen. I seed two or three gen'lemen I knowed well a-standin' by, but I didn't ax nobody to speak fur me; I up an' speaks for myself, an' jes' as soon as I had sensed him wid what I was sayin', he laughs an' says, "Why, Charley, you can have her jes' as she stands fur three hundred and fifty dollars." I tell you I was pleased. Befo' a mule could kick, I jumped round to Mr. Jefferson Balls's office (he was Major Puckett's brother-in-law, an', besides dat, he was de money agent for Colonel Johnson, an' dat's how come he was my agent too). I drawed out three hundred an' fifty dollars, fur I had made a heap dat las' year, more'n I could spend in clo's an' tobacco, more spesherly, too, by reason dat de Colonel always give 'em bofe to me; so as soon as I had drawed de money out I jes' hands it back agin to Mr. Balls for Major Puckett, an' says, "Dis yere sum is for de ackisition of Miss Betsey Dandridge, an' all de chillen we can raise: is dat so, Mr. Balls, sir?" An' he arnsers "yes," an' give me de papers, to hab an' to hole her as long as she behave herself.

So jes' as soon as I could I put back to de Rock Spring farm, an' sho enough we was married at de 'pinted time, an' I tuk her home. I had de best kind of a house ajinin' my trainin' stable, an' you neber seed de like of all de grand things as was give to us. I hauled home three cart-loads o' weddin' presents. Sech furniture an' fixin's was as fine as dey *could* be. Lord! when I look back to dem days an' think 'bout all de money, an' dogs, an' chickens, an' ducks, an' geese, an' pigs I had, an' whole chists full of fine clo's, an' more chaney dan we could eat out of en a year, an' de Colonel ready to hand me out a hundred dollars ebery time I ax fur it, an' think no more 'bout 'em dan 'bout spittin' out a chaw of tobacco! I neber did treat none o' my wives arter dat wid de same respex, kase I was right dar whar all de folks knowed me, an' I had a heap more truck dan I eber could colleck arter I lef' Virginny. I don' know perzackly what year dat was, but it was somewhars 'bout eight year 'fo' I married my second wife down en Kentucky, an' I know de year *dat* happened was de same year Queen Victoriore tuk up wid Prince Albert an' married him, an' made sech a talkin' an' palaveerin' as

neber was heered befo'. Wa'al, dar I was married, an' I mought jes' as well espress my disappintment fust as last. Treatment makes all de respex dat can happen responseful in de world, but a woman ought to tell some of de trufe once a day, ef it's only to limber up her tongue. It was a good while fust befo' I foun' out what make all Betsey's promises an' arnsers all de time fallin' flat and flatter, like bad dough or mean pie-crust, but when I seed how 'twas, I jes' sets to wuk to see ef I could cure her. I tried 'suasion an' finery, birch rods split fine, an' a light hickory stick 'bout as thick as my littlest finger, an' I tried makin' her kin an' my kin dat had religion pray fur her at de big camp-meetin'. But it warn't no use. She had three likely arrs, 'bout a year betwixt 'em, an' I neber had but dat one fault to find wid her; she cooked as good biskits, hoe-cake, bacon fry, hominy mush, an' coffee as any gal I seed; den, moreober, she could iron an' wash my shirts, an' keep things a-goin' right smart; but she couldn't seem to tell de trufe to save her life, an' it got to be so dat I jes' made my mind up to 'vorce her as quick as eber I could. In course an' sartinly I couldn't be out o' pocket for no sech a hussy as she was; an' den de question was wedder it was wuf while to keep de arrs an' raise 'em; but I says, "No, she must ha' come of a bad breed, an' a colt is mos' apt to take arter de dam, anyhow; I better git shet of de whole gang of 'em, an' try a new cross." Dar was a horse-dealer t'other side o' Petersburg by de name of Jones, what had de finest nag I had seen in a year fur sale at jes' de bery price I paid fur Betsey. De horse was named Brown Jim, an' he was wuf de money, I tell you; so I jes' says to Major Puckett dat he could have Betsey back at de same price I paid fur her, an' lowin' fur de war an' tar of de four year I had done kep' her, I would throw de boys into de bargain. Wa'al, I neber was sorry fur dat 'vorcement, nohow, an' dat autumn de Colonel sarnt me out to Kentucky, whar I had Monsieur Tonson an' Medley, 'sides Black Elk, Glencoe, Leviathan, an' yothers.

Our head-quarters was in Paris, Kentucky, an' I staid dar a long time, an' was jes' as happy as a king. In de spring an' fall of de year I would take de horses 'bout fum place to place, en 'cordance wid marster's orders, an' I was jes' as free an' independent as any gen'leman en de land.

I had my helpers an' jockeys, grooms an' stablemen, under me, nobody was ober me, an' de squire or de jedge was always somewhar 'bout to read marster's letters to me. I neber had no book-larnin' myself, kase I neber was willin', fur I knowed my brain was too smart for to stand it. When anybody has got as much sense en de head as I had, dey must take great keer not to be foolin' round tryin' to stuff more en, or de fust thing dey'll bust it open. I lef' all dat fur folks dat wanted fillin' up an' patchin' on to. Yes, I was mighty happy at Paris an' at Bowling Green, whar I staid jes' about de same, 'vidin' my time 'cordin' to de horses. Dar was a heap o' rich gen'lemen all through dat country. Dar was Squire Oglen, whar Monsieur Tonson stood some time, an' was showed in the State Fair, wid me standin' alongside, an' we tuk de prizes of three fifty-dollar tankards. Ole Henry Clay was always aroun', an' mighty peart an' perlite de ole man was, too, an' knowed a horse when he seed him, I tell you. His son, Henry Clay junior, dey called him, he thought dat much of me he offered Colonel Johnson $3500 fur me himself, but de Colonel he tole him money couldn't buy me; an' he made jes' de bery same arnser to Wade Hampton, what offered him de bery same price. I had a heap of people after me, I tell you, an' some on 'em used to beg me jes' to say so as I wanted to go wid 'em an' leave my ole marster; but I would neber 'gree to dat ar scheme wid any of 'em; I was too well off fur dat, an' I heerd folks say as how "betwixt a two-edged sword you falls to de groun'," an' all sech sayin's as has sense en 'em. Whilst I was a-livin' at Paris I foun' anoder good reason fur stayin' jes' how I was an' whar I was. I 'come acquainted wid de likeliest-lookin' an' fa'rest-behavin' light-colored mulatter gal I eber seed in my life. Lord! I tell you dar ain't no sech niggers now as she was! An' dat genteel an' handy, an' sech snappin' black eyes an' coal-black hyar, like an Injun's, an' a pretty slim shape, wid sich a smooth light yaller skin, 'mos' de color of a ripe pumpkin seed. You may sarch dis world ober, but as sho as de Lord is de secret Jedge you won't eber find any 'oman as pretty an' as good as my little Kentucky sweetheart. Her name was Mary Jane Mallory, an' her owner, Mr. Robertson, tole me to marry her an' welcome, an' he would neber say nothin' to part us. She had a

brother dat hired himself out as a locksmith, an' all her folks was nice, pursentable pussons nobody could be shamed by. So I married her, an' tuk her to a little house I had fixed up near de stables, an' she clear-starched an' sewed an' 'broidered an' wukked wid de hand-loom, an' made more pretty things dan I could count. She paid her marster, en course, reg'lar, so much a month fur her hire, but, lor', she neber touched her airnin's fur dat. I had plenty of money to hire as many wives as I wanted, but dis one was de onliest one I eber did want, an' so it was easy enough.

I kin see dat little house now, wid de big white bed, all clean an' sweet an' hung wid ruffled curtains, in one corner, de cupboard full of flowered chaney an' shinin' metal an' glass opposite, an' de bright wood fire, piled up wid hickory an' ash logs, blazin' on de h'arth, an' Mary Jane settin' in front by de candle wid her fine white sewin' an' her pink caliker dress an' slick black hyar, lookin' so kind o' quiet till I speaks to her, an' den you kin see de fire-light a-glimpsin' on her white teeth. Arter a while she had a arr, sech a fine boy it was a picter to see him, an' as smart an' cunnin' as a little 'coon, an' jes' as like his daddy, what was me, you know, as a ole rabbit is like a young one. Dis was little Johnny; we named him arter her folks, her daddy an' her brother; an' I kept on a-reckonin' an' thinkin' dat arter a while when marster sarnt for me to take Monsieur Tonson an' Medley back home to Virginny I would fetch Mary Jane and Johnny along wid me, an' show 'em to my folks in Petersburg, kase my mammy she was livin' dar, an' so was my brothers an' sisters an' a heap of kin, an' I wanted 'em all to see my wife an' boy. But it was 'bout six months arter Johnny was born, an' I was jest beginnin' to think 'bout buyin' Mary Jane in good arnest, so as to be all ready fur de time to start, when I begin to notice dat she hab got a mighty bad-soundin' cough, an' den her mammy says, "Why don't you eat, darter? you don't eat enough." An' den yother folks say, "What make Mary Jane look so poorly an' git so lean?" I was badly skeered, an' I sarnt for de doctor, an' he says she mus' eat a heap an' drink port-wine, an' 'muse herself; so I takes her to see a ole friend at de springs, an' I buys good victuals, an' de gen'lemen, sich as Squire Oglen an' all of 'em, sends her port-wine, an' de doctor gives her quinine an' bark an' everything, but none of it was any use; her time was come, her hour for her to go had done been struck in heaven, an' de time was short. It warn't two year arter our weddin' when I laid her in her coffin, wid her big eyes shet foreber, an' I neber grieved so ober anybody in all de world. She was jes' as fond o' me as I was of her, an' it did 'pear hard luck to lose her jes' as I was makin' up my mind to buy her out an' out, only en course it was a fortunate thing I hadn't bought her, as long as she had to die, kase den I would ha' lost her an' de money too. Arter she was in de ground it jes' 'peared to me like eberything was different; I tuk a dislikement to Paris, an' I didn't feel like goin' home to Virginny. It got so arter a while dat I got de squire to write home to marster an' tell him I wanted to go to some strange place, an' marster he writ back dat "ef I could find *a owner to suit me, dat would pay his price fur me,* I could go, dough he had neber expected to part wid me *by sale.*" It jes' happened 'bout dat time dat Jedge Porter fum 'way down en Louisiana was in de Nu-ninted States, an' trabelling aroun' fur pleasure. He was one of de Washington Sennyters, an' was a great jedge (dey *said* he was a great jedge of de South, an' could make laws like a book, an' I *knows* he was a great jedge of a horse), so when he come to Bowling Green him an' me got acquainted, an' he says to me dat he was lookin' arter a head trainer fur his stables in de South, an' would I like to go wid him ef he would buy me. So I tuk a week or two to consider de mahter, an' him an' me had a heap o' talk, an' de more I thinks to myself 'bout stayin' in Kentucky widout Mary Jane, de more I says to myself dat I can't on no 'count do it.

De eend of de mahter was I tuk sech a likin' to de Jedge dat we fixed it up disaway: I was to go an' stay six months to see how I liked it, an' den, ef I didn't like it, he promised to send me back home, an' ef I did like it, he would pay Colonel Johnson $3500 fur me. Dat's what I sole for when I was young, an' I bet dar ain't many folks wuf dat 'mount o' money Norf or South. Arter dis bargain was made, I went out to Mr. Robertson's, whar my little Johnny was wid his grandmammy; an' Miss Mary Robertson she had jes' tuk sech a likin' to de little feller dat she had him roun' de house harf de time; an' now

when I went up to de house wid Mother-in-law Mallory, what was totin' him in her arms, he reached out his two little fisses to her as quick as he seed her a-settin' on de piazzy. I tole her an' Mr. Robertson all 'bout my new prospex, an' when I was done, de ole gen'leman stretched ober an' picked Johnny up, an' stood him on de little stool by him, and says, "Well, Stewart, I see what you want is dis little man, an' you shall hab-him for $150, an' not one penny more." I tell you I *was* pleased, sho enough, an' I paid de money, an' got de receipt, an' we toted Johnny in to Bowling Green dat bery day. You see, de reason why I neber bought him befo' was dat I had to leave him wid his grandmammy. An' some folks is so cur'ous dat I wa'n't sho dey would let a free nigger, or rader a nigger dat belonged to his own daddy, stay on de place; so Mary Jane's sister she offered to keep him fur me till I could send fur him, kase en course I couldn't trabel wid a baby like dat; but I 'lowed to send fur him jes' as soon as I could git settled. An' de eend of de mahter was I lef' him; an' I ain't neber seed dat chile sence. Wa'al, my new marster an' me we started off for Louisiana, an' I 'clar' to Moses I thought we warn't neber goin' to git dar. We was goin' an' goin', en steamboats an' stages, stages an' steamboats, fur weeks an' days, till we come to New Orleans. It warn't as big as New York, but dar was a sight of oranges an' banarnas, an' more oder kinds of fruit dan I could call de names of. But de wust of de place was ef you axed anybody a question dey arnsered you in French, an' you might screech till you was deef befo' dey would let on dat dey knowed what you was talkin' 'bout. I stood dat kind o' nonsense fust-rate fum white folks: ef dey couldn't talk no Christian langwidge, I jes' felt sorry fur 'em: but when it come to a great big fool nigger a-doin' me dat way, I jes' hits him a lick in his ole black jaws dat shet 'em up fur dat day. So marster an' me we soon left New Orleans, an' come on ober here to de 'Takapas country, whar he got sech a big fine plantation, so much of it, so many trees, an' de fields is so broad, an' de lakes is so big, I felt kind o' skeered an' lonesome de fust week. But it didn't take me long to git ober dat feelin' when I seed de race-course, de stables, an' de horses what was waitin' fur me on de Teche.

It was de prettiest picter of a place,

an' as fine a lot of horses as eber I seed togedder, twelve of 'em always en train-in', wid more brood marrs, outsiders, an' colts dan you could dream 'bout en one night. I had a mighty good large house at de top of de stable yard, an' my bell rung en de oberseer's house, de head help-er's, an' de stable; besides, I had a boy to sleep en ebery stall. I was jes' put right at de head of eberything; nobody could say nothin' to me at all. Ef I said I want-ed *dis*, I got it, or must hab *dat*, I got it too. He was jes' as open-handed an' gin-'rous, but he wouldn't stand no foolin' neither, I tell you. Things had to be jes' so, but dar warn't no naggin' nor scold-in'; it was jes' stiddy management.

Arter my marster, Jedge Porter, died, I belonged to his brother, Mr. James Por-ter, what done arred [heired] de place an' de niggers, an' ef dar eber was a good man walked en shoe-leather, he was one. Dey tells me dat

> " 'Twixt de saddle an' de ground
> De sinner hab salvation found;"

an' en course we all knows 'bout dat dar horse-thief what our Saviour done pardon. arter he was hung up; but I neber had no 'pinion of dis yere way of jumpin' into heaven ober de fence, 'stid of goin' right. 'long by de road an' through de toll-gate, whar St. Peter takes de pennies; but dar was none o' dat wild kind of religion. 'bout Mars' Jeames. He was good all through, both outsides an' down de mid-dle, an' him an' me, an', arter he died, his. folks an' me, we jes' went on peaceful an' happy till de war come an' rooted ebery blessed thing up by de roots.

MISSISSIPPI RIVER PROBLEM

THEY who have, for the past fifty thousand years or so, lived in the Mississippi Valley, have, it is supposed, been studying the problem which the great river presents, with more or less intelligence and care, nearly all that time. But as one human race has succeeded another, the records of the conclusions reached from age to age in regard to the problem have been destroyed by the river itself or buried in the silt which the Father of Waters brings down from the highlands to make his bed withal.

Since the time when the lowlands between the Alleghany and the Rocky mountains were not, but an arm of the sea was in their stead, the steady flow of the rain and spring waters from the mountain heights has been bringing down the grains of its own attrition and dropping them in eddies until the sea has become dry land. Inch by inch the capricious waters have built up barriers to their own flow, and scattered them again, changing the face of the earth sometimes in a night, sometimes in a century, until the great silt bed has become the garden of the world, and the question, "What is the river going to do?" has become one which seriously affects mankind by making its food and clothing cheap or dear. For the land that was made by the river is more productive than any other, at least in the civilized world of to-day. Seventy bushels of wheat will grow on an acre of it in one crop, or two bales of cotton, if cotton be planted, while in the great wheat fields of the Northwest that our fathers thought so rich, thirty bushels to the acre is considered wonderful. And in the Mississippi bottoms the soil is literally inexhaustible. Nature supplies the fertilizers faster than she will turn them into grain or cotton.

So rich a possession as this valley has naturally excited the cupidity of men in all time. Life is easy and pleasant in any spot where it is only necessary to lie down with one's mouth open to have "the co-coa-nuts drop into it." Neither industry nor intelligence is necessary in such a place to obtain wealth. Nowhere else on earth, so far as I know, may a man who literally knows nothing excepting how to drop a cotton seed and how to pick cotton, earn, with only two months' work, his living for a whole year, and from $400 to $600 additional in cash. When La Salle found out how goodly a land it was, his report was the warrant of eviction that drove out the red man to make place for the white, as the Mound-builders had made place for the Indian in what we call the days of old. Yet it must have been only yesterday that the Mound-builders wrought in the valley, for in the few centuries that have elapsed since then the surface of the ground has risen only a few feet—not enough to bury their works out of sight. How long ago, then, must it have been that the race lived there whose pavements and cisterns of *Roman brick* now lie seventy feet under-ground ? And if we can not answer this question, how shall we figure up the sum of the years it has taken for the river to fill the valley a thousand feet deep with silt ? Or, looking forward, and reflecting that the superior races exterminate the lower only to be driven out by another inferior, as the Mound-builders were, how shall we calculate the time until the Chinaman, whose spies are there already, shall drive out the Caucasian, and give place in after-ages to still another race ? And what works shall we leave that shall tell our successors that an intelligent people cultivated the valley before the Chinaman came ?

This is the problem to-day—not that it matters to us to-day whether the works shall remain for the other race to see, but because of the necessity to-day for works of some kind; and since there is little or nothing remaining of the works of our predecessors to tell us of their plans, or of their success or failure, we have to begin as if the problem were new.

The necessity for works of some kind hardly needs a statement. The most ignorant man in the valley who sees the water coming into his cabin and washing away the fruits of his labor, year after year, sees the necessity as plainly as the most skilled engineer. The importance of the works to the human race, however, will bear some words of explanation.

The Mississippi River is nature's highway from the world's farm-land to the world's kitchens. It is easier to put a load of produce on a raft of logs, and let the water carry it toward its destination, than it is to drag it over the ground. Neither of these primitive methods of transportation is in vogue to-day, since science has improved both, but the natural advantage of the one over the other remains. Nature's road lies down the river, and whatever is done to improve it is a step in the easier direction. It is true that science has done far more to develop the other method of transportation, so that in this country to-day the railroads are the formidable rivals of the barge lines, and for many reasons they must always remain so; but the fact remains indisputable that the easiest way, naturally, to carry Minnesota wheat to Europe is down the river. It may not now be the most desirable, but it is one way, and it is naturally the easiest; and since the wheat must be carried, it does not need an argument to show that the roads should be kept in order.

But there is another aspect of the question in which its importance is even more apparent. The river is not only a roadway of navigation, it is also the means by which the valley is made fertile and kept so, and it is also at certain—or rather at uncertain—seasons, a raging, devastating flood, as potent for ill as it is at other times for good. The flood of last spring, which brought death to scores of persons, physical suffering to thousands, and financial disaster to other thousands, was sufficient to impress upon the world the importance of some works of some kind by means of which such disasters should be averted. For it was not only that the dwellers in the valley suffered, but the world suffered a loss in food and clothing—corn and cotton—and this loss was distinctly appreciable.

The problem, then, is: What shall be done to the Mississippi River? The Father of Waters is, in his poetic personality, one of the most valuable individuals on earth, and one of the most troublesome as well as dangerous. What shall we do to encourage his beneficence, and divert his wrath ? No answer that is addressed to either half of the question alone is adequate. Political economists see that it should be answered, and they have demanded of the engineers of the world that they answer it.

Answers are not lacking. Theory after theory has been propounded by thinking men who, from interest or necessity, have given years of study to the question, and yet so intricate and contradictory are the conditions to be considered—the operations of nature that form the factors of the problem—that the different theories are irreconcilable. The doctors differ, and seem now to have agreed to disagree. In the Mississippi Valley all intelligent men study the question, since it is forced upon their attention constantly, and yet, although most of them are theorists, there are very few who do not contradict their own theories in their arguments. Two utterances I heard on the ground, which seemed to embody the very highest intelligence, and both of them I have heard echoed and approved by scores of close thinkers who have studied the question for years.

One man, a veteran river steamboat captain, said: "I have lived on the river, man and boy, for thirty years. I have studied it, because it was my business to, and I am now certain that I don't know anything about it, or about what ought to be done to it."

Another said: "When God put the river into this valley, He told it to go wherever it pleased, and it always has done so, and always will."

Nevertheless, the engineers propose to prescribe its course, and so regulate its forces that it shall stay inside its bed, and keep that bed in good condition.

The difficulties in the way of carrying out this proposition are great. Some of them can be stated readily enough; but he would be a bold man who would undertake to say he could state them all, in view of the declarations of men who have studied the subject for years, and now confess ignorance. One side of the question may be made clear by considering what the course of a drop of water is from the top of the Rocky Mountains to the Gulf of Mexico—perhaps three thousand miles.

Let loose from the snow bank where it has been locked up all winter, it starts with many companion drops on its journey to the sea—its eternity. It rolls through rocky ravines, and over pebbly bottoms, down the mountain-side, loosening the atoms it touches, and perhaps catching one from the decaying trunk of some tree half-way down some hill-side, and carrying it along. So long as it

moves in an unchecked course it will carry that atom. A thousand miles further along its journey it picks up another atom, that millions of other drops have vainly tried to snatch from the smooth surface of some old rock, and, doubly laden, rolls on as swiftly as ever. Still other atoms it picks up—one from a clay bank, three or four from some mud bank, half a dozen from the roots of the grasses that grow by the river-bank, and some, perhaps, that other drops have been unable to carry. When it reaches the lowlands it is heavily laden, yet it is still on its way to the sea, with 1300 miles further to travel. It is opposite St. Louis, and is 408 feet higher than the surface of the sea, for the river is at high water. If it were low water, the drop would have only 369 feet farther to fall on its way. It is now an integer of a flood. The ground over which it has to travel is entirely composed of atoms that other drops have brought down and left, being too heavily burdened to carry their load any farther. Only at three or four places will it touch ground that was not made in this way. As it rolls on, it will pick up atoms or drop them, according as it rolls swiftly or slowly, until, when it reaches the sea, it will drop them all, and take atoms of salt from its neighbors. And it will roll swiftly or slowly according to the resistance it meets from the atoms left by the drops that have gone before.

In other words, the river below St. Louis (for nature keeps it in order above that point) flows through ground it has itself made. There are no confining banks which it has not made for itself, and what it has made, it unmakes still more easily. Carrying with it always the material with which to build its own obstructions, it drops these materials here and there, and continually stumbles over its own burdens.

If the reader can imagine a small stream of molasses running down Broadway for thousands of years, he will see readily the way in which the Mississippi River chokes itself up and changes its course from time to time. The molasses would begin, say, at Union Square, by spreading itself over the ground, and drying up into grains of sugar, making a little hill. Supposing the stream to be always supplied from the top of that hill, and always to flow toward the Battery, it would forever be building up a greater hill at its source, and drying as it flowed down this hill, till it filled Broadway to the tops of the houses. And as it dried up in one place, making an obstruction for itself of sugar, it would flow on the other side of the street until that was filled higher than the first.

Substituting the hills and high lands on either side of the Mississippi Valley for the buildings along Broadway, and water and silt for the sugar-laden molasses, the image is easily formed of the great river and its bed.

As was said, the whole valley is filled with silt at least a thousand feet deep. In order to have deposited this silt thus all over the valley, the river must have flowed in different ages in all parts of the valley, doing for countless centuries just what it is doing to-day—building up sand-bars and mud banks, breaking and cutting them again, and tossing the atoms from place to place, dropping them at low water, and shifting them in floods, but always bringing down more, and building the valley up higher and higher, and carrying the delta out farther and farther to sea. If the supply of material holds out, the Gulf of Mexico must inevitably become dry land as the arm of the sea above it has done.

The character of the silt which forms this "made ground" is an important factor in the problem. It is chiefly mineral in its formation, and is of great specific gravity; but there is a considerable admixture of vegetable matter, which doubtless is the cause of its exceeding fertility. Being formed of heterogeneous atoms brought in solution by the water, and not having amalgamated thoroughly, at least on the surface, or where the water can reach it, it remains soft soluble mud, which is capable of resisting the action of water only by means of gravity. It has almost no cohesion, and offers no proper foundation for any work that is of greater specific gravity than itself. It is used as material for the mud banks called levees, which have been until lately the only engineering works on which reliance has been placed, for there is no other material there to use, but from the fact that it is soluble it is poor material for such works.

These facts, thoughtfully considered, present difficulties enough in the way of engineering works, but the main difficulty is yet untouched. This lies first in the magnitude of the river itself, secondly in

the variations in its volume, and thirdly in its variations in altitude and speed. This may seem like a variety of difficulties instead of one, but that one all lies in the effort to control a vast stream which constantly varies in volume, altitude, lateral position, and speed. It is evident enough that it would be a comparatively simple thing to control a smaller stream of as obstinate a nature, or one equally as large that should not change from month to month in its conditions. One can manage a puddle, or protect himself from the sea, but against a thing that is alternately puddle and sea it is difficult to act.

The stretch of bottom-land over which the river rolls from St. Louis to the sea* is from twenty to two hundred miles wide, and seven hundred miles long. Over this flat surface (for it is almost flat, sloping gently to the sea) the river meanders, cutting a shifting groove in the soft mud, that is 1300 miles long. Why it does not cut for itself a straight line, thus securing a fall of $\frac{58}{100}$ of a foot per mile, instead of $\frac{31}{100}$ of a foot, which it now has, seems strange until we stop to consider that it carries its own obstructions with it until they become too heavy to carry. Then dropping them in its own path, it has to run around them. It thus forever corrects its own tendency to cut away the ground it has made, for if it were straightened and kept straight, as has been proposed by Captain Eads, it would have a direct tendency to do this, which tendency would have to be counteracted by other means. By the increased slope it would acquire increased rapidity, and would carry to the sea as great a burden as it has at St. Louis, if not greater.

As to the variations in the river between high and low water, they are almost inconceivable to one who has not witnessed them. They are as if the Hudson River should once a year flood the second floor of the City Hall in New York city, and occasionally in a "flood year" flow over the third floor; and the problem before the Mississippi engineers is to be compared with the question how, with

* The Ohio River is similar in many respects to the Mississippi, but this paper has reference specially to that part of the country which imperatively needs artificial protection, and comparatively little of the Ohio Valley needs that. With regard to that portion which may be said to need it, very much the same line of remark is applicable that is here applied to the Mississippi.

such floods, serviceable piers could be constructed on our river-front if there were no rock foundation less than one thousand feet deep. One is no more difficult a question than the other, excepting that on the Mississippi there are thirteen hundred miles to look after.

During the floods of last spring the Mississippi River from Cairo to the sea—1100 miles—had an average width of not less than twenty miles, and an average depth from shore to shore of not less than ten feet. Of course much of this was slack water, or the backset caused by the overflow. All this volume of water was not flowing to the sea with the full force that comes of a fall of $\frac{58}{100}$ of a foot. If it had been, there would have been little use in asking to-day what is to be done for the valley, for there would have been very little valley left. But the volume of water was there, and if it could have escaped into the sea as rapidly as it flowed into the valley from above, it would still have been too large to lie in its bed.

The problem in brief, then, is to decide how to keep within fixed bounds a stream that flows in varying volume over a bed of mud, without banks that can be called banks.

Many theories have been advanced in answer to this, and any one who is inclined to labor of that kind can readily construct a theory of his own that will do as well as many that have been urged upon the public with much eloquent and ingenious argument. The writer declines to step in where abler men fear to tread. A brief statement of the main theories advanced, however, is of great interest, especially in view of the fact that the government at Washington has adopted one, and appropriated a few millions for the beginning of a work that is to cost "not more than $46,000,000," its advocates say.

Theorists seek in two directions for an answer. On the one hand, it is urged that by improving the character of the bed and strengthening the banks the river may be kept within its bounds. On the other, it is declared that no works are practically possible that will be sufficient to confine the river in a flood season, and that since it must overflow its banks, the philosophical thing to do is to provide auxiliary channels or outlets that shall guide the surplus water to the sea without damage. Theorists of each school denounce those of the other as incompetent

and radically wrong, and stoop to personal abuse when argument fails. Only a short time ago Mr. Edward Atkinson, in concluding an able argument in favor of the plans adopted by the Mississippi River Commission, said: "It is hardly worth while to consider the projects for relieving the Mississippi River floods by creating new outlets, since these sensational propositions have commended themselves only to unthinking minds, and have no support among engineers."

While this style of argument has been too often relied upon by both sides, the fact remains that the only considerable works undertaken by our race have been in the direction of trying to confine the river, and not of trying to give additional outlets for surplus or flood water. The "levee and jetty" advocates have had their way so far as actual operations have gone, and they seem likely to continue to have it for some time. The present operations are under the direction of the Mississippi River Commission—a body which was created by the Forty-sixth Congress. President Hayes was given the power to create its individuality, which he did by appointing only known and committed advocates of the restrictive theory on the list of members. Efforts were made to secure the appointment of some of the opponents of this theory, but the efforts were unsuccessful.

The outlet theory is one which hardly needs description to be generally understood, though it has been studied and set forth by several persons with much attention to the engineering details involved. By a glance at any large map of the Lower Mississippi, the great number of bayous and natural outlets formed by the natural action of the river will be discerned. Some of these it is proposed to open and clean out, so as to render them available in case of floods, and then, by lock gates at the river side, keep them closed at low water, and open when the water rises too high. The main objection to this theory is on the ground that the real desideratum is a single deep channel, as realizing the least friction between the river and its channel, rather than a multiplicity of channels.

The levee, jetty, and revetment system is not so simple. Its claims are far more elaborate, and the criticisms that are offered are far more complicated than those of the outlet system. The radical idea in-

volved is the building of artificial banks
that shall confine the river within them,
in order to secure the full force and
"scour" of the stream for the improvement of the bed. The obvious effects of
such works—obvious, that is, to all who
have given the subject of river hydraulics
any careful study—are such as to lead to
careful theorizing to justify them; and in
the various steps of this theorizing there is
plenty of room for cavil, if not for sound
criticism.

Without entering the lists either as advocate or critic, it is sufficient to give here
a brief description of what has been done,
what it is decided to do, what it is claimed the benefits will be, and what the ob-
jections are. The public prints, during the
period of subsidence of the recent floods,
were full of references to the proposed
works, and to those which had been constructed, and yet it was difficult, if not impossible, to catch from the discussion a
complete idea of the system.

The first works of which we know definitely were the levees. These are large
banks of earth built to serve as extra banks
when the river should rise, and to keep the
water off the low cultivated lands behind
them. When well built, they undoubtedly serve this purpose, and if kept in repair
they can be made to resist any flood that
is ever likely to come. The whole city of
Cairo, during the floods this year, stood
about fourteen feet below the surface of
the water outside, which rose to the very
top of the surrounding levees. When the
ripples washed on the top of the levees, the
people turned out, and built a temporary
bank above to the height of two feet; and
although the water rose sixteen inches
against this hastily constructed barrier,
the town was saved.

But however well a levee may serve to
protect one spot of land, it does this to the
detriment of other places, since the water
kept from one place flows to another, and,
being out of its banks, is spread to places
that would be untouched if a portion of
its natural overflow were not walled in.
Therefore the levee system, to be perfect,
should be continuous along both sides of
the river. Mathematically speaking, a
defect anywhere would vitiate the whole
system; but practically it is claimed that
the levees constructed by slave labor, and
kept in order before the war, worked fairly
well. It should be remembered, however, that during the years when this system

was in its best condition there were no
such floods as have happened at other
times.

The next work of importance in the
line of restriction was that done by Captain Eads in the South Pass of the Mississippi Delta. He conceived the idea (or, at
least, executed it) of confining a wide
shallow stream within comparatively narrow banks, arguing that if the water could
not pass over the wide space, it would
scour out the bottom, and so deepen the
channel. During the construction of the
jetties it was found that the water, instead
of scouring out the bottom, preferred to
follow its old habit of seeking the line of
least resistance. Finding an obstruction
in its way in the South Pass, it turned off
through the Southwest Pass and the Pas
à l'Outre. It was found that instead of
scouring out the jettied pass, it was scouring out the other two, and there was shortly an additional depth of two feet in each
of these. Captain Eads says: "As soon
as this fact was discovered, submerged
dams were laid across the Southwest Pass
and the Pas à l'Outre, about two feet thick
and about seventy-five feet width of base.
Each of these dams is about three-quarters
of a mile in length."

By thus partially damming the other
two outlets, and by the use of a very powerful dredging machine to assist the stimulated "scour" in the South Pass, Captain
Eads has maintained, and is to-day maintaining, a deeper channel than ever before
existed between New Orleans and the sea.
It is claimed by his critics, however, that
the effect of his work is to retard the flow
of the river above it, and by the consequent settling of the silt held in solution,
to build up the bottom of the river, and
thus increase the danger of overflow.

The plan of the Mississippi River Commission is more elaborate than any other
here described. They propose to narrow
the wide places in the river to a uniform
width of 3000 feet, in order that the bottom shall be scoured out in the shallow
places, and they propose to strengthen
the banks, and regulate the shape of the
bottom by wire and woven brush mattresses, or linings, to be laid in such places
as the river would naturally eat away.
In conjunction with this it is proposed to
strengthen the system of levees, though
this is not a part of the work of the Commission. These wire and brush mattresses
are to be placed in position in such a way

as to encourage the settling of sediment in places where it is desired to have the revetments, and they are to be secured with rubble stone, while in places stone pavements are to be constructed. There are, of course, in a plan of this kind, an enormous number of details that can not be described within the limits of a magazine article, but the general scope of the plan has been fairly told.

As was to be expected, the plan has been severely criticised, and numberless arguments have been made to show the defects in its theory. Whether it is sound or not, however, the theory has been adopted by the government, and the work is in progress. The lowest estimate of its cost by one of the Commission was $33,000,000, and another member said it would be not more than $46,000,000. Its opponents, however, declare that ten times that sum will not complete it satisfactorily. One curious point was made much of in the discussion which was rife last spring. It seems to be regarded as final that the general government has no power to do anything to the river excepting for the purpose of improving navigation on it. Whatever benefits may accrue to the lands along its banks must be purely incidental, and not an object of the work, according to constitutional limitation. This bit of Jeffersonian democracy is not relished by the people of the valley, and during the prevalence of the floods I heard much said there of the possibility of making the question a political issue. "The old flag and an appropriation" is by no means a new political slogan, but it may yet be heard from the Mississippi Valley. If it is once sounded, it will rally a party there that may prove formidable.

CRACKER COWBOYS OF FLORIDA

"A CRACKER."

ONE can thresh the straw of history until he is well worn out, and also is running some risk of wearing others out who may have to listen, so I will waive the telling of who the first cowboy was, even if I knew; but the last one who has come under my observation lives down in Florida, and the way it happened was this: I was sitting in a "sto' do'," as the "Crackers" say, waiting for the clerk to load some "number eights," when my friend said, "Look at the cowboys!" This immediately caught my interest. With me cowboys are what gems and porcelains are to some others. Two very emaciated Texas ponies pattered down the street, bearing wild-looking individuals, whose hanging hair and drooping hats and generally bedraggled appearance would remind you at once of the Spanish-moss which hangs so quietly and helplessly to the limbs of the oaks out in the swamps. There was none of the bilious fierceness and rearing plunge which I had associated with my friends out West, but as a fox-terrier is to a yellow cur, so were these last. They had on about four dollars' worth of clothes between them, and rode McClellan saddles, with saddle-bags, and guns tied on before. The only things they did which were conventional were to tie their ponies up by the head in brutal disregard, and then get drunk in about fifteen minutes. I could see that in this case, while some of the tail feathers were the same, they would easily classify as new birds.

"And so you have cowboys down here?" I said to the man who ran the meat-market.

He picked a tiny piece of raw liver out of the meshes of his long black beard, tilted his big black hat, shoved his arms into his white apron front, and said,

"Gawd! yes, stranger; I was one myself."

The plot thickened so fast that I was losing much, so I became more deliberate. "Do the boys come into town often?" I inquired further.

"Oh yes, 'mos' every little spell," replied the butcher, as he reached behind his weighing-scales and picked up a double-barrelled shot-gun, sawed off. "We-uns

me of the banker down the street. Bankers are bound to be broad-gauged, intelligent, and conservative, so I would go to him and get at the ancient history of this neck of woods. I introduced myself, and was invited behind the counter. The look

A CRACKER COWBOY.

are expectin' of they-uns to-day." And he broke the barrels and took out the shells to examine them.

"Do they come shooting?" I interposed.

He shut the gun with a snap. "We split even, stranger."

Seeing that the butcher was a fragile piece of bric-à-brac, and that I might need him for future study, I bethought

of things reminded me of one of those great green terraces which conceal fortifications and ugly cannon. It was boards and wire screen in front, but behind it were shot-guns and six-shooters hung in the handiest way, on a sort of disappearing gun-carriage arrangement. Shortly one of the cowboys of the street scene floundered in. He was two-thirds drunk,

IN WAIT FOR AN ENEMY.

with brutal shifty eyes and a flabby lower lip.

"I want twenty dollars on the old man. Ken I have it?"

I rather expected that the bank would go into "action front," but the clerk said, "Certainly," and completed this rather odd financial transaction, whereat the bull-hunter stumbled out.

"Who is the old man in this case?" I ventured.

"Oh, it's his boss, old Colonel Zuigg, of Crow City. I gave some money to some of his boys some weeks ago, and when the colonel was down here I asked him if he wanted the boys to draw against him in that way, and he said, 'Yes—for a small amount; they will steal a cow or two, and pay me that way.'"

Here was something tangible.

"What happens when a man steals another man's brand in this country?"

"He mustn't get caught; that's all. They all do it, but they never bring their troubles into court. They just shoot it

out there in the bresh. The last time old Colonel Zuigg brought Zorn Zuidden in here and had him indicted for stealing cattle, said Zorn: 'Now see here, old man Zuigg, what do you want for to go and git me arrested fer? I have stole thousands of cattle and put your mark and brand on 'em, and jes because I have stole a couple of hundred from you, you go and have me indicted. You jes better go and get that whole deal nol prossed;' and it was done."

The argument was perfect.

"From that I should imagine that the cow-people have no more idea of law than the 'gray apes,' " I commented.

"Yes, that's about it. Old Colonel Zuigg was a judge fer a spell, till some feller filled him with buckshot, and he had to resign; and I remember he decided a case aginst me once. I was hot about it, and the old colonel he saw I was. Says he, 'Now yer mad, ain't you?' And I allowed I was. 'Well,' says he, 'you hain't got no call to get mad. I have decided the last eight cases in yer favor, and you kain't have it go yer way all the time; it wouldn't look right;' and I had to be satisfied."

The courts in that locality were but the faint and sickly flame of a taper offered at the shrine of a justice which was traditional only, it seemed. Moral forces having ceased to operate, the large owners began to brand everything in sight, never realizing that they were sowing the wind. This action naturally demoralized the cowboys, who shortly began to brand a little on their own account—and then the deluge. The rights of property having been destroyed, the large owners put strong outfits in the field, composed of desperate men armed to the teeth, and what happens in the lonely pine woods no one knows but the desperadoes themselves, albeit some of them never come back to the little fringe of settlements. The winter visitor from the North kicks up the jack-snipe along the beach or tarponizes in the estuaries of the Gulf, and when he comes to the hotel for dinner he eats Chicago dressed beef, but out in the wilderness low-browed cow-folks shoot and stab each other for the possession of scrawny creatures not fit for a pointer-dog to mess on. One cannot but feel the force of Buckle's law of "the physical aspects of nature" in this sad country. Flat and sandy, with miles on miles of straight pine timber, each tree an exact duplicate of its neighbor tree, and underneath the scrub palmettoes, the twisted brakes and hammocks, and the gnarled water-oaks festooned with the sad gray Spanish-moss —truly not a country for a high-spirited race or moral giants.

The land gives only a tough wiregrass, and the poor little cattle, no bigger than a donkey, wander half starved and horribly emaciated in search of it. There used to be a trade with Cuba, but now that has gone; and beyond the supplying of Key West and the small fringe of settlements they have no market. How well the cowboys serve their masters I can only guess, since the big owners do not dare go into the woods, or even to their own doors at night, and they do not keep a light burning in the houses. One, indeed, attempted to assert his rights, but some one pumped sixteen buckshot into him as he bent over a spring to drink, and he left the country. They do tell of a late encounter between two rival foremen, who rode on to each other in the woods, and drawing, fired, and both were found stretched dying under the palmettoes, one calling deliriously the name of his boss. The unknown reaches of the Everglades lie just below, and with a half-hour's start a man who knew the country would be safe from pursuit, even if it were attempted; and, as one man cheerfully confided to me, "A boat don't leave no trail, stranger."

That might makes right, and that they steal by wholesale, any cattle-hunter will admit; and why they brand at all I cannot see, since one boy tried to make it plain to me, as he shifted his body in drunken abandon and grabbed my pencil and a sheet of wrapping-paper: "See yer; ye see that?" And he drew a circle O and then another ring around it, thus: ◎. "That brand ain't no good. Well, then—" And again his knotted and dirty fingers essayed the brand I O. He laboriously drew upon it and made EO, which of course destroyed the former brand.

"Then here," he continued, as he drew 13, "all ye've got ter do is this—313." I gasped in amazement, not at his cleverness as a brand-destroyer, but at his honest abandon. With a horrible operatic laugh, such as is painted in "the Cossack's Answer," he again laboriously drew ⊕ (the circle cross), and then added some marks which made it look like this: ⊕ And again breaking into his devil's "ha, ha!" said, "Make the damned thing whirl."

I did not protest. He would have shot me for that. But I did wish he was living in the northwest quarter of New Mexico, where Mr. Cooper and Dan could throw their eyes over the trail of his pony. Of course each man has adjusted himself to this lawless rustling, and only calculates that he can steal as much as his opponent. It is rarely that their affairs are brought to court, but when they are, the men come *en masse* to the room, armed with knives and rifles, so that any decision is bound to be a compromise, or it will bring on a general engagement.

There is also a noticeable absence of negroes among them, as they still retain some *ante bellum* theories, and it is only very lately that they have "reconstructed." Their general ignorance is "miraculous," and quite mystifying to an outside man. Some whom I met did not even know where the Texas was which furnishes them their ponies. The railroads of Florida have had their ups and downs with them in a petty way on account of the running over of their cattle by the trains; and then some long-haired old Cracker drops into the nearest station with his gun and pistol, and wants the telegraph operator to settle immediately on the basis of the Cracker's claim for damages, which is always absurdly high. At first the railroads demurred, but the cowboys lined up in the "bresh" on some dark night and pumped Winchesters into the train in a highly picturesque way. The trainmen at once recognized the force of the Crackers' views on cattle-killing, but it took some considerable "potting" at the more conservative superintendents before the latter could bestir themselves and invent a "cow-attorney," as the company adjuster is called, who now settles with the bushmen as best he

can. Certainly no worse people ever lived since the big killing up Muscleshell way, and the romance is taken out of it by the cowardly assassination which is the practice. They are well paid for their desperate work, and always eat fresh beef or "razor-backs," and deer which they kill in the woods. The heat, the poor grass, their brutality, and the pest of the flies kill their ponies, and, as a rule, they lack dash and are indifferent riders, but they are picturesque in their unkempt, almost unearthly wildness. A strange effect is added by their use of large, fierce cur-dogs, one of which accompanies each cattle-hunter, and is taught to pursue cattle, and to even take them by the nose, which is another instance of their brutality. Still, as they only have a couple of horses apiece, it saves them much extra running. These men do not use the rope, unless to noose a pony in a corral, but work their cattle in strong log corrals, which are made at about a day's march apart all through the woods. Indeed,

A BIT OF COW COUNTRY.

COWBOYS WRESTLING A BULL.

ropes are hardly necessary, since the cattle are so small and thin that two men can successfully " wrestle " a three-year-old. A man goes into the corral, grabs a cow by one horn, and throwing his other arm over her back, waits until some other man takes her hind leg, whereat ensues some very entertaining Græco-Roman style.

When the cow is successful, she finds her audience of Cracker cowboys sitting on the fence awaiting another opening, and gasping for breath. The best bull will not go over three hundred pounds, while I have seen a yearling at a hundred and fifty—if you, O knights of the riata, can imagine it! Still, it is desperate work. Some of the men are so reckless and active that they do not hesitate to encounter a wild bull in the open. The cattle are as wild as deer, they race off at scent; and when "rounded up" many will not drive, whereupon these are promptly shot. It frequently happens that when the herd is being driven quietly along a bull will turn on the drivers, charging at once. Then there is a scamper and great shooting. The bulls often become so maddened in these forays that they drop and die in their tracks, for which strange fact no one can account, but as a rule they are too scrawny and mean to make their handling difficult.

So this is the Cracker cowboy, whose chief interest would be found in the tales of some bushwhacking enterprise, which I very much fear would be a one-sided story, and not worth the telling. At best they must be revolting, having no note of the savage encounters which used to characterize the easy days in West Texas and New Mexico, when every man tossed his life away to the crackle of his own revolver. The moon shows pale through the leafy canopy on their evening fires, and the mists, the miasma, and the mosquitoes settle over their dreary camp talk. In place of the wild stampede, there is only the bellowing in the pens, and instead of the plains shaking under the dusty air as the bedizened vaqueros plough their fiery broncos through the milling herds, the cattle-hunter wends his lonely way through the ooze and rank grass, while the dreary pine trunks line up and shut the view.

THE ARCADIAN LAND

IF one crosses the river from New Orleans to Algiers, and takes Morgan's Louisiana and Texas Railway (now a part of the Southern Pacific line), he will go west, with a dip at first southerly, and will pass through a region little attractive except to water-fowl, snakes, and alligators, by an occasional rice plantation, an abandoned indigo field, an interminable stretch of cypress swamps, thickets of Spanish-bayonets, black waters, rank and rampant vegetation, vines, and water-plants. By-and-by firmer arable land, and cane plantations, many of them forsaken and become thickets of undergrowth, owing to frequent inundations and the low price of sugar.

At a distance of eighty miles Morgan City is reached, and the broad Atchafalaya Bayou is crossed. Hence is steam-boat communication with New Orleans and Vera Cruz. The Atchafalaya Bayou has its origin near the mouth of the Red River, and diverting from the Mississippi most of that great stream, it makes its tortuous way to the Gulf, frequently expanding into the proportions of a lake, and giving this region a great deal more water than it needs. The Bayou Teche, which is, in fact, a lazy river, wanders down from the rolling country of Washington and Opelousas, with a great deal of uncertainty of purpose, but mainly southeasterly, and parallel with the Atchafalaya, and joins the latter at Morgan City. Steamers of good size navigate it as far as New Iberia, some forty to fifty miles, and the railway follows it to the latter place, within sight of its fringe of live-oaks and cotton-woods. The region south and west of the Bayou Teche, a vast plain cut by innumerable small bayous and streams, which have mostly a connection with the bay of Côte Blanche and Vermilion Bay, is the home of the Nova Scotia Acadians.

The Acadians in 1755 made a good exchange, little as they thought so at the time, of bleak Nova Scotia for these sunny, genial, and fertile lands. They came into a land and a climate suited to their idiosyncrasies, and which have enabled them to preserve their primitive traits. In a comparative isolation from the disturbing currents of modern life, they have preserved the habits and customs of the eighteenth century. The immigrants spread themselves abroad among these bayous, made their homes wide apart, and the traveller will nowhere find—at least I did not—large and compact communities of them, unalloyed with the American and other elements. Indeed, I imagine that they are losing, in the general settlement of the country, their conspicuousness. They still give the tone, however, to considerable districts, as in the village and neighborhood of Abbeville. Some places, like the old town of St. Martinsville, on the Teche, once the social capital of the region, and entitled, for its wealth and gayety, the Petit Paris, had a large element of French who were not Acadians.

The Teche from Morgan City to New Iberia is a deep, slow, and winding stream, flowing through a flat region of sugar plantations. It is very picturesque by reason of its tortuousness and the great

A PRIMITIVE LOOM.

A LUMBER STATION ON THE TECHE.

spreading live-oak trees, moss-draped, that hang over it. A voyage on it is one of the most romantic entertainments offered to the traveller. The scenery is peaceful and exceedingly pretty. There are few conspicuous plantations with mansions and sugar-stacks of any pretensions, but the panorama from the deck of the steamer is always pleasing. There is an air of leisure and "afternoon" about the expedition, which is heightened by the idle ease of the inhabitants lounging at the rude wharves and landing-places, and the patience of the colored fishers, boys in scant raiment and women in sun-bonnets, seated on the banks. Typical of this universal contentment is the ancient colored man stretched on a plank close to the steamer's boiler, oblivious of the heat, apparently asleep, with his spacious mouth wide open, but softly singing.

"Are you asleep, uncle?"

"No, not adzackly asleep, boss. I jes wake up, and thinkin' how good de Lord is, I couldn't help singin'."

The panorama is always interesting. There are wide silvery expanses of water, into which fall the shadows of great trees. A tug is dragging along a tow of old rafts composed of cypress logs all water-soaked, green with weeds and grass, so that it looks like a floating garden. What pictures! Clusters of oaks on the prairie; a picturesque old cotton-press; a house thatched with palmettoes; rice fields irrigated by pumps; darkies, field hands, men and women, hoeing in the cane fields, giving stalwart strokes that exhibit their robust figures; an old sugar-mill in ruin and vine-draped; an old begass chimney against the sky; an antique cotton-press with its mouldering roof supported on timbers; a darky on a mule motionless on the bank, clad in Attakapas cloth, his slouch hat falling about his head like a roof from which the rafters have been withdrawn; palmettoes, oaks, and funereal moss; lines of Spanish-bayonets; rickety wharves; primitive boats; spider-legged bridges. Neither on the Teche nor the

Atchafalaya, nor on the great plain near the Mississippi, fit for amphibious creatures, where one standing on the level wonders to see the wheels of the vast river steamers above him, apparently without cause revolving, is there any lack of the picturesque.

New Iberia, the thriving mart of the region, which has drawn away the life from St. Martinsville, ten miles further up the bayou, is a village mainly of small oaks. One of them, which with its outside staircases in the pillared gallery suggests Spanish taste on the outside, and in the interior the arrangement of connecting rooms a French château, has a self-keeping rose garden, where one might easily become sentimental; the vines disport themselves like holiday children, climbing the trees, the side of the house, and revelling in an abandon of color and perfume.

A SWAMPER.

frame houses, with a smart court-house, a lively business street, a few pretty houses, and some old-time mansions on the bank of the bayou, half smothered in old rose gardens, the ground in the rear sloping to the water under the shade of gigantic

The population is mixed—Americans, French, Italians, now and then a Spaniard and even a Mexican, occasionally a basket-making Attakapas, and the all-pervading person of color. The darky is a born fisherman, in places where fishing requires no

exertion, and one may see
him any hour seated on the
banks of the Teche, especially the boy and the sun-bon-
neted woman, placidly holding their poles over the muddy stream, and can study, if
he like, the black face in ex-
pectation of a bite.   There too are the
washer-women, with their tubs
and a plank thrust into the water, and a handkerchief of bright
colors for a turban.   These
people somehow never fail to
be picturesque,
whatever atti-
tude they take,
and they are
not   at   all
self-conscious.
The groups on
Sunday   give
an interest to

UNDER THE MOSS.

GOING TO CHURCH.

church-going—a lean white horse, with a man, his wife, and boy strung along its backbone, an aged darky and his wife seated in a cart, in stiff Sunday clothes and flaming colors, the wheels of the cart making all angles with the ground, and wabbling and creaking along, the whole party as proud of its appearance as Julius Cæsar in a triumph.

I drove on Sunday morning early from New Iberia to church at St. Martinsville. It was a lovely April morning. The way lay over fertile prairies, past fine cane plantations, with some irrigation, and for a distance along the pretty Teche, shaded by great live-oaks, and here and there a fine magnolia-tree; a country with few houses, and those mostly shanties, but a sunny, smiling land, loved of the birds. We passed on our left the Spanish Lake, a shallow, irregular body of water. My driver was an ex-Confederate soldier, whose tramp with a musket through Virginia had not greatly enlightened him as to what it was all about. As to the Acadians, however, he had a decided opinion, and it was a poor one. They are no good. "You ask them a question, and they shrug their shoulders like a tarrapin —don't know no more'n a dead alligator;

only language they ever have is ' no' and ' what ?' "

If St. Martinsville, once the seat of fashion, retains anything of its past elegance, its life has departed from it. It has stopped growing anything but old, and yet it has not much of interest that is antique; it is a village of small white frame houses, with three or four big gaunt brick structures, two stories and a half high, with galleries, and here and there a creole cottage, the stairs running up inside the galleries, over which roses climb in profusion.

I went to breakfast at a French inn, kept by Madame Castillo, a large red-brick house on the banks of the Teche, where the live-oaks cast shadows upon the silvery stream. It had, of course, a double gallery. Below, the waiting-room, dining-room, and general assembly-room were paved with brick, and instead of a door, Turkey-red curtains hung in the entrance, and blowing aside, hospitably invited the stranger within. The breakfast was neatly served, the house was scrupulously clean, and the guest felt the influence of that personal hospitality which is always so pleasing. Madame offered me a seat in her pew in church, and meantime

APPROACH TO THE JEFFERSON MANSION.

a chair on the upper gallery, which opened from large square sleeping chambers.
In that fresh morning I thought I never
had seen a more sweet and peaceful place
than this gallery.　Close to it grew graceful China-trees in full blossom and odor;
up and down the Teche were charming
views under the oaks; only the roofs of
the town could be seen amid the foliage
of China-trees; and there was an atmosphere of repose in all the scene.　It was
Easter morning.　I felt that I should like
to linger there a week in absolute forget-
fulness of the world.　French is the ordinary language of the village, spoken more
or less corruptly by all colors.

The Catholic church, a large and ugly
structure, stands on the plaza, which is
not at all like a Spanish plaza, but a veritable New England "green," with stores
and shops on all sides—New England, except that the shops are open on Sunday.
In the church apse is a noted and not bad
painting of St. Martin, and at the bottom
of one aisle a vast bank of black stucco
clouds, with the Virgin standing on them,
and the legend, "*Je suis l'immaculée conception.*"

Country people were pouring into
town for the Easter service and festivities—more blacks than whites—on horseback and in rickety carriages, and the
horses were hitched on either side of the
church.　Before service the square was
full of lively young colored lads crack-
ing Easter-eggs.　Two meet and strike
together the eggs in their hands, and the
one loses whose egg breaks.　A tough
shell is a valuable possession.　The custom provokes a good deal of larking and
merriment.　While this is going on, the
worshippers are making their way into
the church through the throng, ladies
in the neat glory of provincial dress,
and high-stepping, saucy colored belles,
yellow and black, the blackest in the
most radiant apparel of violent pink and
light blue, and now and then a society favorite in all the hues of the rainbow.
The centre pews of the church are reserved for the whites, the seats of the
side aisles for the negroes.　When mass

A LOUISIANA PRAIRIE.

south wind begins to blow.   I think the south wind is the wind of memory and of longing.   I wonder if the gay spirits of the last generation ever return to the scenes of their revelry?   Will they come back to the theatre this Sunday night, and to the Grand Ball afterward?   The admission to both is only twenty-five cents, including gombo filé.

From New Iberia southward toward Vermilion Bay stretches a vast prairie; if it is not absolutely flat, if it resembles the ocean, it is the ocean when its long swells have settled nearly to a calm.   This prairie would be monotonous were it not dotted with small round ponds, like hand-mirrors for the flitting birds and sailing clouds, were its expanse not spotted with herds of cattle, scattered or clustering like fishing-boats on a green sea, were it not for a cabin here and there, a field of cane or cotton, a garden plot, and were it not for the forests which break the horizon line, and send out dark capes into the verdant plains.   On a gray day, or when storms

begins, the church is crowded.   The boys, with occasional excursions into the vestibule to dip the finger in the holy-water, or perhaps say a prayer, are still winning and losing eggs on the green.

On the gallery at the inn it is also Sunday.   The air is full of odor.   A strong

A RUIN ON BAYOU TECHE.

and fogs roll in from the Gulf, it might be a gloomy region, but under the sunlight and in the spring it is full of life and color; it has an air of refinement and repose that is very welcome. Besides the uplift of the spirit that a wide horizon is apt to give, one is conscious here of the neighborhood of the sea, and of the possibilities of romantic adventure in a coast intersected by bayous, and the presence of novel forms of animal and vegetable life, and of a people with habits foreign and strange. There is also a grateful sense of freedom and expansion.

Soon, over the plain, is seen on the horizon, ten miles from New Iberia, the dark foliage on the island of Petite Anse, or Avery's Island. This unexpected upheaval from the marsh, bounded by the narrow, circling Petite Anse Bayou, rises into the sky one hundred and eighty feet, and has the effect in this flat expanse of a veritable mountain, comparatively a surprise, like Pike's Peak seen from the elevation of Denver. Perhaps nowhere else would a hill of one hundred and eighty feet make such an impression on the mind. Crossing the bayou, where alligators sun themselves, and eye with affection the colored people angling at the bridge, and passing a long causeway over the marsh, the firm land of the island is reached. This island, which is a sort of geological puzzle, has a nearly everything one desires of the necessaries of life. A portion of the island is devoted to a cane plantation and sugar-works; a part of it is covered with forests;

DOORWAY OF ST. MARTINSVILLE HOTEL.

very uneven surface, and is some two and a half miles long by one mile broad. It is a little kingdom in itself, capable of producing in its soil and adjacent waters and on the lowlands and gentle slopes, besides thickets of palmetto, are gigantic live-oaks, moss-draped trees monstrous in girth, and towering into the sky with a

" HONORABLE."

and weeds run like waves when the wind blows, great shadows of clouds pass on its surface, alternating dark masses with vivid ones of sunlight; fishing-boats and the masts of schooners creep along the threads of water; when the sun goes down, a red globe of fire in the Gulf mists, all the expanse is warm and ruddy, and the waters sparkle like jewels; and at night, under the great field of stars, marsh fires here and there give a sort of lurid splendor to the scene. In the winter it is a temperate spot, and at all times of the year it is blessed by an invigorating sea-breeze. Those who have enjoyed the charming social life and the unbounded hospitality of the family who inhabit this island may envy them their paradisiacal home, but they would be able to select none others so worthy to enjoy it.

It is said that the Attakapas Indians are shy of this island, having a legend that it was the scene of a great catastrophe to their race. Whether this catastrophe has any connection with the upheaval of the salt mountain I do not know. Many stories are current in this region in regard to the discovery of this deposit. A little over a quarter of a century ago it was unsuspected. The presence of salt in the water of a small spring led somebody to dig in that place, and at the depth of sixteen feet below the surface solid salt was struck. In stripping away the soil several relics of human workmanship came to light, among them stone implements and a woven basket, exactly such as the Attakapas make now. This basket, found at the depth of sixteen feet, lay upon the salt rock, and was in perfect preservation. Half of it can now be seen in the Smithsonian Institution. At the beginning of the war great quantities of salt were taken from this mine for the use of the Confederacy. But this supply was cut off by the Unionists, who at first sent gun-boats up the bayou within shelling distance, and at length occupied it with troops.

The ascertained area of the mine is several acres; the depth of the deposit is unknown. The first shaft was sunk a hundred feet; below this a shaft of seventy feet fails to find any limit to the salt. The excavation is already large. Descending, the visitor enters vast cathedral-like chambers; the sides are solid salt,

vast spread of branches. Scarcely anywhere else will one see a nobler growth of these stately trees. In a depression is the famous salt-mine, unique in quality and situation in the world. Here is grown and put up the Tobasco pepper; here, amid fields of clover and flowers, a large apiary flourishes. Stones of some value for ornament are found. Indeed, I should not be surprised at anything turning up there, for I am told that good kaoline has been discovered ; and about the residences of the hospitable proprietors roses bloom in abundance, the China-tree blossoms sweetly, and the mocking-bird sings.

But better than all these things I think I like the view from the broad cottage piazzas, and I like it best when the salt breeze is strong enough to sweep away the coast mosquitoes—a most undesirable variety. I do not know another view of its kind for extent and color comparable to that from this hill over the waters seaward. The expanse of luxuriant grass, brown, golden, reddish, in patches, is intersected by a net-work of bayous, which gleam like silver in the sun, or trail like dark fabulous serpents under a cloudy sky. The scene is limited only by the power of the eye to meet the sky line. Vast and level, it is constantly changing, almost in motion with life; the long grass sparkling with crystals; the floor is solid salt; the roof is solid salt, supported on pillars of salt, left by the excavators, forty or perhaps sixty feet square. When the interior is lighted by dynamite the effect is superbly weird and grotesque. The salt is blasted by dynamite, loaded into cars which run on rails to the elevator, hoisted, and distributed into the crushers, and from the crushers directly into the bags for shipment. The crushers dif-

drive of twelve miles over the prairie, sometimes in and sometimes out of the water, and continually diverted from our course by fences. It is a good sign of the thrift of the race, and of its independence, that the colored people have taken up or bought little tracts of thirty or forty acres, put up cabins, and new fences round their domains regardless of the travelling public. We zigzagged all about the country to get round these little enclosures. At

VIEW ON THE BAYOU TECHE AT NEW IBERIA.

fer in crushing capacity, some producing fine and others coarse salt. No bleaching or cleansing process is needed; the salt is almost absolutely pure. Large blocks of it are sent to the Western plains for "cattle licks." The mine is connected by rail with the main line at New Iberia.

Across the marshes and bayous eight miles to the west from Petite Anse Island rises Orange Island, famous for its orange plantation, but called Jefferson Island since it became the property and home of Joseph Jefferson. Not so high as Petite Anse, it is still conspicuous with its crown of dark forest. From a high point on Petite Anse, through a lovely vista of trees, with flowering cacti in the foreground, Jefferson's house is a white spot in the landscape. We reached it by a circuitous

one place, where the main road was bad, a thrifty Acadian had set up a toll of twenty-five cents for the privilege of passing through his premises. The scenery was pastoral and pleasing. There were frequent round ponds, brilliant with lilies and *fleurs-de-lis*, and hundreds of cattle feeding on the prairie or standing in the water, and generally of a dun-color, made always an agreeable picture. The monotony was broken by lines of trees, by cape-like woods stretching into the plain, and the horizon line was always fine. Great variety of birds enlivened the landscape, game birds abounding. There was the lively little nonpareil, which seems to change its color, and is red and green and blue, I believe of the oriole family, the papabotte, a favorite on New Orleans tables in the autumn, snipe, killdee, the cherooke (snipe?), the meadow-lark, and quantities of teal ducks in the ponds. These little ponds are called "bull-holes." The traveller is told that they are started in this watery soil by the pawing of bulls, and gradually enlarged as the cattle frequent them. He remembers that he has seen similar circular ponds in the North not made by bulls.

Mr. Jefferson's residence—a pretty rose-vine-covered cottage—is situated on the slope of the hill, overlooking a broad plain and a vast stretch of bayou country. Along one side of his home enclosure for a mile runs a superb hedge of Chickasaw roses. On the slope back of the house, and almost embracing it, is a magnificent grove of live-oaks, great gray stems, and the branches hung with heavy masses of moss, which swing in the wind like the pendent boughs of the willow, and with something of its sentimental and mournful suggestion. The recesses of this forest are cool and dark, but upon ascending the hill, suddenly bursts upon the view under the trees a most lovely lake of clear blue water. This lake, which may be a mile long and half a mile broad, is called Lake Peigneur, from its fanciful resemblance, I believe, to a wool-comber. The shores are wooded. On the island side the bank is precipitous; on the opposite shore amid the trees is a hunting-lodge, and I believe there are plantations on the north end, but it is in aspect altogether solitary and peaceful. But the island did not want life. The day was brilliant, with a deep blue sky and high-sailing fleecy clouds, and it seemed a sort of animal holiday: squirrels chattered; cardinal-birds flashed through the green leaves; there flitted about the red-winged blackbird, blue jays, red-headed woodpeckers, thrushes, and occasionally a rain-crow crossed the scene; high overhead sailed the heavy buzzards, describing great aerial circles; and off in the still lake the ugly heads of alligators were toasting in the sun.

It was very pleasant to sit on the wooded point, enlivened by all this animal activity, looking off upon the lake and the great expanse of marsh, over which came a refreshing breeze. There was great variety of forest trees. Besides the live-oaks, in one small area I noticed the water-oak, red-oak, pin-oak, the elm, the cypress, the hackberry, and the pecan tree.

This point is a favorite rendezvous for the buzzards. Before I reached it I heard a tremendous whirring in the air, and, lo! there upon the oaks were hundreds and hundreds of buzzards. Upon one dead tree, vast, gaunt, and bleached, they had settled in black masses. When I came near, they rose and flew about with clamor and surprise, momentarily obscuring the sunlight. With these unpleasant birds consorted in unclean fellowship numerous long-necked water-turkeys. Doré would have liked to introduce into one of his melodramatic pictures this helpless dead tree, extending its gray arms loaded with these black scavengers. It needed the blue sky and blue lake to prevent the scene from being altogether uncanny. I remember still the harsh, croaking noise of the buzzards and the water-turkeys when they were disturbed, and the flapping of their funereal wings, and perhaps the alligators lying off in the lake noted it, for they grunted and bellowed a response. But the birds sang merrily, the wind blew softly; there was the repose as of a far country undisturbed by man, and a silvery tone on the water and all the landscape that refined the whole.

If the Acadians can anywhere be seen in the prosperity of their primitive simplicity, I fancy it is in the parish of Vermilion, in the vicinity of Abbeville and on the Bayou Tigre. Here, among the intricate bayous that are their highways and supply them with the poorer sort of fish, and the fair meadows on which their cattle pasture, and where they grow nearly everything their simple habits require, they have for over a century enjoyed a quiet existence, practically undisturbed by the agitations of modern life, ignorant of its progress. History makes their departure from the comparatively bleak meadows of Grand Pré a cruel hardship, if a political necessity. But they made a very fortunate exchange. Nowhere else on the continent could they so well have preserved their primitive habits, or found climate and soil so suited to their humor. Others have exhaustively set forth the history and idiosyncrasies of this peculiar people; it is in my way only to tell what I saw on a spring day.

To reach the heart of this abode of contented and perhaps wise ignorance we took boats early one morning at Petite Anse Island, while the dew was still heavy and the birds were at matins, and rowed down the Petite Anse Bayou. A stranger would surely be lost in these winding, branching, interlacing streams. Evangeline and her lover might have passed each other unknown within hail across these marshes. The party of a dozen people occupied two row-boats. Among them were gentlemen who knew the route, but the reserve of wisdom as to what bayous and cut-offs were navigable was an ancient ex-slave, now a voter, who responded to the name of "Honorable" — a weather-beaten and weather-wise darky, a redoubtable fisherman, whose memory extended away beyond the war, and played familiarly about the person of Lafayette, with whom he had been on agreeable terms in Charleston, and who dated his narratives, to our relief, not from the war, but from the year of some great sickness on the coast. From the Petite Anse we entered the Carlin Bayou, and wound through it is needless to say what others in our tortuous course. In the fresh morning, with the salt air, it was a voyage of delight. Mullet were jumping in the glassy stream, perhaps disturbed by the gar-fish, and alligators lazily slid from the reedy banks into the water at our approach. All the marsh was gay with flowers, vast patches of the blue *fleur-de-lis* intermingled with the exquisite white spider-lily, nodding in clusters on long stalks; an amaryllis (pancratium), its pure half-disk fringed with delicate white filaments. The air was vocal with the notes of birds, the nonpareil and the meadow-lark, and most conspicuous of all the handsome boat-tail grackle, a black bird, which alighted on the slender dead reeds that swayed with his weight as he poured forth his song. Sometimes the bayou narrowed so that it was impossible to row with the oars, and poling was resorted to, and the current was swift and strong. At such passes we saw only the banks with nodding flowers, and the reeds, with the blackbirds singing, against the sky. Again we emerged into placid reaches overhung by gigantic live-oaks and fringed with cypress. It was enchanting. But the

ON THE BAYOU TIGRE.

way was not quite solitary. Numerous fishing parties were encountered, boats on their way to the bay, and now and then a party of stalwart men drawing a net in the bayou, their clothes being deposited on the banks. Occasionally a large schooner was seen, tied to the bank or slowly working its way, and on one a whole family was domesticated. There is a good deal of queer life hidden in these bayous.

After passing through a narrow artificial canal we came into the Bayou Tigre, and landed for breakfast on a greensward, with meadow-land and signs of habitations in the distance, under spreading live-oaks. Under one of the most attractive of these trees, close to the stream, we did not spread our table-cloth and shawls, because a large moccason snake was seen to glide under the roots, and we did not know but that his modesty was assumed, and he might join the breakfast party. It is said that these snakes never attack any one who has kept all the ten commandments from his youth up. Cardinal-birds made the wood gay for us while we breakfasted, and we might have added plenty of partridges to our *menu* if we had been armed.

COTTON PLANTATION ON THE TECHE.

Resuming our voyage, we presently entered the inhabited part of the bayou, among cultivated fields, and made our first call on the Thibodeaux. They had been expecting us, and Andonia came down to the landing to welcome us, and with a formal, pretty courtesy led the way to the house. Does the reader happen to remember, say in New England, say fifty years ago, the sweetest maiden lady in the village, prim, staid, full of kindness, the proportions of the figure never quite developed, with a row of small corkscrew curls about her serene forehead, and all the juices of life that might have overflowed into the life of others somehow withered into the sweetness of her wistful face? Yes; a little timid and appealing, and yet trustful, and in a scant, quaint gown? Well, Andonia was never married, and she had such curls, and a high-waisted gown, and a kerchief folded across her breast. And when she spoke, it was in the language of France as it is rendered in Acadia.

The house, like all in this region, stands upon blocks of wood, is in appearance a frame house, but the walls between timbers are of concrete mixed with moss, and the same inside as out. It had no glass in the windows, which were closed with solid shutters. Upon the rough walls were hung sacred pictures and other crudely colored prints. The furniture was rude and apparently home-made, and the whole interior was as painfully neat as a Dutch parlor. Even the beams overhead and ceiling had been scrubbed. Andonia showed us with a blush of pride her neat little sleeping-room, with its souvenirs of affection, and perhaps some of the dried flowers of a possible romance, and the ladies admired the finely woven white counterpane on the bed. Andonia's married sister was a large, handsome woman, smiling and prosperous. There were children and I think a baby about, besides Mr. Thibodeaux. Nothing could exceed the kindly manner of these people. Andonia showed us how they card, weave, and spin the cotton out of which their blankets and the jean for their clothing are made. They use the old-fashioned hand-cards, spin on a little wheel with a foot treadle, have the most primitive warping bars, and weave most laboriously on a rude loom. But the cloth they make will wear forever, and the colors they use are all fast. It is a great pleasure, we might almost say shock, to encounter such honest work in these times. The Acadians grow a yellow or nankeen sort of cotton, which without requiring any dye is woven into a handsome yellow stuff. When we departed Andonia slipped into the dooryard, and returned with a rose for each of us. I fancied she was loath to have us go, and that the visit was an event in the monotony of her single life.

Embarking again on the placid stream, we moved along through a land of peace. The houses of the Acadians are scattered along the bayou at considerable distances apart. The voyager seems to be in an unoccupied country, when suddenly the turn of the stream shows him a farm-house, with its little landing-wharf, boats, and perhaps a schooner moored at the bank, and behind it cultivated fields and a fringe of trees. In the blossoming time of the year, when the birds are most active, these scenes are idyllic. At a bend in the bayou, where a tree sent its horizontal trunk half across it, we made our next call, at the house of Mr. Vallet, a large frame house, and evidently the abode of a man of means. The house was ceiled outside and inside with native woods. As usual in this region, the premises were not as orderly as those about some Northern farm-houses, but the interior of the house was spotlessly clean, and in its polish and barrenness of ornament and of appliances of comfort suggested a Brittany home, while its openness and the broad veranda spoke of a genial climate. Our call here was brief, for a sick man, very ill, they said, lay in the front room—a stranger who had been overtaken with fever, and was being cared for by these kind-hearted people.

Other calls were made—this visiting by boat recalls Venice—but the end of our voyage was the plantation of Simonette Le Blanc, a sturdy old man, a sort of patriarch in this region, the centre of a very large family of sons, daughters, and grandchildren. The residence, a rambling story-and-a-half house, grown by accretions as more room was needed, calls for no comment. It was all very plain, and contained no books, nor any adornments except some family photographs, the poor work of a travelling artist. But in front, on the bayou, Mr. Le Blanc had erected a grand ball-room, which gave an air of distinction to the place. This hall, which

had benches along the wall, and at one end a high dais for the fiddlers, and a little counter where the gombo filé (the common refreshment) is served, had an air of gayety by reason of engravings cut from the illustrated papers, and was shown with some pride. Here neighborhood dances take place once in two weeks, and a grand ball was to come off on Easter Sunday night, to which we were urgently invited to come.

Simonette Le Blanc with several of his sons had returned at midnight from an expedition to Vermilion Bay, where they had been camping for a couple of weeks, fishing and taking oysters. Working the schooner through the bayou at night had been fatiguing, and then there was supper, and all the news of the fortnight to be talked over, so that it was four o'clock before the house was at rest, but neither the hale old man nor his stalwart sons seemed the worse for the adventure. Such trips are not uncommon, for these people seem to have leisure for enjoyment, and vary the toil of the plantation with the pleasures of fishing and lazy navigation. But to the women and the home-stayers this was evidently an event. The men had been to the outer world, and brought back with them the gossip of the bayous and the simple incidents of the camping life on the coast. "There was a great deal to talk over that had happened in a fortnight," said Simonette—he and one of his sons spoke English. I do not imagine that the talk was about politics, or any of the events that seem important in other portions of the United States, only the faintest echoes of which ever reach this secluded place. This is a purely domestic and patriarchal community, where there are no books to bring in agitating doubts, and few newspapers to disquiet the nerves. The only matter of politics broached was in regard to an appropriation by Congress to improve a cut-off between two bayous. So far as I could learn, the most intelligent of these people had no other interest in or concern about the government. There is a neighborhood school where English is taught, but no church nearer than Abbeville, six miles away. I should not describe the population as fanatically religious, nor a church-going one except on special days. But by all accounts it is moral, orderly, sociable, fond of dancing, thrifty, and conservative.

The Acadians are fond of their homes.

It is not the fashion for the young people to go away to better their condition. Few young men have ever been as far from home as New Orleans; they marry young, and settle down near the homestead. Mr. Le Blanc has a colony of his descendants about him, within hail from his door. It must be large, and his race must be prolific, judging by the number of small children who gathered at the homestead to have a sly peep at the strangers. They took small interest in the war, and it had few attractions for them. The conscription carried away many of their young men, but I am told they did not make very good soldiers, not because they were not stalwart and brave, but because they were so intolerably homesick that they deserted whenever they had a chance. The men whom we saw were most of them fine athletic fellows, with honest, dark, sun-browned faces; some of the children were very pretty, but the women usually showed the effects of isolation and toil, and had the common plainness of French peasants. They are a self-supporting community, raise their own cotton, corn, and sugar, and for the most part manufacture their own clothes and articles of household use. Some of the cotton jeans, striped with blue, indigo-dyed, made into garments for men and women, and the blankets, plain yellow (from the native nankeen cotton), curiously clouded, are very pretty and serviceable. Further than that their habits of living are simple, and their ways primitive, I saw few eccentricities. The peculiarity of this community is in its freedom from all the hurry and worry and information of our modern life. I have read that the gallants train their little horses to prance and curvet and rear and fidget about, and that these are called "courtin' horses," and are used when a young man goes courting, to impress his mistress with his manly horsemanship. I have seen these horses perform under the saddle, but I was not so fortunate as to see any courting going on.

In their given as well as their family names these people are classical and peculiar. I heard, of men, the names L'Odias, Peigneur, Niolas, Elias, Homère, Lemaire, and of women, Emilite, Ségoura, Antóinette, Clarise, Elia.

We were very hospitably entertained by the Le Blancs. On our arrival tiny cups of black coffee were handed round, and later a drink of syrup and water, which some of the party sipped with a sickly smile of enjoyment. Before dinner we walked up to the bridge over the bayou on the road leading to Abbeville, where there is a little cluster of houses, a small country store, and a closed drug shop—the owner of which had put up his shutters and gone to a more unhealthy region. Here is a fine grove of oaks, and from the bridge we had in view a grand sweep of prairie, with trees, single and in masses, which made with the winding silvery stream a very pleasing picture. We sat down to a dinner—the women waiting on the table—of gombo filé, fried oysters, eggs, sweet-potatoes (the delicious saccharine, sticky sort), with syrup out of a bottle served in little saucers, and afterward black coffee. We were sincerely welcome to whatever the house contained, and when we departed the whole family, and indeed all the neighborhood, accompanied us to our boats, and we went away down the stream with a chorus of adieus and good wishes.

We were watching for a hail from the Thibodeaux. The doors and shutters were closed, and the mansion seemed blank and forgetful. But as we came opposite the landing, there stood Andonia, faithful, waving her handkerchief. Ah me!

We went home gayly and more swiftly, current and tide with us, though a little pensive, perhaps, with too much pleasure and the sunset effects on the wide marshes through which we voyaged. Cattle wander at will over these marshes, and are often stalled and lost. We saw some pitiful sights. The cattle venturing too near the boggy edge to drink become inextricably involved. We passed an ox sunken to his back, and dead, a cow frantically struggling in the mire, almost exhausted, and a cow and calf, the mother dead, the calf moaning beside her. On a cattle lookout near by sat three black buzzards surveying the prospect with hungry eyes.

When we landed and climbed the hill, and from the rose-embowered veranda looked back over the strange land we had sailed through, away to Bayou Tigre, where the red sun was setting, we felt that we had been in a country that is not of this world.

SOME RICHMOND PORTRAITS

WILLIAM BYRD.

THERE is a glamour of romance and a spirit of adventure around the story of Virginia that charm alike the lover of the poetical and the lover of the heroic. The beauty and bravery of Pocahontas and the daring of Captain Smith have touched a sympathetic chord in the human heart that has caused them to be remembered long after persons of a greater historical importance have been forgotten. Few cities so small as Richmond have occupied so large a place in the world's history. Here Patrick Henry delivered his famous speech, ending with the thrilling words, "Give me liberty, or give me death!" Here Aaron Burr was tried for treason before a court presided over by Chief Justice Marshall, by a jury whose foreman was John Randolph of Roanoke, and in the midst of the most brilliant array of counsel ever assembled in an American court of justice. Here lived men whose fame is world-wide, and women whose beauty and elegance might have added a grace and dignity to courts. Here centred the chief interest of the great American conflict which for four years commanded the attention of the civilized world.

The founder of Richmond was Colonel William Byrd, the second of the name in Virginia. He was of an an-cient English family, whose ancestor, a Norman knight, came in with the Conqueror, but married a Saxon wife, Wierberga Domville, the sole heir of Roger Domville, of the estate of Brexton, in Cheshire, England. Colonel Byrd was born March 16, 1674, and inherited from his father the well-known estate of Westover, on the James River. At an early age he was sent to England for his education, where, under the care and direction of Sir Robert Southwell, he made "a happy proficiency in polite and various learning." After completing his education he was called to the bar in the Middle Temple, and was introduced to many of the most distinguished persons of the age, and particularly contracted an intimate friendship with the illustrious Charles Boyle, Earl of Orrery. He also studied for some time in the Low Countries, and visited the court of Louis XIV. Upon his return to England he was chosen a Fellow of the Royal Society, and being made Receiver-General of his Majesty's revenues in Virginia, came back to America; he was thrice appointed public agent to the court and ministry of England, and after being thirty-seven years a member of the Council of Virginia, at last became president of that body. He was as distinguished for his literary taste as for

EVELYN BYRD.

his public spirit and enterprise. He made a journey to the "Land of Eden," and wrote the result of his experience, also the *History of the Dividing Line between Virginia and North Carolina* — works

existence, and display a richness and elegance unequalled by the most extravagant costumes of the present day. While in England she is said to have been engaged to the celebrated Earl of Peterborough,

JOHN MAYO.

full of wit, humor, and stirring adventure. These books were read and enjoyed by Thackeray and Dean Stanley when they visited Richmond.

Colonel Byrd's first wife was the daughter of Colonel Daniel Parke, the confidential aide-de-camp of the Duke of Marlborough at Blenheim, who was sent to announce the victory to Queen Anne, and presented by her Majesty with a magnificent service of silver, now in the possession of one of his descendants. The sister of Mrs. Byrd was the ancestress of George Washington Parke Custis, of Arlington. By his first marriage Colonel Byrd had two daughters, one of whom, Evelyn, was born at Westover on the 16th of July, 1707. She accompanied her father to England at an early age, and lived there several years in the highest circles of society; she was distinguished for her wit, beauty, and accomplishments. Some of the dresses which she wore at the English court are still in

but as he was a Catholic and she a Protestant, it ended disastrously, and Evelyn returned to Virginia, died unmarried at the age of twenty-nine, on the 13th of November, 1737, and was buried at Westover.

The original portraits of Colonel and Evelyn Byrd, which are reproduced on the preceding page, are now at Brandon, the residence of Mrs. Isabella H. Harrison, on the James River.

Major William Mayo, who laid off the city of Richmond, emigrated from England to the Isle of Barbadoes about 1716, and made an admirable survey of that island between 1717 and 1721; his map is now on file in King's College library. He came to Virginia in 1723, and in 1728, with Professor Alexander Irvin, ran the dividing line between Virginia and North Carolina.

Colonel William Byrd in his history states that a chaplain, the Rev. Peter Fontaine, accompanied the surveying party,

ABIGAIL DE HART MAYO.

"that the people on the frontiers of North Carolina might have an opportunity to get themselves and their children baptized." One of the rivers intersecting the lines was named in honor of Major Mayo, and still retains the name. In 1736 he was appointed surveyor of the Northern Neck of Virginia, in order to settle the disputed boundary between Lord Fairfax and the crown. Early in 1737 he laid off the city of Richmond, and we find in the *Virginia Gazette*, in April of that year, "that lots will be granted in fee-simple on condition of building a house in three years' time of 24 × 16 feet, fronting within five feet of the street." Major Mayo was the most prominent civil engineer in Virginia, and died in 1744. His grandson, Colonel John Mayo, was born October 21, 1760. He was the projector and founder of the celebrated Mayo Bridge, just below the falls of the James River at Richmond. He obtained a charter for the bridge in 1785, and after ineffectual efforts to obtain

State aid or to form a corporation, boldly built it from his own design and at his individual expense. To appreciate his indomitable energy and the progress of bridge-building since that period, it may be mentioned that his petition for a charter was received with ridicule, and Colonel Innis, a prominent member of the Legislature, facetiously observed "that after passing that bill he supposed they would pass one to build a ladder to the moon." But Colonel Mayo's indefatigable resolution overcame all obstacles, and success proved the practicability of his efforts.*

* In William Wirt's celebrated "Letters of a British Spy" (published in the *Virginia Argus*, 1803) we find the following description of the city : "Richmond occupies a very picturesque and most beautiful situation. I have never met with such an assemblage of striking and interesting objects. The town, dispersed over hills of various shapes; the river, descending from west to east, and obstructed by a multitude of small islands, clumps of trees, and myriads of rocks, constituting what are called the Falls; the same river, at the lower end of the town,

Colonel Mayo married Abigail De Hart, daughter of John De Hart, of Elizabethtown, New Jersey, who was a member of the first Continental Congress, that met at Philadelphia in 1774–5, and one of the most prominent lawyers in his State. After his marriage Colonel Mayo bought a beautiful residence in Elizabethtown, called Hampton Place, and his annual advent there in a coach and six, with colored footmen and outriders, was an event long remembered by the inhabitants of that ancient borough. He resided for several years at the Hermitage, a short distance west of Richmond, but in 1816 he bought Bellville, a magnificent seat in the suburbs of the city, and lived there until his death, on the 28th of May, 1818. He was buried at the old Mayo homestead, Powhatan, a short distance east of Richmond; and on the same place, partially protected by an open arbor, is a large rock which marks the last resting-place of the most powerful Indian chief in Virginia, Powhatan, whose principal residence was here, and after whom the place was called. Colonel Mayo served in the State

MARIA MAYO SCOTT.

that ancient borough. He resided for several years at the Hermitage, a short distance west of Richmond, but in 1816 he

bending at right angles to the south, and winding reluctantly off for many miles in that direction, its polished surface caught here and there by the eye, but more generally covered from the view by trees, among which the white sails of approaching and departing vessels exhibit a curious and interesting appearance; then again, on the opposite side, the little town of Manchester, built on a hill, which, sloping gently to the river, opens the whole town to view, interspersed, as it is, with vigorous and flourishing poplars, and surrounded to a great distance by green plains and stately woods—all these objects, falling at once under the eye, constitute by far the most finely varied and most animated landscape that I have ever seen."

troops during the war of 1812, and represented for several years the county of Henrico in the Legislature.

Mrs. John Mayo was one of the most remarkable ladies of her day. She was celebrated for her "personal comeliness and mental endowments," and long occupied a prominent position in Richmond society.

Maria Mayo, the eldest daughter of Colonel John Mayo, was the reigning belle of the day, and as Mr. Mordecai says, in his *Richmond in By-gone Days*, she made the Hermitage anything but a hermitage. She was a great beauty, wrote and repeated poetry charmingly, sang and played on the harp exquisitely, and was so fascinating in manner and agreeable in conversation that she is said to have rejected over one hundred suitors before accepting General Winfield Scott, then in the full glory of his military successes, to whom she was married at Bellville on the evening of March 11, 1817. The festivities were of the most extended and hospitable character, and, as an old letter before us expresses it, "there were splendid doings." It is said that Scott courted Maria Mayo as Mr. Scott, as Captain Scott, and as Colonel Scott without success, but as General Scott, the hero of Lundy's Lane, he carried off the coveted prize.

It would be worth while, had we the space, to present here a characteristic sketch of Richmond society at the beginning of this century. The cravat was the important part of a gentleman's toilet. A Richmond exquisite of the first decade of this century vested himself like a silkworm in the ample folds of his cravat. His valet held one end and he the other of the long thin texture, the former walked round his master till both ends met, when they were tied in a large bow. If the gentleman did not enjoy the luxury of a valet, one end of the cravat was tied to the bed-post, and he walked toward the latter, turning all the while, and wrapping his neck in his cravat till he was wound up like an Egyptian mummy. The stiff collar of the dress-coat stood as high as the ears, and was kept back several inches from the head to enable the wearer to turn to the right or the left. Buckskin breeches and top-boots completed the gentleman's apparel, the perfection of both depending on the tightness of the fit. A quarter of a century earlier—that is, about the time of the American Revolution—Richmond was a smaller town than either Norfolk or Fredericksburg. Its safe and central position caused it to be selected as the capital of the State, but in the year 1775 it was a cluster of villages rather than a town.

The gentlemen of Richmond at that time wore an old-fashioned dress—breeches, stockings, large roomy coats, cocked hats, and knee-buckles. They figured in magnificent waistcoats covered with flowers in gold threads, and reaching to their knees, high-heeled shoes, queues tied with gay ribbons, and a snowy storm of powder on the hair.

The favorite amusement of the most stylish Richmond ladies at that time was a game of cards called loo. The ladies met at each other's houses, and after discussing a dish of tea and another of gossip, the card-table was brought out. Gentlemen were admitted to this entertaining circle, and he who played the most careless and dashing game was the most welcome, provided he was not too successful in his winnings. The stakes were small, but by forfeits, etc., the money in the pool would sometimes accumulate until it amounted to $50, $75, and $100. Then the game became intensely interesting. The practice of gaming became at last a social evil; domestic duties were neglected, mothers forgot their children, wives rifled the pocket-books of their husbands; gentlemen gambled away their gold vest buttons, and ladies their ear-rings and bracelets, carried away by the mad spirit of loo.

The burning of the Richmond Theatre on the 26th of December, 1811, by which seventy-two valuable lives were lost, changed the light tone of society to one of a graver and more serious character.

One of the saddest and most romantic love affairs in the social annals of Virginia was that of Maria Ward and John Randolph of Roanoke. Beginning in his early boyhood, it became the one enthralling passion of his manhood, filling his whole being, until, as he himself said, "he loved her better than his own soul or Him that created it." There is a picture of John Randolph in the rooms of the Virginia Historical Society, taken at the time when he was the accepted lover of Maria Ward. It represents a singularly handsome youth of twenty-five, his eyes dark and full of intellect, his mouth beautifully formed, and over his proud and lofty forehead fell a profusion of dark hair. The breaking off of the affair is wrapped in mystery; all we know is that one summer morning he rode up to the house, and after a long interview in the parlor, the lady left the room in tears, while he rushed from the house, mounted his horse, and rode furiously away. He never saw her again; but one day he approached a house where she was staying while she was singing in the parlor. Fascinated by the sound of her voice, he lingered on the porch, and sent in from time to time a request for her to sing one after another the tender little ballads which were associated with their loves. Maria Ward sang, unconscious of her lover's presence, while he rushed frantically up and down the porch in an agony of grief, waving his arms, and crying in the anguish of his heart: "Macbeth hath murdered sleep; Macbeth shall sleep no more!"

Maria Ward married Peyton Randolph, son of Edmund Randolph, who was Gov-

Maria Ward died in 1826, aged forty-two years. All contemporary accounts unite in describing her as possessing a singular fascination of manners, a charming sweetness and amiability of disposition, an enchanting gayety and *esprit*, and a peculiar, irresistible personal love-

MARIA WARD.

ernor of Virginia, the first Attorney-General of the United States, and Secretary of State under Washington. This lady was distinguished for the exquisite grace and fascination of her manners and her bright wit. Her portrait, a copy of which has been secured for this article through the courtesy of her granddaughter, Mrs. J. L. Williams, of Richmond, represents a lovely girl of sixteen, with wondrous blue eyes, exquisitely delicate complexion, a profusion of sunny brown curls, and in the quaint costume of the last century.

liness. At the time of her death she was still as fresh as the summer rose, as captivating in mind and manners as when she enthralled the passionate heart of John Randolph of Roanoke.

The Richmond bar has always stood high. During the first quarter of the present century John Wickham was not only one of the leading lawyers of Virginia, but of the United States. He was a native of Long Island, but went to Richmond when a youth of sixteen, during the American Revolution. He studied

MRS. JOHN WICKHAM.

law, and rose rapidly in his profession. When Aaron Burr was tried for treason in Richmond, in 1807, Mr. Wickham was the leading counsel for the defense, and gained a national reputation for the brilliant manner in which he conducted his client's case. He was famous for his wit and sarcasm, and was a gentleman of exquisite manners. When Tom Moore visited Richmond, early in this century, he met Mr. Wickham, and said he was "fit to adorn any court." He always declined to enter public life, satisfied to remain at the head of the Richmond bar. He married the daughter of Dr. McClurg, a leading physician and surgeon, who had acted in the latter capacity during the Revolutionary war. Mrs. Wickham was conspicuous in Richmond society for her beauty and personal accomplishments. In delicacy of outline and softness of coloring she was unsurpassed by any woman of her day in Virginia. Their eldest daughter, Julia, married Benjamin Watkins Leigh, one of the most gifted orators and most brilliant men that Virginia has ever produced. He was ready at all times to debate any question. In the United

States Senate he distinguished himself by his splendid talents at a time when Clay, Calhoun, and Webster were members of that body.

In 1790 there arrived in Richmond a French gentleman of polished manners and attractive personal appearance, named Jean Auguste Chevallié. He visited this country as the agent of the celebrated Beaumarchais in his claim against the United States government for moneys advanced during the American Revolution. Charmed by the beauty of Richmond and the cordiality of its people, he determined to settle there permanently. Forming the acquaintance of Joseph Gallego, a native of Malaga, Spain, he joined in the latter in the business of the famous Gallego Mills, which were established in 1796, and have been continued by representatives of the two families ever since.

Mr. Gallego and Mr. Chevallié married two sisters, Mary and Sally Magee. Both of these gentlemen adorned the high society which was so conspicuous in Richmond at the beginning of this century. Compt de Lesseps, the celebrated engineer, is a nephew of Mr. Gallego. Peter Chevallié, son of Jean Auguste, was the father of Miss Sally Chevallié, one of the most elegant women of the day; she married Mr. Abram Warwick, also of the firm which so long and successfully conducted the Gallego Mills. Mrs. Joseph Gallego, forlorn hope at Stony Point under "Mad Anthony" Wayne.

Among the great belles and beauties of Richmond early in the present century few were more distinguished for personal graces and accomplishments than Mary

MRS. JOSEPH GALLEGO.

one of the most admired women that ever lived in Richmond, perished by the burning of the theatre, of which mention has already been made. Upon the same fatal night her niece, Miss Sarah C. Conyers, attended the play with Lieutenant Gibbon, of the navy, to whom she was engaged. Failing to rescue her from the burning building, he determined to share her fate, and they were found locked in one another's arms. Mr. Gibbon was the son of Major Gibbon, the collector of the port, who served with distinction in the Revolutionary war, and gallantly led the

Walker. To a lovely disposition and elegant manners were joined rare intellectual endowments. She was a very particular friend of John Randolph of Roanoke, with whom she corresponded for many years. She was thrice married. Her first husband was John Bell, of the firm of John and William Bell, of Richmond, and William and John Bell, of London. He made a large fortune, but in attempting to monopolize the tobacco trade of Virginia he was ruined. Mrs. Bell had a great taste for architecture, and designed the beautiful seat near Richmond called

Bellville. As an evidence of the magnificence of this mansion it may be mentioned that the drawing-room was so high and large that even the stately form of General Scott looked small in it. After Mr. Bell's death his widow, who was quite young, married Edmund Rootes, a man of wit and of great social distinction. Mrs. Rootes was an accomplished botanist, and corresponded with distinguished persons throughout the United States upon the subject of her favorite study. She was regarded as an authority on the subject, and a gentleman of Richmond re-

of William and Elizabeth Bolling Robertson. He was an eminent lawyer, and one of the social leaders in Richmond, where he was long one of the most honored citizens. He was successively Attorney-General of Virginia, Representative in Congress from 1834 to 1839, and Lieutenant-Governor, and for many years a judge of the Circuit Court at Richmond. He was a member of the Peace Congress of 1861, having previously been sent by the Governor of Virginia as a commissioner to Governor Pickens, of South Carolina, to prevent, if possible, hostile measures be-

MRS. JOHN BELL.

members one bright summer morning seeing Thomas Ritchie, the famous editor of the *Enquirer*, going in to see her with a rare new lily for her to classify. Her third husband was Dr. Starke, of Norfolk, the father of the wife of Admiral Roane. This charming lady died at an advanced age, retaining her many attractions to the last.

One of the most distinguished descendants of Pocahontas in recent times was the late Judge John Robertson, the son

ing adopted until the meeting of the Peace Congress at Washington. Judge Robertson died at his residence, Mount Athos, Campbell County, Virginia, on the 5th of July, 1873.

Miss Elizabeth Lewis Robertson, daughter of Judge Robertson, was not only interesting on account of her great beauty, but because in her features have been preserved unmistakable traits of her descent from Pocahontas. She married Robert Barksdale, the son of Mr. William Barksdale, of Clay Hill, Amelia County, Virginia—a house proverbial for elegant hospitality.

One of the most accomplished literary men of Richmond was the late John R. Thompson. He entered the University of

ing John R. Thompson's management. When Thackeray visited Richmond to deliver his lectures on the Georges, Thompson acted as his chaperon. He was entertained by Conway Robinson, Gustavus

ELIZABETH ROBERTSON BARKSDALE.

Virginia at an early age, and was more conspicuous for his literary tastes and love for reading than for the regular studies. Soon after leaving the university he became associated in the *Southern Literary Messenger*, of which he afterward became the editor. This magazine was established by Thomas W. White in 1834, and edited for eighteen months by Edgar A. Poe, whose brilliant contributions gave it a national reputation, and increased its circulation from seven hundred to five thousand. Its list of contributors included some of the most distinguished American writers: Poe, Longfellow, Donald G. Mitchell, John Esten Cooke, Mrs. Sigourney, William Gilmore Simms, Paul H. Hayne, George D. Prentice, etc. Ik Marvel's "Reveries of a Bachelor" and Baldwin's "Flush Times of Alabama" appeared originally in the *Messenger* dur-

Myers, William H. Macfarland, James Lyons, etc. In 1854 Thompson went abroad, where he was very cordially received by Tennyson, Thackeray, and other English authors. He wrote a book about his travels, which was ready for publication by Harper and Brothers when their establishment was destroyed by fire, and the whole edition was burned.

In 1861 Mr. Thompson went abroad again, and established himself in London as associate editor of *The Index* and *The Cosmopolitan*, of which he afterward became the editor-in-chief. He also wrote for the *Times*, *Standard*, and other leading London journals, thus making his living entirely by his pen. An article of his in the *Standard* struck Carlyle so forcibly that he sent to the paper to ascertain the name of the writer. He was informed that it was a gentleman from Virginia,

JOHN R. THOMPSON.

was daily growing worse, he returned to New York toward the close of April, 1873, and died there a few days afterward. His remains were brought to Richmond and buried at Hollywood, where a beautiful monument has been erected to his memory, chiefly through the active exertions of Miss Mary Pegram and Major Leigh R. Page.

Richmond, with a population of 65,000, has three first-class clubs—the Westmoreland, the Richmond, and the Commercial. All these have been established since the war. There was in the olden time in Richmond an institution called the Buchanan Spring Club, named after the Rev. John Buchanan, to whom the grounds belonged, situated a mile or two from the city. The owner refused to sell the land, but allowed the club to use it free of cost. This club was composed of the leading men of Virginia; they met every Saturday afternoon, and pitched quoits, and had an old-fashioned barbecue under the trees, with mint-julep, broiled shad, etc. The season commenced about the middle of May, and lasted until the 1st of August, when the members dispersed and went to the springs or to their country-seats. Washington, in his visits to Richmond to see his nephew, Bushrod Washington, was a frequent guest; Parson Buchanan, an Episcopalian, and Parson Blair, a Presbyterian, were both members, and pitched quoits together on Saturday, and preached alternately at the Capitol on Sunday. They were both poets and cultivated gentlemen. Parson Buchanan was wealthy, and Parson Blair was poor, and the former gave all his fees to his Presbyterian friend. Chief Justice Marshall was one of the most regular attendants of the club, and would frequently pitch quoits from noon to sunset. He was one of the most famous pitchers in Virginia, and always used the heaviest quoits. Chancellor Wythe, Presidents Madison and Jefferson, John Wickham, and Thomas Mann Randolph were either members or distinguished visitors to this club, which continued in existence for nearly a century. There was another quoit club, the Old Dominion, but that was composed principally of younger and less distinguished men.

The Westmoreland Club was organized in 1877, and numbers among its members

Mr. John R. Thompson, whereupon Carlyle sent him a card, asking him to call, which he did, and from that time was always treated with great kindness. Thompson returned to Richmond early in 1867, but finding nothing for him to do, in the winter of 1868 he removed to New York, where he started a paper called *Every Afternoon*, which failed. Soon after this a friend told him he could get him some literary work which might be of use to him. Thompson told him he would be very glad to get it. His friend then brought him a pile of books to be reviewed, and enjoined upon him to do his best. The manuscript was taken to William Cullen Bryant, at that time the editor of the New York *Evening Post*. After reading it he inquired who was the writer. Being told, he said, "This is the man I have been looking for." An interview was arranged, the result of which was that John R. Thompson became the literary editor of the *Evening Post*. His health failed him from overwork, and Mr. Bryant gave him an unlimited leave of absence. After spending a winter in Nassau and Bermuda he felt so much better that he went to work again. His health again broke down, and he went to Virginia for a while. Deriving no relief, he undertook a journey to the West, and went as far as Colorado. Finding that he most of the leading gentlemen of Richmond. It first occupied the house on Franklin Street, between Seventh and Eighth, which was purchased for General Lee by the City Council of Richmond, and occupied by him, though not accepted as a gift. The club remained there until 1880, when the present quarters, at the corner of Grace and Sixth streets, were secured. It is one of the most attractive club-houses in the South, with its broad piazza, wide halls, spacious rooms, and elegant appointments. The various rooms are adorned with valuable historical portraits, including those of Washington, Patrick Henry, John Randolph of Roanoke, Chief Justice Marshall, Lafayette, Commodore Perry, Black Hawk, Thomas Jefferson, Edmund Pendleton, etc. These pictures are the property of the Virginia Historical Society, which occupies the upper rooms of the house. Mr. Robert A. Brock, the correspondent and librarian of the society, has under his charge many objects of historical interest. Among these may be mentioned the writing-table of George Mason upon which he wrote the famous Bill of Rights of Virginia; the mace used by the Speaker of the House of Burgesses; two maps of Virginia of the date of 1671; the sword of Major Alexander Stuart, of the Revolutionary war; the MS. order-book of Colonel W. Heath, of the Revolution, while encamped at Bound Brook, New Jersey, in 1777; the original MS. records of the colony of Virginia for the five years (1752–1757) of the administration of Lieutenant-Governor Robert Dinwiddie, presented by W. W. Corcoran, Esq. The last is considered the most valuable single acquisition of the society.

We have purposely omitted from this paper any mention of many of the illustrious Virginian families whose descendants have been intimately associated with the material and social life of Richmond. Their record is preserved in the military and political history of the country, and need not be repeated here. Our object has been the less ambitious one of presenting a few characteristic portraits. The Richmond of to-day is the centre of many important industrial interests. Our retrospect has taken us away from this busy modern activity, and brought us face to face with that older Virginian life in which there was much of luxurious leisure, but which also furnished remarkable examples of high intellectual attainment and varied social accomplishment.

KENTUCKY FARMS

WHENEVER a business man gets away from his affairs, and journeys into a far country for even a short time, he may see many things that he would entirely overlook, if, with his mind filled with the every-day cares of life, he passed through the very same sections in the usual unobservant way.

A pity it is that our commercial travellers could not become trained observers, ready and acute as they are in all that pertains to their work, often witty and full of good stories. If they could only learn to spend the many hours which they are obliged to pass wearily in country taverns that are none of the best, and are often of the worst, in reporting what they might observe, what a resource against weariness it would be for them, and what a benefit to all who wish to know what the resources of this country really are, and how they may be developed! The business man who can write at all writes best for other business men. They could also adopt the patent method on which this article is written: in their search after facts they might make the acquaintance of such men as my friend Professor J. R. Procter, the State Geologist of Kentucky, and get them to furnish all the real substance of their reports, and the material to fill up the gaps in their narrative, as he has in this article, so that a part of the interest of the reader would be to find out how much the ostensible writer didn't know of his subject.

At the late meeting of the American Association for the Advancement of Science, in Boston, the writer sought information from the professor about the homespun fabrics that still constitute the common wear of a large population inhabiting the *terra* (almost) *incognita* of the United States, viz., the mountain sides and valleys of Eastern Kentucky and Tennessee, Northern Georgia, Western North and South Carolina, and Southwestern Virginia, and was invited to explore a part of the region by him.

This section is, we may say, somewhat larger than Great Britain, and contains more and purer iron and coal, equal deposits of copper, lead, zinc, and salt, besides corundum and gold in its mines; it enjoys what is probably the finest climate on this continent; it is permeated by the most fertile valleys, and bears upon its hill and mountain sides the heaviest growth and greatest variety of hard-wood timber.

If to this true mountain region be added the Piedmont and Cumberland plateaus on the east and west, the blue-grass section of Kentucky, and the high uplands of Alabama and Georgia, the area will be enlarged to nearly that of France, and it may be affirmed that there is nowhere else to be found in this country, in an equal area, such an opportunity for diversity of employment in agriculture, mining, metallurgy, or variety of manufactures.

Yet in the first two dwellings, built of logs, to which the writer was guided from the new town of Rugby, not only the house, but everything in or about it except iron and crockery ware, had been made by members of the family with their own hands. In the garden grew the little patch of cotton to be ginned on a small roller gin, whittled out with a jackknife; on the hill-side ranged the sheep. Both the wool and cotton were carded with hand-cards, and spun on the spinning-wheel by the house-mother or her children, then woven on the hand-loom, the frame of which had been fashioned with a broad-axe from the oak of their own pasture. The boys were clad in butternut garments, the father in blue jeans, from the same loom. The sheets, bed-quilts, and blankets were truly hand-factured in the same way, while the beds were stuffed with feathers plucked from their own geese.

In the next house I managed to purchase a blue and white quilt of very artistic pattern, and a striped cotton and wool blanket, both woven by the old lady, who seemed to think it *infra dig.* to sell the product of her own hands, and only consented when I explained to her that I wished them to keep as examples of what will soon become one of the lost arts. Her twelve-treddle loom filled about a third of the living-room.

The writer is not a sufficient master of the art of picture-writing to dare to hope to give an impression of the scenes that are to be found in this "land of the sky," as it has been called.

As one passes down that audacious Cincinnati Southern Railroad, built, owned, and operated by the city of Cincinnati and, what is most strange of all about it, promising to be a good investment on its own merits, his mind will be almost harassed by the rapidity with which he must take in the impressions that come upon him. With shuddering enjoyment he will stand on the rear platform as the train passes over a long iron bridge, and he looks down upon the winding river 287 feet below; he will wonder what engineer dared to plan and project the bridge, or what mechanics dared to work upon it as its trusses of 375 feet span were thrown out from each pier and joined in the centre, with no staging or any other support from below, but with only the counterpoise of the parts on solid land to prevent either portion tipping down into the gorge below. As he winds along on a bright October day, watching the red light pass away from the leaves of the blue-gum or the sourwood—more brilliant even than our rock-maples—with eyes surfeited with color, he will welcome the gray shadows of the evening, until another bright light gleams out from the pine knots burning in front of camps of the negro lumbermen, a hundred of whom are there roasting their hoe-cake and frying their bacon, and perhaps wondering when there will be moral capital enough in that land to establish a true savings-bank. In such a bank they could deposit the dollar a day now paid them in gold and silver, which is what they could save after paying the other ten cents of their customary wages for the daily fare; that sum of ten cents being all that their daily and favorite ration of "hog and hominy" costs.

West of the Cumberland plateau, which makes the western flank of this mountain region, lies the "blue-grass" section of the State of Kentucky. When this section is named among those who never visited it, two thoughts may present themselves—sometimes one first, sometimes the other, after the manner of the man. One is Bourbon whiskey, the other fast horses.

The horses that have made the fastest running time, Ten Broeck and Longfellow, and the fastest trotting time, St. Julian and Maud S., were all bred here. The two first named the writer admired in their own persons, he had almost said —they looked intelligent enough to be so called ; the sisters, the cousins, and the aunts of the latter two he did not so much appreciate.

The blue-grass (*Poa pratensis*), which gives the name to a considerable section of the State of Kentucky, is not confined to that State or section, but thrives in many other places; but this particular section is its special home, because the soil is underlain with rotten limestone, constantly disintegrating, and furnishing the elements of fertility. When cultivation ceases, and the ground is allowed to lie fallow, the blue-grass comes in, furnishing almost a perpetual pasture of a most luxuriant description. The only need of turning up the pastures and of occasional cultivation is to remove the fox-tail grass, which, in some seasons much more than others, comes up in the autumn, and injures the winter pasture.

The rotten limestone belongs to the Cincinnati and Trenton groups of the lower silurian formation, and is very rich in fossils. The soils formed from this rock are exceptionally rich in phosphate of lime. Thin bands of phosphatic limestone from Fayette County have been found upon analysis to contain as much as 31.8 per cent. of the weight of rock of phosphoric acid. No wonder this soil should bring forth such bone-producing food!

The Kentuckian who didn't believe that the goodness of the Bourbon whiskey, the speed and endurance of the horses, and the vigor of the people were owing to the peculiarities of the soil and water of this region would be held disloyal to his State.

The trees, consisting mainly of white oak, blue ash, walnut, hard maple, and hickory on the uplands, with the addition of sycamore and elm on the streams, are as grand as any in this country.

One magnificent oak the writer visited on the farm of Major McDowell, near Frankfort, which is over one hundred feet high. There were four in our party; we all touched fingers, tip to tip, and then three more were needed before we could encircle the tree at the height of our shoulders.

There is not much woodland, but what there is is free from underbrush, and well grassed; most of the trees are detached, and give a park-like aspect to the country.

This blue-grass country is the very land where one can farm with brains, withholding his own manual labor, and free from the necessity which is imposed upon our farmers in New England, of working harder than any of their men.

The stone walls are models of good construction, and the substantial post and rail fences impart an air of thrift and prosperity.

This country is furnished with most excellent turnpike - roads. One might ride smoothly on a bicycle from Louisville through Lexington to the eastern edge of the blue-grass region, 130 miles, and from the Ohio River through Lexington for 140 miles, on the best of macadam road; in fact, the whole region is covered with a net-work of these turnpikes, so that every neighborhood is penetrated.

It is a region reminding the traveller of the very richest parts of England, while the frequent comfortable houses will remind him that he is not in England, but in a country where the farmer owns the land, and spends his substance upon it.

The general level ranges from 800 to 1100 feet above the sea, and is claimed to be entirely above malaria; it is watered by many streams rising in the Cumberland Mountains, which, combining, form the Licking and Kentucky rivers.

The monthly mean temperature for the three summer months is 73°, 76°, and 73°, and for the three winter months 27°, 30°, and 35°.

The finest stock and brood mares are wintered on the blue-grass pastures without shelter. It is a cause of much quiet joking among the stock-breeders that the most knowing horse men from other States buy what are apparently their best colts at high prices, leaving what appear to be only second-rates; but the latter, bred on blue-grass and lime-water, and hardened by exposure to the not too severe winters, are apt to win the races, and keep up the Kentucky name, even more than those of the first class, which are more carefully sheltered and trained.

But the point which attracts one most in this region is the fact that crops of grain may be raised year after year, alternating occasionally with hemp and blue-grass, far exceeding the average of most other parts of this country, and without the use of a particle of manure. In fact, the average crop of wheat produced in this section by good farmers without manure is above the average of the high farming of England in a good year.

It is true that some crops appear to have a little temporary effect upon the soil; for instance, when wheat is planted immediately after maize, or Indian corn, the crop is less than when it follows hemp. The land will produce from 800 pounds to 1400 pounds of hemp per acre, and if the stalks are rotted on the field, according to the common practice, the land is left in the best condition for grain, the fibre of hemp being mostly carbonaceous matter drawn from the atmosphere.

What might be done with this land if some experiments were tried with acid fertilizers adapted to releasing the elements of the limestone more rapidly, is one of the problems that may yet yield some astounding results. It would also be an interesting experiment if some of the farmers would subsoil a few acres, and plant wheat in single grains, nine inches apart each way, so that each plant might "tiller" to the utmost extent.

The following statements bear witness to what is now done. Farmer C——, of Franklin County, testifies that he averages twenty bushels of wheat to the acre after corn; but his average on sod land or after hemp is thirty-five bushels, and one year he raised forty-five bushels to the acre on land which had been three years previously in hemp. No manure used. Farmer A——, of Woodford County, averages thirty to forty bushels on clover sod or after hemp. His best crop was fifty-two bushels, on land four years in hemp. No manure. Another farmer in Woodford County had made 4000 bushels of wheat on 100 acres.

As evidence of the inherent fertility of the soil, and the power of restoration without the use of manure, I have the following from a farmer: "Purchased a farm ten years since that had been badly worn by careless tenants for twenty-five years, and at the time of purchase would yield only five barrels of corn to the acre; by rotation with clover, had brought it up to twelve barrels." This farmer gave me his average of wheat after corn at eighteen bushels per acre, and computed the cost per acre as follows:

Seed	$1 00
Ploughing (omitted on hemp land)	1 25
Planting	75
Cutting, threshing, and putting into bags	4 50
Total	$7 50

—or 41⅔ cents per bushel of 60 pounds.

A second farmer's estimate of cost is, on sod land:

Seed	$1 00
Ploughing	2 00
Planting	1 00
Cutting	1 25
Threshing	2 50
Total	$7 75

—25 bushels, or 31 cents per bushel.

On hemp land:

Seed	$1 00
Planting	1 00
Cutting	1 25
Threshing	2 50
Total	$5 75

—at 25 bushels, 23 cents per bushel; at 30 bushels, 19⅙ cents per bushel.

Barley is growing in favor. The foreman of a fine farm showed me a field of blue-grass laid by for winter pasture on which he had made forty bushels of barley to the acre the year before. No manure. Hay is also coming in as a salable and very profitable crop.

Much of the wheat is now carried south over the Cincinnati Southern Railroad, and is distributed from Chattanooga and Atlanta. There is a growing demand for wheat in the South, accompanying the increased prosperity which has ensued from the establishment of free labor.

It may be asked why Kentucky should hold so small a place in the production of wheat, her crop being only five to seven million bushels. The answer is that the land is held by a race of men with whom stock-breeding is almost hereditary. As we have stated, the pasture is practically perpetual, and of the best description, hence most of the blue-grass country is devoted to the raising of horses, mules, and cattle. This occupation is easier, and was much more consistent with the system of slave labor by which the progress of the State was retarded until a period considerably after the surrender of the Confederate army.

The land is now changing hands with considerable rapidity, and, under the impulse of the new forces that have come in with free labor, it seems probable that farming may be substituted for stock-breeding, and that larger crops of cereals, tobacco, and of hemp and flax will ensue. In Kentucky the farms of less than ten acres in size increased in number from 6868 in 1860 to 16,292 in 1870, and the total of farms under 100 acres increased the same period from 58,350 to 92,149, whilst the number of farms of over 500 and under 1000 acres decreased.

Access to the sea-board is now by way of Cincinnati, but other lines are being constructed that will give outlets at the fine harbor of Norfolk and on the York and James rivers, Virginia. This line will be completed to Lexington by June next. From the centre of the blue-grass region to Richmond, Virginia, by this line will be 540 miles, and to Norfolk 640 miles. At present the distance to New York from this section by rail is 830 miles. The completion of projected roads will also give a nearer outlet to the south.

When the railway service is completed, consolidated, and worked as cheaply between this section and the sea-board as it is now between the Western States and New York, the cost of transportation will not exceed $3 50 to $4 per ton, or 11 to 12 cents per bushel. Add to this the freight and charges to Liverpool, and it will appear that it may not be impossible that a time may come when the actual cost in Liverpool of wheat raised in Kentucky will not exceed 60 to 70 cents per bushel of 60 pounds, or at 8⅓ bushels to the quarter of 500 pounds, $5 to $5 84, equal to about 20s. 10d. to 25s. per quarter, all charges paid. At or above 30s. per quarter the production and traffic will be permanently profitable.

This limestone region which I have described, known as "Blue-Grass," comprises 10,000 square miles, or 6,400,000 acres. The area of land now under cultivation in wheat in all Great Britain is less than 5000 square miles, or under 3,000,000 acres, on which a little less than half the flour used by the people is now raised.

It is beginning to appear that no rent can be paid on land devoted to wheat in Great Britain when the price in Mark Lane is less than 40s. per quarter.

Improved farms in this section of Kentucky, furnished with good houses and farm buildings, are now worth $35 to $100 per acre.

The character of the people is one of the main considerations. They are vigorous, very hospitable, old-fashioned, with few exceptions not much given to books, and farming just as their fathers did. They have been a fighting race, but carrying arms secretly is forbidden by law, and the law is rigidly enforced. They are quick to resent an insult, but do not force their ways upon strangers. Much of the land is passing into new hands, and the old duelling and homicidal era is almost a thing of the past.

East of the blue-grass region lies the Kentucky section of the *terra incognita* described in the first part of this article. The portion of the mountain, interior valley, and plateau region in this State comprises about 10,000 square miles, and is of untold wealth. The plateau and the upland valleys are 1500 to 2000 feet above the level of the sea.

The soil is the disintegrated rock of the mountains, rich in all the elements of fertility. The hill-sides are covered with forests of oak, yellow poplar, chestnut, ash, hickory, cherry, pine, etc. In De Friese's report, constituting a part of the geologic survey of Kentucky, a section of the North Cumberland Valley is described; among other facts it is said that in an area of 1250 square yards there were found among other trees six black walnut with an average diameter of forty inches, five buckeye averaging twenty-nine inches, three white ash averaging thirty-four inches, and six linden averaging twenty-three inches.

The coal measures of this section reach a thickness of 2000 feet above the drainage level of the country, containing many beds of very superior quality.

The deposits of the best quality of cannel-coal are more extensive than elsewhere, and iron ore beds of great richness, extent, and purity are very favorably located with reference to the coal.

Various lines of railway are now projected or in process of construction which will soon open this region to colonization.

The State of Kentucky is free from debt, and has a well-established system of common schools, sustained on a method differing in some respects from other States. The school tax is assessed at the rate of twenty cents on the $100 on the property of the State, but is divided according to the number of children, so that the people in the poorer sections or in the mountain districts are aided at their time of greatest need in the support of their schools.

Land in these mountain districts and upland valleys can be bought now in large quantities—in parcels of to 100,000 acres at $1 50 to $3 per acre—and offers great opportunities for the establishment of colonies after the manner of Rugby.

It is a matter of considerable importance that this great section should become more generally known, especially the mountain portion, even the geography of which is not fully comprehended as yet. In the 'far interior of the hills are people who have never seen a wheeled vehicle, and who depend upon the outside world only for steel needles, making even their own iron and pottery.

It has lately been determined to add to the International Cotton Exhibition, which is to be held at Atlanta, Georgia, in the months of October, November, and December, 1881, a building modelled after that which contained the agricultural and mineral products of Kansas and Colorado at the Centennial Exhibition of 1876. In this building will be gathered examples of the minerals, the clays, the timber, the soils, and products of agriculture, and the flora and fauna of this great but almost unknown land, which constitutes the backbone of the eastern portion of our territory.

The tenant-farmers of England and Scotland number about five hundred thousand. Their occupation seems to be approaching its end, as it becomes more and more evident that there is no longer an adequate margin in the prices of the great staple of agriculture from which rent can be paid, and that English land, like our own, must be cultivated by its owners, either in large or small parcels. To this class of tenant-farmers this section will offer the most favorable conditions, where they can buy good land at less than the rent they have been paying.

The marked feature, throughout the Piedmont district especially, is the rapid division of land, and the great increase in the number of small land-owners.

Cotton and tobacco are especially suited to small farms, and if the practice of "ensilaging" green fodder is half as effective as its enthusiastic promoters allege, another force will have been developed, working distinctly in the direction of the good cultivation of moderate parcels of land.

The writer of this article has prepared it con amore, thinking that a Massachusetts man could make no better return for the hospitality of his Kentucky hosts than to describe the two sections in which he passed a few pleasant days, in either of which portions of that great State poor little Massachusetts could be placed, and the part that extended outside her limits wrapped over her so that she could hardly be seen. But for the present old Massachusetts can match the acres of her workshops and factory floors even against blue-grass, and give odds besides; but what will be the conditions of the match in the next century may be a question for the children of the blue-grass farmers and of the coming colonists to determine.

SOUTHERN LITERATURE

LITERATURE as a profession has until quite recently found but few followers in the South. William Gilmore Simms, breaking through the restraints of Southern custom, was a professional man of letters, and as such labored unceasingly, the result being a long line of novels and tales, rich with local color of an older day, and retaining enough of their former hold upon the public to justify a recent edition. Then there was Poe. But his poems and fantastic stories bear no impress of clime, and might have been written under any latitude by a man of his sort. Of Poe's career in Richmond, as editor of the *Literary Messenger*, a record lies before me now in a series of letters from his employer to a man of noted literary ability, for many years the main-stay of the magazine. "He is continually after me for money," he writes. "I am as sick of his writings as I am of him, and am rather more than half inclined to send him up another dozen dollars, and along with them all his unpublished manuscripts," most of which are denominated "stuff." For his "A. Gordon Pym" he demands three dollars a page! "In reality it has cost me twenty dollars per page." And so the pitiful tale goes on from letter to letter. At last: "Highly as I really think of Mr. Poe's talents, I shall be forced to give him notice, in a week or so at the furthest, that I can no longer recognize him as editor of the *Messenger*." So Poe bent his steps northward, passing from one editorial room to another, from each of which in turn issued substantially the same story.

The institutions and traditions of Southern life were unfavorable, if not openly antagonistic, to the establishment of the literary profession. The leisurely and cultivated, among whom literary productiveness would most naturally have its rise, preferred, as their fathers had preferred, the career of the statesman, and its honors were their ambition, to the attainment of which the legal profession was the natural stepping-stone. The art of expressing thought on paper they regarded as an elegant accomplishment, to be cultivated as a gentleman's recreation, not the serious business of his life, for which he was to receive remuneration. That they were a race of polished letter-writers family archives conclusively prove; and able essays on political subjects not infrequently came from their pens. Thus there were men who did literary work, and good work too, to whom the writing of books was neither the prime aim in life nor yet purely a pastime. J. P. Kennedy wrote "Horseshoe Robinson" and "Swallow Barn," both worthy of remembrance for the pictures of Southern life which they contain; but their author was first and principally a lawyer and politician. Aside from works relating to his profession and his duties as a teacher of the law, Beverley Tucker found time to write "The Partisan Leader, a Story of the Future"—a book exciting phenomenal interest at the time of its first appearance, and again at the outbreak of the civil war—and "George Balcombe," which Poe declared "*the best* American novel," and the publisher to whom it was first offered pronounced "above the heads of the novel-reading public." At intervals of a legal career Judge Longstreet jotted down, entirely for his own amusement, a series of delightful character sketches, published under the title of "Georgia Scenes," which would have been no inconsiderable loss had the author succeeded in his subsequent effort to suppress them, though younger writers with greater literary finish have been engaged in the same field. Of verse writers there were many; sweet singers a few, like Philip Pendleton Cooke and Henry Timrod, whose early death was a loss to American literature.

Simms made the prophecy that there would never be a Southern literature worthy of the name under a slave-holding aristocracy. Social conditions were against it. When the result of the war brought about a new state of affairs, and the people of the South, at first stunned by the mightiness of the blow, went bravely to work to meet the demands of the situation, the pen, heretofore a political weapon or the attribute of cultured leisure, was soon made to take its place beside the plough. In Southern life was presently perceived abundant material, rich and varied, possessing high literary value and interest. Letters as a career found a larger following. John Esten Cooke wrote unceasingly, "for bread, not fame." Now, since a little while ago the tireless hand was taken into the cold hand of death, there is no need for bread, the striving for which brought reputation as well. For others too the myrtle wreath is still twined with yew—the three poets, Sidney Lanier, dead in the fulness of a beautiful promise; Paul Hamilton Hayne, dead in the prime of manhood; and Father Ryan, the poet-priest, whose feet, he declared, were less familiar with the steeps of Parnassus than the humble steps leading up to the altar and its mysteries. Of the older and more assured minstrels Mrs. Preston alone remains. But the copse is ringing with a band of younger singers, singing very sweetly withal, whose voices, yet untried, may strike a higher note and a clearer; but time must show.

The first step taken, it has been reserved for the score or more of recent writers, several of whom have already achieved a brilliant success, to firmly establish a worthy and characteristic Southern literature. For the most part they are younger men and women who remember the old, but have come to maturity in the new, era; and the sheaves they have brought were gathered in the luxuriant harvest overspreading the fields about their own dwellings. What Cable saw and heard while connected with mercantile establishments in New Orleans; what Richard Malcolm Johnston remembers of the scenes and people of middle Georgia, where he was born, and the best years of his life were spent; and Miss Murfree's observations during her residence among the mountains of eastern Tennessee—furnished the suggestions for all that is best in their work. Through these and yet more recent writers the profession of letters holds a secure and elevated position among other professions in the South. For this there is great cause to rejoice. Accuracy of observation, delicacy of portraiture and artistic finish, and, above all, their freshness and earnestness, entitle these new writers to no mean rank and the utmost consideration. Through them many and various peoples and dialects have for the first time entered into literature. Novelties of scene and character possess an enhanced charm when portrayed by those to whom they are the surroundings of every-day life, losing nothing of the local coloring and tone through familiarity. The provincial flavor is delightful, and also the ever-present consciousness that the writers are telling us about men and women, possibly unknown and strange to us, with whom they are personally well acquainted, with whom they have walked and talked from day to day.

The number of dialects of various degrees of intelligibility to which we have been treated is somewhat astonishing, and at first glance may deter the general reader. But, with a little perseverance, whatever difficulty there is may soon be overcome—even in the polyglot pages of Mr. Cable's "Dr. Sevier," where French creoles, Spanish creoles, Irishmen, Germans, negroes, and "Américains" meet together, and essay to converse in English—and he will become aware of and fascinated by the charm with which the performances are pervaded. Thus Bret Harte and other writers have made us familiar with pidgeon-English and other dialectic peculiarities of the West. There is, of course, danger lest this sort of thing be carried to excess, and a stress be laid upon it beyond its value. But how long ago was it that the typical Yankee with his peculiar system of phonetics made his bow in literature? How often has he reappeared since? And do we not still find him there?

When "Sieur George" and "Don Joaquin" were published in New York magazines, and were rapidly succeeded by other short stories of the most delicate and exquisite workmanship, picturing new scenes and a highly romantic people, it was immediately recognized that a writer

of no mean ability, with something very well worth the telling, had stepped to the front. The warm Southern glow, wisely tempered and held in restraint, the keen insight into creole character, and the intimate acquaintance with the picturesque streets and by-ways of the French quarter of New Orleans, proclaimed George W. Cable a long resident, if not native, of Louisiana. The son of a Virginia father and a New England mother, he first saw the light December 12, 1844, in the quaint old town whose Old-World physiognomy is made so familiar by his romances, and here, until the past two or three years, has been his home. At an early age, thrown upon his own resources by financial reverses and the death of his father, he left school, and served in various clerical positions until his nineteenth year, when he volunteered for service in the Confederate army. During his career as a soldier every available moment was devoted to self-improvement in the study of Latin, higher mathematics, and the Bible. The war over, he returned to New Orleans absolutely penniless, and began life anew as an errand-boy in a mercantile establishment, after which he studied civil engineering. In 1869 he married, and shortly thereafter was engaged on the staff of the New Orleans *Picayune*, to a special column of which he had already contributed his first literary ventures. Being requested to take charge of the theatrical column, he refused, cherishing scruples against attendance at places of dramatic entertainment, and at one time, strangely enough, against novel-reading. Thus his connection with the *Picayune* was severed, and he accepted the position of accountant and correspondence clerk to a firm of cotton factors, with which he remained until 1879. While in the employ of this firm he did at spare intervals his first serious and not least satisfactory literary work—the short stories afterward collected under the title of "Old Creole Days," and the opening chapters of his first novel, "The Grandissimes." Encouraged by the success of his efforts, he determined to devote himself henceforth exclusively to literature. He has been and still is a most indefatigable worker, going to the desk in his study with the same regularity that he formerly went to his desk in the counting-house, and there remaining until his daily stint is ended. A year or two ago he made a tour through the North with Mark Twain, the two authors giving a series of readings from their works, and about this time made his home in the village of Simsbury, Connecticut, shortly afterward removing to Northampton, Massachusetts. Following "The Grandissimes," and appearing serially, as did its predecessor, came the pathetic, almost tragic story of "Madame Delphine," the most finished, artistic, and perfectly proportioned of Mr. Cable's larger works—a veritable prose poem. His latest novel, "Dr. Sevier," dealing with life in New Orleans before and during the civil war, appeared in 1884, and a somewhat new departure is a series of stories of the Acadians of Louisiana, now in course of publication. In the pages of his fiction are many sombre pictures, tragedy and tears, but the sun is never long obscured, and when the clouds are darkest there comes a burst of humor as delicious as mellow wine, and in all that he has written some underlying purpose is distinctly felt.

The scope and limits of this paper do not permit any investigation of the questions and discussions which have been raised by certain passages in these novels, and occasional articles from the same pen. That Mr. Cable possesses talent—since genius is disallowed in these days—coupled with an extraordinary capacity for painstaking work, from which has resulted some of the most noteworthy contributions to American literature, even those who take the gravest exceptions to any utterance of his are not prepared to deny. For the rest, Mr. Cable has himself said, in more than one instance, "A creole never forgives a public mention." Besides his novels, Mr. Cable has published a history of New Orleans and of the creoles; a volume on the present condition of the negro in the United States, an earnest appeal for its amelioration, but theoretical rather than practical; and a series of articles on creole slave songs and slave dances—a task for which he is peculiarly fitted, since he is an accomplished amateur musician.

Mr. Cable being the recognized master over the enchanted, semitropical realm, beautiful with flowers, yet marked by the trail of the serpent, into which he has introduced us, others have naturally been deterred from following in his footsteps. Something more than a year ago, however, Miss Grace King, a young lady of New Orleans, modestly came forward with a short story, "Monsieur Motte," in which is told the touching self-sacrifice and devotion of a negress for a destitute and orphaned white child. This story, written with no definite idea of publication, was seen by some literary friends, who, immediately realizing its merit, advised sending it to the *New Princeton Review*, then in quest of a tale for its first issue. It won the writer an instant reputation both in this country and in England. Miss King's next venture was "Bonne Maman," which appeared in the pages of this Magazine, followed shortly by a third story of the same general character, "Madame Lareveillière," a development of "Monsieur Motte." These stories are characterized by a warmth of coloring, sometimes increased to a fierce glow, and a delicate and sympathetic treatment, showing perfect familiarity with the people and scenes portrayed. Miss King belongs to an American family, her father, a native of Georgia, having removed to New Orleans many years ago, where he became one of

Grace King

the most prominent lawyers of the section. A man of culture and literary ability, he gave to the education of his children his personal supervision and encouragement; and to him the young author feels that she owes much of her success in the field of letters. Educated at creole schools, the associations and surroundings of her early life were almost entirely French or creole, and to this fact we are indebted for the delightful description of the interior of a young ladies' boarding-school in New Orleans, which forms so effective a setting for the main incident of "Monsieur Motte." In the treatment of her themes, apart from the fine and original quality by which they are marked, Miss King depicts with a delicate touch the passionate and romantic in the life of her native city, contrasting with striking effect the nature of creole, negro, and quadroon, the intensity of which is relieved by a quiet and charming humor. There is in her delineation of character no element of exaggeration, but simply a faithful presentation of the impulsive Southern tem-

R. M. Johnston.

rable character studies continued, and they were finally all brought together and published in a larger volume. Mr. Johnston, while thoroughly identified with the new South, belongs to the old as well, having been born March 8, 1822, in the county of Hancock, in the middle hill country of Georgia, whither, during the childhood of his parents, the two families had removed from Charlotte County, Virginia, where the Rev. Thomas Johnston, great-grandfather of the author, was rector of Cornwall Parish in the later colonial period and during the Revolution. At that time the only educational facilities in the rural districts were offered by the old-field schools, several of which the Johnston children attended, until the family removed to the neighboring village of Powelton—since made familiar to the

perament instinct with the warmth of the Southern sun.

Among the Southern writers who have recently come into prominence, Richard Malcolm Johnston has been the longest before the public, the first issue of his "Dukesborough Tales" having appeared in the old *Southern Magazine*. These stories, published in book form, brought from a New York editor the assurance of their real value, which was confirmed by the enthusiastic appreciation of Sidney Lanier, who was also a Georgian, and who urged the author to continue his work and to seek a wider audience; the subsequent stories of the series were published in Northern magazines. With this enlarged audience the publication of these admi-

reading world as Dukesborough—where a large school had been established by Salem Town, of Massachusetts, who was succeeded by thorough and accomplished teachers from Vermont. Here young Johnston was entered. This school, the most celebrated in the State, as well as the old-field schools, furnished much material afterward turned to good account. After graduation at Mercer College, and a year devoted to teaching, he went to the bar of the Northern Circuit, the judgeship of which he declined in 1857 in order to accept the chair of belles-lettres in the University of Georgia, where he remained until the outbreak of the civil war. Retiring to his country home near Sparta, he opened a boarding-school for boys, which in

1867 he removed to Baltimore County, Maryland, taking forty Georgia boys with him.

During his career as a lawyer, practising in five or six adjoining counties, much of his time was passed at county-seat taverns, where numbers of lawyers would gather together and relate their observations of Cracker life, their person-

to make of literature a career. For the first of the "Dukesborough Tales" he had neither demanded nor expected remuneration; but the altered condition of the Southern people calling forth new resources, he went seriously to work, and produced the long series of stories that at once gained for him a general recognition. Mr. Johnston's character studies are of the

al experiences among the countrymen of middle Georgia, court-house scenes, and the like. These tavern stories, together with his own intimate acquaintance with the people in the old-field schools and as a lawyer, supplied a rich mine of matter for literary work, which as yet it did not occur to him to use. Indeed, it was after the war, when he was forty-five years old, that he first became aware of the power

best, and met with a most favorable reception on their publication in book form. The Georgia cracker, so faithfully portrayed and so lovingly, was a comparatively new figure in literature, except as he had appeared in Judge Longstreet's "Georgia Scenes," a very robust but much less finished performance. A facility for adapting the most commonplace incidents to the purposes of a good story, to which

is added a lively sense of humor, shows the skill of the artist, and the reader cannot fail to feel that the writer is remembering and recording actual events in which he himself was probably a participant. "Old Mark Langston, a Tale of Duke's Creek," published twelve months later, is a story of the same region, possessing the marked characteristics of the shorter stories, its chief strength and charm. "Two Gray Tourists" is his latest production. Mr. Johnston, in conjunction with Dr. William Hand Browne, of Johns Hopkins University, is also the author of a "Biography of Alexander H.

Stephens," and a "History of English Literature." He is still actively engaged in adding to his list of character sketches, the new stories appearing from time to time in different magazines; and he has in contemplation a novel illustrating the higher types of Georgia country and village life.

Another writer who has depicted scenes and life in middle Georgia, though to a less extent, is Joel Chandler Harris, who modestly denies to his performances the merit of literature, counting them simply as "stuff" prepared during the leisure moments of an active journalistic career, and lacking in all that goes to make permanent literature. Mr. Harris's reputation rests mainly upon his delineation of negro character and skilful reproduction of negro dialect in the "Uncle Remus" series, wherein he has preserved the unique and picturesque folk-lore of the Southern plantation. However good his stories of mountaineer and moonshiner, they must yield place to those in which are chronicled the sayings and doings of that abandoned and altogether delightful rep-

mentioned — must offer to Mr. Harris grateful thanks for the preservation of the dear familiar tales, whose quaintness and drollery cannot fail to fascinate less fortunate mortals.

Mr. Harris is yet in the prime of life, having been born, of parents in humble circumstances, in the little village of Eatonton, Putnam County, Georgia, December 9, 1848. His literary career he regards as a thing of accident throughout.

Charles Egbert Craddock

robate Brer Rabbit, and his neighbors of field and thicket. Every man who in his first youth was alternately fondled and tyrannized over by that wellnigh extinct functionary, the old-fashioned black "mammy"—with utmost reverence let her be

"The Vicar of Wakefield," which his mother read aloud when he was a small child, first inspired a desire to express his thoughts on paper, the outcome of this desire being a number of little stories in which the conversational capacity of the characters was limited to the single exclamation, "Fudge!" Though none of these little tales have survived, "since their key-note was 'Fudge!'" says Mr. Harris, "they must have been very close to human nature." Mr. Harris is by profession a newspaper man, having been for

fice of the *Countryman*, a little weekly paper published upon a Georgia plantation ten miles from any post-office. Amid the most peaceful of rural surroundings, broken only by the call of the partridge and the barking of squirrels, he learned to set type. The desire to write, provoked by

M. G. McClelland

many years on the staff of the Atlanta *Constitution*, one of the leading newspapers of the South, upon which he continues to do editorial work. From the editorial sanctum he puts forth no claim to that literary distinction which has deservedly come upon him. His journalistic career was begun in 1862, when, a lad of fourteen, he went as printer's apprentice into the of-

"The Vicar of Wakefield," and stimulated by the "Fudge" stories, still burned within him; so into the columns of the *Countryman* crept certain articles set from the "case" without previous existence in manuscript. This course did not prevent detection; but the editor made no comment, and began lending to the ambitious apprentice many volumes from his large

Frances Courtenay Baylor

and choice library. While engaged upon the *Countryman* he became familiar with the plantation legends of Brer Rabbit and the other "varmints," absorbing the songs and myths of the negroes without any conception of their literary value, unrealized until about ten years ago, when an article upon the subject appeared in one of the Northern magazines. The great bulk of the matter making up his first volume of negro folk-lore—"Uncle Remus, his Songs and Sayings"—was contributed to the columns of the Atlanta *Constitution*. The success of this book was immediate on both sides of the Atlantic, extending even to India, and led to the production of "A Rainy Day with Uncle Remus" and "Nights with Uncle Remus," in which are gathered some of the best of the animal stories, together with some capital touches in the treatment of negro character. These volumes are a unique contribution to literature, done to the life by a faithful and loving hand. In "Mingo and Other Sketches" Mr. Harris introduces the countryman of middle Georgia and the mountaineer with good success; but he is at his best while depicting the old-time negro with his quaint humor and dialect and inexhaustible store of inimitable stories. That picture of "Miss Sally's" little boy and the grizzled old negro

Julia Magruder.

deal with the negro, the one in no wise interferes with the proper appreciation of the other. In Uncle Remus Mr. Harris has possibly given us the truer insight into the character of the type to which he belongs, while the venerable family servant is somewhat idealized by Mr. Page, and, moreover, is made to tell a story possessing a value and interest of its own not entirely dependent upon the personality of the narrator and his race peculiarities. In the matter of dialect Mr. Page has the advantage, though this may be due in part to the difference between the Virginia negro and his brother of Georgia.

Mr. Page comes of one of the oldest, most aristocratic families of his native State, and through both father and mother is third in descent from General Thomas Nelson of Revolutionary fame, signer of the Declaration of Independence, from whom he takes his name. He was born April 23, 1853, at Oaklands, an old family estate in Hanover County, the mansion-house erected nearly a hundred years ago by the slaves, who also felled and prepared the timber. His first instructors were his aunt and the old carriage driver, the former teaching him to read in the Prayer-book of the Episcopal Church and the Waverley Novels. Then came the war, which went far toward increasing a small boy's knowledge of the ways of the world and human nature, while breaking in upon a systematic education. Child as he was, he on several occasions was witness to the horrors of war. His home was situated at the conjunction of two of the great roads leading to Richmond, along which army followed army, and once while with his father, an officer in the Confederate service, in camp near Petersburg, he experienced the sensations of a bombardment.

seated in the light of the blazing pine knots, the grotesque shadows playing among the rafters and along the walls of the cabin, is a perfect bit of *genre*. Then there is the pitiful figure of Free Joe, contrasting so forcibly with the careless happiness and self-importance of Uncle Remus. Mr. Harris has done nothing better than this. "Free Joe and the Rest of the World"—the very title is a sermon.

Three years ago Thomas Nelson Page, a young lawyer of Richmond, Virginia, published "Marse Chan," a story of Virginia before and during the war, related by an old negro man, the former slave and still devoted adherent of a family to which the war had brought utter desolation—a truthful, dramatic, pathetic, and at the same time delightfully humorous representation. Consequently Mr. Page enjoys the reputation of having written the most exquisite story of the war that has yet appeared. In comparison with the work of Mr. Harris, though both authors

The close of the war found the family reduced to poverty, in consequence of which the young son of the house was deprived of many educational advantages; but he had received the indelible impressions out of which "Marse Chan" and "Meh Lady" have grown. At Washington College, now Washington and Lee University, where he was edu-

he has practised his profession in Richmond, no literary work being allowed to interfere. Mr. Page's first published production, other than contributions to college journals and newspapers, was "Uncle Gabe's White Folks," a little dialect poem that appeared in *Scribner's Monthly* in 1876. During the probationary years of a young lawyer's career he turned to

Amélie Rives

cated, he paid less attention to the curriculum than to the debating society, and the college magazine, of which he was editor; after which he went to the University of Virginia, and took his law degree in one year. Since his graduation

his pen as a source of amusement, the subject instinctively chosen being those stirring and trying scenes so vividly imprinted on his mind when a child. The result was "Marse Chan," not published, however, until some years later. Since then other stories have come from his pen in rapid succession—"Unc' Edinburg's Drowndin'," an *ante bellum* tale of Virginia, again with a negro *raconteur*, "Meh Lady," "Ole 'Stracted," and "Polly." These stories have been felicitously characterized as "variant treatments of the same *motif*," for which we feel no disposition to quarrel with Mr. Page, being eager to hear the tale as often as he may find ways to tell it, and grateful to him for such beautiful and faithful pictures of a society now become portion and parcel of the irrevocable past. He is at present engaged on a more ambitious work, a novel of Virginia life since the war, the completion of which has been delayed by ill health. It is hardly just to judge of Mr. Page's capabilities in a field outside his first success by "A Soldier of the Empire," which, though published recently, was his first production.

Possibly not since George Eliot's time has there been so great a literary sensation as that created by the discovery of a feminine personality behind the *nom de plume* of Charles Egbert Craddock. While well known that Craddock was an assumed name, the style, subject-matter, even the handwriting, contained no feminine suggestions. Yet Miss Mary Noailles Murfree is distinctly a woman in the truest sense, possessing feminine accomplishments and attractions that have made her always a social leader and favorite. Speaking of her as a woman, a friend has said, "It is refreshing to find an intellectual woman free from George Eliot's haunting spectre of despair, and the morbid wretchedness of Charlotte Brontë's nervous little body; to see the cheerfulness and vivacity of Jane Austen and Maria Edgeworth once more united to genius and womanly tastes and feelings—to Christian faith, purity, and goodness."

On the paternal side Miss Murfree is descended from a distinguished family of North Carolina, her great-grandfather, Major Hardy Murfree, for whom the towns of Murfreesborough in North Carolina and Tennessee are named, having done good service in the Revolutionary war, and received in return a large grant of land in Tennessee, upon which Charles Egbert Craddock—she prefers to be known by this name—was born. Her grandfather, for many years a member of Congress from North Carolina, removed to Tennessee, where her father, a man of some literary attainments, was, prior to the war, a prominent lawyer possessed of extensive landed estates. Her mother—whose mother was a Murfree—comes of one of the leading and most influential families in the State. Becoming lame from a stroke of paralysis in early childhood, which in no wise dimmed an unusually bright disposition, she was debarred from the ordinary amusements of youth, and developed a reading habit, was always a hard student in school and out, encouraged by an intellectual and cultivated family circle. But doubtless she would never have achieved her brilliant literary success had not the fortunes of war proved disastrous. Mr. Murfree found it necessary to give up his house in Nashville, and Grantlands, Craddock's birthplace, was the battle-field of Murfreesborough. This old homestead and its surroundings she has accurately described in her first novel, "Where the Battle was Fought"—a book of strong parts, but deficient in construction, yet containing one of her most perfectly drawn and finished characters, General Vayne, a portrait from the life. In this emergency the family retired to Murfree's Rock, a small cottage perched upon a crag near Beersheba, a watering-place in the Tennessee mountains, where they were wont to spend the summer months. Here in this elevated region, overlooking miles of valleys, mountains, and undulating hills, peopled with the picturesque and primitive race of her romances, she unconsciously absorbed the material for her future work. Standing on the porch of the little cottage, gazing out over the magnificent landscape at sunset, she formulated in her mind a story which ultimately grew into the exquisite "The Star in the Valley." But it was not written then. About nine years ago, after the family had gone down to live at the sadly altered old homestead near Murfreesborough, before the final move to St. Louis, their present place of residence, the first story of "In the Tennessee Mountains" came into existence. This was "The Dancin' Party at Harrison's Cove," which first saw the light in the *Atlantic Monthly*. Other stories followed, each exhibiting rare descriptive powers—a gift she has since somewhat abused—a strong grasp of a novel subject and dialect, and a style at once bold and delicate. It is little wonder that when collected in a volume their publication was an event, that a sensation resulted from the discovery that a woman of society had written "A-Playin' of Old Sledge at the Settlemint," and "The 'Harnt' that Walks Chilhowee," depicting with masculine force the fierce passions, the minute daily life, of a scant civilization — a seemingly difficult task for a man's accomplishment. But it is characteristic of Miss Murfree's energy and earnestness that no obstacle raised merely by her sex is permitted to block the work in hand; thus she made a careful study of the game of poker for the sake of a scene in "Where the Battle was Fought," and has acquired a knowledge of many abstruse points of law. Her second novel, "The Prophet of the Great Smoky Mountains," in which is unfolded the story of an illiterate mountain preacher and his wrestlings with unbelief, is a series of splendid scenes, somewhat disconnected, abounding in beautiful and graphic descriptions, and dealing entirely with the mountaineers, thus lacking the variety which enhanced the charm of many of the shorter stories. "In the Clouds," her latest work, shows a mastery of construction, in which its predecessors were deficient, possesses their salient features with some new ones, and goes far to establish an already assured reputation.

Miss M. G. McClelland, in her novel "Oblivion," published two years ago, inevitably suggests a comparison with the work of Miss Murfree, though there are certain marked contrasts between the two. Moreover, "Oblivion" was written before Miss Murfree had won her wide reputation, and without knowledge of her writings, and is therefore none the less original for any points of similarity. The mountaineers of Miss McClelland's story are endowed with a tenderness in the intimate relations of daily life, a susceptibility to the refining influences of sentiment, in which those of Miss Murfree are lacking. In the pages of "In the Tennessee Mountains" and its fellows there is seldom, and then very faintly, any evidence of their feminine inception, while in "Oblivion" the hand of the woman is everywhere present.

Lafcadio Hearn

Amid just such scenes as form a background to her story Miss McClelland has dwelt from her youth, though in Buckingham County, Virginia, not western North Carolina, as there represented. Her home is a rambling, old-fashioned frame structure, overshadowed by a magnificent elm-tree, in a wild mountainous country, until quite recently untraversed by a railroad. Cut off from intercourse with others of her age, she grew up an imaginative child, whose dolls were made to personate the characters in Scott's romances, from her love for which grew her early efforts in story-writing. There is yet in the yard a large rock that in her childish imagination was supposed to lie in the path leading to the house of the Landammon of Unterwalden, from which a stick was projected to another rock for the perilous pass across the chasm. Anne of Geierstein was a small doll, for whose cap the old peacock was invited to furnish a feather from his crest. Not entering into the spirit of the performance, and being of a choleric disposition, he took refuge on the roof of the barn, and screamed exultantly at the ineffectual efforts to dis-

Robert Burns Wilson

lodge him by hurling stones. The war brought financial embarrassment upon the family, which the young author of "Oblivion" has met most nobly. Fortunately for her, she was the daughter of cultivated parents, people of the old *régime*, and her mother has served as school-mistress, playmate, companion. A day of systematic schooling she has never had until now, when, with indomitable energy and determination, she is pursuing a prescribed course of study. With the outside world she has little personal acquaintance. With these serious drawbacks she has achieved that most dangerous of successes, a successful first book. Her first experience with type was the appearance in 1879 of two bits of verse in the columns of a newspaper, one of these written while churning with the left hand, the other composed while pursuing a turkey hen to her hidden nest in the woods. "Princess," her second novel in point of publication, was in point of fact written several years before "Oblivion," but, owing to the extreme stand taken against divorce, it could not find a publisher. Modified and rewritten, it has now done so; but we refuse to take it as a successor to "Oblivion," as in reality it is not, and are justified in demanding the fulfilment of the promise which that exquisite mountain idyl held forth, a promise partially kept in her latest story, "A Self-made Man."

The work of the writers heretofore mentioned gives strong internal evidence of

Southern origin—scene, *dramatis personæ*, and treatment being redolent of the soil—a provincial flavor altogether fresh and delightful. But Miss Frances Courtenay Baylor, another Southern woman whose pen has recently brought her into prominence, has put forth a book none the less charming because its racy and sparkling pages proclaim the author an American at large, and identify her with no particular section of a very extensive country. Miss Baylor's name has long been one of high social distinction in Virginia, and she herself is essentially a Virginian, though born in Arkansas, and prior to the war a resident of San Antonio, Texas. At the close of the war she went abroad, and again in 1873. After a residence of two years in England she returned to America, and made her permanent home near Winchester, Virginia—an old town retaining much of its pristine social estate, from which the aroma of the old *régime* has not entirely passed away. In this atmosphere, undisturbed by the rushing currents of the nineteenth century, her breezy book was written. But Miss Baylor is something of a cosmopolite as well as a Virginian. "On Both Sides" is not strictly a novel, there being no plot nor effort to sustain the reader's interest by the unfoldings of a story. Indeed, the two parts of which the book consists were written at different times, and published independently, the one part treating of the experiences of a party of Americans domiciled in England; the other, in which many of the same characters are brought forward, narrating the experiences of some English people travelling in America. As a whole, "On Both Sides" is a charmingly witty and clever production, and Miss Baylor shows a wonderful facility for portraying local characteristics, contrasting her Englishmen with the multiform types and phases of American life, from New England to New Orleans, from Virginia to California. In "Juan and Juanita," a story for younger readers, she enters upon a new field, made familiar to her by her residence in the far South.

Another young novelist whose home is in the vicinity of Winchester is Miss Julia Magruder, who has given us in "Across the Chasm" a study of social conditions since the war, contrasting certain types of the North and South. She was for some years a resident of Washington and Baltimore, with the society of which cities

her story deals. The book is well written, containing some delightfully humorous scenes and touches, though Miss Magruder, in a conscientious effort to be impartial, has scarcely done full justice to her own section. All that she says is true; but there is much besides that she might have said without incurring the accusation of partiality. The fault is one of omission, not of commission; and such a book, coming from such a source, is a pleasant sign of the new era, not in Southern literature alone, but in sectional good feeling.

Miss Amélie Rives, of Virginia, has burst into prominence with a single short story. Coming of distinguished lineage, and possessing rare personal attractions, she had already won an extended social reputation, not only in her native South, but at the North as well. Indifferent to social triumphs, she has always preferred the life of her ancestral home, Castle Hill, among the red hills of Albemarle, an estate that has been in the family since the original royal grant, the mansion-house having been erected in part far back in the last century. Here, with her horses, her dogs, her dumb-bells, and her studio, the young authoress, upon whom so many talents have been bestowed, is in the element she loves best. Like Miss McClelland, though for another reason, she has never crossed the threshold of a schoolroom, her governess receiving instructions to permit her charge to study how and when she would. Thus has resulted a knowledge of the beautiful and attractive in literature and art, and not unnaturally her ungoverned methods of work. When the inclination seizes her she will shut herself in her studio, and stand before the easel ten hours at a time; or else, having read everything bearing upon the subject chosen, write as many hours with a rapidity and exactness wellnigh inconceivable. The latter quality is exemplified in her sixteenth-century story, "A Brother to Dragons." In this manner, though just entered upon her twenties, she has written, heretofore for her own pleasure alone, dramas, poems, and stories covering many pages of manuscript, and embracing a wide range of subjects, from the deluge to our own time. From these a visiting friend selected "A Brother to Dragons," and submitted it without comment to the *Atlantic Monthly*, in an early number of which it appeared anonymously. This story, showing an imaginative power unequalled in contemporary fiction save in some of Blackmore's best work, and that bold yet delicate quaintness which characterized the finest productions of the Elizabethan era, at once arrested the attention of critics. The most difficult test for all judgment of her future work is that which she has herself furnished in her first published story.

The limits of this paper do not permit extended mention of many recent Southern writers whose names are familiar to readers of this and other magazines, as well as of current volumes of prose and verse, who, nevertheless, are rendering effective service in the general awakening. Mrs. Mary Spier Tiernan is favorably known as the author of "Homoselle" and "Suzette," conscientious and sympathetic pictures of Virginia in *ante bellum* days. In "Women" Miss Mary Tucker Magill treats of the war period, and has written, besides, a "History of Virginia" and some good character sketches. Through for some years a resident of New York, Mrs. Burton Harrison is a Southern woman who has made contributions to Southern literature. In addition to those already mentioned are Mr. James Lane Allen, whose series of papers descriptive of his native Kentucky were a notable feature of this Magazine during the past year, and Mr. H. S. Edwards, of Macon, Georgia, whose humorous short stories have won for him a well-deserved reputation. Besides this very creditable array of names, there are writers of extended reputation to whom the South may lay some sort of claim, as Frank R. Stockton, seeing that he is the son of a Virginia mother and the husband of a Virginia wife, and the author of many Virginia stories; and the American novelist of English birth, Mrs. Frances Hodgson Burnett.

From the realm of poesy the South's stronger singers, those who may be crowned by the name of poet, have with a single exception passed beyond the gates of the unseen land. Mrs. Margaret J. Preston, who long ago received her just recognition, still sings, and none the less cheerfully and hopefully because of her blindness. Those who would follow these along the paths of Parnassus are for the most part young men, whose work thus far has not justified collection between the covers of a book. Though now identified with the West, Maurice Thompson in his "Songs of Fair Weather" gives token of his Southern youth and training. Samuel Minturn Peck, of Alabama, has recently gathered his songs and *vers de société* under the felicitous general title of "Cap and Bells"; and upon the shoulders of William H. Hayne a portion at least of his father's mantle seems to have fallen.

Among the younger verse writers is Robert Burns Wilson, of Kentucky, of whom Paul H. Hayne, shortly before his death, spoke most hopefully and kindly: "The old man whose head has grown gray in the service of the Muses, who is about to leave the lists of poetry forever, around whose path the sunset is giving place to twilight, with no hope before him but 'an anchorage among the stars,' extends his hand to a younger brother of his art with an earnest *Te moriturus saluto*." Mr. Wilson was born at the home of his grandfather, in Washington County, Pennsylvania, October 30, 1850; but his earliest recollections are of an apple orchard in full blossom among the Virginia hills, and a ploughman, with long beard and kindly gray eyes, who allowed him to ride on the beam of the plough and watch the turning furrows. It must have been near sunset, for with just such scenes Mr. Wilson's poems are full—transcripts from the gentler side of nature, with now and then a great storm; and when the sun does shine it is apt to be just before he goes down at the death of another day. This all-pervading melancholy is in a measure to be accounted for and excused by many circumstances of his life. His father, an architect and builder, being much impoverished, the early education of the artist-poet devolved upon his mother, through whom he is descended from the Nelson family of Virginia, whose talent for drawing and painting enabled her to sympathize with the tastes of her son. After her death he had several years of regular schooling, and the age of nineteen found him making portraits for a livelihood, and doing such other artistic work as came in his way. When twenty-two he went to Louisville, shortly afterward removed to Frankfort, Kentucky, among whose beautiful and picturesque hills he has since resided. And a more suitable environment for poet or painter would be difficult to find. Several of his pictures attracted much attention at the Louisville Exposition in 1883, and again at the New Orleans World's Fair. Mr. Wilson's love for nature was developed when, a lad of fourteen, he would wander over hill and field declaiming epics of his own composition, tinctured doubtless with that brooding spirit pervading almost every product of his pen. Despite this persistent note of sadness, he shows himself a close student of nature, and has learned well to portray her many moods in melodious verse. "June Days" and "When Evening Cometh On," first printed in this Magazine, are replete with delicate word pictures, and may possibly be counted the best of his published work. When his verses, now scattered through the newspapers and magazines of the past few years, have been gathered in a volume, the showing, while it would not discredit an older singer, will give high promise of a golden maturity.

A middle position between fictionist and verse-writer is that occupied by Lafcadio Hearn, of Louisiana, by virtue of his volume of poetical prose, "Stray Leaves from Strange Literature." Mr. Hearn was born in 1850 in Santa Maura, of the Ionian Islands, his mother a native Greek, his father a surgeon in the British army, whose regiment was stationed in the Grecian islands during the English protectorate. After receiving a liberal education in England, Ireland, and France, he came to America, his father having died in India, and the family become involved in a disastrous business failure. Like Mr. Harris, he is a journalist. Immediately on his arrival in America he learned the printer's trade in Cincinnati, held various subordinate positions in a printing-office, and finally was engaged as reporter and travelling correspondent on several newspapers of the city. It was on a vacation journey that he first came to the South, leaving, as he himself has expressed it, "sleet and gloom to sail into the warmth and perfume of a Louisiana autumn day—into a blaze of violet and gold." The Southern blood in his veins answered with a thrill, and he determined to remain. In New Orleans he found more congenial journalistic employment, leaving him greater time for the cultivation of literary tastes, which had been denied full gratification in the North, though he had already translated and published "One of Cleopatra's Nights,"

a volume of stories from the French of Théophile Gautier. "Stray Leaves from Strange Literature," inspired by some words of Baudelaire—"*le miracle d'une prose poétique, musicale sans rhythme et sans rime*"—a happy description of the book, by-the-way—is an interpretation of certain Eastern stories and legends in English poetical prose. From exhaustive studies in Oriental literature, a subject which has always possessed for him a strong fascination, resulted this volume of exquisite exotics, gathered from the rich treasures of ancient Egyptian, Indian, and Buddhist literature, the same which supplied the material for Edwin Arnold's "The Light of Asia." The weird and beautiful myths, as interpreted by Mr. Hearn, though lacking the metrical form, are veritable poems, heavy with the perfume and glamour of the East, delicate, fragrant, graceful. A second effort in the direction of poetical prose is a little volume, read in the proof by the present writer, entitled "Chinese Ghosts." In his treatment of the legend lore of the Celestial Empire Mr. Hearn has, if possible, been even more delicate and charming than in the stories which go to make the previous volume, so much so, indeed, that one is persuaded to full belief in the beauty and witchery of the almond-eyed heroines of his pages.

From this synoptical presentation of some of the more recent Southern writers, besides the main fact of the establishment of a characteristic Southern literature, developing along an independent line from which old obstructions and restrictions have been removed, two great points are made distinctly apparent—the rich variety of the new fields worked by men and women native to the soil, and the wonderful possibilities of the magazine short story. By short stories Mr. Johnston, Mr. Cable, Mr. Harris, and Miss Murfree won unreserved recognition; Mr. Page, Miss King, and Miss Rives have as yet given us nothing else.

Whatever there is to be said by way of criticism hardly comes within the province of this article. And the critics, in almost every instance, have found only kind words to say for these men and women, who have not only succeeded in building up a Southern literature worthy of the name, but have infused a stream of rich warm blood into our national literature.

PLANTATION LIFE

THE Boré plantation was situated on the left bank of the Mississippi, about six miles above New Orleans, taking as a point of departure the Cathedral, then the centre of the city, and following the public road that ran along the river in all its windings. The next one above was the plantation of Pierre Foucher, the son-in-law of Boré, and a portion of it is now the City Park, on which the "World's Exposition" lately took place, succeeded by the present "American Exposition." It is a spot round which cluster more historical souvenirs than about any other in Louisiana. The plantation above Foucher's, and on which has since sprung up the town of Carrollton, belonged to Lafrénière, Attorney-General under the French government, who was the principal leader in the revolution that drove away, in 1768,

the first Spanish Governor, Don Antonio de Ulloa, who had come to take possession of Louisiana, transferred by France to Spain. Lafrénière had two sons-in-law —Noyan, Bienville's nephew, executed by Governor O'Reilly for rebellion against the King of Spain, and Lebreton, who had been a *mousquetaire*, or guardsman, in the King's household troops. He became proprietor of the plantation after his father-in-law had been shot by the same authority. The son of this Lebreton married a daughter of Boré. On his being assassinated by a petted and pampered slave, the plantation passed into the hands of Macarty, who had been the tutor of the children of the defunct, and has since become the town of Carrollton. The youngest and last daughter of Boré married Don Carlos Gayarré, the grandson of the *real contador*, or royal contador, Don Estevan Gayarré, whose mission was to take possession of Louisiana with Governor Ulloa. This third son-in-law resided on the plantation of Boré; so that all those families were grouped in a tribe-like fashion around a central point—the head and patriarch of the family and its branches.

On the Foucher plantation, and near its upper limit, there was a very large house, occupied by one Lefort, who kept a school that was very well attended by the children of the planters on both sides of the river. It was there that I learned my A B C, before I was sent to the College of Orleans, situated where to-day stands the Church of St. Augustin, corner of St. Claude and Bayou Road, *alias* Hospital Street. This Lefort was a man of culture, but rather rough, and unmercifully addicted to striking his pupils. I was six years old when I attended his school, and I have not yet forgotten, after so many years, the blows which he used to give me because my young and imperfect organs of speech could not properly pronounce the English *the*. He was very fat and pot-bellied. When the river was high, and covered the batture in front of the levee, he took us to bathe twice a week. The way in which he floated on the river without any effort, and like a bag of wind, was to me at the time a cause of wonder and speculation. To dive would have been for him as impossible as to fly like a bird.

Indigo had been the principal staple of the colony, but at last a worm which attacked the plant and destroyed it, through consecutive years, was reducing to poverty and to the utmost despair the whole population. Jean Étienne de Boré determined to make a bold experiment to save himself and his fellow-citizens, and convert his indigo plantation into one of sugar-cane.

In these critical circumstances he resolved to renew the attempt which had been made to manufacture sugar. He immediately prepared to go into all the expenses and incur all the obligations consequent on so costly an undertaking. His wife warned him that her father had in former years vainly made a similar attempt; she represented that he was hazarding on the cast of a die all that remained of their means of existence; that if he failed, as was so probable, he would reduce his family to hopeless poverty;

that he was of an age—being over fifty years old—when fate was not to be tempted by doubtful experiments, as he could not reasonably entertain the hope of a sufficiently long life to rebuild his fortune if once completely shattered; and that he would not only expose himself to ruin, but also to a risk much more to be dreaded—that of falling into the grasp of creditors. Friends and relatives joined their remonstrances to hers, but could not shake the strong resolve of his energetic mind. He had fully matured his plan, and was determined to sink or swim with it.

Purchasing a quantity of canes from two individuals named Mendez and Solis, who cultivated them only for sale as a dainty in the New Orleans market, and to make coarse syrup, he began to plant in 1794, and to make all the other necessary preparation, and in 1795 he made a crop of sugar which sold for twelve thousand dollars—a large sum at that time. Boré's attempt had excited the keenest interest; many had frequently visited him during the year to witness his preparations; gloomy predictions had been set afloat, and on the day when the grinding of the cane was to begin, a large number of the most respectable inhabitants had gathered in and about the sugar-house to be present at the failure or success of the experiment. Would the syrup granulate? would it be converted into sugar? The crowd waited with eager impatience for the moment when the man who watches the coction of the juice of the cane determines whether it is ready to granulate. When that moment arrived the stillness of death came among them, each one holding his breath, and feeling that it was a matter of ruin or prosperity for them all. Suddenly the sugar-maker cried out with exultation, "It granulates!" Inside and outside of the building one could have heard the wonderful tidings flying from mouth to mouth and dying in the distance, as if a hundred glad echoes were telling it to one another. Each one of the by-standers pressed forward to ascertain the fact on the evidence of his own senses, and when it could no longer be doubted, there came a shout of joy, and all flocked around Étienne de Boré, overwhelming him with congratulations, and almost hugging the man whom they called their savior—the savior of Louisiana. Ninety years have elapsed since, and an event which produced so much excitement at the time is very nearly obliterated from the memory of the present generation.

In 1796 a stirring event occurred at the plantation of Étienne de Boré. The French General Collot, on his way to New Orleans from the Western States and Territories, had stopped to visit that gentleman. As soon as this was known in the city, the Governor, Baron de Carondelet, who had received from Philadelphia a confidential communication informing him that General Collot was intrusted by the French government with a secret mission, against which the Spanish authorities were to be on their guard, sent up an armed boat by the river and fifty dragoons by land to arrest him. The General was put in the boat and taken down to New Orleans, where he was imprisoned in Fort St. Charles, situated about the spot where now stands the United States Mint. On the next day he was called upon by the Spanish Governor, who proposed to him a house in town which he might occupy on parole, and with a soldier at his door. Having accepted the proposition, he left the fort in the Governor's carriage. Shortly after, on the 1st of November, the General, from whom some of his maps, drawings, and writings had been taken away, was conveyed on board of one of the King's galleys, and accompanied by a captain of the regiment of Louisiana, who was not to lose sight of him, was transported to the Balize, where he was detained a prisoner in the house of the chief pilot, Juan Ronquillo, "situated," he said, "in the midst of a vast swamp, and from which there was no egress except in a boat." He remained at that dismal spot until the 22d of December, when he embarked on board of the brig *Iphigenia* for Philadelphia.

Étienne de Boré was extremely indignant at the arbitrary arrest of General Collot, who was his guest at the time. He considered it an insult to himself, and he expressed his feelings loudly and without restraint. He was known for his intense attachment to French interests, and it is said that the Baron seriously thought of having him arrested and transported to Havana, but that he was deterred by the fear of producing a commotion by inflicting so harsh a treatment on so distinguished a citizen, who, by his personal character, his rank, his family connections, and the benefit he had lately conferred on his country by the introduction

of a new branch of industry, commanded universal sympathies and exercised the widest influence.

In the beginning of 1798, when Gayoso de Lemos was Governor of Louisiana, the Boré plantation was visited by three illustrious strangers, the Duke of Orleans and his two brothers, the Count of Beaujolais and the Duke of Montpensier, of the royal house of France, who, driven into exile after the death of their father on the scaffold, were striking examples of those remarkable vicissitudes of fortune with which the annals of history are so replete. When a *mousquetaire*, or guardsman, in the household troops of Louis XV., and watching over the safety of the Majesty of France, little did De Boré dream that the day would come when three princes of the blood would be his guests on the bank of the Mississippi.

This plantation was sagaciously and tastefully laid out for beauty and productiveness. The gardens occupied a large area, and at once astonished the eye by the magnificence of their shady avenues of orange-trees. Unbroken retreats of myrtle and laurel defied the rays of the sun. Flowers of every description perfumed the air. Extensive orchards produced every fruit of which the climate was susceptible. By judicious culture there had been obtained remarkable success in producing an abundance of juicy grapes, every bunch of which, however, when they began to ripen, was enveloped in a sack of wire to protect them against the depredations of birds. The fields were cultivated with such a careful observance of the variable exigencies of every successive season that there was no such thing known as a short or half crop, or no crop at all. This was reserved for much later days. But under the administration of Étienne de Boré, during a period of about twenty-five years, from the first ebullition of a sugar kettle in 1795 to the time of his death in 1820, every crop was regularly the same within a few hogsheads. When, however, he ceased to exist, this seat of order and prosperity became a chaos of disorder and ruin, and the estate finally passed away from the family into the hands of strangers.

It was a self-sufficient little domain, exporting a good deal, and importing but meagrely, so that the balance was very much in its favor. It was largely supplied with sheep and their wool, with geese, ducks, turkeys, guinea-fowls, and every variety of poultry without stint. Eggs were gathered by the bushel. Pigeons clouded the sun, and when the small black cherries (called *merises* in French) were ripe, those feathered epicures ate them voraciously, got royally drunk, and falling from the trees, strewed the ground beneath. A numerous herd of cattle, under the inspection of old Pompey and a black youngster called *Souris* (in English *mouse*), on account of his diminutive figure, pastured luxuriously and grew fat. What a quantity of fresh butter, rich cheese, milk, cream, and clabber! Vast barns gorged with corn, rice, and hay; hives bursting with honey; vegetables without measure, and so luscious; a varied and liberal supply of carriages always ready for use, and horses for the saddle or for driving, all glossy and sleek; spirited mules, well fed and well curried— the pride of the field hands; shrimps and fish from the river; multitudes of crawfish from the deep ditches; raccoons and opossums to gladden the heart of the most surly negro. Boré had made of his estate both a farm and plantation. Every day before dawn cart-loads departed for New Orleans with diversified produce, most of which was handed over, when it reached its destination, to two old women, Agathe and Marie, who were the occupants and guardians of the town house of Boré. They admirably understood the art of selling, and were well known to the whole population, whose confidence they possessed. Going to market with baskets full, they generally brought them back empty. Josephine, a handsome, strong-limbed, and light-footed mulattress, with another female assistant of a darker color, sold the milk and butter with wonderful rapidity, and both were back at the plantation at half past 10 A.M., with the mail, the daily papers, and whatever else they had to bring. It was clock-work in everything on that plantation of the old *régime*. Hence the *farm* produced at least six thousand dollars per annum, besides supplying all the wants of those who resided on it, black or white, and the product of the *plantation* was almost all profit.

The Boré town house of which I have spoken was situated at the corner of Conti and Chartres streets, where, after its demolition, there was erected the tall brick building known as the Sarrasin Tobacco Manufactory. In front, across the street at the south corner, on the right hand in Conti Street going toward the river, there was the house of Destréhan, his brother-in-law, who was the first Senator the State elected to Congress on her becoming a part of the Union in 1812, but he declined to take his seat. This will appear strange to our modern politicians.

The house of Destréhan has also been demolished, and in its place there has been erected a vulgar three-story building with a whitewashed front, as frigid-looking as a tomb, although at night it becomes a *café chantant*. The ancient Louisiana name of Destréhan has also disappeared forever. As to the defunct house of Boré, its architecture was strikingly French, and had it continued in existence would have attracted the attention of those modern tourists who are so fond of antiquities. It was a massive two-story brick house, built under the Spanish government by a M. Voltaire de Fonvergne. There was a large gate-yard in Conti Street. Most of the rooms were also large, and with marquetry floors of oak—a rare thing in Louisiana, which I do not remember having seen in any other house. Everything was broad in it— broad doors, broad windows, broad chimneys, high ceilings. As to the main flight of stairs with its fantastically worked iron rails, it seemed to my young eyes to be as broad as the street itself. The roof was a solid terrace with a stone balustrade. During the summer months it was a pleasant place late in the evening when the floor had sufficiently cooled down under the fresh breeze coming from the river. The first story was occupied by a druggist named Tolozan, a man of polished and engaging manners, whose store was well patronized by the *élite* of the city, and where gossips of that class used to meet. Altogether the house had a peculiar physiognomy of its own. I was about seven years old when Étienne de Boré sold it to his son-in-law, Pierre Foucher. This old mansion at the corner of Conti and Chartres was inherited by Foucher's daughter, Madame de Lachaise, whose husband pulled it down, and substituted for it the ugly red thing which looks like a rampant lobster.

But to return to the plantation from which I have digressed. The discipline established on it was a sort of military one. At dawn, when it was time to go to the field and to the other labors of the day, the big bell rang. The whole gang of negroes came to the house, in front of which they all kneeled, and a short prayer was said, always in the presence of a male member of the family, who stood up with head uncovered. The same ceremony was performed in the evening before they went to their supper and their rest for the night. I vividly remember how I felt when, being about eight years old, I was for the first time called upon to preside over the prayers of the dark assemblage.

Those who administered the plantation under M. de Boré's vigilant eye were his two grandsons, Jean Baptiste and Deschapelles Lebreton, and two Frenchmen as overseers. One of them was Klein d'Alberg, a kinsman of General Klein, who subsequently became a peer of France under Louis Philippe, and whose son, many years after, I met at the palatial residence of the Baroness of Pontalba in Paris—the same lady whose name is so well known in Louisiana, and is connected with the public square on which stands in New Orleans the equestrian statue of General Jackson. The other employé, very small in stature, almost feminine in manner and appearance, the gentlest-tempered, the most modest, the most tender-hearted man I ever knew, was the son of General Duphot, who under the first French republic was assassinated in a riot in Rome, of which the French had taken possession. Each one of those gentlemen had his post of duty assigned to him, and his particular department of supervision, for which he was responsible. Every evening those subordinates came to the "lord and master of all that he surveyed," and rendered him an account of their stewardship. Then they received his orders for the next day.

I do not remember having seen a negro whipped, but I remember having been present when occasionally one of them, for some delinquency, was put in the stocks for the night or during a whole Sunday. This is the principal punishment that I have known to be inflicted. Basile, the commander of the gang, and the most boastful, the most self-important negro who ever trod the earth, although he was invested with but very limited power, was armed with an enormous whip, at least twenty feet in length, which from time to time he cracked portentously over his head with the most terrific emphasis of sound, whilst goading with threatening words

some laggard who he thought did not wield his hoe with sufficient diligence; but I never saw that whip fall on the back of any of the hands. In the field when at work they used to sing in chorus or concert, and there was in those songs a melody which lingers to this day in my heart. I now wish that I had noted down the words and the music which seemed to enliven so much those sons of Africa, and which certainly were their own composition.

This landlord of the old *régime* never raised hogs. I never saw one ranging and grunting at liberty on any portion of his domains. Hog-raising was a monopoly which he left to his negroes. Leading to the sugar-house and its dependencies there was a long and fine avenue of pecan-trees. In a parallel line to it there were the negro quarters, comfortable cabins with fireplaces, and drawn in a double row. Each 'negro had a hog-pen behind his cabin, and his small poultry-yard; each one had also a lot of ground for raising corn, pumpkins, and anything else he pleased. When fat, the hogs were sold at the market price to master or mistress, or to any other bidder, when not slaughtered by their owners for their own alimentation.

The Mississippi in those days, when high, used to carry an immense quantity of drift-wood. On Sundays many of the negroes would draw ashore with ease a quantity of logs, which they cut into cords, and sold to their master for a dollar per cord. If at any time they were forced, for the good of the crop, to do more than their usual task, they were liberally paid for it, or the number of extra hours during which they worked was returned to them out of their ordinary days of labor. They caught catfish, sheep's-head, shrimps, eels in abundance, raccoons, opossums, etc., and in my boyhood, when rambling about their quarters at the time they cooked their meals, my nostrils were frequently regaled with a savory smell. It is certain that they all looked fat and sleek, and none ran away. Therefore they must have been gently treated and well fed. There were among them masons, carpenters, blacksmiths, cartwrights, every other mechanic that might be wanted, and even an excellent shoemaker. So we were perfectly independent of the outward world.

But the negroes did not wear shoes at that antediluvian epoch. They protected their feet with what they called *quan-tiers*, made in this way: The negro would plant his foot on an ox-hide that had undergone a certain preparatory process to soften it. Armed with a flat and keen blade, another negro would cut the hide according to the size and shape of the foot, leaving enough margin to overlap the top of it up to the ankle. Holes were bored into it, and with strips of the same leather this rustic shoe was laced tight to the foot. It was rough and unsightly, but wholesome, like the French *sabot*, or wooden shoe. The foot in a woollen sock, or even bare, when encased in a *quantier* stuffed with rags or hay, was kept remarkably warm and dry. Twice a year there came numerous bales of merchandise—blankets and warm clothing at the beginning of winter, and lighter articles of dress at the beginning of spring. The thick *capot de couverte* was universally used by the negroes, and frequently even by their masters. It was a sort of frock with a hood, and made out of a blanket.

This population of black laborers was for a long time composed only of natives of Louisiana called creole negroes, and of natives of Africa called Banbaras, or by whatever other names that designated the tribes they had belonged to in their country. There were distinct peculiarities and idiosyncrasies among them. On the Boré plantation there was one who pretended that he was a prince, and had ruled over numerous subjects. He was so proud and fiery that he was named Achilles. He looked upon the other negroes as his inferiors, and exacted from them all great demonstrations of respect. When the American negroes, as they were called, began to be introduced—meaning those who came from the United States, to which Louisiana was not yet annexed—they were treated with the utmost contempt, and even deep-rooted aversion, by the creole and African negroes with whom they had to associate. They were looked upon as thieves, and capable of every sort of villanous tricks. Whenever any theft was perpetrated or any other delinquency committed, it was immediately alleged that it was the *Méricain coquin* (the American rogue) who had done it. So they had at first a hard time of it. On the other hand, the *Méricain coquin*, being generally more intelligent than the creole *nigger* and the imported African, was disposed to treat them as fools, and openly asserted his own su-

periority. Thus those black immigrants, when they first came to a Louisiana plantation, rather put things out of joint, from a want of affinity with the sable company into which they were introduced.

On a certain occasion one of those Africans, named Big Congo, a field hand, was the hero of an amusing anecdote. The overseer had sent him to M. de Boré with a message to which an answer was desired. The barbarian returned after a while and informed the overseer that he had found *master* in the parlor, that he had delivered the message, that the *old man* had looked at him straight in the face, but had not answered anything.

"Brute! what story is this?" exclaimed the overseer, getting angry.

"It is true," insisted the negro, in his peculiar lingo, which I translate into English. "Master was in a gold window. He looked at me good, but would not talk."

"What! what! are you drunk?" said the overseer, who was fast losing his temper.

But the negro stuck to it. "Pray come with me," he said, imploringly. "Don't get angry. I will show you master in the gold window."

The overseer went with him, and entering the saloon, found hung up to the wall an oil portrait of Boré in a gilt frame that had just been brought home from the city. The African pointed to it with intense satisfaction in proof of his having told the truth. "*A la li*," he said; "here he is."

It was a living likeness and a fine specimen of art, executed by a most skilful painter named Mouchette, who was on his travels, and merely passing through Louisiana. Big Congo was comically bewildered when assured that no flesh and blood stood before him.

I have already intimated that the former *mousquetaire*, or member of the royal body-guard, and ex-captain of cavalry in the French army, kept up a complete military discipline on his plantation. It is true to the very letter. Every evening after supper sentinels were stationed at every point where depredations might be committed. They were two by two, armed with stout clubs — never a sentinel alone. At midnight they were relieved and replaced by others, and so on in turn, going through the whole gang successively, a new set every night. Thus every trespass, every violation of law or order, was well guarded against.

One day, however, the habitually quiet denizens of the Boré plantation were thrown into commotion. Boré had bought a magnificent pair of carriage-horses. They had not been one week at home when they disappeared at night. The stables were found locked. All the gates of the yard in which stood the stables looked as if their padlocks and bars had not been tampered with. There was not the slightest sign of *effraction* anywhere. The walls could not have been overleaped. The sentinels had seen and heard nothing, and their fidelity was not doubted. The whole affair was extremely mysterious and puzzling. One thing, however, was certain. The thief, who evidently was a most expert one, had only the choice between two roads in his flight—down to the city or up along the bank of the river. On close inspection, tracks were discovered on the way up, and the pursuit began. But the thief had the advantage of several hours in his favor. The stolen horses were fleet, and the thief managed to keep ahead in the race. He had been seen by many, but not suspected. The pursuit ceased at Baton Rouge without success. Unfortunately there were no telegraphs in those days. Our bewildered negroes, unable to account for this bold and extraordinary deed, which appeared marvellous to their superstitious imagination, attributed it to Zombi or Bouki, who rank among the mischievous spirits in which they believe.

A magnificent avenue of pecan-trees led from the public road alongside the bank of the river to the vast enclosure within which stood the house of M. de Boré, with its numerous dependencies. That part of the enclosure which faced the river presented a singular appearance when approached from the public road through the avenue of pecan-trees. It was that of a fortified place, for there was to be seen, with a revetement of brick five feet high, a rampart of earth about fifteen feet in width and sloping down to large moats filled with water and well stocked with frogs, fish, and eels. The rampart was clothed in clover, and at its foot, on the edge of the moats, there grew a palisade of the plant known in Louisiana under the name of "Spanish-daggers," through which it would not have been easy to escalade the parapet. In their

season of efflorescence their numerous clusters of white flowers were beautiful. They stood in bold relief from their background of green clover, and towered proudly above the stout and sharp-pointed leaves by which they were protected. This picturesque and uncommon line of fortified enclosure extended a good deal more than three hundred feet on both sides of the entrance gate that opened into the court-yard at the end of the pecan avenue. This may have been in reminiscence of France, where such château-like sights were frequent. On the opposite side, in front of this line of enclosure, there was another, consisting of a well-trimmed and thick orange hedge four feet in height. Beyond were the gardens and several alleys of superb grown-up orange-trees, gorgeous in turn, according to the season, with their snowy blossoms and their golden apples, reminding one of the fabled ones of the Hesperides.

Whenever the pecans began to ripen, this grand avenue from the public road to the house was invaded by thousands of crows, which broke the shells of the nuts with their strong beaks, and ate the luscious substance inside. The incessant *caw, caw*, could have been heard, it seems to me, at the distance of a mile or two. No Englishman could have boasted of a more splendid rookery. The crows were as talkative and boisterous as politicians on election day.

Among the sensational occurrences which I remember whilst a boy, and enjoying the sweet spring life of youth on the Boré plantation, was the shock of an earthquake, which was distinctly felt in lower Louisiana—the same which so terrified New Madrid, further up on the Mississippi. Next came the tremendous hurricane which did so much damage below the city, in the parish of Plaquemines, by causing the river to overflow, and by precipitating the waters of the Gulf upon the low lands, whereby many families were drowned. This hurricane was a fine specimen of the kind, and raged on our plantation with fearful sublimity. It began early in the morning. A dense pell-mell mass of white and dark clouds, strangely mixed, under the whip and spur of a furious wind, was driven in a helter-skelter race so close to the earth that a tall man might have fancied that he could touch it with his hand. I remember to have repeatedly and gleefully jumped up as if to accomplish it myself, although a little boy, and whenever the irresistible grasp of the hurricane, lifting me above the ground, carried me onward ten or twelve feet, and tumbled me down heels over head on the greensward, I shrieked with delight. There was not a drop of rain; it was all blow. When night came, the battering blows of the giant became more terrific. The house shook to its very foundations, and in every point of its structure. It seemed to be assailed by an infuriated multitude of winds that rushed from every quarter of the horizon to engage in a demoniacal conflict on our premises. Notwithstanding this war of the elements, I had fallen asleep, when my father waked me up suddenly, and apparently in great alarm carried me in his arms to what was probably thought a safer portion of the building.

My family was at the Boré plantation when, in the afternoon of the 23d of December, 1814, General Jackson was informed that the British had landed in Louisiana, and that a portion of their troops had been seen on the Villeré plantation below the city. I was then at the College of Orleans, corner of St. Claude and Bayou Road, *alias* Hospital Street, when, at 3 o'clock P.M., a great commotion was observed within its learned precincts. All studies were suspended; the class-rooms shut up; the pupils hurrying to and fro in evident alarm; parents pouring in and taking their children away. My cousin, Frédéric Foucher, the son of Pierre Foucher, and myself were beginning to fear our being forgotten and left to shift for ourselves, instead of being as well cared for as most of our companions —both our families being six miles above the city, and ignorant of the exciting news —when there came a messenger from Madame Porée, the sister of Pierre Foucher, and the aunt of Frédéric, to tender us the shelter of her house at the corner of Dumaine and Royal streets, which is still in existence, with the same antiquated front painted yellow, and with the same balcony on which the two boys stood and saw Major Plauché's battalion of uniformed, well-equipped, and well-drilled militia pass under it. That corps was composed of the *élite* of the young men of the city— *la jeunesse dorée*—and it seems to me that I see now as vividly as I saw then the handsome Edmond Foucher conspicuous

in the ranks of those who were thus marching rapidly to meet the enemy. Looking up to the balcony, he saluted his old aunt with a cheerful smile and a wave of the hand that seemed intended to comfort her and dispel her alarms.

At seven o'clock the battle began, and the roar of the artillery, with the discharges of musketry, was almost as distinctly heard as if in our immediate neighborhood. There was not the slightest noise in the apparently dead city. It held its breath in awful suspense. There was not a human being to be seen moving in the streets. We, the two boys and the ladies of the household, petrified into absolute silence by the apprehensions of the moment, stood on the balcony until half past nine, when the firing gradually ceased. But still we continued to remain on the same spot; for what was to happen? Were our defenders retreating, pursued by the enemy? These were hours of anxiety never to be forgotten. About eleven o'clock the oppressive silence in the city was broken by the furiously rapid gallop of a horseman shouting as loud as he could, "Victory! victory!" He turned from Chartres Street into Dumaine, and from Dumaine into Royal, still shouting "Victory!" The voice had become hoarse, and yet no human voice that I ever afterward heard was fraught with more sweet music. That night we went to bed with thankful hearts. The two boys soon slept soundly, as boys sleep, with that blissful unconcern which appertains to their age. But I doubt if our kind hostess and her daughters closed their eyes, for they had husbands, brothers, sons, on the battlefield, and they did not know at what cost to them the victory had been achieved.

Early the next morning the two boys departed to meet their respective families, one on the Foucher plantation and the other on the adjacent plantation of Boré. The 9th of January was to be the tenth anniversary of my coming into this world. In the morning of the preceding day the famous battle of the 8th was fought on the plains of Chalmette, four miles below the city. In a bee-line the distance must have been very short between the field of action and the Boré plantation, six miles above New Orleans by the windings of the river, for the furious cannonading and the discharges of musketry were prodigiously distinct. The ladies of the family, pale with the natural emotions of fear produced by the dangers of the situation, were grouped on the broad gallery in front of the house. No man was visible, for the only one who had remained at home (on account of his age) had, when the battle began, ascended with slow but firm steps a flight of stairs which led to the top of the portico. At every volley of artillery or musketry I flung myself on the floor, exclaiming, "Ten Englishmen killed!" "Twenty Englishmen flat on the ground!" and so on. I continued rejoicing in the fancied destruction of our invaders, notwithstanding the remonstrances of my poor mother, in whose alarm I very little participated. The battle had not yet ended when my grandfather Boré came down from his post of observation with the same measured step and the same self-possession with which he had ascended, and said to his daughters, who anxiously interrogated his looks, "Dismiss your fears; the Americans are victorious."

"But, father, how do you know it?" inquired my mother.

"You forget, my dear child," replied M. de Boré, with a calm smile, "that I have some military experience. My practised ear has not been deceived, I am sure. The American guns have silenced the English guns. The enemy is defeated."

These words had hardly been spoken when, in the long avenue of pecan-trees that led to the river, there appeared a troop of about a hundred men rushing toward the house. "The English! here come the English!" was the simultaneous cry of the women. M. de Boré stretched himself up to his full height, shaded his eyes with his hand, and after having looked steadily at the advancing crowd, said, contemptuously, "These men the English! bah!"

They came rapidly to the piazza, about six feet high, on which we stood, and along which ran a wooden balustrade. M. de Boré did not understand one word of the language spoken by these unexpected visitors, whose ragamuffin appearance was no recommendation. But if they were bandits, it was comfortable to see that they all were unarmed.

"Who are they, and what do they want?" inquired M. de Boré, surveying them evidently with no friendly eye. He was informed by one of his family that they were fugitives who reported that the Americans had been completely routed, that they themselves were a portion of the defeated, and that they begged

for food. The blood ran to the cheeks of the old soldier, his eyes flashed, and he shouted in French to the men: "You lie! The Americans are victorious. You have run away; you are cowards. Never shall it be said that I gave a hospitable welcome to dastardly fugitives from the battle-field. Hence, all of you, or I will call my negroes to drive you away." His words were not comprehended, but his indignant wrath was visible, and his pantomime was expressive. One of the beggarly crew seemed to apprehend his meaning, for he took off his hat and pointed with his index finger to a hole which looked as if made by a ball. He no doubt intended to intimate that he had faced danger, and that he was not as cowardly as supposed. In making this exhibition he had approached close to the piazza and held his hat aloft. The old gentleman retreated a few steps; then rushing back to the balustrade of the piazza, on which he leaned forward, and looking down upon the suppliant below, shouted: "In thy hat! in thy hat!"—striking his breast violently—"*there* is where the ball should have been received, and not through thy hat, when probably thy back was turned to the enemy. No! no food for cowards. There is food in the British camp; go and get it."

He was superb at that moment, and turning his back upon the pitiful-looking postulants, he kept up pacing the piazza like a chafed lion in a cage. My mother followed him a few feet behind, as he walked to and fro with a hurried step, and thus expostulated all the while:

"Father, they look so miserable."

"No! no food for cowards. I have said it."

"They seem to be so jaded and hungry."

"No! I say no!"

"Father, they are so wet, and shivering with cold."

"No! no food for fugitives from the field of honor."

"But, father," continued my mother, in a piteous tone, "they may not have fled, after all. Perhaps they only retreated."

Grandfather, wheeling round, with a smile on his lips, and with the usual expression of benevolence on his face, said: "Daughter, I am inflexible. No food shall *I* give to those wretches. But I am going away, and in my absence *you* may deal as you please with those heroes of retreat" (*avec ces héros de la retraite*). True to his word, he disappeared, and was not seen for the remainder of the day.

Meanwhile the little boy, who has grown up to be the octogenarian who writes these lines, had a grand time of it, for big fires were lighted over the vast court-yard, calves and sheep were killed and roasted, huge pots of hominy and of rice were prepared; and he keenly enjoyed the *barbecue*, if he may be permitted to use this well-known modern expression, that was given to those men, who were a detachment of the Kentuckians that had fled from Colonel Thornton's attack upon General Morgan's command on the right bank of the river, as related in history.

When the war was over, the Tennesseeans, before they were permitted to go home, encamped for some time on the plantation adjacent to the lower line of the Boré plantation. That plantation then belonged, or had belonged, to the Ducros family, and subsequently became the property of Captain Beale, who at the head of the Orleans Riflemen had distinguished himself under General Jackson in the defence of our city. Beale had married a daughter of the Spanish Governor, Don Carlos de Grandpré.

Generals Coffee and Carroll, who commanded the division of the Tennessee troops, together with their military suite, were tendered by M. de Boré the hospitality of his house, where they were luxuriously entertained for several months. General Jackson was a frequent visitor, and the writer of these lines, although more than once kindly patted on the head by the hero, remembers that he stood much in awe of the warrior who was reported to have killed so many men. I remember even to have been considerably excited on one occasion, when he, jestingly no doubt, proposed to my mother to take me with him to Tennessee. On that day I felt strongly inclined to begin hostilities against the hero.

As a social incident, I may be at liberty to mention that at dinner, the dessert being over and coffee served, M. de Boré would rise and retire with the ladies, after having with a bow taken leave of his military guests, whom he left to the enjoyment of their bottles of wine placed on the "bare mahogany," after the American fashion. The same formality was observed every day. This convivial privilege seemed to be relished by those officers, who frequently would linger an hour round the board, conversing freely together in a language entirely unknown to the family of whose hospitality they partook. They were courteous and tolerably well-bred, gentlemanly in many respects, but some of them had peculiar habits, among which the most eccentric was for one of them to throw himself back in his chair and elevate his feet to the level of the table, on which these extremities of the human body were made to repose in apparent comfort. If anybody happened to indulge in a sneering remark on the subject, M. de Boré would deprecatingly say, with a gentle smile: "*Eh bien! Que voulez-vous? Ils n'en savent pas davantage. C'est la coutume de leur pays.*" As to General Jackson, he was conspicuous for his courtly manners. It was due to instinct or inspiration. He was nature's nobleman.

Breakfast was at eight in the morning, dinner at two P.M., and supper at seven in the evening. It was seldom that there was not some guest or guests at every one of those meals, either from the immediate neighborhood or from distant parts. In those days travelling between New Orleans and Baton Rouge, now the capital of the State, and both situated on the left bank of the Mississippi, was generally on horseback, or in a land vehicle of some sort; rarely by water. Some of the planters who lived at a distance of thirty or forty miles from New Orleans drove to it with four in hand, and it was not merely for show, considering that the road was occasionally in a very poor condition. All of them knew very well that they would offend if they passed by the Boré plantation without stopping to rest for the night, or at least to take refreshments. Peddlers going up or down what was then called the "Coast," carrying their wares on their backs or in carts, and in boats pulled up against the current *à la cordelle*—that is to say, by a rope thrown over the shoulders of men who footed it on the levee—frequently halted at Boré's gates with full reliance on the hospitality of the old *mousquetaire*. They always found a comfortable room at their service, and were kindly admitted to the family table. They belonged by virtue of their white skin to the aristocratic class, and it was the prevailing feeling not to degrade the poorest and humblest of the Caucasian race by lowering him to the level of the servile blacks.

In this matter there was no difference of treatment in the homes of our wealthiest planters. This democratic hospitality was universal. Was it because there was no democracy, and because social position was unquestionably better defined than at present? Certain it is that those who at a more recent epoch were qualified with the appellation of "white trash" never or seldom suffered in the old *régime* from the insolence of birth, rank, or wealth. Almost all of those peddlers were foreigners, and it has been more than once my pleasant luck, in the course of years, to meet them or their descendants in palatial mansions both in New York and in Paris, or to hail their elevation to high official station in Louisiana.

Before retiring for the night all the members of the family respectfully saluted M. de Boré, and affectionately greeted one another. The same ceremony was repeated in the morning. It was a rule not to be infringed, and it had the good effect of preventing quarrels from being of long duration, for a reconciliation not merely apparent, but real, no doubt, would soon have been a forced conclusion. As to myself, boy that I was, in return for a kiss on my forehead I imprinted my lips on his caressing and paternal hand morning and evening, as if he had been a monarch to whom I paid a willing homage. I never heard him use a harsh word. His blue eye was calm and benevolent; but although I was inclined to have too strong a will of my own, yet such was the loving awe with which I regarded him that I would have preferred facing an infuriated bull than incur his displeasure, and I am conscious that the same feeling of veneration was shared by all those who approached him and fell within the reach of his moral influence.

He occupied at the table of refection a seat larger than any other, and appropriated to his own special use. It was placed at the centre of the long table, my mother sitting in front. When the bell rang, he was very punctual. His habit was to stand up a minute or two, until everybody was at his respective post. Then he waved his hand as an invitation to sit, and all sat down. After this had been done, any vacant seat remained unoccupied, because the slothful delinquent shrank from encountering a cold rebuke.

It was a fundamental rule that the Police Jury of the parish should meet at the sugar-house of M. de Boré, and after adjourning, repair to his mansion for dinner. Whilst waiting for the convivial hour, the guests either remained gossiping on the broad piazza—I will not say *smoking*, for I never saw on such occasions the indulgence of so rare a habit at that epoch—or entertained themselves in the billiard-room. For any one of them to have retired before having staid to dinner would have been an infraction of decorous regard not to be thought of for one instant. Once, however, after the sitting of the Police Jury was over, and most of its members had assembled on the piazza, waiting for the grateful sound of the dinner-bell, one of that body, who had lingered at the sugar-house, was seen approaching on horseback, and wheeling into the pecan avenue which led to the public road, instead of coming to the house, where was the rest of the company.

"Who is he that is going away without taking leave of us?" asked M. de Boré, shading his eyes with his hand, the better to see.

"It is Mr. Avart," answered somebody.

"Well," exclaimed the old gentleman, "I will favor him with a lesson that will, I hope, turn to his profit." He jumped on a chair, on which he stood as erect and conspicuous as possible, and shouted to the horseman who was slowly trotting away, "Mr. Avart! Mr. Avart!" The person thus addressed stopped and turned round as if to respond to the call. "No, no!" continued M. de Boré; "don't come back! don't come back! I hailed you merely to request you to carry my respects to your family"—with still greater emphasis—"my respects to your family! That's all. Now you may go."

M. de Boré, although of the old *régime*, was an enthusiastic admirer of Napoleon. He had in his parlor a fine engraving of the battle of Austerlitz at the moment when General Rapp, on horseback and bareheaded, rushes with fiery haste into the presence of the Emperor, shouting, "Victory! victory! the enemy is annihilated!" To which Napoleon replies, "I never saw thee, Rapp, looking so handsome." My father, born in Louisiana, was of Spanish origin, and loyal to his race to the very core of his heart. At the head of his bed there was hung up in a wooden frame his old coat of arms, in which figured the crowned head of Sultan Abderahman, defeated in the valley of Roncal, in Navarre, when attempting to cross the Pyrenees and penetrate into France, about the year 800 of our Lord. When Napoleon pushed his legions into Spain, Don Carlos Gayarré suppressed his feelings in the presence of his father-in-law, and out of respect for him. But at the announcement of any French triumph in the land of his ancestors he would retire moodily to the privacy of his bedchamber; then the angry tones of a guitar were heard, and a manly voice sang all those patriotic hymns which responded to the popular cry of "Death to the foe! war to the knife, and the knife to the hilt!" Thus the same family presented a rather strange compound. M. de Boré, the noble of the old *régime* and *mousquetaire* in the household troops of a Bourbon king, carried away by military enthusiasm, had become an imperialist and Bonapartist; Pierre Foucher, one of his sons-in-law, was a red republican, who had no liking for kings and priests; the other son, my father, was an intense royalist. And yet they all lived in perfect harmony, which shows that they possessed at least a large fund of good-breeding and forbearance.

There bubbles up in my memory at the present moment the recollection of an anecdote concerning this *mousquetaire* grandfather of mine. There was in France, under the reign of Louis XV., a bright-complexioned and educated mulatto from San Domingo or some other French West Indian island. He was named St.-George, and is mentioned in some of the memoirs of the epoch as the most wonderful fencer that had ever appeared since the famous Creighton. Like this prototype, so far as manly exercises went, he was as skilful a shot as a swordsman. At twenty paces he never failed to hit a small nail on the head. He swam like a fish; and as to his feats of horsemanship, they were prodigious. One night, at a theatre in Paris, M. de Boré having the bad luck of displeasing a gentleman who occupied the next seat to his, they went out and crossed swords in the street by the light of the lamp-post. This was the way at that epoch to settle the slightest unpleasantness of this kind. M. de Boré was soon run through the body and stretched on his back. He was, however, consoled by the information that if vanquished, it had been by the invulnerable St.-George. This col-

ored duellist, who acquired quite a reputation for his exploits, as such, never was even scratched in his innumerable encounters. But it is reported that, on his having succeeded in obtaining a commission in the French army, he showed the white feather in the first general engagement with the enemy. On that occasion he felt, no doubt, that the marvellous skill on which he had hitherto so successfully relied could be of no avail to parry death.

M. de Boré was about thirty-two years old when he obtained permission to pay a second visit to Louisiana, where he was destined to settle at last and end his career. He was ready to embark, when he received the following note from the Comtesse de Rochechouart Montboissier, the wife of the Minister of War, addressed to him as *Mousquetaire Noir, à la Rochelle, Hôtel du Bien Nourri* (hotel of the well fed). These guardsmen were called black on account of the color of the horses they mounted.

"Paris, 9th January, 1772.

"It is with great pleasure, sir, that I have undertaken to inform you that the commission of Captain which you seemed so much to desire has been granted to you *par le dernier travail de M. de Montboissier*. When the brevet is ready, he will forward it to you. He is very glad to have been able to render you this service. We both wish you a happy voyage and a speedy return to us, after having arranged your affairs in that country sufficiently to your satisfaction. If it should be possible for you to send me a hundred feathers like those with which you had the kindness to favor me, my obligation to you would be very great. The trimming of my dress is finished; it is superb; and as I am afraid of losing some of the feathers, I should be happy to be able to replace them. I beg to be excused for thus taxing too much your gallantry and generosity, for you have given me such a large quantity of those feathers that it looks as if I needed no more. I return to you my thanks in advance, and I entreat you to be convinced of the very great sincerity of the sentiments with which I have the honor to be, sir, your very humble and very obedient servant.

"Rochechouart de Montboissier.

"P.S.—M. de Montboissier requests me to address to you a thousand compliments on his behalf."

Now that it is the raging fashion for women to adorn themselves so much with feathers of all sorts, it would probably interest our Louisianians of the fair sex to know, if possible, what were those colonial feathers which so vividly excited the gratitude of Comtesse Rochechouart de Montboissier, and no doubt the admiration of the court of Versailles in the days of Louis XV., one hundred and fourteen years ago.

On the Boré plantation, midway between the river bank and the cypress swamp, there was a depression in the land, where, in consequence of it, a large pond of standing water had been formed. All around this pond to some distance the soil was of a marshy nature, full of tall weeds, sheltering a multitude of wild game, such as snipes, water-hens, rails, etc. The portion of the ground beyond the marsh, extending to the forest, with another gradual depression, was cultivated, and called *La Terre Haute* (the high land), although it was not more elevated than the other part running to the public road and the river on the other side of the pond and its immediate surroundings of reeds. This expression was used, we suppose, as a mere designation of the locality situated beyond the intervening low lands. This pond and marshy ground was a famous shooting spot at that epoch. During the winter it was the resort of innumerable flocks of ducks, that successively came to it in the evening until it was completely dark. As they passed over their expected shelter, probably for examination before alighting, the ambuscaded hunters rose from their concealment and emptied their guns. Hence this was called *La Passée.*

This pond, known far and wide, was called *La Mare à Boré* (the Boré pond). In any other country this sporting ground would have been jealously guarded, but in Louisiana this would have been looked upon with extreme disfavor. Hence this pond, or *Mare à Boré,* was treated as public property, without any interference from the owner. On Saturdays in particular, late in the afternoon, there used to come quite a battalion from New Orleans, mostly composed of the *élite* of the population of that city—lawyers, physicians, commission merchants, brokers, bankers, *e tutti quanti.* Among the members of the bar, Mazureau and John R. Grymes, who were celebrities, and Morel, also distinguished, may be cited as the most prominent. On such occasions we could hear from our dwelling-house a lively rattle of gun-firing, as if a skirmish was going on. Some even camped there, to be ready for the sport early on the next morning.

Fires were lighted, tents erected, and the comforts and wants of the human body attended to with proper care. Sober and grave heads of families of high social standing, when in their hunting dress, not unfrequently thought themselves free to assume the liberties of a somewhat rakish crew; jokes were cracked, tales related by the blazing piles, pranks perpetrated, and to speak the unpleasant truth, there ensued, although rarely, quarrels that led to duels. Page after page could be written about the many occurrences which in those days contributed to the fame of *La Mare à Boré.* The negroes themselves had all sorts of tales to relate about it. Their superstitious imagination, which is always at work, connected that spot with hobgoblins and apparitions, among others the ghost of a colossal raccoon that seems to have claimed special jurisdiction over *La Mare à Boré.*

Once or twice a year there was on the plantation an occurrence which excited the most intense interest, particularly among the youthful portion of the population, white and black. It was when a drove of wild horses came from Texas or some other Mexican territory. Those animals looked so fiery and ungovernable that they seemed to have the devil himself in their bodies, and the men who led and owned them were evidently the denizens of some weird wilderness. They wore the broad Spanish *sombrero,* or hat; their faces were bronzed, and their eyes dark and piercing. They wore soft leather gaiters up to the knee, and that part of their breeches which was destined to an inevitable friction when they rode was lined also with leather. Stout and rough-looking brogans enveloped the foot up to the ankle, and their heels were armed with spurs six inches long, called *rakachias.* At their sight the joyous exclamation was heard, "Here are the *ouachinangs!*" All the juvenility of the locality and its neighborhood clapped their palms and shouted in anticipation of fun. These horses were for sale, and driven from plantation to plantation, where a market for some of them was always found.

It is remarkable how trifling events, apparently not worth remembering for more than a day, remain fresh in one's memory during a long life. Who knows what subtle influence for good or for evil such things may have ? May not what appeared to the youthful mind but an un-

meaning incident yet contribute by an
unfelt process to the formation of character, and to habits of deportment in after-
years? One day as our family, seated on
the front piazza, was enjoying the balmy
atmosphere of a bright May morning,
there came on a visit from New Orleans
M. de Boré's favorite nephew, whose
name was Bernard de Marigny. He was
one of the most brilliant and wealthiest
young men of the epoch. He drove in a
dashing way to the house in an elegant
equipage drawn by two fiery horses. Full
of the buoyancy of youth, he jumped out
of his carriage and ran up the broad steps
of the brick *perron* that ascended to the piazza. As he reached the top of it he said,
with a sort of careless and joyous familiarity, "*Bonjour, mon oncle, bonjour,*" and
bowed slightly round to the family without removing his hat. "*Chapeau bas,
monsieur!*" responded a calm voice of
command. "*Toujours chapeau bas de-
vant une femme, et il y en a plus d'une
ici.*" (Hat off, sir! Always hat off before a woman, and there are more than
one here.) A fitting apology was instantly made by the youthful delinquent. Was
the old *mousquetaire*, or guardsman, in-
fluenced on that occasion, unknowingly
to himself, by the remembered example
of Louis XIV., the gorgeous "*roi soleil,*"
who never failed to bow to any woman,
whatever her condition, whom he chanced
to meet?

As to Madame de Boré, I was so young
when she died that I have no distinct recollection of her. There remains in my
mind but a sort of dim vision of a lady
seated near a small round table with a
white marble top encircled by a diminutive copper railing of half an inch in
height. On that table there used to be a
work-basket, and also a beautiful gold
snuff-box in what is called the style Louis
Quinze. I long preserved that snuff-box
with infinite care; but during the war of
secession a light-colored slave of the name
of Wilson, whom I had drilled to be as accomplished a servant as could be found in
any luxurious home, logically came to
the conclusion that I was getting too poor
to need his talents any more, and to satisfy his own epicurean tastes by high living. He had taught himself to read and
write, and having by this means risen
above the prejudices of his former ignorance, he determined to secede from me,
and with much prudential foresight he

suddenly and clandestinely departed, with
my grandmother's snuff-box, together
with an additional supply of diamonds
and other trinkets. Being tender-footed
and accustomed to ride like a gentleman,
he considerately took two of my best
mules, one for himself and one for a companion whom he invited to join him, for
he always was very fond of society. After having disposed of the mules in a way
of which I know nothing, he carried the
rest of his plunder to New York, where he
completed his education, and then returned to New Orleans. He now flourishes
here like a green bay-tree, and is constantly employed as an indispensable attendant
at balls and dinner parties given in the
fashionable world. Considering his in-
contestable abilities, the seduction of his
winning manners, and his everlasting
smile, which would have secured him
much profitable success in a certain line
of business, I feel under no small degree
of obligation to him for not having turned politician, and plundered the State with
as much dexterity and impunity as he
plundered me. It shows great modera-
tion on his part, for which he is to be commended.

But to return to Madame de Boré, who
had been educated at Versailles in the
St.-Cyr Institution, founded by Madame
de Maintenon. She must have been a
prodigy of fascination, if I am to believe
the old men who so frequently described
her to me. One of them once exclaimed
in a fit of enthusiasm, interrupted by an
octogenarian cough, "*Cela eut valu la
peine de faire cinquante lieues seule-
ment pour voir Madame de Boré prendre
une prise de tabac*" (it would have been
worth while to travel fifty leagues merely
to see Madame de Boré take a pinch of
snuff).

Another admirer related to me the following anecdote as a specimen of her tact
and dignity. In those days, which we may
call remote, because between that past and
the present there seems to be a lapse of
five hundred years, it was the invariable
custom at a set dinner to have the dessert
enlivened by songs from the male guests.
Once it happened that one of them hazarded a song which would not have been
objectionable to a generation familiar with
La Belle Hélène and *La Fille de Madame
Angot.* It seemed indelicate to Madame de
Boré. She hastened to interrupt the singer with these words: "Sir, I am so charm-

ed with your song that I cannot resist the impulse to toast you at once. Ladies and gentlemen, fill your glasses, and let us drink to the singer's health." It was difficult to convey reproof more gracefully.

Years had elapsed. I was in Paris, and visiting an aged relative of mine, a Louisianian, in her palatial mansion, Avenue de Marigny. I was alone with her in the reception saloon. In front of us, in a smaller saloon, in sight but not within hearing, there were two of her married daughters with the Comte de Talvande and the old Prince de Bethune—he whose red tomato face, strikingly framed with a profusion of snow-white beard and hair, was so exquisitely and amusingly reproduced in terra-cotta by Cham, the artist, and exposed in so many of the glass windows of Parisian shops. I noticed that my relative would now and then cast an uneasy glance at the group, who were talking and laughing a little rompishly. At last she said to me: "I am thinking of Aunt Boré. What would she have thought of such manners? One day a gentleman offered me a bouquet in her presence. She intercepted it before I could take it, and said to him, 'I thank you on behalf of my niece; but it would have been better to have presented the bouquet to me with a request to hand it over to her." I have mentioned these anecdotes as illustrative of an epoch which has passed away forever. I close what I have to say about this lady of the old *régime* by mentioning that my mother assured me of her never having been able to discover the smallest speck of a cloud in the conjugal sky of her parents.

M. de Boré had two male cooks with the necessary aids; one was a negro, and the other of a lighter color. The negroes are born cooks, as other less favored beings are born poets. The African brute, guided by the superior intelligence of his Caucasian master, in the days of slavery in Louisiana, gradually evolved into an artist of the highest degree of excellence, and had from natural impulses and affinities, without any conscious analysis of principles, created an art of cooking for which he should deserve to be immortalized. And how is it possible to convey to this dyspeptic posterity of our ancestors, to a thin-blooded population whose stomach has been ruined by kitchen charlatans, sauce and gravy pretenders, kettle and pot druggists, any idea of the miracles of the old creole cooking transmitted from colonial days, and growing fainter and fainter in dim traditions which have no meaning and no sense for this coarse-feeding generation? It had nothing in common with the much-vaunted culinary science of France. It was *sui generis;* it was not imitative; there was no traditionary lore about its origin; it had no ancestry; it sprang from itself. Pierre or Valentin, the colored cook, had not been taught by any missionary from foreign climes; he had not studied the records of roasting, baking, and boiling from the age of Abraham to the days of Master Jean or Mistress Jeanne on the banks of the Mississippi. He could neither read nor write, and therefore he could not learn from books. He was simply inspired; the god of the spit and the saucepan had breathed into him; that was enough. Good heavens! with what supreme, indescribable contempt would Aunt Henriette or Uncle Frontin have looked down upon the best French *cordon bleu* that had presumed to teach her or him! Sufficient to say that Marc Antony, if he had known a creole cook of the old *régime*, would have given him two or three of his best Asiatic provinces as a reward for feasting Cleopatra.

Gombo file! Gombo févis! Gombo aux herbes! Gombo chevrettes, ou aux huitres! What do these things mean at present but vapidity of taste, instead of the licking of one's lips? And the soups? —the soups! not a ghost of them lingering on earth. Who knows how to roast? Who knows how to season *juste à point?* And the flavor?—the flavor! whither has it evaporated? How many delicious dishes have vanished forever of which the best cooks of France have never dreamed! To invent them it had required the constantly improving genius of several generations of apron-girt Sambos. Where is the last of them? What of a turkey fattened, stuffed, and roasted by him? Who but Sambo knew how to bake rice in an iron pot? I say *iron*, because it must be nothing else, and that rice must come out solid, retaining the exact shape of the pot, with a golden crust round its top and sides. You think this easy, presumptuous mortal. Well, try it, and let us see if your farinaceous production will have its required shape and color, and its precise proportion of salt and lard. I give it to you in a thousand. Who but Sambo ever made *grillades de sang de dinde,* looking and tasting like truffles? What a sauce! Where did he get that sublime composition? But time and space do not permit me to continue a description which, after all, is inadequately descriptive. I will content myself with saying that black Pierrot or yellow Charlotte, as a cook in the days of the Egyptian flesh-pots in Louisiana, is not within the comprehension of any one born since the firing of the first gun against Fort Sumter. The effort must be given up. It would be attempting to grasp the infinite space. The last Brutus, alas! perished with the liberties of Rome, and what is perhaps more deplorable, the last creole cook could not survive the acquisition of his own liberty in Louisiana.

The furniture of M. de Boré, although abundant and comfortable, was very plain when compared with the exigencies of modern times. It was in the style of simplicity which prevailed in the dwellings of the wealthiest planters; but the table and the wines were superb. Every Sunday there were regularly, without any special invitation, a dozen or two of guests, who generally came from New Orleans. Among them the most assiduous were some Knights of St. Louis, who on such occasions never failed to carry their decoration dangling from the button-hole, such, for instance, as the Hazures, two brothers who dwelt, I believe, near Bayou St. John, on the Gentilly road. There was something in all those waifs of another age—in their appearance, in their dress, in their physiognomy, in their manners, in their peculiarities of conversation and language, in their bows and greetings, in their accent and modulations of voice— something which produced on me the most vivid impressions. They were monuments of the past, pyramids not in stones and cement, but in flesh and bones. There was in them what might have been called a lofty *je ne sais quoi*, to use a French locution. These men of the old *régime* seemed to entertain more esteem and respect for one another than we do now for our contemporaries. They evidently loved more to look up than to look down. They were not prodigal of their demonstrations of regard, but when expressed, it could be relied on as sincere, for they never hesitated to manifest their feeling of antipathy, reprobation, or opposition when necessary. As I grew in years I became

more deeply struck with the faith which the men of that epoch reposed in one another, the more so because of the universal distrust of man's honor and integrity which I have observed spreading in later times over the whole surface of our community, like a stain of oil over a piece of carpeting. Well do I recollect when, in my youth, I delighted to listen to the conversation of those old men who still lingered on the stage after the days for acting were past. When they engaged in discussions on some point or other, I have sometimes seen the controversy settled at once by one of them observing, "I remember M. de Boré having said so and so on this matter." "Ah, indeed! did he say so?" "Certainly." "Well, then, of course—" And there was no more questioning of this and that.

"A change has come over the spirit of my dream." The scenes I have witnessed, the things I have seen, have vanished forever. There is not a vestige, not a wreck's fragment, left of the Boré plantation, save myself, standing alone in the arid and parched wilderness of the past, forgotten, but trying in vain to forget and to close my eyes to the shapeless shadows that beckon me away. But enough. M. de Boré died seventy-eight years old. When on his death-bed, at his very last moments, he summoned me, boy that I still was, to his presence. Putting his hands on his grandson's head, he blessed him, and gave him his parting instructions and recommendations with a firm voice, a serene brow, a clear limpid eye, through which his soul eloquently spoke. I will repeat only his very last words: "Let no temptation ever betray you out of the path of honor and virtue. Keep your conscience always free from self-reproach, so that your death may be as calm as mine. Trusting in the mercy of God, I fear not to appear before His tribunal, where I hope not to grieve for you, when in due time we are to meet again, and when you shall render your accounts to Him. Farewell! Let your motto in this world ever be, '*Sans peur et sans reproche.*'"

M. de Boré ordered that his funeral and his tomb be as plain as could decently be, but that a thousand dollars, which might be spent in these vanities, be saved for a better use, and given to the Charity Hospital of New Orleans. It was done according to his request.

THE SOUTH REVISITED

IN speaking again of the South in this Monthly, after an interval of about two years, and as before at the request of the editor, I shrink a good deal from the appearance of forwardness which a second paper may seem to give to observations which have the single purpose of contributing my mite toward making the present spirit of the Southern people, their progress in industries and in education, their aspirations, better known. On the other hand, I have no desire to escape the imputation of a warm interest in the South, and of a belief that its development and prosperity are essential to the greatness and glory of the nation. Indeed, no one can go through the South, with his eyes open, without having his patriotic fervor quickened and broadened, and without increased pride in the republic.

We are one people. Different traditions, different education or the lack of it, the demoralizing curse of slavery, different prejudices, made us look at life from irreconcilable points of view; but the prominent common feature, after all, is our Americanism. In any assembly of gentlemen from the two sections the resemblances are greater than the differences. A score of times I have heard it said, "We look alike, talk alike, feel alike; how strange it is we should have fought!" Personal contact always tends to remove prejudices, and to bring into prominence the national feeling, the race feeling, the human nature common to all of us.

I wish to give as succinctly as I can the general impressions of a recent six weeks' tour, made by a company of artists and writers, which became known as the "Harper party," through a considerable portion of the South, including the cities of Lynchburg, Richmond, Danville, Atlanta, Augusta (with a brief call at Charleston and Columbia, for it was not intended to take in the eastern seaboard on this trip), Knoxville, Chattanooga, South Pittsburg, Nashville, Birmingham, Montgomery, Pensacola, Mobile, New Orleans, Baton Rouge, Vicksburg, Memphis, Louisville. Points of great interest were necessarily omitted in a tour which could only include representatives of the industrial and educational development of the New South. Naturally we were thrown more with business men and with educators than with others; that is, with those who are actually making the New South; but we saw something of social life, something of the homes and mode of living of every class, and we had abundant opportunities of conversation with whites and blacks of every social grade and political affinity. The Southern people were anxious to show us what they were doing, and they expressed their sentiments with entire frankness; if we were misled, it is our own fault. It must be noted, however, in estimating the value of our observations, that they were mainly made in cities and large villages, and little in the country districts.

Inquiries in the South as to the feeling of the North show that there is still left some misapprehension of the spirit in which the North sent out its armies, though it is beginning to be widely understood that the North was not animated by hatred of the South, but by intense love of the Union. On the other hand, I have no doubt there still lingers in the North a little misapprehension of the present feeling of the Southern people about the Union. It arises from a confusion of two facts which it is best to speak of plainly. Everybody knows that the South is heartily glad that slavery is gone, and that a new era of freedom has set in. Everybody who knows the South at all is aware that any idea of any renewal of the strife, now or at any time, is nowhere entertained, even as a speculation, and that to the women especially, who are said to be first in war, last in peace, and first in the hearts of their countrymen, the idea of war is a subject of utter loathing. The two facts to which I refer are the loyalty of the Southern whites to the Union, and their determination to rule in domestic affairs. Naturally there are here and there soreness and some bitterness over personal loss and ruin, life-long grief, maybe, over lost illusions—the observer who remembers what human nature is wonders that so little of this is left—but the great fact is that the South is politically loyal to the Union of the States, that the sentiment for its symbol is growing into a deep reality which would flame out in passion under any foreign insult, and that nationality, pride in the republic, is everywhere strong and prominent. It is hardly necessary to say this, but it needs to be emphasized when the other fact is dwelt on, namely, the denial of free suffrage to the colored man. These two things are confused, and this confusion is the source of much political misunderstanding. Often when a Southern election "outrage" is telegraphed, when intimidation or fraud is revealed, it is said in print, "So that is Southern loyalty!" In short, the political treatment of the negro is taken to be a sign of surviving war feeling, if not of a renewed purpose of rebellion. In this year of grace 1887 the two things have no relation to each other. It would be as true to say that election frauds and violence to individuals and on the ballot-box in Cincinnati are signs of hatred of the Union and of Union men, as that a suppressed negro vote at the South, by adroit management or otherwise, is indication of remaining hostility to the Union. In the South it is sometimes due to the same depraved party spirit that causes frauds in the North—the determination of a party to get or keep the upper hand at all hazards; but it is, in its origin and generally, simply the result of the resolution of the majority of the brains and property of the South to govern the cities and the States, and in the Southern mind this is perfectly consistent with entire allegiance to the government. I could name men who were abettors of what is called the "shot-gun policy" whose national patriotism is beyond question, and who are warm promoters of negro education and the improvement of the condition of the colored people.

We might as well go to the bottom of this state of things, and look it squarely in the face. Under reconstruction, sometimes owing to a tardy acceptance of the new conditions by the ruling class, the State governments and the municipalities fell under the control of ignorant colored people, guided by unscrupulous white adventurers. States and cities were prostrate under the heel of ignorance and fraud, crushed with taxes, and no improvements to show for them. It was ruin on the way to universal bankruptcy. The regaining of power by the intelligent and the property owners was a question of civilization. The situation was intolerable. There is no Northern community that would have submitted to it; if it could not have been changed by legal process, it would have been upset by revolution, as it was at the South. Recognizing as we must the existence of race prejudice and pride, it was nevertheless a struggle for existence. The methods resorted to were often violent, and being sweeping, carried injustice. To be a Republican, in the eyes of those smarting under carpet-bag government and the rule of the ignorant lately enfranchised, was to be identified with the detested carpet-bag government and with negro rule. The Southern Unionist and the Northern emigrant, who justly regarded the name Republican as the proudest they could bear, identified as it was with the preservation of the Union and the national credit, could not show their Republican principles at the polls without personal danger in the country and social ostracism in the cities. Social ostracism on account of politics even outran social ostracism on account of participation in the education of the negroes. The very men who would say, "I respect a man who fought for the Union more than a Northern Copperhead, and if I had lived North, no doubt I should have gone with my section," would at the same time say, or think, "But you cannot be a Republican down here now, for to be that is to identify yourself with the party here that is hostile to everything in life that is dear to us." This feeling was intensified by the memories of the war, but it was in a measure distinct from the war feeling, and it lived on when the latter grew weak, and it still survives in communities perfectly loyal to the Union, glad that slavery is ended, and sincerely desirous of the establishment and improvement of public education for colored and white alike.

Any tampering with the freedom of the ballot-box in a republic, no matter what the provocation, is dangerous; the methods used to regain white ascendency were speedily adopted for purely party purposes and factional purposes; the chicanery, even the violence, employed to render powerless the negro and "carpet-bag" vote were freely used by partisans in local elections against each other, and in time became means of preserving party and ring ascendency. Thoughtful men South as well as North recognize the vital danger to popular government if voting and the ballot-box are not sacredly protected. In a recent election in Texas, in a district where, I am told, the majority of the inhabitants are white, and the majority of the whites are Republicans, and the majority of the colored voters voted the Republican ticket, and greatly the larger proportion of the wealth and business of the district are in Republican hands, there was an election row; ballot-boxes were destroyed in several precincts, persons killed on both sides, and leading Republicans driven out of the State. This is barbarism. If the case is substantiated as stated, that in the district it was not a question of race ascendency, but of party ascendency, no fair-minded man in the South can do otherwise than condemn it, for under such conditions not only is a republican form of government impossible, but development and prosperity are impossible.

For this reason, and because separation of voters on class lines is always a peril, it is my decided impression that throughout the South, though not by everybody, a breaking up of the solidarity of the South would be welcome; that is to say, a breaking up of both the negro and the white vote, and the reforming upon lines of national and economic policy, as in the old days of Whig and Democrat, and liberty of free action in all local affairs, without regard to color or previous party relations. There are politicians who would preserve a solid South, or as a counterpart a solid North, for party purposes. But the sense of the country, the perception of business men North and South, is that this condition of politics interferes with the free play of industrial development, with emigration, investment of capital, and with that untrammelled agitation and movement in society which are the life of prosperous states.

Let us come a little closer to the subject, dealing altogether with facts, and not with opinions. The Republicans of the North protest against the injustice of an increased power in the Lower House and in the Electoral College based upon a vote which is not represented. It is a valid protest in law; there is no answer to it. What is the reply to it? The substance of hundreds of replies to it is that "we dare not let go so long as the negroes all vote together, regardless of local considerations or any economic problems whatever; we are in danger of a return to a rule of ignorance that was intolerable, and as long as you wave the bloody shirt at the North, which means to us a return to that rule, the South will be solid." The remark made by one man of political prominence was perhaps typical: "The waving of the bloody shirt suits me exactly as a political game; we should have hard work to keep our State Democratic if you did not wave it." So the case stands. The Republican party will always insist on freedom, not only of political opinion, but of action, in every part of the Union; and the South will keep "solid" so long as it fears, or so long as politicians can persuade it to fear, the return of the late disastrous domination. And recognizing this fact, and speaking in the interest of no party, but only in that of better understanding and of the prosperity of the whole country, I cannot doubt that the way out of most of our complications is in letting the past drop absolutely, and addressing ourselves with sympathy and good-will all round to the great economical problems and national issues. And I believe that in this way also lies the speediest and most permanent good to the colored as well as the white population of the South.

There has been a great change in the aspect of the South and in its sentiment within two years; or perhaps it would be more correct to say that the change maturing for fifteen years is more apparent in a period of comparative rest from race or sectional agitation. The educational development is not more marvellous than the industrial, and both are unparalleled in history. Let us begin by an illustration.

I stood one day before an assembly of four hundred pupils of a colored college—called a college, but with a necessary preparatory department—children and well-grown young women and men. The buildings are fine, spacious, not inferior to the best modern educational buildings either in architectural appearance or in interior furnishing, with scientific apparatus, a library, the appliances approved by recent experience in teaching, with admirable methods and discipline, and an accomplished corps of instructors. The scholars were neat, orderly, intelligent in appearance. As I stood for a moment or two looking at their bright expectant faces the profound significance of the spectacle and the situation came over me, and I said: "I wonder if you know what you are doing, if you realize what this means. Here you are in a school the equal of any of its grade in the land, with better methods of instruction than prevailed anywhere when I was a boy, with the gates of all knowledge opened as freely to you as to any youth in the land—here, in this State, where only about twenty years ago it was a misdemeanor, punishable with fine and imprisonment, to teach a colored person to read and write. And I am brought here to see this fine school, as one of the best things he can show me in the city, by a Confederate colonel. Not in all history is there any instance of a change like this in a quarter of a century: no, not in one nor in two hundred years. It seems incredible."

This is one of the schools instituted and sustained by Northern friends of the South; but while it exhibits the capacity of the colored people for education, it is not so significant in the view we are now taking of the New South as the public schools. Indeed, next to the amazing industrial change in the South, nothing is so striking as the interest and progress in the matter of public schools. In all the cities we visited the people were enthusiastic about their common schools. It was a common remark, "I suppose we have one of the best school systems in the country." There is a wholesome rivalry to have the best. We found everywhere the graded system and the newest methods of teaching in vogue. In many of the primary rooms in both white and colored schools, when I asked if these little children knew the alphabet when they came to school, the reply was: "Not generally. We prefer they should not; we use the new method of teaching words." In many schools the youngest pupils were

taught to read music by sight, and to understand its notation by exercises on the black-board. In the higher classes generally the instruction in arithmetic, in reading, in geography, in history, and in literature was wholly in the modern method. In some of the geography classes and in the language classes I was reminded of the drill in the German schools. In all the cities, as far as I could learn, the public money was equally distributed to the colored and to the white schools, and the number of schools bore a just proportion to the number of the two races. When the town was equally divided in population, the number of pupils in the colored schools was about the same as the number in the white schools. There was this exception: though provision was made for a high-school to terminate the graded for both colors, the number in the colored high-school department was usually very small; and the reason given by colored and white teachers was that the colored children had not yet worked up to it. The colored people prefer teachers of their own race, and they are quite generally employed, but many of the colored schools have white teachers, and generally, I think, with better results, although I saw many thoroughly good colored teachers, and one or two colored classes under them that compared favorably with any white classes of the same grade.

The great fact, however, is that the common-school system has become a part of Southern life, is everywhere accepted as a necessity, and usually money is freely voted to sustain it. But practically, as an efficient factor in civilization, the system is yet undeveloped in the country districts. I can only speak from personal observation of the cities, but the universal testimony was that the common schools in the country for both whites and blacks are poor. Three months' schooling in the year is about the rule, and that of a slack and inferior sort, under incompetent teachers. In some places the colored people complain that ignorant teachers are put over them, who are chosen simply on political considerations. More than one respectable colored man told me that he would not send his children to such schools, but combined with a few others to get them private instruction. The colored people are more dependent on public schools than the whites, for while there are vast masses of colored people in city and country who have neither the money nor the disposition to sustain schools, in all the large places the whites are able to have excellent private schools, and do have them. Scarcely anywhere can the colored people as yet have a private school without white aid from somewhere. At the present rate of progress, and even of the increase of tax-paying ability, it must be a long time before the ignorant masses, white and black, in the country districts, scattered over a wide area, can have public schools at all efficient. The necessity is great. The danger to the State of ignorance is more and more apprehended. And it is upon this that many of the best men of the South base their urgent appeal for temporary aid from the Federal government for public schools. It is seen that a state cannot soundly prosper unless its laborers are to some degree intelligent. This opinion is shown in little things. One of the great planters of the Yazoo Delta told me that he used to have no end of trouble in settling with his hands. But now that numbers of them can read and cipher, and explain the accounts to the others, he never has the least trouble.

One cannot speak too highly of the private schools in the South, especially of those for young women. I do not know what they were before the war, probably mainly devoted to "accomplishments," as most of girls' schools in the North were. Now most of them are wider in range, thorough in discipline, excellent in all the modern methods. Some of them, under accomplished women, are entirely in line with the best in the country. Before leaving this general subject of education it is necessary to say that the advisability of industrial training, as supplementary to book-learning, is growing in favor, and that in some colored schools it is tried with good results.

When we come to the New Industrial South the change is marvellous, and so vast and various that I scarcely know where to begin in a short paper that cannot go much into details. Instead of a South devoted to agriculture and politics, we find a South wide-awake to business, excited and even astonished at the development of its own immense resources in metals, marbles, coal, timber, fertilizers, eagerly laying lines of communication, rapidly opening mines, building furnaces, founderies, and all sorts of shops for utilizing the native riches. It is like the dis-

covery of a new world. When the Northerner finds great founderies in Virginia using only (with slight exceptions) the products of Virginia iron and coal mines; when he finds Alabama and Tennessee making iron so good and so cheap that it finds ready market in Pennsylvania, and founderies multiplying near the great furnaces for supplying Northern markets; when he finds cotton-mills running to full capacity on grades of cheap cottons universally in demand throughout the South and Southwest; when he finds small industries, such as paper-box factories and wooden bucket and tub factories, sending all they can make into the North and widely over the West; when he sees the loads of most beautiful marbles shipped North; when he learns that some of the largest and most important engines and mill machinery were made in Southern shops; when he finds in Richmond a "pole locomotive," made to run on logs laid end to end, and drag out from Michigan forests and Southern swamps lumber hitherto inaccessible; when he sees worn-out highlands in Georgia and Carolina bear more cotton than ever before by help of a fertilizer the base of which is the cotton seed itself (worth more as a fertilizer than it was before the oil was extracted from it); when he sees a multitude of small shops giving employment to men, women, and children who never had any work of that sort to do before; and when he sees Roanoke iron cast in Richmond into car irons, and returned to a car factory in Roanoke which last year sold three hundred cars to the New York and New England Railroad—he begins to open his eyes. The South is manufacturing a great variety of things needed in the house, on the farm, and in the shops, for home consumption, and already sends to the North and West several manufactured products. With iron, coal, timber contiguous and easily obtained, the amount sent out is certain to increase as the labor becomes more skilful. The most striking industrial development to-day is in iron, coal, lumber, and marbles; the more encouraging for the self-sustaining life of the Southern people is the multiplication of small industries in nearly every city I visited.

When I have been asked what impressed me most in this hasty tour, I have always said that the most notable thing was that everybody was at work.

In many cities this was literally true : every man, woman, and child was actively employed, and in most there were fewer idlers than in many Northern towns. There are, of course, slow places, antiquated methods, easy-going ways, a-hundred-years-behind-the-time makeshifts, but the spirit in all the centres, and leavening the whole country, is work. Perhaps the greatest revolution of all in Southern sentiment is in regard to the dignity of labor. Labor is honorable, made so by the example of the best in the land. There are, no doubt, fossils or Bourbons, sitting in the midst of the ruins of their estates, martyrs to an ancient pride; but usually the leaders in business and enterprise bear names well known in politics and society. The nonsense that it is beneath the dignity of any man or woman to work for a living is pretty much eliminated from the Southern mind. It still remains true that the purely American type is prevalent in the South, but in all the cities the business sign-boards show that the enterprising Hebrew is increasingly prominent as merchant and trader, and he is becoming a plantation owner as well.

It cannot be too strongly impressed upon the public mind that the South, to use a comprehensible phrase, "has joined the procession." Its mind is turned to the development of its resources, to business, to enterprise, to education, to economic problems; it is marching with the North in the same purpose of wealth by industry. It is true that the railways, mines, and furnaces could not have been without enormous investments of Northern capital, but I was continually surprised to find so many and important local industries the result solely of home capital, made and saved since the war.

In this industrial change, in the growth of manufactures, the Southern people are necessarily divided on the national economic problems. Speaking of it purely from the side of political economy and not of politics, great sections of the South —whole States, in fact—are becoming more in favor of "protection" every day. All theories aside, whenever a man begins to work up the raw material at hand into manufactured articles for the market, he thinks that the revenue should be so adjusted as to help and not to hinder him.

Underlying everything else is the negro problem. It is the most difficult ever given to a people to solve. It must, under our Constitution, be left to the States concerned, and there is a general hopefulness that time and patience will solve it to the advantage of both races. The negro is generally regarded as the best laborer in the world, and there is generally good-will toward him, desire that he shall be educated and become thrifty. The negro has more confidence now than formerly in the white man, and he will go to him for aid and advice in everything except politics. Again and again colored men said to me, "If anybody tells you that any considerable number of colored men are Democrats, don't you believe him; it is not so." The philanthropist who goes South will find many things to encourage him, but if he knows the colored people thoroughly, he will lose many illusions. But. to speak of things hopeful, the progress in education, in industry, in ability to earn money, is extraordinary—much greater than ought to have been expected in twenty years even by their most sanguine friends, and it is greater now than at any other period. They are generally well paid, according to the class of work they do. Usually I found the same wages for the same class of work as whites received. I cannot say how this is in remote country districts. The treatment of laborers depends, I have no doubt, as elsewhere, upon the nature of the employer. In some districts I heard that the negroes never got out of debt, never could lay up anything, and were in a very bad condition. But on some plantations certainly, and generally in the cities, there is an improvement in thrift, shown in the ownership of bits of land and houses, and in the possession of neat and pretty homes. As to morals, the gain is slower, but it is discernible, and exhibited in a growing public opinion against immorality and lax family relations. He is no friend to the colored people who blinks this subject, and does not plainly say to them that their position as citizens in the enjoyment of all civil rights depends quite as much upon their personal virtue and their acquiring habits of thrift as it does upon school privileges.

I had many interesting talks with representative colored men in different sections. While it is undoubtedly true that more are indifferent to politics than formerly, owing to causes already named and to the unfulfilled promises of wheedling politicians, it would be untrue to say that there is not great soreness over the present situation. At Nashville I had an interview with eight or ten of the best colored citizens, men of all shades of color. One of them was a trusted clerk in the post-office; another was a mail agent, who had saved money, and made more by an investment in Birmingham; another was a lawyer of good practice in the courts, a man of decided refinement and cultivation; another was at the head of one of the leading transportation lines in the city, and another had the largest provision establishment in town, and both were men of considerable property; and another, a slave when the war ended, was a large furniture dealer, and reputed worth a hundred thousand dollars. They were all solid, sensible business men, and all respected as citizens. They talked most intelligently of politics, and freely about social conditions. In regard to voting in Tennessee there was little to complain of; but in regard to Mississippi, as an illustration, it was an outrage that the dominant party had increased power in Congress and in the election of President, while the colored Republican vote did not count. What could they do? Some said that probably nothing could be done; time must be left to cure the wrong. Others wanted the Federal government to interfere, at least to the extent of making a test case on some member of Congress that his election was illegal. They did not think that need excite anew any race prejudice. As to exciting race and sectional agitation, we discussed this question: whether the present marvellous improvement of the colored people, with general good-will, or at least a truce everywhere, would not be hindered by anything like a race or class agitation; that is to say, whether under the present conditions of education and thrift the colored people (whatever injustice they felt) were not going on faster toward the realization of all they wanted than would be possible under any circumstances of adverse agitation. As a

matter of policy most of them assented to this. I put this question: "In the first reconstruction days, how many colored men were there in the State of Mississippi fitted either by knowledge of letters, law, political economy, history, or politics to make laws for the State?" Very few. Well, then, it was unfortunate that they should have attempted it. There are more to-day, and with education and the accumulation of property the number will constantly increase. In a republic, power usually goes with intelligence and property.

Finally I asked this intelligent company, every man of which stood upon his own ability in perfect self-respect, "What do you want here in the way of civil rights that you have not?" The reply from one was that he got the respect of the whites just as he was able to command it by his ability and by making money, and, with a touch of a sense of injustice, said he had ceased to expect that the colored race would get it in any other way. Another reply was—and this was evidently the deep feeling of all: "We want to be treated like men, like anybody else, regardless of color. We don't mean by this social equality at all; that is a matter that regulates itself among whites and colored people everywhere. We want the public conveyances open to us according to the fare we pay; we want privilege to go to hotels and to theatres, operas and places of amusement. We wish you could see our families and the way we live; you would then understand that we cannot go to the places assigned us in concerts and theatres without loss of self-respect." I might have said, but I did not, that the question raised by this last observation is not a local one, but as wide as the world.

If I tried to put in a single sentence the most wide-spread and active sentiment in the South to-day, it would be this: The past is put behind us; we are one with the North in business and national ambition: we want a sympathetic recognition of this fact.

SAVANNAH

NO city of the Union blends more palpably the old and the new than Savannah. The place has to a large extent kept its early individuality. It has broad shaded streets rolling in primitive sand, and lined with old-fashioned residences, with a stately flavor of the aristocratic about them, and even the new and more elegant homes avoid the gorgeous phylactery of modern fashion. The past is a living presence in this beautiful old city. The statues and monuments greet one with their historic memories, and tell mutely, yet with eloquence, of eventful annals.

The city and commonwealth were coeval with each other, founded together, and with their annals honorably linked. Savannah enjoys the distinction of long being the germ of the State, and could the noble knight, statesman, and gentleman, Sir James Oglethorpe, the heroic founder of both, have been able to look into the future, and have seen his modest little municipal venture become the first naval stores station in the world, the second cotton port of the American continent, and the head-quarters of the greatest railway and steam-ship transportation system of the South, as it has, his great heart would have throbbed with pride, and he would have felt that he had planted well.

On the afternoon of the first day of February, 1733 (O. S.), Oglethorpe landed at Yamacraw Bluff, on the Savannah River, with 112 colonists. This spot, in a direct line, is only twelve miles from the sea, but the winding of the river lengthens the distance to eighteen miles. The site is the first elevation above the stream, and consisted of a lofty bluff of sand, with a dense pine forest extending back. Into this forest the colonists cut an opening and arranged a quaint little plan of a place, reminding one of a child's toy town, with everything precise and rectangular—streets, houses, and squares laid off mathematically and alike. The system of commodious public parks at regular intervals is the glory of this "Forest City," and constitutes one of its most beautiful and healthy features. As the city extended, these open spots were continued in the same beneficent plan, until there are dozens of them,

shady with great trees, green with velvety swards, threaded by broad walks, and many of them ornate with monuments and fountains. The broader streets strike them in the centre, and narrow streets pass by them, while they are confronted by homes and churches.

The bluff upon which Savannah reposes rises abruptly some forty feet, and extends a mile on the river from which it receives its name. On each side of the city on the river the land consists of low swamps and creeks that have admitted of little improvement, and only of rice culture, and that have bred disease and invited epidemics. In the writer's recollection there were destructive visitations of yellow-fever in 1854, 1858, and 1876, paralyzing business and destroying life. But in the year 1877 the Legislature of Georgia made an appropriation of one-third of the tax of the county of Chatham, in which Savannah lies, amounting to $27,633 73, for the drainage of these swamps. The low, dank, unhealthy marshes were converted into smiling truck farms and rich vegetable gardens. The beautiful city no longer wrestles with the burden of malarious environment that surrounded it with baleful vapors, and bred deadly sickness at intervals. Aside from the moral and sanitary effects so immeasurable, it has in the transformation of black bogs into oases of fertility created a growing and profitable truck industry. From the records of the Ocean Steam-ship Company, that valuable scheme of transportation, we learn that in 1881 the steamers carried north 93,000 packages of vegetables. The business has grown to 236,000 packages, and the local production has increased to 92,000.

In laying off the city the central leading thoroughfare, beginning at the river, centrally in the bluff, and extending out through the squares to the beautiful enclosure now called Forsyth Park, was named Bull Street, after Colonel William Bull, a Charleston engineer and officer sent over by the Governor of South Carolina to aid Oglethorpe in planning the new town. The Greene and Pulaski monuments are located in the squares on this street, the former in Johnson Square, the nearest to the river, and the latter in Monterey Square, the nearest to Forsyth

NOTABLE MONUMENTS IN SAVANNAH.

priate ceremonies, during the week devoted to the centennial celebration of the Chatham Artillery. General Greene was second in command under Washington, and was identified with Georgia and Savannah by a donation from Georgia of a valuable landed interest here in recognition of his distinguished services and heroic patriotism. He died and was buried in Savannah.

The commercial activity of Savannah began early. Settlements sprang into existence,

Park. The Greene monument was completed in 1829. It was a tall, plain shaft uninscribed, resting on a granite base, and enclosed with an iron railing. Not until May, 1886, were the proper inscriptions placed upon the historic shaft and unveiled with appro-

steadily increasing the trade importance of the new place, as it was the only point of entry for all importations, and from its river-bank were shipped skins, lumber, and other articles not needed for home use. Savannah was the commercial metropolis of the colony. The first effort to ship a Georgia cargo was in 1749, and was accomplished by the house of Harris and Habersham. The articles exported were mainly deer-skins, hogs, poultry, rice, staves, tar, and pitch, unconsciously forecasting in the latter articles Savannah's supremacy in lines of trade in which she now leads the world. To this firm is due the enterprise of first establishing well-approved export and import relations with Europe, and it is an honorable fact that the Habersham descendants of that pioneer firm in the colony's commerce rank to-day among the strongest merchants of the present Savannah. This sterling family gave to the colony one of its best Governors, and later to President Washington an able Postmaster-General in his cabinet. The Habersham rice-mills have been the leading industrial establishment of the city from an early period. Her first wharf was built in 1757, and in 1758 forty-one vessels entered the new port. To-day her shipping nearly reaches a million of tonnage. Her first exports were of the value of ten thousand dollars; they now amount to fifty millions. Her first cotton bale was exported by Thomas Miller in 1788, one hundred years ago, and now she is the second cotton port of the American continent, having handled as high as 896,681 bales, worth forty millions of dollars.

The two most potent agencies of Savannah's advancement have been the Central Railroad and Ocean Steam-ship Company, and the Savannah, Florida, and Western Railway.

The Central Railroad system has a gigantic claim to the admiration, the gratitude, and support of all Georgians. It is the most powerful instrumentality of both Savannah's and Georgia's growth. Its magnificent scheme of commercial links, its fleet of noble ocean steamers, its massive system of wharves, elevators, presses, depots, and structures, its immense facilities for the easy and speedy doing of a prodigious business, the perfect method and efficiency of its management, and the peculiarly solid character of its stocks and securities, so largely owned in the homes and rooted in the confidence of the people, and not speculatively reposing in great blocks for capricious manipulation by the capitalists of the financial world—all of these remarkable features go to make the Savannah Central a pride and benefaction for city and State. This corporation, with its more than 1500 miles of track, covering the State with its network of steel, and linking Georgia to its neighbors, worth from forty to fifty millions of money, doing fifty millions of shipments, employing thousands of laborers, and its superb line of the finest ocean steam-ships, owned and controlled by Southern money and genius, and tapping Philadelphia and New York, and making the vast current of commerce for the whole South pour through Savannah and Georgia, enriching both, is a factor of power and progress, whose beneficence, great as it has been, is in its infancy.

The originator and genius of this important enterprise was W. W. Gordon, whose powerful energy and resources carried it through to completion under many and discouraging difficulties.

The wharves of the railroad are a revelation of enterprise. They constitute a scale of business method and activity that

MOUTH OF THE SAVANNAH RIVER.

LOADING COTTON AT THE WHARF.

would do credit to London and New York. In 1871 the place was a marsh. There are thirty acres of improvement, ten acres of platform on piles, five acres of shed under cover, 4000 feet of wharf front and 500 more projected, 750 feet of timber wharf, cotton wharf for 12,000 bales and projected wharf for 25,000 more, storage houses for 100,000 tons of guano, ten miles of track threading the wharves, three great cotton warehouses holding 30,000 bales, a grain elevator holding 270,000 bushels at one time, a cotton compressor pressing 2400 bales a day, scales everywhere that will weigh cars in bulk, smaller scales at each car, six at one track, for loading a train simultaneously. The wharves take 800 hands when a full force is required, and the company employs eighteen special policemen. Often there are forty ships and steamers at a time loading and unloading. The Savannah, Florida, and Western Railroad has a special track. The Philadelphia steamers have an inlet between sections of the wharf. The great piles of freight are astonishing. Every conceivable product of commerce is there.

The writer saw huge crates of cabbage, curiously enough those raised in Florida and Massachusetts meeting on a common ground and in friendly rivalry. The immense ocean steamers towered up their vast bulks like huge marine monsters taking in and giving out cargoes. These steamers carry 6000 bales of cotton and 100 first-class passengers, and are palaces in luxury.

The Savannah, Florida, and Western Railway, known as the Plant railroad system, is a worthy contemporary of the Central as a potential factor of progress and expansion for Savannah.

The line runs from Charleston through Savannah to the Chattahoochee River and to Jacksonville, with branches to Albany, Bainbridge, Gainesville, and Brunswick, and has a steam-ship line from Tampa to Havana and Key West. It combines over 800 miles of track under the single masterly administration. The policy of the management has been comprehensive, far-seeing, and sagacious. No dividends have been paid, but the whole profits have been invested in extending and perfecting the

HOUSE WHERE WASHINGTON AND LAFAYETTE WERE ENTERTAINED.

system. It is one of the best equipped railways in the Union, and handles the large winter travel to and from Florida admirably. It has made new connections, opened up new industries, tapped fresh regions of trade, and created remunerative business. Its iron tentacles have penetrated and gleaned the orange-laden realm of Florida.

Like the Central road, this railway has vast wharves on the river at the right of the city that are a revelation of activity and enterprise. The company owns 326 acres, which it is improving. It has a mile and a half of river-front, three-quarters of a mile of massive wharves, and it will extend them a full mile. These vast improvements are a fitting companion to the mammoth wharves of the Central. These wharves, with their great masses of lumber, rosin, turpentine, and guano, afford some conception of the magnificent commerce Savannah is enjoying, and of the superb railway agencies that have evoked this commerce into fructifying existence. Acres of ground are covered with the barrels of rosin and turpentine.

The business in naval stores was the creation of this railway company. In 1875 the receipts at Savannah were 9555 barrels of turpentine and 41,797 barrels

of rosin, and have reached the present annual figure of 133,139 barrels of turpentine and 564,026 barrels of rosin, showing a steady and large increase.

An event in railway matters was the extension from Bainbridge Junction to Chattahoochee, connecting with the new Pensacola and Atlantic Railroad of 160 miles to Pensacola, making a shorter route from the sea-coast cities to Pensacola, Mobile, and New Orleans. From its local traffic in Florida, the orange El Dorado of the world, that attractive sanitarium of the invalid, it is now the vital part of a great trunk line and the channel for foreign travel. The road has been the beneficent instrumentality of new and vast vegetable, melon, and fruit industries, and its future cannot be estimated. It is in the infancy of its traffic. Savannah has handled a million melons in a season, 1,040,315 barrels and packages of vegetables, 83 million feet of lumber, 2 million hides, 742,748 bushels of rice, and 160 million pounds of guano.

The sea inlets on the coast abound in excellent oysters, crabs, and shrimps, which are peddled through the city. Early in the crisp mornings are heard the colored venders of oysters, fish, and vegetables moving briskly along the sidewalks in the balmy air, with their baskets and buckets of commodity on their heads, crying their wares in a crooning, sweet-voiced accent that musically enlivens the quiet. These African pavement merchants are of both sexes, but chiefly female, and they all have plaintive expression, and use the same rising inflection on the last word.

ilies, rich from commerce or planting, at the head of great cotton houses or baronial plantations of slaves, with large incomes and the opportunity and taste for leisure, luxury, and culture, brought home life to a degree of polish and elegant exclusiveness that could not be surpassed anywhere. The prohibition

LIBRARY IN THE GEORGIA HISTORICAL SOCIETY.

Their voices have the peculiar melody of the low-country black, an intonation that subtly recalls in a suggestive way the original African in his primitive simplicity, and by some unconscious association also suggests the earliest past of the old town.

From an early period the social lines of demarcation were very broadly marked. As much of an aristocracy was built up as this country will allow. Old fam-

against slavery and spirits was early removed, it being found on trial that the colony was at a disadvantage in rivalry with its neighbors, and the people soon became the possessors of great estates of slaves, and practised a refined conviviality. Hospitality ripened into a fine art, and never flowered to more exquisite display than in this city. The men were lordly, honorable, chivalric, and thorough-bred. They were college-educated, well-read and well-travelled, unpractised in labor—that is, the planters—lavish with money, dressed fashionably, and were noted for their courtesy and respect to women. A European lady said she would know a Savannah-raised gentleman anywhere. They were quick-blooded, given to the professions, naturally eloquent, and fond of pleasure. The women were pure, luxurious, modest, and thoroughly feminine. They were absolutely helpless, so far as the practical world was concerned, and wholly dependent upon father, husband, brother, or son. It was part of this civilization that the male members of a family cared for the females, and the result has been an ornamental type of womanhood. Every social and educational advantage was enjoyed by young women. They were protected from rude associations, tenderly nurtured, taught accomplishments, their morals and manners cultivated, and every feminine grace fostered and developed. There has never been a finer strain of ladies. And they were trained for presiding as house-keepers as well as for shining in the parlor. While screened from hardship, labor, and exposure, they were taught the management of servants and domestic administration of large households, requiring tact and energy. The bond between the old and young mistresses and their family servants was a close and tender one, and the domestic help of that *régime* was peculiarly faithful and skilled, and noted for its deference and devotion. It is fast passing away, and the house service under the later civilization cannot compare to it. In the olden time wealthy and even ordinary homes were stocked with servants who did but one thing.

The new era has much changed the old condition. When, in the vicissitudes of the city's varied career, the dainty denizens of the palatial mansions were forced to peddle ginger-cakes from the basements, the servants gone, it was a pathetic spectacle. The old social aristocracy has been thinned. New ideas have come in, and the old baronial civilization is gone; but the fragrance of the broken vase lingers there still. There is the same social purity and refinement without its extreme exclusiveness. To gain admission to the best homes the stranger must still be satisfactorily vouched for. The old-fashioned spirit of elegant hospitality yet prevails. Entertainment is still

an art, and the best social characteristics of the former *régime* continue under the best practical forms.

No city in the Union has had a higher class of commercial men than Savannah, and its cotton merchants have been noted for their enterprise and integrity. They have been safe, energetic, and far-seeing, and to their sagacious efforts, with the aid of the Central and Gulf railroads, is due the city's stand as a cotton mart. In the ten years from 1871 to 1881 the cotton business of the place grew under the work of those men from 455,796 to 896,681 bales. Of the latter crop 881,161 were upland, or short-staple, and 15,520 bales were sea-island, or long-staple cotton. Of the aristocratic long-staple variety of cotton but an average of 40,000 bales is raised in the South, Georgia leading, with Florida second, and South Carolina third. Georgia is first in cotton acreage and second in cotton production in the South. There is no ground for doubting that Savannah will continue to expand commercially. Her population has grown since 1880 over 12,000, reaching a total of 45,000 people. Her property has in two years increased nearly three millions, surpassing in its growth any city in the State, reaching a total of over twenty-two millions. Her new buildings will average yearly seven hundred in number since 1883. Her naval stores trade has more than doubled since 1880. Her retail trade runs to sixteen millions, and wholesale to seventeen millions. Her banking operations amount to one hundred and fifty millions. The whole business of the city reaches the gratifying figure of one hundred millions of dollars.

While Savannah's main strength lies in her commercial advantages, she has been enterprising in manufactures. The census of 1880 gave her seventy-three establishments, with a capital of $995,950, working 1048 hands, and creating $3,099,416. The increase in the classes of establishments enumerated in the census has run to 104. The leading manufacture was and is the rice industry. The city had in 1880 three rice-mills, with a capital of $263,000, working 219 hands, and turning out $1,488,769 of products. The number has been increased to four mills. Georgia is the second rice-producing State in the South, ranking next to South Carolina. Savannah's receipts of rice have reached the figure of 742,784 bushels. The census list did not include all the manufactures. It omitted 175 small industries, including nineteen blacksmiths, six cabinet-makers, one cracker factory, four harness-makers, one paper-mill, one stereotype establishment, six wheelwrights, etc. Since then there have been new industries added—barrel, boat, frame, pattern, pump, truck, trunk, and stamp makers. The city has now an aggregate of 316 establishments, with $2,250,000 of capital, working 2200 hands, and creating near five millions of products. This estimate does not include the great railroad shops of the Central and Gulf railroads. Among the manufactures that have not been mentioned may be stated cotton yarns, tin-ware, lithographs, furniture, blacking, stone, iron, engines, cultivators, cigars, shingles, mill gearing, stills, sashes, doors, iron railings, candy, blank books, patent medicines, colognes, corn-mills, ploughs, guano, flour, roller compound, etc. There is a dry-dock and marine railway to repair ships, also packing houses, planing-mills, cotton-presses, grain elevator, and all cosmopolitan conveniences. Six cotton-presses employ 600 hands, and can press 6900 bales a day. The founderies use 200 tons of pig-iron, the corn-mills grind 2100 bushels of grain daily. The rice-mills store 670,000 bushels of grain, and turn out 510 barrels of clean rice a day.

The picturesque points of attraction in and near Savannah

ORIGINAL GROWTH OF PINES IN FORSYTH PARK.

TELFAIR ACADEMY.

are many and of rare beauty. Forsyth Park is the most lovely spot in the city, terminating Bull Street. It contains twenty acres in the park proper, enclosed with an iron fence. It was named after one of our most brilliant Georgians, John Forsyth, United States Senator in 1818 and in 1830, and Governor in 1827. This enclosure presents a unique appearance, its basic element being a forest of stately pines that contrast strikingly with the exquisite scheme of garden beneath, laid tastefully off into winding walks, grass swards, vivid groupings of bright plants and flowers, such as coleus, roses, cacti, and dahlias, and fantastic mounds of luxuriant vines. The central fountain is a gem of its kind, and leaves a living memory of poetic picturesqueness. The park extension contains thirty acres, and is adorned with a tall soldiers' monument, unveiled in 1876. There are other parks not so attractive as Forsyth — Battery Park, for picnics, the inevitable base-ball park, Concordia Park, and Ten Broeck Race-course and Thunderbolt Race-track, the former course famous for many a celebrated race under the auspices of the Sa-

vannah Jockey Club. In the slavery days the Forest City was noted for its turf spirit. The Ten Broeck Course is three miles out on the Central road. Under the new *régime* Savannah cares little for racing.

The most beautiful and romantic suburb of Savannah is her Bonaventure, now known as Evergreen Cemetery. It is on an arm of the river, some four miles from the city. It rises in terraces from the river, the terraces supported by blocks of shell and lime, and great broad avenues of gigantic live-oaks, draped in massive festoons of pendent gray moss, give the spot its glory. Among the other attractive river suburbs may be mentioned the Isle of Hope, six and a half miles out on the Skidaway River, where "Wormsloe," the home of the Jones family, so well known in Revolutionary annals, was located; "Bewlie," or "Beaulieu," on the Vernon River, the home of William Stephens, the first Governor after Oglethorpe, and now the delightful summer residence of citizens; Montgomery, ten miles from Savannah, on the Vernon River, and the terminus of the Seaboard Railroad, a delightful little village, and the head-quar-

SCULPTURE GALLERY, TELFAIR ACADEMY.

ful bathing. The road-stead offers secure anchorage for ships in stormy weather on the sea. It is suited for a "calling station." There is a light-house on the north end, and the government has a signal station communicating with Savannah by telephone and telegraph. Excellent hotels and boarding-houses have been built to entertain the thousands of summer visitors that go to the island for the sea-breezes and the ocean baths. There are many handsome residences that have been erected by the wealthy. Excursions go to Tybee from all parts of the State.

The city early began the improvement of the river. It has spent $120,000 of its own money on this valuable water thoroughfare. An appropriation was secured from Congress of $26,000 in 1826, one of $161,000 in 1855, another of $483,000 in 1873; and in 1882, on an estimate of $730,000 as necessary to complete

ters of the "Regatta Association of Georgia," under whose auspices annual yacht contests are held; Schuetzen Park, three miles from the city, on Warsaw River, east of Bonaventure, the sporting ground of the large German element of the city; and Thunderbolt, the terminus of the four miles of shell road that is the favorite summer drive of the citizens, and whose waters are the chief source of supply of oysters, crabs, fish, and shrimps.

Tybee Island, at the entrance of the Savannah River, must in time become the most popular and valuable suburb of the city. There is no reason why it should not become the Cape May of the South Atlantic coast. It has a lovely beach, four miles long, where the Atlantic Ocean surf invites to safe and delight-

the improvement of the river, and secure twenty-two feet depth at mean high-water from the city to Tybee Roads, annual appropriations have been given for the work. The channel has been straightened, widened, and deepened, the bar lowered, the river lighted at night, and every obstruction to navigation for the largest ships is being removed. At the bar nineteen and a half feet depth at low-water has been obtained. The work is being conducted under a United States engineer. And through this fine channel established lines of steamers run to Boston, New York, Baltimore, Philadelphia, Augusta, Jacksonville, Charleston, and other home points, and to Liverpool, England. As an aid to her trade, the city, with enterprise characteristic of her business men, organized fifty years ago the Savannah, Ogeechee, and Altamaha Canal Company, and invested a quarter of a million of money in a canal for the shipment of lumber, timber, and rice. In addition to the two great Central and Gulf railroad lines, the city has two seaboard railroads, and the Tybee Railroad and Savannah, Dublin, and Western Railroad under way, the latter opening up new local territory to the thriving seaport.

The city has had some notable visitations of fire and of distinguished guests. A great conflagration in 1796 burned 229 houses ; another, in 1820, destroyed 463 dwellings ; a sweeping fire levelled a large part of the place in 1864, while in 1882 the old dilapidated Yamacraw section of the city was beneficially burned out of existence. These great destructions of property have but stimulated growth and improvement. Formal visits with great ceremony were made to Savannah by President Washington in 1790, Aaron Burr in 1802, President Monroe in 1819, General Lafayette in 1825, Daniel Webster in 1848, and President Fillmore in 1854.

It is an illustration of Savannah's enterprise that she can claim the credit of building and sending over the first steam vessel that ever crossed the Atlantic Ocean.

The wholesale and commission business thoroughfare of Savannah is Bay Street, which runs parallel with the river and along the bluff. The leading retail trade street is Broughton, running parallel with Bay, and the fourth from it. On the left of Johnson Square, where the Greene monument rises on Bull Street, is Christ Church, on whose site stood the chapel in which John Wesley first ministered as chaplain to the colonists. It has since 1743 been an Episcopal church, the first in the colony, and was destroyed in succession by fire and hurricane, and the third structure now stands on the ground. The Independent Presbyterian church on Bull Street, corner of South Broad Street, cost $160,000 in 1819, is 200 feet high, and at its consecration President James Monroe assisted. The theatre fronts Chippewa Square and Bull Street, and was built in 1818, and is said to be the oldest house of histrionic art in use in the United States. All of the great dramatic and operatic stars have figured within its walls. The Oglethorpe Barracks cover two blocks, and front on Bull Street,

and were built in 1833, and are models of comfort. The Hebrews have a synagogue, fronting the Pulaski monument and Bull Street, in Monterey Square. It is entitled "Mickva Israel," and the society was chartered in 1790. West of Franklin Square, between St. Julian and Bryan streets, is a noted colored Baptist church. The Rev. Andrew Marshall, its pastor, a celebrated colored preacher, a slave, bought his own freedom, and his funeral in 1856 was one of the largest ever held in the city. The City Market occupies a square between Congress and Bryan streets, and is a model of a brick structure. The Catholics have a fine cathedral of "Our Lady of Perpetual Help," 100 feet by 212, corner of Abercorn and Harris streets ; the hospital of the Sisters of Mercy, known as the St. Joseph's Infirmary, on Taylor Street ; and the Convent of Saint Paul de Vincent, corner of Abercorn and Liberty streets, founded in 1842. The convent covers a whole block. The Custom-house is a plain granite building, corner of Bay and Bull streets, 110 by 52 feet, and 52 feet high. It is inadequate to the Federal business, and Congress has provided for a new public building.

Savannah has always been famed for its military spirit. It has had more martial organizations in proportion to its population than any city in the South. It has to-day a full regiment, and a battalion of infantry, artillery, and horse companies, white, all flourishing, and a large number of colored companies. The Chatham Artillery was organized May 1, 1786, and has two cannon, given to it by President Washington. This company did service in the war of 1812–15, and in the Florida war. The corps celebrated its hundredth anniversary with a week's festivities, entertaining companies from all parts of the Union, and illustrating characteristically the lavish and native hospitality of the city. The Georgia Hussars was formed in 1799 ; the Volunteer Guards in 1802 ; the Republican Blues in 1808 ; the Phœnix Riflemen in 1830 ; the Jasper Greens in 1843 ; the German Volunteers in 1846, etc. ; and these organizations and others are vital to-day.

Journalism in Savannah has ever been conservative and strong, typifying the people. It has now two dailies, the *Morning News*, edited and owned by Colonel J. H. Estill, and the *Afternoon Times*, under charge of B. H. Richardson, aided by W. G. Waller. The *News* was established in 1850, and its editor for over thirty years was W. T. Thompson, the author of that popular book of humor, *Major Jones's Courtship;* and for years the only eight-page evening daily in the State, and well conducted. The educational standard in this city has always been high. Its free - school system is among the finest in the South, and affords the best tuition to the white and colored

ART GALLERY, TELFAIR ACADEMY.

one of the workers on this journal was Joel Chandler Harris, another well-known Georgia humorist, and author of the "Uncle Remus" sketches. The *News* is a powerful and wealthy newspaper, and Colonel Estill ranks among the foremost of the Southern press men. The *Times* is children. There are also excellent Catholic schools, and a Business College and a Vocal Academy. The Chatham Academy, on South Broad and Bull streets, covering a block, dates back to 1788.

As may be naturally expected from an old city of such distinguished antecedents

"RELICS OF THE BRAVE."
From the painting by Carl Hacker in the Telfair Academy.

and hereditary culture, there is a cultivated taste for literature and art, and it
has taken a conspicuous public direction.
The place has had many connoisseurs in
the highest realms of taste. At the corner of Jones and Bull streets is a spacious
and costly brick building, formerly the
residence of the late Alexander A. Smets,
now used as the German Harmonic Club-
house. Mr. Smets, a gentleman of fortune, made one of the finest private collections in the South of rare books of literature, science, and art, and of drawings and
engravings, and his library was known to
scholars in America and Europe. On the
corner of Liberty and Bull streets is a
handsome modern residence, the home of
the late G. W. J. De Renne, now occupied
by his widow. Mr. De Renne was a millionaire, whose life was devoted to cultured
leisure. The State owes him a large debt
of gratitude for his public-spirited service
and liberality in preserving and publishing valuable early records of the colony
and State and of the city.

Fronting Forsyth Park, at the corner
of Whitaker and Gaston streets, is the
handsome building called Hodgson Hall,
94 by 41 feet, containing the library of
12,000 volumes of the Georgia Historical
Society. The building was erected by
Mrs. Margaret Telfair Hodgson in memory of her husband, who was a zealous
member of the society. Mrs. Hodgson
was a Miss Telfair, a descendant of Governor Telfair, and a member of a family
distinguished in Georgia annals. The
hall was completed by Miss Mary Telfair,
sister of Mrs. Hodgson, and dedicated at
the thirty-seventh anniversary of the society, February 14, 1876.

But to the public-spirited Telfair family
is due a still larger meed of gratitude for a
liberal and exalted art benefaction to the
city. One hundred years ago, in 1786,
Edward Telfair was elected Governor of
Georgia. Through the munificent generosity of Miss Mary Telfair, a descendant
of that patriotic and distinguished Chief
Executive, the costly and aristocratic
home of the family in Savannah was dedicated and opened, Monday, May 3, 1886, a

century later, as the "Telfair Academy of Arts and Sciences." Miss Telfair died June 2, 1875, and gave the family homestead, with her books, pictures, and statuary, to the Georgia Historical Society, in trust, for a perpetual Art and Science Academy. The will was contested, but the bequest prevailed. The bequest amounted to $150,000, of which nearly two-thirds was in money to execute the purpose. The Society Directory, under General Henry R. Jackson's lead, placed the matter in the hands of Mr. Carl N. Brandt, the artist, who has discharged his delicate trust faultlessly.

His idea was to bring to Savannah the best in art, and thereby awaken a love which would in time give expression in an art school with all its branches of industrial execution. He remodelled the building and added to it with consummate judgment and prevision of needs. He has created an art museum for the pleasure of the people and for the inspiration and instruction of art students that fills the purpose, obtaining the most perfect specimens, having new models of peculiar value made under great difficulty, and gathering many objects not generally seen in such collections.

Miss Telfair desired the main features of her ancestral home preserved. The old mansion was 65 by 60 feet. Mr. Brandt has enlarged the building to 168 by 60 feet, adding sculpture and picture galleries, the director's dwelling, and two studios. Five heroic stone statues of Phidias, Raphael, Michael Angelo, Rubens, and Rembrandt, in Marzina stone on granite pedestals, greet the visitor in front of the Academy. The main hall is imposing. The old wooden stairway leading to the second floor has been removed, and an iron and marble staircase made, with a 50-foot skylight above, and it connects the old and new buildings. The sculpture gallery is 60 by 60 feet, and 78 feet high, and the picture gallery of the same dimensions and 32 feet high, both with skylights, a glass dome being placed in the centre and ceiling of the lower gallery. The seats around the dome, 16 feet in diameter, furnish room for visitors to sit down. The effect of the colorings and decorations is rich, quiet, and soothing. They are all in a subdued tone, to show the art objects to the greatest advantage. Everything is substantial. The sculpture hall has marble tiling, and the other

rooms hard-wood double flooring. The beautiful frieze, by Director A. Schrandolph, of the Stuttgart Academy of Fine Arts, with the large gilded laurel wreath modelled by Professor Brandt, surrounding the entire gallery above the frieze, deserves special attention. The lighting and ventilation are perfect.

Professor Brandt spent four months in Europe in 1883 securing his purchases. Mr. W. W. Astor, United States Minister to Italy, obtained permission to have certain of the sculptures, of which there were reproductions in the Vatican collection and in other museums, moulded, and casts of these are in the Telfair collection. The British Museum in London, the Louvre Palace in Paris, the Berlin Museum, the Uffizi Palace in Florence, the Naples Museum, and others, have furnished famous works of art. The art library has received due attention.

The arrangement of the casts and reproductions from the original marbles of Phidias in the Parthenon Temple and of the frieze in the front hall shows them to great advantage. This academy has, in fact, in this branch of plastic art, a larger collection, better arranged, than any other institution in this country. The hall of painting is very beautiful. Its exquisite tapestried panellings have been much admired: they were brought from Munich. The collection of paintings is not large, but of high merit. Mr. Brandt has contributed three excellent portraits of his wife, General Henry R. Jackson, and General A. R. Lawton. There are Hacker's "Relics of the Brave," Bruett's "Farmer's Protest," from the Düsseldorf Gallery, Oesterly's "Sheep Grazing," Braith's "Fjord in Norway," reproductions of Werner's pictures of the Nile, the Acropolis of Athens, and Hildebrandt's "World Travels," and others. Mr. Brandt's intention is to add modern pictures of a high standard of art for the education of students and the people, and to assist in the development of connoisseurs who will know the good from the mediocre.

The creation of an art school is the next step in this enterprise. The foundation has been laid in a comprehensive collection of the best art achievements of the world for appreciation and study. This institution, properly managed, developed, and utilized, must make Savannah the art centre of the South.

CRUISING ON THE GULF COAST OF FLORIDA

IT is now a score of years since the hospitable *Karena,* known to the natives as " The Ark," threaded most of the waterways and ran aground on all the bars of the west coast of Florida, from Cedar Keys to Key West. It was the prototype of the cruising house-boat of that coast of to-day, and, as its owner with prophetic instinct once remarked, lacked only a little steam-tender to run its errands. In place of the *Karena* we now see floating houses, with every attribute of a home, from a *chef* to a canary, from a library to a pet cat, with sixty-horse-power engines in the basement, in which the owner changes his residence while he sleeps, and only knows where he is living when his captain tells him. Glittering launches, polished dinghies, and a uniformed crew go with this outfit, which suggests yachting rather than the cruising I care for. Stately yachts at stated times rattle their anchor-chains just within Boca Grande, while near by their chartered craft lodge the guides who know the tricks of the tides and the tarpon and reduce the labor of the fisherman to a minimum. I have seen a well-known yachtsman quietly enjoy his magazine and cigar on the deck of his boat while his guide trolled for tarpon within a few hundred feet. When a tarpon was hooked, the sportsman laid aside his magazine and was rowed out to the skiff of his guide, from which he captured what was left of the fish. There are house-boats of simple construction which are moved about by tugs, and often anchored for the season in one place. They make inexpensive homes with attractive features, but they are not cruisers. Occasionally, a should-be cruiser becomes conventionalized, and goes back and forth from Fort Myers, to Punta Rasa, and Boca Grande, fishing in orthodox fashion on the predetermined dates.

The interest of a cruise is often in inverse ratio to its cost. Two young men, with some knowledge of sailing and a genuine love for the camp-fire, arrived on the west coast of Florida with two months in time and two hundred dollars to spend. They bought a sloop with a small skiff for one hundred dollars, enlarged and fitted up the cabin at a cost of seventy-five dollars, invested twenty-five dollars in supplies, and buried themselves among the Ten Thousand Islands. Two months later they emerged with clothing in tatters, faces and arms red as the Indians with whom they had consorted, bodies rugged, and stores of experience sufficient to illuminate their lives. They sold their outfit at cost, reducing their net expenses for two months to the twenty-five dollars paid for supplies, to which the wilderness had contributed, without cost, fish, game, and fruit.

My latest cruise began as a family affair, with the girl, the camera-man, and a captain. Another girl was needed, so we borrowed the tree-lady, who, having just evolved from her inner consciousness a tree-book, which was counted authoritative, was now anxious to see some real trees.

Our equipment was the result of compromises between the requirements of deep-water cruising and shallow-bay exploration, and between cabin capacity and seaworthiness. It consisted of a yawl-rigged, flat-bottomed boat 37×14, with a draught of three feet, a cabin 20×12×6 feet, two skiffs, and a small launch. Fittings and furnishings were severely practical, and included dark room, tools for all ordinary repair-work, and fishing, hunting, and photographic outfits.

Starting from Marco, we gave the tree-lady her choice between tarpon and crocodiles, and as she selected the former, sailed for Charlotte Harbor and the tarpon resorts of Captiva Pass and Boca

THE HOUSEBOAT AT ANCHOR

Grande, where the season was at its height. On the first day at Captiva Pass the tarpon scored. The tree-lady was in a skiff with the camera-man, making tarpon jump while he photographed them; the girl was on Captiva beach gathering shells, leaving me to fish by myself, which I did by placing my tarpon-rod on the seat beside me, with the bait trolling behind the skiff as I rowed in the swift current of the pass. There came a highly pitched buzz of the reel, a wild leap six feet in air of a frightened tarpon, and my rod flew over the stern of the skiff, leaving a straight wake to the Gulf. I fancy that the whole outfit—rod, massive reel, and six hundred feet of costly line—was an exhibit that night at some club of tarpon devoted to the baiting of fishermen. I should like to see the legend attached to it, to know the estimate of my weight, and to hear the account of the contest, that I might compare the stories told by fish with those told about them.

We were fishing for the camera, and when the hooked tarpon ceased to pose they were turned loose, with a single exception. The tree - lady wanted some tarpon scales big enough to weigh the fish-stories she was preparing for her family. At Boca Grande we anchored north of the pass, safe from everything but a gale from the northeast, which is what came to us with the going down of the sun. A strong tide held the boat in the trough of the sea, and a wicked roll caused havoc in the cabin, where a bottle of oil breaking on the floor made walking thereon distressing. As the tide rushed past, it created a wake of phosphorescent fire, and an occasional wave breaking over us bathed the boat in liquid moonshine, while filling the cockpit with water that had to be bailed out. We hoisted the jigger to hold the boat across the seas, and gave the hurricane-anchor a few more fathoms of chain. Our captain was on shore unable to join us. Four times he dragged his skiff through the surf and tried to row to us, but four times he was capsized and swept back. As the night wore on, the launch filled and sank, and the remaining skiff was swamped, broke her painter, and was washed ashore. In the morning the captain succeeded in reaching us, although his skiff sank under him just as he caught the line we threw him. We made tackle fast to the launch, lifted it until it could be bailed out, and then hoisting a sail with many reefs, spent an exciting quarter of an hour in clawing away from the beckoning beach. Following the storm, the fishing at Boca Grande was marvellous. The mile-wide pass was filled with minnows by the thousand million, making dark patches upon the water, often many acres in extent. Among them porpoises rolled, thousands of tarpon leaped, the fins of hundreds of great sharks cut lanes through them, uncountable cavalli, Spanish mackerel, bluefish,

ladyfish, and other predatory small fry, devouring and being devoured, beat the water into surflike waves; while, moved by a single impulse, here, there, and everywhere, minnows by the yard or acre were leaping three feet in the air, filling it with rainbow-tinted masses of spray. Everywhere the water was covered with dying minnows and spangled throughout with their scales. As our skiff was rowed among them, tarpon leaped about it, drenching us with water and throwing hundreds of minnows and other little fish into the boat. A small fish, which had fallen aboard, was put upon a tarpon-hook, and as it dropped overboard was swallowed by a jack-fish, which in turn was seized by a tarpon. A great shark took up the trail of the tarpon, and a moment later had bitten him in two, at the same time striking the skiff so vicious a blow that I was glad to remember that, contrary to current superstition.

COCOA AND DATE PALMS NEAR SHELL MOUNDS
Relic of the Aborigines

SHARK PURSUING TARPON
A fraction of a second lost a record picture. The wake of the pursuing shark may be seen, but the camera was
too late to catch the fish himself

the shark in this country never attacks a human being.

Tarpon - fishing with the camera is the apotheosis of sport. There is yet to be discovered anything more picturesque and thrilling than the leap of the near-by tarpon, filling the air with prismatic drops, and the gleaming silver of its gracefully contorted body brilliantly reflecting the rays of the sun.

Only less spectacular, because of its Lilliputian scale, is the leap of the lady-fish, which rises to a fly and gives an acrobatic performance that makes the best work of any known game-fish look very tame. Sea - trout, Spanish mackerel, channel - bass, and other game-fish kept the larder full and gave continuous sport at every pass in Charlotte Harbor and Pine Island Sound from Gasparilla to Punta Rasa. Half an hour with a landing-net on the shore would fill a bucket with crabs, while on any moonlight night from May to July great turtles could be found crawling on the beach, and turned over for stews and steaks, or followed to their crawls for the one hundred and thirty to one hundred and eighty eggs which would be there in the morning. We beach-combed for shells from Gasparilla to Big Marco Pass — all but the tree - lady, who explained that she was under contract to produce a standard work of reference

on conchology and must approach the subject with a mind that was blank. Later when she sailed for the north from Marco, we turned south for the crocodile country. From Coon Key to Sand-fly Pass our course lay outside the keys, and we ran before a gale under jib and jigger, landing disgracefully among the bushes when we tried to stem the tide that flowed from Chokloskee Bay. Here we found a party of Seminole Indians, paved the way for a visit to their camp, and obtained a full-grown wild-cat, or lynx. We made a cage for "Tom," who day by day grew more ferocious and had to be fed at the end of a stick. He nearly ate up his cage in his efforts to get free, but when his door was opened, hesitated long before he came out. He then walked slowly, growling at everybody, but so surprised by the indifference with which he was regarded that he soon began to make advances, and finally laid a tentative paw upon the hand of the captain as he stood at the wheel. Thereafter he became friendly, sometimes too friendly, occasionally playfully jumping upon any one who happened to be sleeping on deck, which, until we got used to it, was exciting.

From Pavilion Key south the coast is one vast bank of clams, perennially inviting the cruiser to go overboard and tread for them. One night when anchored with light tackle a few miles below Pavilion, a gale from the southwest dragged the anchor, a big wave lifted us, and at the very top of a spring-tide dropped us on a high coral reef. The next morning we were many yards from water, with the chances that we were settled for a month; but happily a favoring wind that day raised the water enough to enable us to haul the boat back into her element. As our cruise led us through crooked channels in the shallow water of the Bay of Florida, we often ran aground, but by promptly going overboard could usually push off into deeper water. Once we had to dig the boat out, loosening the mud under it with a hoe and washing it away by a current from the propeller of the launch.

At Madeira Hammock we anchored for a crocodile-hunt, in the interest of the camera, and for ten days in skiffs explored creeks and bays in the pursuit. Once we turned aside to follow with a harpoon three big fins travelling tandem that belonged to a thirteen-foot sawfish, whose thousand pounds propelled a broad four-foot saw, armed with fifty-two teeth, through schools of smaller fish. He belonged to the detested shark family, and we wasted no sympathy on him as he towed us at racing speed through a mile of creek and bayou. We caught a number of crocodiles, but their story belongs to the camera-man. We took with us for shipment to the Bronx Zoological Gardens, at Bronx Park in New York, one ten-foot specimen which we had captured in his cave, and sailed for Marco, where the camera-man left us for New York. On the way up the coast the cat and the crocodile quarrelled, and to save the eyes of the saurian we put him overboard one evening with a rope around his body. During the night he died—mysteriously. The lynx swam ashore in response to the crowing of a cock, and perished in a hen-roost, but not mysteriously. Both had been prematurely promised to the Zoo in New York, and I was mortified; so I visited a rookery, captured and shipped a dozen pelicans for the Zoo, and again sailed for the crocodile country. We started on Friday, wherefore the girl predicted disaster, and reminded us thereof on the following day when a heavy

rain-squall struck us, shut us up in semi-darkness and proceeded to box the compass with the boat. When the squall got through with us we were under bare poles, with the jib our only hoistable sail. Two days later at Madeira Hammock I stood again, harpoon-pole in hand, in the bow of the skiff, which my perspiring boatman patiently sculled among the keys, over the flats, and through the labyrinthic rivers that lie between the Bay of Florida and the saw-grass of the Everglades. The harpoon was simply a pointed bit of barbed steel, only capable of penetrating one inch beyond the barb, and intended merely to maintain communication with the quarry until it could be secured by other means.

One morning, just after we had started on our daily cruise, a series of swirls in the water near us, the language of which was then unfamiliar, seemed to tell of a frightened crocodile and that the hunt was on. We followed the zigzagging trail of muddy water as fast as we could scull and pole, getting occasional glimpses of a fleeing something, until the full view of it under the bow of the skiff gave me the chance I was seeking. As the harpoon struck a broad back, which was not that of a crocodile, the creature rose above the surface, and a big beaverlike tail deluged me with half a barrel of water as it struck and nearly swamped the skiff, and told me that I had at last found the manatee which I had vainly hunted during many years. For hours we chased the creature, keeping a light strain on the harpoon-line, frightening him as he came up to breathe, until, exhausted, he rose more and more frequently, and I made a score of unsuccessful casts of a lasso at this specimen of the wild cattle of the sea. Finally the manatee came to the surface to breathe so near the skiff that I put my left arm around his neck as far as it would go and tried to slip the noose over his head with my right. The sudden lifting of his head threw me upon his back, while a twist of his big tail sent me sprawling. We were swamped four times while working the manatee into shallow water, where we got overboard, fastened a line around him, and soon had him under control, although when the captain got astride of the creature he was promptly made to

LOOKING FOR SHELLS ALONG THE BEACH

turn a back somersault. Docile as our captive had become, he was yet eleven feet long, of massive proportions, and a weight which was difficult to handle. We tore the seats out of the skiff, sank it, and succeeded in getting the creature over it. Then, having bailed out the water, we were paddling the overladen craft out in the bay, when a cataclysm left us swimming side by side, while a submerged skiff was being towed Gulfward by a rejoicing manatee. We soon recaptured and persuaded him into shallow water, where I herded him while the captain went to the big boat for an anchor and cable, with which we made our captive fast, giving him two hundred feet of rope in an excellent seacow pasture.

We were now candidates for a dungeon and liable to a big fine because of our unlawful detention of a highly protected mammal, so we sailed for Miami in pursuit of an *ex post facto* permit. The authorities were good to me when convinced of the educational destiny of the manatee, and in a week I returned with permits in my pocket, promises of free transportation by rail and steamer to the New York Aquarium, telegrams of congratulation from the Zoo people, and lumber for a tank for the manatee, only to find no trace of anchor, cable, or captive. Our boat had been struck by lightning in Miami, but the shock to our nerves, although serious, was light in comparison with this.

For a day we followed the zigzag trail of the anchor flukes, through a water glass over half a mile of the bottom of the bay, until we came upon the anchor, cable, and worn-through harness from which the manatee had escaped. I returned to Marco; here I left the girl, took aboard gasoline for a thousand miles' trip, four weeks' provisions for two, and sailed south with my boatman to capture a manatee. We explored the waterways between the

Everglades and the Gulf from Capes Romane to Sable. We sailed up broad rivers which narrowed until the bowsprit plunged into the bushes at every tack and the towed skiff gathered oysters from overhanging mangrove branches as it swung against the bank. We followed the contracting channels with the launch, until we were flying at full speed through crooked creeks, with bushes from the banks sweeping our craft on either side. When the branches closed over the stream, we dragged the skiff under them to the everglades or the end of the creek. We struck waterspout weather off Shark River, when conical clouds sent swirling tails dancing over the surface of the water, which they sometimes touched and drew upward in huge swaying columns. The next day our boat lay becalmed at the mouth of the Rogers River, which we explored in the launch.

As we started, graceful frigate-pelicans floated high above us with motionless wings, while on the water about us their awkward namesakes filled pouches with food for their families, and flew homeward with the curious intermittent strokes peculiar to these birds. The round head and bright eyes of the grass-eating green turtle bubbled up for a moment above the water, in pleasing contrast with the grosser head of his loggerhead cousin. Water-turkeys dropped heavily in the river as we passed, then quickly thrust snakelike heads above its surface to gaze at us. Herons, big and little, blue, white, and green, flapped lazily out of our way with discordant cries; brown curlews, roseate spoonbills, and white ibises sat undisturbed upon nearby trees; egrets and long whites forgot the bitter lessons that man's cupidity and woman's vanity had taught them, and even a monkey-faced owl, big and white, unknowing how rare a specimen he was, turned goggle-eyes upon the gun beside me. At the head of the river a tropical storm burst upon us, followed by a calm, and filled the western sky with massive clouds wonderfully colored, which were duplicated in the mirror of the water, until the illusion of a sky beneath us of infinite depth made me cling to the boat for dizziness. At the end of a long vista the middle ground of slim palmetto

THE PET WILDCAT

CRANES FEEDING ON MUD-FLATS

and towering royal palms completed an unforgettable picture.

We had explored Lossmans River to the Everglades, and were cruising the bays near its head, when, about dusk, we saw a big rattlesnake swimming towards a mangrove key. To cut him off compelled us to run the launch full speed into the key. The skiff in tow came surging up beside us, and the snake was between the two boats. We got the snake in the skiff, where the captain held him down with an oar until I had him safely by the neck. After extracting the fangs of the reptile, which was six and a half feet long and had ten rattles, I tied him in the boat to be skinned for mounting the next morning. Sometimes, as we cruised, the big eyes of a wondering deer gazed upon us from a bit of meadow; once I snapped the camera-shutter on a black face with white eyeballs, framed in an opening in the mangrove bushes, and on the same day in the depth of the wilderness we exchanged nods of half recognition with an alligator-hunter upon whose head was a price.

The days left us were few. Sweet bay-leaves had supplanted coffee, palmetto-cabbage was our vegetable, cocoa-plums, custard-apples, wild limes and lemons our fruit, and hour by hour we measured the gasoline left in the tank. One morning, with scant two inches in the launch, I estimated that we could go through Shark to Harney River, up that to the Everglades, and return. Far up the river we went, among beautiful keys, between richly wooded banks, past Golgotha camps of alligator-hunters and trappers of otter; in channels choked with moss and grass, which had to be cleared from the propeller every few minutes; along shores covered with wading birds; over waters alive with alligators and thickly dotted with the heads of fresh-water terrapin, until the launch was stopped by a solid mass of lily-pads, covering the stream and held in place by stems eight feet long, through which startled alli-

SUNSET OVER THE GULF

gators made their way along the river-bed, setting the pads above to dancing mysteriously. Forcing our way in the skiff through half a mile of pads, we reached the Everglades, and following an Indian trail, pushed far out on its surface for a final interview with a region which, although desolate, was yet strangely fascinating. When but a mile of our return trip was left, a frightened manatee, just ahead of our launch, rolled his body half out of water, like a porpoise, and throwing his tail in the air, started down the river. This was our last chance, and we followed his every turn. When he headed up-stream to escape us, we were so near that again he leaped half out of water, and soon was so exhausted that he rose for breath every few seconds. My hopes, which had died, were resurrected, and already I was drawing up the skiff for the final act, when the engine stopped, with its last drop of gasoline, and the manatee-chase was ended.

As we silently poled the launch home-ward, my mind ran over the results of the hunt. We had seen a dozen manatee and had a calling acquaintance with half that number. We were familiar with their slightest appearance above the water and with the signs they left beneath it. We had seen them as Romeos and Juliets, and often when within a few feet of one had only been thwarted by the darkness of the water which in the rainy season pours from the cypress and man-grove swamps. A tiller-rope broken dur-ing the excitement of a quick turn had saved one from probable capture, and as I remembered that an impulse of emotional insanity had held my hand when a mother manatee with an unweaned calf pressed close to her side rose beside me, I thought with bitterness of the poet who wrote, "The quality of mercy is not strained." But I knew where the creatures lived, and when we reached our boat, just as the stars came out, I had determined that in the hunt for a manatee it was only the first chapter that had closed.

THE SALZBURGER EXILES, IN GEORGIA

THE colonial currents to the American continent were of great variety. The Spanish and Portuguese were ostentatious in the extreme. The English settlers, dividing between the Plymouth and the James River colonies, cared but little what the great world said about them or saw of them. They were intent on a permanent home, among new and more roomy conditions. The French colonists aspired for possession of the territory. But the missionaries who accompanied them were occupied solely in introducing the gospel among the native races. The Dutch, all aglow with their new independence at home and with their maritime successes on the Eastern seas, labored to open new lines of commerce by a firm occupation along the Atlantic coast of the Western hemisphere.

But apart from all these prominent colonial settlements in the newly discovered America, there were smaller deposits which attracted no general European notice. The general edict of Pedro Moya, of Contreras, dated Mexico, November 3, 1571, issued on the establishment of the Holy Inquisition in Mexico, condemns the Jews, the followers of Mohammed, and the sect of Martin Luther. We have, therefore, the remarkable fact that in the very body of the original Spanish conquerors there were those three classes of heretics. President Stiles, of Yale, in his sermon before the General Assembly of Connecticut in 1783, declares that there is a "Greek Church brought from Smyrna." But his statement is not definite as to its habitat. He says, "I think it falls below these States"—that is, south of the Middle States and Georgia. There was an important colony of Jews in the new province of Georgia. They came over directly from London. Governor Oglethorpe was importuned to protest against their welcome. But that wise and liberal founder of the province inquired into their character and purposes, and being satisfied, gave them a cordial welcome. These Jews justified his confidence, and became an important and valuable factor in the new population.

Among these minor colonial groups, whose purpose was simply a safe home for conscience and person, must be reckoned the Salzburger exiles. Their whole history had been a thrilling romance. Their real ancestors had been the Waldenses of the Piedmontese Alps. That little body of independent believers, whose history had been marked by ten persecutions, and whom the Dukes of Savoy had failed to repress, suffered an occasional thinning of its ranks. But whenever a scion was lopped off, it was only a transference of faith and stubborn existence. So, when one of these small bodies emigrated eastward, and settled in the quiet little Tyrolese nook of Tieffereck, a valley of the Salzburg principality, they thought that at last they were safe from the lash of persecution. But they no sooner became thrifty, and developed in numbers, and their Protestant principles became public, than they were summoned before the reigning bishop, and were ordered to renounce their Lutheran sentiments.

This they refused to do. A universal

CHURCH IN NEW EBENEZER.

persecution was ordered. But for the kindly intervention of the Elector of Brandenburg, the ancestor of the present ruling family of Prussia, and of other Protestant rulers, it is probable that the Salzburger Protestants would have been put to death. They were offered the opportunity of exile, and gladly embraced it. They set out on foot in search of friends and liberty. It was a pilgrimage of sublime faith. They were received with open arms in many towns. The farther north they went, the more pronounced was their welcome. Some reached Berlin, where, like the Huguenots from France, they were accorded a hearty reception.

That portion of the fugitive pilgrims which became the first Salzburger colony to Georgia followed the course of the Rhine down to Holland. Their journey was tedious, and the future uncertain. They enlivened their journey by the singing of hymns, born of their sorrows. One of the most familiar was the one commencing thus:

"I am a wretched exile here—
 Thus must my name be given—
From native land and all that's dear,
 For God's Word I am driven.

"Full well I know, Lord Jesus Christ,
 Thy treatment was no better;
Thy follower I now will be;
 To do Thy will I'm debtor.

"Henceforth a pilgrim I must be,
 In foreign climes must wander;
O Lord, my prayer ascends to Thee,
 That Thou my path wilt ponder."

Already in December, 1732, the invitation had been extended from the Trustees of the new colony of Georgia to fifty families of the Salzburger Protestants, to come to England and join the English colony to Georgia. On the 27th of November of the following year this first band reached Rotterdam. Here their future pastors, Rev. John M. Bolzius and Rev. Israel C. Gronau, met them. Both had been teachers in Francke's Orphan House at Halle, but resigned their positions for the purpose of casting in their lot with the emigrants to the wilds of America. The Trustees of the province of Georgia had ships in waiting. In these the exiles embarked and sailed to Dover, England. On reaching that port the Trustees met them, and were greatly pleased with them. An oath was administered to each Salzburger of "strict piety, loyalty, and fidelity." Solemn parting services were held, after which the *Puris-burg*, bearing the exiles, set sail for Georgia.*

The interest of the Trustees of the new colony in the persecuted Salzburgers was no new passion. It is probable that from the first moment when their sorrows became known to the British public, the humane Oglethorpe determined upon assisting them. Who knows but that when he was a brave soldier under Marlborough, and won his laurels in Germany, he came across some of the persecuted Protestants on the Bavarian plains, and hoped that when the peaceful days should come, he might succor them or their brothers? This at least is certain, that the Trustees of the colony of Georgia, who were simply Oglethorpe and a few helpers, regarded the Salzburgers as of special importance. Indeed, one of the real designs of the new colony, as named in the charter, was to furnish "a refuge for the distressed Salzburgers and other Protestants." The Salzburgers consisted at first of only fifty families.

Oglethorpe was already in Georgia when the *Purisburg*, with its precious freight of Salzburgers, arrived, on March 12, 1734. He gave them a cordial welcome, and assigned them a tract up the Savannah River, at a distance of twenty-four miles from his town of Savannah.

The land where the Salzburgers settled was not directly on the river, but on a creek connecting with it. They called their settlement Ebenezer. Here they constructed dwellings, a house of worship, a mill, and indeed all the buildings necessary for their new life in the wilderness. They were in the midst of an immense pine forest. Their joy knew no bounds. They were at last safe from persecution.

The Salzburgers at first breathed freely in their Ebenezer among the pines; but their life was one of long and patient trial. There were marshy places and stagnant pools, which produced malaria. The people were too remote from metropolitan Savannah, which only a few years before, in February, 1733, had been laid out by Oglethorpe, and consisted at first of only "a few tents under four pine-trees." The "river" on whose banks they had built their mill, and where they had gathered in the evenings to talk of the

* Strobel, *The Salzburgers and their Descendants*, pp. 54ff.

best means of getting far-off partners in language and faith to join them, was merely a lazy creek, which in a direct line to the Savannah River was only six miles, but was so tortuous that the distance to row a boat was twenty-four miles.

The settlers resolved to apply to Oglethorpe to give them another grant of land. Their request was complied with, and they were permitted to remove a few miles to the bank of the Savannah River. Here, at last, they were truly happy. They still adhered to the name of their first settlement, and called their second home New Ebenezer, the former settlement ever afterward retaining the name of Old Ebenezer. It is only in the locality itself that these distinctions of Old and New are known. Their stay at the first place being short, and the settlement on the bank of the Savannah permanent, the Ebenezer of history, the Mecca of the Salzburgers in America, has borne the general name of Ebenezer.

When the Salzburgers were at last established on the bank of the river, nothing was needed to complete their happiness but the companionship of their brethren whom they had left in sorrows at home. They applied to General Oglethorpe for direct aid in securing the passage to America of those with whom they had been in correspondence, and who wished to join their far-off companions in faith.

The life of the community at Ebenezer was one of Acadian simplicity. The herdsmen took their cattle out into the woods for grazing, and returned with them in the evening. There was no court of justice. Whenever differences occurred, the senior minister, the Rev. Mr. Bolzius, called three or four of the eldest together and settled the dispute. All parties submitted willingly to the decision. There was public worship every Wednesday evening, and twice on Sundays. The people very early built a church and an orphan-house. It was this orphan-house which so pleased Whitfield, when he visited the place, that he made it the model for his celebrated orphanage at Bethesda, for which he made collections along the Atlantic coast, and toward which the quiet Benjamin Franklin one day emptied his pockets of their contents of copper, silver, and gold. One of the most important departments of the Salzburger life was their industries. They paid special attention to the raising of cattle, and seem to have kept up a stock farm at Old Ebenezer long after their removal to the new settlement. They also had a bell-foundry, and in those days the fame of the sweet-toned Salzburger bell went far and wide, and, for aught we know, some of them are still heard in the pine groves of Georgia.

But the most distinctive industry of the Salzburgers was the culture of the silk-worm and the weaving of silk. Even as far north as Virginia much care was bestowed on silk. General Oglethorpe

abandoned the silk industry. But the Salzburgers persevered, and in 1751 they sent over to England one thousand pounds of cocoons and seventy-four pounds of raw silk, which brought them a return of one hundred and ten pounds sterling. The Trustees of the province encouraged the industry by giving to each female who should learn the art of spinning a reeling-machine and two pounds sterling in money.

All about the old church at the present Ebenezer there are still mulberry-trees,

LUTHERAN SALZBURGER CHURCH IN SAVANNAH.

shared in this general enthusiasm, and encouraged the industry among the colonists. As far back as 1733 the Trustees of the province induced Nicolas Amatis, of Piedmont, to remove to Georgia. Besides his family, Amatis took with him his servant, Jaques Camuse, for the special purpose of rearing silk-worms and manufacturing silk. In 1736 the Salzburger pastor, the Rev. Mr. Bolzius, led in introducing the industry among his people. In 1742 five hundred mulberry-trees were sent to Ebenezer, and a machine was erected for preparing the silk. By the year 1750 nearly all the English had

no doubt the neglected descendants of the original planting a century and a half ago. Indeed, the present Salzburgers have not quite given up the working in silk. I stopped at the home of a venerable couple where I saw the plain and well-worn spinning-reels used for this purpose. There is, however, no longer any weaving of silk in all the region. The only article manufactured is fishinglines. These are of the finest and strongest quality, and are in great demand in Savannah.

Some of the silk goods manufactured by Oglethorpe's colonists commanded a high price in the markets of the Old World. The Queen of England on one occasion surprised her guests by wearing a dress made entirely of the silk woven by the Georgia weavers.

The colonists developed steadily. Their pastors were active in promoting both spiritual and temporal interests, and were the real leaders in all things. They had places of worship and separate societies in Savannah, Ebenezer, Zion, Bethany, and Goshen. They paid strict attention to establishing schools. Their life was in almost every respect a separate

A SALZBURGER HOUSE BUILT OF CYPRESS BLOCKS.

one from that of the English colonists, but on all public questions there was perfect harmony. When the disturbances occurred which led to the Revolution, it was not long a question on which side the Salzburgers would cast their lot. They espoused the cause of independence with great fervor. The few who adhered to the royal standard lost the sympathy of the great body of the community. In the Provincial Congress held at Savannah, July 4, 1774, to take measures for supporting the people of Boston in their opposition to the Stamp Act and other causes of offence, there were many Salzburger delegates. Among them were John Sterk, John A. Truetlen, Jacob Waldhaur, John Floerel, and Christopher Craemer.

This early devotion to the cause of independence brought its severe penalty. Ebenezer lay on the highroad from Au-

gusta to Savannah, and was frequently a stopping-place for marauders and regular troops. The British, apparently fully aware of the adverse sentiments of the people, spared nothing. The Salzburger church was at first used as a hospital, but was for a time converted into a stable. During the whole war the Salzburgers were in a condition of great distress. The settlement was threatened with total extinction. But with the achievement of national independence the people again gave proof of their original vitality, and organized their industries and their stately little institutions with all the old fervor and persistence. With the beginning of the present century we find them still adhering to their severe morality and their industrious habits. In 1824 they ceased to hold worship in the German language, and adopted the English. About the same time the financial support which had come from Germany and England was entirely cut off, and the Salzburgers were left to support their schools and worship entirely by their own contributions. Their pastors were as remarkable for their longevity as for their devotion to the spiritual and material interests of the people. Bolzius served thirty-two years, Rabenhorst twenty years, and the elder Bergmann thirty-six years.

One of the most curious parts of the life of the Salzburger colony during its entire history was the literary means employed to make known its fortunes to friends and lookers-on in Europe. The Rev. Samuel Urlsperger, pastor of St. Ann's Lutheran Church in Augsburg, continued his interest in them long after he had bidden farewell to them while on their foot journey from Salzburg to the sea. He arranged that correspondence be kept up with him after the arrival of the exiles in America. The principal correspondent was Pastor Bolzius. He kept a minute journal of the daily life of the community, and this, with all public matters relating to the English and the Indians, he reported regularly to his friend in Augsburg. Urlsperger edited this vast mass of information with great care, and issued it from the Orphan-house Press of Halle, Germany. With the exception of Stevens's *Journal*, the *Ausführliche Nachrichten* is the most valuable storehouse of facts during this period of the history of the colony of Georgia. It was published in parts as they arrived from Georgia. The first part is ornamented with a map of Georgia and a portrait of Tomo Chachi Mico, the friendly Indian chief who gave Oglethorpe a cordial welcome, and afterward made a journey to England. The *Nachrichten* is now a very rare book. While the copy in my possession comprises over four thousand pages, small folio, it is far from complete.

The celebrated *Hallische Nachrichten*, while not dealing with the Salzburgers, is of equal importance with the Urlsperger *Nachrichten*, because of its minute treatment of the settlement and historical development of the Evangelical Lutherans of Pennsylvania. The correspondent was Muhlenburg, and his communications were received at Halle, and were published by the press of the celebrated Orphan-house of Francke. The *Hallische Nachrichten* is about as rare as the Urlsperger *Nachrichten*, but this want is now supplied by a new edition, which is now appearing in this country.

These two detailed reports of Germans in this country to their friends in the Old World occupy a unique place in the literature of the colonies. The disposition of the Puritans to sustain close relations with their brethren in England was manifested by separate treatises on church government, monographs on the Indians, and brief historical and biographical accounts. The Swedes, settling on the Delaware, reported descriptive accounts, such as the excellent works of Acrelius and Campanius. The Salzburgers, however, while one of the smallest of all the fugitive societies from Europe, stand before the world as the authors of the most circumstantial report ever sent from a Protestant religious body in colonial America to their helpful and loving co-religionists in Europe. It must not be forgotten, however, that for minute reporting to the authorities in Europe, the *Relations* of

the Jesuit fathers from France excel all other accounts of missionary laborers in the New World.

Within the last half-century there has been no material increase in the Salz-

SECTIONAL VIEW OF A SALZBURGER HOUSE, SHOWING MANNER OF DOVETAILING.

burger community. The mission of these humble people has not been to be ministered unto, but to minister. Their religious life has been an important factor in the development of Georgia, not alone as a colony, but as a State. Their spirit has penetrated all communions. Especially the Baptists and the Methodists have been strengthened by the accession of members from the Salzburger societies. Among the Methodists in Effingham County today are the Hineleys, Sherrans, Bergsteiners, Neidlingers, Zittraners, and Zettlers; while among the Baptists are the Rohns, Dashers, Waldhaurs, Wisenbakers, Bergsteiners, and others. The constant tendency on the part of the young is to affiliate with the churches distinctively American. I learned in Savannah that many of the most thriving citizens are direct descendants of the original Salzburgers. Their ancestry has been of such honorable character that it is not surprising that the present Salzburger generation should be held in especial esteem.

The Salzburgers took great care to provide themselves with books. The present pastor, Austin, invited me to examine a box and a barrel, both of which were filled with remnants of books used by the exiles. Huge folio copies of Bibles had become dilapidated by much use, and later by neglect resulting from the use of more convenient copies. Arndt's *True Christianity* was a permanent book, and, indeed, is still in use by the Germans of America, as by their brethren in the fatherland. I saw a copy of *Spener's Selections from the Holy Scriptures*, published in Frankfurt-on-Main in 1713; Madai's *Brief Information on the Utility and Use of Medicines*, prepared in the Francke Orphan-house, published in Halle in 1779; Luther's *Smaller Catechism*, published by Carl Cist in Philadelphia in 1795; *Reading-book for Small Children*, also published by Cist in 1795; and Bachmair's *Complete German Grammar*, published by Henry Miller in Philadelphia in 1772. The most unaccountable of all the dead books in this mass of printed matter in Pastor Austin's barn was a fiery work in German bearing the title of *A Meditation on the Crime of Drunkenness*, published "in the year 1741." Neither place nor author is given. From the presence of many anglicized German words, and from the excellent paper, less flexible than the German printing-paper of the last century, I was of the opinion that the pamphlet was printed in this country, and was not without suspicion that it had come from the press of Benjamin Franklin. On consulting Mr. Charles R. Hildeburn, of Philadelphia, the author of *A Century of Printing: the Issues of the Press in Pennsylvania, 1685-1748*, he replied that he had little doubt that it was issued from the press of Christopher Saur. If this be the case it must be admitted that it is not found in Mr. Charles G. Sower's list of the *Publications of Christopher Sower*. Whoever was the publisher of this little work, it gives ample proof that while spirituous liquors were at that early date prohibited in the province of Georgia, the Salzburger exiles were so well satisfied with the regulation that they were determined that no change should be made in it.

The land of the Salzburgers is now most easily reached by taking the railroad from Savannah for the little station of Guyton. This rural village is in Effingham County, which takes its name from Lord Effingham, who was associated with Pitt, Burke, and others of the day in befriending the oppressed American colonies. I had telegraphed for a conveyance, and found one ready on my arrival. But the driver had little acquaintance with the territory, and no sympathy with its charming historical associations. So we soon parted. Mr. Mannette, a shopkeeper of Guyton, was good enough to serve me as both driver and guide for the long day through the calm pine forests. His French name awakened my curiosity, and I found him to be a descendant of both Huguenot and Salzburger ancestry. He knew every path over all the country, and was well acquainted with the humble and honest folk scattered here and there in the woods.

It is difficult to imagine a more weird and suggestive scene than is presented by a ride in early spring through the country made memorable by the exiles. The silence is almost painful. After leaving Guyton, I had not ridden a mile in our primitive wagon before the wilderness began. Now and then we passed a house which bore the unmistakable traces of the early period, or was modelled after the original houses. The mode of construction was various enough. The weather-boarding consisted of sawn logs, which were dovetailed at the corners of the house. A hole was bored through the logs at these corners, and a long wooden pin was driven through from top to bottom. For long stretches the pine forest cannot show a clearing. In one case a little school-house, quite dilapidated, relieves the monotony. But the wonder is where the children lived who ever attended it. The pines stand up in straight and tall shafts. They bear a large amount of wounding. To extract the turpentine, the axeman *boxes* them. His process is to make a deep incision, which is so shaped as to serve as a cup or box for receiving the turpentine. Hundreds of boxed pines are constantly in sight. The tree is afterward cut down if it is at all an advantage to convert it into lumber and haul it to market. There are large sections of burnt pines, which have been caught in a woods fire, and are charred and dead from trunk to the utmost branch. The road winds gracefully through this great forest, with no sound but that of the insects.

After going many miles through the

forest, in an atmosphere densely laden with the perfume of the pines, we turned abruptly to the left. Here we drove over an old road, now overgrown with shrubbery almost strong enough to arrest our progress. I was now on the site of Old Ebenezer, the first resting-place of the Salzburgers, whence they removed to the present settlement, or New Ebenezer. A careful examination resulted in finding no trace whatever of a building, or even of a place where it could be seen that one had stood. That historical sawmill, the first in all the region to convert the primeval pines into lumber, and which had cost fifteen hundred pounds sterling to establish, had entirely disappeared. Talifer says that it was already a ruin in 1740,* and it is not surprising that my hope to discover at least the place where it had stood and done its good work was without proper warrant. But the dull and narrow little creek was still there. This was the *river* on whose banks the exiles first settled, and where they remained until their removal to New Ebenezer.

We now returned to the main road, and proceeded on our way through the forest in a general course toward the permanent settlement on the Savannah River. The forest becomes less dense. Now and then a cottage comes into view, where a Salzburger family lives. We draw up before the home of the present senior pastor of the district, the Rev.

* *Narrative of the Colony of Georgia in America,* London, 1740, p.102.

Jacob Austin. He has an assistant, and these two perform the pastoral work for the four Salzburger churches of the entire region. Pastor Austin accompanied me to the present Ebenezer, and gave me much interesting information concerning his parishioners and their beautiful and simple life. On reaching the Savannah, I was for the first time in the presence of memorials of the first generation of the exiles. The most important of all is the church. It is a large structure, and bears evidence of long and faithful service. The present seats, although not over-comfortable, are newer than the building proper.

Along the river near the church one can easily see the fragments of rude masonry, now covered with luxuriant growths of underwood and creepers, which the British erected for protection during the Revolutionary war. The grounds about the church are ample. The graveyard is the same as was used in the early days, but has been enlarged and beautified in the later years. The graves of the pastors, who served the flock with great fidelity, are marked with appropriate stones. The inscriptions on the graves deal but little in praise, and are mostly confined to dates of birth and death. This whole God's-acre is a beautiful picture of simplicity, and is thoroughly German. As one strolls along its walks, and lingers beneath its trees, and reads the touching memorials to the beloved dead, he can easily imagine himself back in little Tyrolese Tieffereck, the cradle of the Salzburg exiles in Georgia.

THE NEW ORLEANS BENCH AND BAR

TWENTY years had elapsed since the cession of Louisiana to the French by the Spaniards, and by the French to the United States, and yet very few of the ancient population of the Latin race who had witnessed that event, or who had been born since, had acquired any knowledge of the English language, and still fewer among the new-comers of Anglo-Saxon origin had made any effort to learn to speak French, or even to understand it, so that intercourse between the two races, either for pleasure or business, was not a thing of easy accomplishment. The great majority of the ex-colonists were French in language, in blood, in feelings, in ideas, in manners, habits, and temperament. They were intensely anxious to retain an autonomy which they fondly believed to have been guaranteed by the treaty of cession. They keenly resented the act of the Federal government which made the English language the official one, and they clung the more tenaciously to the language of their ancestors. Those who had succeeded in mastering the "foreign idiom," as the English was then called, affected to use it only when they could not do otherwise, and only on rare occasions. On the other hand, the Americans, the *aventuriers* (adventurers), as they were designated at that epoch, were intent upon assimilating to themselves as quickly as possible what they looked upon as an extraneous element, which had no right to a prolonged existence. They wanted a fusion in which they would predominate and control. They were determined to absorb, but not to be absorbed. Hence, on the part of the primitive colonial inhabitants, a vigorous resistance to this projected effacement of all the old landmarks of the past *régime* of European domination. Hence also frequent collisions of an unpleasant nature; every friction between these two antagonisms emitted sparks that showed the combustibility of the materials at hand. This want of homogeneity of language and feelings manifested itself in a striking manner in the courts of justice. We proceed, as an illustration of it, to describe faithfully some of the scenes which we witnessed at the New Orleans bar a few years after that

city had become the capital of the State of Louisiana.

For a long while it was almost of absolute necessity that the judges should understand both the English and French languages, and in consequence of the motley composition of our cosmopolite population there was in every court a permanently appointed interpreter, who, as a sworn and regular officer thereof, translated the evidence, the testimony of the witnesses, and, when necessary, the charges of the judge to the jurors. Our jurisprudence was based on the laws of Spain and on the Napoleon Code, which had been adopted by our Legislature with such modifications as had been thought advisable. The commentaries of French and Spanish jurists, with decisions of the tribunals of the two countries of which Louisiana had successively been the colony, were daily and extensively quoted as authorities. The juries being composed of men some of whom did not understand one word of French, and others equally as ignorant of the English, it became imperative on litigants to employ in each case on both sides two lawyers, one speaking French, the other English, and supposed to command individually the sympathies of that portion of the population to which they belonged. Under such circumstances and exigencies the trial of cases was necessarily long and expensive. The petitions and answers, the citations, and all writs whatever, were usually in both languages, and the records containing the testimony of witnesses, and original documents with their indispensable translations, were oppressively voluminous.

Will the reader accompany me to one of the district courts of the old *régime*, and witness some of the judicial proceedings of the epoch? The presiding judge is Joshua Lewis, a high-minded gentleman, if not a profound jurist, who commands universal esteem in the community where he has come to reside. As irreproachable in his private as in his public life, Judge Lewis was born in Kentucky, and did honor both to his native and to his adopted State. When the British invaded Louisiana he hastened to descend from the bench, shouldered his rifle, and

bravely met them on the plains of Chalmette. Associating much with the ancient population, he had learned but a
little of their language, sufficient, however, to state in a few words, clearly if not
grammatically, to a jury who understood
only French, what law was applicable to
the case on which they were to decide.

The lawyers retained in the case to be
tried are Alfred Hennen for the plaintiff,
an Anglo-Saxon American, and Étienne
Mazureau for the defendant, a French
creole. Hennen is from New England.
He is a tall, well-formed, massive man,
with a handsome, benevolent face, glowing with the warm tints of a florid complexion, which denotes his Northern origin. He is invincibly self-possessed, and
no provocation can throw him off his
guard in his fortress of cold and passion-
less reserve. Nothing can ruffle his temper; and if the attempt is made he turns
it off with a good-natured laugh, which
blunts the edge of his adversary's weapon. ·
He is an erudite, but plain, dry, plodding,
practical lawyer, who never aims at any
fancy flight of eloquence. He has a large
and well-furnished library, which he liberally puts at the disposal of his friends.
He is laboriously industrious, and always
comes into court with a long string of authorities, which he uses as a lasso to throw
round the neck of his opponent. He is
not much addicted to urge upon the court
argumentative deductions from the broad
principles of jurisprudence, but prefers
relying on an overwhelming avalanche
of precedents and numerous decisions,
gathered from far and wide, in cases
which he deems similar to his own. His
fees amount to a large income, of which
he takes thrifty care, although he lives
according to the exigencies of his social
position. He is a conspicuous and worthy
member of the Presbyterian Church. He
is abstemious in his habits, very fond of
exercise on horseback and on foot, and a
strict observer of the rules and prescrip-
tions of hygiene. Like all members of
the legal profession from the other States
of the Union, he much prefers the common
to the civil law, the latter being looked
upon by them as an abortive creation of
the Latin mind, which they hold, of
course, to be naturally inferior to the
Anglo-Saxon intellect.

The lawyer on the other side is Étienne
Mazureau, a native of France, who has
emigrated to Louisiana in search of a
better fortune, and who in a few years
has risen to be one of the magnates of
the New Orleans bar. Of a medium
size, compactly built, with flashing dark
eyes, intensely black hair, and a brown
complexion, he is a perfect specimen of
the Southern type, as if to the manner
and to the manor born. He is of an ardent temperament, and the sacred fire of
the orator glows in his breast. He is
an adroit and most powerful logician, but
on certain occasions his eloquence becomes tempestuous. He delights in all the
studies appertaining to his profession, and
possesses a most extensive and profound
knowledge of the civil law, from the
twelve tables of Rome and the Institutes
of Justinian to the Napoleon Code. He
is also thoroughly familiar with the Spanish jurisprudence, which is derived from
the same source. He is deeply versed in
the common law, which, however, when
the opportunity presents itself, it is his
special pleasure to ridicule and treat with
spiteful depreciation. He is not free from
a certain degree of arrogance, based on
the consciousness he has of his learning
and of the superiority of his splendid intellectual powers. When irritated by
what he thinks futile contradiction, he
has a provoking way of throwing back
his head, and of superciliously lifting at
a right angle with surrounding objects a
nose whose nostrils dilate with contempt.
He is particularly elated when in his forensic conflicts he triumphs over an Anglo-Saxon member of the bar to whom he
happens to have taken a special dislike.
His voice is superb, now calmly argumentative, now tremulous with passion, and
frequently derisive, with sneers and sar-
casms as sharply pointed as the savagest
arrow. Aggressive by nature, he sometimes affects the most dulcet tones of con-
ciliatory placidity, and when he thus
transforms himself he is more to be
dreaded than when he is apparently in
one of his fiercest moods. ċ He is a terror
to the witnesses of the adverse party,
whom he likes to browbeat and to keep
broiling on the gridiron of his torturing inquisition. His invectives, when prompted by indignation, wrath, or any other
cause of excitement, are a sort of tropical
hurricane. He is too proud and lofty to
ever have recourse to the petty trickeries
and snap judgments of the minnows of
his noble profession, and never takes any
undue and ungentlemanly advantage of

his brethren at law. He is equally great and successful in civil and criminal cases. Hence his income is very large; but he has a peculiar knack at getting into debt and parting with his money in the most unaccountable manner. He has this characteristic in common with many men of splendid abilities, through whose pockets silver and gold run as through a sieve, much to the mortification of their creditors.

These were the two men pitted against each other in the case to which we call the attention of the reader. The plaintiff had bought a tract of land measuring, as stated in the act of sale, twenty arpents, fronting the Mississippi, and running on that line from an oak on the lower limit to a willow on the upper one. After the completion of the sale and payment of the price, it was discovered that the front of the tract measured twenty-five arpents instead of twenty. The purchaser claimed these twenty-five arpents, but the defendant was willing to surrender only twenty. Hence the suit brought by the plaintiff to be put in possession of what he claimed to have bought and paid for, and therefore his property.

Hennen had made himself acquainted with the French language, and Mazureau spoke English with great fluency, so that, contrary to what habitually took place, there was but one lawyer employed on either side.

"Oyez! oyez! The honorable First District Court of the State of Louisiana is in session!" cries the sheriff in a loud and clear voice. "Gentlemen of the jury summoned in this case," says the clerk, "please answer to your names." After this is done, the jurors are called to the sacred book.

Here a struggle ensues between the two lawyers about the composition of the jury. Hennen challenges as many of the creoles and naturalized French as he can, and Mazureau does the same with the Americans. At last the jury is formed—nine of the Latin race, and three of the Anglo-Saxon. On Mazureau's lips may be seen a smile of satisfaction. Hennen has a troubled look. Let us give a little of our attention to the manner in which that jury had been sworn.

Clerk to the first juror: "You swear that—"

1st Juror: "*Je n'entends pas. Parlez français.*" (I don't understand. Speak French.)

Clerk: "All right."

And the oath is administered in French. 2d Juror approaches to qualify.

Clerk: "*Vous jurez que—*"

2d Juror: "I don't understand. Speak English."

Clerk: "All right."

And the second juror, duly sworn in his vernacular, takes his seat; and so on to the last of the twelve, each one insisting on being addressed in his own maternal tongue.

Judge: "Mr. Augustin Macarty, I appoint you foreman of this jury."

On hearing which, Mazureau allows again an expression of approval to beam all over his face. Macarty is of an ancient and high-toned family. He has served several years as Mayor of the city, and is uncompromisingly conservative in all his views and feelings—the very embodiment of the old *régime*. It was he who, in his official capacity, as reported, and backed by public opinion, had caused the first cargo of ice brought to New Orleans to be thrown into the river as a measure of public safety, because cold drinks in the summer would affect throats and lungs, and would make consumptive the whole population. He might have added, perhaps with more propriety, that liquor refrigerated by ice might become more tempting, more provocative of thirst, and that the sweet indulgence might lead to a habit injurious to health. Be it as it may, we will venture to say something in support of the objection of dear old Macarty to the introduction of this new crystallized luxury. Are we sure that he was as absurdly ridiculous as some people may think, when we recollect that consumption, now so common among us, was almost unknown before the arrival of that ill-fated ship with its load of hyperborean product, which was soon succeeded by more welcome importations of the same kind? But let us return to the trial.

Hennen rises, and after a slight bow to the court and jury, reads to them the petition and answer, written in English and French as required. Then he says: "This case, as your honor sees, is founded on article 2495 of the Civil Code, which reads as follows:

"'*There can be neither increase nor diminution of price on account of disagreement in measure when the object is designated by the adjoining tenements and sold from boundary to boundary.*'

"This is the law on which is based the claim of my client. As to the facts alleged in the plaintiff's petition, they are admitted by the defendant, who demands five thousand dollars more for the five arpents fronting the river, with the usual depth of forty arpents; but he is not entitled to that increase of price, considering that the extent on the front line was designated by an oak and a willow that clearly marked the boundaries of the tract. If there were between these designated limits only fifteen arpents instead of twenty, the purchaser, my client, would be entitled to no diminution of the price to be paid by him, and on the same principle, when there are twenty-five arpents instead of twenty, the defendant cannot claim an increase of the sum for which the sale has been effected. This is made so plain by the words of the article of the Civil Code cited by me that I cannot conceive the object of the defendant in incurring the expenses of this litigation. He cannot but know that the verdict of this jury, confirmed by your honor, will be against him, and probably he only aims, for some purpose which I cannot imagine, at retaining possession as long as he can of the property for which he has received the stipulated price."

Then turning to the jury, he said: "Gentlemen, as the facts in this case are admitted, I have no evidence to introduce. It now becomes your duty to apply the law to those facts, and its text is so plain that its meaning cannot be a matter of doubt in anybody's mind."

During this address, which we summarily reproduce, the French and creole members of the jury had been showing signs of impatience, and it ended in this interrogation from Foreman Macarty: "Mr. Hennen, do you really presume to induce us to grant twenty-five arpents to your client when the act of sale only says twenty?"

Hennen: "The words of the contract are that the plaintiff bought a tract of land of twenty arpents, with the usual depth, extending, on the line fronting the river, from a certain oak to a certain willow that indicated the boundaries. As to the law, it says that the designation of visible limits, and not the specification of the number of arpents mentioned, is the criterion to ascertain the area of the land intended to be transferred by the seller to the purchaser."

Foreman Macarty, after having exchanged, in a whisper, a few hasty words with his French colleagues, takes a square attitude in his seat, with all the indications of a man who is going to assert an irrevocable decision. He fixes a steady eye on Hennen, and says, in a peremptory tone:

"Mr. Hennen, we are satisfied that the defendant never intended to sell, nor the plaintiff to buy, more than twenty arpents fronting the river. We don't care for your oak and your willow. It is useless for you to trouble us with such a preposterous claim. Your client is not honest, sir. It is wrong on his part to try to avail himself of an evident mistake of the defendant as to the quantity of land he thought he was selling. He certainly would have asked a larger sum if he had not been deceived on the subject. We are indignant, sir!"

Hennen, blandly: "I regret, Mr. Macarty, your misconception of the case. Allow me to say to you that I regret it for the sake of the two parties to this suit. If you persist in your views, if a verdict is rendered against the plaintiff, I will certainly appeal to the Supreme Court, who will reverse it. Meanwhile you will have done an injury to my client, whose taking possession of the land he has paid for will be delayed to his detriment, and by the prolongation of this litigation you will be the cause of inflicting on the defendant heavier costs than he would otherwise have had to pay. I beg the court to instruct the jury as to the law which is to govern their final decision."

Judge: "Gentlemen of the jury, Mr. Hennen has correctly quoted the law to you. Your duty is to enforce its application in accordance with the legislative will, and not to suit your own individual notions of the just or unjust."

Macarty: "We beg leave to remain mindful of a higher law than the one which we are desired to enforce, a law implanted in our hearts by God himself—the law of honesty, the law of conscience."

Judge: "I feel bound to tell you that I believe the Supreme Court will not sanction your views, and will probably reverse your verdict."

Macarty: "That is the affair of the Supreme Court. Ours is to act according to our conscience."

This conversation had been carried on

in French. All the while the three Anglo-Saxon members of the jury looked vacantly at every object in the court-room, and probably were wondering at the cause and meaning of all this hubbub. As to Mazureau, he seemed to be in a satisfactory condition of mind, and had been repeatedly giving nods of approbation whenever Macarty spoke. Raising his spectacles high up on his forehead above his brows, which with him was known to be a sign that he considered his work done, and that he could rest contented, he had thrown himself back on his chair, which he caused to tilt on its hind legs, and it was evident that he was keenly enjoying his adversary's prompt defeat, when it had not been necessary for him even to utter a single word to bring about this result.

But Hennen was not a man to be easily discouraged, and getting a little more animated than was his habit, he said: "Gentlemen of the jury, allow me, under the pleasure of the court, to state to you respectfully that it is the conscience of the law that you are bound to consult here, and not your self-assumed notions of right and wrong, or what you call your conscience, in administering justice in the courts of your country in conformity with the obligations of the solemn oath which you have taken. There is not a lawyer at the bar who will not tell you that this is the correct doctrine to be adopted by you in the discharge of your duties as jurors. I even appeal on this point to the eloquent orator, to the profound jurist, to whom we all look as a safe guide in all matters of law. I appeal to Mr. Mazureau himself, who appears here for the defendant."

A sneering expression of cynical triumph which had spread over Mazureau's face immediately vanished; he put on an air of sympathetic compassion for the embarrassment in which his opponent found himself, and in that ominously most dulcet tone of voice which he sometimes assumed, and which was generally indicative of the forth-coming of some fatal thrust, he said: "Mr. Hennen, will you permit me to address you one question?"

Hennen: "Certainly, sir; at your pleasure."

Mazureau: "Are you not from New England?"

Hennen: "Yes, sir."

Mazureau: "Well, in that land of your nativity, was it not lawful to burn old women as witches?"

Hennen, looking somewhat perplexed, stammered out: "It occasionally happened—in former times."

Mazureau sprang up with flashing eyes, shaking his fist dramatically at Hennen, and with a loud burst of his sonorous voice he thundered out: "Would you have executed that law? Would you have burned old women at the stake? Would you have lighted up the fire? Which of the two authorities would you have obeyed on that occasion—that conscience which God has placed in your heart, or the fanatical dictate of an impious legislation? I will not insult you by doubting your choice. And now how is it that you expect these high-minded men, these intelligent jurors, to do what you would not yourself have done? Why should they not in these days follow the example which you would have given them in former times, which is, to trample upon any immoral and nefarious law that violates the most sacred feelings of conscience and the principles of common justice between man and man?"

He paused, as if to take breath and allow his emotion to subside. Then, with calm dignity: "May it please the court, I have no more to say. The case is closed on my part." And he looked significantly at the French and creole members of the jury, who could hardly refrain from loudly expressing their applause.

Hennen stood bewildered for a minute or two, but recovering himself, he said: "May it please the court, I have only a few words to address to those members of the jury who do not understand French." After this had been done, a short charge was delivered by the judge in English and in French, and the jury retired to their room. Everybody present thought that they could not possibly agree.

In their chamber, as soon as they entered it, the jurors of the Latin race grouped themselves in a corner, talking excitedly, and looking doggedly determined not to yield an inch to the Yankees, who had sought the opposite corner, and were whispering together. This is what one of those Yankees said to his colleagues: "I cannot stay here long. I have most pressing business to attend to, and you also, I presume." There was an assenting movement of the head from those who were thus addressed. "Well," continued he, "this is a plain case. There should be a verdict for the plaintiff. But those French and creoles have no sense, you know. They are the creatures of prejudice or whim. They are not practical. Besides, they are particularly obstinate, and as they never have anything to do, they will keep us here locked up God knows how long. Had we not better humor them? It will do no harm to the plaintiff, for, as Hennen says, the Supreme Court will surely reverse our verdict."

This suggestion being accepted, the Anglo-Saxon, advancing toward Macarty and pointing to the record which that gentleman held in his hand, said, with a look and tone of interrogation, "*Vous, monsieur*, for plaintiff, eh?" Macarty shook his head negatively. "For defendant?" Macarty gave an affirmative nod. "*Eh bien, nous aussi*" (Well, we too), continued the Saxon, calling to his assistance these French words, which he recollected, and which he put together as well as he could, whilst he pointed to his two friends as concurring in his opinion.

Macarty understood the words and the action. His face became radiant, and he exclaimed, "Je vois avec satisfaction, messieurs,que vous avez de l'honneur et de la conscience, et que vous n'êtes pas hommes à donner vingt-cinq arpents à qui n'en a acheté que vingt. Allons, c'est bien; c'est très bien." (I see with satisfaction, gentlemen, that you are men of honor and have a conscience, and that you are not the men to give twenty-five arpents to one who has bought only twenty. It is well; it is very well indeed.)

Whereupon there was a general shaking of hands, and the jury returned to the court-room. The clerk announced, "Verdict for the defendant."

"Mr. Sheriff, discharge the jury," said the astonished judge.

Hennen: "May it please the court, I beg leave to file my motion of appeal from this extraordinary verdict."

The judge nods assent, and descends slowly from the bench. Mazureau approaches Hennen, who is handing some papers to the clerk. They look at each other face to face, and both laugh heartily. They seem to be much amused at something.

Mazureau pulls out his watch: "Oh! oh! already four o'clock. It is dinner-time. Hennen, my house is close by. I have to-day a fat turkey *aux truffes*, and exquisite claret just received from Bordeaux. Suppose you join me?"

"Willingly."

And the two eminent lawyers went away arm in arm.

Let us witness another jury trial, in which it happens that the two races are again divided. This contingency has been provided for, and it has been thought prudent on both sides to employ two lawyers, one speaking English and the other French. John R. Grymes, of Virginia, and Dominique Seghers, of Belgium, for plaintiff; Edward Livingston, of New York, and Moreau Lislet, of France, for defendant.

John R. Grymes claims to belong to one of the first families of Virginia, and of course is not destitute of a coat of arms. He is an elegant, *distingué* looking man, above the middle size, always fashionably well dressed, always systematically courteous. He brings to the bar some of the etiquette and forms observed in the saloons of refined society. He is never boisterous, loud, passionate, and rough in his tone and gesticulations. As an orator he could not rise to the altitude where dwell the thunder and lightning of heaven; he remains on earth, where, whatever may be for him the disadvantage of the sandy plain on which he stands, he wields with admirable effect the light, flexible, brightly polished, but cold Damascus steel blade of Saladin. As a lawyer he has a lucid, logical mind, and speaks with the richest fluency, never being at a loss or hesitating about a word, but that word, although presenting itself with the utmost ease and confidence, is not always the proper one. His style is far from being classical, or even grammatical, but it is effective, it is persuasive, and the meaning which it intends to convey is understood without effort, even by the dullest. His pronunciation denotes at once his Virginian origin, but his voice is musical, and his easy, pleasing flow of speech leaves no time and no desire to the hearer to analyze its constructive elements.

There is nothing of the scholar in Grymes; his collegiate education has been imperfect; his reading is not extensive as to legal lore, nor anything else. But there is infinite charm in his natural eloquence, and his powerful native intellect knows how to make the most skilful use of the materials which it gathers at random outside of any regular course of study and research. He has the reputation of never preparing himself for the trial even of important cases, and he seems pleased to favor the spreading of that impression. He affects to come into court after a night of dissipation, and to take at once all his points and all the information which he needs from his associate in the case, and even from what he can elicit from his opponents during the trial. It is when he pretends to be least prepared, and has apparently to rely only on intuition and the inspiration of the moment, that his brightest and most successful efforts are made. Many have some doubts about the genuine reality of this phenomenon, and believe that Grymes works more in secret than he wants the public to know.

No man was ever more urbanely sarcastic in words or pantomime. If the court disagrees with him on any vital point, and lays down the law adversely to his views, he has a way of gracefully and submissively bowing to the decision with a half-suppressed smile of derision, and with an expression of the face which clearly says to the by-standers: "I respect the magistrate, as you see, but what a goose that fellow is!" There is in his habitual sneers a sort of amiability, a good-natured love of piquant fun, which protects them against the suspicion of malignity; the shafts of his gilded bow scratch gently the skin with a perfumed steel point. He is a Chesterfield in his deportment toward all his colleagues of the bar; but if too much chafed by any of them he snorts once or twice, as if attempting to expel some obstruction from his nostrils. This is a sign in him of rising hostility, and without losing his temper he becomes politely aggressive, and his usually edulcorated language assumes a sort of vitriolic pungency. No one possesses better than he does the art of ridiculing without giving positive offence. But he is careful to use it sparingly in court, although profusely addicted to it in social intercourse. He is extremely fond of advocating with the utmost gravity wild paradoxes, which he frequently makes the amusing subjects of conversation. He stands among the highest in his profession, and exercises great influence over judges and jurors.

He has a decided taste for luxurious living, for horse-racing, cock-fighting, and card-gambling. He would not brook the shadow of a word of disparagement,

and on a point of honor would immediately, like all Southern gentlemen, appeal to the arbitration of the duello. Notwithstanding this sensitiveness, and the considerable fees which he annually receives for his services as a very able and popular member of the bar, there are few men known to be more dunned than he is. But he possesses privileges and immunities to which nobody else could aspire; he is the Richard Brinsley Sheridan of New Orleans. For instance, as an example of the liberties which he takes, if dunned too actively, he will give a check on any bank of which he bethinks himself at the moment, and the person who presents it becomes an object of merriment. It is looked upon as done in fun. There is not, of course, any idea of swindling or of doing any real impropriety. It is only one of Grymes's practical jokes. He will pay in the end, as everybody knows, with any amount of interest in addition, and without questioning the rate.

In those days of strongly marked individualities in New Orleans there was a man famous for collecting money from the most obdurate debtors, and he therefore was the favorite agent of creditors. His name was Dupeux. He was a terror to all those who indulged in the fancy that they could escape from the payment of what they owed. It might have been possible if there had been no Dupeux in the world, but as there was a Dupeux, it was impossible. He was the constable of one of our justices of the peace, but he never himself resorted to law. He had other means of coercion in his bag. Once on the track of a debtor, he never lost sight of him. That debtor felt at once that he was doomed, for he soon discovered that he was haunted more frightfully than by a ghost. Wherever he was, by day and by night, if there was any imaginable access to him, there suddenly stood in his presence the inevitable Dupeux, with his pale, supplicating face, expressive of the agony of too long deferred hope of payment, and with the same Gorgon bill in his hand. No tempest of curses and threats could frighten him away never to return, and when his bodily presence could be avoided, still his mournful, piteous face and its mute appeal remained visible through the debtor's imagination. It became an insupportable obsession, and it sometimes happened that, to get rid of it, the persecuted victim of debt would in a fit of desperation start in pursuit of Dupeux to hasten a payment which had been hitherto pertinaciously delayed or absolutely refused.

Such was the individual who, one morning very early, met Grymes sallying from a house where he had gambled with friends during the whole night. Dupeux approached reverentially the great lawyer, and with a pathetic gesture presented the bill for which he had been dunning that personage for several months. "Ah, my friend!" exclaimed Grymes, "what a lucky coincidence! You happen to meet me when I am flush. By-the-bye, put off that doleful face of yours; it gives me the chills. Well, how much is the bill, Dupeux—my poor Dupeux ?"

"Twenty-five dollars, Mr. Grymes."

"Is that all ? My conscience smites me for having made you wait so long, and you have been so patient, too ? You are an angel, Dupeux—my poor Dupeux!" And he pulled out of his pocket a very large bundle of bank-notes, from which he extracted one, that he handed over to the collector, saying, "Pay yourself."

"This is a one-hundred-dollar note, Mr. Grymes. How can I get change at this hour when all the banks and shops are closed?" said Dupeux, in a whining tone. "Have you not smaller notes?"

"Trouble not yourself about the change, my friend; keep it all, Dupeux—my poor Dupeux! Let the balance of seventy-five dollars go toward indemnifying you for all the shoes that you have worn in your perambulations after me. Good-by, and may you have an appetite for breakfast, Dupeux—my poor Dupeux!"

Such was John R. Grymes, the most careless of men about money, coining it by the bushel, and squandering it in the same way. But toward the end of his life he became more economical, honorably paid all his debts, and left to his family a competency when he died at a ripe old age.

Dominique Seghers, his colleague in the suit, was a perfect type of the red tape old French *avoué* of the ancient *régime*. He looked into every case intrusted to his care *con amore*, almost with paternal affection. For, was he not to give it a legal existence, a judicial shape or form, that would be faultless? Besides, he loved to handle and manipulate the law, so as to show what his skill could do with it. Such is the love of the artist for the instrument

to which he is indebted for his fortune and his fame. The very moment a subject of litigation was placed in his hands, he doubted not of its being founded in law, and if that law was not apparent, he felt convinced that by dint of patient researches he would discover in the end that the projected suit could be based on some article of the Civil Code, some special statute, some applicable precedent, some decision of court, if not on the broad principles of jurisprudence. For him professionally there was no right or wrong outside of the text of the law. Everything else was vaporous sentimentality, sheer romance.

He was essentially practical. To go to court was to go to war, and the participants in it were to take the consequences. Strategic manœuvres ending in a surprise that defeated a too confident or inexperienced adversary were, according to his views, nothing but fair play. As to himself, he went into the conflict armed to the teeth with every offensive and defensive weapon, from the big gun of massive argument to the penknife quibble of the smallest size. For who knows but what the feather may be adjudged of weight, when the granite block will be declared to have none? Who knew this better than Seghers? And thus he neglected nothing to insure success. It was his business to gain his case: that of the court or of the jury was to decide correctly. If they erred, whose responsibility was it? Not his surely if in duty to his client he had misled them by some *ignis fatuus*. Within the precincts of the court, within the range of his profession, he proceeded with the caution of an Indian creeping stealthily into the territory of a hostile tribe, and looking anxiously for an enemy behind every bush and tree. He gave no quarter, and asked for none.

There never was a microscope more effective than the one with which Seghers examined every word, every syllable, every comma, in his adversary's pleadings, and there never was any false step, any negligence, any defect or omission of legal formalities, of which old Seghers hesitated to take immediate advantage. I say "old Seghers," because in my youth I never heard his name mentioned without the addition of that adjective. It seemed as if he had never been suspected of ever having been young.

Nothing could have been more instructive for a young practitioner than to study attentively every petition or answer that Seghers ever filed in court. They were written with a skill and minute care that defied criticism. It was evident that he had left no loop-hole through which his opponent could stick a pin, and woe to that opponent if he got entangled in the spider's web against which he bumped his head! As to himself, he never entered any battle-field of litigation unless encased in a double-plated suit of armor ten inches in thickness, and without having protected his position, whenever it was possible, with all sorts of pitfalls and traps.

He had to contend against a peculiar and very serious impediment for a man of his profession. It was the extreme difficulty which he had to express himself. In court he painfully struggled for words. They stuck in his throat; and when at last they came out, it was as if they had forced their way through an obstructed passage. It was in a jumbling sort of way. There was an elbowing, a pushing, a trampling upon one another, as people generally do when in a too closely packed crowd. But he patiently took his time to evolve order out of confusion. No interruptions from court or jury, or from the adverse party, however frequently repeated, could put him out of countenance. If continued too long, for the evident purpose of increasing the disarray of his words, if not of his ideas, and enfeebling his laboriously uttered arguments, he would stop, and phlegmatically show his annoyance at it by merely turning up his eyes to heaven, seemingly as a mute appeal for the grant of sufficient patience to support him under the inflicted vexations. But after a while he would start again, in his humdrum style, precisely from the point where the thread of his discourse had been cut off.

I need not mention, for it might be easily inferred, that in his every-day life Seghers was as methodical and precise as in his professional one. His physical appearance would easily have denoted the inward man to a physiognomist. There was a great deal of character in his features. They were strongly marked — a sharp long face; a large mouth; a much-protruding and big nose; gray eyes participating of the elongated olive shape, with furtive and oblique glances to detect anything suspicious, from whatever part of the horizon it might come, large flat ears that stuck close to the sides of the head, and for which no approach of a velvet-footed cat would have been noiseless. This gentleman acquired by his profession a considerable fortune.

Among the Americans who had come to New Orleans to better their fortune, none was so distinguished as Edward Livingston. He was of an illustrious family, and before emigrating to the extreme South he had been Mayor of the city of New York. He had not been long in the place which he had chosen for his new sphere of action before he gave ample evidence of his superb talents. He at once became one of the leading members of the bar, notwithstanding his having enemies who spread evil reports against him, and his having incurred a great deal of unpopularity in consequence of the part he took in the famous "batture case," which gave rise to riots in New Orleans and to an acrimonious controversy between Thomas Jefferson and himself, in which he showed that he was at least equal, if not superior, to his great adversary. He, however, manfully and successfully battled against the numerous obstacles which he met in his way. He was possessed of too much genius and firmness of nerve to be kept down and prevented from rising up, eagle-like, to the altitude where he could freely expand his wings and breathe in his native empyreal element. Conquering prejudices, calumnies, and envy, he grew rapidly, as he became better known and appreciated, upon the esteem and confidence of his fellow-citizens in his newly elected home, and was sent to represent Louisiana in the Senate of the United States. His career as such, as Secretary of State under the Presidency of General Jackson, and as Minister Plenipotentiary in France, is well known For the present I have only to deal with him as a member of the New Orleans bar, where he towered up as one of its giants.

Edward Livingston was tall and spare in body, and with strong, clear-cut features, which denoted his Scotch ancestry. The habitual expression of his face was meditative and rather austere, but his smile was indicative of the benignity of his heart. He was mild in manner, courteous, dignified, and indefatigably laborious. The pleasures of society did not seem to have much attraction for him. To change the nature of his occupation was sufficient relief and rest for his temperament, and even a diversion much more to his taste than any other. He was a profound jurist and an accomplished scholar. Which of the two predominated, it would have been difficult to tell. He managed his cases in court with admirable self-possession. It was the calm consciousness of strength; it was the serene majesty of intellect. There was no sparring, no wrangling, no browbeating. When he rose to speak, the attention of the judge, jurors, members of the bar, and everybody in court was instantly riveted. All knew that they were to listen to what was worth hearing. There were no flashy declamations, no unbecoming carpings, no hair-splitting, no indecorous clap-trap, no tinsel ornament, no stage thunder, no flimsy sophistical argumentation, no idle straggling words. His discourse was compact and robust; his language was terse and pure. His eloquence was of the classical order, and uniformly elegant. It would, in forensic debates, flow at first with the modesty of a gentle stream, but by degrees, swelling and rushing like the mighty tide of the ocean, it would overflow far and wide, and leave to opposition not an inch of ground to stand upon.

Moreau Lislet, his associate in the case which we have supposed ready for trial, is a rotund Frenchman past the meridian of life. His eyes sparkle with good-natured wit under the large spectacles which bestride his small nose. Everything seems soft in him, even his bones. His flesh is tremulous, like blancmange or a jelly, and as yielding under the touch. His hands are diminutive and plump. He does not look formidable, does he? No. Well, you had better beware of him. He is an Artesian-well of legal lore—deep, very deep. He is one of those two or three jurists who were intrusted by the Legislature with the work of adapting the Napoleon Code to the wants and circumstances of Louisiana under her new institutions. He has no pretensions to oratory. He addresses the court or the jury in a sort of conversational, familiar way. He is always in a good humor, which is communicative. He is a very great favorite with the judges, the clerks, the sheriffs, the jurors, the members of the bar—in fact, with everybody. He is so kind, so benevolent, so amiable in all his dealings and sayings! His *bonhomie* is so captivating! Of so sympathizing a nature is he that, for instance, he sometimes takes up his adversary's side of the question, admits that there is a good deal to say in his favor, and says it and shows it too. He will even go so far as to present it to the court in its very best aspect. But after having thus acted with such kindness and impartiality toward his opponent, he pathetically apologizes for destroying all his hopes and illusions, regrets that his claim is not founded on the law and evidence applicable to the case, demonstrates it beyond the shadow of a doubt, and finally exterminates the poor fellow with a sigh of compassion over his hard fate. Ho! ho! beware of Moreau Lislet and of his *bonhomie!*

The case in which these four gentlemen were engaged was a jury one. It was in the latter part of June, and exceedingly hot. When Grymes, for the plaintiff, rose to address the jury in English, one of its members who did not understand a single word of that language, speaking in the name of such of his colleagues as were in the same predicament, begged the judge on that ground to allow them to leave their seats, and be permitted to inhale the fresh air under the arcades of the building in which the court held its session. This was graciously permitted, and during one hour that Grymes spoke the Gallic portion of the jurors enjoyed their promenade and their cigars in the cool breeze that came from the river. When Grymes had done, and Seghers, on the same side, rose in his turn, the voice of the sheriff was heard crying loudly, "Gentlemen of the jury who are outside, please come into court." They immediately filed in and gravely resumed their seats. Seghers had hardly said a few words in French when the Anglo-Saxon jurors, on their application for a similar favor, were also permitted to stretch their legs under the same arcades, and to pass their time as comfortably as they could. The repetition of this scene took place when Livingston and Moreau Lislet spoke alternately. This was of daily occurrence at that epoch.

After a little while everybody became reconciled to what at first had been thought an intolerable inconvenience or annoyance. In the course of time the high-spirited and light-limbed Latin genet and the massive, slower-tempered Saxon horse, being both harnessed to the car of justice, learned to pull together, and contrived by some means or other to make its wheels work smoothly, notwithstanding the natural difficulties of the road. The qualifications to be a juror were then of a higher order than those which have been since required, and if the echoes which are wafted to me in my retreat from our courts of justice are faithful expressions of the public sentiment on the subject, I must come to the conclusion that trials by jury sixty years ago, notwithstanding certain eccentricities from which they were not free, gave rise to fewer complaints than those of the present day.

On a certain occasion there was great excitement in the city. Two eminent citizens had quarrelled about a hog. It was a question of the identity of the animal, and impossible to doubt their good faith. They became irritated and more obstinate in proportion to the prolongation of their dispute. At last it was evident that there would be no yielding on either side, and they went to law. Moreau Lislet was retained for plaintiff, and Mazureau for defendant—two of the magnates of the bar—and fees were paid them immensely larger than the value of the hog. On the day of trial the court-room was crowded to suffocation, for much fun was expected. It was, of course, a jury case. Moreau Lislet read the petition, in which the hog was minutely described and asserted to be a blooded one, worth five hundred dollars. The answer was a general denial, putting plaintiff on full proof of what he alleged. It seems there was but one witness to identify the hog. That witness was sworn, and confirmed the description in the petition. He was a farmer of the parish of St. Bernard, about sixty years old, of ponderous frame. He evidently was very little accustomed to the position he had been called to. His whole face was expressive of primitive innocence. After this witness had concluded his testimony in favor of the plaintiff, Moreau Lislet said, "The witness is yours, Mr. Mazureau."

Mazureau fixed on the witness his dark imperious eyes, and said, with affected emphasis and in his most effective dramatic style: "Sir, remember that you are here, on oath, to testify in a case of the utmost importance, although it may appear trifling to your simple understanding. It is not merely a hog question; it is a question of honor, whether one of our most respected fellow-citizens unjustly, unlawfully, and fraudulently retains in his possession property that belongs to another. I put you on your guard for your own sake. You may be indicted for perjury if the slightest wilful inaccuracy in your evidence shows that you do not speak the truth, the whole truth, and nothing but the truth. Besides, you may be sued for damages in consequence of the injury you may do to the defendant's reputation.

"Now," continued Mazureau, "I compliment you, sir, on your minute description of the plaintiff's hog, which is missing from his pen. I will not cross-examine you on the subject. I am full of admiration for your memory, and I want you to be equally particular about defendant's hog. It won't do to say in general terms that they are exactly alike." At this point the implacable tormentor began to puncture and scarify the witness, much to the merriment of the by-standers. "What do you know of hogs? Whence your extraordinary faculty to discriminate among them, and so vividly to remember their respective physiognomy? How long have you lived with them? What opportunity had you to examine the defendant's hog and the peculiarities of its formation? Have you measured its ears, its tail, its legs, its nose, the length and height of its body? I want to know whether in all these details the defendant's hog is exactly like the plaintiff's missing one."

All these questions and many others had been successively put to the witness, who had been driven almost to the verge of desperation. At last, being made conscious by the incessant bursts of laughter from the audience that he was an object of ridicule, he exhibited symptoms of marked irritation. It exploded when Mazureau said to him: "Well, sir, all these details are very confused and unreliable. Give us the *tout ensemble* of the hog. Group all these details together, and tell us how the entire hog exactly looked."

The witness measured Mazureau from head to foot slowly and deliberately, and said, "You want a *fac-simile* of defendant's hog?"

"Yes, sir."

"You want the court, the jury, and the whole audience to know how the animal looks, altogether, from its nose to its tail, and from its tail to its feet?"

"Yes, sir; you fully comprehend my meaning and desire."

." Well, sir, that hog looks exactly like you, and both you and the hog could not be more alike if you were twins."

There was a roar of laughter in the audience, but this time at the expense of Mazureau. The judge himself, the jurors, the members of the bar, and all other persons present were convulsed with laughter.

Mazureau calmly waited for the restoration of order. Then he blandly said to the witness, "If I understand you correctly, the most accurate description you can give this court and jury of defendant's hog is his being so like me that you could not tell one from the other?"

"Yes, sir," doggedly answered the witness, who was much encouraged by the effect he had produced on the audience.

"I thank you, sir, for the precision of your language. I have no more questions to ask;" and the witness withdrew from the stand.

By this time Moreau Lislet had become serious. He knew Mazureau's temper, whose unnatural calm portended nothing good.

"Mr. Moreau Lislet," said Mazureau, with the kindest intonation, "will you do me the favor to hand me your petition?"

After having read it loudly and distinctly, so as to be heard by everybody present, he said: "May it please the court, gentlemen of the jury, it is plain that the plaintiff has failed to make out his case. You have heard me read from his petition the most minute description of his missing hog, and his own witness has just given you what he thinks the best and most faithful representation or portraiture of the one alleged to be in defendant's possession. Well, it is unquestionable that there is no point of resemblance between the two animals, one of which you see now standing before you in my person. I rest my case here. The plaintiff must be put out of court on the evidence which he has himself adduced."

Moreau Lislet looked blank, and was no longer inclined to laugh, and well he might, for there was an instantaneous verdict against his client. Mazureau walked up to his defeated adversary, and opening his gold snuffbox, offered him a pinch, saying, "Moreau, what do you think of the old dictum, '*He laughs the best who laughs the last*'?"

A LUMP OF SUGAR

IT is almost impossible in these days of "sweetness and light," when the comfort and prosperity of a people are fairly tested by its consumption of sugar *per capita*, and this one article contributes more than any two or three others to the expenses of government, to look back to the times when those gracious dames our great-grandmothers, seated about the tea-table, took their delicate nibbles of the new luxury from a lump of sugar suspended in their midst by a string, or, still further in the past, to imagine a sugarless world. Yet sugar was little known to "our ancients." The Chinese date their use of sugar to that same remote and provoking antiquity which they forever fling in the face of the upstart Caucasian, and it is claimed by the apostles of the newest American industry—sorghum-growing—that it was the sorghum plant, rather than the sugar-cane proper, which furnished them with sweetness from its juice, as well as bread from its seeds. From China sugar-growing came, it would seem, to India and Arabia, and the Arabian confections were among the costly luxuries of Greece and Rome. Theophrastus mentions the juice as "honey in reeds," and the solid form is spoken of by Pliny, who describes it as a gravelly substance dissolving in the mouth, and by Dioscorides, the Greek physician who travelled about the world with the Roman armies, in his "Materia Medica," as a medicine. The inevitable Crusaders, who were to Europe what the *Mayflower* Pilgrims are to us, brought the sugar-cane to Europe amongst their many importations of antiquities and novelties, but it had probably been earlier introduced into Spain and Sicily, coming from Arabia by way of Nubia, Egypt, and Northern Africa, by the Moors and Saracens. The Venetian merchants early became interested in its product; they were probably the earliest refiners, and loaf-sugar was first made in Venice in the sixteenth century. A learned treatise on sugar-making, the "Saccharologia" of Sala, appeared in that century, and we have a notice of a refinery existing in Dresden in 1597. From the Mediterranean the sugar-cane emigrated to Madeira, and thence across the Atlantic to San Domingo and the other West Indies, probably early in the sixteenth century. About the middle of last century certain Jesuit priests, coming from San Domingo to Louisiana, are said to have brought the sugar-cane first to our own shores, but it was many years before it was grown commercially. A dramatic tradition exists at New Orleans of the first refining at a plantation near that city, which was made the occasion of a public festival, at which, when the word was given, "It grains," a shout of joy went up from the crowd. Our word "sugar" can be traced by its various forms of middle English *sugre*, French *sucre*, German *zucker*, Spanish *azucar*, Arabic *sakkar* or *sokkar*, and *assokar*, Persian *shakar* (whence the Greek *sakcharon*—Latin *saccharum*), all the way back to the Sanskrit *çarkara*, which originally meant "gravel"—a circumstance which points to the early knowledge of crystalline sugar in Asia as a "sweet gravel." "Jaggery," the name of the crude sugar imported from Asia, is another form of the same word.

Sugar is found in many plants, but the great sugar mines are the sugar-cane, the sorghum grass, and the beet root. The date-palm in the far East and our own maple-tree add to the supply, and some sugar or syrup has been made in southern California from the water-melon. Besides these natural sugars, large quantities of starch sugar or glucose are made by chemical treatment of starch. These are the great commercial sources of sweetness. A sugar which is not sweet is made in small quantities from milk, for use chiefly in medicine, milk sugar being the substance of the homœopathic powders and pellets.

The world's production of sugar is probably well toward eight million tons a year. Of this, British India and China produce and themselves consume over a million tons each of cane sugar, their exports being small, and these of very low grade sugars. The estimated product of all countries available for export was, in 1884-5, a year of large production, 2,162,000 tons of cane and no less than 2,557,800 of beet sugar. It is estimated that the cane-sugar crop marketed this year will increase to 2,218,000 tons, and that the beet-sugar crop will fall off 520,750 tons—partly the result of a lower acreage resulting from the low prices of last year. Cuba produces more than a quarter of the whole export supply of cane sugar, last year's product being 627,000 tons, while this year's will probably equal her largest crop (1875), which was 699,000 tons. Of this, more than half (in 1885, 339,536 gross tons) comes to this country, which gets nearly half its total supply for refining from that island of revolutions. Louisiana produced last year but 94,000 tons, but its normal product is nearer 125,000 tons, to which Texas, our other chief sugar-growing State, adds 10,000 tons more. Five other States contribute some cane sugar. The Sandwich Islands crop, under the stimulus of the treaty which permits its sugar to enter duty free, reaches 65,000 tons, but it is said that the use of all the available land, and the poor quality of native labor, the prohibition of Chinese, and the high price of white labor, fix the limit at the present figure. Of the beet-sugar supply, Germany produced last year 1,155,000 tons, Austria 557,000, Russia 380,000, France 325,000, Belgium 90,000, and Holland 50,000 tons. Our chief contribution to this crop is from a factory at Alvarado, California, producing about 1000 tons, but it is believed that this will become an important Pacific coast industry. Beet sugar is largely imported into this country for refining purposes, and we get also some date-palm sugar, called commercially "date jaggery." Our yield of maple sugar, in which Vermont still leads, was about 25,900 tons last year. Sorghum, although large quantities of syrup are made from the large acreage at the West, has not yet come into the market as an important commercial source of crystallizable sugar, the largest crop having been but 5000 tons; our scientific agriculturists, who give good reasons for looking to this as one of the great American crops of the future, have yet to justify their faith by their works. The manufacture of commercial glucose, or artificial starch sugar, has of late years reached enormous proportions in this country, amounting in value to a third of our cane-sugar crop.

All sugars, as well as starch and gum, belong chemically to the class of carbohydrates, that is, they are a combination of carbon (C) with hydrogen (H) and oxygen (O) already combined in the proportion in which these two form water (H_2O or Aq). There are three groups of these: the true crystalline sugars or *sucroses* ($C_{12}H_{22}O_{11}$), including cane sugar, milk sugar, maltose (the sugar of malt), etc.; the *glucoses* ($C_6H_{12}O_6$ or $C_{12}H_{24}O_{12}$),

CUTTING SUGAR-CANE.

or inverted sugars, which contain one more atom of water, including grape sugar or dextrose, fruit sugar or lævulose, etc.; and the *amyloses* ($C_6H_{10}O_5$ or $C_{12}H_{20}O_{10}$), which contain one less atom of water, and are found in irregular granules instead of crystals, including starch, dextrine (the "sticking-stuff" used for postage-stamps), the gums, and cellulose, or vegetable fibre, of which cotton is the most noteworthy example, being almost pure cellulose. Thus a lump of charcoal (C) and a glass of water (H_2O) contain together all the elements of a lump of sugar, a pint of syrup, a pound of starch, or a spool of thread. By chemical treatment either the sugar group or the starch group can be turned into the glucoses, and, by fermentation, into alcohol (C_2H_5OH). Thus a chemist will make sweetness out of your cotton handkerchief, a manufacturer will transform the starch of tons of corn into glucose, and a brewer or distiller will produce from barley malt or corn and rye gallons of beer or whiskey. Stranger still, from these same carbo-hydrates powerful explosives can be made: a mixture of sugar with chlorate of potash makes a "white gunpowder," which a drop of acid will touch off; and by soaking cotton (cellulose) with nitric and sulphuric acids, gun-cotton is produced, which may be spun and woven into unsuspicious thread or cloth or paper that will explode at a flash, or solidified into the useful but highly inflammable celluloid. Dissolved in alcohol and ether, gun-cotton becomes the collodion which on drying produces the film so useful in surgery as a temporary skin. At a temperature of 320° F. true sugar becomes the transparent substance known as barley sugar; at 400° F. it loses part of its water and becomes "caramel" or burnt sugar, the coloring matter of molasses, of brown candies, and of some liquors.

Within each of the three carbo-hydrate groups there are numerous substances, which are, as the chemists phrase it, *isomeric* (of *equal parts*), that is, containing exactly the same kind and number of atoms, but *allotropic*, that is, with these atoms arranged in *different ways*. In the "spelling game" you can arrange the same letters A, E, M, N into the quite different words, Mane, Mean, Name, Amen. Nature has the same trick. She puts her C's (carbon) together to make coal, graphite (of "lead" pencils), or the diamond. Thus out of six C's, ten H's, five O's, she makes starch, or gum, or cellulose; out of $C_{12}H_{22}O_{11}$, she makes a number of different sugars; out of $C_6H_{12}O_6$, she makes dextro-glucose or dextrose, lævo-glucose or lævulose, and still other glucoses. These have different qualities, but are chiefly to be distinguished apart by the curious effect they have in turning aside a ray of light which has first been "polarized," or made to vibrate on one plane only. Dextrose, indeed, is so called because it turns the ray to the right (*dexter*), and lævulose because, though exactly of the same atoms, it turns the ray to the left (*lævus*), or inverse direction. Cane sugar, pure, dissolved in its weight of water at a temperature of 59°, rotates the ray 73.80 to the right, whereas trehalose, a true sugar made from Turkish manna, rotates it under the part of the instrument, and with the help of an eye-piece at the other end of the tube the degree of deviation is read off on a little scale above, marked to show the actual percentage of sugar. The key to this useful and wonderful provision of nature is probably the simple fact that the different combinations of atoms give different reflecting or refracting surfaces to the different crystals or granules.

The man who, by the patient plodding of scientific investigation, or by the inspiration of genius which is its equivalent, will some day read the secret of an atom of carbon, in its protean combinations with its intimates oxygen and hydrogen,

A PRIMITIVE SUGAR-MILL IN ARKANSAS.

same conditions 220° to the right. If the sugar is less pure, or the solution stronger, it has a different effect on the ray, and this fact is the basis of the commercial test of sugars by the scientific instrument called the polariscope, in which a ray of light, polarized as it is admitted into the instrument, passes through a solution of sugar, carefully weighed and dissolved in a definite amount of water, and placed in a long tube, closed with glass at both ends. The deflection of the ray is counteracted by interposing a wĕdge of quartz, forming a will achieve one of the great triumphs of mankind. Out of the corn which gives us the daily bread for which we daily pray comes also the spirit which crazes men; out of the wholesome peach, the deadly acid one drop of which will kill. The same simple atoms are in each, and our rudest manufacturing processes can give them the change of form which is the difference between life and death; but science has not yet reached below the surface of the mystery, and to the wisest eye the transformation is still a miracle.

SUGAR-CANE MILL, LOUISIANA.

Science long ago reached beyond the telescope and microscope, which disclose their secrets to the eye, and turns now to the spectroscope and the polariscope, which reveal to the scientific imagination those infinitesimal secrets evident only in the effects of atoms, unknown and unseen, on the delicate and tremulous beam of light. The beam of the polariscope is not unlikely to become the divining-rod of the Columbus, yet to come, of organic chemistry, who will prove one of the great benefactors of mankind. So far, man, for the most part, has had to be content with undoing what nature has done, as in breaking up starch into glucose or alcohol. Some "organic" substances, as indigo and the aniline dyes, have, however, been made by man. When, if ever, he succeeds, directly or indirectly, in converting the carbon about us, the hydrogen and oxygen of water, the free nitrogen of the air, into the organic products we now get, in roundabout fashion, only through nature's laboratory, the plants, the whole problem of food supply will be solved.

For the plants are the great sugar-makers. By what mysterious force each extracts from the soil and the air, by help of sun and wind and rain, the exact proportions of carbon, hydrogen, and oxygen which it combines into its characteristic sugar, we can only conjecture. Still more mysterious is the transfer of "the principle of life" and of growth at certain periods of plant development from the production of fibre throughout the plant to the production of sugar in the cells, or the misdirection of that principle, under certain ill conditions of weather, to the production of "invert sugar," which provokes fermentation and the ruin of the crop.

The sugars produced by animals come chiefly, probably entirely, from the carbohydrates of the plants. The bee collects the true sugar lodged infinitesimally in two and a half millions of flowers, so it is said, to make his pound of honey, the sugar of which is really a glucose. It is a glucose also, called diabetic sugar, which is produced abnormally by the human body in the disease known as *diabetes* (or "pouring through"), from the excessive excretion of the kidneys, which holds great quantities of sugar in solution. This excessive production of sugar, which can be partially held in check by the use of non-saccharine or diabetic food, was long supposed to be a disease of the kidneys, but physicians are now inclined to consider it more a disease of the nervous system, originating at the base of the brain, which the kidneys are trying in vain to correct. In fact, it has been artificially produced in animals by experiments on the brain, and brain-workers are found to be peculiarly subject to it. Somehow or other the nerves fail to do their work, or the right orders are not given through them from the nerve centres, the processes of life go wrong, and sooner or later comes death. This is about all that medicine can tell us now; some day it will know more.

Among the sugar-producing plants, the sugar-cane, the sorghum grass, and our Indian corn, or maize, are near cousins in vegetable society, belonging all to the family of the grasses. They look down from a superior height of a dozen feet, more or less, upon their humbler second cousins twice removed, the wheat, rye, barley, oats, and common grasses of our fields, modest but very useful members of another group of the same family. There is no "set" of the vegetable kingdom to which humankind and all kinds of animal life owe more than to these humble folk and their big cousins. We get the greater part of our own food and a fiery portion of our drink from their seeds, most of the fodder for our beasts from their stalks, bedding for man and beast from the dry straw and husks, sweetness from the juice, and finally cleanliness, which is next to godliness, and so gives the family a connection with spiritual things, from the broom-corn variety of sorghum, which does most of our sweeping. The sorghum, sugar-cane, and maize are magnificent plants, with their broad green leaves, their tall stems, and the clustered spikes or tassels atop, reaching in the case of some varieties a height of thirty feet. They are distinguished from the other groups of grasses by having pithy instead of hollow stems, in which pith nature stores her sweetness. All of them require abundant moisture, more or less heat and sunshine, and a soil containing some organic matter—potash, silica, phosphoric and sulphuric acids, lime and magnesia, and oxides of iron and manganese. They seem to have the property of extracting most of their nutriment from the air, so much so that some investigators look upon them, especially maize, when ploughed in, as nature's great means of recuperating poor soil and of turning inorganic matter into organic food. Sorghum, it is said, will produce crop after crop from the same ground, and cane will grow in the tropics fifteen years consecutively without exhausting the soil.

Although sorghum is generally considered an upstart thrusting itself into sugar-cane society, it has claims to be considered the more ancient and aristocratic of the two. It is said that sorghum, which is the *durra* of the East, was the plant originally used by the Chinese in making sugar. The differences between the two plants are many and vital, despite their botanical grouping. The sugar-cane (*Saccharum officinarum*, Linn.) is a perennial plant, growing in favorable localities sometimes

THE CRUSHERS.

for fifty years from the same roots, propagated not by seed but from cuttings, of slow growth, and requiring in the tropics often from fourteen months to two years for its development. The sorghum (*Sorghum vulgare*, Pers.), which is really a cereal, and much more like maize than like sugar-cane, is an annual, grown from seed, and maturing often within three months. The sugar-cane is of thick and sturdy growth, with a great deal of woody fibre in its outer envelope, and with a tough and dense internal structure. The sorghum is taller and more slender, of a softer outer structure, and less dense pith. The sorghum, unlike the sugar-cane, is crowned with a cluster of edible seeds, the "seed head," used as food for men as well as for cattle. There are a number of species of sugar-cane, although all are supposed to have developed by cultivation from a single progenitor, whose *habitat* is unknown; the varieties of the sorghum are less marked, and are all definitely within one species.

The process of "sugar-making," in its essentials, is a simple enough matter of cookery. The first care of the producer is to get all the sugar possible out of the cane or grass or root, either by squeezing out the juice or washing out the sugar; the sugar-maple saves the sugar-maker this trouble, delivering the sap ready for the boiler. The juice is then cleared of its impurities, as coffee is cleared by the white of an egg, or water is filtered through charcoal; it is then boiled, to evaporate as much of the water as possible, and crystallize the solid sugar; it is then cooled, and the molasses drained off, leaving the soft dark sugars, in which each crystal has its thin coating of molasses, or dried by a centrifugal machine, as clothes are dried in the whirling drier, whence the water flies out, or further clarified and left to crystallize in white loaves, which are sawed or crushed or ground or powdered into the several varieties of fine white sugar. Most of these earlier processes are performed on the plantations, but in many cases they are repeated and the sugar carried through the final process in the great refineries. "Refining" is, in fact, little more than a finer repetition of the processes of "making," and to do these simple things on a great scale and in the best way is the sole purpose of those enormous beehives of industry.

The sugar planter requires for his cane plantation a warm, moist climate, with intervals of hot, dry weather, with little danger from frost; a soil not too rich, containing lime and magnesia, and of good drainage; and the benefit of sea-breezes, salt in the air being better for him than salt in the soil. The sugar plantations of Louisiana find these conditions in the alluvial soil of the lower Mississippi Valley. In laying out an estate, drainage must be carefully provided for, and in some countries irrigation is much used. From one to four cuttings are set out together in holes about two feet apart. As the canes grow they must be well weeded and "trashed," *i. e.*, all dry, dead leaves removed. They begin to grow in Louisiana in February, and are harvested from October to January. After the first cutting of the new plants the stole or stool left sends up another growth of cane, called "ratoons," which with each cutting grow smaller in size and closer in joints, and are said to yield sweeter juice and finer sugar. The one planting will last many years, but Louisiana sugar-growers reckon only on three years' product, planting a third of the sugar ground anew each year. Rats, white ants, lice, "borers," and some minute animals producing "rust" and "must," fight against the growing plant, as also do wind and frost. When cutting-time comes, the cane is cut with a hatchet close to the stole, the top is chopped off, and the leaves stripped; the canes are then bundled up and carried to the mill, often, on the large plantations, on narrow donkey railways, or placed in windrows, on the fields, so that the juice may not ferment until they can be handled.

Louisiana plantations, when the crop is in full vigor, are indeed a lovely sight, with their broad expanse of leafy cane. Some of them are of great extent, the Magnolia Plantation, now owned by ex-Governor Warmoth, which claims to be one of the banner plantations of the State, having 492 acres in cane last year. In 1883-4 over 172,400 acres of cane were harvested in the State, the total crop of 128,000 tons of sugar being one of the best ever made in the State; but in 1884-5 floods spoiled so much of the crop that only 118,650 acres were harvested, producing 94,000 tons of sugar. The crop of 1885-6 is estimated at 110,000 tons. About 20,000 freedmen are kept busy in the sugar fields and mills. The plantations are expected to yield from twenty to twenty-five tons of cane per acre, though the average of the State in the short crop of 1884–5 was but seventeen tons. A good crop should produce 3,000,000 tons of cane, and be worth to the State from $12,500,000

the tropics, contains a much larger proportion of juice, much richer in sugar, than the Bourbon cane, commonly grown in Louisiana. It is seldom that as much as half of this sugar is utilized. The Magnolia Plantation this past year indeed produced 163¾ pounds per ton, but

WEIGHING SUGAR ON THE DOCKS.

up. To this Texas and the five other States which dabble in cane-growing add little over ten per cent.

The census returns of 1880 reported 227,776 acres in sugar-cane, of which 181,592 were in Louisiana. The crop was 178,872 hogsheads of sugar and 16,573,273 gallons of molasses, of which Louisiana's entire return was 171,706 hogsheads of sugar and 11,696,248 gallons of molasses. The cane is ninety per cent. juice, and the juice contains about fifteen per cent. of sugars, so that a hundred pounds of cane hold about thirteen and a half pounds of sugar. These figures vary greatly, however, with the variety of cane and the character of the season. The Otaheite cane, requiring a much longer hot season to ripen it, and therefore grown only in

the average for Louisiana was, with the vacuum process, 130 pounds, by other processes 87 pounds, per ton of cane. Great progress has been made in sugar-growing in recent years through an improved levee system to keep the waters of the Mississippi under control, better means of transportation, more scientific treatment of the land, and more complete processes of manufacture; but there is still an enormous margin for increased production by improved scientific methods, and an increase of half as much again in the yield of sugar per acre ought to be within the possibilities of the near future. The crop now costs $2 50 per ton of cane, or $50 or so per acre, and should yield about $500 total return. This would add over $5,000,000 yearly to the wealth of the State. So much for statistics, and their word to science.

The sugar-maker's first aim is to get from the cane as much of its percentage of juice as it can be induced to give up. The juice is enclosed in little cells of lignose, or woody fibre, which make the other tenth of the cane's weight. There are three ways of extracting the juice—by crushing, by soaking out the sugar by the process of "diffusion," or by a combination of crushing and of maceration in water. Crushing or grinding the cane is a process in use from the earliest times, as is seen in the primitive sugar-mills of the East, which consist of the hollowed stump of a tree, within which is a grinding pestle worked by oxen treading their round, driven from the arm of the bar by one man, while another feeds in pieces of cane, one by one, and takes out the crushed remains. A mill almost as primitive as this is still in use in Arkansas.

The sugar-house on a great plantation is a large, high building, the centre of the farm, to which roads or tramways lead from all directions. As a load of cane comes up, it is fed upon an endless belt or railway, which carries it up slowly to the crushing-mill, an affair of simple construction but of enormous power. The crushers are great rollers of cast-iron, in pairs or triplets, sometimes one set, sometimes more, working at a pressure of from fifty to eighty pounds to the square inch, and so arranged as to give slightly before any extraordinary strain. There are all sorts of opinions as to whether it is better to crush rapidly or slowly, and to crush once only or to repeat the operation with increasing pressures. The juice flows from the crushers in one direction; the residual cane, now known as "begass," is carried off in another by an endless belt, to be used either for dressing for the cane fields or as fuel in the heating processes which the juice is next to undergo. One of the great improvements in modern sugar-making has been the development of furnaces which get most of their fuel from the begass.

There have been several attempts to extract a greater proportion of juice by purely mechanical means, as by defibrators, shredding the cane into pulp, by raspers also tearing it into shreds, and by the curious press invented by Bessemer, but never much used, in which the canes were crushed endwise by a plunger working in a cylinder. Another method slices the canes lengthwise before crushing. The process of maceration consists in wetting or steaming the cane, either before crushing or after a first crushing.

The "diffusion" process is used somewhat in cane and commonly in beet-sugar making. Cane-cutters first slice the cane diagonally about one-sixteenth of an inch thick in pieces three or four inches long. These slices go to the diffusion "battery," a series of ten or a dozen tanks, in one of which the fresh slices are subjected to steaming and then to a flow of fresh water, which carries into the next tank the first extraction of sugar. The solution goes from tank to tank until it is nearly saturated, when it is withdrawn from the battery, while from another tank the now exhausted chips drop through a slide valve into begass carts below, and are saved for manure, or sometimes for paper-making. About eighty-three per cent. of the juice is thus saved. This process has, however, not met with favor in this country.

The juice has now to be purified (or "defecated") and clarified, going first through a preliminary straining, by means of an endless sieve of wire-gauze, which lets the strained juice through into gutters beneath, and delivers the scum at the end of the machine. It is then heated in pans or steam-coil boilers to about 210° F., "milk of lime" being added to neutralize the acid in the juice. A scum rises and a sediment falls; the cleared juice is run off by itself. An excess of lime has to be corrected by the use of acids, sulphuric or sulphurous, a delicate process known as "tempering." The liquid must then be filtered, and finally crystallized into sugar.

These processes, in the old-fashioned plantation sugar-houses, are effected by what is known as a "battery" of open pans or "taches." The first two pans are the clarifiers; below these, copper pans are set in masonry on a descending plane, the lowest of which is the "striking tache," under which is the furnace. The temperature of the upper pans is lower according to their distance from the fire. The juice is ladled from one pan to another down the scale, becoming of course more concentrated from the greater heat as it descends, until at the striking pan it is on the point of crystallization. If syrup from sour canes has got into the pan, producing a sticky proof, some buckets of lime-water are let in; on the other hand, dilute sul-

THE MIXING-ROOM.

phuric acid is introduced to clear a dark sugar. Now, after six or eight hours of boiling, the *masse-cuite* (cooked mass), as the concentrated juice is called, of a reddish gold-color, is ready for the "strike." Here the skill of the sugar-maker, standing half naked by the pan, his eye alert on the mass, must be tested. He must "strike," that is, dip off the liquid, at exactly the moment when it is ready to crystallize in the coolers. Perhaps half the contents of the pan is "struck out," or "cut." The rest is left in the pan for "doubling," or adding new syrup to make still larger crystals. Sometimes four or five cuts are made before the boiling is finished.

Most of the better plantations now use, however, the vacuum pan, which will be described as we reach the refineries. By reducing the pressure of the air, this enables the sugar to be boiled at a lower temperature, so that there is less danger of loss from burning or overheating. The "triple effect" process, very largely in use, is a combination of three steam pans, in which the pressure is less and the syrup denser in the second than in the first, and in the third than in the second, as the liquid passes continuously through the series. As the exhaust steam of one pan is used for heating another, the saving of fuel is considerable. But the vacuum processes can best be explained by making a sudden journey (on paper) from the plantations of Louisiana to the great refineries of New York, where the methods of sugar-making are repeated on a grand scale, in the most scientific manner.

The great refineries which line the water-front of Brooklyn and Jersey City are enormous piles of brick, often more than a hundred feet high, with a dozen or more rows of windows one above the other, with no pretentions to architectural show, but by their very size and massiveness making an impressive feature of the river landscape. They are contrived so as to take the sugar as it is landed, and carry it through one process after another with the least possible waste of power, time, and space, until the "shining sand" emerges purified and ready for consumption. Accordingly the refineries are alongside deep water, and at their wharves vessels of all sorts, from West Indian coasters to the great steam "tramps" that roam the world over in search of a job, may be seen, three and four together, unloading their cargoes into the voracious maw of the great cookshop. The dock presents a busy scene. Great hogsheads or stacks of bags are swung by derricks over the ships' sides, or a constant line of hurrying men bustle down the gang-planks with barrow-loads of bags. Uncle Sam has first to make sure that he gets his share in the shape of duties, and the refiner must also have a care that he himself gets what he is paying for, and that Uncle Sam does not get more than his dues. The first work, therefore, is that of weighing and sampling. Two huge scale beams confront each other on the dock, one marked "U. S.," the other that of a city weigher, paid by and representing the refiner. Each hogshead is trundled along in a hurry to Uncle Sam's scale; the chain grips it; two stout pair of arms at the other end of the lever swing it into the air; a quick eye and a quick hand note the gross weight; a sampler runs his gauge through the bung, and turns out the sample into a tin can with the others, presently to be sent on to the examiners for testing. Then the cask is turned over to the second weigher, who repeats the process on the refiner's part, and compares notes with the government's weigher. After the sugar has been turned out, one hogshead out of every three or four is weighed for "tare," and allowance made accordingly on the weigher's books.

On the wharf-level are the mixing-rooms, dark kitchens, misty and mysterious with clouds of steam, where brawny men rush about half naked on the edge of seething pits of muddy broth. The floor is sloppy and treacherous, and one shudders at the horrid possibilities of a fate which has more than once overtaken the workers at this cyclopean cookery. Suddenly there comes trundling in an enormous hogshead weighing 1500 to 2000 pounds. Two men, springing fiercely at it with big hammers, knock in the head, while others attach the chains from a big derrick above, which by the pull of a lever raises the cask above the open mouth of the "mixer," and dumps its contents into the steaming syrup below. These "mix-

ers" or "blow-ups" are really great stew-pans set in the ground, heated by steam, which melt the crude sugar into a syrup, and mix together the various caskfuls and bagfuls. They are tanks made of wrought or cast iron, and inside are a vertical revolving shaft on which are the mixing arms, and coils of steam-pipe whence live steam is blown into the seething mixture. Before the raw sugar is dumped in, clear water, or "sweet water" from the washings of bags, is run in, and heated nearly to boiling. These tanks hold 3000 to 4500 gallons, and treat nine to thirteen tons of sugar at a time. The heating occupies half an hour or so, during which a scum of impurities rises to the top, and is skimmed off, while other dregs, sometimes precipitated, if the mixture shows a tinge of acidity, by a few buckets of lime-water, sink to the bottom, and are cleaned out after the liquor is run off. From the mixers run pipes connecting with force-pumps, which raise the liquid to the very top of the enormous building, whence, percolating downward, it goes through the refining process, reaching the lower stories as clear sugar.

A rude elevator takes us up to the top. For company we have the "beer man," who rings his hand-bell vigorously at each landing, and sets out a line of little pails of beer. Brawny fellows they are who come to drain them, sweating at every pore, for it is hard and hot work they do, and "moistening up" is a necessary process within as the moisture pours from them without. At last we reach the top, whence the open windows command a far view of the river, the great city silent below, the two-legged midgets which skip to and fro on the wharf right beneath us. In sharp contrast with the place we have left, this is a great silent room, where nothing seems to be going on. We are in the defecating-room, fitted with banks or ranges of square tanks about six feet high, which are the "defecators." These are filled with the liquid pumped up from the "mixers," kept at about 170° temperature, undergoing the same process used by the house-keeper in clearing coffee with the white of an egg. What happens in the coffee-pot is simply that the albumen of the egg, as it diffuses itself and sinks slowly to the bottom, makes a kind of mesh which takes along with it the solid particles of dregs or lees which have not dissolved, leaving the coffee solution clear. Bullock's blood or

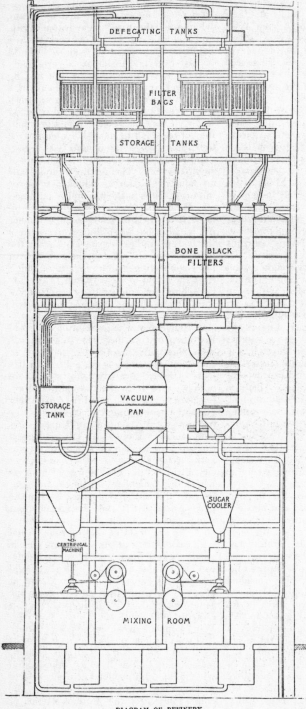

DEFECATING TANKS

FILTER BAGS

STORAGE TANKS

BONE BLACK FILTERS

STORAGE TANK

VACUUM PAN

SUGAR COOLER

CENTRIFUGAL MACHINE

MIXING   ROOM

DIAGRAM OF REFINERY.

some other form of albuminous matter performs the same service for the sugar in these defecators. After from twenty minutes to half an hour the clear liquor is drawn off, and the dregs separately removed.

The good house-keeper will not only clear, but also strain her coffee; the refiner does the same with his sugar. On the next stage below, the floor seems to be a series of gutters, underneath which, it will be presently seen, hang, in great compartments holding four or five hundred bags each, the bag filters, of coarse, thick cotton twill, four or five feet long, and but a few inches round. The liquor from the defecators flows through the gutters into these filters, and thence to the floor of the compartments, where it is collected again, and carried off into vats. After the liquor has run through the bags, there remains in them much good sugar; consequently the gutters are flushed with clean warm water, which running through the bags brings the sugar with it, making a weaker liquor called "sweet water," and leaving behind only the insoluble dregs. These are washed out, by turning the bags inside out, by stout-armed washermen, whose work is not confined to Monday mornings, but lasts day in and day out.

The liquor has now been freed from its organic and insoluble matters, and is a bright but brown-colored syrup, containing still some soluble impurities. It must now be rid of these. The means employed is similar to the charcoal filter screwed on a faucet to purify drinking water, but the filter becomes a Brobdingnag affair, an enormous circular tank two stories deep (or about twenty feet) and eight feet across. Finely powdered charcoal, particularly

tom, perforated, over which a blanket is fitted to prevent the bone-black from flowing through with the liquid. A stream of bone-black is then turned on, which must be distributed evenly through the filter. To do this, a workman descends into this atmosphere of powdered blackness, first fitting a sponge over his mouth and nostrils. He fastens to the rim of the man-hole a hanging ladder of linked

THE BONE-BLACK FILTER.

the animal charcoal called bone-black, made by calcining and pulverizing bone, has a peculiar power which the most skilled chemists do not fully understand. It decolorizes syrup by retaining the soluble impurities, letting the cleared liquid pass through. The filters, of which a large refinery may contain a hundred or more, open through man-holes at the top to the filter-room floor. When a filter is to be refilled, the first work is to rinse it thoroughly clean. The tank has a false bot-

steel, takes an electric lamp suspended from a flexible wire, and disappears into the black pit. The largest filters hold thirty to forty tons of the bone-black. When they are filled, the man-hole is closed, and the syrup from the cisterns below the bag filters is turned on. It percolates slowly down, is allowed some time to settle, and after about seven hours the drawing off begins through a narrow discharge pipe. The syrup is at first crystal clear, and is discharged into a tank from which the whitest and purest sugars will be made. As it exhausts the powers of the bone-black it becomes more and more amber-colored, as is seen by the rows of tiny glasses set in a frame against the light, filled with samples taken at in-

eral stories of the great buildings are given up. As a matter of fact, reburning is just what is not done; the bone-black is not burned, otherwise it would disappear in vapor; it is expressly prevented from burning by being treated in red-hot

THE VACUUM PAN.

tervals from the flow. Each shelf in this frame represents one filtering, and the successive glasses side by side represent a gamut of tone, from brilliant transparency to a strong gold-color. A skilled workman, as the syrup begins to lose its clearness, turns the discharge at the fitting moment into a second tank, and thus different grades of sugars are separated. After about twenty hours the charge is run out; the sugar remaining in the charcoal is washed out by running through fresh or sweet water, and the bone-black must be "reburned" before it can again be used. A ton of bone-black filters about a ton of sugar.

The "reburning" of the bone-black, though purely a side process, is part of the work of all large refineries, and to it sev-

pipes from which the air is carefully excluded, between which a hot flame plays. The impurities are, however, burned, and go off as vapor. The damp charcoal is run out or shovelled out of the filters at the bottom; it is washed, sometimes permitted to ferment, partly dried, and then delivered into the burners or pipes referred to, heated by enormous fires in the story below. It comes out "revivified" through these cleansing fires and as good as new, indeed better, for bone-black four to six months in use is said to give the best results. Some time after this it deteriorates, and must be mixed with new charcoal or cast aside.

The liquor is now refined; it remains to crystallize the sugar into solid form. This is accomplished in the vacuum pan, or striking pan. The principle is another application of science to kitchen cookery. The housewife who is making sugar-candy boils down her syrup till it is thick, and then lets it cool: the result is that it crystallizes more or less perfectly, and produces solid candy. If strings are strung across a pan as the mass slowly cools, large crystals of rock-candy form on them. The cook's trouble usually is that as the syrup becomes thicker, it takes a hotter fire to keep it boiling, and it is very likely to "catch" and burn. When it burns, it makes caramel; if it is not boiled enough it makes a molasses, and will not "pull" or solidify, but remains sticky.

The sugar refiner has the same difficulties to avoid and the same purposes to accomplish.

about forty tons of syrup. Inside the boiler are coils of steam-pipe, which do the heating. Now in boiling, the bubbles of vapor which rise to the top are kept down by the pressure of the outer air, and as a liquid grows thick these bubbles find it harder to force their way to the top, and so it requires more heat to boil a dense liquid. If, therefore, the pressure above is relieved, the bubbles rise easier, and boiling commences at a lower temperature, at which also a liquid is less likely to burn. The vacuum pan has an opening through its cover into a great pipe connected with an air-pump, which pumps the air and vapor from the top of the heated syrup, and thus permits it to boil at a lower temperature, and prevents

FILLING THE CONES.

The vacuum pan—invented by Charles E. Howard, an Englishman, in 1813—is an enormous copper boiler, covered with a copper cover or dome, both parts being fastened together, air-tight and steam-tight, along the rim. The larger ones are twenty feet high, holding

the formation of caramel. This pump is set at work, and as soon as the pressure is reduced, a feed-cock at the side is opened and syrup sufficient to cover the first coil of pipe is let in. The pipe is charged with steam, and the syrup begins to concentrate. At short intervals a new supply of syrup is let in, the upper steam coils are heated, and presently the liquid begins to "grain," or crystallize. Now comes the critical time when the skill of the sugar-maker is tested. There are several devices to show him what is going on inside the pan without breaking the vacuum: a thermometer and a vacuum gauge stand out from the top; there is a sight glass set hermetically into the side through which he may peep in; and an ingenious device, called a "proof stick," enables him to take out samples at any time. This is a hollow rod of brass or gun-metal fitting closely into a larger tube, which extends into the pan and is closed at the end by a sort of stopcock. When the proof stick is run into this tube and turned half-way round, the stopcock is opened and the stick is filled with the liquid. It is then turned back and withdrawn, and the quick eye of the sugar-maker makes "proof" by noticing against the light the crystals adhering to the stick, or by cooling the *masse-cuite* on a plate of glass. If the sugar-maker desires a large regular grain, he uses a thin syrup and concentrates it quietly and slowly. As each new charge is let in,

it boils up to the bull's-eye, or sight glass, and then subsides, adding its contribution to the existing crystals, which gradually "grow." If the sugar-maker makes mistakes, the new syrup, instead of depositing on the existing crystals, starts a new set of minute crystals of its own, making a "false grain," and injuring the quality of the sugar. When the proof will scarcely run out of the socket of the proof stick, the temperature is reduced below 150° F.; a slide at the bottom of the pan is opened, and the contents are run out into a receptacle below.

After the *masse-cuite* has left the pan, the crystallization is completed by cooling, and the sugar must then be cured. The processes are quite different for "mould" and for "soft" sugars. The best grades of syrup, boiled to an even, good-sized grain, are used for the former, whether loaf, cut, crushed, or pulverized. As the syrup cools it is run into conical moulds, with a small aperture at the bottom or smaller end, through which the uncrystallized liquid may drain off. As this drains off at the bottom, fresh liquid is poured in at the top, which washes the

SAWING SUGAR.

crystals as it slowly filters through. After some days the moulds are turned over, and the brilliant white cone of the "sugar-loaf" is turned out, solid to the last degree. This has disappeared, in its old-

is so sugary that one tastes the sweetness as he breathes. The crushed sugar is literally "crushed" by merely smashing the loaves; the pulverized sugar is simply ground fine from the dust of the other

THE DANCING BARRELS.

fashioned blue paper wrappings, from the grocer's shelves, but the finest sugars are still made from it.

The square lump-sugar is made by sawing up these loaves, first into round plates or disks, then into square rods, and then into the little cubes, by successive gangsaws, like those of a big saw-mill on a small scale, enclosed in covers like Dutch ovens to prevent waste of the sugar dust. Nevertheless, the air of the sawing-room

kinds, and sifted out by a long vibrating sieve. Granulated sugars may be made from loaf by tearing the crystals apart, but it is now mostly the product of the centrifugal machines.

The "soft" sugars are cured mostly by the centrifugal machines, which act on the familiar principle of the rotary clothes-drier. The centrifugal machines are claimed as the invention of a Massachusetts man named Hurd, in 1844, although

SORGHUM FACTORY AT HUTCHINSON, KANSAS.

it is said that the principle had previously been applied in England. They are practically two tubs or drums set one within the other, the inner one pierced with fine holes and revolving at great speed, reaching a thousand revolutions a minute. Over each centrifugal is a discharge pipe from the coolers; the brown syrup is let in, the inner drum is started, and as it whirls a change of color is seen in its inner wall, from dark to light brown, gradually to yellow, and then suddenly, if the sugar is of high grade, to brilliant white. The reason is simple. As the drum gains speed, the liquid flies off by centrifugal force, first the free liquid, and finally, as clean water is introduced for a final washing, even the delicate film of syrup or molasses coating each crystal, leaving its intrinsic whiteness to shine forth. The solid crystals remain, and fall to the bottom as the machine is stopped.

The sugar is now ready for barrelling. Most of the large refineries have cooper shops of their own, and as the barrels are delivered it is amusing to see the dexterity of those practised in handling them, as they start them spinning a hundred yards away, rounding a post or a corner, and bringing up exactly where they are wanted. The sugar is delivered slowly from spouts above the barrels, each of which "stands on its own bottom," in a separate frame, which is by eccentric machinery given just the irregular motion a man gives a barrel in "settling" it. It is droll enough to see these rows of barrels bobbing and nodding and making lunges toward each other, as though they were a set of tipsy topers holding hands in a row to keep themselves steady, and singing "We won't go home till morning!" This is the method of packing granulated sugars; the softer kinds are packed, like flour, by a screw press.

Sorghum sugar making is, in this country, rather a matter of prophecy than of experience, yet there seems to be no good reason why the work of the Department of Agriculture, of which this industry is a pet nursling, should not result in developing an important interest. The first sorghum seed was sent to this country in 1853, and the department has ever since "lent a hand" to encourage sorghum-growing, scattering over the country in a recent season, from the experimental sorghum farm established near Washington, over 60,000 pounds of seed. The growing of sorghum received its first impetus during the war, when the supply of Louisiana molasses was cut off, and all through the Western country farmers planted their half-acre of sorghum, and produced a few gallons of syrup. The first methods of manufacture were primitive enough. The first crushers were upright wooden rollers, worked by an old horse, and fed by a lad who thrust each stalk by itself through a hole in front of the rollers, dodging the beam each time the old horse went by. While it was in operation its dreadful crunching and screeching might be heard the country round, and the relief was great when, as often happened, the horse stalled and the mill stuck. Then iron mills of two-horse-power were made, and great was the demand. Farmers possessing them would "make up" their neighbors' crops on shares. The ordinary maple-sugar pans were used for boiling, and from the earliest daylight of frosty October, when the crusher would be started, until late at night, when the boiling was completed, the farmer and his men worked hard at his syrup crop. The crop was, in fact, chiefly syrup, for in the census year, 1879–80, when forty States and Territories reported sorghum, but 12,792 pounds of sugar were made, against 20,444,402 gallons of molasses. In 1881 New Jersey established a bounty of one dollar per ton of cane and one cent per pound of merchantable sugar grown in the State, and though only one establishment was the result, that at Rio Grande, this produced 375,869 pounds of sugar in 1884. The State has paid out in four years $22,275 for cane and $11,219 24 for sugar. Besides this, there are considerable factories at Sterling, Ottawa, and Hutchinson, Kansas, and as much as a million pounds of sugar has been produced in a season.

The sugar sorghum is planted from seed in April or May, and at first grows slowly, very like its cousin the broom-corn sorghum. The botanists distinguish only one species, but the farmer finds a good deal of difference between the "Early Amber cane," which is the favorite, the Orange, also much planted, Link's Hybrid, the Honduras, Liberian, and other kinds, which ripen later than the Early Amber, and are therefore less suited to high latitudes. After the plant gets its real start, it grows wonderfully, and with remarkable independence of season and climate, in wet times or dry times, when Indian corn would be drowned out or burned up, and from Minnesota to Texas, where it has been known to develop a second crop from the stubble after the first has been cut. Profitable growing for sugar is, however, confined to lower latitudes than at first supposed, and the isothermal lines of 70° for the three summer months is now thought by the best authorities to mark the sugar limit, though syrup may be profitably made further north. This includes Missouri, Tennessee, Kentucky, Illinois—which led in syrup production in the census year in the order named—Kansas, southern Indiana, etc., as probable sugar-producing States. The crop ripens at the North in September and October, and at its maturity presents a fine picture, with its deep green leafage, and the red or dark tops of ripening seed. Its great enemies are early frosts and the equinoctial storm, which is apt to strike the plant just as it is ready to harvest, top-heavy with its cone of seed, and bend it to the ground. In 1883 the storm played sad havoc with the ripened crop. The Western farmers, who grow mostly for syrup, report a yield of from 150 gallons of syrup per acre up, costing about $24 per acre to raise, in addition to use of land and outfit. At fifty cents per gallon, this would give a profit of about $30 per acre; but the trouble is that this syrup must come into competition with other syrups selling at scarcely above half that price.

Sugar-making from sorghum follows the same processes as with cane. The most notable plantation and mill in the country is that started in 1881 at Rio Grande, New Jersey, which occupies a stretch of four miles along a narrow peninsula near Cape May. The cane is brought to the mill on a tramway, a contractor who works the plantation delivering it stripped and taking away the begass at $2 12 the ton. The begass is sent to the pig-pens, which are a most noteworthy feature of the place, where the pigs, after getting out a part of the remaining sugar, tread it into excellent manure. These pigs are fed chiefly from the sorghum seed, which is neatly chopped off the bundles of cane by a mammoth guillotine, threshed out, and boiled till the starch granules burst, making a pasty mass, which in turn makes excellent pork. This has led to the prophecy that the breakfast-table of the future may depend largely upon the sorghum plant, which supplies good bread or "cakes" and capital pork from its seed, and sugar or syrup—with a flavor of its own, easily removed, however, by bone-black—from its juice.

At Rio Grande the diffusion process now replaces crushing. The waste is still considerable, but it is claimed that the diffusion process, though costly, saves thirty per cent. more sugar, and experiments conducted at Ottawa, Kansas, last year, by Professor H. W. Wiley, of the Agricultural Department, obtained, it is claimed, ninety-eight per cent. of the sugar in the cane. How great this crop may be in the future no one can prophesy.

The beet-sugar industry has scarcely made a start yet in this country, though in Europe it has attained such proportions as to furnish half the marketed sugar of the world, and about a third of the total production. The production of beet sugar is a commercial triumph of the man of "mere science." A Berlin apothecary, Marggraf, first drew attention to the beet root as a possible sugar mine, and a Prussian chemist, Achard, first successfully extracted the sugar. It was not, however, until the Napoleonic wars and the blockade of Continental ports raised the prices of sugar that the industry was started. Napoleon in 1811 offered bounties for the production of beet sugar, and made the chemistry of the process a specialty in scientific schools. Germany followed the example, and even now the industry is fostered by the government through experimental stations and by means of bounties on sugar protection. The German law of 1869 laid a tax on beets of $4 (16 marks) per ton, to compensate for the loss of revenue from imported sugars, and gave a drawback of $42 to $47 per ton of sugar exported. As by the improved processes the yield of beet root is over nine and a half per cent. of merchantable sugar, besides more than two per cent. of molasses, this law guaranteed a profit to manufacturers for export, and the production has been very great.

The beet commonly used in Europe is the White Silesian, weighing from one and a half to two and a half pounds, and producing fifteen to twenty tons to the acre. It succeeds best where there is dry, unclouded autumn weather. The juice is extracted either by rasping the beet into shreds, and pressing out the juice, or by the diffusion process. As the beet contains much less sugar in proportion than cane, its transportation is a serious matter, and in France and Belgium under-ground pipes are in use, through which the juice is sent to a central factory. The process of extracting the sugar from the juice is essentially the same as in the treatment of cane, except that the process of carbonation, which is coming into use also with sorghum, is very generally used. The method proposed by the Department of Agriculture and practiced for one season at Ottawa, Kansas, with success, is a modification of the process used for beet juices, and consists in adding a large excess of lime to the tepid juice, and afterward precipitating the excess by carbonic acid. After passing through a filter press the clear juice is saturated with sulphurous acid, and again filtered. This process gives a juice perfectly limpid and of great purity. The production of beet sugar, where bounties are not paid, will probably be limited by the fact that, with improving scientific processes, the larger proportion of sugar in cane and sorghum will give them an increasing advantage to the planter and consumer. The census of 1880 reported four beet-root factories, with $365,000 capital, employing 350 hands, to whom it paid $62,271 wages, or $177 each, and producing $282,572 product.

Everybody has eaten maple sugar, and a good many of us have helped in sugar frolics, but few know that we produced in the census year from twenty-three States 36,576,061 pounds of sugar, besides 1,796,048 gallons of molasses, and a still larger crop in later years, reaching in 1885 25,900 tons. Vermont and New York are the States whose groves of rock or sugar maple give the chief supply. The sap begins to rise in February, after the first break-up of the long frost, and the "sap days" continue off and on for six weeks, into March or April. But the tree is like a sensitive-plant: during south winds and when a storm is coming the sap ceases to flow, and a dozen or so good sap days are a fair average. The trees are notched with an axe or tapped with an auger about three or four feet up the trunk, the sap flows into troughs, whence it is taken to open kettles in or near the grove, over fires fed with the dead branches of the maple-trees. Three gallons or more of sap will flow from a good tree during a day, producing a pound or less of sugar, but some trees have produced forty pounds of sugar in a single season. The date-palm sugar of the East is collected in much the same way. During boiling the sugar is stirred with a wooden spoon, and fresh juice added; when it thickens and becomes golden yellow, it is strained, cooled, settled with a little lime or soda, and cleared with milk or white of egg, and put in pans to crystallize. Then, as sugar or syrup, it is ready for the buckwheat cakes.

Different lines of sugar have different names, varying with the country of origin, the quality, and the process used. "Melada" is the name of the concentrated cane juice, just on the point of graining, in which shape some refining material is imported. "Jaggery" is the very crude East Indian sugar, containing a great deal of dirt. "Muscovado" sugar is that cured by simple drainage, the sticky mass from the coolers being put in casks with perforated bottoms, loosely filled with rushes, whence the molasses drains into a cask below. "A" sugar is simply a term to designate the higher grades of soft sugar, various fancy names being used by various refineries. "B" sugar is more brown.

Molasses and syrups are by-products both of the farm and the refinery in every kind of sugar-making. The molasses of the beet is too unpalatable, however, for food, and can be used only for distillation and like processes. Molasses is really a mixture of crystalline and uncrystallized sugar, with some impurities, colored by caramel or burnt sugar. The name comes by way of *melasse* (the same as *melada*), from the word *mel*, honey, and means honey-like. The sugar-maker's object is to get as much sugar and as little molasses as possible from a given quantity of juice, and with the improvement of processes the world over, less molasses is produced. The distillation of molasses makes rum, in which shape "Jamaica" in especial sends us her sugar crop. Syrup, as has been seen, is the leavings of refined sugar, that is to say, a superior grade of molasses, but most of that nowadays sold is a mixture with glucose.

Glucose, or the sugar made from starch, has become of late years an enormous industry, the chief seat of which is at Buffalo, New York. Thousands of bushels of corn are converted by these factories, in which the essential process is the boiling of the fresh starch of the grain, in vats holding about a ton and a half each, in water with one or two per cent. of sulphuric acid. The starch granules burst, take up the extra atom of water, and so make 238 pounds of sugar out of 220 pounds of starch. The purification of the sugar from the acid and its crystallization are processes similar to those already described. This kind of sugar can be marketed at from two to three cents, and it is much used by confectioners and brewers, as food for bees in making artificial honey, but most of all for the production of table syrups. It is simply a substitute for cane sugar, less sweet, but very much cheaper. It is probably not unhealthy, since the common notion that because acid is used in its formation it must be poisonous has no foundation, and the old objection that it is commonly sold for what it is not no longer holds true, glucose being now a recognized article of demand. The census of 1880 reported seven glucose factories, with $2,255,000 capital, employing 1193 hands, to whom it paid $605,802, or $508 each, and from material valued at $3,044,450 producing a product valued at $4,551,212, or about a third of our cane-sugar crop.

A considerable portion of the refined sugars find their way to the candy shops. The word candy comes to us from the Arabic and Persian *qand*, another name for sugar. Candy-making is a considerable trade in itself. The census of 1880 reported 13,692 confectioners. There are eight or ten large factories in New York alone, employing perhaps a hundred people each, and using a hundred barrels or more of sugar a week, besides quantities of glucose.

The "stick" candy, which seems to be an indigenous American product, is of ordinary "A" sugar, boiled down with water and a little cream of tartar to prevent crystallization. The mass is taken in batches of about fifteen pounds to a marble table, where it is kneaded like bread, and the flavoring and coloring worked in. The paste then goes to the "pulling-hooks," where for five or six minutes it is pulled and twisted and repulled and retwisted at the hands of a workman who certainly earns his living. Thence it returns to the marble table, at one end of which is a metal plate, kept hot, on which he works the candy into its final shape. Stripes are pressed into the batch, two feet long and a foot thick, and it is then drawn and twisted out till it is the proper size of the penny "stick," the right length of which is clipped off by huge scissors. Clear candy is not kneaded or pulled. Flat candy is run into pans, and a knife is run across where it is to be broken into sticks or squares. The drops, fishes, and other fancy shapes are made by passing the paste through a machine, which cuts and presses it to the proper size and shape.

Lozenges are rolled out like pie-crust, sometimes printed in carmine with a hand-stamp, and then cut out with dies. "Sugar-plums" and sugared almonds are made in a very interesting way, by throwing the nut, seed, or other nucleus with boiling sugar into great copper pans, which are shaken by hand or revolved by machinery over a hot fire. Rolled over and over in the moist sugar, the plums soon begin to grow, and are "polished off" by each other, while, above, steam-worked fans carry off the dry dust. Gum drops are made of gum-arabic and sugar, boiled and mixed, seven or eight hundred pounds at a time, in huge copper steam-kettles, whence the mixture is taken out into smaller kettles to be flavored and colored. The cheap gum drops and "marsh-mallows" are now made chiefly from glucose. Cream or soft candies are made in a simple way, from sugar mixed with cream of tartar to prevent crystallizing. To give them their fancy forms, a flat tray is filled with starch, which is pressed into moulds by a series of plaster-of-Paris models—a drop, hand, face, berry, or what it may be—arranged on a long stick. Into these starch moulds the hot cream is poured, and then allowed to dry. Some factories have as much as 50,000 pounds of starch in this use. The drying-room is kept at a high temperature, in which the "creams" soon become dry and solid. They are then separated from the starch by huge sieves. If they are to be glossed, they are placed in huge tin pans and a cold solution of sugar poured over them to stand overnight. In the morning the ice of sugar on top is broken, and the "creams" are found coated with fine crystals. The liqueur drops are a very curious product. The syrup is mixed with brandy or flavored water, and is poured into the starch

moulds. As it cools at the top and on the mould, the crystals make a continuous case, imprisoning the liquor within.

The adulteration of candy is chiefly by the use of *terra alba*, or white clay. This harmful stuff can be detected by dissolving the suspected candy in water, when the clay falls to the bottom undissolved. An ounce roll of cheap lozenges will sometimes contain three-quarters of an ounce of this injurious stuff. The coloring of candies is, for the most part, not dangerous, since a piece of red coloring matter the size of a gum drop will color 5000 pounds of candy. Unscrupulous manufacturers, however, sometimes use mineral instead of the safe vegetable colors, and cart-loads of such candy have been seized and destroyed by the health-officers in New York. For the most part, carmine and cochineal are used for red, saffron for yellow, caramel or burnt sugar for brown, and this with carmine for orange. Green and blue candies are to be avoided. These colors are used sometimes, however, in "decorating"—a surface treatment of fine candies by hand, in which a water-color artist is employed to do art work at wholesale according to the model set him. As for this purpose the proportion of coloring matter to sugar is about one-millionth, the result of swallowing paint is not so disastrous as might be expected. In flavoring, essential oils are used, about a pound to a thousand pounds of sugar, and this is worked in during the boiling or kneading. Licorice colors and flavors both at once.

The consumption of sugar is a chief test of a nation's prosperity. This country consumed of cane sugar in 1885 about 1,170,000 tons. There are no figures to show how our consumption has increased, but it is known that its use in Great Britain more than trebled in about forty years, being reported in 1846 at $20\frac{7}{8}$ pounds, and in 1882 at $70\frac{1}{2}$ pounds, per head of population. The duty was removed from sugar in that country in 1874. In our country it is the most prolific source of customs revenue, sugar and molasses constituting over 13 per cent. of our total importations, and paying 29 per cent. of all duties. The 2,578,993,335 pounds of sugar imported in 1884–5, valued at $69,078,857, produced a revenue of $50,845,916, or 73.66 per cent. The duty on sugars is, for those not above No. 13 Dutch standard in color, testing not above 75 degrees by the polariscope, $1\frac{4.0}{1.0.0}$ cents per pound, or if above 75 degrees, $\frac{4}{100}$ for each additional degree or part of a degree; for those above No. 13, and net above No. 16, $2\frac{75}{100}$ cents; for those not above No. 20, 3 cents; for those above No. 20, $3\frac{50}{100}$ cents per pound. The Dutch standard is an arbitrary scale of shades of brown adopted by other nations as a matter of convenience, sugars below No. 13 being the cheap, dark sugars mostly used for refining. Confectionery, or tinctured, colored, or adulterated sugar, valued at not over 30 cents a pound, pays 10 cents a pound duty; if over 30 cents, 50 per cent. *ad valorem.* Hawaiian sugar not above No. 20 is free from duty under the reciprocity treaty, but the combination of the transcontinental railroads and steam-ship lines to keep up sugar freights gave to the controllers of this crop so strong a hold that the Pacific coast has had up to this year no benefit from the remission of the duty nor from the low prices at the East. The imports of 32,183,026 gallons of molasses, valued at $4,413,492, produced, at four cents per gallon, $1,287,321, or 29.17 per cent. Molasses testing above 56° by the polariscope is subject to 8 cents per gallon duty, but this is not imported to any extent. The government pays a drawback of from $1\frac{1}{4}$ to $3\frac{18}{100}$ cents per pound on sugar exported, to encourage the importation of raw sugars for refining here, and it is alleged that this, like the German bounty, is so much above the import tax as to guarantee a profit to our refiners, who are now, in fact, doing much of the refining for England and the world. We exported of refined sugar in the year 1884–85, 252,574,335 pounds, valued at $16,071,699.

There is no industry in which the tendency to industrial concentration is more clearly shown, for whereas the census of 1880 found only 49 refineries, with a capital of $27,400,000, the product returned, $155,400,000, despite great reductions of prices, was nearly half as much again as that in 1870, when the census included the plantation mills as refineries and counted up 1091. Some of the great refineries now turn out 250,000 tons of syrup yearly. The refineries, by the census of 1880, employed 5857 hands, an average of 120 each. The ordinary hands in a New York refinery get from $35 per month up, and a sugar-boiler as much as $100 per month.

In 1864, during the war, when gold was at a premium, raw sugar averaged $17\frac{1}{4}$ cents a pound, and indeed reached 25 cents. In 1885 it averaged 5.18 cents, or in bond 3.06 cents, showing an average difference of price because of the duty of 2.12 cents per pound. The average of refined sugars in 1885 was $6\frac{1}{2}$ to 7 cents per pound, and some kinds, as granulated, fell below 6 cents during the spring. These were the lowest prices since thirty years ago, but it is to be noted that in those years raw sugar ruled on the whole as low as now, so that the demand seems to have kept fully apace with the greatly increased supply.

Note.—The material for the portion of this article relating to the sorghum industry has been supplied chiefly by Professor H. W. Wiley, of the Agricultural Department. Mr. Isaac A. Hedges, President of the Mississippi Valley Cane [Sorghum] Growers' Association, and a devotee of sorghum, has published a book on sorghum under the somewhat misleading title of *Sugar-canes and their Products, Culture, and Manufacture* (St. Louis, 1881); Peter Collier is the author of a later treatise on *Sorghum . . . . as Source of Sugar, Syrups, and Fodder* (Cincinnati, 1884); and there are other earlier American works. The reports and bulletins of the United States Department of Agriculture, and the reports for 1883 and 1884 of the New Jersey Bureau of Labor Statistics, give valuable information as to sorghum. The most recent and highest English authority on *Sugar-growing and Refining* in general is the very comprehensive book of that title by Charles G. W. Lock, F.L.S., and others (London and New York, 1882), condensed in *Spon's Encyclopedia of the Industrial Arts, Manufactures, and Commercial Products* (London and New York, 1882), edited by the same writer. Two works on beet sugar are by E. B. Grant (Boston, 187-), and by L. S. Ware (Philadelphia, 1880). Reference may also be made to papers in this Magazine on the "Sugar Regions of Louisiana," before the war, by T. B. Thorpe (Vol. vii., p. 746); on "Sugar-making in Cuba," by H. B. Auchincloss (Vol. xxx., p. 446), and on "Sugar-making Machines," by E. H. Knight (Vol. I., p. 385). An "Annual Statement of the Sugar Trade of the United States" is issued in January of each year by the *Shipping and Commercial List*, New York.

MEMPHIS AND LITTLE ROCK

THE State of Tennessee gets its diversity of climate and productions from the irregularity of its surface, not from its range over degrees of latitude, like Illinois; for it is a narrow State, with an average breadth of only a hundred and ten miles, while it is about four hundred miles in length, from the mountains in the east—the highest land east of the Rocky Mountains—to the alluvial bottom of the Mississippi in the west. In this range is every variety of mineral and agricultural wealth, with some of the noblest scenery and the fairest farming land in the Union, and all the good varieties of a temperate climate.

In the extreme southwest corner lies Memphis, differing as entirely in character from Knoxville and Nashville as the bottom-lands of the Mississippi differ from the valleys of the Great Smoky Mountains. It is the natural centre of the finest cotton-producing district in the world, the county of Shelby, of which it is legally known as the Taxing District, yielding more cotton than any other county in the Union except that of Washington in Mississippi. It is almost as much aloof politically from east and middle Tennessee as it is geographically. A homogeneous State might be constructed by taking west Tennessee, all of Mississippi above Vicksburg and Jackson, and a slice off Arkansas, with Memphis for its capital. But the redistricting would be a good thing neither for the States named nor for Memphis, for the more variety within convenient limits a State can have, the better, and Memphis could not wish a better or more distinguished destiny than to become the commercial metropolis of a State of such great possibilities and varied industries as Tennessee. Her political influence might be more decisive in the homogeneous State outlined, but it will be abundant for all reasonable ambition in its inevitable commercial importance. And besides, the western part of the State needs the moral tonic of the more elevated regions.

The city has a frontage of about four miles on the Mississippi River, but is high above it on the Chickasaw Bluffs, with an uneven surface and a rolling country back of it, the whole capable of perfect drainage. Its site is the best on the river for a great city from St. Louis to the Gulf; this advantage is emphasized by the concentration of railways at this point, and the great bridge, which is now on the eve of construction, to the Arkansas shore, no doubt fixes its destiny as the inland metropolis of the Southwest. Memphis was the child of the Mississippi, and this powerful, wayward stream is still its fostering mother, notwithstanding the decay of river commerce brought about by the railways; for the river still asserts its power as a regulator of rates of transportation. I do not mean to say that the freighting on it in towed barges is not still enormous, but if it did not carry a pound to the markets of the world it is still the friend of all the inner continental regions, which says to the railroads, beyond a certain rate of charges you shall not go. With this advantage of situation, the natural receiver of the products of an inexhaustible agricultural region (one has only to take a trip by rail through the Yazoo Valley to be convinced of that), and an equally good point for distribution of supplies, it is inevitable that Memphis should grow with an accelerating impulse.

The city has had a singular and instructive history, and that she has survived so many vicissitudes and calamities, and entered upon an extraordinary career of prosperity, is sufficient evidence of the territorial necessity of a large city just at this point on the river. The student of social science will find in its history a striking illustration of the relation of sound sanitary and business conditions to order and morality. Before the war, and for some time after it, Memphis was a place for trade in one staple, where fortunes were quickly made and lost, where no attention was paid to sanitary laws. The cloud of impending pestilence always hung over it, the yellow-fever was always a possibility, and a devastating epidemic of it must inevitably be reckoned with every few years. It seems to be a law of social life that an epidemic, or the probability of it, engenders a recklessness of life and a low condition of morals and public order. Memphis existed, so to speak, on the edge of a volcano, and it cannot be denied that it had a reputation for violence and disorder. While little or nothing was done to make the city clean and habitable, or to beautify it, law was weak in its mobile, excitable population, and differences of opinion were settled by the revolver. In spite of these disadvantages, the profits of trade were so great there that its population of twenty thousand at the close of the war had doubled by 1878. In that year the yellow-fever came as an epidemic, and so increased in 1879 as nearly to depopulate the city; its population was reduced from nearly forty thousand to about fourteen thousand, two-thirds of which were negroes; its commerce was absolutely cut off, its manufactures were suspended, it was bankrupt. There is nothing more unfortunate for a State or a city than loss of financial credit. Memphis struggled in vain with its enormous debt, unable to pay it, unable to compromise it.

Under these circumstances the city resorted to a novel expedient. It surrendered its charter to the State, and ceased to exist as a municipality. The leaders of this movement gave two reasons for it, the wish not to repudiate the city debt, but to gain breathing-time, and that municipal government in this country is a failure. The Legislature erected the former Memphis into The Taxing District of Shelby County, and provided a government for it. This government consists of a Legislative Council of eight members, made up of the Board of Fire and Police Commissioners, consisting of three, and the Board of Public Works, consisting of five. These are all elected by popular vote to serve a term of four years, but the elections are held every two years, so that the council always contains members who have had experience. The Board of Fire and Police Commissioners elects a President, who is the executive officer of the Taxing District, and has the power and duties of a mayor; he has a salary of $2000, inclusive of his fees as police magistrate, and the other members of his board have salaries of $500. The members of the Board of Public Works serve without compensation. No man can be eligible to either board who has not been a resident of the district for five years. In addition there is a Board of Health, appointed by the council. This government has the ordinary powers of a city government, defined carefully in the act,

but it cannot run the city in debt, and it cannot appropriate the taxes collected except for the specific purposes named by the State Legislature, which specific appropriations are voted annually by the Legislature on the recommendation of the council. Thus the government of the city is committed to eight men, and the execution of its laws to one man, the President of the Taxing District, who has extraordinary power. The final success of this scheme will be watched with a great deal of interest by other cities. On the surface it can be seen that it depends upon securing a non-partisan council, and an honest, conscientious President of the Taxing District—that is to say, upon the choice by popular vote of the best eight men to rule the city. Up to this time, with only slight hitches, it has worked exceedingly well, as will appear in a consideration of the condition of the city. The slight hitch mentioned was that the President was accused of using temporarily the sum appropriated for one city purpose for another.

The Supreme Court of the United States decided that Memphis had not evaded its obligations by a change of name and form of government. The result was a settlement with the creditors at fifty cents on the dollar; and then the city gathered itself together for a courageous effort and a new era of prosperity. The turning-point in its career was the adoption of a system of drainage and sewerage which transformed it immediately into a fairly healthful city. With its uneven surface and abundance of water at hand, it was well adapted to the Waring system, which works to the satisfaction of all concerned, and since its introduction the inhabitants are relieved from apprehension of the return of a yellow-fever epidemic. Population and business returned with this sense of security, and there has been a change in the social atmosphere as well. In 1880 it had a population of less than 34,000; it can now truthfully claim between 75,000 and 80,000; and the business activity, the building both of fine business blocks and handsome private residences, are proportioned to the increase in inhabitants. In 1879-80 the receipt of cotton was 409,809 bales, valued at $23,752,529; in 1886-87, 663,277 bales, valued at $30,099,510. The estimate of the Board of Trade for 1888, judging from the first months of the year, is 700,000 bales. I notice in the comparative statement of leading articles of commerce and consumption an exceedingly large increase in 1887 over 1886. The banking capital in 1887 was $3,360,000—an increase of $1,560,000 over 1886. The clearings were $101,177,377 in 1877, against $82,642,192 in 1886.

The traveller, however, does not need figures to convince him of the business activity of the town; the piles of cotton beyond the capacity of storage, the street traffic, the extension of streets and residences far beyond the city limits, all speak of growth. There is in process of construction a union station to accommodate the six railways now meeting there and others projected. On the west of the river it has lines to Kansas City and Little Rock and to St. Louis; on the east, to Louisville and to the Atlantic seaboard direct, and two to New Orleans. With the building of the bridge, which is expected to be constructed in a couple of years, Memphis will be admirably supplied with transportation facilities.

As to its external appearance, it must be said that the city has grown so fast that city improvements do not keep pace with its assessable value. The inability of the city to go into debt is a wholesome provision, but under this limitation the city offices are shabby, the city police quarters and court would disgrace an indigent country village, and most of the streets are in bad condition for want of pavement. There are fine streets, many attractive new residences, and some fine old places, with great trees, and the gravelled pikes running into the country are in fine condition, and are favorite drives. There is a beautiful country round about, with some hills and pleasant woods. Looked at from an elevation, the town is seen to cover a large territory, and presents in the early green of spring a charming appearance. Some five miles out is the Montgomery race-track, park, and club-house—a handsome establishment, prettily laid out and planted, already attractive, and sure to be notable when the trees are grown.

The city has a public-school system, a Board of Education elected by popular vote, and divides its fund fairly between schools for white and colored children. But it needs good school-houses as much as it needs good pavements. In 1887 the tax of one and a half mills produced $54,000 for carrying on the schools, and

$19,000 for the building fund. It was not enough—at least $75,000 were needed. The schools were in debt. There is a plan adopted for a fine High-School building, but the city needs altogether more money and more energy for the public schools. According to some reports the public schools have suffered from politics, and are not as good as they were years ago, but they are undoubtedly gaining in public favor, notwithstanding some remaining Bourbon prejudice against them. The citizens are making money fast enough to begin to be liberal in matters educational, which are only second to sanitary measures in the well-being of the city. The new free Public Library, which will be built and opened in a couple of years, will do much for the city in this direction. It is the noble gift of the late F. H. Cossitt, of New York, formerly a citizen of Memphis, who left $75,000 for that purpose.

Perhaps the public schools of Memphis would be better (though not so without liberal endowment) if the city had not two exceptionally good private schools for young ladies. These are the Clara Conway Institute and the Higby School for Young Ladies, taking their names from their principals and founders. Each of these schools has about 350 pupils, from the age of six to the mature age of graduation, boys being admitted until they are twelve years old. Each has pleasant grounds and fine buildings, large, airy, well planned, with ample room for all the departments—literature, science, art, music—of the most advanced education. One finds in them the best methods of the best schools, and a most admirable spirit. It is not too much to say that these schools give distinction to Memphis, and that the discipline and intellectual training the young ladies receive there will have a marked effect upon the social life of the city. If one who spent some delightful hours in the company of these graceful and enthusiastic scholars, and who would like heartily to acknowledge their cordiality, and his appreciation of their admirable progress in general study, might make a suggestion, it would be that what the frank, impulsive Southern girl, with her inborn talent for being agreeable and her vivid apprehension of life, needs least of all is the cultivation of the emotional, the rhetorical, the sentimental side. However cleverly they are

done, the recitation of poems of sentiment, of passion, of love-making and
marriage, above all, of those doubtful dialect verses in which a touch of pseudo-
feeling is supposed to excuse the slang
of the street and the vulgarity of the
farm, is not an exercise elevating to the
taste. I happen to speak of it here, but I
confess that it is only a text from which
a little sermon might be preached about
"recitations" and declamations generally,
in these days of overdone dialect and
innuendoes about the hypocrisy of old-
fashioned morality.

The city has a prosperous college of
the Christian Brothers, another excellent
school for girls in the St. Agnes Academy, and a colored industrial school, the
Lemoyne, where the girls are taught
cooking and the art of house-keeping,
and the boys learn carpentering. This
does not belong to the public-school system.

Whatever may be the opinion about
the propriety of attaching industrial training to public schools generally, there is
no doubt that this sort of training is indispensable to the colored people of the
South, whose children do not at present
receive the needed domestic training at
home, and whose education must contribute to their ability to earn a living.
Those educated in the schools, high and
low, cannot all be teachers or preachers,
and they are not in the way of either social elevation or thrifty lives if they have
neither a trade nor the taste to make neat
and agreeable homes. The colored race
cannot have it too often impressed upon
them that their way to all the rights and
privileges under a free government lies in
industry, thrift, and morality. Whatever
reason they have to complain of remaining discrimination and prejudice, there is
only one way to overcome both, and that
is by the acquisition of property and intelligence. In the history of the world
a people were never elevated otherwise.
No amount of legislation can do it. In
Memphis—in Southern cities generally—
the public schools are impartially administered as to the use of money for both
races. In the country districts they are
as generally inadequate, both in quality
and in the length of the school year. In
the country, where farming and domestic
service must be the occupations of the
mass of the people, industrial schools are
certainly not called for; but in the cities

they are a necessity of the present development.

Ever since Memphis took itself in hand
with a new kind of municipal government,
and made itself a healthful city, good
fortune of one kind and another seems
to have attended it.   Abundant water it
could get from the river for sewerage purposes, but for other uses either extensive
filters were needed or cisterns were resorted to.   The city was supplied with water, which the stranger would hesitate to
drink or bathe in, from Wolf River, a
small stream emptying into the Mississippi
above the city.   But within the year a
most important discovery has been made
for the health and prosperity of the town.
This was the striking, in the depression of
the Gayoso Bayou, at a depth of 450 feet,
perfectly pure water, at a temperature of
about 62°, in abundance, with a head sufficient to bring it in fountains some feet
above the level of the ground.   Ten wells
had been sunk, and the water flowing was
estimated at ten millions of gallons daily,
or half enough to supply the city.   It was
expected that with more wells the supply
would be sufficient for all purposes, and
then Memphis will have drinking water
not excelled in purity by that of any city
in the land.   It is not to be wondered at
that this incalculable good fortune should
add buoyancy to the business, and even to
the advance in the price, of real estate.
The city has widely outgrown its corpo-
rate limits, there is activity in building
and improvements in all the pleasant suburbs, and with the new pavements which
are in progress, the city will be as attractive as it is prosperous.

Climate is much a matter of taste. The
whole area of the alluvial land of the
Mississippi has the three requisites for malaria—heat, moisture, and vegetable de-
composition.   The tendency to this is
overcome, in a measure, as the land is
thoroughly drained and cultivated. Memphis has a mild winter, long summer, and
a considerable portion of the year when
the temperature is just about right for enjoyment.   In the table of temperature for
1887 I find that the mean was 61.9°, the
mean of the highest by months was 84.9°,
and the mean lowest was 37.4°.   The cold-
est month was January, when the range
of the thermometer was from 72.2° to 4.3°,
and the hottest was July, when the range
was from 99° to 67.3°.   There is a preponderance of fair, sunny weather.   The rec-

ord for 1887 was: 157 days of clear, 132
fair, 65 cloudy, 91 days of frost. From
this it appears that Memphis has a pretty
agreeable climate for those who do not
insist upon a good deal of "bracing," and
it has a most genial and hospitable society.

Early on the morning of the 12th of
April we crossed the river to the lower
landing of the Memphis and Little Rock
Railway, the upper landing being inaccessible on account of the high water.
It was a delicious spring morning, the
foliage, half unfolded, was in its first flush
of green, and as we steamed down the
stream the town bluffs, forty feet high,
were seen to have a noble situation. All
the opposite country for forty miles from
the river was afloat, and presented the appearance of a vast swamp, not altogether
unpleasing in its fresh dress of green.
For forty miles, to Madison, the road ran
upon an embankment just above the
flood; at intervals were poor shanties
and little cultivated patches, but shanties,
corn patches, and trees all stood in the
water. The inhabitants, the majority colored, seemed of the sort to be content with
half-amphibious lives. Before we reached Madison and crossed St. Francis River we ran through a streak of gravel.
Forest City, at the crossing of the Iron
Mountain Railway, turned out to be not
exactly a city, in the Eastern meaning of
the word, but a considerable collection of
houses, with a large hotel. It seemed, so
far in the wilderness, an irresponsible sort
of place, and the crowd at the station
were in a festive, hilarious mood. This
was heightened by the playing of a travelling band which we carried with us
in the second-class car, and which good-
naturedly unlimbered at the stations.
It consisted of a colored bass-viol, vio-
lin, and guitar, and a white cornet. On
the way the negro population were in
the majority, all the residences were shabby shanties, and the moving public on
the trains and about the stations had not
profited by the example of the commercial
travellers, who are the only smartly dressed people one sees in these regions. A
young girl who got into the car here told
me that she came from Marianna, a town
to the south, on the Languille River, and
she seemed to regard it as a central place.
At Brinkley we crossed the St. Louis,
Arkansas, and Texas Road, ran through

more swamps to the Cache River, after
which there was prairie and bottom-land,
and at De Valle's Bluff we came to the
White River. There is no doubt that
this country is well watered. After White
River fine reaches of prairie-land were encountered—in fact, a good deal of prairie
and oak timber. Much of this prairie had
once been cultivated to cotton, but was
now turned to grazing, and dotted with
cattle. A place named Prairie Centre had
been abandoned; indeed, we passed a good
many abandoned houses before we reached Carlisle and the Galloway. Lonoke
is one of the villages of rather mean
appearance, but important enough to be
talked about and visited by the five aspirants for the gubernatorial nomination,
who were travelling about together, each
one trying to convince the people that
the other four were unworthy the office.
This is lowland Arkansas, supporting a
few rude villages, inhabited by negroes
and unambitious whites, and not a fairly
representative portion of a great State.

At Argenta, a sort of railway and factory suburb of the city, we crossed the
muddy, strong-flowing Arkansas River
on a fine bridge, elevated so as to strike
high up on the bluff on which Little
Rock is built. The rock of the bluff,
which the railway pierces, is a very shaly
slate. The town lying along the bluff has
a very picturesque appearance, in spite of
its newness and the poor color of its
brick. The situation is a noble one, commanding a fine prospect of river and
plain, and mountains to the west, rising
from the bluff on a series of gentle hills,
with conspicuous heights further out for
public institutions and country houses.
The city, which has nearly thirty thousand
inhabitants, can boast a number of handsome business streets with good shops and
an air of prosperous trade, with well-
shaded residence streets of comfortable
houses; but all the thoroughfares are bad
for want of paving, Little Rock being
forbidden by the organic law (as Memphis is) to run in debt for city improvements. A city which has doubled its
population within eight years, and been
restrained from using its credit, must expect to suffer from bad streets, but its
caution about debt is reassuring to in-
tending settlers. The needed street improvements, it is understood, however,
will soon be under way, and the citizens
have the satisfaction of knowing that

when they are made, Little Rock will be a beautiful city.

Below the second of the iron bridges which span the river is a bowlder which gave the name of Little Rock to the town. The general impression is that it is the first rock on the river above its confluence with the Mississippi; this is not literally true, but this rock is the first conspicuous one, and has become historic. On the opposite side of the river, a mile above, is a bluff several hundred feet high, called Big Rock. On the summit is a beautiful park, a vineyard, a summer hotel, and pleasure-grounds—a delightful resort in the hot weather. From the top one gains a fair idea of Arkansas—the rich delta of the river, the mighty stream itself, the fertile rolling land and forests, the mountains on the border of the Indian Territory, the fair city, the sightly prominences about it dotted with buildings—altogether a magnificent and most charming view.

There is a United States arsenal at Little Rock; the government post-office is a handsome building, and among the twenty-seven churches there are some of pleasing architecture. The State - house, which stands upon the bluff overlooking the river, is a relic of old times, suggesting the easy-going plantation style. It is an indescribable building, or group of buildings, with classic pillars of course, and rambling galleries that lead to old-fashioned, domestic-looking State offices. It is shabby in appearance, but has a certain interior air of comfort. The room of the Assembly—plain, with windows on three sides, open to the sun and air, and not so large that conversational speaking cannot be heard in it—is not at all the modern notion of a legislative chamber, which ought to be lofty, magnificently decorated, lighted from above, and shut in as much as possible from the air and the outside world. Arkansas, which is rapidly growing in population and wealth, will no doubt very soon want a new State-house. Heaven send it an architect who will think first of the comfortable, cheerful rooms, and second of imposing outside display! He might spend a couple of millions on a building which would astonish the natives, and not give them as agreeable a working room for the Legislature as this old chamber. The fashion is to put up an edifice whose dimensions shall somehow represent the dignity of the State, a vast structure of hallways and staircases, with half-lighted and ill-ventilated rooms. It seems to me that the American genius ought to be able to devise a capitol of a different sort, certainly one better adapted to the Southern climate. A group of connected buildings for the various departments might be better than one solid parallelogram, and I have a fancy that legislators could be clearer-headed, and could profit more by discussion, if they sat in a cheerful chamber, not too large to be easily heard in, and open as much as possible to the sun and air and the sight of tranquil nature. The present Capitol has an air of lazy neglect, and the law library which is stored in it could not well be in a worse condition; but there is something rather pleasing about the old, easy-going establishment that one would pretty certainly miss in a smart new building. Arkansas has an opportunity to distinguish itself by a new departure in State-houses.

In the city are several of the State institutions, most of them occupying ample grounds with fine sites in the suburbs. Conspicuous on high ground in the city is the Blind Asylum, a very commodious and well-conducted institution, with about 80 inmates. The School for Deaf-Mutes, with 125 pupils, is under very able management. But I confess that the State Lunatic Asylum gave me a genuine surprise, and if the civilization of Arkansas were to be judged by it, it would take high rank among the States. It is a very fine building, well constructed and admirably planned, on a site commanding a noble view, with eighty acres of forest and garden. More land is needed to carry out the superintendent's idea of labor, and to furnish supplies for the patients, of whom there are 450, the men and women, colored and white, in separate wings. The builders seem to have taken advantage of all the Eastern experience and shunned the Eastern mistakes, and the result is an establishment with all the modern improvements and conveniences, conducted in the most enlightened spirit. I do not know a better large State asylum in the United States. Of the State penitentiary nothing good can be said. Arkansas is still struggling with the wretched lease system, the frightful abuses of which she is beginning to appreciate. The penitentiary is a sort of depot for convicts, who are distributed about the

State by the contractors. At the time of my visit a considerable number were there, more or less crippled and sick, who had been rescued from barbarous treatment in one of the mines. A gang were breaking stones in the yard, a few were making cigars, and the dozen women in the women's ward were doing laundry-work. But nothing appeared to be done to improve the condition of the inmates. In Southern prisons I notice comparatively few of the "professional" class which so largely make the population of Northern penitentiaries, and I always fancy that in the rather easy-going management, wanting the cast-iron discipline, the lot of the prisoners is not so hard. Thus far among the colored people not much odium attaches to one of their race who has been in prison.

The public-school system of the State is slowly improving, hampered by want of constitutional power to raise money for the schools. By the constitution, State taxes are limited to one per cent.; county taxes to one-half of one per cent., with an addition of one-half of one per cent. to pay debts existing when the constitution was adopted in 1874; city taxes the same as county; in addition, for the support of common schools, the Assembly may lay a tax not to exceed two mills on the dollar on the taxable property of the State, and an annual *per capita* tax of one dollar on every male inhabitant over the age of twenty-one years; and it may also authorize each school district to raise for itself, by vote of its electors, a tax for school purposes not to exceed five mills on the dollar. The towns generally vote this additional tax, but in most of the country districts schools are not maintained for more than three months in the year. The population of the State is about 1,000,000, in an area of 53,045 square miles. The scholastic population enrolled has increased steadily for several years, and in 1886 was 164,757, of which 122,296 were white and 42,461 were colored. The total population of school age (including the enrolled) was 358,006, of which 266,188 were white and 91,818 colored. The school fund available for that year was $1,327,710. The increased revenue and enrolment are encouraging, but it is admitted that the schools of the State (sparsely settled as it is) cannot be what they should be without more money to build decent school-houses, employ competent

teachers, and have longer sessions. Little Rock has fourteen school-houses, only one or two of which are commendable. The High-School, with 50 pupils and 2 teachers, is held in a district building. The colored people have their fair proportion of schools, with teachers of their own race. Little Rock is abundantly able to tax itself for better schools, as it is for better pavements. In all the schools most attention seems to be paid to mathematics. and it is noticeable how proficient colored children under twelve are in figures.

The most important school in the State. which I did not see, is the Industrial University at Fayetteville, which received the Congressional land grant and is a State beneficiary; its property, including endowments and the university farm, is reckoned at $300,000. The general intention is to give a practical industrial education. The collegiate department. a course of three years, has 77 pupils; in the preparatory department are about 200; but the catalogue, including special students in art and music, the medical department at Little Rock of 60, and the Normal School at Pine Bluff of 215, foots up about 600 students. The university is situated in a part of the State most attractive in its scenery and most healthful, and offers a chance for every sort of mental and manual training.

The most widely famous place in the State is the Hot Springs. I should like to have seen it when it was in a state of nature; I should like to see it when it gets the civilization of a European bath place. It has been a popular and even crowded resort for several years, and the medical treatment which can be given there in connection with the use of the waters is so nearly a specific for certain serious diseases, and going there is so much a necessity for many invalids, that access to it ought by this time to be easy. But it is not. It is fifty-five miles southwest of Little Rock, but to reach it the traveller must leave the Iron Mountain Road at Malvern for a ride over a branch line of some twenty miles. Unfortunately this is a narrow-gauge road, and however ill a person may be, a change of cars must be made at Malvern. This is a serious annoyance, and it is a wonder that the main railways and the hotel and bath keepers have not united to rid themselves of the monopoly of the narrow-gauge road.

The valley of the Springs is over seven hundred feet above the sea; the country is rough and broken; the hills, clad with small pines and hard-wood, which rise on either side of the valley to the height of two to three hundred feet, make an agreeable impression of greenness, and the place is capable, by reason of its irregularity, of becoming beautiful as well as picturesque. It is still in the cheap cottage and raw brick stage. The situation suggests Carlsbad, which is also jammed into a narrow valley. The Hot Springs Mountain—that is, the mountain from the side of which all the hot springs (about seventy) flow—is a government reservation. Nothing is permitted to be built on it except the government hospital for soldiers and sailors, the public bathhouses along the foot, and one hotel, which holds over on the reserved land. The government has enclosed and piped the springs, built a couple of cement reservoirs, and lets the bath privileges to private parties at thirty dollars a tub, the number of tubs being limited. The rent money the government is supposed to devote to the improvement of the mountain. This has now a private lookout tower on the summit, from which a most extensive view is had over the well-wooded State, and it can be made a lovely park. There is a good deal of criticism about favoritism in letting the bath privileges, and the words "ring" and "syndicate" are constantly heard. Before improvements were made the hot water discharged into a creek at the base of the hill. This creek is now arched over and become a street, with the bath-houses on one side and shops and shanties on the other. Difficulty about obtaining a good title to land has until recently stood in the way of permanent improvements. All claims have now been adjudicated upon, the government is prepared to give a perfect title to all its own land, except the mountain, forever reserved, and purchasers can be sure of peaceful occupation.

Opposite the Hot Springs Mountain rises the long sharp ridge of West Mountain, from which the government does not permit the foliage to be stripped. The city runs around and back of this mountain, follows the winding valley to the north, climbs up all the irregular ridges in the neighborhood, and spreads itself over the valley on the south, near the Ouachita River. It is estimated that there are 10,000 residents in this rapidly growing town. Houses stick on the sides of the hills, perch on terraces, nestle in the ravines. Nothing is regular, nothing is as might have been expected, but it is all interesting, and promising of something pleasing and picturesque in the future. All the springs, except one, on Hot Springs Mountain are hot, with a temperature ranging from 93° to 157° Fahrenheit; there are plenty of springs in and among the other hills, but they are all cold. It is estimated that the present quantity of hot water, much of which runs to waste, would supply about 19,000 persons daily with 25 gallons each. The water is perfectly clear, has no odor, and is very agreeable for bathing. That remarkable cures are performed here the evidence does not permit one to doubt, nor can one question the wonderfully rejuvenating effect upon the system of a course of its waters.

It is necessary to suggest, however, that the value of the springs to invalids and to all visitors would be greatly enhanced by such regulations as those that govern Carlsbad and Marienbad in Bohemia. The success of those great "cures" depends largely upon the regimen enforced there, the impossibility of indulging in an improper diet, and the prevailing regularity of habits as to diet, sleep, and exercise. There is need at Hot Springs for more hotel accommodation of the sort that will make comfortable invalids accustomed to luxury at home, and at least one new and very large hotel is promised soon to supply this demand; but what Hot Springs needs is the comforts of life, and not means of indulgence at table or otherwise. Perhaps it is impossible for the American public, even the sick part of it, to submit itself to discipline, but we never will have the full benefit of our many curative springs until it consents to do so. Patients, no doubt, try to follow the varying regimen imposed by different doctors, but it is difficult to do so amid all the temptations of a go-as-you-please bath place. A general regimen of diet applicable to all visitors is the only safe rule. Under such enlightened rules as prevail at Marienbad, and with the opportunity for mild entertainment in pretty shops, agreeable walks and drives, with music and the hundred devices to make the time pass pleasantly, Hot Springs would become one of the most important sanitary resorts in the world. It is now in a very crude state; but it has the water, the climate, the hills and woods; good saddle-horses are to be had, and it is an interesting country to ride over; those who frequent the place are attached to it: and time and taste and money will, no doubt, transform it into a place of beauty.

Arkansas surprised the world by the exhibition it made of itself at New Orleans, not only for its natural resources, but for the range and variety of its productions. That it is second to no other State in its adaptability to cotton raising was known; that it had magnificent forests and large coal fields and valuable minerals in its mountains was known; but that it raised fruit superior to any other in the Southwest, and quite equal to any in the North, was a revelation. The mountainous part of the State, where some of the hills rise to the altitude of 2500 feet, gives as good apples, pears, and peaches as are raised in any portion of the Union; indeed, this fruit has taken the first prize in exhibitions from Massachusetts to Texas. It is as remarkable for flavor and firmness as it is for size and beauty. This region is also a good vineyard country. The State boasts more miles of navigable waters than any other, it has variety of soil and of surface to fit it for every crop in the temperate latitudes, and it has a very good climate. The range of northern mountains protects it from "northers," and its elevated portions have cold enough for a tonic. Of course the low and swampy lands are subject to malaria. The State has just begun to appreciate itself, and has organized efforts to promote immigration. It has employed a competent State geologist, who is doing excellent service. The United States has still a large quantity of valuable land in the State open to settlement under the homestead and pre-emption laws. The State itself has over 2,000,000 acres of land, forfeited and granted to it in various ways; of this, the land forfeited for taxes will be given to actual settlers in tracts of 160 acres to each person, and the rest can be purchased at a low price. I cannot go into all the details, but the reader may be assured that the immigration committee make an exceedingly good showing for settlers who wish to engage in farming, fruit raising, mining, or lumbering. The constitution of the State is very democratic, the statute laws are stringent in morality, the limitations upon town and city indebtedness are severe, the rate of taxation is very low, and the State debt is small. The State, in short, is in a good condition for a vigorous development of its resources.

There is a popular notion that Arkansas is a "bowie-knife" State, a lawless and an ignorant State. I shared this before I went there. I cannot disprove the ignorance of the country districts. As I said, more money is needed to make the public-school system effective. But in its general aspect the State is as orderly and moral as any. The laws against carrying concealed weapons are strict, and are enforced. It is a fairly temperate State. Under the high license and local option laws, prohibition prevails in two-thirds of the State, and the popular vote is strictly enforced. In forty-eight of the seventy-five counties no license is granted, in other counties only a single town votes license, and in many of the remaining counties many towns refuse it. In five counties only is liquor perfectly free. A special law prohibits liquor selling within five miles of a college; within three miles of a church or school, a majority of the adult inhabitants can prohibit it. With regard to liquor selling, woman suffrage practically exists. The law says that on petition of a majority of the adult population in any district the county judge must refuse license. The women, therefore, without going into politics, sign the petitions and create prohibition.

The street-cars and railways make no discrimination as to color of passengers. Everywhere I went I noticed that the intercourse between the two races was friendly. There is much good land on the railway between Little Rock and Arkansas City, heavily timbered, especially with the clean-boled, stately gum-trees. At Pine Bluff, which has a population of 5000, there is a good colored Normal School, and the town has many prosperous negroes, who support a race-track of their own, and keep up a county fair. I was told that the most enterprising man in the place, the largest street-railway owner, is black as a coal. Further down the road the country is not so good, the houses are mostly poor shanties, and the population, largely colored, appears to be of a shiftless character. Arkansas City itself, low-lying on the Mississippi, has a bad reputation.

Little Rock, already a railway centre of importance, is prosperous and rapidly improving. It has the settled, temperate, orderly society of an Eastern town, but democratic in its habits, and with a cordial hospitality which is more provincial than fashionable. I heard there a good chamber concert of stringed instruments, one of a series which had been kept up by subscription all winter, and would continue the coming winter. The performers were young Bohemians. The gentleman at whose pleasant, old-fashioned house I was entertained, a leading lawyer and jurist in the Southwest, was a good linguist, had travelled in most parts of the civilized globe, had on his table the current literature of France, England, Germany, and America, a daily Paris newspaper, one New York journal (to give its name might impugn his good taste in the judgment of every other New York journal), and a very large and well-selected library, two-thirds of which was French, and nearly half of the remainder German. This was one of the many things I found in Arkansas which I did not expect to find.

THE SOUTH AND THE SCHOOL PROBLEM

BEFORE the late war there was not in the Slave States of the Union any general or efficient system of education for the masses of the people. How different was the conception of the subject that then had favor from the American doctrine of the "common school for the elementary education of the children of all the people at public expense," is indicated by the phrases that in many parts of the South in the old days described the schools carried on for short periods with public money: they were "poor schools," or "free schools," according to the fancy of the locality where the poor things existed. They were for white children whose parents were too poor to provide even the most rudimentary education. Very naturally they were despised by the very people for whose benefit they were conducted. Negro children were not considered in these meagre plans for the education of the children of the poor.

With reconstruction came to the South the common school, one of the best issues of the revolution. With the new order the American doctrine of the common school was sure to prevail. If the Southern people had been left to themselves it would have come, but Reconstruction brought it sooner than natural evolution would have developed it. The financial break-down that, in the South, followed the long and exhausting war, as well as the social and political disruptions, made anything like an effective school system for several years impossible. But the principle was recognized; the common school was anchored in the reconstruction constitutions. So much the South owes to the carpet-bag governments; they did not give to the Southern people common schools, but they began them. The over-ruling providence that, in wondrous ways, "saved a remnant alive," brought out of that period of Southern history the beginnings of common-school education for the children of all the people—a blessing that can never depart from them.

It was natural that the interest of Southern white people in the common school suffered semi-paralysis at the beginning; State laws forbidding the education of the black people had just been repealed, and the white people paid nearly all the taxes that supported schools open to both races. That the common school held its place after the white people had regained control of their affairs shows how rapidly and deeply the roots of conviction as to its utility and necessity had gone down into the Southern mind.

It was in the logic of events that the common school, if it existed at all, must offer its advantages to both races. It was certain that sooner or later all distinctions in the systems of public education adopted by the Southern States growing out of race, color, or previous condition of servitude would disappear, with the single exception, also certain, that the two races would not be taught, at public expense, in the same schools. No system of public schools requiring the races to be taught together could have been begun, much less maintained. As one man, the Southern people said, " We will have separate schools or no schools." As to the two races involved in this question of public schools the difference is this: the negroes do not wish mixed schools; the white people will not have them. Doctrinaires could not settle such questions; they had to be settled on the ground by the people most concerned in their right settlement.

The common school has not only had to win its way in the face of hostile tradition; it has not only had to contend against the mistaken economy that refused enough money to do thorough work; it has not only suffered from the real poverty of the people; it has been handicapped by the popular prejudice against negro education, and by the reluctance of the white people to maintain schools for two races while only one race bore nearly all the burdens. But the common school holds its place, steadily gaining ground, while as late as 1884 there was in only two States, Maryland and Kentucky, discrimination against the colored schools. There is none, as I am informed, in 1889.

If it shall appear that any real progress has been made in public education in the South during the last ten years, it will, to say the least, be encouraging for the future. Every Southern State has a system of public schools. As "systems" there is little to say against them; they are modelled after the best in our country. The leading features are copied from the most approved systems in the Northern and Eastern States. That the great majority of the public schools, outside the cities and a few larger towns, are inefficient and altogether unsatisfactory is conceded on every hand. The Southern people in the rural districts, where most of them live, and the small villages, have now reached the most difficult and discouraging period in the development of the common schools. They have greatly interfered with private schools, but have not yet taken their place. It is the country and village school that is now being considered; the larger cities of the South, without exception, have thorough-going systems of graded schools; hundreds of the larger towns and a few of the richer counties are following the example set by the cities.

The common school in the South concerns, for the most part, the village and rural population. The urban population is small, though it is now fast outgrowing the old proportions. Of 560,281 children of school age in Georgia, 490,270 do not live in towns and cities. The case of Georgia as to the distribution of the children of school age is the case of the South.

In the statements and illustrations that follow in this paper "the South" is considered as including Virginia, North Carolina, South Carolina, Georgia, Florida, Alabama, Mississippi, Louisiana, Texas, Arkansas, Tennessee, and Kentucky. So far as the grave questions growing out of race problems and other conditions characteristic of the South are concerned, Delaware, Maryland, West Virginia, and

Missouri are not Southern States. What of the common school in the States here considered as making up the South?

The term is short, the average being in 1883 for all these States (substantially unchanged), in days, 81.6; the average for the Union in 1883 was 119.63 days. In many instances private subscription enables the teacher to "keep school" longer than the three or four months that make up the State's term.

The school buildings are, as a rule, inferior. They are without modern appliances; most of them have what their fathers had — rough benches, a few elementary books, and a good supply of hickory switches. A small number have wall maps, cheap globes, or charts of some sort. Many lack the cheapest blackboards. The text-books used by the children in these schools are such as are used in other portions of the Union.

The salaries paid the teachers will indicate, to some extent, the quality of the public schools. Texas is already better off than her sisters; her more than fifty millions of acres of school lands promises for the future an endowment for public education unmatched in the world. The average monthly salary paid teachers in the rural districts in Texas, 1888, was only $39 04. In other States it ranges from $20 to $30.

Many of these schools are much better than these poor salaries indicate; the struggle for bread has driven many, especially women, who come of families once rich, but broken down by the issues of war, to school-teaching, and in log houses, on pitiful salaries, some of the best school-work is done. But some of these schools are worse than the lowest salary would indicate.

Outside the cities and more progressive larger towns the Southern people are not yet educated to the point of taxing themselves for the education of their own children; with many the specious objection that "one citizen should not be taxed to educate another citizen's children," as if feeding, clothing, and educating a child belong to the same category, still has force; in every Southern Legislature are obstructionists of the worst possible Bourbon type, who devote themselves to saving the people from spending their own money for their own benefit. Nothing proves the sore need of education more than the influence exerted by such men.

But throughout the South there is promise of better things. The subject of education, especially the education of the masses, is everywhere a matter of earnest discussion. Teachers, editors, candidates for office, preachers, farmers, mechanics, white and black people, all classes, are discussing the subject. How wide-spread this awakening has been is illustrated by the interest shown in the subject by the country press. When a Southern county town weekly, depending for life chiefly on county advertising, takes an abiding interest in a matter of general concern, it is proof that the people are beginning to be aroused. The South is beginning to awake to the perils that lie but partially concealed in the ignorant classes, both white and black, that make up so large a part of the population. It is time to awake; there is reason to be alarmed when the tenth census reports in the twelve States under consideration in this paper 332,733 white voters and 886,905 negro voters as "unable to write." If in a union of States like ours, which binds all into one, this alarm should not extend to States more fortunate than these twelve Southern States, it would indicate an indifference to common interests and common dangers more alarming than ignorance itself.

The illiteracy brought to view by the census of 1880 is simply appalling, but comparison with the census of 1870 shows just enough gain to stimulate zeal and inspire hope. Including Delaware, Maryland, the District of Columbia, West Virginia, and Missouri, the percentages of illiteracy are as follows: 1870, white illiteracy, 19.4 per cent.; in 1880, 16.6 per cent.; 1870, colored illiteracy, 88.9 per cent.; 1880, 78.9 per cent. These figures show the status of persons "twenty-one years and upward." The gain is real, not imaginary, but when we consider the swift movement of our times, it is slow; when we consider the material recuperation of the Southern States since 1870—to say nothing of the amazing development of the resources of the whole country—this gain upon illiteracy in the South is small and disappointing. Nor should we forget that the census reports on illiteracy are always rose-colored when at their worst. There is enough education in the country, or at least knowledge of its lack, to make people ashamed to confess illiteracy. Candor compels the sorrowful admission at this point that Georgia leads the procession of illiterates. In 1880 Georgia returned a greater number of persons "ten years old and upward" as "unable to write" than any State in the Union. In a total population, "ten years old and upward," of 1,043,840, there were whites 128,934, and negroes 391,482, total 520,416, who could not sign their names. Alabama shows a total of 433,447 "unable to write"—whites, 111,767; colored, 321,680. In white illiteracy Tennessee leads with 216,227, with Kentucky close by with 214,497.

What are these States doing to educate their illiterate hosts? Detailed statements as to all of them would extend this paper beyond reasonable limits. A few illustrative statements must suffice

Take Georgia to begin with. The figures for 1887 are used, the returns for 1888 not being all in hand when this statement was prepared. The entire sum raised in Georgia in every way by the State and by cities and counties under local laws for 1887 was $795,987 26. Of this sum the cities and counties, under local law and for local use, raised $302,477 74. But of the whole school population of 560,281 there are 490,270 who do not live in such cities and counties as made special provision for their children — that is, Georgia, for her children not helped by local taxation, expended in 1887 considerably less than $1 for each one of school age.

During the last twelve months the State of Georgia has done more thinking on the subject of illiteracy and popular education than during twenty years past. The subject has filled the papers; it has been a leading topic in not a few Church Assemblies. The two Georgia Conferences of the Methodist Episcopal Church South, after stirring debate, delivered their minds upon the Legislature in favor of six months' public schools.

The General Assembly during the winter session gave unwonted attention to the subject. Public education was never so earnestly or so ably discussed by a Georgia Legislature, and an act was passed almost unanimously providing four months schools for 1889, and five for 1890. It means six months public schools for white and colored children in 1891.

Alabama has taken an advanced step, adding to the appropriation of 1888 $100,000. In every one of these States are indications of awakening.

To return to the question, "What are these States doing?" a few general statements must answer at this time. The total amount expended by Tennessee for public education in 1887 was $1,023,893 23; by Arkansas, 1888, $901,190 58; by North Carolina, 1888, $691,188 20; in Kentucky, for 1886, the "Auditor's estimate of the total net resources of the white and colored school fund was $1,042,899 18; by South Carolina, total expenditures for public education for 1885, $549,857 69; by Virginia, 1887, $1,535,289 11; by Texas, 1888, $2,007,808 94; by Florida, 1888, $484,110 23 —and there is no more creditable showing made by any Southern State.

Putting all together, taking the exact figures in the latest reports, and the best possible estimates based on preceding reports of late years, these twelve States have expended upon the public-school systems since the war the sum of $122,-497,219 59—a stupendous amount of money, considering the conditions of life and business in these States since April 9, 1865.

One of the tables in the tenth census makes a grouping of States that places Missouri among the "Western States," and Delaware, Maryland, and the District of Columbia in the "Middle States," placing West Virginia among the "Southern States." In this table the total "valuation of real estate and personal property" of New York was $2,651,940,006; of the thirteen Southern States here grouped together, $2,370,923,269, or nearly $300,000,-000 less than the total for New York. These figures do not fairly indicate comparative ability to raise the sums needed to meet the expenses of government. In 1880 in all the Southern States there were barely 2000 persons holding United States non-taxable bonds, and they were holders of small amounts, while in New York alone there were 14,803 holders of such bonds, and it is almost certain that three of these persons held larger amounts than all the Southern holders put together.

To me it is clear that the soundest political and business economy has indicated that the Southern States should have expended more of the comparatively little they had in the education of the people, but it is not discreditable that the tenth census shows a total expenditure for public education in 1880 by New York of $9,936,662, and by these Southern States, for 1880, of $7,812,693. And in considering what the census tells us on all these subjects, it should be remembered that the expenses of government in the South are met, for the most part, by something more than half the people.

This paper would be incomplete if we were to omit all mention of higher education. Most of the colleges and universities suspended and crippled by the war have been re-established. Of them all, scarce a dozen have anything like adequate endowments. In no country are there as many thoroughly capable and devoted teachers doing college work on as small salaries as these Southern institutions can show. There is not in the entire South one woman's college sufficiently endowed to lift it above the perils that come with the fluctuation of patronage. Most of the Southern colleges lack the appliances that modern investigation and modern methods make necessary for the best work.

One striking and inspiring fact should be mentioned here to the honor of the Southern faculties; notwithstanding poverty, the work of the colleges is far broader and much better than before 1860. The courses of study are not only more thorough, they are more liberal, and more in harmony with the best thought and best tendencies of our times.

Of true normal school work there has not been much in the South outside the splendid work done in the best of the higher institutions for the negroes. But the need of normal schools is more and more realized; the influence of the Peabody fund is being felt in every Southern State; every well-trained teacher aided by this foundation, so wisely and patriotically administered by trustees and agents, goes forth an incarnate argument for normal school training. The Peabody Fund has accomplished incalculable good in another way; it has put a great premium on local enterprise, and so has done more than anything known to me to foster sentiment in favor of local taxation for local needs.

A marked feature in recent discussions in the South as to education has been tool craft in connection with training in books. Georgia has stepped ten paces in front, and has established a technological school of high grade in the city of Atlanta, placing at its head a man eminently fitted for his work, the Rev. D. I. S. Hopkins, the late president of Emory College. Mississippi has established at Columbus a school for girls that unites industrial training to education in books. The success of the experiment has challenged attention throughout the entire Southern country.

In this connection it should be said that the higher institutions for negro youth in the South have almost without exception introduced industrial training as part of the course of study. The late John F. Slater, of Norwich, Connecticut, in 1882 gave one million dollars, as he said, "to aid in the Christian education of the lately emancipated race and of their descendants in the South." Mr. Slater desired that the interest of the money he gave should be used to make more efficient the work of schools established by others. It was intended to help as many, and to help them as rapidly, as possible, so as to help them truly. So in carrying out the founder's wish those institutions have been aided that were known to do such work as made their students good teachers, and the agent was instructed to "prefer those schools that joined to instruction in books some form of industrial training." The result is that every important school for negro youth in the South has adopted industrial training, and with the most beneficent and every way gratifying results.

The most unique and altogether wonderful chapter in the history of education is that which tells the story of the education of the negroes of the South since 1865.

The friends of the negro's education really began during the war. The work was taken hold of with a vigor the world never saw before as soon as hostilities ceased. The government expended through the Freedmen's Bureau large sums; Northern benevolence poured many millions of dollars into the South to teach, enlighten, lift up, and better christianize the emancipated people. Presently most of the Southern States began to make appropriations of public money to institutions that best prepared colored men and women to teach in the common schools. The churches of the North organized great societies to raise money and carry on the work of education among the colored people. Counting all the higher schools, whether called universities, colleges, institutes, or seminaries, there are about one hundred and fifty able to prepare men and women to teach in the common schools, some of them fitted to do thorough college work. In these institutions, working on small salaries, I have met many times men and women "of whom the world is not worthy," graduates of the foremost schools in America—Harvard, Yale, Princeton, Colby University, the University of Boston, University of Michigan, Oberlin, Wellesley, Vassar, Mount Holyoke, and the best of them all. Among these teachers some of the best are colored men and women who were taught during the first decade of this great Christian experiment.

There has been some prejudice excited by the over-naming of the institutions established for the colored people. Many are called "university," but not one does university work, nor is there now occasion for such work; many more are called colleges, but the least part of the work they do is college work. I had occasion to look carefully into this matter. In 1883–4, in the schools receiving aid from the "John F. Slater Fund," there were employed 303 teachers, and enrolled 7273 students. They were in colleges, universities, institutes. An actual count, as the catalogues classed the students, resulted in the following conclusion: "The percentage of the whole number engaged in classical studies, the higher mathematics, and other college studies, and studies preparatory to admission to the college classes, was less than five per cent. of the whole number." The ninety-five in each hundred were learning just what they should have been learning; they were fitting themselves to be intelligent men and women, and to teach in the public schools for their people. The president of one of the best of these institutions tells me that "more than 1000 of his former students have taught in the public schools."

In connection with some of the best of these institutions are professional schools. The negro preacher has abundant opportunity to use his gifts. The negro lawyer has not much encouragement. The negro doctor is rapidly winning his way. There are three really admirable medical schools for colored men in the South: Medical Department, Howard University, Washington city; Meharry Medical College, Nashville, Tennessee; and Leonard Medical School, Raleigh, North Carolina.

No people were ever helped so much in twenty-five years, and no illiterate people ever learned so fast. The most painstaking and long-continued investigations justify me in making the following statements, using the round numbers nearest the actual facts:

1. There are in the South, in 1889, 16,000 common schools conducted by colored teachers; in these schools about one million colored children receive elementary instruction from three to four months per annum at public expense.

2. Not less than two millions of the colored people can at least read.

3. In higher education the best ones succeed as well as other people with the same sort of preliminary training.

4. The African churches in the South are fired with commendable zeal to do what they can in the education of their people. In some enterprises they have done notably well, justifying the firm persuasion that some day they will be capable of conducting their own institutions.

5. The introduction of industrial training into all the leading institutions for the colored people has been an unmixed blessing. It has helped scholarship, discipline, and the building up of self-reliant, self-maintaining manhood and womanhood.

6. There is a growing friendliness toward the cause of negro education. Grants of money are made with less reluctance; the States and cities are putting every year larger sums in the work of educating the negro, and those who teach him are beginning to receive something like Christian recognition.

7. The white churches of the South are beginning to move in the actual work of teaching the negro. What they have begun they will carry on.

8. There is substantial progress. Investigation in every available direction, with the best helps I could get from the highest official sources in each of the twelve States specially considered in this paper, led to these results, comparing 1882 and 1888: Total colored school population, 1888, 2,057,990, an increase from 1882 of fourteen per cent.; total colored enrolment for 1888, 985,522, an increase of thirty-four per cent. This is hopeful; the gain in numbers at school is relatively more than the gain in the population.

Comparing the case of the white people with the case of the negroes in these respects, we find: For 1888, total white school population, 3,383,618, an increase from 1882 in six years of nineteen per cent.; total white enrolment, 1888, 1,997,-558, an increase of thirty-seven per cent.

9. What the higher-grade institutions

for colored people now most need is endowment sufficient to secure for many years to come thoroughly efficient instruction.

I conclude this review of a very broad field with a condensed statement of the sources of revenue for carrying on this vast undertaking, the education of a race. Into this cause have gone the following amounts:

Freedmen's Aid Society (Methodist)....	$2,225,000
Baptist Home Mission...............	2,000,000
Presbyterian Home Mission.........	1,542,746
American Missionary Association.....	6,000,000
The different women's societies......	500,000
John F. Slater.....................	1,000,000
Daniel Hand......................	1,000,000
Other individual gifts..............	1,000,000
Quakers and others................	500,000
Total.....................	$15,767,746

By the States, in aid of normal schools and in maintaining the common schools, the following amounts:

Alabama...............	$3,404,293 24
Arkansas	3,409,110 00
Florida	849,000 00
Georgia...............	2,702,276 00
Kentucky.............	1,362,873 00
Louisiana	2,150,000 00
Mississippi...........	7,136,800 00
North Carolina........	2,441,062 00
South Carolina........	3,000,000 00
Tennessee.............	2,358,000 00
Texas	4,064,259 00
Virginia	4,500,000 00
Total...........	$37,377,673 24

More and more this disproportion will increase. It costs much more to maintain 16,000 public schools, although with short terms and low salaries, than to conduct many more colleges than have been established or will be needed.

To make these 16,000 schools what they should be requires more money than the Southern States can at this time furnish.

DECATUR, GEORGIA, *March* 30, 1889.

ALONG THE BAYOU TECHE

MR. HORACE FLETCHER, of New Orleans, has an irresistible way, which perhaps he caught from the general irresistibleness of all New Orleans, though it is more likely that it was born with him in Massachusetts. At all events when he said to Mr. Smedley the artist and myself that no one could pretend to have seen New Orleans until he had also seen the Teche or Acadian region, he said it in such a way that it was difficult to wait from Saturday until Tuesday for the steamboat—a steamboat, by-the-way, which has its name painted up in its cabin, with a stove-pipe in front of the letter "c," so that its passengers cannot help but read the name "Te—he," and feel sure that they are bound upon a very merry boat, and certain of a jolly time. The *Teche* and her sister boats go into the 'Cajun (Acadian) country in the old way, the way of befo' de wa' and befo' de railroads, taking a journey of hundreds of miles to fetch them where the cars go in less than a hundred; taking days where the cars take hours.

The course is by two loops whose sides are nearly parallel. One is made by going up the Mississippi until the mouth of the Red River is reached, then down the Atchafalaya toward New Orleans again, and then up the Teche away from New Orleans and almost parallel with the route up the Father of Waters. The three lines of waterway are so nearly beside one another that points upon them which are actually close together by wagon road are great distances apart by the boat journey; for instance, one place which is forty-four miles from another as the crow flies, is 376 miles from it by the boat route.

"Take your roughening with you," said the captain, "for we do not sell anything to drink on the boat." Mr. Fletcher does nothing by halves, so that along with a little "roughening" he took a case of mineral water, a mule-load of bananas to be fried in crumbs by the darky cooks, a copy of Charles Dudley Warner's *West and South*, the current copies of *Harper's Weekly* and of *Puck* and *Life*. We had a dismal, cold, rainy day to start with, and no ladies aboard. The men huddled around the stove at the masculine end of the saloon, and smoked and swapped stories. It was a perfect reproduction of a day in a cross-roads tavern, such as every man who follows a gun or a rod and has been storm-stayed in the country has experienced. The red-hot stove, the circle of men, the wind scolding at the windows and thrashing them with rain, the door opening to allow some one to be shot in with a blast of chilling air, like a projectile out of a pneumatic gun, the weary and worn old newspapers, the gradual torpor that the heat produced among the men—nothing was lacking. In the evening, after supper, we heard subdued music working a difficult way through a stateroom door.

Music! It was inspiration! It was precisely what was wanted to atone for the beastly weather and the imprisonment indoors. I knocked on the stateroom door, and found that the musician was the mulatto "texas-tender," which is to say the man in charge of the rooms of the pilots and petty officers on top of the saloon roof. Would he stop hiding his melody under a bushel and come out and play for us? "Certainly, sah, if dat wuz what we wished." So he came out, appearing to us with a guitar in one hand and the upper part of his body enmeshed in a strange arrangement of heavy wire that went around each upper arm and across his chest and up to his mouth, where it was solid and black like a gag. He looked as if he was pinioned and gagged and walking out to a gallows to be hanged with a guitar in his hand. Perhaps that was what would happen to him if he played in a centre of civilization, but we were resolved to be tolerant, though critical. He sat in a chair, and lo! the "strange device" of wire proved to be a patent concertina-holder. The gag was the concertina. For an hour he played for us, very much to our satisfaction, though there were features of dear old "Annie Rooney" that we did not recognize, and "Comrades" became a trifle quarrelsome and discordant at times. We asked the captain if there were no negroes in the crew who could sing or dance.

"I don't know," said he. "They are all in the St. Charles now."

"The St. Charles?"

"'TAKE YOUR ROUGHENING WITH YOU,' SAID THE CAPTAIN."

"Oh," said the captain, "you don't understand. That is what we call the place where the roustabouts sleep, on the main-deck under the boilers."

In the morning the light broke upon a wet and depressing scene. The broad yellow river, so glorious in sunlight, was a hurrying sheet of mud enclosed between lines of dripping willows and mounds of wet Cherokee rose-bushes not in bloom. The great reaches of the levees more than ever suggested earth-work fortifications against the forces of Neptune. The sky was dark and cheerless. Of signs of population there would be none for miles, and then we would see scores of negro cabins, and close by the usually white mansion

of their white employer. The smoke-stacks of an occasional sugar-refinery rising above the trees told us that we were in the sugar country, but rice plantations were plentiful. Now and then a vagabond house-boat was seen, nose up on the bank, or drifting down with the current. Usually the after-part of such an ark was covered over by a projection of the roof of the house, and in that shelter we nearly always discovered the shiftless proprietor, fishing or mending his lines or whittling, or, more often than anything else, smoking and letting his mind take a vacation. We heard much that was interesting about these and other Southern craft from the pilots and the captain.

The house-boats, it appears, are a survival of one among many kinds of boats which were very much more numerous upon the great river before the era of steam navigation than steamboats are now. Among the earlier forms of boats were the famous "Kentucky flats," or "broad-horns," and family boats of this pattern were an early modification of their general plan, which was that of a strong-hulled ark, long and narrow, and covered with a curving roof. I have read that "family boats of this description, fitted up for the descent of families to the lower country, were provided with a stove, a comfortable apartment, beds, and arrangements for commodious habitancy, and in them ladies, servants, cattle, sheep, dogs, and poultry, all floating on the same bottom, and on the roof the looms, ploughs, spinning-wheels, and domestic implements of the family, were carried down the river." Fulton's *Clermont*, which proved its usefulness as the first practicable adaptation of steam-power to water travel in 1807, must have been quickly copied on the Mississippi, for in one list of notable passages up that river I have seen a note of a trip by a steamboat in 1814. But long after that the barges, skiffs, horse-boats, broad-horns, and family boats must have remained very numerous. They floated down stream with the current, and were pulled up again by means of wheels worked by horses or cattle, and by the toilsome and slow processes known as warping and bushwhacking. A boat which was warped up the river kept two row-boats ahead of her, carrying hawsers, which were made fast to the trees on the shore, and then pulled in as the bigger vessels were thus hauled along. When the length of one cable had been pulled in, the other boat had fastened the other cable far ahead, and so the vessel "inched" along against the five-mile current of the stream a little more quickly than a house moves when its owner has decided to move it down a country road to a distant cellar he has dug for it. It took a day to go six or eight miles by that method. Smaller boats were propelled against the current by rowing, sailing, or poling them along; and when the water was high and overflowed the banks, they bushwhacked up stream—that is, they pulled the vessels along by hauling on the bushes that brushed the sides of the craft.

At last came the Mississippi steamboats, those queer creations which seem to be made by house-carpenters who have forgotten how to build houses, and yet never knew the ship-joiner's art. They are huge, flat-bottomed, frail houses floated on box-like hulls, but they are as comfortable as the Southern barons demanded that they should be in the glorious days when they revelled like kings. We cannot tell what sort of boats will travel the great river in the surely coming day when it shall be all walled in and kept in its place, but it is no more likely that the railroads will crush out passenger travel on that majestic and interesting river than that they will upon the Thames or the Hudson. Just now there is a spell upon the traffic. The war interrupted it, and the people of the North and East must rediscover the fact that the journey from St. Paul or St. Louis is one of the greatest delights and wonders of our continent. However, Mississippi steamboating has stood still for more than twenty years. The rocket of its glory burst with the famous *Lee* and *Natchez* race in 1870. They still talk of that world-famous brush in the river pilot-houses, and I heard it referred to more than once during the nine or ten days I spent upon the river. One of the captains in that test of speed, historic old Captain Leathers, who commanded the *Natchez*, is still in the service, though he has a son who is a man beyond the age of thirty, and in command of a boat unkindly named the *Natchez*, after the famous racer the old man captained years ago. The talk of record-breakings and of quick runs is all of what we in New York would call long voyages, since these consume the time of ocean journeys, and our longest steamboat trips are to Albany and Fall River, and are accomplished in a night.

The quickest run from New Orleans to Cincinnati, made by the *R. R. Springer* in 1881, was done in 5 days, 12 hours, and 45 minutes. The fastest time over the course of 1013 miles from the Crescent City to Cairo, Illinois, was that made by the *R. E. Lee* in 1870, in 3 days and 61 minutes, and was therefore run at the rate of about 14 miles an hour—against the current, to be sure. The *Lee*, the competitor of the *Natchez*, reached Natchez, during their memorable race, in 16 hours, 36 minutes, and 47 seconds, making the distance of 272 miles at the speed of about 16½ miles

"SCORES OF NEGRO CABINS."

an hour. The speed per hour during the whole race of 1278 miles to St. Louis figures at about 13½ miles.

The race took place in the summer of 1870. Captain Leathers with the *Natchez* completed a run to St. Louis in 3 days, 21 hours, and 58 minutes, and Captain Cannon, of the other and rival king-boat on the river, the *R. E. Lee*, at once announced his intention to beat her on the return trip. The *Natchez* returned to New Orleans in due time, and her captain found that the *Lee* was going to refuse all freight and passengers during the race. More than that, the *Lee* had taken out all her light upper work that could be removed, in order to lessen her draught in the water. Captain Leathers of the *Natchez* affected not to need such advantages. He took aboard a small cargo of freight and some passengers, and the two mighty packets were cast loose from the New Orleans levee on June 30, 1870. Away they went, with their huge white bodies throbbing and their trails of jet smoke curling behind them. The *Lee* made no landings for coal. She had engaged a tender to precede her 100 miles up the river to give her a supply of whatever fuel she needed. Farther along, flat-boats with wood and coal awaited her in mid-stream. They were warped to her as she slowed up alongside of them, were emptied as she

swept them along, and then were flung off to drift where they might after they had served their purpose. The *Natchez* copied this method after a time.

The race made a wonderful stir. Boats loaded with spectators preceded and tried to accompany the racers from New Orleans, and everywhere along the river it was said to seem as if the interior had been depopulated, so numerous were the persons who crowded the shores to look on. The *Lee* was lucky, and made the trip in 3 days, 18 hours, and 14 minutes, arriving in St. Louis when thirty thousand persons were assembled on the levee and on the house-tops to cheer her. The *Natchez* had met with unusual detentions by fog and groundings. The time of the boats as they reached each principal city on the way was cabled to Europe, and it was estimated that a million of dollars was wagered on the race.

Thus, with talk of the historic and picturesque past, surrounded by what might be called "the local color," we drove the wretched weather out of mind until we reached a watery corner and turned out of the mighty river into the Atchafalaya. This we called the "Chafferlyer," to be in harmony with our acquaintances. It is fed out of the Mississippi where the Red River joins the Father of Waters, and immediately that we entered it a new scene was presented—a view of a narrow stream between groves which grow not merely to the water's edge, but into the water. It does not look like any river that we know in the North; it is rather like water running through woods, as a flood might appear, or a greatly swollen stream. Suddenly what is called the Grand pours into it, but the Grand is merely a wider belt of liquid mud flowing through a wilderness. Next the land begins to rise, higher banks are formed, and with these come views of cottages, freight-houses, ruins of old brick sugar-mills, fishermen's tents, negro cabins, bits of greensward, banks of rose-bushes, and patches of cultivated farm land. Our first stop was at a honey

The Mate of a Teche boat.

plantation, where the half-acre lot filled with beehives, novel as the sight proved, was not as peculiar as the honey-planter himself. He is famous up and down the Teche route as a man who so loves to argue that nothing can possibly happen which will not arouse his instinct for debate. He has some little learning, and even in his worn old suit of homespun suggested traces of gentle blood and breeding as he stood on the river-bank flinging long sentences and uncommon words up at our captain on the main-deck, while his daughter, the only other white person for miles around, leaned her spare form against the side of the cabin doorway, and smiled with affectionate pride as she reflected upon the good time her father was

having with his vocal organs. Something which had been ordered by him from New Orleans had not come, and he was begging leave to differ with the captain, no matter how the captain sought to account for the delay. I think I remember that the sum of this man's income each year was computed at five hundred dollars, which proved, it seemed, that he was in very comfortable circumstances, could well afford to go to New Orleans twice a year, and was able to support the position of a man of consequence in that region.

Presently we saw our first Acadians—nowhere spoken of in their own country otherwise than as 'Cajuns. The first one on the route keeps a low gin-mill, a resort for bad characters. The next one we saw was a swarthy, stalwart man with a goatee *à la* Napoleon III., who was catching bait with a net. Moss hangs from the cypress and oaks in great and sad profusion in this part of the route. The wilderness is only occasionally broken by a clearing, and after each interruption it seems to snap shut again as if not even man could overcome the force of the rank growth of vegetation, except here and there, and for a mere geographical instant. There was a fuzz of disappointingly small scrub palmettoes on the ground, and wherever there was a cabin or a man there was also a dugout canoe or pirogue. These boats were not such as men have made in almost every known part of the world by merely scooping out the heart of a log and fashioning its ends. They were the lightest and prettiest boats of the kind I ever saw, mere shells or dishes, very skilfully and gracefully modelled, but so shallow as to be likened to nothing so closely as to half a pea-pod. Bait-catching was the business carried on with them. The men were after shrimp, but very often caught crawfish, those relentless allies of the Mississippi River which eat into the levees and let the river through behind them. They are a tenth the size of lobsters, and look like lobsters "out of drawing," as the artists would say—that is, they appear disproportioned, with their tails too small for their bodies. They are red and greenish-red, but some are as rosy as one of the old masters is said to have painted lobsters in the sea after he had become acquainted with them on the dinner table. They have blue lobster eyes and fierce claws.

In time we came to the mouth of a

bayou which was closed during the war, but which, were it opened, would take us to Plaquemine, twenty-five miles across a country around which we had gone 190 miles to get where we were. Farther on we came to the openings into two or three other bayous, and thus gradually were brought to realize that this region of the mouths of the Mississippi is a land that is nine-tenths covered with water. Travellers by the cars do not comprehend the character of Louisiana, or see, with anything like the view of a steamboat passenger, with what profusion the surface of the earth is littered with bayous, branches, canals, ditches, lakes, and swamps. Lake Chico was a notable incident of this second day's progress. It is merely a swelling of the Atchafalaya or Grand into a sheet of yellow water thirty miles long and twelve miles wide. It is picturesquely littered with snags and floating logs and channel stakes. The narrow entrance to it, where wooded promontories all but block the way, is much admired by persons afflicted with the fever for kodaking everything out of doors. The Spanish-moss is so abundant there that if I were a sufferer from the epidemic I would have been tempted to photograph some of the trees that carried the greatest burdens of the weed, and looked as if they had been washing out their worn and faded winter garments and were hanging them up to dry. But a far better picture would be one that showed how we felt our way into the lake, being so uncertain whether there was sufficient water that we wedded our steamboat to a great scow with ropes, gave our spouse the task of carrying a good part of our load of freight, and sent a mate ahead of us in a small boat to prod the mud with a pole. Whatever the mate

'CAJUNS.

discovered he discreetly kept to himself; but we, not to be retarded by his reticence, posted a darky on the upper deck with a sounding-line to chant the musical lingo of the Southern pilots, in which we often heard the phrase "mark twain," which gave the humorous Mr. Clemens his *nom de plume*.

Our first notable stop occurred a little after dusk, at Pattersonville, where we went ashore for a cake of shaving-soap, and saw vaguely by the yellow light of a few scattered kerosene lamps that we were the only souls adrift in a long wide street, which boasted here and there a dwelling, and here and there a neglected shop. We asked for the soap in one store, and the clerk treated us to a Southern expression that we had not yet heard upon its native soil. "I'm sorry, sah," said he, "but I've done run plumb out of it." We added that to our notes. We had grown quite used to hearing size and distance expressed with the phrases, "A right smart of a plantation," "a smart distance," or "a right smart hotel"; also to hearing every one say, "Where is he at now?" and "I dun'no' where I left my hat at." When night fell, thick and black, our two powerful electric search-lights were utilized with weird and theatrical effect to throw great shafts of daylight at whichever bank we were searching for a landing. Each light cut a well-defined path through the night, and when it picked out a grove of trees or a clutter of negro cabins or a landing, it created a veritable stage-picture. These lamps bothered the pilots so much in steering their way through the water that they were only lighted for viewing the bank, and for helping the roustabouts to see while loading and unloading the cargo. The pilots so quickly shut off the light when they had nothing to do but to pick out an uncertain course, through water and air that were equally black, that they seemed to me like water-cats that could see very well in their element, but were helpless upon land.

In the morning, after many hours spent in throwing spectacular landings on the blank wall of night, and then carrying freight out to them, and wiping them out of existence by turning off our lights, we awoke to find the Atchafalaya basking in the sun and in quite another country. We had travelled from the swamps and cypress brakes of Louisiana to something like the Thames in England—to a pastoral country watered by a narrow, pretty river of clear water that loafed along between patches of greensward, rows of oaks, white manor-houses, cabins set among roses, magnolias, and jasmines, and with great clearings, and men at work ploughing on either side. White bridges that invariably broke apart as the boat approached them, and that were often set upon pontoons, still further domesticated and civilized the scenery. Every plantation had a bridge for itself, it seemed. It was a little jarring to have a man come aboard with two rattlesnake-skins, each large enough to make into two pairs of Chicago slippers; five inches wide and a yard in length the skins were. We had pointed out to us the Calumet Plantation, which is said to be the most orderly and completely appointed sugar farm in Louisiana. The rows of whitewashed negro cabins were formed of houses better than the 'Cajun houses we had been seeing.

Daniel Thompson is the planter here, and his son, Mr. Wibrey Thompson, came aboard and talked very interestingly of the experiments he and his father are making in the analyses of many sorts of cane, the breeding of the best varieties, the perfecting of refining processes, and the broadcast publication of the results of the work in the laboratories, where as many as three chemists are sometimes at work together. Such men are the representatives of the new type of farmers who are numerous in the West and who are multiplying in the South. They do not farm by prayer, or take land on shares with luck or nature, after the old plan. Chemistry is their handmaiden, and she rules in the place of chance. One whom I knew went to Germany and France to study the beet-sugar industry there before he bought his ranch in Kansas, and he mastered French and German so that he could read all that is known of the industry. Others learn chemistry or employ chemists to analyze everything they deal with. These new-school farmers publish all that they learn; they write reports for the government to publish, and they lecture to farmer audiences in the winter, in which season, by-the-way, they are generally as busy as the old-time luck farmers used to be idle. They keep the most minute accounts of outlay and income, crediting the refuse they burn to the fuel account, the stuff cattle eat to the saving of fodder, offsetting their earnings with their fixed charges, wear and tear of machinery, interest on the principal invested, and, in short, tabulating everything. These are mainly Eastern and Northern men, but the new generation of Southerners is not without representation in the scientific class. We shall find, before we leave the Teche country, that there are great districts wherein every plantation is owned by Northern or Eastern men. The cultivation of semitropical fruits has been a failure in Florida because the land there was taken haphazard by men who are trying to farm with Providence and dumb luck for partners. Agriculture there was based on the theory that if an invalid who could not endure Northern winters had money to buy land he could grow oranges in white sand. The new school of scientific, take-nothing-for-granted farming is already taking root there, and will in time make more money out of oranges than dumb luck has sunk in planting them where they did not belong.

Mr. Wibrey Thompson, while he was aboard the *Teche*, said that he was con-

studied, and people have not known how to rid the juice of its impurities. All this is overcome, and it is seen to be the best producer; but in the mean time the sorghum farmers have lost money, and, worse yet, have lost their faith in the cane.

Farther along, from the boat's deck we saw Acadian men and women gathering Spanish-moss from the trees. Our first sight of this peculiar Louisiana in-

FELLOW-PASSENGERS.

vinced that the future source of sugar will be sorghum. It may not be in his time, he says, nor in five hundred years, but the fact that he has demonstrated that it is the most practicable product and economical cane, and that it yields most readily to the processes of selection, satisfies him that the world will in time turn to it for its sugar supply. Sorghum in the rough yields twelve per cent. of sugar, the same as sugar-cane, but in three years, by choosing the best cane and "breeding it," he raised the yield to twenty and a half per cent. He is certain he can plant it and get fourteen per cent. off-hand from a whole crop, and in a short time can get sixteen per cent. Potentially or technically, sorghum is now in the best position it has ever held yet; actually, it is bankrupt and dead. This year only one concern in the country will make sorghum sugar. The reason for this is that it has always been grown from poor seed. It has not been bred or

dustry was of a 'Cajun man high up in an oak-tree, half hid in a mass of waving gray moss. How he got into it we did not see, but now he was tearing his way out of it, cutting and ripping it, and tossing it down upon the river-bank, where it lay in soft, rounding mounds, as the clouds of the sky might do if they were treated in the same violent way. This moss is sold in New Orleans, where it is so highly prized for stuffing mattresses that they say nothing in the bed line can equal one that is made of a moss mattress and a hair mattress on top of a wire-spring mattress. Such a bed, I was told, would even satisfy the princess in Andersen's tale who was bruised black and blue by the three pease the peasant woman put under the mattresses in order to discover whether she really was a princess. The moss-gatherers of Louisiana heap the soft fibrous stuff upon the ground, pour water upon it, and leave nature the task of rotting it into a black dry mass.

A SUGAR-CANE PLANTATION.

This moss, which is found as far north as Asbury Park on the Atlantic coast, is a very peculiar growth. It is said not to be a parasite and not to live upon anything it gets from the trees. It is believed in most parts of the South that it rids the atmosphere, of malarial poison, and where it grows the people boast that fevers and chills are as rare as in the mountains. The weight of testimony favors this theory, but frankness compels me to add that in Florida the tourist will read in the circular of one hotel that the presence of Spanish-moss "attests the healthfulness of the climate," while at another hotel he will be told that the peculiar merit of that locality lies in the fact that Spanish-moss does not grow there. This moss, so green and littered with pinkish blossoms when in its prime, dies on a dead tree when the bark fails to hold it, and then it becomes the color of cigar ashes. Patient study of a mass of it will, it is said, show no root, beginning or end to it, and any piece of it which is blown from one live-oak to another may take hold and breed a bedtick filling of it.

We entered the Bayou Teche on a glorious day, and thought it part of a drowsy, dreamy, gentle, semitropic scene. It runs through the heart of a broad savanna. Afar off, on either side, we saw the forests of the neglected South that has so long awaited the now approaching multitude from Europe, but the land beside the bayou was every acre cultivated or built upon. We could not have found ourselves amid stranger scenes had we gone to the French part of Canada or to England or France. Often there was an edging of reeds or a grove of oaks that would have resembled an old orchard of the North but for the abundance of the funereal moss that bearded every limb. Then we passed villages with funny little Grecian-looking stores and banks and court-houses, all pillared and with pointed roofs. Then there were splendid planters' homes, white and neat, with rows of Corinthian columns in front and a brigade of whitewashed negro cabins in dependent nearness, as little chickens cluster near the mother-hen. There were pretty white bridges here and there, as ornamental amid the greenery as statues on a lawn. On these the "quality folks" always gathered to see the boat, apart from the colored folks, who huddled upon the shore in barbaric colors, every wench wearing something red, and chewing tobacco or snuff, and all giggling and skylarking like the children that they remain until they die. Two sets of sugar-houses were the great monuments of the industry of the region, the old more or less ruined refineries of ante-bellum days, and the unpicturesque but practical factories of to-day.

When the boat stopped, as it did with the frequency of a milk-cart on a busy route, we were taken to a country club, sometimes, and the bar-tender was formally introduced as Mr. Belden or Mr. Labiche, whereupon everybody "passed the time of day" with him, as the Irish put it, before ordering the toddy. In one town there had been a ripple of excitement that had not quieted when we landed there. An insult had been offered to a prominent old citizen, "who was as brave as a lion," by a young man whose courage was not questioned. Seconds were appointed, and they found that the young man had made a mistake and ought to apologize.

"We have reached a stage of civilization where a duel would be impossible," said a citizen who was discussing the affair. Then he added, "This would have been peculiarly distressing, as there are at least ten friends of the old gentleman armed and awaiting the outcome of the deliberations, while the younger man has at least six friends who have their rifles in readiness."

The kind of hospitality that obtained along the bayou was simply astonishing to a Northern man. We were begged to leave the boat and visit the homes of friends of five minutes, to stay a week or till the next boat; in one case, to take a month of fishing and hunting. Often when we tore away from these kindly persons they followed us up with bundles of cigars and bottles of good cheer. To have doubted their sincerity would have been like doubting the cause of daylight,

and yet, like that phenomenon, it was almost past comprehension. Ah! but it was also a land of pathos and tragedy. The wounds made by the war may almost be said to bleed yet. The clerk of our boat never made a trip without stopping at the noble plantation that his father owned and lost; the mate on every voyage sees the great acres that his parents were obliged to surrender. Everywhere one journeys in the South such are the sights; every time men talk (I had almost said), that is what one hears. It is not true that the war spirit is alive anywhere except in the talk of politicians, and mainly of those in the North, but it is wonderful that it is not true; it is wonderful how the South has adjusted itself to its altered condition.

Through the broad and golden savanna we zigzagged all day, eating only three meals in the cabin, yet seeming to be forever at it. At close intervals everything aboard ship moved forward with a lurch, and we knew that the vessel had grounded her nose at a landing. Down went the great landing-stage that rides before her like an upraised claw, and that grabs the bank when she stops as a swimmer might hold himself up with one hand. Whenever the claw went out to catch the bank a bunch of ragged negroes scrambled off, and fell into the reeds and bushes, weighted down with the boat's hawser, and stumbling, slipping, and falling as they fought their way to the trees or the clear ground. Hallooing, swearing, and crashing they made their way, working, as all negroes do (when they have to), harder than any other laborers in America. The boat made fast, order was resumed, and took the shape of a rolling line of blacks, shouldering bags and packages, and shambling to and from the shore as softly as so many animated bundles of rags naturally would, for they were ragged from their tattered hats down to their gaping, spreading, padlike shoes. The length of stay at each place was computed by the number of "packages" on the clerk's list. Fifty meant no time at all, 200 indicated a chance to stretch one's legs on the bank, and 1000 or 2000 carried the opportunity to go to town and shake hands with the hearty folk in the law-offices, the court-houses, or the clubs. When the last "package"—which might be a broom or a steam-engine—was put ashore, the scramble of the roustabouts

"WORKING AS ALL NEGROES DO."

was repeated. The line was cast off, the claw began to rise by steam-power, and the darkies rushed down the bank, and hung on to it, and climbed up at the greatest possible risk of being left, and losing as many dollars or dollars and a half as they were days from the city. No officer of the boat ever considered them at all.

These were incidents of a day's travel along the Bayou Teche. Towards bedtime we stopped at one place where the clerk's list of packages assured us we might go ashore and visit a planter whose house was near the bayou. The place proved a typical old manor-house, and yet what a change had befallen it! Instead of the bustling household of before the war—the queenlike mistress, the young ladies with Parisian finish, the little children, the governess, the ever-numerous guests, the troop of servants, the bird and fox hounds, and the pleasure-loving Southern lord—only one room showed a light. The rest of the house was dark. We went in, and found a log fire blazing cheerily on an open hearth in a bachelor's paradise, bare-floored, with magazines, pipes, cigar-boxes, and newspapers scattered all about, and a general tone of disorder and settled loneliness. The planter said that his wife was in Chicago, where he also spent much of his time.

At daybreak we were awakened to find the boat at the plantation of Messrs. Oxnard and Sprague, new-found New Orleans friends who had invited us to visit them. Although it was but daylight, the great colonnaded and galleried mansion, as fine as a lord's country-seat in England, was the seat of a welcoming bustle. Breakfast was spread in the great dining-room upon a snow-white cloth, before a blazing log fire. Again the proprietors were Northerners and bachelors, and the floors and walls were bare, while literature, guns, and smoking implements made picturesque disorder.

I found next day that the plantations lay side by side up and down the bayou for miles, as farms do along a Jersey pike, or cottages neighbor each other on a village road. Were they all maintained by Northern men and bachelors? The inquiry brought the response that not one of the old Southern planters had managed to keep his acres, and that of the new Northern ones only one in that particular neighborhood had his wife with him. Profitable as sugar-planting is, it can only be carried on after a great primal outlay. A modern, well-equipped, economical sugar-house, with its machinery, costs at least $300,000, independent of the cost of the hundreds and perhaps thousands of acres of land bought at $40 each, at an average. Men who have the means to venture upon such an outlay can afford to live where they will, and, as a rule, their homes are in New Orleans or other cities, and the old manor-houses which came with the acres are considered as mere conveniences or business headquarters.

These are the earnest and the scholarly latter-day planters of whom I have spoken—self-instructed plodders or favored

college graduates who have learned that the laboratory of to-day, and the scientific reports and periodicals of the age, are better from a business point of view than the wine-cellars and French novels of the departed era. These new-comers will make Louisiana rich, and America royal over princely nations of Christendom. But to find these people and this new condition actually within the walls of the feudal palaces of slavery days sent a sentimental chill to my very marrow. In Mr. Sprague's great house, over and above all the kindness and hospitality he showered around him, and stronger than the kindliness of his very atmosphere, was the sadness of having the dead, assassinated past so persistently thrust into the mind. He will not mind my using his house to point the tale of the revolution in the South, for he knows that it is a thing apart from the merry time he made for me, and from the friendships that were engendered by his kindness. He must himself have felt that it was strange to walk about the great wide halls and through the immense high rooms of the house, with doors and windows a dozen feet high, and with fireplaces framed in marble, and to think what such a mansion was intended for, of the departed state and pride of which such a house is the emptied cage, the violated tomb. Between rows of moss-curtained oaks and great pecans was the avenue where the horses and carriages brought the gentry to the broad galleries and broader halls, where they disported an aristocracy that was not out of place in their days.

If the lower Atchafalaya suggested England, the Teche country was like Holland, with its extended flat vistas, far along which the sky met the plough-tracked, water-riddled land. But on high were the Southern buzzards, noisome to the sight and to another sense, but ever-beautiful when on the wing. Apparently no Southern view omits them. I could almost say I never looked up in the daytime without seeing them soaring, with the grace of better birds, eternally. The mules, the buzzards, and the negroes broke the Hollandish similitude. Near the Oxnard-Sprague house was a street of negro cabins in a double row, from which came the varied sounds of jews-harps, laughter, and quarrelling. The cabins were of one sort—the single type all over the South—one-storied, often one-roomed, and with a rude brick chimney outside and a gaping fireplace within. Nearly all the white folks who trudged along the highway were Acadians, all but hallowed by the magic of Longfellow, and it was strange indeed to hear that we must not call them 'Cajuns to their faces lest they be offended, that the term is taken as one of reproach, and that the negro farm hands taken care of on the white men's places look down upon these people who have to take care of themselves, as the darkies elsewhere look down upon "poor whites." Among the Acadians along the Bayou Teche are very many who are ignorant, untidy, and unambitious, though nearly all are saving of what they get. Some perform odd jobs, as work is offered to them, and some work the land for those planters who have more than they can manage, and who guarantee a certain sum which leaves a margin of profit for the crops they are able to raise. We saw some rather pretty Acadian girls, dark-skinned, and just missing beauty because of the heaviness of their faces, and we asked them where we could find a certain group of Choctaw Indians' houses where we might buy Indian basket-work. They did not understand us at all until I bethought me that Indians were *sauvages* to the French mind. I tried the girls with that word, and they brightened up and led us to the Indian cabins, which were in no wise different, exteriorly, from the near-by homes of the girls themselves.

The last of the Acadians to reach this new home of theirs came only a little more than a century ago, yet they were only a thousand strong then, while now they number forty thousand. Whether any of their "Evangelines" wedded Choctaw bucks I do not know, but a sufficient number of the French Nova-Scotians married Indian squaws to lend the Acadian faces of to-day a strong trace of kinship with the people they call savages. Yet I never, outside of British Columbia, saw Indians so uncouth as were many of the

THE CLERK.

swarthy yet kindly and simple exiles from Grand Pré, who here have found a drowsy, luxuriant, flowery, and sunny land just suited to their natures.

I spent twenty-four hours on the plantation, and every wakeful hour brought a new delight, found sometimes in the great bare house, sometimes in the fields, and sometimes in the near-by village. There was no unfriendliness toward the newcomers that I could see; indeed, in the village there were only a few cottages half buried amid flowers along a bowery perfumed road, a somnolent shop or two, a lazyman's hotel, and two restful-looking churches. To turn from that slow-going, placid settlement, moss-grown like its trees, to the huge pulsating refineries of the invaders was to be reminded of a sudden change in a disordered dream.

Yet just such companions as these two forces are found throughout the region. Thus the new South works side by side with the old one, the one vigorous and promising, the other placid, picturesque, and doomed.

COUNTY COURT DAY IN KENTUCKY

I.

THE local institutions of the Kentuckian have one deep root in his rich social nature. He loves the human swarm. The very motto of the State is a declaration of good-fellowship, and the seal of the commonwealth the act of shaking hands. Divided, he falls. To be happy, the Kentuckian must be one of many; must assert himself, not through the solitary exercise of his intellect, but the senses; must see men about him who are fat, grip his friend, hear cordial, hearty conversation, realize the play of his light and deep emotions. Society is the multiple of himself.

Hence his fondness for large gather-ings; most of all for open-air assemblies of the democratic sort—great agricultural fairs, race-courses, political meetings, barbecues and burgoos in the woods—where no one is pushed to the wall, or reduced to a seat and to silence, where all may move about at will, seek and be sought, make and receive many impressions. Quiet masses of people in-doors absorb him less. He is not usually fond of lectures, does not build splendid theatres or expend lavishly for opera, is almost of Puritan excellence in the virtue of church-going, which in the country is attended with neighborly reunions.

This large social disposition underlies much of the history of the most social of all his days—a day that has long had its observance imbedded in the structure of his law, is invested with the authority and charm of old-time usage and reminiscence, and still enables him to commingle business and pleasure in a way peculiarly his own. Hardly more characteristic of the Athenian was the agora, or the forum of the Roman, than is county court day characteristic of the Kentuckian. In the open square around the court-house of the county-seat he has of old had the centre of his public social life, the arena of his passions and amusements, the rallying-point of his political discussions, the market-place of his business transactions, a civil unit of his institutional history.

It may well be that some stranger has sojourned just long enough in Kentucky to have grown familiar with the wonted aspects of a county town. He has remarked the easy swing of its daily life:

amicable groups of men sitting around the front entrances of the hotels; the few purchasers and promenaders on the uneven brick pavements; the few vehicles of draught and carriage scattered along the level white thoroughfares. All day long the subdued murmur of patient local traffic has scarcely drowned the twittering of English sparrows in the maples. Then comes some Monday morning when the whole scene changes. The world has not been dead, but only sleeping. Whence this sudden surging crowd of rural folk— these lowing herds in the streets? Is it some animated pastoral come to town? some joyful public anniversary? some survival in altered guise of the English country fair of mellower times? or a vision of what the little place will be a century hence, when American life shall be packed and agitated and tense all over the land? What a world of homogeneous, good-looking, substantial, reposeful peo-

WET GOODS FOR SALE—BOWLING-GREEN.

CONCLUDING A BARGAIN.

ple with honest front and amiable meaning! What bargaining and buying and selling by ever-forming, ever-dissolving groups, with quiet laughter and familiar talk and endless interchange of domestic interrogatories! You descend into the street to study the doings and spectacles from a nearer approach, and stop to ask the meaning of it all. Ah! it is county court day in Kentucky; it is the Kentuckians in the market-place.

II.

They have been assembling here now for nearly a hundred years. One of the first demands of the young commonwealth in the woods was that its vigorous, passionate life should be regulated by the usages of civil law. Its monthly county courts, with justices of the peace, were derived from the Virginia system of jurisprudence, where they formed the aristocratic feature of the government. Virginia itself owed these models to England; and thus the influence of the courts and of the decent and orderly yeomanry of both lands passed, as was singularly fit-

ting, over into the ideals of justice erected by the pure-blooded colony. As the town meeting of Boston town perpetuated the folkmote of the Anglo-Saxon free state, and the Dutch village communities on the shores of the Hudson revived the older ones on the banks of the Rhine, so in Kentucky, through Virginia, there were transplanted by the people, themselves of clean stock and with strong conservative ancestral traits, the influences and elements of English law in relation to the county, the court, and the justice of the peace.

Through all the old time of Kentucky State life there towers up the figure of the justice of the peace. Commissioned by the Governor to hold monthly court, he had not always a court-house wherein to sit, but must buy land in the midst of a settlement or town whereon to build one, and the contiguous necessity of civilization — a jail. In the rude court-room he had a long platform erected, usually running its whole width; on this platform he had a ruder wooden bench placed, likewise extending all the way across; and on this bench, having ridden into town, it may be, in dun-colored leggings, broadcloth pantaloons, a pigeon-tailed coat, a shingle-caped overcoat, and a twelve-dollar high fur hat, he sat gravely and sturdily down amid his peers, looking out upon the bar, ranged along a wooden bench beneath, and prepared to consider the legal needs of his assembled neighbors. Among them all the very best was he; chosen for age, wisdom, means, weight and probity of character; as a rule, not profoundly versed in the law, perhaps knowing nothing of it—being a Revolutionary soldier, a pioneer, or a farmer—but endowed with a sure, robust common-sense and rectitude of spirit that enabled him to divine what the law was; shaking himself fiercely loose from the grip of mere technicalities, and deciding by the natural justice of the case; giving decisions of equal authority with the highest court, an appeal being rarely taken; perpetuating his own authority by appointing his own associates: with all his shortcomings and weaknesses a notable historic figure, high-minded, fearless, and incorruptible, dignified, patient, and strong, and making the county court days of Kentucky for wellnigh half a century memorable to those who have lived to see justice less economically and less honorably administered.

But besides the legal character and intent of the day, which was thus its first and dominant feature, divers things drew the folk together. Even the justice himself may have had quite other than magisterial reasons for coming to town; certainly the people had. They must interchange opinions about local and national politics, observe the workings of their own laws, pay and contract debts, acquire and transfer property, discuss all questions relative to the welfare of the community—holding, in fact, a county court day much like one in Virginia in the middle of the seventeenth century.

III.

But after all the business was over, time still hung idly on their hands, and being vigorous men, hardened by work in forest and field, trained in foot and limb to fleetness and endurance, and fired with admiration of physical prowess, like riotous school-boys out on a half-holiday, they fell to playing. All through the first quarter of the century, and for a longer time, county court day in Kentucky was, at least in many parts of the State, the occasion for holding athletic games. The men, young or in the sinewy manhood of more than middle age, assembled once a month at the county-seats to witness and take part in the feats of muscle and courage. They wrestled, threw the sledge, heaved the bar, divided and played at fives, had foot-races for themselves, and quarter-races for their horses. By-and-by, as these contests became a more prominent feature of the day, they would pit against each other the champions of different neighborhoods. It would become widely known beforehand that next county court day "the bully" in one end of the county would whip "the bully" in the other end; so when court day came, and the justices came, and the bullies came, what was the county to do but come also? The crowd repaired to the common, a ring was formed, the little men on the outside who couldn't see, Zaccheus-like, took to the convenient trees, and there was to be seen a fair and square set-to, in which the fist was the battering-ram and the biceps a catapult. What better, more time-honored, proof could those backwoods Kentuckians have furnished of the humors in their English blood and of their English pugnacity? But, after all, this was only play, and play never is perfectly satisfying to a man who would rather fight; so from playing they fell to harder work, with a more indemnifying motive, and throughout this period county court day was the monthly Monday on which the Kentuckian regularly did his fighting. He availed himself liberally of election day, it is true, and of regimental muster in the spring and battalion muster in fall—great gala occasions; but county court day was by all odds the preferred and highly prized season. It was periodical, and could be relied upon, being written in the law, noted in the almanac, and registered in the heavens.

A capital day; a most admirable and serene day for fighting. Fights grew like a fresh-water polype—by being broken in two: each part produced a progeny. So conventional did the recreation become that difficulties occurring out in the country between times regularly had their settlements postponed until the belligerents could convene with the justices. The men met and fought openly in the streets, the friends of each standing by to see fair play and whet their appetites.

Thus the justices sat quietly on the bench inside, and the people fought quietly in the streets outside, and the day of all the month set apart for the conservation of the peace became the approved day for carrying on individual war. There is no evidence to be had that either the justices or the constables ever interfered.

These pugilistic encounters had a certain law of beauty: they were affairs of equal combat and of courage. The fight over, all animosity was gone, the feud ended. The men must shake hands, go and drink together, become friends. We are touching here upon a grave and curious fact of local history. The fighting habit must be judged by a wholly unique standard. It was the direct outcome of racial traits powerfully developed by social conditions.

IV.

Another noticeable recreation of the day was the drinking. Indeed the two went marvellously well together. The drinking led up to the fighting, and the fighting led up to the drinking; and this amiable co-operation might be prolonged at pleasure. The merchants kept barrels of whiskey in their cellars for their customers. Bottles of it sat openly on the counter, half-way between the pocket of the buyer and the shelf of merchandise. There were no saloons separate from the taverns. At these whiskey was sold and drunk without screens or scruples. It was not usually bought by the drink, but by the tickler. The tickler was a bottle of narrow shape, holding a half-pint—just enough to tickle. On a county court day wellnigh a whole town would be tickled. In some parts of the State tables were placed out on the sidewalks, and around these the men sat drinking mint-juleps and playing draw poker and "old sledge."

Meantime the day was not wholly given over to playing and fighting and drinking. More and more it was becoming the great public day of the month, and mirroring the life and spirit of the times—on occasion a day of fearful, momentous gravity, as in the midst of war, financial distress, high party feeling; more and more the people gathered together for discussion and the origination of measures determining the events of their history. Gradually new features encrusted it. The politician, observing the crowd, availed

A "TICKLER."

THE QUACK-DOCTOR.

himself of it to announce his own candidacy or to wage a friendly campaign, sure, whether popular or unpopular, of a courteous hearing; for this is a virtue of the Kentuckian, to be polite to a public speaker, however little liked his cause. In the spring, there being no fairs, it was the occasion for exhibiting the fine stock of the country, which was led out to some suburban pasture, where the owners made speeches over it. In the winter, at the close of the old or the beginning of the new year, negro slaves were regularly hired out on this day for the ensuing twelvemonth, and sometimes put upon the block before the court-house door and sold for life.

But it was not until near the half of the second quarter of the century that an auctioneer originated stock sales on the open square, and thus gave to the day the characteristic it has since retained of being the great market-day of the month. Thenceforth its influence was to be more widely felt, to be extended into other counties and even States; thenceforth it was to become more distinctively a local institution without counterpart.

To describe minutely the scenes of a county court day in Kentucky, say at the end of the half-century, would be to write a curious page in the history of the times; for they were possible only through the unique social conditions they portrayed. It was near the most prosperous period of State life under the old *régime*. The institution of slavery was about to culminate and decline. Agriculture had about as nearly perfected itself as it was ever destined to do under the system of bondage. The war cloud in the sky of the future could be covered with the hand, or at most with the country gentleman's broad-brimmed straw hat. The whole atmosphere of the times was heavy with ease, and the people, living in perpetual contemplation of their superabundant natural wealth, bore the quality of the land in their manners and dispositions.

When the well-to-do Kentucky farmer got up in the morning, walked out into the porch, stretched himself, and looked at the sun, he knew that he could summon a sleek kindly negro to execute every wish and whim—one to search for his misplaced hat, a second to bring him a dipper of ice-water, a third to black his shoes, a fourth to saddle his horse and hitch it at the stiles, a fifth to cook his breakfast, a sixth to wait on him at the table, a seventh to stand on one side and keep off the flies. Breakfast over, he mounted his horse and rode out where "the hands" were at work. The chance was his overseer or negro boss was there before him: his presence was unnecessary. What a gentleman he was! This was called earning one's bread by the sweat of his brow. Whose brow? He yawned. What should he do? One thing he knew he *would* do—take a good nap before dinner. Perhaps he had better ride over to the blacksmith shop. However, there was nobody there. It was county court day. The sky was blue, the sun golden, the air delightful, the road broad and smooth, the gait of his horse the very poetry of motion. He would go to county court himself. There was really nothing else before him. His wife would want to go too, and the children; so away they went, he on horseback or in the family carriage, with black Pompey driving in front and yellow Cæsar riding behind. The turnpike reached, the progress of our family carriage is interrupted or quite stopped, for there are many other carriages on the road, all going in the same direction. Then pa, growing impatient, orders black Pompey to drive out on one side, whip up the horses, pass the others, and get ahead, so as to escape from the clouds of white limestone dust, which settles thick on the velvet collar of pa's blue cloth coat and in the delicate pink marabou feathers of ma's bonnet, which Pompey can't do, for the faster he goes, the faster the others go, making all the more dust; so that pa gets red in the face, and jumps up in the seat, and looks ready to fight, and thrusts his head out of the window and knocks off his hat; and ma looks nervous, and black Pompey and yellow Cæsar both look white with dust and fear.

A rural cavalcade indeed! Besides the carriages, buggies, horsemen, and pedestrians, there are long droves of stock being hurried on toward the town—hundreds of them. By the time they come together in the town they will be many thousands.

For is not this the great stock-market of the West, and does not the whole South look from its rich plantations and cities up to Kentucky for bacon and mules? By-and-by our family carriage does at last get to town, and is left out in the streets along with many others to block up the passway according to the custom.

The town is packed. It looks as though by some vast suction system it had with one exercise of force drawn all the country life into itself. The poor dumb creatures gathered in from the peaceful fields, and crowded around the court-house, send forth, each after its kind, a general outcry of horror and despair at the tumult of the scene and the unimaginable mystery of their own fate. They quite overflow into the by-streets, where they take possession of the sidewalks, and debar entrance at private residences. No stock-pens wanted then; none wanted now. If a town legislates against these stock sales on the streets and puts up pens on its outskirts, straightway the stock is taken to some other place, and the town is punished for its airs by a decline in its trade.

As the day draws near noon, the tide of life is at the flood. All mixed in with the tossing horns and nimble heels of the terrified, distressed, half-maddened beasts, are the people. Above the level of these is the discordant choir of shrill-voiced auctioneers on horseback. At the corners of the streets long-haired—and long-eared —doctors in curious hats lecture to eager groups on maladies and philanthropic cures. Every itinerant vender of notion and nostrum in the country-side is there; every wandering Italian harper or musician of any kind, be he but a sightless fiddler, who brings forth with poor unison of voice and string the brief and too fickle ballads of the time, "Gentle Annie," and "Sweet Alice, Ben Bolt." Strangely contrasted with everything else in physical type and marks of civilization are the mountaineers, who have come down to "the settlemints" driving herds of their lean, stunted cattle, or bringing, in slow-moving, ox-drawn "steamboat" wagons, maple-sugar, and baskets, and poles, and wild mountain fruit—faded wagons, faded beasts, faded clothes, faded faces, faded everything. A general day for buying and selling all over the State. What purchases at the dry-goods stores and groceries to keep all those negroes at home fat and comfortable and comely—cottons, and gay cottonades, and gorgeous turbans, and linseys of prismatic dyes, bags of Rio coffee and barrels of sugar, with many another pleasant thing! All which will not be taken home in the family carriage, but in the wagon which Scipio Africanus is driving in; Scipio, remember; for while the New-Englander has been naming his own flesh and blood Peleg and Hezekiah and Abednego, the Kentuckian has been giving even his negro slaves mighty and classic names, after his taste and fashion. But very mockingly and satirically do those victorious titles contrast with the condition of them that wear them. A surging populace, an in-town holiday for all rural folk, wholly unlike what may be seen elsewhere in this country. The politician will be sure of his audience to-day in the court-house yard; the seller will be sure of the purchaser; the idle man of meeting one still idler; friend of seeing distant friend; blushing Phyllis, come in to buy fresh ribbons, of being followed through the throng by anxious Corydon.

And what, amid all this tumult of life and affairs—what of the justice of the peace, whose figure once towered up so finely? Alas! quite outgrown, pushed aside, and wellnigh forgotten. The very name of the day which once so sternly commemorated the exercise of his authority has wandered away into another meaning. "County court day" no longer brings up in the mind the image of the central court-house and the judge on the bench. It is to be greatly feared his noble type is dying. The stain of venality has soiled his homespun ermine, and the trail of the office-seeker passed over his rough-hewn bench. So the new constitution of the commonwealth comes in, to make the autocratic ancient justice over into the modern elective magistrate, and with the end of the half-century to close a great chapter of wonderful county court days.

V.

Since then what changes—the last decade of the old South and a quarter of a century of the new! How has it fared with the day meantime? What development has it undergone? What contrasts will it show? For assuredly it has rolled onward as a stone in the path of State progress, always dropping the most of the past and gathering the most of present growth and usage.

Undoubtedly, as seen now, the day is not more interesting by reason of the features it wears than for the sake of comparison with the others it has lost. A singular testimony to the conservative habits of the Kentuckian, and to the stability of his local institutions, is to be found in the fact that it should have come through all this period of upheaval and downfall, of shifting and drifting, and yet remained so much the same. Indeed it seems in no wise liable to lose its larger meaning of being the great market and general business day, the great social and general laziness of the month and the State. Perhaps one feature has taken larger prominence—the eager canvassing of voters by local politicians and office-seekers for weeks, sometimes for months, beforehand. Is it not known that even circuit court will adjourn on this day so as to give the clerk and the judge, the bar, the witnesses, an opportunity to hear rival candidates address the assembled crowd? And yet, for all the general similarity, if we look closely enough and deeply enough we shall discover momentous differences. These people—these groups of twos and threes and hundreds, lounging, sitting, squatting, taking every imaginable posture that can secure bodily comfort—are they in any vital sense new Kentuckians in the new South? If you care to understand ever so little whether this be true, and what it may mean if it is true, you shall not find a better occasion for doing so than a contemporary county court day.

The Kentuckian is not come in to county court to-day to pick a quarrel or to settle one. He *has* no quarrel. His fist has reverted to its natural use and become a hand. Nor does he go armed. Positively it is true that gentlemen in this State do not now get satisfaction out of each other in the market-place, and that on a modern county court day a three-cornered hat is hardly to be seen. And yet you will go on defining a Kentuckian in terms of his grandfather, unaware that he has changed faster than the family reputation. The fighting habit and the shooting habit were both more than satisfied during the civil war. Nevertheless, it is necessary to make a sectional discrimination in this respect, and to draw the line of peaceableness along the base of the mountains.

Another old-time feature of the day has

disappeared—the open use of the pioneer beverage. Merchants do not now set it out for their customers; in the country no longer is it the law of hospitality to and sales of which have in consequence declined. Railways have touched the eastern parts of the State, and broken up the distant toilsome traffic with the steam-

LORDS OF THE SOIL.

offer it to a guest. To do so would commonly be regarded in the light of as great a liberty as to have omitted it once would have been considered an offence. The decanter is no longer found on the sideboard in the home; the barrel is not stored in the cellar.

Some features of the market-place have disappeared. The war and the prostration of the South destroyed that as a market for certain kinds of stock, the raising boat wagons of the mountaineers. No longer is the day the general buying day for the circumjacent country as formerly, when the farmers having great households of slaves sent in their wagons, and bought on twelve months' credit, knowing it would be twenty-four months' if they desired. The doctors too have nearly vanished from the street corners, and the itinerant venders, though on the highway one may still happen upon the peddler with his pack; in the midst of an eager throng still may find some monsieur lecturing to the Kentuckians on the art of making and eating waffles; and still meet the swaying, sightless old fiddler, singing to ears that never tire the gay ditties of cracked and melancholy tone.

Through all changes one feature has remained. It goes back to the most ancient days of local history, and appertains to the local historian as a phenomenon of manners. The Kentuckian *will* come to county court "to swap horses"; it is in the blood. In one small town may be seen fifty or a hundred countrymen assembled during the afternoon in a back street to engage in this delightful recreation. Each rides or leads his worst, most objectionable beast; of these, however fair-seeming, none is above suspicion. It is the potter's field, the lazar-house, the beggardom, of brute conditions. The stiff and aged bondsman of the glebe and plough looks out of one filmy eye upon the hopeless wreck of the erewhile gallant roadster, and the poor macerated carcass that in days gone by bore its thankless burden over the glistening turnpikes with the speed and softness of the wind has not the strength to return the contemptuous kick which is given him by a lungless, tailless rival. Prices range from nothing upward. Exchanges are made for a piece of tobacco or a watermelon to boot. You may not care for the business, but here are curious ethics of trade, and argument and humor, and human nature at a rare angle.

But always let us return from back streets and side thoughts to the central court-house square and the general assembly of the people. Go among them; they are not dangerous. Do not use fine words, at which they will prick up their ears uneasily; or delicate sentiments, which will make you less liked; or indulge in flights or sallies of thought, which they despise. Remember here is the dress and the talk and the manners of the street, and fashion yourself accordingly. Be careful of your speech; they are human. If you can honestly praise them, do so. How they will glow and expand! Censure, and you will get the rough cold shoulder. For to them praise is friendship and censure enmity. They have wonderful solidarity. Sympathy will on occasion flow through them like an electric current, so that they will soften and melt, or be set on fire. There is

a Kentucky sentiment, expending itself in complacent, mellow love of the land, the people, the institutions. You speak to them of the happiness of living in parts of the world where life has infinite variety, nobler general possibilities, greater gains, harder struggles; they say, "We are just as happy here." "It is easier to make a living in Kentucky than to keep from being run over in New York," said a young Kentuckian, and home he went.

If you attempt to deal with them in the business of the market-place, do not trick or cheat them. Above all things they hate and despise intrigue and deception. For one single act of dishonor a man will pay with life-long aversion and contempt. The rage it puts them in to be charged with lying themselves is the exact measure of the excitement with which they regard the lie in others. This is one of their idols—an idol of the market-place in the true meaning of the Baconian philosophy. The new Kentuckian has not lost an old-time trait of character: so high and delicate a sense of personal honor that to be told he lies is the same as saying he has ceased to be a gentleman. Along with good faith and fair dealing goes liberality. Not prodigality; we have changed all that. The fresh system of things has produced no more decided result than a different regard for material interests. You shall not again charge the Kentuckians with lacking either "the telescopic appreciation of distant gain," or the microscopic appreciation of present gain. The influence of money is active, and the illusion of wealth become a reality. Profits are now more likely to pass into accumulation and structure. There is more discussion of costs and values. Small economies are more dwelt upon in thought and conversation. Actually you shall find the people higgling with the dealer over prices. And yet how significant a fact is it in their life that the merchant does not, as a rule, give exact change over the counter! At least the cent has not yet been put under the microscope.

Perhaps you shall not accept it as an evidence of progression toward these that so many men will leave their business all over the country for an idle day once a month in town—nay, oftener than once a month; for many who are at county court in this place to-day will attend it in another county next Monday. But do not be deceived by the appearance of the streets. There are fewer idlers than of old. You may think this quiet group of men who have taken possession of a buggy or a curb-stone are out upon a costly holiday. Draw near, and it is discovered that there is fresh, eager, intelligent talk of the newest agricultural implements and of scientific farming. In fact the day is to the assembled farmers the seed-time of ideas, to be scattered in ready soil—an informal, unconscious meeting of grangers.

You shall not forget, either, that the occasion is very democratic. There seems to be a striking equality of stations and conditions. Having travelled through many towns, and seen these gatherings together of all classes, you will be pleased with the fair, attractive, average prosperity, and note the almost entire absence of paupers and beggars. Somehow misfortune and ill fortune and old age save themselves here from the last hard necessity of asking alms on the highway. But in regard to the other social extreme, the appearance of the people will easily lead you to a wrong inference. They are at least much less democratic than they seem when thus meeting, and their dress and speech and manners in the market-place are not their best equipment. You shall meet with these in their homes. In their homes, too, social distinctions begin and are enforced, and men who find in the open square a common footing may never associate elsewhere. But even among the best of the new Kentuckians will you hardly observe fidelity to the old social ideals, which adjudged that the very flower of birth and training must bloom in the bearing and deportment. With the crumbling and downfall of the old system fell also the structure of fine manners, which were at once its product and adornment.

Naturally there is little room for women among the crowds of the day. It has ceased to be an in-town gala occasion for the rural members of this sex. Sweet, artless Phyllis was long ago chased out of the street by the cattle, which liked not her fluttering ribbons and the hues of her bright attire; and as for finding her aristocratic urban contemporary shopping on such a day, why, one might equally have expected to catch the noble Aspasia higgling for stale fish in the most disreputable quarter of the agora, or the high-born Lucretia bartering for beccafichi and surrounded by the parasites of Rome.

VI.

A new figure has made its appearance in the Kentucky market-place, having set its face resolutely toward the immemorial court-house and this periodic gathering together of freemen, beyond comparison the most significant new figure that has made its way thither and cast its shadow on the people and the ground. Writ all over with problems that not the wisest can so much as even read. Stalking out of a fiery awful past into what far uncertain future? Clothed in hanging rags, it may be, or a garb that is a mosaic of strenuous patches. Ah! Pompey, or Cæsar, or Cicero, of the days of slavery, where be thy family carriage, thy master and mistress, now?

He comes into the county court, this old African, much because he is a colored Kentuckian and must honor the stable customs of the country. He will not buy and sell; he is not a politician; he has no debt to collect, and no legal business. Still example is powerful and the negro imitative, so here he is at county court. It is one instance of the influence exerted over him by the local institutions of the Kentuckian, so that he has a passion for fine stock, must build amphitheatres and hold fairs and attend races. Naturally, therefore, county court has become a great social day with his race. They stop work and come in from the country, or from the outskirts of the town, where they have congregated in little frame houses, and exhibit a quasi-activity in whatever of business and pleasure is going forward. In no other position of life does he exhibit his character and his condition more strikingly than here. Always comical, always tragical, light-hearted, sociable; his shackles stricken off, but wearing those of his own indolence, ignorance, and helplessness; the wandering Socrates of the streets, always dropping little shreds of observation on human affairs and bits of philosophy on human life; his memory working with last Sunday's sermon, and his hope with to-morrow's bread; citizen, with so much freedom and so little liberty—the negro forms one of the conspicuous features of a county court day at the present time.

A wonderful, wonderful day this is that does thus always keep pace with civiliza-

GENTLEMEN OF LEISURE.

tion in the State, drawing all elements to itself, and portraying them to the interpreting eye. So that to paint the scenes of the county court days in the past is almost to write the history of the contemporary periods; and to do as much with one of the present hour is to depict the oldest that has survived and the newest that has been born in this local environment. To the future student of governmental and institutional history in this country, a study always interesting, always important, and always unique will be county court day in Kentucky.

THE OLD WAY TO DIXIE

IT was quite by accident that I heard, while in St. Louis, that I could go all the way down the Mississippi to New Orleans in one of a fleet of packets that differ in no material way from

those which figure in a score of *ante bellum* novels like *Uncle Tom's Cabin*, and which illuminate our Northern notions of life in the South when its planters basked in the glory of their feudal importance.

I could see the mighty river during a journey as long as that from New York to Liverpool; could watch the old-fashioned methods of the Simon Pure negro roustabouts at work with the freight; could gossip and swap stories with the same sort of pilots about whom I had read so much; could see many a slumbering Southern town unmodernized by railroads; could float past plantations, and look out upon old-time planters' man-

sions; and could actually see hard winter at St. Louis merge into soft and beauteous spring at Vicksburg, and become summer with a bound at New Orleans.

More wonderful than all besides, I could cast my lines off from the general world of to-day to float back into a past era, there to loaf away a week of utter rest, undisturbed by a telegraph or telephone, a hotel elevator or a clanging cable-car, surrounded by comfort, fed from a good and generous kitchen, and at liberty to forget the rush and bustle of that raging monster which the French call the *fin de siècle*.

"And how many do it?" I asked.

"Very few indeed," was the reply; "not as many on the best boat in a season as used to take passage for a single trip. The boats are not advertised; the world has forgotten that they are still running."

The only company that maintains these boats is the old Anchor Line, and there are no departures for New Orleans except on Wednesdays; but this was Saturday, the sailing day for Natchez, only 272 miles from the end of the route, and therefore serving well for so bold an experiment. I packed up at the Southern Hotel, and was on board the *City of Providence*, Captain George Carvell, master, an hour before five o'clock, the advertised sailing hour. The strange, the absolutely charming disregard for nineteenth-century bustle was apparent in the answer to the very first question I asked.

"Does she start sharp at five o'clock?"

"No, not sharp; a little dull, I expect."

The *City of Providence* lay with her landing-planks hoisted up ahead of her like the claws of a giant lobster. She was warped to a wharf-boat that was heaped with barrels, boxes, and bags, and

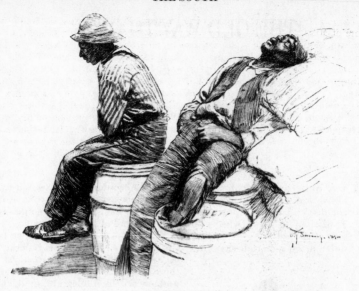

ROUSTABOUTS.

alive with negroes. At a rough guess I should say there were 125 of these black laborers, in every variety of rags, like the beggars who "come to town" in the old nursery rhyme. Already they interested me. Now they would jog along rolling barrels aboard with little spiked sticks, next they appeared each with a bundle of brooms on his shoulder, and in another two minutes the long, zigzagging, shambling line was metamorphosed into a wriggling sinuosity formed of soap-boxes, or an unsteady line of flour-bags, each with ragged legs beneath it, or a procession of baskets or of bundles of laths. As each one picked up an article of freight, an overseer told him its destination. The negro repeated this, and kept on repeating it, in a singsong tone, as he shambled along, until one of the mates on the boat heard him and told him where to put it down, the study of the mate being to distribute the cargo evenly, and to see that all packages sent to any given landing were kept together. It seemed to me that all the foremen and mates were selected for their conscientious intention to keep their hands in their trousers pockets under all circumstances, for their harsh and grating voices, and for their ability to say a great deal and not have a word of it understood by your humble servant, the writer.

The roustabouts looked all of one hue from their shoes to the tops of their heads. Their coffee-colored necks and faces matched their reddish-brown clothes, that had been grimed with the dust of everything known to man; which dust also covered their shoes and bare feet, and made both appear the same. When a huddle went off the boat empty-handed they looked like so many big rats. They loaded the *Providence's* lower deck inside and out; they loaded her upper deck where the chairs for the passengers had seemed to be supreme; and then they loaded the roof over that deck and the side spaces until her sides were sunk low down near the river's surface, and she bristled at every point with boxes, bales, agricultural implements, brooms, carriages, bags, and, as the captain remarked, "Heaven only knows what she 'ain't got aboard her." The mates roared, the negroes talked all the time, or sung to rest their mouths, the boat kept settling in the water, and the mountains of freight swelled at every point. It was well said that twenty ordinary freight trains on a railroad would not carry as much freight as was stowed aboard of her, and I did not doubt the man who remarked to me that when such a boat, so laden, discharged her cargo loosely at one place, it often made a pile bigger than the boat itself.

The *City of Providence* was one of a long line of Mississippi boats edging the broad, clean, sloping levee that fronts busy St. Louis. She was by far the largest and handsomest of the packets; but all are of one type, and that is worth describing. They are, so far as I remember, all painted white, and are very broad and low. Each carries two tall black funnels, capped with a bulging ornamental top, and carrying on rods swung between in front of the "Texas." The pilot-house is always made to look graceful by means of an upper fringe of jig-saw ornament, and usually carries a deer's head or pair of antlers in front of it. We would call it enormous; a great square room with space in it for a stove, chairs, the wheel, the pilots, and, in more than one boat that I saw, a sofa or cushion laid over the roof of the gangway from below. The sides and back of the house are made

THE "TEXAS."

the funnels the trade-mark of the company cut out of sheet-iron—an anchor or an initial letter, a fox or a swan, or whatever. There are three or four stories to these boats: first the open main-deck for freight and for the boilers and engines; then the walled-in saloon-deck, with a row of windows and doors cut alternately close beside one another, and with profuse ornamentation by means of jig-saw work wherever it can be put; and, last of all, the "Texas," or officers' quarters, and the "bureau," or negro passengers' cabin, forming the third story. Most of the large boats have the big square pilot-house on top of the "Texas," but others carry it as part of the third story principally of sliding window-sashes. The front of the house, through which the pilots see their course, is closable by means of a door hinged into sections, and capable of being partially or fully opened as the state of the weather permits. The wheel of one of these great packets is very large, and yet light. It is made as if an ordinary Eastern or Northern wheel had been put in place and then its spokes had grown two feet beyond its rim, and had had another rim and handles added. There are many sharp bends in the river, and I afterward often saw the pilots using both hands and one foot to spin the big circle, until the rudder was "hard over" on whichever side they wanted it.

ROUSTABOUTS GETTING UNDER WAY.

and the "Texas" and "bureau" had followed on the second roof. Pictures of the packets scarcely show how unlike our boats these are, the difference being in the methods of workmanship. Each story is built merely of sheathing, and in the best boats the doors and fanlights are hung on without frames around them; all loose and thin, as if they never encountered cold weather or bad storms. All the boats that I saw are as nearly alike in all respects as if one man had built them. I was told that the great packets cost only $70,000 to $100,000, so that the mere engine in a first-class Atlantic coast river or sound boat is seen to be of more value than one of these huge packets, and a prime reason for the difference in construction suggests itself. But these great, comfortable vessels serve their purpose where ours could not be used at all, and are altogether so useful and appropriate, as well as picturesque and attractive to an Eastern man, that there is not room in my mind for aught than praise of them.

These Mississippi packets of the first and second class are very large boats, and roominess is the most striking characteristic of every part of them. They look light, frail, and inflammable, and so they are. The upright posts that rise from the deck of such a boat to support the saloon-deck are mere little sticks, and everything above them, except the funnels, is equally slender and thin. These boats are not like ours at any point of their make-up. They would seem to a man from the coast not to be the handiwork of ship-builders; indeed, there has been no apparent effort to imitate the massive beams, the peculiar "knees," the freely distributed "bright-work" of polished brass, the neat, solid joinerwork, or the thousand and one tricks of construction and ornament which distinguish the work of our coast boat-builders. These river boats—and I include all the packets that come upon the Mississippi from its tributaries—are more like the work of carpenters and house-builders. It is as if their model had been slowly developed from that of a barge to that of a house-boat, or barge with a roof over it; then as if a house for passengers had been built on top of the first roof,

It was after six o'clock when the longshore hands were drawn up in line on the wharf-boat and our own crew of forty roustabouts came aboard. To one of these I went and asked how many men were in the long brown line on shore.

"Dam if I know, boss," said the semibarbarian, with all the politeness he knew, which was none at all, of word or manner. It occurred to me afterwards that since everybody swears at these roustabouts, an occasional oath in return is scarcely the interest on the profanity each one lays up every year.

In a few moments the great island of joiner-work and freight crawled away from the levee and out upon the yellow, rain-pelted river, with long-drawn gasps, as if she were a monster that had been asleep and was slowly and regretfully waking up. How often every one who has read either the records or the romances of our South and West has heard of the noise that a packet sends through the woods and over the swamps to strike terror to the soul of a runaway darky who has never heard the sound, or to apprise waiting passengers afar off that their boat is on its way! It is nothing like the puff! puff! of the ordinary steam motor;

was a chair and a marble-topped washstand, a carpet, and there were curtains on the glazed door and the long window that formed the top of the outer wall. The supper-bell rang, and I stepped into the saloon, which was a great chamber, all cream-white, touched with gold. The white ribs of the white ceiling were close together over the whole saloon's length of 250 feet, and each rib was upheld by most ornate supports, also white, but hung with gilded pendants. Colored fanlights

THE SALOON OF A MISSISSIPPI STEAMBOAT.

it is a deep, hollow, long-drawn, regular breathing—lazy to the last degree, like the grunt of a sleeping pig that is dreaming. It is made by two engines alternately, and as it travels up the long pipes and is shot out upon the air it seems not to come from the chest of a demon, but from the very heels of some cold-blooded, half-torpid, prehistoric loafer of the alligator kind. To the river passenger in his bed courting sleep it is a sound more soothing than the patter of rain on a farm-house roof.

I had been in my state-room, and found it the largest one that I had ever seen on a steamboat. It had a double bed in it, and there was room for another. There

let in the light by day, and under them other fanlights served to share the brilliant illumination in the saloon with the state-rooms on either side. At the forward end of the saloon were tables spread and set for the male passengers. At the other end sat the captain and the married ladies and girls, and such men as came with them. The chairs were all white, like the walls, the table-cloths, and the aprons of the negro servants, who stood like bronze statues awaiting the orders of the passengers. The supper proved to be well cooked and nicely served. As the fare to New Orleans was about the same as the price of a steerage ticket to Europe, it was pleasant to know that the meals, which were included in the bargain, were going to be as admirable as everything else.

After supper I was asked to go up into the pilot-house, then in charge of Louis Moan and James Parker, both veterans on the river, both good story-tellers, and as kindly and pleasant a pair as ever lightened a journey at a wheel or in a cabin. That night, when a dark pall hung all around the boat, with only here and there a yellow glimmer showing the presence of a house or government light ashore, these were spectral men at a shadowy wheel. In time it was possible to see that the house was half as big as a railroad car, that Captain Carvell was in a chair smoking a pipe, that the gray sheet far below was the river, and that there was an indefinable something near by on one side which the pilots had agreed to regard as the left-hand shore. They said "right" and "left," and spoke of the smoke-stacks as "chimneys." But over and through and around the scene came the periodic gasp—shoo-whoo—from the great smoke-stacks, as gusts of wind on a bleak shore would sound if they blew at regular intervals.

SALOON ORNAMENT.

Back in the blaze of light in the cabin I saw that the women had left their tables, and were gathered around a stove at their end of the room, precisely as the men had done at theirs. The groups were 200 feet apart, and showed no more interest in one another than if they had been on separate boats. I observed that at the right hand of the circle of smoking men was the neatly kept bar in a sort of al-

cove bridged across by a counter. Matching it, on the other side of the boat, was the office of Mr. O. W. Moore, the clerk.

SALOON ORNAMENT.

To Mr. Moore I offered to pay my fare, but he said there was no hurry, he guessed my money would keep. To the bartender I said that if he had made the effervescent draught which I drank before supper I desired to compliment him. "Thank you, sir," said he; "you are very kind." How pleasant was the discovery that I made on my first visit to the South, that in that part of our Union no matter how humble a white man is he is instinctively polite! Not that I call a bartender on a Mississippi boat a humble personage; he merely recalled the general fact to my mind.

The boat stopped at a landing, and it was as if it had died. There was no sound of running about or of yelling; there was simply deathlike stillness. There was a desk and a student-lamp in the great cabin, and, alas for the unities! on the desk lay a pad of telegraph blanks—"the mark of the beast." But they evidently were only a bit of accidental drift from wide-awake St. Louis, and not intended for the passengers, because the clerk came out of his office, swept them into a drawer, and invited me to join him in a game of tiddledywinks. He added to the calm pleasures of the game by telling of a Kentucky girl eleven feet high, who stood at one end of a very wide table and shot the disks into the cup from both sides of the table without changing her position. I judged from his remarks that she was simply a tall girl who played well at tiddledywinks. No man likes to be beaten at his own game, the tools for which he carries about with him. Even princes of the blood royal show annoyance when it happens.

I slept like a child all night, and mentioned the fact at the breakfast table, where the men all spoke to one another and the clerk addressed each of us by name as if we were in a boarding-house. Every one smiled when I said that the boat's noise did not disturb me.

"Why, we tied up to a tree all night," said the clerk, "and did not move a yard until an hour ago."

At this breakfast we had a very African-looking dish that somehow suggested the voudoo. It appeared like a dish of exaggerated canary seed boiled in tan-bark.

"Dat dere," said my waiter, "is sumping you doan' git in no hotels. It's jambullade. Dey done make it ob rice, tomatoes, and brekfus' bacon or ham; but ef dey put in oysters place ob de ham, it's de fines' in de lan'."

I had not been long enough in the atmosphere of Mississippi travel to avoid worrying about the loss of a whole night while we were tied up to the shore. There had been a fog, I was told, and to proceed would have been dangerous. Yet I was bound for New Orleans for Mardi-gras, and had only time to make it, according to the boat's schedule. But I had not fathomed a tithe of the mysteries of this river travel.

"It's too bad we're so late," I said to Mr. Todd, the steward.

"We ain't late," said he.

"I thought we laid up overnight," I said.

"So we did," said he. "But that ain't goin' to make any difference; we don't run so close to time as all that."

"Don't get excited," said Captain Car-

THE PILOT.

vell. "You are going to have the best trip you ever made in your life. And if we keep a-layin' up nights, all you've got to do is to step ashore at Cairo or Memphis or Natchez and take the cars into New Orleans quicker'n a wink. You can stay with us till the last minute before you've got to be in New Orleans, and then the cars 'll take you there all right. I only wish it was April 'stead of February. Then you leave a right cold climate in the North, and you get along and see flowers all a-blooming and roses a-blushing. Why, sir, I've been making this run thirty-nine years, and I enjoy it yet."

"Come up in the pilot-house," said Mr. Moan. "Bring your pipe and tobacco and your slippers, and leave 'em up there, so's to make yourself at home. You're going to live with us nigh on to a week, you know, and you ought to be friendly."

It was by this tone, caught from each officer to whom I spoke, that I, all too slowly, imbibed the calm and restful spirit of the voyage. Nothing made any difference, or gave cause to borrow trouble —not even hitching up to the river-bank, now and then, for a night or two.

We had been at Chester for nearly an hour. The clerk went ashore, visiting, and disappeared up the main street. We were to take on 500 barrels of flour, and for a long while these had been jolting and creaking and spurting out little white wisps of powder as the black crew rolled them aboard. The pilot remarked, as he looked down at the scene, that when we came to leave we would not really get away, because we must drop down to a mill half a mile down stream, and then to a warehouse farther along, and then, "if there are any other stops near by, some one will run down with a flag, or a white handkerchief, and call us."

I alone was impatient—the only curse on the happy condition. In the middle of a lifetime of catching trains and riding watch in hand I found that I did not know how to behave or how to school myself for a natural, restful situation such as this. I felt that I belonged in the world, and that this was not it. This was dreamland—an Occidental Arabia. True, we were moved by steam, we lifted the landing-stages by steam, and swung red farm wagons to the hurricane-deck and blew whistles, all by steam; but it was steam hypnotized and put to sleep. Could I not hear it snore through the smoke-stacks whenever the engineer disturbed it? As we swung away from Chester, Mr. Moan pointed across the river and said:

"That's Claraville over there. It's a tidy place. Been that way since I was a boy. It don't grow, but it holds its own."

I harbored the hope that I would appreciate that remark, and the spirit which engendered it, in five days or so of life on the lazy boat. Even then I could see that it was something to "hold one's own." It was an effort, and perhaps a strain. It is more than we men and

women are able to do for any length of time.

We pushed high up a stony bank at a new place. Again the clerk went ashore, and this time the captain followed him. Another wabbling stream of flour-barrels issued from a warehouse and rolled into the boat. I think I began to feel less forced resignation and more at ease. I was drifting into harmony with my surroundings. It was still a little strange that the voices on shore were all using English words. Spanish or Arabic would have consorted better with the hour. As a happy makeshift a negro came out and sat on a barrel and played a jews-harp. He was ragged and slovenly, and was the only black man not at work; but perhaps a man cannot work steadily and do justice to a jews-harp at the same time. He turned his genius upon a lively tune, and the serpentlike stream of barrels began to flow faster under the negroes' hands, as if it were a current of molasses and the music had warmed it. The church bells—for it was Sunday—broke upon the air at a distance; at just the right distance, so that they sounded soft and religious. The sun was out. Only one other thing was needed—tobacco.

When I went to get my pipe, the youngest of the ladies in the saloon was at the piano, and "A Starry Night for a Ramble" was trickling from her fingers' ends. I dropped into a chair to listen, and to think how prone the Southern folk are to insist upon a recognition of caste in every relation of life. First, the captain at the head of all, then the ladies and their male escorts—these were the aristocrats of the boat. The lonely male passengers were the middle class, graciously permitted to sleep on the saloon-deck. Finally, the negro passengers and the petty officers were sent up above, to quarters far from the rest. But the young lady saw me sitting there, and the music stopped. She left the piano stool with a flirt of her skirt; not a violent motion of the whole back of her dress, as if she was really "put out" by my intrusion, but just a faint little snap at the very tail of the eloquent garment. How many languages women have! They have one of the tongue, like ours; one of the silent, mobile lips, as when school-girls talk without being heard; one of the eyes; one of their spirits, that rise into vivacity for those they love or seek to please, and that sink into moodiness or languor near those they don't care for; and finally, this of the skirts.

But that was only a faint whip of the very tail of the skirt, down by the hem. It hinted to me that we were to become acquainted soon. There was plenty of time; I would not hurry it.

I went to my great comfortable room and experimented with the locked door which was opposite the entrance. It opened, and led out upon the outer deck, past all the other state-room doors. That was exquisite. It was like part of a typical Southern home, with the parlor opening out on a veranda over a river. I was reminded of the first true Southern house I ever stopped at, in the Blue Ridge Mountains. There were two long arms in front of the main building, and the rooms in these arms had a door and a window at each end. I was enraptured with my good fortune until night came, when I discovered that neither window sported a catch and neither door had a lock. I might as well, I might better, have been put to bed in the fields. All the stories of murder I had heard during the day— and they were plenty—came back, and sat on the edge of the bed with me. I complained in the morning, and the proprietor laughed, and said there was not a lock on a door in the county. They murdered there, but they did not rob. That was a consolation.

The Mississippi proved not so unlike a Northern river as might have been expected. The Hudson is as wide in some places, and I have seen parts of Lake Ontario with just such shores. Fields of grain ran to the edge of the bluff, and here and there were houses and patches of trees. The Illinois side was a long reach of wooded bluff. The water itself was mud. As Senator Ingalls is quoted as saying, it was "too thick for a beverage and too thin for food." Everywhere the yellow water, running the same way as the boat, seemed to outstrip our vessel. Everywhere it was dotted with logs, twigs, and little floating islands of the wreckage of the cottonwood thickets of Dakota and Montana, perhaps of the forests at the feet of the Rocky Mountains. That was the main peculiarity of the river—the presence of thousands of tons of débris floating behind, beside, and ahead of the steamboat. Here and there we saw a "government light," a little lantern on a clean

"I'S FIXED FOR LIFE, BOSS, IF DE GOV-ER'MENT DONE HOLD OUT."

white frame-work, suggesting an immaculate chicken-coop. Men who live in nearby houses get ten or fifteen dollars a month —the lights being of two grades—for lighting them every night and putting them out every morning. Mr. Moan told of a negro down below where we were who gets fifteen dollars a month for keeping a difficult light, and who, on being asked how he was getting along, replied that it was money enough for the keep of his wife and himself. "I's fixed for life, boss," he said, "if de gover'ment done hold out."

I noted with keen pleasure that neither Pilot Moan nor Pilot Parker blew the whistle as the boat was backed off the mud at a landing. In New York they would surely whistle and shriek "good-by." In France they would blow all the time. The Mississippi plan is better. There they

A MISSISSIPPI STEAMBOAT CAPTAIN.

puffing and splashing up to them for freight.

At one stop which we did make, Captain Carvell ordered a barge pushed out of the way—"so's we sha'n't make a bunglesome landing," he said. The nearest great landing-stage, a long gang-plank hung by the middle from a sort of derrick, and capable of connecting the boat with a hill or a flat surface, was let down on the bank. The unavoidable flour-barrels came head foremost along a wooden slide this time, and a darky on the boat sang an incessant line, "Somebody told me so," as a warning to the men below that another and another barrel was coming. They are fond of chanting at their work, and they give vent to whatever comes into their heads, and then repeat it thousands of times, perhaps. It is not always a pretty sentence, but every such refrain serves to time their movements. "O Lord God! you know you done wrong," I have heard a negro say with each bag that was handed to him to lift upon a pile. "Been a slave all yo' days; you 'ain't got a penny saved," was another refrain; and still another, chanted incessantly, was: "Who's been here since I's been gone? Big buck nigger with a derby on." They are all "niggers" once you enter the Southern country. Every one calls them so, and they do not often vary the custom among themselves.

These roustabouts are nothing like as forward as the lowest of their race that we see in the North. Presumably they are about what the "field hands" of slavery times were. They are dull-eyed, shambling men, dressed like perambulating rag-bags, with rags at the sleeves, up and down the trousers, at the hems of their coats, and the rims of their caps and hats. A man who makes six changes

whistle only when approaching a landing, "to notify the labor."

For miles and miles we floated out in the channel and were alone in the world—we and the distant blue hills, the thin bare forests, and the softly speeding stream. Not a house or a fence or a ploughed acre was in sight. What a country ours is! How much room it offers to future peoples! They are not hurrying—they who have so much more at stake than we on that boat. Why, then, needed we to hurry? When a house or a village hove in sight, it was not always wooden, as in the West. Often the warehouses, the mills, and even the manor-houses were of stone or brick. Some of these places were inaccessible to so big a boat as the *Providence*, but from its decks could be seen little waggle-tailed stern-wheelers

of his working attire every year by contract with a tailor would be surprised at
how long these men keep their clothes.
Some wear coats and vests and no shirts;
some wear overcoats and shirts and no
vests; some have only shirts and trousers—shirts that have lost their buttons,
perhaps, and flare wide open to the trousers band, showing a black trunk like
oiled ebony. They earn a dollar a day,
but have not learned to save it. They
are very dissipated, and are
given to carrying knives,
which the mates take away
from the most unruly ones.
The scars on many of their
bodies show to what use these
knives are too often put.
"Who's dat talkin' 'bout cuttin' out some one's heart?" I
heard one say as he slouched
along in the roustabout line.
"Ef dar's goin' to be any
cuttin', I want to do some."
Though they chant at their
work, I seldom saw them
laugh or heard them sing a
song, or knew one of them
to dance during the voyage.
The work is hard, and they
are kept at it, urged constantly by the mates on shore and
aboard, as the Southern folks
say that negroes and mules
always need to be. But the
roustabouts' faults are exces-
sively human, after all, and
the consequence of a sturdy
belief that they need sharper
treatment than the rest of us
leads to their being urged to do
more work than a white man.
There were nights on the
Providence when the landings ran close together, and
the poor wretches got little or
no sleep. They "tote" all the
freight aboard and back to land again on
their heads or shoulders, and it is crushing work. Whenever the old barbaric
instinct to loaf, or to move by threes at
one man's work, would prompt them, one
of the mates was sure to spy the weakness
and roar at the culprits.

The mates showed no actual unkind-
ness or severity while I was on that boat.
But they all—on all the boats—have fear-
some voices, such as we credit to pirate
chiefs on "low, rakish, black boats" in

yellow-clad novels. Any one of them
would break up an opera troupe. They
rasp at the darkies in their business
voices, with a "Run up the plank, nigger;
now, then, nigger, get wood"—and then
they turn and speak to the passengers in
their Sunday shore-leave voices, as gently
as any men can talk.

Mr. Halloran, an up-river pilot of
celebrity who was studying the lower
river, told me that he remembered when

THE MATE OF A MISSISSIPPI BOAT—"NOW, THEN, NIGGER."

it was the custom for the mates to hit
lazy negroes on the head with a billet of
wood, "and knock them stiff." The
other negroes used to laugh (presumably
as the sad-faced man laughed when the
photographer clapped a pistol to his head
and said, "Smile, —— you, or I'll shoot
you"). When the felled negro came to,
the others would say, "Lep up quick an'
git to work, nigger; de mate's a-coming."
They do not urge the help with cord-
wood now—so the mate of the *Providence*

THE CHICAGO MAN.

told me — because the negroes get out warrants and delay the boat.

I have said that the blacks all call themselves "niggers." The rule has its exceptions. I went ashore at a plantation called "Sunnyside," and saw a cheery old "aunty" standing near a cabin doorway from out of which pickaninnies were tumbling like ants out of an ant-hill.

"How many children have you got, aunty?" I inquired.

"I 'ain't got none yere," she said; "mine's all out in de fiel'. Dese yer two is my gran'chillen; de oders I'm takin' car' of fer de ladies ob de neighborhood."

There is a fine barber shop and "washroom" on the packet, and the barber and I often conversed, with a razor between us. He asked me once how I liked my hair trimmed, and I said I always left that to the barber.

"Dat's c'rect," said he; "you kin leave it to me safely; and you kin bet I'm more dan apt to do it in de mos' fashionablest manner." Then he turned, and called to his assistant, a coal-black boy who was working his way to New Orleans. "Hey, dere! you nigger! Git me a high stool outen de pantry. How you 'spect I's gwine cut de gemmen's ha'r ef I doan' hab no stool?"

I mentioned the fact that the roustabouts were working very hard.

"Dat dey is," said the barber. "We call 'em 'roosters' on de ribber, but rous'about is more correc'. Dey wuk hard night an' day, an' dey git mo' kicks dan dollars. Ef I got rejuced so's I had to do manual labor, I'd go to stealin' 'fo' I'd be a rooster. Certain su' I would, 'cause dey couldn't wuk a man no harder in de penitentshuary ef he got caught dan dey do on dese boats."

At supper on the second night I began to find fault with the custom of separating the ladies and the gentlemen by the length of an enormous saloon. The gulf between the men and women was yet as wide as ever. There they sat at their separate table. Later they would make a ring around a stove of their own, or retire to an especial saloon called "the nursery," which spans and shuts off the whole back end of the boat—the most attractive part of our Northern steamboats. There were four women on this boat and a little baby girl. The tiny woman, though only four years old, had been to visit me during the afternoon, and had told me her own peculiar version of Cinderella. Poor little tot! She was with a man and woman whom she called papa and mamma, but they made the cruel mistake of telling everybody that she was a little orphan waif, the child of a pauper, and that they had adopted her—the last thing, one would think, that they would noise abroad. I wondered whether her name might not be Cinderella, and that led me to think that I did not know even the name of the youngest of the grown women, who, by-the-way, was only eighteen or nineteen, with jet hair, coal-black laughing eyes, and a smiling mouth set with pearls. She was perfectly formed, and being beautiful, was also amiable, for there can be no true beauty in a woman who is not sunny-hearted. It was she who played the piano for the women—until a man listened. Perhaps another time I may be able to enjoy such a restful break in my life to the uttermost, and not draw comparisons or seek faults to find, yet on this second night I was unable to help recalling the only other trip I had then made on a Southern river. It was on the Ohio. Half the passengers were

We stopped at Cairo on the second morning out, and were pulling away from there while I ate my breakfast. I told Captain Carvell that I was sorry to have missed seeing that important town, but I found that, as before, my regrets

THE MAN FROM PROVIDENCE.

Kentuckians. As soon as the boat started, a negro roustabout was hired to fiddle in the saloon, and every man sought a partner and fell to waltzing. It was idyllic; it was a snatch of Arcadian life, of Brittany or Switzerland imported to America. A young Kentuckian, who introduced himself to me and then to all the women, kindly introduced them all to one another and then to me. That was better than this Mississippi plan of putting a whole boat's length between the sexes. It suggested a floating synagogue.

were groundless. Nothing is missed and nothing makes any difference on that phenomenal line. "You won't miss Cairo," said the captain; "we are going up a mile to get some pork, and down half a mile to get some flour. We shall be here some hours yet." I ate a leisurely breakfast, saw the town to my heart's content, and was back on the boat an hour before it got away for good. A railroad train whizzed along above the levee like a messenger from the world of worry and unrest, and I looked at it as I have often

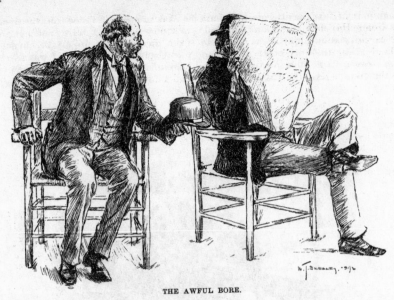

THE AWFUL BORE.

looked at a leopard caged in a menagerie. It could not get at me, I knew.

The beautiful black-eyed girl had kept in the ladies' end of the saloon, wrapped up in Cinderella, the Chicago man's tiny daughter, but on this day, as I was on the upper deck, I could not help seeing her mount the ladderlike stairs to the pilot-house. It is amazing that four women and half a dozen men should have been together so long and not become acquainted. To be sure, I could have followed the pretty brunette to the pilot-house and been introduced by one of the pilots; but there was no hurry. Besides, at the time, a young commercial traveller from Providence was telling me of his uncertainty whether or not he was in love. The subject of his doubts was a young lady whose portrait he carried in a locket which he kept opening incessantly.

I spent much time every day in the pilot-house. I heard very much about the skill and knowledge the river-pilot's calling required, but I saw even more than I heard. This giant river does not impress those who study it with its greatness so much as with its eccentricities. It runs between banks that are called earth, but act like brown sugar; that cave in and hollow out, and turn into bars and islands, in a way that is almost indescribable. Islands in it

which were on one side one year are on the other side another year. Channels which the steamboats followed last month and for years past are now closed. Bars no one ever saw before suddenly lift above the surface. Piloting on the Mississippi is a business no one ever learns. It is a continual subject of study. It is the work of years to understand the general course of the channel, and then the knowledge must be altered with each trip. The best pilot on the river, if he stops ashore a few months, becomes greener than a new hand. The pilots not only report their new experiences for publication in the newspapers, but they make notes of remarkable changes, and drop them into boxes on the route for the guidance of others in the business.

In the lower part of the river, below Tennessee, the whistle of a boat may often be heard between twelve and fifteen hours before the boat reaches the point where the sound came. This is because of the manner in which the river doubles upon itself. A town which may be only four or five miles across one of these loops will hear the boat, but the distance around the bend, and the stops the boat makes, may allow a prospective passenger to do a day's business before he boards the vessel.

Nothing could be more primitive than many of the boat-landings. The vessels

simply "run their nozzles agin the shore,"
as John Hay has sung that they did.
Villages, planters' depots or mills, are
found on the edge of a rude bank, and
the boats run up close as they can and
lower the stages. The darkies tumble
up and down the bluff, the spectators
line its edge. There is no staircase, pier,
or wharf-boat, sea-wall, or anything. If
there was, it is a question whether it
would last out a single season. I seldom
looked long at such a bank that I did
not see a piece of it loosen and crumble
and fall into the rushing, yellow river.

dinary river. Any one may see Island
Number Ten, and call to mind its exciting part in the late war; but it had no
part in it, for old Island Number Ten disappeared years ago, and this is a new one,
not on the site of its predecessor. Yet the
true Island Number Ten bore very ancient, heavy timber, and many fine plantations. The new one is already timbered with a dense growth of cane and
saplings.

At Fort Pillow we saw the river's most
stupendous ravages of that particular time.
The famous bluff, fifty feet high at least,

ROUSTABOUTS UNLOADING A MISSISSIPPI BOAT.

Sometimes it was only a ton that fell in;
sometimes it was a good fraction of an
acre. Captain Carvell told me that once
he was looking at as noble and large a
tree as he ever saw in his life, standing
inshore and away from the edge of a
bluff. Suddenly the land slipped away
from around it, and it fell and crashed
into his steamboat. At many and many
a stopping-place the pilots call to mind
where the banks were when they began
piloting, and always they were far out
in the present stream. One pointed out
to me an eddy over the wreck of a steamer that sunk while warped to the shore.
She was now in the middle of the extraor-

was sliding down in great slices and bites
and falling into the river. One great
mound was in the water, another had
fallen just behind it, and these had carried the trees that were growing in the
earth flat down in the mixed-up dirt.
But beyond these a huge slice many rods
long and many yards thick was parting
from the bluff and leaning over toward
the water, with huge trees still standing
on it, and reaching their naked roots out
on either side like the fingers of drown-
ing men. Below, at what is called Centennial Cut-off, the eccentric river has re-
versed its original direction. It used to
form a letter S, and now it flows down

the central curve of the S where it used to flow northward. The two loops are grown with reeds, and form a vast amphitheatre, at the sides of which, five miles off, one sees the distant banks covered with big timber.

Still farther down the river, in places where the men of the River Commission had been at work, we saw the banks cut at an angle like a natural beach, and sheathed with riprap. In places the water is said to have got under the sheathing and melted the work away, but there was no disposition among the navigators I was with to criticise the government work, so great has been the continually increasing improvement of the waterway. We saw few of those snags which were once as common as the dollars of a millionaire, but we did see many places where the crews of the snag-boats had been at work. The men chop down the trees so that when the bank caves the trees and their roots will both float off separately. If left to pursue the wicked ways of inanimate things, the trees would be carried out into the stream to sink butt downward, and project their trunks up to pierce the bottom of the first boat that struck one. The government boats have done splendid work at pulling up snags. It is said that their tackle is strong enough for any snag they ever find, and that "they could pull up the bottom of the river, if necessary."

Down on the Mississippi State and Arkansas shores we began to note the consequences of former high stages of water. The water-marks were often half-way up the cabin and warehouse doors, and tales were told of families that take to the second stories of their houses on such occasions, not forgetting to put their poultry and cattle on rafts tied to trees, to keep them until the flood subsides.

It was on the third day that I became acquainted with the beautiful nunlike pianist. I found her in distress among the firkins and brooms and boxes on the upper deck, among which the boat's cat had fled from the too violent endearments of little Cinderella. My hands and those of the pianist met in the dark crannies of the freight piles, and we fell to laughing, and became so well acquainted that soon afterward she dropped into a chair beside me. In fifteen minutes she had told me her name, age, station, amusements, love affairs, home arrangements, tastes, hopes, and religious belief. The manner of the narrative was even more peculiar than the matter. Her mother, then on board with her, was an Arkansas widow who kept a hotel to which commercial travellers repaired in great force, and at which —so I judged from what the young woman had imbibed—they paid their way with quite as much slang as cash. As I have seen such girls before in my travels in the Southwest, and have always found them different, in a marked way, from the girls in large towns, I will try to repeat what I jotted down of her observations.

"You're married, ain't you?" She was a pretty girl, as I have said, and she had large deep black eyes. These she set, as she spoke, so as to give a searching glance that showed her to be expectant of a denial of my happy state, yet confident she was right. "I knew it. Well, the married kind are the worst that come to our hotel. My mother keeps a hotel at ——, you know; the captain's told you, I suppose. It's a village; but I know a few things. The band plays 'Annie Rooney' where I live, but it ain't up to me, for I know 'Comrades,' and 'Maggie Murphy's Home,' and the very latest songs the boys bring to the house. That Providence feller's in love, ain't he? Well, I say, I thought it was either love or dyspepsia that was ailing him. Say, do you believe in— pshaw! I was going to ask if you believed in love, but of course you're married, and you've got to say 'yes.' I always call 'rats' when I hear of anybody being in love. Ain't it dull on this boat? I never see such men. I believe if a woman knocked 'em down they wouldn't speak to her. You're the only one that ain't glued to the bar; you and Admiral Farragut; that's what I call the captain. He's nice, ain't he? I think he's too cute. I love old men, I do."

A pause, and a rapt expression of a face turned upon the river-bank as if in enjoyment of the tame scenery.

"Say! what's the latest slang in New York? The boys—travellers that stop at our house, you know—ain't brought in anything new in a long while. You're from New York, ain't you? Can't help it, can you? My! what a jay-bird I'd look like in New York! Well, you needn't get scared. I ain't a-going. I'm going to stay where I'm on top. Bob Ingersoll lives in New York, don't he? He's im-

DECK OF A MISSISSIPPI BOAT—"YOU'RE MARRIED, AIN'T YOU?"

mense, ain't he? No, I see you ain't stuck on him. Well, neither am I, and I'm going to tell you the truth. Everybody my way is crazy to read everything he writes and says, but I'm going to stick to my little old Bible till a good deal smarter man than he is comes along. If I was Ingersoll, and knew for sure that I was right, I wouldn't stump the country to try and take away the comfort of every poor old widow and young girl and decent man; because our belief in religion is close on to all that most folks has in this world."

I spoke of my surprise that she should believe in religion and not in love.

"Say!" said she; "I help run a hotel, and I agree with everybody that comes along—for the price. But I ain't in a hotel now, and you're married, and I'll give myself away. I made fun of love, but, gee whiz! I didn't mean it. I reckon a girl don't fool you talking that way. I'm in love, right smart in love, too; up to my neck.

"My mother hates him. You see, we used to be well off, and father's people were 'way up, and mother keeps in with all her old friends. They're all as poor as we, but they're prouder'n Lucifer, and mother'd rather we'd marry poor quality folks than see us rich and happy if our husbands were common stock. Well, I want to do what's right, but what must I go and do but fall in love with a German. He's a civil engineer, and he was laying out a railroad and come to our house. You'd think he was a chump to look at him, but, say! he's just splendid. Ma saw what was going on, and she ordered me not to write to him. I told him that, and he said for us to run away. Oh, he's immense, if he is a German. I let on I was real angry. I told him I was going to mind my mother, and he shouldn't put such ideas in my head. I scared him pale; but I liked him all the better; he was so cut up. But he said 'All right,' and we don't write—except he writes to my aunt, and I see the letters. We are waiting two years till I'm twenty-one, and I'm telling ma I love him three times a day so as to get her used to it. She's praying for everything to happen to Jake, but, say! it takes more than prayer to kill a German, don't it?"

Our remarkable tête-à-tête was interrupted by the announcement of dinner, and we put the length of the cabin between us. I never more than "bade her the time of day," as the Irish say, after that, for it seemed more profitable to divide my time between the pilot-house and the towns ashore. At Columbus, Kentucky, we saw the first true Southern mansion, with its great columns in front and its wide hall through the middle. We began to make many stops in midstream to deliver the mail by a yawl, manned most skilfully by the second mate and several roustabouts. At Slough,

Kentucky, we saw cotton fields and corn fields opposite one another, and felt that we were truly in the South. At every village the houses were emptied and the levee was crowded. Darkies were in profuse abundance, and forty were idle to every one who worked. Every woman and girl, white and black, had put on some one bright red garment, and the historic yellow girls made no more effort to hide the fact that they were chewing tobacco or snuff than the old negresses did to conceal the pipes that they smoked.

Down and down we went with the current, and no longer noticed the deep snoring of the engine, or thought of the rushing world to the north and east. The table fare remained remarkably good, the nights' rests were unbroken; never did I stop marvelling that the boat was not crowded with the tired men of business, to whom it offered the most perfect relief and rest. The hotel-keeper and her frank and beautiful daughter got off at a picturesque town fronted by great oaks. The daughter waved her hand at the pilot-house and called out, "Ta-ta."

There was mild excitement and much blowing of whistles when we passed our sister-boat the *City of Monroe*—the prize Anchor liner from Natchez.

"Hark!" said the first mate in his society voice. "Stop talking. Listen to her wheels on the water. It's music. It's for all the world like walnuts dropping off a tree. When she made her first big run the roustabouts got up a song about her: 'Did ye hear what the *Monroe* done?'"

As the days went by it was apparent that the woods extended along both sides of the turbid river, with only here and there a clearing for a town or farm or house. The population does not cling to the shore ; it is too often overflowed. At Pecan Point (pecan is pronounced "pecarn" along the river) we saw the first green grass on February 23d, and the first great plantation. It was, as we have all read, a great clearing, a scattering of negro cabins, and then the big mansion of the planter, surrounded by tidy white houses in numbers sufficient to form a village. Here a darky put a history of his life into a sentence. Being asked how he got along, he said: "Oh, fairly, fairly, suh. Some days dere's chicken all de day, but mo' days dey's only feathers." We saw the first cane-brake in great clumps, and as each cane was clad with leaves from top to bottom, the distant effect was that of thickets of green bushes. We saw many little plantations of a few acres each, usually with a government river light on the bank, and consisting of a couple of acres of corn and as much more of cotton. We learned that in this way thousands of negroes have kept themselves since the war. We saw their log huts, their wagons, and the inevitable mule, for a mule and a shotgun are the first things that are bought, by whites and blacks, in this region.

Memphis proved an unexpectedly lively town, with a main street that was rather Western than Southern. Here the freight from and for the boat was handled in surprisingly quick time, by means of an endless belt railway something like a tread-mill. We left the dancing lights of the city, and moved out into a pall of smoke suspended in fog, and then I saw how well and thoroughly the men in the pilot-house knew the mighty river. After a run of a few miles the captain declared it unsafe to go farther. The electric search-light was thrown in all directions, but only illuminated a small circle closed in by a fog-bank. In absolute, black darkness the pilot and the captain discussed the character of the shores, to hit upon a hard bank with heavy timber to which it would be safe to tie up. They agreed that some unseen island across the stream and lower down would serve best.

"Look out for the bar just above there," said the captain.

"Yes," said the pilot; "I know where she is."

The wheel was spun round, the boat turned into a new course, and presently the search-light was thrown upon the very timber-studded reef they sought—as fine an exhibition of knowledge, experience, and skill as I ever witnessed.

We now had Mississippi on the left and Arkansas on the right, and saw the first commercial monuments of the great industry in cotton seed and its varied products. This was at Helena, Arkansas, and already, two days after Washington's birthday, the weather had become so hot that the shade was grateful. The negroes warmed to their incessant, laborious work, and the black processions to and from the shore at the frequent landings became leaping lines of garrulous toilers. The river becomes very wide, often miles wide, in long reaches, and at one part the boat's officers pointed to where it is eating its way inland, and said that a mile in the interior snags are found sitting up in the earth, far beneath the roots of the present trees, as they did in the old bottom, showing either that the river was once many times wider than now, or that it has shifted to and fro as it continues to do.

To tell in detail what we saw and did during two more days; how we saw green willows and then dogwood and jasmine in bloom, or even how Captain Carvell got out his straw hat at Elmwood, Mississippi, would require a second article. We often heard the familiar cry of "Mark twain," which Samuel D. Clemens took as his *nom de plume*, and a line about that may be interesting. The *Providence*, laden down till her deck touched the water,

A RAFT OF LOGS.

drew a little more than four feet, and though the river has a depth of 80 to 120 feet, there are places where bars made it necessary to take soundings. Whenever this was done a negro on the main-deck heaved the lead, and another on the second deck echoed his calls. These are the cries I heard, and when the reader understands that a fathom, or six feet, is the basis of calculation, he will comprehend the system. These, then, were the cries:

"Five feet." "Six feet." "Nine feet." "Mark twain" (12 feet).

"A quarter less twain" (10½ feet)—that is to say, a quarter of a fathom less than two fathoms.

"A quarter twain" (13½ feet).

"Mark three" (18 feet).

"A quarter less three." "A quarter three" (19½ feet). "Deep four." "No bottom."

The tows that we saw were too peculiar to miss mention. On this river the loads are "towed before" instead of behind. The principle underlying the custom is that of the wheelbarrow, and is necessitated by the curves in this, the crookedest large river in the world. The barges and flats are fastened solidly ahead of the tug-boat in a great fan-shaped mass, and the steamer backs and pushes and gradually turns the bulk as if it had hold of the handles of a barrow in a crooked lane.

We saw a famous boat, the *Wilson*, from Pittsburg, come along behind a low black island. It proved to be a tow of large, low, uncovered barges, thirty of them, each carrying 1000 tons. She was therefore pushing $105,000 worth of freight, for the coal sells in New Orleans at $3 50 a ton. The work of propelling these tows is so ingenious that the pilots are handsomely paid. They cannot drive their loads; they merely guide them, and a mistake or bad judgment in a bend may cost thousands of dollars through a wreck. The barges are made of merely inch-and-a-half stuff, cost $700 each, and are seldom used twice. They are sold to wreckers.

This is in the region where the levees, that are said to have cost $150,000,000, line the river-side through whole States—mere banks of earth such as railways are built on where fillings are required. Some of these are far away from the water, and some are close beside it; some are earthy, some are grassy, and some are heaped up with banks of Cherokee roses that blossom in bouquets of hundreds of yards in length. These are the levees into which the crawfish dig and the water eats, and we read of crevasses that follow and destroy fortunes or submerge counties. But they are mere incidents in the laziest, most alluring and refreshing, journey that one tired man ever enjoyed.

COLONIAL VIRGINIA

BY the famous bull of the infamous
Pope Alexander VI. the whole of
North America was given for evermore
to Spain. But our forefathers in England in the days of Queen Elizabeth had
little respect for popes, and still less respect for their bulls. England, though
not esteemed in those days the equal in
military strength of France or Spain, nevertheless occupied an impregnable position; and when such a monarch as Philip
II., with the papal blessing on his enterprise, sent an Invincible Armada to her
shores, with declared intent to enrich her
polity with an Inquisition, and to enliven
the monotony of her social life with periodical *autos-da-fe*, she possessed ample
means of proving practically that the in-
vincibleness of the royal armada was as
much a matter of doubt as the infallible-
ness of the papal decree. Our doughty
ancestors had a theory of their own about
these things, and one of the ways in which
they sought to carry their theory into
practice was by hampering and forestall-
ing the Pope and his lieutenant the Most
Catholic King in the occupancy of the
New World. Of course they had no idea
of the immensity of the victory their proceedings were destined one day to achieve.
But they were guided by a very sound instinct, and they builded better than they
knew.

After the exploring voyages of the Ca-
bots—which were not diligently followed
up—the earliest expeditions of English
mariners to the American coasts were undertaken in great part as measures of hostility to Spain. Here was an excellent
poaching ground for them. Elizabeth's
valiant sea-kings, with swift and sudden
attack invading the harbors of the West
Indies and the Spanish Main, carried off
many a richly laden galleon. Sometimes
they were even bolder than this. In 1587,
Sir Francis Drake sailed with flying colors into the port of Cadiz itself, and burned, sank, or captured more than a hundred vessels designed for the service of
the Invincible Armada of the following
year. Such dangerous exploits used to
be quaintly called "singeing the King of
Spain's beard." But these great men—
the fathers of the English navy, and as
hardy mariners as ever existed—were not
mere privateers. A spirit of scientific curiosity and enthusiastic dreams of com-

mercial empire were joined with their adventurous courage. In 1576, Sir Martin
Frobisher set sail for the Arctic Ocean in
search of a northwestern passage to India.
In a vessel of twenty-five tons burden—
not much larger than the barge of a modern man-of-war—he penetrated as far as
the entrance to Hudson Bay. In 1579,
Sir Francis Drake, having singed the Most
Catholic beard all along the coasts of Chili
and Peru, struck across the equator, and
sailed as far as the coast of Oregon, in the
hope of finding a passage northeasterly
into the Atlantic. Failing in this, he
crossed the Pacific, after having named
our western coast New Albion, and returned home in 1580 by way of the Cape
of Good Hope. This was the second cir-
cumnavigation of the earth, sixty years
after Magellan. In 1583, Sir Humphrey
Gilbert conducted a small company to
Newfoundland, and took possession of the
country in the name of Queen Elizabeth.
As they then proceeded southward toward
the New England coast in search of a favorable place for a settlement, their principal vessel crushed its bows against a
sunken rock, and nearly all hands were
lost. The other two vessels, which in size
were hardly superior to modern pleasure-
yachts, set out to return to England; but
on the way they were overtaken by a terrible storm, and Gilbert's tiny craft was
swallowed up in the waves.

The enterprise in which Gilbert thus
unfortunately perished was prosecuted on
a much wider scale by his half-brother,
the still more famous and still more unfortunate Sir Walter Raleigh. Gilbert's
colony was designed for little more than
a station from which to worry the Spaniards. Raleigh's plan included the founding of a state, the development of agriculture, and the acquisition of immense revenues. He obtained from Elizabeth a grant
of a vast territory, to be called Virginia,
extending vaguely from the Hudson River to the confines of what is now Georgia.
Though he did not visit his new domains
in person, his vessels explored the coast
below Chesapeake Bay, and made on Roanoke Island the first English settlement
in America. Raleigh had learned the art
of war in France under Coligny, and it
was the terrible story of Ribaut and Me-
nendez and Dominique de Gourgues that
first turned his attention to this part of

the world. He thought that he might succeed where Ribaut had failed; and indeed he aroused such interest in England through his explorations and the descriptions of them by Hariot and Hakluyt, that it is hardly improper to regard him as the first founder of the colony of Virginia. Nevertheless, his immediate attempts at making a self-supporting settlement were so disastrous that, after five years of incessant labor, and having lost £40,000 in the enterprise, he made up his mind that such an undertaking was too great for the resources of a single individual, and in 1589 he assigned his rights and privileges to a joint-stock company of merchants and adventurers.

Raleigh's subsequent career shows of how little avail are the brightest talents and most faithful services to insure their possessor against ruin if he happen to have incurred the ill-will of a despotic and unscrupulous ruler. In 1595 Raleigh conducted a voyage of exploration to the Orinoco. In 1596 he was rear-admiral in the fleet which captured Cadiz, and it was chiefly to his sagacity and bravery that the victory—such a humiliating blow to Philip II.—was due. In 1597 he commanded the fleet which captured Fayal. Yet, in spite of all this, one of the first things James I. did on succeeding to the English crown was to arrest Raleigh for high treason, on the charge that he (of all men!) had been plotting with Spain. One of his friends, Lord Cobham, had, in fact, engaged in a conspiracy to dethrone James in favor of his cousin Arabella Stuart, and he had endeavored to obtain money from the Spanish king in aid of his undertaking. On the discovery of the plot, Raleigh was at once suspected, partly because of his acquaintance with Cobham, partly because his old rival the Earl of Essex had years before so poisoned James's mind against him that the king now gladly seized upon the first opportunity to get him into trouble. In seeking to clear himself, Raleigh made some statements which reflected upon Cobham; and when Cobham, who was a selfish and cowardly creature, heard the report of what Raleigh had said, he flew into a rage, and accused Raleigh of having been the prime instigator of the plot. This accusation Cobham soon afterward retracted, and, besides this, the utmost diligence of the crown lawyers could discover no evidence whatever against the great admiral.

But in reading the state trials of the Stuart period, one often has occasion to feel that the common-law maxim, that a man must be presumed innocent until he is proved to be guilty, was read backward, as witches read the Lord's Prayer when they wished to summon the devil. Too often the maxim practically in vogue was that the prisoner must be presumed to be guilty until proved to be innocent; with the further proviso that no amount of evidence could possibly be held to establish his innocence. The bench in England was then as corrupt as it was in New York under the rule of the "Tweed Ring." Judges, and jurymen too, were quick to detect the bent of the royal mind and act in accordance therewith. The scenes at Raleigh's trial were such as to disgrace the memory of the famous Attorney-General Coke, as well as of the time-serving judges who refused to confront Cobham with the prisoner, and without any further evidence, and in spite of the absurdity of the whole charge, condemned him to die the death of a traitor. But the wrath of the people was such that James did not venture to carry out the sentence. The grand old knight was kept shut up in the Tower for more than twelve years, and solaced himself by writing that delightful *History of the World* which has given him a foremost place among the worthies of English prose literature. In 1616, on the intercession of Buckingham, he was at length set free, and placed in command of an expedition to Guiana for the purpose of opening a gold mine. Raleigh had some misgivings about starting on a doubtful adventure without first obtaining a pardon in set form. But Lord Bacon is said to have assured him that the king, having under his broad seal made him admiral of a fleet, with power of martial law over sailors and officers, had substantially condoned all offenses, real or alleged. But in this case I doubt if the worldly-wise and selfish Bacon came much nearer than the sincere and generous Raleigh toward sounding the unfathomable perfidy of the Stuart character. James always cherished a perverse fondness for Spain, and now in particular he had taken it into his head that his son Charles ought to marry the daughter of Philip III. So the Spanish ambassador, Gondomar, wormed out of him all the minutest details of the Guiana expedition, and sent the intelligence without delay to

Madrid. So when the English fleet reached the Orinoco, their exploring party was attacked by the Spaniards, and in the fight which ensued Raleigh's son Walter was slain. Though the English were victorious, the approaches to the mines were too strongly guarded to be carried by the force they had at command; and in such wise was this expedition defeated through the treachery of its own sovereign. Nothing was left for the baffled and brokenhearted admiral but to make his way back to England. His friends the earls of Pembroke and Arundel had guaranteed his return in any event; and he could not run the risk of getting them into trouble. After reaching England, his wife, keenly alive to the danger he was incurring, prevailed upon him to escape to France; but just as the escape was successfully achieved, his chivalrous scruples overcame him, and he returned with sweet serenity to meet the fate which was but too surely threatened. The Spanish court now clamored for Raleigh's death, on the ground that he had undertaken a piratical excursion against a Spanish colony; and now it is worth our while to observe the desperately complicated villainy of the king. It would never do for James to admit this claim of the Spaniards, because he regarded the country about the Orinoco as his own, on the strength of Raleigh's own discoveries twenty years ago. But Gondomar's influence was now supreme, and Spain must be propitiated at whatever cost. So, in utter defiance of common decency, Sir Walter Raleigh was seized and beheaded on the old charge of complicity in the Cobham conspiracy — a charge of which he had already been virtually condoned, and of which, doubtless, neither the king nor any other man in England had ever really believed him to be guilty. Thus, at the hands of the treacherous and cowardly son of Elizabeth's archenemy and rival, perished the last and greatest of the sea-kings who had made her reign illustrious—the statesman whose far-seeing genius first directed the efforts of England toward the colonization of the Western world.

The enterprise which had proved too arduous for Raleigh's unaided powers was nevertheless carried out during Raleigh's lifetime under the leadership of a man who has immortalized the homeliest of names, not only by solid work which no one can fail to rate highly, but also by romantic adventures of the most astonishing sort, for which we have only his own word to go by. The life of Captain John Smith reads like a chapter from *Gil Blas* or *The Cloister and the Hearth*. If half of what he says is true, we may fairly call him the American Roland or Cid, albeit many critics, more shrewd than genial, have felt more like characterizing him as an American Munchausen. Perhaps it is well that it should be so. Perhaps it is well that, even in American history, which for the most part began under the blazing midday sun of historical testimony, there should be left at least one little trace of the twilight of heroic legend. At all events, the historic basis of Smith's career is such that he can never in the remotest future run any serious risk of getting identified with Odysseus, or Indra, or Jack the Giant-Killer; and his historical importance is great enough to justify us in recalling for a moment some of the scenes of his autobiography. Born of a good family in Lincolnshire, he ran away from his studies at the age of sixteen or seventeen, and served some three years in the Netherlands against the Spaniards. Returning to his native place, tired of the society of his fellow-creatures, he made himself a tent of boughs by a brook in the woods some distance from any town, and lived there awhile as an anchorite, not meditating on his sins, however, but on the political affairs of Europe and on the art of war. As the result of these meditations, he made up his mind to go and fight the Turks. In passing through France he was robbed of all he had about him, but his life was saved by a peasant who found him lying, half starved and half frozen, in the forest. He made his way to Marseilles, and embarked with a company of pilgrims for the Levant; but a violent storm arose, which they attributed to their having a heretic on board, and so, like Jonah, the young adventurer was thrown into the sea. He swam ashore, however, and made his way to the Austrian camp in Hungary, near Limbach, which the Turks were besieging. Here he invented a sort of fire-work, called the "fiery dragon," which so annoyed the barbarians that they withdrew. In single combat, for the amusement of the ladies, says the narrative, he slew and beheaded three Turkish champions, one after the other; but in a bloody battle which ensued he was taken prisoner, carried to

Adrianople, and sold as a slave in the market-place, and finally carried off to the Crimea. Here he was dressed in the skin of a wild beast, had an iron collar fastened about his neck, and was cuffed and kicked about like a dog; but one day he rose in rebellion, broke his master's skull with a threshing-stick, dressed up in his clothes, mounted his horse, and fled through the Russian wilderness to Poland, whence he made his adventurous way, with various disguises, through Germany, France, and Spain, to Morocco, where he was at last picked up by an English man-of-war, and after taking part in a fierce battle with two Spanish galleons, made his way back to England just in time to start in the first squadron sent out in 1606 by the London Company for the colonization of Virginia. Through the incompetency of the first two governors, Wingfield and Ratcliffe, the management of the enterprise fell naturally into Smith's hands, and it was only through his sagacity and energy that the colony was prevented from perishing within the first three years through privation and mutiny. In the course of an exploring journey up the Chickahominy, which it was thought might be a strait leading into the Pacific Ocean, an incident occurred which throws some light on our adventurer's character for truthfulness. It is clear that he was captured by the Indians, and was set at liberty or escaped. But he has left two accounts of the affair, one published in the following year, 1608, the other published in 1624. These two accounts are inconsistent with each other in many details, but in particular the first one makes no mention of any danger incurred by Smith, and says nothing whatever about Pocahontas; on the contrary, the Indians are described as having been extremely kind and courteous toward their prisoner. In 1613, Pocahontas was married to an Englishman, and three years afterward she accompanied her husband to England, and at once became the principal object of interest to the fashionable world by reason of the absurd misconception which saw in her an Indian princess, daughter of the "mighty emperor" Powhatan. After a year of fashionable excitement she died; and it is to be observed that in all the frequent contemporary allusions which refer to Pocahontas, down to the time of her death, there is not a word which relates to her heroic rescue of the English explorer. But in Smith's second account of his adventures in Virginia, published in 1624, seven years after the death of the Indian girl, the full story of the rescue is to be found. The natural inference from all this is hardly favorable to the author's credit as a historian. The story in itself, however, is not only not extraordinary, but it is substantially in accordance with Indian usage, so much so that the romance with which it has always been invested is the outcome of a misconception no less complete than that which led the fair dames of London to make obeisance to the dusky squaw as to a princess of imperial lineage. Where a prisoner was about to be put to death, not from any feeling of personal hatred or revenge, or from considerations of savage policy, but merely from the spirit of wanton cruelty in which the Indians' tiger-like nature delighted, it was no very uncommon thing for some one of the tawny gang, moved by pity or admiration, or some unaccountable freak, to interpose in behalf of the victim. Many a poor wretch, already tied to the fatal tree, while the firebrands were heating for his torment, has been rescued from the jaws of death, and adopted either as husband or as brother by some laughing young squaw, or as a son by some bereaved old wrinkled warrior. In such cases the new-comer was allowed entire freedom, and treated like one of the tribe, and opportunities for escape were usually not difficult to find.

Smith left the Jamestown settlement in 1608, ascended Chesapeake Bay, and explored the Potomac, Patapsco, and the Susquehanna, travelling some two thousand miles in an open boat with half a dozen companions; and, first of Englishmen, meeting in friendly parley the invincible Mohawks, whose fleet of bark canoes encountered him upon the Chesapeake. In the following year he was badly wounded by an accidental explosion of gunpowder, and obliged to return to England for surgical treatment. The colony which he left at Jamestown, numbering some five hundred souls, relapsed into anarchy after his departure. Famine and desertion thinned their ranks until scarcely a hundred were left. The fate which had overtaken Raleigh's colony of Roanoke seemed to be awaiting them, and in their despair they were even about to abandon the country, when, in June, 1610, Lord Delaware arrived with re-enforcements. In the following year Sir Thomas Dale brought over more men and supplies, the thieves and mutineers were checked with a high hand, and systematic cultivation of the soil was begun in earnest. It was not long before negro slaves were introduced. The land was laid out in large plantations, and the tobacco crop became a prolific source of wealth. Emigrants began to come over at the rate of more than a thousand a year; and so strong had the colony grown by 1622 that a terrible massacre, directed by the successor of Powhatan, in which nearly four hundred persons lost their lives, produced but a slight and temporary effect.

By this time the prosperity of the colony had begun to excite the jealousy of the king. With his perverse friendship for Spain, James was not inclined to look favorably upon the attempts of his subjects to colonize America, but one consideration had prevailed upon him to allow such attempts to proceed. It was generally understood that colonies founded in America were to be under the direct control of the king, and that Parliament had no authority to meddle with their affairs; and from this the king was not unnaturally led to infer that in course of time the crown might gain assistance from its loyal colonies in carrying on its perennial struggle with the representatives of the people at home. Accordingly James had consented to the formation of the Virginia Company with ample powers; but by 1623 he had come to regard these powers as too extensive to be intrusted to any private company, and so he ordered the directors to give up their charter. On their refusal the king brought suit against the company on a writ of *quo warranto*, and at the same time illegally seized upon their papers, so that they might have no means of defending themselves. Commissioners were sent to Virginia to collect evidence against the good management of the company. No such evidence was procured. But in those evil days of Stuart tyranny one of the worst features was the subserviency of the courts, whereby the king could generally obtain almost any decision upon which he had set his heart.

So the company was dissolved; and henceforth the affairs of the colony were administered by a governor and two councils, one sitting in Virginia and the other in England. The governor and the members of both councils were all appointed by the king, and in the absence of a charter the colonists had no security whatever against arbitrary government. This suppression of the Virginia Company was the first high-handed act of tyranny perpetrated by the English crown in relation to American affairs; but events turned in such a way that it probably favored, instead of checking, the independent spirit of the colony. For the next sixty years the Stuart kings had so much to occupy their attention at home, and found it such hard work to keep on the throne, that the Virginians were left pretty much to themselves, and probably enjoyed a greater share of liberty than they would have done under the continual supervision of a private company interested in making money out of the colony. Indeed, in 1639 they expressed themselves as unwilling to have the company revived. Unlike the settlers of New England, the Virginians were in the main loyal in their feelings toward the Stuart kings. But after the execution of Charles I. they submitted without remonstrance to be governed by a Parliamentary commission. In fact, they cared very little by whom they were technically governed, so long as they were allowed practically to govern themselves. The internal political constitution of Virginia at that time was in some respects the most liberal the world had yet seen. As Mr. Bancroft observes, "Virginia was the first state in the world, composed of separate boroughs, diffused over an extensive surface, where representation was organized on the principle of universal suffrage."[*] The colony taxed itself, and enjoyed practical freedom of trade; and under such conditions it flourished so that by the end of the seventeenth century it had become a really powerful state, as colonial states were then reckoned, with a white population of nearly 60,000, and perhaps 2000 negroes. During the first half of the eighteenth century, however, the growth of the colony became still more conspicuous. At the time of the Seven Years' War the population exceeded 400,000 souls, of whom more than half were negroes.

From the beginning the white population of Virginia was almost entirely English, and such it seems to have remained. A few Huguenots came over from France toward the close of the sev-

---

[*] Bancroft, *Hist. U. S.*, i. 175.

enteenth century, and these were followed, within a few years, by a considerable number of Scotch Presbyterians from the north of Ireland, who made for the frontier, and began to settle upon the eastern slope of the mountains. Some Germans, too, came in from Pennsylvania. But all these foreign elements taken together can hardly have amounted to two per cent. of the white population, and in no way produced any appreciable effect upon the character of the colony, which was thoroughly English in blood, as well as in manners and laws.

The first colonists, who came over with Smith, were for the most part idle adventurers, like the Spaniards who in the preceding century had flocked to the standards of Cortez and Pizarro, drawn thither mainly by the belief that America was a sort of fairy-land, where great riches could be obtained without labor. It was not these adventurers, however, that laid the foundations of the greatness of Virginia. As soon as it had become apparent that solid wealth was to be obtained from large plantations of tobacco, a very different class of people began to come in. The great planters of Virginia were for the most part men of high social position—younger sons of noble and powerful families, such as England from that day to this has been continually sending forth to play a prominent part in all the outlying regions of the world. The smaller planters were mostly recruited from the ranks of that self-reliant, indomitable yeomanry which for so many ages was the pride and strength of the mother country. Many of these settlers were Puritans; but after the overthrow of Charles I. the royalist party sent out an increasing number of emigrants, until the Cavaliers acquired the ascendency in the colony. In 1651, the Governor, Sir William Berkeley, even suggested that Charles II. himself should seek a refuge among his loyal Virginians.

The tendency toward an aristocratic type of society, thus already faintly manifested in these early days, was made irresistible by the economic conditions under which the colony was established. Not only was the labor of Virginia purely agricultural, but the only agriculture worth speaking of was the raising of tobacco. In this pursuit the entire energies of the colony were absorbed to an extraordinary degree; and from this fact have flowed many of the peculiarities by which Virginian society has always been characterized. The cultivation of tobacco on a great scale required immense plantations and an abundance of cheap labor; and as among the white immigrants cheap labor was not forth-coming in sufficient quantity, recourse was at once had to the slave-trade. The first negro slaves were brought into the colony in 1619. For some time their numbers increased but slowly, but toward the end of the seventeenth century the increase became very rapid, until in the middle of the eighteenth, as already observed, they had come to outnumber the white population. At this time the rapidity of the increase had begun to awaken serious alarm, and it was felt that something must be done to restrict the importation of slaves. At the time of the Revolutionary war projects of negro emancipation were freely discussed in Virginia; but nothing came of the discussion, and after the abolition of the foreign slave-trade in 1808 had increased the demand for Virginia-bred slaves in the States further south, the very idea of emancipation faded out of memory. It is generally admitted that the treatment of the slaves by their masters was mild and humane. The cultivation of tobacco in Virginia did not work such a terrible drain on human life as the cultivation of sugar in the West Indies, or the raising of cotton in the Gulf States after the invention of the gin. It was more profitable to take care of the slave than to work him to death. At the same time the negro was not regarded as having any rights which the white man was bound to respect: he was regarded simply as a beast of burden. Slaves were not allowed to leave their plantations except with passports duly signed by the master. Absconding slaves were formally outlawed, and a price was set upon their heads; or, if caught by the sheriff, they were to suffer death or nameless mutilation at his good pleasure. There was no penalty attached to the murder of a slave by his master, but if he were killed by any one else, the master could recover his value, just as in case of damage done to a dog or a horse.

Viewed in connection with the generally mild treatment of slaves by their masters, the ferocious character of these legislative enactments bears witness to the alarm with which the rapid increase of the colored population was regarded. Until the end of the seventeenth century, as already observed, there were but few negroes in Virginia, and cheap labor was obtained from other sources. Convicted criminals were sent over in great numbers from the mother country, as in later times they were sent to Botany Bay, until the system was made the subject of serious complaint on the part of the colony. On their arrival they were indented as servants for a term of years. Kidnapping was also at this time in England an extensive and lucrative business. Young boys and girls, usually of the lowest class of society, were seized by press-gangs on the streets of London and Bristol and other English ports, hurried on board ship, and carried over to Virginia to work on the plantations or as house servants. These poor wretches were not, indeed, sold into slavery, but they passed into a state of servitude which might easily be prolonged almost indefinitely by avaricious or cruel masters. The period of their indenture was short—usually not more than four years; but the ordinary penalty for serious offenses, such as were very likely to be committed, was a lengthening of the time during which they were to serve. Among such offenses the most serious were insubordination or attempts to escape, while of a more venial character were thievery, or unchaste conduct, or attempts to make money on their own account. Their lives were in theory protected by law, but where an indented servant came to his death from prolonged ill-usage, or from excessive punishment, or even from sudden violence, it was practically impossible to get a verdict against the master. The lash was inflicted upon the indented servant with scarcely less compunction than upon the purchased slave; and in general the condition of the former seems to have been nearly as miserable as that of the latter, save that the servitude of the negro was perpetual, while that of the white man was liable to come to an end. For him Pandora's box had not quite spilled out the last of its contents.

In the majority of cases, however, it may be questioned whether the release of the indented white servant brought with it any marked improvement in his fortunes. In England, indeed, there was an impression that the aristocracy of Virginia was recruited from the ranks of these kidnapped paupers and convicts, as is shown not only in the writings of Defoe

and Mrs. Aphra Behn, but even in works of a more serious character, pretending to scholarly research. Malachi Postlethwayte, author of several works on commerce, wrote, in 1750 or thereabouts: "Even your transported felons, sent to Virginia instead of Tyburn, thousands of them, if we are not misinformed, have, by turning their hands to industry and improvement, and, which is best of all, to honesty, become rich, substantial planters and merchants, settled large families, and been famous in the country; nay, we have seen many of them made magistrates, officers of militia, captains of good ships, and masters of good estates."* A few years ago, in the time of our great civil war, one used to meet with illustrations of the survival of this false impression in occasional statements of English newspapers to the effect that "the citizens of the United States were the offspring of the vagabonds and felons of Europe."† It is needless to say that the worthy Postlethwayte had been grossly misinformed. Now and then one of this wretched class of indented white servants recruited from the jails and slums of London may, through superior ability and under exceptional circumstances, have succeeded in working his way up to the ownership of a plantation, so that his descendants would be reckoned in with the good society of the colony; but such instances must have been extremely rare. As a general rule, these persons on their release from servitude became irreclaimable vagabonds. The fact that manual labor was a badge of servitude, while they were by nature and experience unfitted to perform any work of a higher sort, was of itself sufficient to prevent them from doing any work at all, save when compelled by actually threatening starvation. And as manual labor came to be more and more completely relegated to an inferior race of men, this wretched position of the mean white men became worse and worse. They were a lazy, shiftless set, whom even the negroes regarded with contempt. The negro slave might at least take a certain sort of pride in belonging to the establishment of a powerful or wealthy master, and from this point of view society might be said to have a place for him, even though he possessed no legal rights. But

* Postlethwayte's *Dictionary of Commerce*, vol. ii., p. 319.

† Whitmore, *The Cavalier Dismounted*, p. 17.

the white freedman was little better than an outcast. The negro might be like a Sudra, but the mean white was simply a Pariah. On the frontier he relapsed into savagery, if such a change could in his case be properly called a relapse. In the midst of the colony he was wont to earn a precarious livelihood or a violent death by gambling, betting, and thieving, now and then engaging in bolder enterprises of arson or highway robbery. At his best he was but a lounger in taverns or at horse-races. Crimes against person and property, which were much more frequent in Virginia than in the Middle and Northern colonies, were usually committed by men of this class. In these characteristics we may easily recognize the attributes of an order of humanity which has not yet become utterly extinct on American soil, though its days have for some time since been numbered. This order of humanity, as I shall show hereafter, grew up in the other Southern colonies as well as in Virginia, and from precisely the same causes. These felons from Newgate and these victims of the kidnappers, sent over to be flogged and starved for a while on tobacco plantations, and then turned adrift to prey upon society, were undoubtedly in great part the progenitors of the most degraded portion of the English race—the so-called "white trash" of the Southern States.

The great planters, the small planters, the negro slaves, and the half servile, half outlawed "white trash" may thus be regarded as constituting four classes of society in the colony of Virginia. But between the upper two classes it would be difficult to draw a hard and fast line. In origin, as already observed, the great planters were mainly English rural gentry, the small planters were mainly English yeomen. Even in England these two classes shaded into one another; there was not so very much difference between a small country squire and a wealthy farmer. What difference there was might consist in the fact that the squire's great-grandfather might have been fourth or fifth son of a peer, while the yeoman's ancestry would be reckoned back to some Saxon or Danish freeholder; but both alike were descended from men who had never known what it was to bow down before a task-master or a despot. In Virginia both alike became land-holders and owners of slaves, they mingled together in society, and their families intermarried.

It was otherwise with those middle-class Englishmen who came to the colony to engage in trade. Like all rural aristocracies, the Virginia planters despised tradesmen and manufacturers, and looked upon the management of country estates as the only occupation worthy of gentlemen. But the tradesmen and merchants were few in numbers, and of manufacturers there were none. The absorption of the people in tobacco-planting was so complete that there was no room for the development of manufactures and commerce.

One principal result of this devotion to tobacco culture was the absence of town life. In 1765 there was nothing like a city in the colony. The largest town was Norfolk, with about 7000 inhabitants; Jamestown consisted of half a dozen houses; Williamsburg, which was at once capital and university town, contained some 200 wooden houses, and its streets were unpaved. Richmond had hardly a more substantial existence than Martin Chuzzlewit's "Eden." The Legislature, thinking this state of things hardly creditable to the colony, labored assiduously to cure the evil; but its attempts met with no better success than ordinarily awaits the efforts of legislatures to guide the progress of society. Neither bounties nor direct orders to build were of any avail. To make towns on paper was as easy as to make a promissory note; but nobody would settle in the towns. Most of the county seats consisted simply of the court-house, flanked by the jail, the wretched country store, and the still more wretched country inn. As there were no centres of business, the tradesmen were in the habit of travelling about from plantation to plantation and peddling their wares. One would suppose that the necessity for exporting the great quantities of tobacco that were raised would of itself have given rise to a considerable class of thriving merchants. But the manner in which the Virginia planter disposed of his crops was peculiar. Most of the greater plantations lay near the wide and deep rivers of which Virginia has so many; and each planter would have his own wharf, from which his own slaves might load the tobacco on to the vessels that were to carry it to England. If the plantation lay at some distance from a navigable river, the tobacco was conveyed to the nearest creek, and tied down upon a raft of canoes, and so floated and paddled down stream until some head of navigation was reached, where a warehouse was ready to receive it. The vessels which carried away this tobacco usually paid for it in all sorts of manufactured articles that might be needed upon the plantations. Every manufactured article that required the least skill or nicety of workmanship was imported in this way from England, in ships of which the owners, masters, and crew were generally either Englishmen or New-Englanders. In the colony no manufacturing was done, and such rude carpentry or smithery as was needed was taken in hand either by specially trained slaves on the plantations, or by white mechanics who travelled about the country in quest of jobs. As the traders were mostly peddlers, so the artisans were for the most part tinkers.

We have just seen how the rivers and creeks were used as highways of traffic: for a long time they were the only highways, and the vessel or the canoe was the only kind of vehicle, public or private, in which it was possible to get about with ease and safety. Until after the middle of the eighteenth century there were but few roads save bridle-paths, and such as there were became impassable in rainy weather. There were also but few bridges, and these were very likely to be unsound, while the ferry-boats were apt to be leaky. It was often necessary for the traveller to swim across the stream, with a fair chance of getting drowned, and more than a fair chance of losing his horse. The course of the bridle-path often became so obscure that it was necessary to blaze the trees. It was not uncommon for people to lose their way and find themselves obliged to stay overnight in the woods, perhaps with the howls of the wolf and panther sounding in their ears. The highway robber was even a more uncomfortable customer to meet than these beasts of prey; and in those days, when banking was in its infancy, and travellers used to carry gold coins sewed under the lining of their waistcoats, the highwayman enjoyed opportunities which in this age of railways and check-books are denied him. In 1777, a young Rhode Island merchant, Elkanah Watson, armed with a sabre and pair of pistols, journeyed on horseback all the way from Providence to Charleston in South Carolina, with several hundred pounds in gold quilted into his coat. In

seventy days he accomplished the whole distance of 1243 miles, fortunately without encountering any more serious mishaps than being arrested as a British spy in Pennsylvania, and having a fight with a large bear in North Carolina; and he has left us a narrative of his journey, which is as full of instruction as it is of interest.

The Virginian traveller, however, in colonial times, was not likely to carry any very large sums of money concealed on his person, for he dealt in a circulating medium too bulky for that. The current money of the Virginian was tobacco. The prices of all articles of merchandise were quoted in pounds of tobacco. In tobacco taxes were assessed and all wages and salaries were paid. This use of tobacco as a circulating medium and as a standard of values was begun in the earliest days of the colony, when coin was scarce, and the structure of society was simple enough to permit a temporary return to the primitive practice of barter. Under such circumstances tobacco was obviously the most convenient article by which to estimate values. But with the further growth of the colony the financial and social results of the use of such a medium became disastrous. People rushed to the cultivation of tobacco in somewhat the same spirit as that which in recent days prompted the rush to the gold mines of California and Australia; and cereal crops, which might here and there have been introduced with great benefit to the colony, as the example of Maryland well shows, were entirely neglected. But, besides this, tobacco was a highly speculative crop. The returns were usually immense, but they fluctuated considerably from year to year, and this fluctuation affected the value of every article that was bought and sold throughout the colony. No one could estimate from one year to another, with any approach to accuracy, what the purchasing power of his income was going to be. The inevitable result of this was wild extravagance in living, chronic debt, relieved by frequent bankruptcy, persistent evasion of creditors, and the destruction of that trait of character which among a commercial people is known as financial integrity, and prized as one of the cardinal virtues.

This extravagance in living was further stimulated by the regal hospitality for which the great planters early became famous. Apart from politics, these country squires found but little business wherewith to occupy their time. The direct supervision of the slaves was ordinarily intrusted to overseers, and the masters were thus secured in the enjoyment of ample leisure, which men of noble ambition, such as Jefferson and Madison, could turn to good profit in cultivating their minds. But to men of more common mould this ample leisure became monotonous, and in such a society as that here depicted, with no town life, no roads or inns worth speaking of, and no amusements save horseracing, the entertainment of guests by the month together was regarded both as a duty and as a privilege. Every planter kept open house, and provided for his visitors with unstinted hand. The style of living was extremely generous, and often splendid. The houses were spacious and solidly built, sometimes of brick or stone, but more often of wood. Panelled wainscots of oak and carved oaken chimneypieces were common, and the rooms were furnished with the handsomest chairs and tables and cabinets that could be brought over from England. The dress, too, of both men and women was rich and costly, and the latest London fashions were carefully followed. Silver plate, elegant china, and choice wines were commonly to be found at these great manor-houses, and the stables were stocked with horses of the finest breed.

The part of the house that was least amply provided for was, no doubt, the library, which usually contained a few English classic authors, with perhaps Montaigne and Le Sage. The Virginians were not a reading people, and nothing could be much poorer than the sort of education that was provided for the children. The long distances between the plantations, and the absence of towns, made it impossible to establish such a system of public schools as flourished in New England. In 1671, Sir William Berkeley, the friend of the Stuarts, said he thanked God that there were no free schools in the colony, and that there were not likely to be any. In 1692, James Blair, a Scotch clergyman of considerable learning and great energy and public spirit, succeeded in establishing William and Mary College, the second in age among American universities, and so long as he remained its president the institution flourished, and its influence seems to have been good so far as

it extended; but it stood quite alone, unsupported by any schools, and it seems to have degenerated sadly as soon as the strong hand of its founder was taken off, until it came to be merely a second-rate high school. There was no intellectual life in the colony, and previous to the Revolutionary war there was absolutely no literature worthy of notice. The first newspaper did not appear till 1736.

The intellectual stimulus which schools failed to furnish to the colony was not supplied by the clergy. The parson in old Virginia belonged to the class of fox-hunting, wine-bibbing parsons, of which there were so many examples in the mother country at the same time. The general tone of the English Church during the first half of the eighteenth century was very low, even in England; and the peculiar conditions of existence in Virginia did not tend to raise the tone of the clergy. The Episcopal Church was supported by the government in Virginia until the Revolution, the governor, as vicegerent of the sovereign, being the head of the Church. The country was divided into parishes, after the English fashion, and the same functions of local government were discharged by the vestries in Virginia as in England. The vestries corresponded to the New England town-meetings as far as was possible in view of the vast difference between the concentrated life of New England and the scattered life of Virginia. Even under the conditions under which they worked in Virginia, the political value of these vestry meetings was very great; and we may point to them as the one great benefit which came to the colony from the attempt to establish the English Church system there. From no other point of view can the attempt be said to have wrought any good. The degraded condition of the Church and its ministers afforded an excellent field for the labors of the Wesleyans, and to such good purpose did they work that by the time of the Revolution two-thirds of the people in the colony had become Dissenters. When the Revolution came, the Dissenters were all to be found on the patriotic side, while in the Episcopal Church were many loyalists; and this contrast was all that was needed to break down the Church establishment entirely, and to cast upon it irredeemable discredit.

The other learned professions in Virginia, before the middle of the eighteenth century, stood at no higher level than the clerical profession. Medicine was perhaps in the most degraded condition of all, its practice being largely left to itinerant barbers and quacks. The lawyers, too, were at first men without learning or character. But shortly before the Revolution a great change had been wrought in this department; and we find the profession graced by such names as those of Henry and Jefferson, until at last in John Marshall the old colony gave to the United States one of the very greatest jurists that the English race has ever produced.

One chief cause of this rapid and splendid development of legal talent in the colony was undoubtedly the close connection which obtains between legal and political activity. The political life of Virginia was always healthy and vigorous. Unlike the men of New England in many respects, the men of Virginia yielded not a jot to them in their hatred of despotism, or in the value which they set upon self-government. They were fully imbued with all the deep and sound political instincts by the aid of which the English race has learned to rule itself and to guide the world. And the royal government of the colony afforded them an excellent school for political training. The whole political history of Virginia down to the time of the Stamp Act is a dreary history of bickerings between the governor appointed by the crown and the Assembly elected by the people. A dreary history one may well call it, inasmuch as its details can have no more interest, either from a dramatic or from a philosophical point of view, than the details of any petty lawsuit about a breach of contract or a disputed right of way across a field. To mention the names of the commonplace men who were sent over from time to time to govern Virginia, and to recount their paltry squabbles, would be to write history after a fashion which is happily becoming obsolete. Chronological tables and the monographs of local antiquarians are the places where facts of this sort may best be found specifically stated. The value of such facts as materials is very great; but the business of the historian is to set forth their import, not to recount them in detail, unless they possess some human interest of their own. Looking at the matter in this light, the colonial annals of Virginia may be passed over with little ceremony. The point which chiefly in-

terests us to-day is that all these dismal bickerings were of signal use to the people in training them to ascertain what their rights were under the English constitution, and to defend themselves in the possession of these rights with intelligence and dignity. The remarkable advance in political skill achieved by the Virginians during the first half of the eighteenth century is illustrated by the contrast between the management of Bacon's rebellion and the management of the great constitutional struggle which culminated in the independence of the United States. The rebellion headed by Nathaniel Bacon in 1676 is the one conspicuous event that breaks the dead monotony of Virginian history down to the time of the French war. It was a rebellion in which the passions of the people were strongly enlisted, and for good reason, yet it instantly collapsed upon the loss of its leader.

Bacon's rebellion was a consequence of the oppression wrought in the colony by the infamous government of Charles II., and by the hands of that Sir William Berkeley who took such pleasure in the thought that the Virginians were not likely to possess any means of educating themselves. Charles began by enforcing the Navigation Act, prohibiting the importation of any merchandise into the colony except in English vessels navigated by Englishmen. An attempt was next made to do away with the popular election of representatives. Under the influence of the loyalist feeling called forth by the restoration of the monarchy, the Assembly elected in 1661 contained a large majority of friends of the Stuarts—of men who believed in prerogative and in divine right; and the governor, having thus secured a legislature which was quite to his mind, kept it alive for fifteen years, until 1676, simply by adjourning it from year to year, and refusing to issue writs for a new election. The first act of this royalist Assembly was to institute such a vigorous persecution against all Dissenters as to lead within two years to an abortive Puritan conspiracy and the hanging of several of its leaders. In 1669, the king granted the whole of Virginia to Lords Arlington and Culpepper for the remainder of the century, at the same time giving them the right of appointing all public surveyors, so that the very titles of the colonists to the lands which they occupied were thrown into jeopardy. Thus threatened in their religion, in their trade, and in their homes, the colonists were ripe for rebellion, when all at once the horrors of the tomahawk and scalping-knife were added to their other troubles. In 1672, after a fearful struggle of twenty years' duration, the Senecas of New York had overthrown their kinsmen the Susquehannocks, and driven them from their territory at the head of the Chesapeake. Slowly retreating southward, the defeated savages at first engaged in a war with Maryland, and afterward, in the summer of 1675, invaded Virginia. They spread themselves all over the country, from the Potomac to the James, burning and murdering, and carrying terror to every household. After this state of things had lasted several months, and driven the colonists into frenzy, the sagacious governor, for reasons best known to himself, suddenly disbanded a large force that had been gathered for the purpose of chastising the Indians, and "as a consequence the country was laid waste; one parish in Rappahannock County, which on the 24th of January, 1676, consisted of seventy-one plantations, was within the next seventeen days reduced to eleven."* At last, after nearly four hundred scalps had been taken by the savages, the people raised a small volunteer force without authority from the governor, and by acclamation put it under the leadership of Nathaniel Bacon, a wealthy young Englishman of good family and liberal education, who had but just come over to Virginia. As Bacon marched against the Susquehannocks, Governor Berkeley proclaimed him a rebel, and started with a small force in pursuit of him. This insane conduct aroused the whole country to rebellion, and Berkeley was obliged not only to retreat, but to issue writs for a general election, and to promise a redress of grievances. Bacon was elected to the new Assembly, which was decidedly anti-Stuart in temper, and it was not long before he had come to control it entirely. An eloquent memorial was sent to the king, recounting the oppressions under which his faithful subjects in Virginia had suffered, and Bacon once more marched against the Indians. In the midst of a brilliant campaign he learned that Berkeley had once more proclaimed him a rebel, whereupon, leaving his work on the frontier, he instantly marched upon Jamestown, and took possession of the government, while

Berkeley fled in dismay. A third time, after settling affairs at the capital, did Bacon set forth to overwhelm the Indians, and no sooner had he got out of sight than Berkeley came forward and resumed the administration of the colony. Again Bacon returned to Jamestown, captured the sixteen or eighteen houses of which the capital consisted, and burned them to the ground, that the town might no longer afford a shelter to the tyrant. His two principal supporters, Drummond and Lawrence, who owned the best two houses, set on fire each his own dwelling with his own hand. But a few days after this, Bacon was seized with a malarial fever, and died, and so the rebellion instantly collapsed. Virginian politics were still in that undeveloped condition in which everything depended upon the fate of the leader. Bacon's principal followers were tried by court-martial, and hanged as soon as sentence was pronounced. "You are very welcome," said Berkeley, with a low bow, as the wealthy Drummond was brought before him. "I would rather have had a visit from you than from any other man in Virginia. You shall be hanged in half an hour." Drummond and twenty-one others were put to death, and three died of cruel treatment received in prison. On hearing of these troubles, Charles II. issued a proclamation in which Berkeley was roundly censured for his cruelty, and especially for acting too much on his own discretion. "The old fool," observed the king, "has taken away more lives in that naked country than I for the murder of my father."* The too zealous governor was recalled in disgrace, but not a single point was gained by the people of the colony. The political results of the disturbance were rather disastrous than otherwise. Assemblies were henceforth to be called together only once in two years, and were to sit but fourteen days, while the universal suffrage was restricted by a property qualification. All the acts of Bacon's Assembly were repealed, all the old grievances were renewed, and many estates were confiscated into the bargain. The governors who succeeded Berkeley were as a rule no better than he, and from this time down to the passage of the Stamp Act the political history of Virginia is simply the story of a protracted brawl between the governors and their Assemblies. But this brawl-

* Bancroft, i. 545.

* Bancroft, i. 556.

ing, as I have said, afforded an admirable political discipline for the people. The government of England, moreover, was felt to be a continual source of irritation. In the arduous work of securing the independence and providing for the future stability of the American Union her part was second to none.

THE SOUTHERN GATEWAY OF THE ALLEGHANIES

IT is the custom to speak of this continent as the New World, but modern science has discovered it to be in reality the old one. The rocks give evidence that it was in existence anterior to the time when Europe and Asia first emerged from their long bath of salt-water; and hence it is in America that the explorer must look for the remains of really old cities. Here, accordingly, he finds them "older than the hills"—being entombed in them—and strewn so thickly over the Ohio and Mississippi valleys as to bespeak a population acquainted with many of the arts of civilization long before the age of history.

Of these remains, among the most remarkable are those which have been discovered at and near Chattanooga, in Tennessee. The early settlers found here, near the site of the present depot of the Western and Atlanta Railroad, an immense mound filled with human bones and warlike implements, evidently the relics of some great battle fought in very ancient times for the possession of this pass through the mountains. Here, too, are traces of a large city, which doubtless existed far back in the twilight ages, before Troy was founded, or the Asiatic people began the study of the dead languages at the Tower of Babel. These facts are interesting, as they point to the conclusion that Chattanooga has been the home of three successive races, with perhaps an unbroken existence since the time of the mound-builders. They also indicate that those vanished people chose this as the site of a city for the same reason that the Cherokees made it a stronghold, and the modern engineer has laid here the tracks of eight important railways—because it is the southern gateway of the Alleghanies.

The Appalachian chain of mountains divides in West Virginia into two parallel ranges—the Alleghanies on the east, and the Cumberland on the west, and these, converging again at Chattanooga, are broken through by the Tennessee, which is here a broad river, already fed by half a dozen navigable streams that drain wide and fertile regions. The course of the river from this point to the Ohio is northwest, and hence it must form a link in any through line of water communication between the Northwestern and South Atlantic States. Chattanooga commands this river, and also the great Appalachian valleys which extend through Virginia, Tennessee, Georgia, and Alabama; and the topography of the country is such that no practicable connection between the southwest and northeast can be had except at this crossing of the Tennessee. The location is the apex of an inverted triangle, whose diverging lines reach to the far northeast and northwest, and hence nature has distinctly marked it out as the site of a great city.

Though itself only seven hundred feet above the sea, Chattanooga is surrounded by mountains, and in the midst of natural scenery as grand and picturesque as any in this country. The best near view of the town is from Cameron Hill, but from the summit of Lookout Mountain, only two and a half miles away, the prospect is of almost unparalleled magnificence. The eye there ranges over portions of five States, across spreading forests, cultivated fields, scattered farm-houses, and thickly settled towns, nestling among high mountains, which roll away in gigantic billows, as if they were the crested waves of some fearfully disturbed ocean, arrested and petrified in its onward sweep ages before man was created. The tall cliffs of Cumberland Gap, one hundred and thirty miles northeast, may be distinctly seen, and through the whole wide landscape winds, like a silver thread, the beautiful Tennessee—now hidden by some overhanging wood, now emerging into some grass-covered valley, and ever broadening as it comes, till it sweeps past the city in a rushing torrent half a mile in width. Then, as if loath to leave the abodes of men, it turns back upon itself in a sharp curve, forming what—from its resemblance to a human foot—is called Moccasin Bend, and then it plunges into a narrow gorge between the jutting crags of Walden's Ridge and Raccoon Mountain, and winds again its tortuous way till it is lost to sight in the far northwest, amid scenery that is beautiful beyond description. In a broad plain at the base of Lookout lies the scattered city, bathed for a distance of four miles by the winding river, and encircled completely with mountains—Walden's Ridge on the north, towering upward a thousand feet, Missionary Ridge on the east, rising in sharp acclivities only two and a half miles away, and Lookout, at the same distance on the south, soaring nearly eighteen hundred feet into the air. Beautiful the scene is in repose; but how sublime it must have appeared in war! So grand was it that Sherman says, "Many a time, in the midst of the carnage and noise, I could not help stopping to look across that vast field of battle to admire its sublimity."

Every acre of land and water within a radius of ten miles of the present city is pregnant with events worthy of a place in the nation's history. I refer not only to the conflicts of recent years, on which hung the fate of the Union, but to those also of an earlier time, when the white man met the red, and John Sevier, with a handful of riflemen, routed the "hosts of Wyuca" on the identical spot where, eighty years later, Hooker had the skirmish with the Confederates which is known as the "battle above the clouds." The actors in those early events were few; but some of them were of the order of heroes. Their story, if rightly written, would form one of the most thrilling pages in our history; and what they did had a most important bearing on American destiny, for it was they—this handful of riflemen in buckskin leggings and hunting shirts—who decided the long conflict between civilization and savagery which was waged beyond the Alleghanies.

This is not the place to tell their history, but without straying from my subject I may briefly refer to one of their achievements, for it led directly to the subsequent transfer of this region to the whites, and thus opened Chattanooga to civilized settlement.

In the time of the Revolution this region was tenanted by a fierce tribe of Indians called Chickamaugas. The first settlers of Nashville came into collision with them when they took their perilous way down the Tennessee to that remote outpost of civilization, and for many years they waged an unrelenting war upon the whites. Time and again Sevier invaded their strongholds at and near Chattanooga, burned their towns, destroyed their crops, and drove the bravest of their warriors like frightened deer to the mountains. But they could not be subdued until Sevier could discover their secret fastnesses. Hiding in them till the storm was over, the miscreants would again emerge into the daylight, rebuild their birch-bark cabins, and resume their barbarous warfare.

For eighteen years they were the terror of the entire border. Sevier was wellnigh everywhere, but even his sleepless vigilance could not guard every scattered dwelling. Issuing in small parties, these wretches would fall at midnight upon some unprotected farm-house, plunder and slay the occupants, and be back in their inaccessible haunts before pursuit could be undertaken. Every white man prayed for vengeance upon them, but until their secret haunts were known the prayer could not be answered. At last, however, came the stripling David who was to meet this Goliath of Gath, and through him the power of the Chickamaugas was broken.

LOOKOUT MOUNTAIN AND MOCCASIN BEND FROM THE PINE WOODS OF CAMERON HILL.

He was a boy of fifteen, named Joseph Brown, and his story is a remarkable instance of long-studied vengeance in one so young; but space will allow me to refer to only two of its incidents. His father had been awarded some lands in the vicinity of Nashville for services in the Revolution, and in 1788 he set out, with his family, to settle upon them. Within a few miles of Chattanooga his boat was suddenly surrounded by about forty Indian canoes, and in a few moments his headless body lay at the bottom of the Tennessee. His two oldest sons and four other young men were at once murdered, and his wife and four younger children made prisoners. Joseph's captor was a young half-breed brave named Chia-chatt-alla, who spared his life that he might be the slave of his mother, a degraded French woman who had been brought up and married among the Chickamaugas. He took Joseph to her cabin, and then returned to the boat to secure his share of the plunder. He had scarcely gone when there appeared at the door of the cabin Cutte-atoy, the head chief of the small town of Tuskegee, opposite Chattanooga, with a dozen of his warriors, demanding the boy from the French woman. He said the lad was old enough to notice everything, and if allowed to live would escape, and some day pilot there an army to destroy them all. The boy could not understand his words, but he did his actions, for the savage very soon drew his knife and stepped forward to despatch him. But the woman threw herself between them, declaring the lad should not be killed in her cabin. To this the chief assented, and seizing Joseph, he pitched him headlong among a circle of warriors who stood outside the doorway. The boy thought his last moment had come, and fell upon his knees, saying the words of Stephen, "Lord Jesus, receive my spirit." A dozen knives and tomahawks gleamed in the air above him, but they did not fall, for again the woman sprang before the boy, declaring now that he should not be murdered. The Indians tore her away, but just then one of them proposed that the lad should be stripped of his clothes, lest they should be stained, and so ruined, by his execution. All this while Joseph had been upon his knees; and now the woman, regardless in her fury of her personal safety, turned fiercely upon the chieftain, and threatened him with the vengeance of Chia-chatt-alla if he should take the life of his captive. At last she had hit upon the right argument. By Cherokee law the boy's life could not be taken without consent of his captor. Life for life was their code; hence the chief's own life would be forfeit to Chia-chatt-alla. Incited by his hag of a mother, might he not exact of Cutte-atoy the penalty? This is probably what the chief thought, for he suddenly lifted the boy from his knees and handed him over to the woman, retaining, however, his clothes, all but his trousers.

For more than a year the boy was a prisoner among the Chickamaugas, enduring all sorts of hardships, but meanwhile discovering all their hiding-places in the mountains. Then he was liberated by John Sevier, and returned to his friends in South Carolina.

Then the words of Cutte-atoy came to him: "He is old enough to notice everything, and some day he will escape and pilot an army here." Again and again the words came to the boy, till the idea became his controlling thought. Gradually then it began to dawn upon him that God had saved his life for a purpose, and that purpose was vengeance upon the Chickamaugas.

But he kept his thoughts to himself, for experience had taught him to be silent and patient and wary. So he waited till he was nearly nineteen, and had grown to the stature of manhood. Then he proposed to his mother to carry out his father's intention of settling on their lands near Nashville. This he did to be within striking distance of the Chickamaugas.

They travelled overland to Nashville, and on his father's lands the boy, not yet nineteen, built a cabin, and assumed the duties of head of the family. Soon the Cherokees were reported to be marauding over the country; and on the morning of October 1, 1792, word was brought to the boy that they were besieging Buchanan's Station, four miles south from Nashville. Seizing his rifle, he hurried to the fort. The fight was over, but there at the entrance, just as he had fallen, with a burned-out torch in his grasp, lay the man at whose hands he had suffered so much wrong and indignity, the French woman's son, Chia-chatt-alla. He had been shot while attempting to set fire to the building.

Now the youth thought himself old enough to take a part in the bloody drama that was being enacted everywhere about him. He repaired to James Robertson, who had military command of the Nashville district, and told him that he knew the secret fastnesses of the river Indians, and could pilot an army to their rear which might destroy them. Robertson heard him gladly, but shook his head, saying that he could do nothing. The orders of the government were imperative that both he and Sevier should act strictly on the defensive, and under no circumstances again invade the Cherokee country. Spain held Louisiana and the mouths of the Mississippi, and was in alliance with the Creeks and Cherokees. An attack upon them would provoke a collision with her, and that the infant republic was not prepared for, while all the wisdom and prudence of Washington were required to avoid another war with Great Britain. So for two years Sevier and Robertson held their hands, while death lurked beside every man's dwelling. The farmer could not fell a tree, gather a crop, or sit in his doorway without a loaded rifle beside him. In a population of 7040 in the Nashville district the killed were from sixty to seventy yearly. At last, when some of the first men in the district had fallen, the Nashville people rose, enrolled themselves, and demanded to be led against the Chickamaugas. Then Robertson gave way, and sending for young Brown, asked him to find a route for an army through the woods to Nicojack.

It was more than a hundred miles, through a trackless forest where never white man had been, and behind every tree might lurk a Chickamauga; but with

NICOJACK CAVE.

two or three companions the young man went and returned in safety. By the route he had blazed, a force of five hundred and fifty men soon followed, and the rest is history. The head chief of the Chickamaugas was killed, and seventy of his warriors, and their towns were laid in ashes. But more than this—the Indians were shown that their secret haunts had been discovered, and hence that further conflict with the whites would result in their own extermination.

In the fight young Brown was intrusted with the command of a company detailed to intercept a flight of the Indians to the cave of Nicojack. When it was over he returned to the town, and asked if any prisoners had been taken. He was directed to a cabin where about twenty were confined, and entering it, found there, crouching in a corner, his former mistress, the old French woman. All the captives recognized him, and were terror-stricken, for they remembered his murdered kindred. The woman was the only one to speak. She pleaded for their lives, reminding Joseph that she had saved him

when he was about to be murdered by Cutte-atoy. "We are white people," he answered; "we do not kill women and children." "Oh, co-tan-co-ney" (Oh, that is good news to the wretched), she cried.

Brown at the age of eighty-six wrote out the narrative from which the foregoing is taken. He had then, as in his youth, the feeling that he was God's avenger. "The judgment of Heaven," he says in his narrative, "fell upon the Indians."

From this time forward the fact that their hiding-places were known to the whites restrained the Chickamaugas; and soon a new generation of them sprang up who learned the arts of peace, and "walked not in the ways of their fathers." Piece by piece they sold their lands to the government, till in 1817 their once broad territory was reduced to a narrow mountain tract on the south side of the Tennessee. Here they hoped to plant their corn in peace; but "manifest destiny" had its eye upon this pass through the mountains, and in another score of years the last Cherokee took his farewell look at the

JOSEPH BROWN LEADING HIS COMPANY TO NICOJACK.

graves of his ancestors, and wended his way beyond the Mississippi. Then (in 1838) Chattanooga came into possession of the whites—the last of the three races who have held this gateway of the Alleghanies.

No sooner had the white man come in contact with the beautiful valley of the Lookout than Chattanooga sprang into being. In April, 1839, the site was divided into lots, and in 1841 the place was an incorporated town, with a considerable population. The first settlers had regard to its position as a commercial centre, and expected that the grain

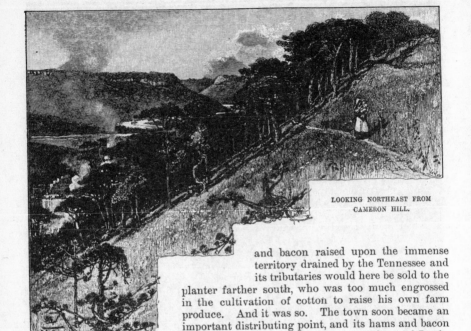

LOOKING NORTHEAST FROM
CAMERON HILL.

and bacon raised upon the immense territory drained by the Tennessee and its tributaries would here be sold to the planter farther south, who was too much engrossed in the cultivation of cotton to raise his own farm produce. And it was so. The town soon became an important distributing point, and its hams and bacon acquired a celebrity second only to those of Louisville and Cincinnati.

But the trade of the town was at first altogether barter. In the years succeeding the financial crisis of 1837 there were no banks in Tennessee, and the "shinplasters" in circulation lacked the stability of the famous 'coon-skin currency of 1784–88. They would not "keep overnight," and the countryman from Powell's River or the north fork of the Holston, though rude of manner and uncouth of garb, had a large stock of "horse-sense," and all the shrewdness of his Scotch-Irish ancestors. He was altogether too "smart" to stuff his wallet or his wife's stocking with "irresponsible paper money." So it was a flitch of bacon for a pair of brogans, and a whole hog for five gallons of whiskey. This total lack of a circulating medium might be supposed to embarrass trade, and restrict it to very narrow limits. But it did not, for the "trading animal" can accommodate himself to almost any circumstances. The business of Chattanooga grew to large dimensions. The spring and fall freshets, which render navigable streams that in midsummer may be crossed without wetting one's feet, brought down such fleets of flat-boats from the "up-country" that they were often crowded together along the entire river frontage. In these boats the countryman brought to market his surplus produce, and took back his year's supply of tea, coffee, salt, whiskey, wearing apparel, and "fancy fixin's" for the goddess of his household. The prices exacted of him were high; but what was that to him, so long as he manufactured his own currency? Like the bank officials of "wildcat" times, who issued their notes so long as they could find strength to affix their signatures, his exchequer could not be exhausted while he could use his right hand in creating a surplus.

Prices *were* high. Salt, for instance, during many years, ranged at from six to ten dollars a barrel. In 1839 fifteen hundred barrels were sold at Chattanooga for eight dollars each. All of this indispensable article consumed in East Tennessee and Northern Alabama was manufactured on the north fork of the Holston, in Virginia, and floated in flat-boats to the various landings along the river. This could be done only during freshets, and hence boats and cargoes were gotten ready in advance, and when the rise of water came were despatched, often in large fleets.

Grain and other produce were brought to market in the same way. Logs were usually cut and hauled in summer-time to the banks of streams, often a long distance "up-river"; and these, at low-water, were made into rafts, on which a booth of poles was erected, where the raftsmen could prepare their meals, and sleep when anchored for the night to some large tree that stood upon the river-bank. Often the rafts, one following another, would extend along the stream for miles, looking, to the unfamiliar eye, as they wound their devious way down the winding river, like a company of "great American sea-serpents" out for a holiday excursion. The voyage frequently occupied several days, and when it was over, and the logs disposed of, the raftsmen took their way on foot through the woods to their homes, sometimes as far away as the borders of Virginia. Steam has brought about a revolution in all other kinds of business carried on at Chattanooga, but its timber trade is still conducted in this primitive fashion. The traveller will see in the

river there, after every considerable freshet, enough oak, walnut, and poplar to roof, if sawed into boards, the entire State of Rhode Island.

And so Chattanooga bought and sold, and traded in timber and swine's flesh, like other Gentile towns, till 1850, by which time its business had greatly increased, and its population numbered about fifteen hundred. But not ten of these people knew of the infinite wealth which nature had stored away among its mountains, or dreamed of its future as a great iron-manufacturing centre.

The year 1849 was an important era in the history of Chattanooga. A few men had for some time dreamed of a rail communication which should supersede the slow and hazardous water transportation; but the wiseacres had shaken their heads, and asserted that no railroad could be built among these mountains that would ever pay interest upon the expenditure. While they were saying this, the State of Georgia went quietly to work, and one pleasant December day in 1849 drove the iron horse snorting into the valley of Lookout. It bore a bottle of water from the ocean, and

FLAT-BOATS ON THE TENNESSEE RIVER.

this, poured into the Tennessee, symbolically wedded Chattanooga to the Atlantic. This road, which connected the town with Atlanta, was soon followed by others that gave it direct communication with Nashville, Memphis, and Norfolk.

Chattanooga felt at once the influence of this increase in its transportation facilities. The river trade was so largely augmented that the Atlanta road could not move the south-bound produce nearly as fast as it arrived. In this emergency the road adopted the barbers' rule of "first come, first served," and required shippers to register the arrival of their produce in a book kept in its office; but it was generally weeks before grain could be sent forward, and often as many as 200,000 bushels were waiting upon the wharf, shielded only by rude sheds from the weather. Manufacturing also sprang into being under the new facilities. A foundery and machine shop was erected for the manufacture of freight cars, which soon demonstrated that no better car wheels can be made than from the cold-blast charcoal iron of East Tennessee. Other founderies and manufacturing establishments soon followed, and by the close of the decade the population of the town had nearly doubled, and its business increased in a much larger proportion.

Then came the war, and Chattanooga suffered severely. The engineers of both armies saw its vast advantages as a depot of supplies and base of operations; and hence it was contended for, till its inhabitants were scattered and its industries swept away. But, the war over, it rose from its ruins, and then was exhibited the surprising energy of the Southern character. Men and women who had been brought up to despise labor, and were wholly unacquainted with it, displayed an adaptiveness to circumstances and an extent of practical resources that wrought miracles, created something out of nothing, and in an incredibly short time built up a thriving city. In 1865 the place was a military post, though there were many permanent residents; in 1870 it had a population of 6093.

On the 19th of February, 1866, Andrew Johnson announced by proclamation that the civil war in America was ended. The forces of the Union were rapidly disbanded, and within three months Chattanooga, which had been the rendezvous of twenty thousand men, contained only a few hundred bluecoats, who had resolved to remain and become permanent citizens. With them, however, lingered some of the débris of the army—the human scum which gathers upon the surface of hostile operations. Then returned many of the former residents, some of whom had served in the Confederate ranks.

The inhabitants of the new city had not only to begin anew; they had to clear away the wreck of former things—a stranded social and labor system—and with totally disorganized materials "build again the waste places."

The task was Herculean, and it was made the greater by the presence of a disorderly white element, and a numerous black population, who, reversing Judge Taney's opinion, thought the white man had no rights the negro is bound to respect. Moreover, the civil authorities were composed of such creatures as come to the front in times of transition and disorder. They were wellnigh powerless to protect life and property. It was difficult to preserve even semblance of social order; but still it was done, for the majority were cool, determined, clear-headed men, who had belonged to both armies. Acting together, they kept the anarchical elements in subjection; but they resorted to no violence, for they recognized that the town would soon outgrow its superficial disorder, and slough off its worthless and criminal population. The emergency brought Northern and Southern men into close connection, and thus it was that in Chattanooga was the first exhibition of the absolute reconstruction which now so happily prevails throughout the Union.

The marvellous growth of Chattanooga is shown by the rapid increase of its population, which, from almost nothing in 1865, sprang to 6093 in 1870, to 13,000 in 1880, and by a census of May 1, 1885, numbered 25,101, and is growing at the rate of nearly three thousand yearly. Much of this rapid growth is, of course, due to its natural advantages, but more, I think, to the wonderful energy of its men and women—its men who have done the work, and its women who have inspired the doing. It is the Southern women who have made the New South. When husbands and brothers came out of the war, broken in health and fortune, and disheartened by defeat, it was their wives and sisters who bade them hope, infused into them new life and energy, and transformed a

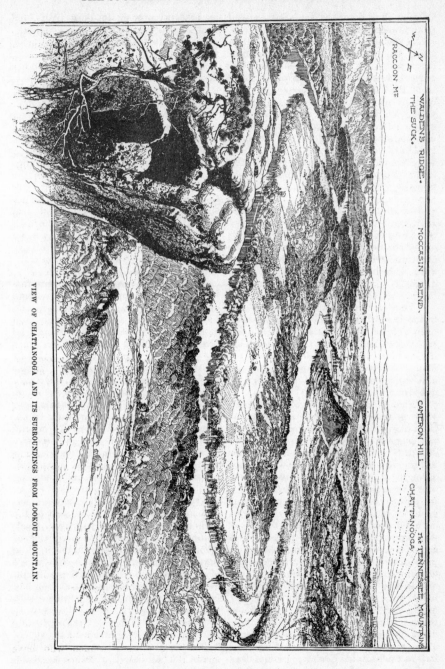

VIEW OF CHATTANOOGA AND ITS SURROUNDINGS FROM LOOKOUT MOUNTAIN.

multitude of idle, spendthrift youth, who had never done a useful thing in their lives, into earnest, active, enterprising men, who have rebuilt the waste places, and made the South of to-day the most prosperous section of the Union.

Let us catch a brief glimpse of the Chattanooga of to-day. Major George C.

Connor thus describes the view as seen from Cameron Hill:

"A carriageway of easy grades winds along the western brow of this natural observatory. From your seat you will observe the dark clouds of smoke rushing from the stacks of the Roane Iron and Steel Works; on your left, and just beyond, the beautiful Tennessee, flowing gently around the 'Moccasin Bend,' whose beauties are fully seen from the 'Point' of Lookout.

"Soon you reach the lower ridge of the hill, and a partial view of the city is obtained. Right at this point, on the left-hand side of the road, stood the platform and catafalque on the 22d of September, 1881, when the greeting to the Society of the Army of the Cumberland was extended by the Society of ex-Confederate Soldiers, and where the solemn requiem services were held in memory of President James A. Garfield, whose remains then lay in state at the national capital.

"Your carriage continues up to the extreme summit, where the flag-staff stands on which the United States flag was hoisted, by both Federals and Confederates, on the memorable occasion just referred to. You will now descend from your carriage and enjoy the exquisite panorama spread out around you.

"First glance at old Lookout, for the view is more imposing from this point than any other. Then move along over the rugged valley, through which the railroads struggle out from among the tall mountains, by the narrow gateway through which the Tennessee escapes, along the rocky bluff of Walden's Ridge, up northeasterly, catching occasional glimpses of the silvery curves of the river, until you halt at the base of the elevation known as Missionary Ridge. Just there, of a sunny day, you see the white piers of the magnificent iron bridge of the Cincinnati Southern Railway.

"Just in front, beyond the city, which lies at your feet, is the Citizens' Cemetery, on the farther side of which you can see the tall shaft of the Confederate monument, lifted above the dense shrubbery. Then your eyes pass over Fort Wood, and halt at the National Cemetery, whose flag-staff stands on the summit of the beautiful knoll where sleep the ashes of the Federal dead. Beyond is clearly seen the narrow valley on which the serried hosts manœuvred in the days of war, but which is

as peaceful now in its corn, fruits, and flowers as if the angel of peace and concord had always hovered over its fertile fields.

"To the right the Stanton House looms up sharply, and further still are the smoke-stacks of the rolling-mill, cotton factory, car-works, pipe-works, boiler-works, nail-works, plough factory, steam-tannery, blast-furnace, and fire-brick works, and the somewhat straggling section of the city known as the Fifth Ward.

"Facing directly to the east, we glance down at the city. Bounding it on the north is the beautiful broad river, from the centre of which comes up an immense stream into the city reservoir, a few feet below, on the eastern brow of the hill. The view is very effective, especially when the shade trees are covered with foliage, and the warmth of summer prevents the emission of smoke from the chimneys."

Northern men have been important factors in the development of Chattanooga, and without disparagement to others who have shown perhaps equal enterprise and energy, I may speak of one of them who has been identified with the town since the close of the war, and whose operations illustrate its industrial progress. He was a general officer in the Union service, a practical iron-worker, and somewhat acquainted with geology and mineralogy. While going about on army duty he observed the surface indications of iron and coal throughout this region, gathered specimens, and made a record of various outcrops and their localities. The war ended, he resigned his commission, and mounting his horse, explored the Cumberland range. Everywhere he found abundant ore, but at a locality about five miles west of the Clinch River, and seventy north of Chattanooga, he hit upon immense fields of iron, coal, and limestone in such close juxtaposition as to be within rifle range of one another. Returning to the North, he formed an iron company, and soon had in operation here a furnace of about 9000 tons yearly capacity. Before the war only seven small furnaces—"blast-pots" they were called—having a total capacity of 20,000 tons, were in operation in all Tennessee. They used charcoal for smelting, but this gentleman began with coke, and thus was the pioneer in the making of coke iron south of the Ohio River. His enterprise was a success from the start. In 1869 the company bought the government roll-

ing-mill at Chattanooga, erected puddling furnaces there, and began the manufacture of 40,000 tons of iron rails yearly, and in 1871 they put up a larger furnace at Rockwood—their up-country location—which augmented their annual production of iron to 20,000 tons. This they soon enlarged to 40,000 tons. Their capital was at first $125,000, was soon increased to $600,000, and has since been forced up by the expansion of their business to $1,000,000. Chattanooga is the head-quarters of their operations, and all their

AMONG THE IRON WORKERS.

iron is shipped there, but at
Rockwood they have built
up a thriving town, with hotels,
churches, and schools, and a population of more than a thousand.   The operatives are nearly all negroes.

Growing out of the manufacture of pig-iron there are
in Chattanooga rolling-mills, nail, stove, pipe, and plough
factories, and machine shops, which have, exclusive of
the monstrous Roane Iron-works, an annual producing
capacity of 150,000 tons.   The Roane Company is building steel-works, now nearly completed, which will at
once add six hundred men to the present working force

RAFTS ON THE TENNESSEE.

of Chattanooga. This establishment in operation, the total iron product of the place will not be less than $6,000,000 annually.

In addition, other branches of manufacture in which iron is not the only factor are successfully prosecuted at Chattanooga. Among these, besides the lumber and flouring mills, are cotton and furniture factories, marble-works, and two tanneries, the larger of which turns out three million dollars in leather yearly—more, it is said, than any similar establishment in the country. All told, these establishments yield an annual product of $5,000,000. Besides these, there are within a radius of fifty miles of the town various mills, furnaces, and machine shops, which are tributary to Chattanooga, and have helped to build up its wholesale trade to a yearly volume of $7,500,000. Ten years ago there were only two wholesale houses in the city; now they number eighty-eight, and are being added to yearly. Recent statistics show the annual business in various branches to be as follows: Agricultural implements, $650,000; produce, $300,000; furniture, $200,000; grain, $1,250,000; groceries, $1,500,000; hardware and iron supplies, $1,750,000; liquors, $260,000; and house-furnishing goods, $450,000. The comparatively small amount of spirits sold indicates that an "intolerable deal of sack" does not enter into the household supplies of the Tennessee country people. The total business of the town is estimated at $15,000,000, and it is said that eighty per cent. of its manufacturing capital of $7,500,000 is from the North. Of its business men, there is about an equal proportion from the North and from the South, those from the North being chiefly engaged in manufacture, and those from the South in mercantile pursuits.

The business men are mostly of the active, enterprising character usually seen in new communities. They have been drawn here by the favorable climate and business possibilities, and have found that skill, energy, and industry, acting in a fair field, are sure to be rewarded. Some of them have built up considerable fortunes, and fewer failures are reported to occur among them than among any similar number of mercantile men in the country.

Chattanooga is very favorably situated for commerce. Its location midway between the cotton-growing and grain-raising States gives it decided advantages as a wholesale market. By direct lines of railway it now has trade with northern Georgia, Alabama, Mississippi, southern Kentucky, and East and West Tennessee, and by river with East Tennessee and northern Alabama. The removal of the obstructions to the Tennessee at Muscle Shoals will give it water communication nine months in the year with the Ohio, Cumberland, Missouri, and Mississippi rivers, and bring New Orleans and St. Louis as near to it as they are now to Pittsburgh, Pennsylvania. Already the general government has expended nearly $5,000,000 upon these obstructions, and another $300,000 will complete the work. Chattanooga will then have transportation facilities unsurpassed by those of any inland city in the Union.

According to Buckle, there is no instance in history of a people attaining to a high degree of civilization without the help of a fertile soil and a genial climate. The soil of Chattanooga is fertile in iron. It underlies the very city, and everywhere ribs the vast mountains which surround it and stretch away on every side as far as the eye can reach. But iron dug out of the ground is mixed with impurities that need to be purged away before it is fit for its multitudinous uses. These auxiliary materials are generally found at such distances from the ore as to involve a heavy cost in transportation. But in this section they lie side by side and all together, the iron with the coal needed for coke, the limestone for smelting the ore, and the fire-clay and sandstone for the construction of furnaces. An idea of these mineral resources thus tributary to Chattanooga cannot better be given than in the words of General John T. Wilder, the founder of the iron-works at Rockwood, and the gentleman of whom I have spoken as having fully explored the whole territory. He says:

"The coal-field of Tennessee extends entirely across the State, from Kentucky to Georgia and Alabama, being an extension of the Appalachian coal-fields, whose northern extremity is in northern Pennsylvania, and extends southwesterly across Pennsylvania, West Virginia, eastern Kentucky, Tennessee, and ends in central Alabama. The coal-field of Tennessee covers 5100 square miles, there are about 4000 square miles in Alabama, and 250 square miles in Georgia, all belonging to the lower coal measures; all these broad

NORTH END OF CHATTANOOGA.

acres, excepting a small area in Alabama, form a covering for the Cumberland table-land, raised above the surrounding country, with an outcrop above the drainage of the valleys on either side, easily opened, ventilated, and drained."

Throughout this extensive region are wonderful beds of fossiliferous red hematite iron ore, none of it more than fifteen miles from the eastern outcrop of the coal measures, and all of it covered by the great limestone beds of the subcarboniferous period. "All these formations lie like the leaves of a book, flat, bedded on each other, and generally tilted up and broken into high ridges, or folded into deep synclinal troughs or valleys, in either case exposing the edges of the ore beds, making it easy to find, ready to mine, abundant in quantity, always accessible. These beds usually average four to five feet in thickness, sometimes more." The General adds in regard to one species of the timber of this region: "The largest forests of chestnut-oak in the United States, producing the

best quality of tan-bark, cover the coal-fields of Tennessee, Georgia, and Alabama, supplying the largest oak tannery on the continent, at Chattanooga, and furnishing tan-bark for the towns of St. Louis, Louisville, and Cincinnati. They are sufficient in area to supply 300,000 cords per year for an indefinite period without exhaustion, as the tree reaches maturity in our climate in forty years, and grows on an area of over 7,000,000 acres, and if cut once in forty years, and producing only two cords per tree, it would produce perpetually 350,000 cords each year. One cord of chestnut-oak tan-bark grown in this latitude produces thirty-three per cent. more tannin than all the bark grown north of the Kanawha River."

Other woods equally valuable surround Chattanooga. The city is in the midst of a vast forest, where not one-sixth of the land has yet been subjected to cultivation. Besides oak, there are chestnut and black-walnut standing there in almost inexhaustible supply and primeval grandeur. Here, too, is hickory enough to make the wagons of a continent, and a sufficient supply of red cedar is growing on the Clinch River alone to furnish hollow-ware to every American house-keeper for another century.

More need not be said to show that the country of which Chattanooga is the centre fulfils the first of the two requirements which Buckle deems essential to the attainment of a high civilization. Of the other, it may be affirmed that the climate of Chattanooga is genial beyond description. The town is in a happy mean between extremes. Flowers bloom in March; and May is the New England June, when, "if ever, come perfect days." Then are the mocking-birds carolling among the trees, and the barefooted little black boys crying the luscious red strawberries about the streets. The days are simply delightful, and the nights—one needs only a quiet conscience to sleep soundly through them if an earthquake should be rumbling beneath him. And this is true of all the year, except, it may be, the latter part of July and the month of August.

Then, when the blazing sun has drawn the great river up to the clouds, it comes down again at night in drops of scalding steam, as hot as a Russian bath, and not nearly so invigorating. But there is an easy escape from this in a tramp to the top of Lookout Mountain. Three hundred feet of altitude is equivalent to one degree of latitude, so, by a walk of two and a half miles, and an ascent of eighteen hundred feet, one may here transport himself to the climate of the Hudson Highlands. Up there, when all the world is sweltering below him, he may rest at night as cool as if packed in a refrigerator; and by day may revel in scenes that are all alive with poetry and history.

Here the visitor may wander through Rock City, a product of nature's own handiwork, through streets paved with natural stone, and beneath domes and pinnacles that nature itself has erected to its great Creator. Near here are the statues of the "Sisters," carved in stone, and the profile of "The Old Man of the Mountain," a huge rock on the ledge forming what is known as the Natural Bridge.

BROAD STREET, CHATTANOOGA.

STREET IN ROCK CITY.

The stranger should visit the national cemetery, on the slope of the mountain, where sleep thirteen thousand Union soldiers. The enclosure, approached through a lofty gateway of Alabama limestone, includes seventy-five acres. The ground rises toward a central eminence one hundred feet above the avenue which winds around the cemetery. From a flag-staff one hundred and fifty feet high on the top of this mound floats the ensign of the Union. Driving on around the eastern side of the cemetery, and past Fort Wood, we come to the Confederate cemetery, where, under the weeping-willows, lie thousands of soldiers who wore the gray in the late war. The monument on the hill above, with a shaft thirty feet high, bears the simple inscription, "Our Confederate Dead." Mrs. G. C. Connor was president of the association under whose auspices it was constructed. The larger portion of the funds for this object was given by Northern-born citizens, and United States troops participated in the laying of the corner-stone.

From Lookout Point one looks down on the theatre of events that will never go out of this nation's history. Up that narrow pass climbed John Sevier with his riflemen; and across that deep gorge marched General Hooker and his blue-coated army, each to do efficient battle on the same cloud-capped field for their country; yonder, where the clustering grape now hangs thick and red with the life-blood of more than a thousand heroes, Sheridan scaled the beetling heights of Missionary Ridge, and turned the scale to victory; and farther east, across that broad, stream-threaded field, Garfield rode in hot haste to warn Thomas that Longstreet was coming to Chickamauga. But all this, and more, is already history. It is written in these hills of iron, these mountains of coal, and these forests of timber that Chattanooga has a great future. In the very nature of things it cannot be many years before it is the metropolis of the central South, and the iron emporium of the whole country.

THE BLUE-GRASS REGION OF KENTUCKY

I.—BLUE-GRASS.

ONE might well name it Saxon grass, so much is it at home in favorable localities of Saxon England, so like the loveliest landscapes of green Saxon England has it made other landscapes on which dwell a kindred race in America, and so near is itself to the type of nature that is peculiarly Saxon: being a hardy, kindly, beautiful, nourishing stock; loving rich lands, and apt to find out where they lie; uprooting inferior aborigines, but stoutly defending its new domain against all fresh invaders; paying taxes promptly and well, with some profits to boot; thriving best in temperate latitudes and checkered sunshine; benevolent to flocks and herds; and allying itself closely to the history of any people whose content lies in simple plenty and habitual peace—the perfect squire-and-yeoman type of all grasses.

In the earliest spring nothing is sooner afield to contest possession of the land than the blue-grass. Its little green spear points are first to pierce through the soft rich earth, and array themselves in countless companies over the rolling landscapes, while its creeping roots reach out in every direction for securer foot-hold. So early does this take place, that a late hoar-frost will now and then mow all these bristling spear points down. Sometimes a slow-falling sleet will incase each emerald blade in glittering silver; but the sun by-and-by dissolves it away, leaving the temper of the blade unhurt. Or a light snow-fall will cover tufts of it over, making pavilions and colonnades with white roofs resting on green pillars. The roofs vanish anon, and the columns go on silently rising. But usually the final rigors of the season prove harmless to the blue-grass. One sees it most beautiful in the spring, just before the seed stalks have shot upward from the flowing tufts, and while the thin, smooth, polished blades, having risen to their greatest height, are beginning to bend over, or break and fall over, on themselves and their nether fellows, from sheer luxuriance. The least observant eye is now constrained to note that blue-grass is the great characteristic element of the Kentucky turf—the first element of beauty in the Kentucky landscape. Over all the stretches of woodland pastures, over the meadows and the lawns, by the road-side edges of turnpike and lane, in the fence corners—wherever its seed has been allowed to flourish — it spreads a verdure so soft in fold and fine in texture, so entrancing by its freshness and fertility, that it looks like a deep-lying, thick-matted emerald moss. One thinks of it, not as some heavy green velvet-like carpet spread over the earth, but as some great, light, seamless veil that has fallen delicately around it, and that might be rolled off and blown away by a passing breeze.

After this you will not see the blue-grass so beautiful. The seed ripens in June. Already the slender seed stalks have sprung up above the uniform green level, bearing on their summits the fuzzy, plumy, purplish seed-vessels, and save the soft, feathery undulations of these as the wind sweeps over and sways them, the beauty of the blue-grass is gone. Moreover, certain robust and persistent weeds and grasses have been growing apace, roughening and diversifying the sward, so that the vista is less charming. During July and August the blue-grass lies comparatively inactive, resting from the effort of fructification, and missing, as well, frequent showers to temper the summer sunshine. In seasons of severe drought it even dies quite away, leaving

the surface of the earth as bare and brown as a winter landscape or an arid plain. Where it has been closely grazed, one may, in walking over it at such times, stir such a dust as one would raise on a highway; and the upturned, half-exposed rootlets seem entirely dead. But the moderated heats and the gentle rains that usually come with the passing of summer bring on a second vigorous growth, and in the course of several weeks the landscape is covered with a verdure rivalling the luxuriance of spring.

There is something seemingly incongruous in this marvellous autumnal rejuvenescence of the blue-grass. All nature appears content and resting. The grapes on the sunward vineyard slopes have received their final colorings of purple and gold; the heavy mast is beginning to drop in the forest, followed by the silent lapse of the russet and crimson leaves; the knee-deep aftermath has paled its green in the waiting autumn fields; the plump children are stretching out their nut-stained hands toward the first happy fire-glow on chill dark evenings; and the cricket has left the sere dead garden for a winter home at the cheery hearth. Then, lo! as if by some freakish return of the vanished spring to the very edge of winter, the pastures are suddenly as fresh and green as those of May. The effect on one who has the true landscape passion is transporting and bewildering. Such contrasts of color it is given one to study nowhere but in blue-grass lands. It is as if the seasons were met to do some great piece of brocading. One sees a new meaning in Poe's melancholy thought — the leaves of the many-colored grass.

All winter the blue-grass continues green—it is always *green*, of course, never *blue*—and it even grows a little then, except when the ground is frozen. Thus, year after year, drawing all needful nourishment from the constantly disintegrating limestone below, flourishes here as nowhere else in the world this wonderful grass.

But what of all this, in view of its economic value? Even while shivering in the bleak winds of March, the young lambs frolicked away from the distent teats of the ewes, with growing relish for its hardy succulence, and by-and-by they were taken into market the sooner and the fatter for its superior developing qualities. During the long summer, foaming

SWEET-POTATO FIELD.

pails of milk and bowls of golden butter—retaining its pure flavor—have testified to the Kentucky housewife with what delight the cows have ruminated on the capacious stores gathered each plentiful day. The Kentucky farmer knows, too, that the distant metropolitan beef-eater will in time have good reason to thank him for yonder winding herd of sleek young steers that are softly brushing their rounded sides with their long white silky tails, while they plunge their puffing noses into its depths and tear away huge mouthfuls of its inexhaustible richness. Thorough-bred sire and dam and foal, also, in paddocks or deeper pastures, have drawn from it their unequalled form and quality and organization: hardness and solidity of bone, strength of tendon, firmness and elasticity of muscle, power of nerve, and capacity of lung. Even the Falstaff porkers, their little eyes gleaming with gluttonous enjoyment, have looked to it for the shaping of their posthumous hams and the padding of their long backbones in depths of snowy lard. In winter, mules and sheep and horses paw away the snow to get at the green shoots that lie covered over beneath the full, rank growth of autumn, or they find it attractive provender in their ricks as hay. Still, for all that live upon it, here it is perennial and abundant, beautiful and benefi-

cent—one of the direct causes of the superiority of Kentucky live stock, the first great natural factor in the prosperity of the Kentucky people. What wonder if the Kentuckian, like the Greek of old, should wish to have even his paradise well set in grass, or that, with a knowing humor peculiarly his own, he should smile at David's expense for saying, "He maketh his grass to grow upon the mountains," inasmuch as the only grass really worth speaking of grows on a certain well-known plain!

II.—THE BLUE-GRASS LANDSCAPE.

But if grass is the first element in the lovely Kentucky landscape, as it must be in every other one, by no means should it be thought sole or chief. In Dante, as Ruskin points out, whenever the country is to be beautiful, we come into open air and open meadows. Homer, too, places the sirens in a meadow when they are to sing. Over the blue-grass, therefore, one walks into the open air and open meadows of the blue-grass land.

This has long had some reputation for being one of the very beautiful spots on the face of the earth, and it is worth while, therefore, to consider for a moment those elements of natural scenery wherein alone the beauty could consist. Or perhaps it would be wise to ask whether this reputation be not a mere local prejudice—one of those local illusions of landscape which involve the transference of the beholder's own tender feelings to the objects of the natural world. The answer will best be given by beginning to describe this country without reference to human presence or interference.

One might well say, first of all, that the landscape possesses what is so very rare even in beautiful landscapes—the quality of gracefulness. Nowhere does one encounter vertical lines or violent slopes, nor, on the other hand, are there perfectly level stretches like those that make the green fields monotonous in the Dutch lowlands. The dark, finely sifted soil lies deep over all the limestone hills, filling out their chasms to evenness, and rounding their jagged or precipitous edges, very much as a heavy snow at night will leave the morning landscape with mitigated ruggedness and softer curves. The long slow action of water has further moulded everything into symmetry, so that the low ancient hills descend to the valleys in exquisite folds and uninterrupted slopes. The whole great plain undulates away league after league toward the distant horizon in an endless succession of gentle convex surfaces—like the easy swing of the sea—presenting a panorama of subdued swells and retiring surges. Everything in the blue-grass country is billowy and afloat. The spirit of it is intermediate between that of violent energy and complete repose; and the effect of this mild activity is kept from becoming monotonous by the accidental perspective of position, creating fresh vistas with an infinite variety of charming details.

One traces this quality of gracefulness elsewhere—in the labyrinthine courses of the restful streams, in the disposition of forest mosses, in the free, unstudied succession of meadow, field, and lawn. Surely it is just this order of low hill scenery, just these buoyant undulations, that should be covered with the blue-grass. Had Hawthorne ever looked on this landscape when most beautiful, he could never have said of England that "no other country will ever have this charm of lovely verdure."

The most characteristically beautiful spots on the blue-grass landscape are the woodland pastures. A Kentucky wheat field, a Kentucky meadow, a Kentucky lawn, may be found elsewhere; but a Kentucky sylvan slope has a loveliness unique and local. Rightly do all poets make pre-eminently beautiful countries abound in trees. John Burroughs, writing with enthusiasm of English woods, has said that "in midsummer the hair of our trees seems to stand on end; the woods have a frightened look, or as if they were just recovering from a debauch." This is not true of the Kentucky woods, unless it be in some season of protracted drought. The foliage of the Kentucky trees is not thin nor dishevelled, the leaves crowd thick to the very ends of the boughs, and spread themselves full to the sky, making, where they are close together, under-spaces of green-lighted gloom scarcely shot through by some shafted sunbeam. Indeed, one often finds here the perfection of tree forms. I mean that exceedingly rare development which enables the extremities of the boughs to be carried out to the very limit of the curve that nature intends the tree to define as the peculiar shape of its species. Any but the most favorable conditions, of course, leaves the outline jagged, faulty, and untrue. Here and there over the blue-grass landscape one's eye rests on a cone-shaped, or dome-shaped, or inverted pear-shaped, or fan-shaped tree. Nor are fullness of leafage and perfection of form alone to be noted; pendency of boughs is another distinguishing feature. One who loves and closely studies trees will note here the comparative absence of woody stiffness. It is expected that the willow and the elm should droop their branches. Here the same characteristic strikes you in the wild cherry, the maple, and the sycamore—even in great walnuts and ashes and oaks; and I have occasionally discovered exceeding grace of form in hackberries (which usually look paralytic and as if waiting to hobble away on crutches), in locusts, and in the harsh hickories—loved by Thoreau.

But to return from these details to the woodland pastures as wholes. They are the last vestiges of that unbroken primeval forest that, together with cane-brakes and pea vines, covered the face of the country when it was first beheld by the pioneers. No blue-grass then. In these woods the timber has been so largely cut out that the remaining trees often stand out clearly revealed in their entire form on the landscape, their far-reaching boughs perhaps not even touching those of their

A SPRING-HOUSE.

nearest neighbor, or else interlacing them with ineffectual fondness. There is something pathetic in the sight, and in the thought of those innumerable stricken ones that in years agone were dismembered for cord-wood and kitchen stoves and the vast fire-places of old-time negro cabins. In the truly blue-grass pasture all undergrowth and weeds are annually cut down, so that the massive trunks are revealed from a distance; all the better because the branches seldom are lower than from ten to twenty feet above the earth. Thus in its daily course the sun strikes every point beneath the broad branches, and nourishes the blue-grass up to the very roots. All savagery, all wildness, is taken out of them; they are full of tenderness and repose—of the utmost delicacy and elegance. Beneath, over all the graceful earth, spreads the flowing green, uniform and universal. Above this stand the full, swelling trunks—warm browns and pale grays—often lichen-flecked or moss-enamelled. Over these expand the vast domes and canopies of impenetrable leafage. And falling down upon these comes the placid sunshine through a sky of cerulean blueness, and past the snowy zones of gleaming cloud. The very individuality of the tree comes out as it never can in denser places. Always the most truly human object in still, voiceless nature, it here throws out its arms to you with gestures of imploring tenderness, with what

Wordsworth called "the soft eye-music of slow-waving boughs." One can not travel far, no matter where he be in the blue-grass country, without coming upon one of these woodland strips.

Of the artistic service rendered the landscape of this region by other elements of scenery—atmosphere and cloud and sky—much might, but little may be said. The atmosphere is sometimes crystalline, sometimes full of that intense repose of dazzling light which one, without ever having seen them, knows to be on canvases of Turner. Then, again, it is amber-hued, or tinged with soft blue, graduated to purple shadows on the horizon. During the greater part of the year the cloud sky is one of strongly outlined forms; the great white cumuli drift over, with every majesty of design and grace of grouping; but there come, in milder seasons, many days when one may see three cloud belts in the heavens at the same time, the lowest far, far away, and the highest brushing softly, as it were, past the very dome of the inviolable blue. You turn your eye then downward to see the light wandering wistfully among the low distant hills, and the sweet tremulous shadows crossing the summer meadows with timid cadences. It *is* a beautiful country; the Kentucky skies are not the cold, hard, brilliant, hideous things that so many writers on nature among us broadly style American skies (usually meaning New England skies,

KENTUCKY RIVER, FROM HIGH BRIDGE.

however), as contrasted with skies European. They are at times ineffably
warm in tone and tender in hue, giving
aerial distances magical and fathomless
above, and throwing down upon the
varied soft harmonious greens of the
landscape below, upon its rich browns
and weathered grays and whole scheme
of terrene colors, a flood of radiance as

bountiful and transfiguring as it is chastened and benign.

But why make a description of the blue-grass region of Kentucky? What one sees may be only what he feels—may be only intricate affinities between nature and self that were developed long ago, and have become too deep to be viewed as relations or illusions. What two human beings find the same things in the face of a third, or in nature's? Descriptions of scenery are notoriously disappointing to those whose taste in landscape is different, or who have little or no sentiment for pure landscape beauty at all. So one coming hither might be sorely disappointed. No mountains; no strips of distant blue gleaming water nor lawny cascades; no grandeur; no majesty; no wild picturesqueness. The chords of landscape harmony are very simple; nothing but softness and amenity, grace and repose, delicacy and elegance. One might fail at seasons to find even these. This is a beautiful country, but no paradise; there come days when the climate shows as ugly a temper as is possible in even a perfectly civilized human being. No little of the finest timber has been lost to it by storms. The sky is sometimes for days one great blank face of grewsome gray. In winter you laugh with chattering teeth at those who call this "the South," the thermometer in your hand perhaps registering from twelve to fifteen degrees below zero. In summer it occurs to you that the name was no mistake, but only a half-truth. It is only by visiting this region during some lovely season, or by dwelling here from year to year, and seeing it in all the humors of storm and sunshine, that one can fall in love with it.

III.—BLUE-GRASS FERTILITY.

But the ideal landscape of daily life must not be merely beautiful, it should be also useful. With what may not the fertility of this region be truthfully compared? With the valleys of the Schuylkill, the Shenandoah, and the Genesee; with the richest lands of Lombardy and Belgium; with the most fertile districts of England. The evidences of this fertility are everywhere apparent. Nature, even in those places where she has been forced for nearly a hundred years to bear so much at the hands of a not always judicious agriculture, unceasingly struggles to cover herself with bushes of all sorts and nameless annual weeds and grasses. Even the blue-grass contends in vain for complete possession of its freehold. One is forced, living here year after year, to note, even though without the least sentiment, the rich pageant of transitory wild bloom that *will* force a passage for itself over the landscape: firmaments of golden dandelions in the lawns; vast beds of violets, gray and blue, in dimmer bosky glades; patches of flaunting sunflowers along the road-sides; purple thistles, and, of deeper purple still, and far denser growth, beautiful iron-weed in the woods; with many clumps of alder bloom, and fast-extending patches of perennial blackberry, and groups of delicate May-apples, and whole fields of dog-fennel and golden-rod. And why mention coarser things—indomitable dock and gigantic poke, burrs and plenteous nightshade, and mullein and plantain, with dusty gray-green ragweed and thrifty fox-tail?—an innumerable throng!

Maize and pumpkins and beans grow together in a field—a triple crop. Nature perfects them all, yet must do more. Scarcely have the ploughs left the long furrows before there springs up a varied wild growth, and a fourth crop, morning-glories, festoon the tall tassels of the Indian corn ere the knife can be laid against the stalk. Harvest fields usually have their stubble well hidden by a rich, deep aftermath. Garden patches, for all that persistent hoe and rake can do, commonly look at last like spots given over to weeds and grasses. Sidewalks quickly lose their borders. Pavements would soon disappear from sight; the winding of a distant stream through the fields can be readily followed by the line of communistic vegetation that rushes there to fight for life, from the minutest creeping vines to forest trees. Every neglected fence corner becomes an area for a fresh colony. Leave one of these sweet, humanized woodland pastures alone for a short period of years, it runs wild with a dense young natural forest; vines shoot up to the tops of the tallest trees, and then tumble over in green sprays on the heads of others.

A kind, true, patient, self-helpful soil if ever there was one! Some of these lands after being cultivated, not always scientifically, but always without artificial fertilizers, for more than three-quarters of a century, are now, if properly treated, equal in productiveness to the best farming lands of England. The farmer from one of these old fields will take two different crops in a season. He gets two cuttings of clover from a meadow, and has rich grazing left. A few of these counties have at a time produced three-fourths of the entire hemp product of the United States. The State itself has at different times stood first in wheat and hemp and Indian corn and wool and tobacco and flax, and this although half its territory is covered with virgin forests. When lands under improper treatment have become impoverished, their productiveness has been restored, not by artificial fertilizers, but by simple rotation of crops, with nature's own help. The soil rests on decomposable limestone, which annually gives up to it in solution all the essential mineral plant food that a judicious system of agriculture should ever remove.

The transition from material conditions to the forms of life that they insure is here natural. Soil and air and climate, the entire aggregate of influences happily co-operative, make this region beyond question the finest grazing district in the world. The Kentucky horse has carried the reputation of the country into regions where even the people could, perhaps, have never made it so well known. Your expert in the breeding of thorough-breds will tell you that the muscular fibre of the blue-grass animal is to that of the Pennsylvania-bred horses as silk to cotton, and the texture of his bone, when compared with the latter's, much as ivory beside pumice-stone. If taken to the Eastern States, in twelve generations he is no longer the same breed of horse. His blood fertilizes American stock the continent over. Jersey cattle brought here increase in size. Sires come to Kentucky to make themselves and their offspring famous. The people themselves are a fecund race. Out of this State have gone more to enrich the citizenship of the nation than all the other States together have been able to send into it. So at least your loyal-hearted Kentuckian looks at the rather delicate subject of inter-State migration. Let all the forces of nature receive their due share of credit, likewise. By actual measurement the Kentucky volunteers during the civil war were found to surpass all others (except Tennesseeans) in height and weight, whether coming from the United States or various countries of Europe. But for the great-headed Scandinavians, they would have been first, also, in circumference around the forehead and occiput. Still it is conceded that Kentucky has little or no literature.

One element that should be conspicuous in all very fertile countries does not strike the observer here—much beautiful water; no other State has a frontage on navigable rivers equal to that of Kentucky. But in the blue-grass region there are few limpid, lovely, smaller streams. Wonderful springs there are in places, and vast stores of water there must be in the cavernous earth below; but the landscape lacks the charm of this element—clear, rushing, musical, abundant. The water-courses, ever winding and graceful, are apt to be either swollen and turbid or insignificant; of late years the beds seem less full also—a change consequent, perhaps, upon the denudation of forest lands. In a dry season the historic Elkhorn seems little more than a ganglion of precarious pools.

IV.—AGRICULTURAL AND DOMESTIC ASPECTS OF RURAL LIFE.

The best artists who have painted cultivated ground have always been very careful to limit the area of the crops. Undoubtedly the substitution of a more scientific agriculture for the loose and easy ways of primitive husbandry has changed the key-note of rural existence from a tender Virgilian sentiment to a coarser strain, and as life becomes more unsophisticated it grows less picturesque. When the old work of the reaper is done by a fat man with a flaming face, sitting on a cast-iron machine, and smoking a cob pipe, your artist will leave the fields as soon as possible. Figures have a terrible power to destroy sentiment in pure landscape; so have houses. When one leaves nature, pure and simple, in the blue-grass country, he must accordingly pick his way circumspectly or go amiss in his search for the beautiful. If his taste lead him to desire in landscapes the finest evidences of human labor, the high artificial finish of a minutely careful civilization, he will here find great disappointment awaiting him. On the other hand, if he delight in those exquisite rural spots of the Old World with picturesque bits of homestead architecture and the perfection of horticultural and unobtrusive botanical details, he will be no less aggrieved. What he sees here is

NEGRO CABINS.

neither the most scientific farming, simply economic and utilitarian—raw and rude—nor that cultivated desire for the elements in nature to be so moulded by the hand of man that they will fuse harmoniously and inextricably with his habitations and his work.

The whole face of the country is taken up by a succession of farms. Each of these, except, of course, the very small ones, presents to the eye the variation of meadow, field, and woodland pasture, together with the homestead and the surrounding grounds of orchard, garden, and lawn. The entire landscape is thus caught in a vast net-work of fences. The Kentuckian retains his English ancestors' love of inclosures; but the uncertain tenure of estates beyond a single generation does not encourage him to make them the most durable. One does, indeed, notice here and there throughout the country stone walls of blue limestone, that give an aspect of substantial repose and comfortable firmness to the scenery by their solid masonry. But the farmer dreads their costliness, even though his own hillsides furnish him an abundant quarry.

He knows that unless the foundations are laid like those of a house, the thawing earth will unsettle them, that water, freezing as it trickles through the crevices, will force the stones out of their places, and that breaches will be made in them by boys on a hunt whenever and wherever it shall be necessary in order to get at a lurking or a sorely pressed rabbit that has crept within. It is ludicrously true that the most terrible destroyer of stone walls in this country is the small boy hunting a hare, with an appetite for game that knows no geological impediment. Therefore one hears of fewer limestone fences being built of late years, even of some being torn down and superseded by plank fences or post-and-rail fences, or by the newer barbed-wire fence—an economic device that will probably become as popular in regions where stone and timber were never to be had as in others, like this, where timber has been ignorantly, wantonly sacrificed. It is a genuine pleasure to know that one of the most expensive, and certainly the most hideous, fences ever in vogue here is falling into disuse. I mean the worm-fence—called worm because it wriggled over the landscape like a long brown caterpillar, the stakes being the bristles along its back, and because it now and then ate up a noble walnut-tree close by, or a kingly oak, or frightened, trembling ash—a worm that decided the destiny of forests. A pleasure it is, too, to come occasionally upon an Osage orange hedge-row, which is a green eternal fence. But you will not find many of these. It is generally too much to ask of an American, even though he be a Kentuckian, to wait for a hedge to grow and make him a fence. When he takes a notion to have a fence, he wants it put up before Saturday night.

If the Kentuckian, like the Englishman, is fond of walling himself around, though with but a worm-fence, like the Frenchman, he loves long, straight roads. You will not find elsewhere in America such highways as the Kentuckian has constructed all over his country—broad, smooth, level, white, glistening turnpikes of the macadamized limestone. It is a luxury to drive upon them, and also an expense, as one will discover before he has passed through many toll-gates. He could travel more cheaply on the finest railway on the continent, though of course it will not be himself, but his horses and vehicle, that are paid for. What Richard Grant White thought it worth while to record as a rare and interesting sight—a man on an English highway breaking stones—is no uncommon occurrence here. All limestone for all these hundreds of miles of roads, having been quarried here and there, almost anywhere, near each of them, and then having been carted and strewn along the road-side, is broken by a hammer in the hand of a man. By the highway he sits —usually an Irishman—pecking away at a long rugged pile as though he were good to live for a thousand years. Somehow, in patience, he always gets to the other end of his hard row. But if, some bright Easter morn, you sit for a moment beside him, and speak to him sympathetically of labor and of life, his tears will sprinkle his dusty hands, showing his heart is elsewhere.

One can not sojourn long here without coming to conceive an interest in this limestone, and loving to meet its rich warm hues on the landscape. It has made a deal of history: limestone blue-grass, limestone water, limestone roads, limestone fences, limestone bridges and arches, limestone engineering architecture, limestone water-mills, limestone spring-houses and homesteads—limestone Kentuckians! Outside of Scripture no people was ever so like to be founded on a rock. It might be well to note, likewise, that the soil of this region is what scientists call sedentary— called so because it sits quietly on the rocks, not because the people sit quietly on it.

Undoubtedly the most picturesque bits in the blue-grass country, architecturally, are those old stone water-mills and old stone homesteads — landmarks each for separate trains of ideas that run to poetry and to history. The latter, built some of them by descendants of pioneers nearly a hundred years ago, stand gray with years, but good for nameless years to come: great low chimneys, deep little windows, thick walls, mighty fire-places; situated usually with keen discretion on an elevation near a spring, just as a Saxon forefather would have placed them centuries ago. Happily one will see the water of this spring issuing still from a recess in a hill-side, with an overhanging ledge of rock—the entrance to this cavern being walled across and closed with a gate, thus making, according to ancient fashion, a simple natural spring-house and dairy.

Something like a feeling of exasperation is apt to come over one when he turns from these to the typical modern houses. Nowhere, certainly, in rural America, are there, within the same area, more substantial, comfortable homesteads than here. They are nothing if not spacious and healthful, frame or brick, two stories, shingle roofs. But they lack characteristic physiognomy; they have no harmony with the landscape, nor with each other, nor often with themselves. They are not beautiful when new, and can never be beautiful when old, for the beauty of newness and the beauty of oldness alike depend on beauty of form and color, which here is lacking. One longs for the sight of a rural Gothic cottage, which would harmonize so well with the order of the scenery, or for a light, elegant villa that should overlook these light and elegant undulations of a beautiful and varied landscape. It must be understood that there are notable exceptions to these statements even in the outlying districts of the blue-grass country, and that they do not at all apply to the environs of the towns, nor to the towns themselves.

Nowhere does one see masses of merely beautiful things in the country. The slumbering art of interior decoration is usually spent upon the parlor, which constitutes does not seem to have any compelling, controlling sense of the beautiful. She invariably concedes something to beauty, but not enough. You will find a show

OLD FARM-HOUSE.

the usual ceremonial dessert of American entertainment. The grounds around the houses are not kept in the best order. The typical rural Kentucky housewife of flowers at the poorest houses, though but geranium slips in miscellaneous tins and pottery. But, on the other hand, you do not generally see around more prosperous homes any such parterres or beds as there is money enough to spend on, and time enough to tend, and grounds to justify.

A like spirit is shown by the ordinary blue-grass farmer. His management strikes you as not the pink of tidiness, not the model of systematic thrift. Exceptions exist—many exceptions—but they care for themselves; the rule holds good. One can not travel here in summer or autumn without observing that weeds flourish where they can possibly do nothing but harm and create ugliness; fences often go long unrepaired; gates may be found swinging on one hinge. He misuses his long-cultivated fields; he cuts down his scant, precious trees. His energy is not tireless, his watchfulness not sleepless. Why should they be? Human life here is not massed and swarming. The occupation of the soil is not close and niggard. The landscape is not even compact, much less crowded. There is room for more, plenty for more to eat. No man here, like the ancient Roman prætor, ever decided how often one might, without trespass, gather the acorns that fall from his neighbors' trees. No woman ever went through a blue-grass harvest field gleaning. Ruth's vocation is gone. By nature the Kentuckian is no rigid economist. By birth, education, tradition, and inherited tendencies he is not a country clout, but a rural gentleman. His ideal of life is neither vast wealth nor personal distinction, but solid comfort in material conditions, and the material conditions are easy: fertility of soil, annual excess of production over consumption, comparative thinness of population. So he does not brace himself for the tense struggle of life as it goes on in centres of fierce territorial shoulder-pushing. He can afford to indulge his slackness of endeavor. He is neither an alert aggressive agriculturist, nor a landscape gardener, nor a purveyor of commodities to the green-grocer. If the world wants vegetables, let it raise them. He'll not work himself to death for other people, though they pay him for it. His wife is a lady, not a domestic laborer; and it is her privilege, in household affairs, placidly to surround herself with an abundance which the straining lifelong female economists of other regions not necessary to name would regard with conscientious and furious indignation.

In truth, there is much evidence to show that this park-like country, intersected by many beautiful railroads, turnpikes, and shaded picturesque lanes, will become less and less an agricultural district, more and more a region of unequalled pasturage, and hence a thousand times more park-like still. One great interest abides here, of course—the manufacture of old Bourbon whiskey. Another interest has only within the last few years been developed—the cultivation of tobacco, for which it was formerly thought that the blue-grass soils were not adapted. But as years go by, the stock interests invite more capital, demand more attention, give more pleasure—in a word, strike the full chord of modern interest by furnishing an unparalleled means of speculative profit.

Forty years ago the most distinguished citizens of the State were engaged in writing essays and prize papers on scientific agriculture. A regular trotting track was not to be found in the whole country. Nothing was thought of the breeding and training of horses with reference to development of greater speed. Pacing horses were fashionable; and two great rivals in this seductive gait having been brought together for a trial of speed, in lieu of a track, paced a mighty race over a river-bottom flat! We have changed all that. The gentlemen no longer write their essays. The trotting horse will soon, undoubtedly, be admitted to manhood suffrage here, much as beef once won the spurs of knighthood. He has already, even without the right of voting, been styled the first citizen. The great agricultural fairs of the State have modified their exhibits with reference to him alone, and fifteen or twenty thousand people give afternoon after afternoon to the contemplation of his beauty and his speed. His one rival is the thorough-bred, who goes on running faster and faster. By-and-by time will be no more. One of the brief code of nine laws for the government of the young Kentucky commonwealth that were passed in the first legislative assembly ever held west of the Alleghanies dealt with the preservation of the breed of horses. Nothing was said of education. The Kentuckian loves the memory of Thomas Jefferson, not forgetting that he once ran race-horses. These great interests, not overlooking the cattle interest, the manufacture of whiskey, and the raising of tobacco, will no doubt constitute the future determining factors in

HARRODSBURG PIKE.

the history of this country. It should not be forgotten, however, that the Northern and Eastern palate at once becomes kindly disposed at the bare mention of the many thousands of turkeys that annually fatten on these plains. But it is now well that we should for a moment come face to face with these blue-grass Kentuckians.

V.—THE BLUE-GRASS KENTUCKIANS.

"In Kentucky," writes Professor Shaler, in his recent history, "we shall find nearly pure English blood. It is, moreover, the largest body of pure English folk that has, speaking generally, been separated from the mother country for two hundred years." They, the blue-grass Kentuckians, are the descendants of those hardy, high-spirited, picked Englishmen, largely of the squire and yeoman class, whose absorbing passion was not religious disputation, nor the intellectual purpose of founding a State, but the ownership of land and all the pursuits and pleasures of rural life, close to the rich soil, and full of its strength and sunlight. They have to this day, in a degree perhaps equalled by no others living, the race qualities of their English ancestry and the tastes and habi-

tudes of their forefathers. If one knows well the Saxon nature, on the one hand, and has, on the other, been a close student of Kentucky life and character, stripped bare of the accidental circumstances of local environment, he may amuse himself endlessly with laying the two side by side and comparing the points of essential likeness. It is a question whether he is not more like an English ancestor than a New England contemporary. This is an old country, as things go in the West. The rock formation, a geologist will tell you, is very old; the soil is old; the race qualities here apparent are old. Is not the last true? In the Sagas, in the Edda, a man must be overbrave. "Let all who are not cowards follow me!" cried McGary, putting an end to all prudent counsel on the eve of the dreadful battle of the Blue Licks. The Kentuckian winced under the implication then, and has done it in a thousand instances since. Overbravery! The idea runs through all the anachronistic pages of Kentucky history, drawing them back into the past centuries of his race. It is this quality of temper and conception of manhood that has operated to build up in the mind of the world the ridiculous figure of the typical Kentuckian. Hawthorne conversed with an old man in England who told him that the Kentuckians flayed Tecumseh where he fell, and converted his skin into razor-strops. Collins, the Kentucky Froissart, speaking of Kentucky pioneers, relates of the father of one of them that he knocked Washington down in a quarrel, and received an apology from the Father of his Country on the following day—a little man, too. His son was the second Pepin of the house coming to this State, and here faithfully nourishing his family and his temper so long as he lived—the representative of many. I have been quick to mention this typical Hotspur figure, and to cast upon it the sulphurous side light of historic reminiscence, because I knew it would come foremost into the mind of the reader whenever one began to speak with candor of Kentucky life and character. Better have it up and be done with it. It was never a faithfully true face: satire bit always into burlesque along lines of coarseness and exaggeration. Much less is it true now, except in so far as it describes a kind of human being found the world over.

But I was saying that old race qualities are apparent here, because this is a people of English blood with hereditary agricultural tastes, and because it has remained to this day largely uncommingled with foreign strains. Here, for instance, is the old race conservatism that expends itself reverentially on established ways and familiar customs. The building of the first great turnpike in this country was opposed on the ground that it would shut up way-side taverns, throw wagons and teams out of employment, and destroy the market for chickens and oats. Prior to that, immigration was discouraged because it would make the already high prices of necessary articles so exorbitant that the permanent prosperity of the State would receive a fatal check. True, however, this opposition was not without a certain philosophy of Attic savor; for in those days people went to some distant lick for their salt, bought it warm from the kettle at seven or eight cents a pound, and packed it home on horseback, so that a fourth dropped away in bitter water. Coming back to the present, the huge yellowish-red stage-coach rolls to-day over the marbled roads of the blue-grass country. Families may be found living exactly where their pioneer ancestors effected a heroic settlement—a landed aristocracy, if there be such in America. Family names come down from generation to generation, just as a glance at the British peerage will show that they were long ago being transmitted in kindred families over the sea. One great honored name will do nearly as much here as there to keep a family in peculiar respect, after the reason for it has ceased. Here is that old invincible race ideal of personal liberty, and that old, unreckoning, truculent, animal rage at whatever infringes on it. They were among the very earliest to grant manhood suffrage. Nowhere in this country are the rights of property more inviolable, the violations of these more surely punished: neither counsel nor judge nor any power whatsoever can acquit a man who has taken fourpence of his neighbor's goods. Here is the old land-loving, land-holding,

HEMP FIELD.

home-staying, home-defending disposition. This is not the lunching, tourist race that, to Mr. Ruskin's horror, leaves its crumbs and chicken bones on the glaciers. The simple rural key-note of life is still the sweetest. Now, after the lapse of more than a century, the most populous town they have built contains less than twenty thousand white souls. Along with the love of land has gone comparative content with the fair annual increase of flock and field. No man among them has ever got immense wealth. Here is the old sense of personal privacy and reserve which has for centuries intrenched the Englishman in the heart of his estate, and forced him to regard with inexpugnable discomfort his nearest neighbor's boundaries. This would have been a densely peopled region, the farms would have been minutely sub-divided, had sons asked and received permission to settle on parts of the ancestral estate. This filling in and too close personal contact would have satisfied neither father nor child, so that the one has generally kept his acres intact, and the other, impelled by the same land hunger that brought his pioneer forefather thither, has gone hence into the younger West, where lie broader tracts and vaster spaces. Here is the old idea, somewhat current still in England, that the highest mark of the civilized gentleman is not cultivation of the mind, not intellect, not knowledge, but elegant living. Here is the old hereditary devotion to the idea of the State. Write the biographies of the men who have been engaged in national or in local politics, and you have largely the history of the State of Kentucky. Write the lives of all its scientists, artists, musicians, actors, poets, novelists, and you find many weary mile-stones between the chapters.

Enter the blue-grass region from what point you choose—and you may do this, so well traversed is it by railways—and you become sensitive to its influence. If you come from the North or the East, you say: "This is not in a broad sense typical modern America. Here is something local and unique. For one item, nothing goes fast here." By-and-by you see a blue-grass race-horse, and note an exception. But you do not also except the rider or the driver. The speed is not his, remember. He is a mere bunch of mistletoe to the horse. Detach him, and he is not worth timing. Indeed, with all the tracks in this country, there is not a general race-course

for the human race. Speed for the most part lies fallow. Every man starts for the goal at his own natural gait, and if he sees that it is too far off for him to reach it in a lifetime, he does not run the faster, but has the goal moved nearer him. I do not mean that the Kentuckians are provincial. As Thoreau said, no people can long remain provincial in character who have a propensity for politics, whittling, and rapid travelling. I do not mean that they are inaccessible to modern ideas, for they are not. I mean that the shock of modern ideas has not electrified them. They have walled themselves around with old race instincts and habitudes, and when the stream of tendency rushes against this wall, it recoils upon itself instead of sweeping away the barrier. Undoubtedly great breaches are here and there effected, and much constantly percolates through. I do not mean that civilization has ever suffered an arrest here, but that the old race momentum has carried its development along peculiar lines, and to the working out of characteristic effects.

One will not suppose, however, that there is here that modern American plague—Anglomania. The typical Kentuckian regards himself an American of the Americans, and thinks as little of being like the English as he would of imitating the Jutes. In nothing is he more like his transatlantic ancestry than in strong self-content. He sits on his farm as though it were the pole of the heavens—a manly man with a heart in him. Usually of the blonde type, robust, well formed, with clear, fair complexion, that grows ruddier with age and stomachic development, full neck, and an open, kind, untroubled countenance. He is frank, but not familiar; talkative, but not garrulous; full of the genial humor of local hits and allusions, but without a subtle nimbleness of wit; indulgent toward all purely masculine vices, but intolerant of petty crimes; no reader of books nor master in religious debate, faith coming to him as naturally as his appetite, and growing with what it is fed upon; loving roast pig, but not caring particularly for Lamb's eulogy; loving his grass like a Greek, not because it is beautiful, but because it is fresh and green; a peaceful man with strong passions, and so to be heartily loved and respected or heartily hated and respected, but never despised or trifled with. An occasional barbecue in the woods, where the saddles of South-Down mutton are roasted on spits over the coals of the mighty trench, and the steaming kettles of burgoo lend their savor to the nose of the hungry political orator, so that he becomes all the more impetuous in his invectives; the great agricultural fairs; the race-courses; the monthly county court day, when he meets his neighbors on the public square of the nearest town; the quiet Sunday mornings, when he meets them again for rather more clandestine talks at the front door of the neighborhood church—these and his own fireside are his characteristic and ample pleasures. You will never be under his roof without being deeply touched by the mellowest of all the virtues of his race—simple, unsparing human kindness and hospitality.

. The women of Kentucky have long had a reputation for beauty. An average type is a refinement on the English blonde—greater delicacy of form, feature, and color. A beautiful Kentucky woman is apt to be exceedingly beautiful. Her voice is almost uniformly low and soft; her hands and feet delicately formed; her skin quite pure and beautiful in tint and shading; her eyes blue or brown, and hair nut brown or golden brown; to all which is added a certain unapproachable refinement. It must not for a moment be supposed, however, that there are not many genuinely ugly women here, as elsewhere.

CHARLESTON, SOUTH CAROLINA

PERHAPS there are no two States which stand more as representatives of their two sections than Massachusetts and South Carolina. In the history of the country they have never been silent, and they have spoken with no uncertain sound. Though they have often been bitterly opposed, yet in their sturdy and uncompromising allegiance to what each has believed to be the right way of acting they have found a certain sympathy with each other, and a certain large measure of mutual respect. Each has felt that in the other she had a foeman worthy of her steel when in opposition, and when in conjunction a friend not to be misunderstood or distrusted. In the same way it might be said that their two largest cities are worthy antagonists, and now heartily respected friends. Boston is Massachusetts boiled down, and Charleston may be spoken of as a very strong decoction of South Carolina. Both think what they must, and say what they think. The people of both have a very strong attachment for and a hearty pride in their city, and an injury to it, an insult aimed at it, or even a humorous remark bearing on any of its peculiarities, is sure to call to their feet a host of indignant defenders. More than all others, these are the feminine cities of the Union, being all through and everywhere just what they are anywhere, and, like women, arousing a chivalric love. Both have a glorious past and a living present, such as in kind and intensity of personal life can scarce be easily found elsewhere—at any rate in the East, or in the original thirteen colonies. There is among their merchants a fine sense of honor, which holds itself high for the sake of the city as well as from personal motives, and in social life an aristocracy not based upon wealth. Both have a line of noble names, the very possession of which is a presumption of breeding and refinement. Both are the holders of the kind of firmness that begins with "O," and are ready to maintain their opinion with any and all arms. Both have strongly marked peculiarities in their English, and hold to these as firmly as to any other characteristic. They are noble and consistent members of the great family of cities, standing proudly side by side in spite of their well-marked differences, and acting as constant foils to the beauty of each other. While seeming to be opposed, they understand each other, and hold alike to the old motto concerning the obligations resting on a real nobility.

In the old times it was especially Boston that hated slavery, and it was Charleston, above all other cities, that hated anti-slavery. It has always been the boast of Boston that her public schools were absolutely perfect, and one would hardly have expected that any resemblance could be found to them, or to the spirit which runs through them, in the public schools of Charleston, differing as did the two cities for so long in the very principles of their existence. But there is a story about the public schools of Charleston before the war which is worth telling, and worthy of the noble city, and which shall not go untold so long as I, who was a part of it, do not forget the duty of recognizing noble deeds.

It was easy in Boston to carry on the schools. They were a part of the tradition of the city, and it took no great amount of courage to support and defend them. They were filled by the children of rich and poor alike, and it was the boast of the city that the child of the mechanic sat side by side with the children of the richest and noblest families. To be a teacher had always been to be respected, if not honored, and there was no thought of accepting charity in the children who enjoyed their advantages. This was generally the case in the Northern States. But in the South it was different. The public schools were supposed to be only for those who could not afford to pay for education, and consequently they had many of the characteristics of charity schools. The teaching in them was poor and far behind the times, and none of the families of breeding ever thought of sending their children to them. These were educated in small private schools, or at home under tutors and governesses, or were sent North. But about the year 1857 some of the best men in Charleston became dissatisfied with this state of things, and determined to see if it could not be bettered. They studied the ways of other cities, and the outcome of the movement was the building of three large school-houses after the New York plans, having each one accommodations for primary and grammar departments, and of one noble house of different idea, to be called the Girls' High and Normal School. They meant to have good schools, and they were determined to have good teachers, and in time to have them educated in their own city. The men who initiated the movement and who gave it their personal attention, and not merely the weight of their names, were the men who should begin such enterprises. They were a power in the community, and commanded universal respect and confidence. They made up their minds that as to schools they must learn of the North, and they faced the necessity of the situation with a noble courage. Their ultimate purpose was to supply their city with good schools, taught by native teachers, and they hesitated at no sacrifice of their life-long prejudices to attain their end. They must have large and convenient houses. They built them, sparing no expense and no trouble to make them as good as any. They needed teachers in line with the best theories, and familiar with the most tested practice of the profession. They took them from the principals of New York and Providence grammar-schools. They demanded the best, and they offered those men and women salaries sufficient to draw them from their positions in those two cities, and to make the question of their acceptance of the offers only a matter of time. They made these schools free to all the children of the city, and bought the books which were to be used. They furnished the rooms with everything that could make them attractive and healthful. They sought in the city for the best teachers, men and women, that they could find, and made them assistants to the Northern principals, to learn of and to be trained in their ways; and when all this had been done they put their own children, not only boys, but girls, into these public free schools, side by side with any who might choose to come. Never was there a nobler instance of entire singleness of purpose and of the sacrifice of preconceived opinions to conviction. It seems worth while to give the names of the Commissioners for the year 1860 as a testimony. Some of the names will be easily recognized as

familiar: C. G. Memminger, chairman; William C. Bee; W. J. Bennett; G. P. Bryan; George Buist; W. G. De Saussure; C. M. Furman; William Jervey; Hon. A. G. Magrath; Hon. W. A. Pringle; F. Richards; John Russell; E. Montague Grimké, secretary.

Of the building for the Girls' High and Normal School something more should be said. Situated in St. Philip Street, a square, three-story building with a crowning dome, it attracted the eye of whoever passed that way. Below there were wardrobes, and a large room for the use of the girls at recesses in stormy weather. The second story was filled by a hall and classrooms leading therefrom, while above was a still larger hall, to which the increased size of the school drove the daily sessions in the second year of its life. The glory of the place, however, was the garden in the midst of which it was set, and which, surrounded by a high stone wall, gave perfect freedom and seclusion to the pupils. This garden was overflowing with all sorts of roses and flowering plants, was laid out with gravelled walks, and well cared for by the Irish janitor, who had a little house on the premises. Dan was very proud of the garden and his care of it, though he used often to assure us that, for real beauty, now, there was no place like Ireland, adding, "And sure if ye were there now, I could show yez a spot where this blessed minute ye could stand knee-deep in clover." In the second story, and fronting this garden, was a piazza two stories in height, with lofty pillars reaching to the roof—a pleasanter spot than which, during the heats of the early summer, I have never found.

For this school, in which was the hope of the entire system, the teachers were all selected from the Northern States—the most convincing proof, if anything further were needed, of the noble courage and fearlessness of purpose which characterized every act of the Board of Commissioners. The principal was a teacher of long experience in the public schools of Boston, a native of New Hampshire; two of the assistants were Massachusetts born and bred, and one came from Pennsylvania. To show how conservative and wise were the board, it may be stated that of the seventy-seven teachers in all the public schools, only nine were of Northern birth and home. But in the Normal School, where the future teachers were to be trained, they were all Northern, that the very best and most modern work might be done there.

Of those three women, coming thus into a new home and a strange city, I was one, and am therefore telling what I know and saw.

It was a fresh experience, the voyage thither in one of the beautiful steamers which then ran between Charleston and the Northern cities—the *Massachusetts* and the *South Carolina*. But stranger to our Northern eyes was Charleston itself, with the cross on old St. Michael's rising high above it as the steamer came in view of the garden-loving city. The harbor is bad, like those of all the sand-line cities; and the steamers, though drawing at the utmost only sixteen feet, were often obliged to lie outside waiting for high water, and had always to time their departures by the almanac. But, once within the bars and on shore, there were no bars in the welcome of the people. Not only by our personal friends, but by all connected with the schools, were we made to feel at home. The exquisite breeding of the city asserted itself, and at once took us, though from an alien land and a different civilization, into its charmed circle. The commissioners who had invited us there spared no pains to make our stay pleasant, making us welcome to their homes as well as to those of all the best people in the city. Courtesies of all kinds were offered to us. How beautiful and strange it all was—the rides about the country, where, while our Northern homes were still shivering in frost and snow, the Cherokee rose spread its white petals along the dusty roads, and we picked the yellow jasmine where the gray moss hung from the live-oaks! Camellias blossomed unafraid in the open air, and our desks at school were beautiful with them and magnolia blooms, or weighted with daintily arranged baskets of the purple or the large lemon figs which our girls had picked as they came to school from before their doors. The memory even now lies in my mind, sweet and still, persistent as the odor of orange blossoms from the Charleston trees. The orange-tree is not safe in that latitude; a sudden frost might stifle its life; but they were sometimes planted, and were of course found in conservatories or raised in parlors.

It was with a curious interest that we studied the buildings and customs of the town, so different in every way from those of our Northern homes. The long, airy houses with their three stories of piazzas, the negro quarters in the yards, often much larger and more imposing than the dwelling of the master and mistress, swarming with happy and careless life, as the many servants passed to and fro between house and quarters; and the little darkies of all ages were free to play and tumble to their hearts' content, unless, indeed, a sweet-voiced call came from the rear of the piazza, "George Washington and Columbus, come notice Miss Elvira!" followed by the rush of perhaps half a dozen small darkies of varying ages, all eager to play with and care for the heiress of the house and of them. And the loving and reverent care which they did take of the little Elvira was beautiful to see! Then the long stretch of the yard, with its pump in the middle, where a buxom serving-maid was filling her pails of water, which came into the house afterwards, one poised on her stately head, while she carried two in her hands; the queer wooden shutters, and the bewildering arrangement of the numbers of the houses on the street, where it was said that every citizen, if he moved, carried his number with him as a part of his personal property; the inevitable negro everywhere, waiting on and serving us at every turn; the beautiful gardens, whose high gates opened mysteriously and swiftly by invisible hands at the appeal of the loud-echoing bell. While one negro led us up the path, another opened the front door, a third escorted us to the drawing-room, while a fourth announced our arrival to the gracious mistress, and a fifth chubby little girl or boy appeared before we were fairly seated with a tray of cooling drink! And the procession of servants from the kitchen when dinner was in course of serving, one servant for each dish, so that everything was smoking hot, though it had come some distance in the open air! The queer and fascinating dialect of the negroes, and the altogether fascinating accent of the Charlestonians, the flare and live sighlike breath of the pitch-pine knots in the fireplace in the evening or the early morning, when the servant who came to make our fire entertained us all the time of her stay by her remarks, and never quitted the room—which she did half a dozen times during the process—leaving us in doubt as to what her errand might be, but announcing encouragingly each time, as she opened the door and disappeared, "Now I'm going for the matches," "Now I'm going for to fetch the dust-pan," etc. All was new, and full of interest and suggestion.

The regulations under which it was considered necessary to keep the colored population were to us new and interesting. The law at that time forbade their being taught to read. A colored woman could not wear a veil in the street, nor were two negroes allowed to walk arm in arm except at funerals. A curious and suggestive thing happened, therefore. Every negro funeral was largely attended, and the corpse was sure to be followed to the grave by an imposing line of mourners, all walking arm in arm. One very marked figure in the city was the old man at the ladies' entrance of the Charleston Hotel. I think I have never seen a man who had more the appearance of being somebody's grandfather than this kindly old Marcus. One day he had disappeared, and there was no one at the door. After long and futile search for him, a messenger brought word that he wanted the loan of money in order to return, and the mystery was finally solved by the discovery that he could not come, not because he had bought either oxen or land or married a wife, but for the simple reason that, having become more than specially interested in his one only pastime of gambling the night before, he had, in a fit of noble rage at his persistent ill luck, rashly hazarded his clothes—and lost the game. A contribution from his friends at the hotel soon restored him, clothed and in his right mind, which was a very positive one. There was a tradition current that one evening, as a party of lately arrived Northerners were having a pleasant conversation in the parlor somewhat late, they were surprised by the appearance of Marcus, who gravely informed them that he had come to sweep the parlors, and that "our folks in dis house always goes to bed by half past ten, sah!" The intimation was humbly heeded. Of course no one could resist the law of the hotel when the decisions were handed down from such a height.

Old St. Michael's Church was well worth a visit, with its tiled aisles and square pews. In its steeple, 193 feet in height, were the chimes which marked the quarters of the hour, and here too were

rung, morning and evening, the bells which regulated the negroes in their perambulations. In winter the evening bells ring from quarter of six to six, and for a quarter of an hour before nine. This last was called the "last bell-ringing," and after it had ceased to sound any unfortunate negro found in the streets, unless he could show a pass from his master, was summarily deposited in the guard-house for the remainder of the night. During the ringing of the last bell two men regularly performed on the fife and drum on the corner opposite where the guard-house was situated, and the negroes who came out to listen to the music dispersed in quick time as the last tap was given the drum, and the last stroke of the bell lingered in the air. The watchman in the tower called the hour, and all relapsed into silence again. I give a literal copy of one of these passes:

"CHARLESTON, March 12, 1855.
"Paris has permission to pass from my residence in Beaufain St., near Rutledge, to the corner of Vanderhorst's wharf and East Berry, and from thence back again to my residence, before drum-beat in the morning, for one month.
"JAS. B. CAMPBELL.
"J. L. HUTCHINSON, Mayor."

One of the most interesting places was the church of Rev. J. L. Girardeau, a very large building, capable of seating perhaps fourteen hundred persons. In the morning the lower floor was occupied by the white congregation, and the negroes, as in the other churches, sat in the galleries, but in the afternoon the negroes filled the body of the house, the whites being seated only at the sides and in the galleries. To one not accustomed to the sight, the church then presented a striking appearance, and we had an opportunity of seeing all shades and varieties of color, in both complexion and dress. The old and staid negro women generally wore bright handkerchiefs twisted around the head, sometimes with the addition, though not the amendment, of a bonnet perched upon the top thereof, crown uppermost; but the younger and gayer portion of the community wore bonnets of all styles, from the most fashionable to the most obsolete. The only music was by the negroes, and it was really worth hearing. As of course they could not read, the hymn was retailed, two lines at a time, by the minister, who usually began the singing, and it welled out refreshingly strong and true. Before the services commenced the audience sometimes struck up a voluntary, greeting the ear as we entered in the form of some grand old tune sung by the assembled throng. The courtesy which surrendered the main part of the church to the negroes for half the time was only one out of many customs in the city which testified to the general kind feeling existing between master and slave, where true nobility asserted itself in relation to inferiors as well as to equals. In the homes of Charleston the negroes were treated like a sort of children of the household, and this because of a real affection.

The strength of family feeling on the part of the negroes was often queerly put, as thus: "Law sakes! Balaam Preston Hamilton Smith," a venerable old negro was heard to exclaim to a young man who was understood to be thinking of marrying, "don't say you'd go fur to 'liberate fur to take up wid any middlin' set. If you want a wife, you'd better marry into de Middleton family. De Middletons is a mighty good family. Hm! De Roses is 'spectable too; but jes look at me! I married into de Middleton family!"

The closeness of the relation was amusingly illustrated by an incident which occurred in school when we insisted that certain words should be pronounced according to authority, and not in the way in which the girls had been accustomed to sound them. "But," they said, "you know we grow up with the negroes, they take care of us, and we hear them talk all the time. Of course we can't help catching some of their ways of talking. It sounds all right to us." They were told that if they could find in any dictionary the least authority for the pronunciation dear to them, there would be no objection to it; that we were only trying to give them the best, and that it was not for any notion of ours that we insisted. "But," they said, quickly and sadly, "the dictionaries are all Northern dictionaries!" and so the matter came to an end. For it was by no means nothing but flowers and fruit from their gardens that these Southern maidens were in the habit of bringing to us, their Northern teachers; they brought to our aid every morning the sweetest docility, the greatest eagerness to learn, and the most perfect breeding. Even in the days after the *Star of the*

West had been fired on, and the whole city was full of devotion to the Palmetto State and of denunciations of the North and of the people there; when for a Northern woman it was sometimes difficult to be calm; when we could neither listen to the prayers offered from the pulpits nor read the newspapers; when threatening anonymous letters came to our hand, and we grew tired with the constant strain and uncertainty—even then, and perhaps even more than before, to cross the threshold of that school-room was to pass at once into an atmosphere of peace and unfailing courtesy. Those girls came from homes that were full of bitter feeling and opposition to the North, but there was never an ungentle look or word from them to their Northern teachers. The school-room was an asylum, a safe and sure place for us; and what this meant of good-breeding and loyalty is comprehensible perhaps only to those who have spent their lives in contact with young and warm-hearted girls. There is nothing but sweet and dear memories of those girls, light-hearted and happy then, but with heavy clouds of war and trouble hanging over them — war and trouble which in more than one instance broke up happy homes, and struck down at their sides the brothers and the friends whom they so loved. I have before me now a card on which the girls of the first class wrote their names together for me, and to look it over is to recall much of sadness, though much of devotion, faithfulness, and high courage. The planning of this work is exquisitely neat, as was all the work that they did. Here are the names of two sisters, who afterwards became teachers in our places when we came away. Underneath, a name that recalls all gentleness and grace; next it, that of a girl whose parents had been born in New England, and who showed it in every fibre. Then comes Sallie, tall and slender, full of dash and fire, and the indescribable charm of the Southern girl, with her haughty, "Who'd stoop to quarrel?" so often said when some difference arose in the class; then Lizzie, with her beautiful dark eyes and her no less beautiful disposition, whose after-life was so full of sadness and sorrow; then the carefully written signature of the girl who took up the teacher's life, drawing her inspiration from what we brought her in those long-past days, and who has become a tower of strength to a new generation in her chosen profession; and then Celia, who, leaving her gracious and luxurious home, gave up her life to caring for the poor and suffering, and died at her post, mourned by the whole city. Sweet and strong they pass before me in memory, the girls of that first class, with the happy days in which we lived together in the close relation of teacher and taught. They had never before been in a large school, and its life and regulations were new and striking to them. They grew mentally like plants given a new sun and soil, and the work to the educator was beyond measure delightful, yielding a rich harvest.

We had visitors, men and women, to all of whom our work was of the greatest interest, and to whom it was a comparative novelty to be allowed to visit a school, and to see the work going on. I was greatly puzzled at first by the saying, which I heard often, that they had come to "see the system," as if we had some patent method of conveying information and of training, which had to be applied in some well-defined manner. I have since learned that this idea is not peculiar to the South.

Not different from the cordiality with which we were welcomed to the city homes was the thoughtful kindness which provided for our Christmas holidays. To see the rice plantation, with its long avenue of live-oaks, and the noble mansion standing on the wide lawn; to go over the store-house, where were kept goods of all kinds ready to be distributed to the field hands, the piles of dress goods and provisions, and all presided over by the gracious mistress of the house; to watch the men laborers, tall and brawny, splendid animals, with their fully developed muscles, and their rows of perfect white teeth, and the not-so-fortunate negro women, who also toiled in the rice-fields, bent and knotted with the labor; to see the great supper provided for them on Christmas eve, and to listen to their rejoicing and songs—all this was a great pleasure and a great lesson.

But it all was to pass away. The Democratic Convention in April, 1860, to which we devoted all our spare time, was a highly interesting and significant event. Political meetings grew more common and more enthusiastic. Then followed the election of President Lincoln, and the immediate resignation of the Federal judge, one of our commissioners, the Hon. A. G. Magrath, and of the district attorney. The streets bloomed with palmetto flags, and with a great variety of mottoes, and the air grew more and more charged with electrical feeling. The banks all suspended November 30, 1860. The convention met December 16th, and the act of secession was passed on the 20th, between one and two o'clock. The firing of guns and the ringing of bells announced the fact to the eager populace, and we began to live in a scene of the wildest excitement—a double-distilled Fourth of July. Business was at once suspended, and stores were closed. The chimes of old St. Michael's rang merrily at intervals all the afternoon. Fire companies of both colors paraded the streets, noisily jingling their bells, and one continually met members of the Vigilant Rifles, the Zouaves, the Washington Light-Infantry, or some other of the many companies, hurrying in a state of great excitement to their headquarters. Boys in the street shouted, "Hurrah! Out of the Union!" with all the strength of their lungs; and the negroes, who, on hearing any unusual noise, always made their appearance at all the gates, stood in groups at every passageway. The young men devoted themselves to drinking the health of the State, and exhibited indubitable evidence of having done so as they walked or drove furiously along. On Meeting and King streets in several places the sidewalks were covered with the remains of Indian crackers, and the whole air was redolent of gunpowder.

The excitement by no means came to an end as the day wore to its close, with a rosy sunset over the rippling waters of the Ashley, and when the twilight had died away an illumination of the principal business streets by means of blazing tar-barrels produced a strong and bodeful light. Meeting Street, from above the Charleston Hotel to below Institute or "Secession" Hall, was ablaze with burning tar, which overflowed so that sometimes the whole width of the street was aflame.

Ladies as well as gentlemen crowded Secession Hall at an early hour. About half the floor was reserved for members of the convention and the Legislature, the remainder being filled with an excited crowd of men. The meeting was opened with a prayer, short but comprehensive, acknowledging the possibility of suffering and privation, but asking, after that was passed, that their sails might whiten every sea, and their agriculture and commerce be greatly prospered. The ordinance of secession was then handed to the president, and by him read from a large parchment with the seal of the State hanging therefrom. At its close tumultuous applause shook the building, and the delegates, called in the order of their districts, were summoned to affix their names. The table upon which the signing was done was that upon which the ratification of the Federal Constitution had been signed. The whole evening there was a constant discharge of fireworks, crackers, and fire-arms in the street below, so that during the prayer it was at times impossible to hear what was being said. Bands of music passed at intervals, and the crowd outside shouted and cheered without intermission.

At last the signing was over, and the president, taking up the parchment amid profound silence, said, "The ordinance of secession has been signed and ratified, and I proclaim the State of South Carolina to be an independent commonwealth." This was the signal for an outburst of enthusiasm such as is not often witnessed. Every one rose to his feet, and all broke forth into tumultuous and ever-renewed cheering. Handkerchiefs waved, hats were swung round and wildly tossed into the air, or they were elevated on canes, swords, or muskets, and spun round and round. The act of secession was then read to the crowd on the outside of the building, who greeted it with their shouts. The two palmetto-trees which stood on either side of the platform were despoiled of their leaves by the audience as mementos of the occasion, and the meeting slowly dispersed.

It was in the assembly-room of the old school-house, early on the morning of January 9, 1861, as I sat at the desk bending over my books preparing for the day's work, that I heard the report of the first gun which was fired at the *Star of the West*, and lifted my head to listen, with a great fear at my heart, and an effort to persuade myself that the sounds were only the effect of my excited imagination as they came again and again. On the morning of April 12th I was twenty miles away, in one of the beautiful homes where we had been so often welcome guests, and on coming down to breakfast found anxious faces and much excitement among the servants, who reported that they had heard firing all the night in the direction of Charleston. We ate breakfast almost in silence, our only thought being whether we could get to the city that day; and after the meal was over stood on the broad piazza waiting till the big strong farm wagon could be arranged to take us to the railroad station. At last it appeared.

The driver went to the kitchen for a last word, and detailed one of the house-servants who stood looking on to stand in front of the horses till he should return. The latter, attracted by the play of two children, turned away to watch them; some sudden noise startled the horses, and away they went, big wagon and all, in a mad run round and round over the great field, in and out among out-houses, sheds, and trees, while we stood helplessly looking on, and heard the sound of the guns. It seemed a long time before they made for the opposite sides of a tree, which they saw stood directly in their way, and smashing the pole of the wagon on its trunk, were brought to a standstill. There was the wagon hopelessly ruined, so far as any journey in it for that day was concerned, dripping as to its back end with broken eggs; there was the terrified negro, tears streaming down his face, and crying out, "Oh, I only looked away from dose horses one minute, and now I have done more harm dan I can pay for all my life long!" And again and again we heard the sound of the far-off guns. The brother of one of our company was on duty at one of the forts; the families of all of them were there whence came the ominous sound. But there was absolutely nothing to do on that isolated plantation but to sit still or pace up and down while the servants hunted for some other vehicle in sufficient order to be trusted to carry all of us over the roads, floating with the spring rains. They worked at an old carry-all, which they found stored away in a shed, till they thought it safe to trust, and it was some time after dinner before we finally set off for the railroad station miles away. When we reached there in safety, in spite of the ominous groans and creaks of the crazy old carriage in which we sat crowded, the air was full of rumors, but we could hear nothing definite. At last came the train, delayed, and with troops on board, whose number was augmented at several stations where we stopped, to be still farther delayed, and when we were finally landed in a shed on the side of the river opposite Charleston, we found it swarming with citizen soldiery. We crossed the river, and said hasty good-byes. I rushed to my boarding-place, flung down my packages, and hastening through the streets, filled with an excited crowd, reported myself to the principal of the school as being in the city, to be greeted as soon as seen by the exclamation, "By Jove! I knew you'd get here somehow."

The night came and passed, and the sun rose cloudless and bright on one of the April days which are like the June days of New England, but the wind had shifted, and we heard no reports. It was believed that the firing had ceased—why, no one could tell—but at the Battery the smoke still showed that it had not, even though there it was almost impossible to hear the sound.

Let us go thither. Many of the stores have their doors open, but no shutters are unclosed, and only necessary business is transacted. We go down Meeting Street, past Institute or Secession Hall, and remember the scene of the 20th of last December there. Saddled horses stand waiting at the door, and remind us that General Beauregard's office is within. As we turn down Water Street towards the East Battery the crowd becomes visible, lining the sidewalk. Making our way between the carriages which fill the street, we mount the steps leading to the walk, and taking up our position at the least crowded part, turn our attention to the harbor. The reports come deadened to the ear, though one can easily tell whence the shot come by the smoke.

The crowd increases, and is composed of all materials. Women of all ages and ranks of life look eagerly out with spyglasses and opera-glasses. Children talk and laugh and walk back and forth in the small moving-space as if they were at a public show. Now and then a man in military dress goes hastily past. Grave men talk in groups. Young men smoke and calculate probabilities and compare conflicting reports, and still the guns send forth their deadly missiles, and the light clouds suddenly appearing and hanging over the fort till dispersed by the wind tell of the shells which explode before they reach their destination.

"There goes Stevens again! He gives it to 'em strong!" and a puff of white smoke rises from the iron-clad battery.

"Look! Did you see the bricks fly then from the end of the fort? She struck that time!"

"What is that smoke over Sumter? Isn't it smoke?" and all glasses and eyes are turned in that direction and watch eagerly. It increases in volume and rolls off seaward. What can it be? Is he going to blow up the fort? Is he heating shot? What is it? Still the batteries keep up their continual fire, and Anderson's guns, amidst a cloud of smoke, return with two or three discharges. Suddenly a white cloud rises from Sumter, and a loud report tells of the explosion of some magazine—"Probably a magazine on the roof for some of his barbette guns" —and the firing goes on.

"Look out! Moultrie speaks again!" and another puff of smoke points out the position of that fort, followed by one from the floating battery of the others. We listen and watch.

"I don't believe Anderson is in the fort. He must have gone off in the night and left only a few men. It was a very dark night."

"See the vessels off there? No, not there; farther along to the right of Sumter. That small one is the *Harriet Lane*."

"Yes, I can see them plain with the naked eye. Ain't they going to do anything? The large one has hauled off."

"No; they are still."

"Look! Can you see those little boats? Three little boats a hundred yards apart. They are certainly coming."

"Yes," said a woman, an opera-glass at her eyes, "the papers this morning said they were to re-enforce with small boats, which were to keep at a great distance from each other." Another, incredulous, says they are nothing but waves, and you can see plenty anywhere like them. "Doubleday is killed," remarks another. "They saw him from Moultrie, lying on top of the ramparts."

This is set at naught by a small boy, who says, "Look, do you see that mosquito just on the corner of that flag in Sumter?" and a dignified silence follows.

Now the smoke rises over Sumter again, black smoke, and curls away, but no other signs of life. We watch, and as we watch it grows blacker and thicker. The fort must be on fire!

"Yes! Can't you see the flame? There

at the south angle! You can see it through this glass. Look now!"

The smoke hides all one side of the fort, and the leaping flames leave no room for doubt. They spread till it seems as if the whole fort must be a sheet of flame within, and the firing goes on as if nothing had happened, but no signs of life at Fort Sumter. Why doesn't the fleet do something? How *can* men with blood in their veins idly watch the scene and not lend a helping hand when they have the power? They must be armed vessels! Is Anderson still in the fort? No signal comes from there, and the firing continues, and the shells explode around and within, and the dense black smoke rolls away, and the flames leap round the flag-staff.

"Now you'll see that old flag go down!" cries a boy with a spy-glass.

"*That old flag!*"

I listen and watch in mournful silence, and hear the beating of my heart as the flames rise higher and higher. What does it mean? Anderson can't be in the fort! He must be on board the fleet, or they could not stand idly by.

"He has probably left slow matches to some of his guns. He means to burn up the fort—to blow it up!"

"Captain Foster intimated that it was undermined," says another.

Still the flag-staff stands, though the flames are red around it.

"It would be a bad omen if the flag should stand all this fire," says a gentleman at my side as he hands me his glass. I level it and look.

A vessel has dropped anchor just between, and the flag of the Confederate States, fluttering from the fore, completely conceals the staff at Sumter. I move impatiently to the right to get rid of it, and see with throbbing heart the flag still safe, and watch with sickening anxiety.

Another explosion, which scatters the smoke for a while.

"He is blowing up the barracks to prevent the fire from spreading," says one.

Can it be that he is still there?

Still the flag waves as of old. The flames die down, and the smoke somewhat clears away, and the shells explode as before, and Major Stevens fires continually.

"It is West Point against West Point to-day," says one.

"Stevens was not at West Point."

"No, but Beauregard was a pupil of Anderson's there."

The tide has turned and is going out, and now the vessels cannot come in. What does it mean? Still the people pass and repass; the crowd thins a little; they jest idly and remark on the passers, and conversation goes on. Friends meet and greet each other with playful words. Judge Magrath stands in a careless attitude, a red camellia in his button-hole, at the window of one of the houses overlooking the scene. Beauregard passes, observant. Carriages drive by. People begin to leave.

"The flag is down!" A shot has struck the staff and carried it away. "Look! the flag is down!" and an excited crowd rush again through the streets leading to the Battery, and a shout fills the air.

The flag of the United States has been shot down in the harbor of Charleston, South Carolina.

"It is up again on a lower staff!" "Yes!" "No!" "It is a white flag!"

A white flag waves from the walls of Fort Sumter, and the colors which have been repeatedly lowered to-day as a signal of distress in vain have fallen at last.

The firing ceases, and Anderson surrenders unconditionally, with the fort a blazing furnace.

The school went on, and everything there was as usual, except perhaps a shade of added gravity, and a sense of sorrow for the parting which flung its shadow over teachers and taught; if it had been possible, an increased docility and loving gentleness on the one hand, a greater tender watchfulness and earnestness on the other. The shadow grew heavier and the parting nearer as the months went on, full of stir, till the day in early June when I left my class to meet the chairman of the special commissioners for our school in the dome-room, not to stand there again. Mr. Bennett had brought me my salary, then due; he paid me as usual *in gold*, and he said: "We are very sorry that you feel you must go. We want you to say that when this trouble is over you will come back to us," and he reached out his hand for a leave-taking with the old-time courtesy of which we had so much since we had made our home in Charleston. I said: "Mr. Bennett, I am so sorry to go! But I cannot promise to come back. I am afraid that neither you nor I nor any one knows how long this trouble is going to last, and I cannot say anything about coming back."

And so I had to turn away from my girls, and travel to Massachusetts by way of Georgia, Tennessee, Kentucky, Indiana, Ohio, Pennsylvania, and New York. I have the notes of that journey still, kept in pencil as we went, full of excitement and wonder. As the war went on, the schools had to stop; all the beautiful fabric so wisely and so nobly planned was destroyed, and the labor seemed to have been in vain. The shells went ploughing their way through the roof into the old class-rooms, so full of sweet and gracious memories, and fell in the flower-planted garden where we had walked with the eager girls. Trouble and anguish fell upon the dear old city. And when her people fled to Columbia, fire and destruction met them there, such realities as we at the North never knew, even with all that came to us. That was the time when a young woman remarked to my friend one evening, "Well, whatever happens, I am sure that we shall not be utterly ruined, for my father has put our goods in seven different places in the city, so that we shall be sure to have something," and said "Good-night." In the lurid glare of the next morning, before daybreak, the same girl knocked at the same door with the piteous appeal: "Have you got a dress you can lend me to wear? I have not one thing left." That was what war meant to those people. We thought it was hard!

I turn over the relics in my possession with gratitude and affection never wavering and with profound respect—the pass for gray-headed "Paris," in its faded ink, with the strong, manly signature of his master at the foot; letters, records, and, given to me long after, postage-stamps bearing the name of the Confederate States; sheets of note-paper with the palmetto flag and the Confederate flag in colors at the head; a newspaper printed on wall-paper, bearing date, "Vicksburg, July 4, 1863"; and bank-bills of all denominations, from five hundred dollars to five cents. These are coarse in execution and on a poor quality of paper; but they used the very best they had. I know that no New York bank will take them on deposit, for I tried them once at the desk of the receiving-teller of the Sixth National, with as inexpressive a face as I can command from a long experience in teaching—which is saying a great deal—

and much to the astonishment of that functionary. But they are not valueless, for all that. There are many things which the banks will not take, and yet which are worth more than all the silver in the Treasury vaults at Washington, and realer than real estate in New York. These bills stand to-day for such assets as those, for "he who can prevail upon himself to devote his life for a cause, however we may condemn his opinions or abhor his actions, vouches at least for the honesty of his principles and the disinterestedness of his motives. . . . He is no longer a slave, but free. The contempt of death is the beginning of virtue." And surely the old South needed no lessons in virtue from us.

But the work on those schools was not lost, for one by one they who had been our girls took up the task with the spirit we had helped to inspire in them, and one of them has made not only on her city, but on the wide Southern country from which her girls come to her wise guidance, an abiding mark. After the war was over, and the time of mismanagement and misuse, the seed that had been sown in earnest faith, unswerving purpose, and singleness of spirit brought forth a hundredfold.

And the two cities, so alike in so many ways, so different from all the other cities of the land, even through the bitter war learned to know each other better, and to recognize more fully their common character. As is the case often with two human sisters, they repelled each other simply because they were at heart and in all that constitutes true nobility so much alike. But as two sisters, taught better to understand each other by the experience of life, find their former repulsion changed into attraction, and finally into a complete unity that no outside influence can in the least affect, so is it with Boston and Charleston. When fire and earthquake fought for the possession of their beauty and their old and sacred places, they reached out tender hands to each other; for in the new dispensation the Lord was in both fire and earthquake. The great and strong wind bears now only peace and good-will for message on its Northern and Southern way, and if ever henceforth there be need of defending "that old flag," no two States will stand closer shoulder to shoulder than Massachusetts and South Carolina.

DRAINAGE OF THE EVERGLADES

THE first proposal to drain the over-flowed lands of South Florida was made in 1847 by Hon. J. D. Westcott, based upon the reports of General W. S. Harney, who had explored the Everglades in the Indian wars, and General Thomas S. Jesup, who had thoroughly scouted the valley of the Kissimmee and the region west and south of Peace Creek. Mr. Buckingham Smith, in the same year, made an interesting report to the Secretary of the Treasury upon the practicability of the scheme. Upon the strength of this and confirmatory reports of the army and navy officers, an act of Congress, August 12, 1848, granted the swamp and overflowed lands to the State of Florida, on condition of draining the same, the act being incorporated in a general law dedicating the proceeds from the sales of such lands, in any State where they lay, after the expense of drainage was paid, to purposes of internal improvement and education.

But Indian hostilities delayed active operations for ten years, and the outbreak of the civil war remanded the enterprise to the study of theorists. The slow percolation of population into South Florida, accelerated by the investment of Hon. W. M. Randolph, of Louisiana, and Hon. H. S. Sanford, ex-Minister to Belgium, in the county of Orange, which abuts upon the drainage area, was followed by the building of the South Florida Railroad, from the new town of Sanford, on the upper waters of the St. John's, to Orlando, the thriving county seat. Under Mr. James E. Ingraham's administration the road was pushed through to Lake Tohopeka-liga, the summit reservoir or source of

Kissimmee River. Practical and economical interests revived the study of the theorists. Careful surveys of engineers of steamboat, railway, and canal companies were re-enforced by those of the United States Topographical Corps, under an act of Congress, and the general features of the country were mapped. These, however, were disconnected, and pertaining to other interests or enterprises. Under a charter of incorporation from the State, March 5, 1879, Mr. James M. Kramer, civil engineer of the Drainage Company, entered upon a more thorough and practical survey of the area subject to drainage south and west of Peace Creek, or south of Township 25, and west of Range xxvii., including the valley of the Kissimmee and the great basin of the Okeechobee and the Everglades.

Of this region the agent of the State, Mr. S. L. Niblack, says, in his report, June 27, 1882, that the water of Lake Okeechobee does not overflow the country around the lake, except on the south, where it spreads out over the Everglades, and that the flooding of the flats of the Kissimmee River is caused by the rain-fall. In the dry season, from October to May, these vast prairies are partially drained, and pastured with thousands of wild cattle, which feed on the rich, nutritious grasses. The extent of the area south of latitude 28° thus subjected to periodic inundation from the rain-fall is estimated by Mr. Kramer at 1000 square miles in excess of the combined areas of the States of Rhode Island, Connecticut, New Jersey, and Delaware. The problem submitted to the engineers, therefore, was simply to relieve this vast territory, of which a large proportion is not subject to inundation, but is susceptible of immediate cultivation, of the surplus water of the rainy season. This, from estimate of observations extended over eight years at Punta Rassa, near Charlotte Harbor, is annually an average of three feet eight and a half inches. In the interior the average is probably in excess of this. This quantity, distributed over a season from May to September, through sunshiny or windy forenoons and rainy evenings, is not abnormal. Any soil properly drained and aerated will rapidly absorb and utilize its daily proportion before the rainy afternoon follows. The cause of this superficial accumulation lies in the physics and topography of South Florida, and complicates the engineering problem, but without rendering it more difficult. Indeed, when it is understood, the practicability of drainage by parts becomes easy and simple in solution.

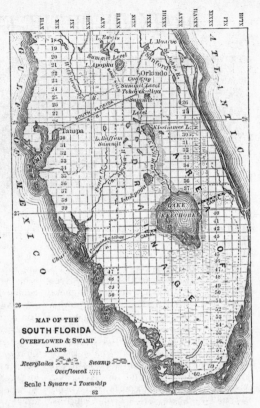

MAP OF THE
SOUTH FLORIDA
OVERFLOWED & SWAMP
LANDS
Everglades   *Swamp*
Overflowed
Scale 1 *Square* = 1 *Township*

From an average elevation of two hundred feet above the sea, on the 30° 30′ parallel of latitude, the peninsula slopes by a slow, easy descent to the keys. But this incline, fifty miles wide by three hundred long, is broken into longitudinal and transverse sections of terraces. The St. John's, gathering its waters into a chain of lakes about the twenty-eighth parallel, flows north along the eastern flanks of the interior table-land, from a maximum elevation of twenty feet above the sea, to the Atlantic, near Jacksonville. A depression of a maximum elevation of eighty-seven feet above the sea divides the long slope of the interior table, in the latitude of Lake George, extending up the irregular valley of the Ocklawaha and across to the Wicassisa, emptying into the Gulf. South of this the land rises again to an elevation of one hundred and forty-six feet above the sea on the sand-hills west of Orange. This ridge, holding Lake Apopka between its arms, latitude 28° 40′, extends south sixty miles, rising, above Lake Buffum, in Polk County, to an elevation of one hundred and sixty-three feet. From this ridge and the terraces of lakes about it the Ocklawaha and the Wekiva flow north and east;

the Withlacoochee north and west; the Charley Apopka and Peace Creek south and west; and the Kissimmee and Blue Jordan, a swamp river, south into Okeechobee. The rivers east of the ridge discover the peculiar terrace form of the topography; that is, the water, seeping down, pools and fills a shallow trough at the foot of the ridge, from which it overflows into a lower terrace, pooling again, and thus successively develops the chain of linked lakes exhibited by the St. John's.

The western valley shore of this river below Lake Monroe, 10.976 feet above the sea, is less than three miles wide. Sanford is fourteen feet higher; and Belair Grove, three miles inland, forty feet higher. So, going west from Lake Winder, ninety miles up the St. John's, and 18.737 feet above the sea at Charlotte Harbor, the head of Wolf Creek, ten miles in the interior, is at an elevation of 61.989 feet; and Lake Conway, on the highest terrace of Orange County, one hundred feet above the sea, having no visible outlet, seeps through

MAP OF THE TOHOPEKALIGA SUMMIT LEVEL.

swamp and marsh to Little Tohopekaliga, a fall of twenty-nine feet in less than ten miles. These various examples of river marsh or upland lake indicate that the terrace form of the topography of South and East Florida is not a local incident, but a general characteristic. Of this simple explanation of that accumulation of superficial water the engineer avails himself in order to drain these terraces successively. Otherwise, if the flooding of the prairies was caused by the overflow of a single grand reservoir of the valley at Okeechobee, the drainage would be accomplished by enlarging its outlets. Over these the long rain cloud from May to September unburdens its fruitful showers, filling and overflowing terrace over terrace, from each of which the freshet falls, not into the single channel of one mighty river, but down broad, shallow valleys, overspreading the wild pastures that fringe the central basin; and, combining with its gathered volume of increase, stays the slow drainage and evaporation mayhap from season to season. When this occurs, and the redoubled freshets of each successive terrace unite with the combined volume of the Kissimmee River in Lake Okeechobee, the overburdened banks give way to the impetuous floods, which in 1841, '48, '55, '62, '69–'70, and '74 drowned the palm groves of the Caloosahatchee.

But when the dynamics of this system of terraces is understood, it becomes a key

to the solution of the problem of drainage. The engineer is not left to the alternative of reducing the volume spread over twenty thousand nine hundred square miles at once. He can proceed from terrace to terrace, reclaiming the higher ones by successive descent, step by step, while the drainage of the central basin proceeds as an independent operation. This can be best illustrated by the maps. The one above includes the region west from Lake Winder, on the St. John's, Township 26, Range xxxv., and extends westward six townships. The general elevation of this table above the sea at Charlotte Harbor is 66.82 feet. The highest basin is the small lake in Township 26, Range xxxii. The summit ridge is in Range xxxiii. The general contour of the terrace is represented by the topographical chart below, reduced from the surveys of Assistant-Engineer W. G. Williamson, of the United States Topographical Corps. It does not represent an airline, but the depression of lake surfaces, after crossing the divide between the valley of the St. John's and the summit level. The distances from Lake Winder and the elevations above the sea at Charlotte Harbor are given in the following table.

	Distance from Lake Winder in Miles.	Elevation above the Sea at Charlotte Harbor in Feet.
Lake Winder	00.0	18.787
Head of Wolf Creek .	10.11	61.989
Alligator Lake	28.40	71.484
Isabel Lake	31.41	71.804
Little Tohopekaliga .	37.32	70.812
Tohopekaliga	52.98	64.593
Cypress Lake	58.81	64.593
Hatchenaha	66.81	60.235

Neither of these represents the topography in its general character, until we understand that, as the Tohopekaliga sum-

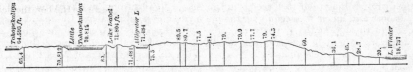

SECTION OF TOHOPEKALIGA SUMMIT LEVEL.

mit level is a terrace of the high table-lands of Orange and Polk counties, it is itself divided into subterraces sixty feet above the sea, extending like a flare edge from the head of Wolf Creek (61.989 feet) to Lake Hatchenaha (60.235 feet).

The lake surface of this summit level is fifty-three square miles, but swamp and "bay" (the word applied in Florida to slough and water-grass meadows) amplify the area to 250 square miles. It is 45.856 feet above the valley of the St. John's, and is succeeded on the south by the lower terrace of the Kissimmee lake and river.

The fall from the summit level to the escarpment of Wolf Creek and Lake Hatchenaha, or Turkey Lake (to render the Indian into English), is nearly five feet in three and a half miles. A canal forty feet wide and six feet deep was projected, and has been completed, connecting the latter with Tohopekaliga. This furnishes a fall of nearly two feet to the mile. Omitting the figures, it is calculated the discharge of such a current will require an area of rain-fall in this region over three thousand square miles, independent of evaporation, to keep it supplied. A most important function of such an aqueduct is its service as a catch basin for the supersaturated soil.

The Drainage Company was reorganized in 1881, under the presidency of Mr. Hamilton Duston, who had previously invested heavily in the reclamation and settlement of South Florida. The preliminary surveys under Mr. Kramer were completed in the summer of 1882, and Captain Rose, an experienced engineer, organized his company, and built the hull for his dredge in the raw woods on Lake Tohopekaliga. The patent (Allan's) is on the continuous ladder principle. A chain of buckets, suspended from an upright of forty feet, is drawn under a drum at the extremity of an arm extending forty feet horizontally from the foot of the upright, and over an incline to its top. The whole has some resemblance to a figure 4, having a short foot resting on the bow of the scow. The chain of buckets revolves over the drum, sinking their steel scoops in the soft ooze and muck, to ascend over the incline to the top of the 4, where they are met by a washer from the two-inch nozzle of a force-pump as each bucket falls over, with a jerk, discharging its contents on a sluice-gate, at right angles to the keel, ex-

tending beyond the edge of the cutting, and building its levees as it progresses. The long arm swings on the stem of the 4 from side to side, controlled by levers, so that each bucket sinks beyond the previous one, digging or cutting a swath of thirty-seven feet, as a mower swings his scythe. A tow-rope over a drum, attached to a stake properly set for the width and rectilineal edge of the cutting, controls the progress by means of levers. The huge crane swings; the timbers groan; steel and iron rattle and clang; the cough of the engine is broken by shouts of the men up to their waists in water; the anvil clinks; the sharp word of command cracks like a cow-whip; the constant stream of black ooze pours over the sluices; and as the huge iron and steel megatherium, like its prototype, toils deep in the marsh, behind it is the clean-cut edge and levees of the new canal. The scow on which these operations are conducted is a stern-wheel steamboat, having a narrow cabin for the accommodation of the men, and a smithy. Only white labor is employed.

The scenery is like its prototype of the coal period, a sea of maiden cane embroidered with bay and cypress where Reedy Creek and the tortuous Kissimmee cross the watery prairie. Here we find ferns, and pig-weed six inches in stem, and wearing a huge flower like a hat; while saffron, morning-glory, jasmine, water-lily, sparkle among the green of vines and the gray of tillandsia. The ardor of vegetation is everywhere magnificent in its richness and variety of color and tones. The drainage has already reclaimed nearly 400,000 acres, acknowledged by grants under the contract, chiefly in this summit level.

The terrace of Orange County south of Township 25 abuts upon the superior table-land of the adjacent area in Township 29, Range xxx. This territory, as indicated by the range lines on the map, lies southwest of that which we have examined, which it overlaps. It includes an area of 576 square miles, containing numerous small bodies of water, arranged on ascending subsidiary terraces as we go west from Lake Kissimmee. The average elevation above the sea at Charlotte Harbor is 106 feet. In the vicinity of Lake Buffum the high peak of the sand-hills divides the waters of Peace Creek and Charley Apopka from the water-shed of the Kissimmee Valley. The larger lakes,

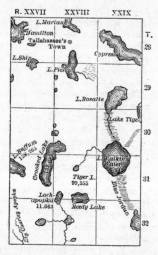

MAP OF THE LAKE BUFFUM SUMMIT LEVEL.

outlets by vegetation. It is entirely apart from the relation of the adjacent terraces to the system; but the chart shows its peculiar adaptation to practical irrigation by means of locks and dams. The planter and fruit-grower may here, as in Orange County, be made independent of the weather by these small adjacent bodies of water situated on different levels.

In the angle between the regions mapped, Townships 29 of Ranges xxx. and xxxi., lie the beautiful lake and valley of the Kissimmee, extending eastward to the St. John's. Nothing appears more striking to the observant explorer than the sharp distinction in nature between adjacent territories through which he passes. As he goes southward from Lake Kissimmee he leaves behind the prevailing characteristics of high pine level, hummock, and prairie of crab-grass. Before him, like a sea, rolls the lustrous pale yellow cane, having a long silky plume, through which the river winds, inextricable errors involute, like a labyrinth. In the remote horizon is the bronze fringe of red bay, the deep green of live-oak, tufts of palm, or the tawny fronds of the pine, melting into the kaleidoscope of cloud-land, by which the trained eye distinguishes at a glance elevation above the water. On that sallow or gamboge ground-work the courses of streams embroider an arabesque in green willow and custard-apple. The heavens are opened, tinged with iridescent hues, like the nacre of a shell; the abundance and plumage of wild fowl increase. The deer feed with a "shocking tameness," wild turkey seem domesticated, and fish are taken without trouble or skill.

A low swell of the ground, rich in crab-grass, extends south, by Fort Drum, Range xxxv., Township 34, to the vicinity of Fort Van Swearingen, and the heads of Taylor and Cow creeks, which empty into the Okeechobee. Of this Mr. Niblack, in his report to the State Board, June 27, 1882,

in order from the north, are Pierce, Rosalie, Walk-in-Water, Kotsa, Crooked, Buffum, Reedy, and Lochapopka. It includes the farm lands proper of the Tallahassee Indians, removed south of Micanopy half a century since, of which a remnant survives.

The topographic chart below, reduced from Mr. W. G. Williamson's report, exhibits a cross section of the pools and narrow longitudinal valleys into which the region is subdivided. The following table gives the heights and distances:

	Distance from Lake Kissimmee in Miles.	Height above the Sea at Charlotte Harbor in Feet.
Tiger Lake	2.01	59.384
Walk-in-Water . .	5.51	67.942
Lake Lenore	16.76	92.104
Lake Little Tiger .	18.18	99.355
Crooked Lake	21.73	132.683
Lake Buffum	26.16	138.265

The engineering in this region is reduced to the drainage of the long accumulation of surface water by the gradual filling of its

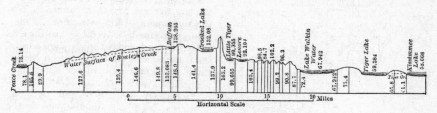

SECTION OF THE LAKE BUFFUM SUMMIT LEVEL.

says, "Within this limit there is, in the vicinity of Fort Drum, a pine ridge, five miles in length and one-half to three-quarters in width, that might with light drainage be cultivated." There is, he adds, a ridge about Fort Davenport, west of the Kissimmee, T. 29, R. xxvii., four or five miles wide, extending south to Lake Istokpoga, T. 36, R. xxx., said to be barren and uninhabitable. All the rest, according to Mr. Niblack's report, is subject to overflow.

But on an excursion in probably the more favorable season of December, 1882, the writer found pine levels and arable land quite down to the vicinity of Okeechobee. The most singular curiosity of his exploration was a swine-herd brought up in that wild, trackless region, and yet whom no curiosity, or the chance wandering of his herds, had led to the mouth of the Kissimmee, a few miles below. He had "had no 'casion for to go thar," and he never went. I fancy it was a more vigorous race than the swine-herd held these watery fastnesses for forty years against the combined army and navy.

Nothing could appear more queenly and magnificent than Lake Okeechobee as we came upon it. The closing day was drawing the soft veils of dusk over the pinnate and pointed foliage set clear against the dying lights.

The river is one hundred and twenty feet wide at the mouth, flowing with a

LAKE KISSIMMEE.

mean velocity of two feet per second, ten feet deep, discharging 207,360,000 cubic feet every twenty-four hours. On an estimated evaporation of one-eighth of an inch per day, the exhalation would aggregate 290,400,000 cubic feet, or 83,040,000 in excess of the inflow of the Kissimmee. Hence it is estimated that in only abnormal conditions the great lake overflows its margins. But these estimates do not include the inflow from other terraces, which fill the valley of Fish-eating Creek on the west, and Cow Creek and Taylor's Creek on the north and east, whose combined volume will probably counterbalance the normal evaporation of three-eighths of an inch per day.

To control this, a proposed canal from Cahoney Bay, in Okeechobee, to the St. Lucea, is to be cut one hundred and twenty feet wide and ten feet deep, having a fall of one foot per mile, with a mean velocity of 3.86 lineal feet per second, capable of lowering the estimated thousand square miles of surface four feet in a season.

It would require too much space to distinguish the botanical characters of vegetation in this virgin area; but the economy of nature is exhibited in the increase of leaf surface by atmospheric nutrition, displayed in gigantic ferns, palms, and the massing of delicate pinnate foliage in the bay, cypress, and their congeners, like the refinement of art in nature. These, shining, pointed, or darkly varnished in the willow and custard-apple, show a thousand tones and shades of green, which catch the lights and shadows in innumerable angles and surfaces, developing an extraordinary brilliance and softness. The great basin is a shallow pool on the oolitic limestone, in a frame of saw-grass,

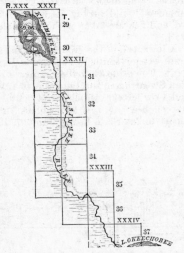

VALLEY OF THE KISSIMMEE.

MAP OF OKEECHOBEE DRAINAGE CANAL.

ond canal through the soft chalk rim of the outer basin. Curiously Captain Menge, engineer of the dredge, found here the remains of an old cut of the Spaniards, showing that even the project of drainage of Governor Westcott was not the first.

An earlier United States survey makes the fall from Fort Thompson, at the southern extremity of Lake Flirt, to Charlotte Harbor, less than two feet. This would make a descent from the chalk ridge of the outer basin of Okeechobee—a distance of ten miles—two feet to the mile. It was found necessary to dam at that point in order to get water to float the dredge-boat.

South of Fort Thompson is the beautiful current of the Caloosahatchee, flowing between high banks, terraced in the characteristic manner of the topography.

whose pale straw-color is brought out against the distant vaporous, velvety bronze and green of the red bay. It sits on a stool twenty-five feet above the sea, and five feet above the terrace of the Everglades. We crossed under a high wind, December 9, from the Kissimmee to the mouth of the Drainage Canal.

The axe-men had penetrated the fringe of custard-apples, and revealed through the opening the welcome pillar of smoke

CHARLOTTE HARBOR AND THE VALLEY OF THE CALOOSAHATCHEE.

of the dredge. The stratification as developed in the cutting beginning from the bed-rock is clay and marl under white sand, overlaid by a deep bed of muck. The depth and rankness of this superficial deposit are extraordinary. It needs no scientific acumen to discover that the successful drainage of such a deposit will develop an area of fertility unrivalled even by the loamy bottoms of the Mississippi.

A canal twenty-two feet wide, having an average fall of one foot to the mile, connects Okeechobee with Hiokpochee, and this is connected with Lake Flirt by a sec-

This feature, peculiar to all river valleys, indicates the manner in which the grand trowels of nature have built up the watershed of all South Florida. Here in the soft marl or loam are exhibited everywhere the escarpments seen in the harsher features of parallel roads in the geology of more northern latitudes. In that is the explanation of the overflowed lands of Florida, and the key to their successive drainage, terrace by terrace, to the Everglades.

Again the scenery has changed. The tall silken plumes of the saw-grass and

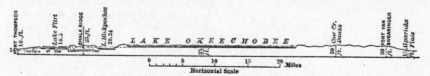

SECTION OF BASIN OF LAKE OKEECHOBEE.

bamboo-like cane give way to forests of live-oak, palm, myrtle, and mangrove islands. In the valley of Peace Creek are found the bones of huge pachydermata of the swamp epoch. In the groves and gardens, among fig and olive, grow the date, betel-nut, cocoa, and cabbage-palm. The sugar-cane tassels, and ratoons, or grows from one planting, from seven to sixteen years. Cotton becomes perennial.

When our little party first penetrated from Orange County by interior waters to the Gulf, it was all raw, wild, unknown; but since then a little steamer has gone through the Drainage Canals down the Caloosahatchee, and in another season the Northern tourist can explore the described region, and pronounce for himself upon the accuracy of the proposed theory, and the character of the land reclaimed.

IN SUNNY MISSISSIPPI

WE say we like London because of its historic associations and haunts, and we think of them so often that we come to regard our country as lacking the things which awaken reverent emotion. A mere tomb in an English graveyard, or a lettered slab in the pavement of one of the Inns of Court, sends us back a century or two as we ponder what some poet did and how he lived and what were his surroundings. And yet the sentimental mind may find plenty of this sort of delight here in America—delight that should be extreme to an American. I thought of that in Richmond when I saw the portrait of poor Pocahontas in the Capitol, close to that of Light-horse Harry Lee and to those of some of the famous royal Governors. And I thought of how there was a Virginia known to Shakespeare, as well as a "vexed Bermoothes." And so it was again when I found myself in Charleston, with its museum of ante-Revolutionary buildings, and its French traces that point back to the earliest Protestant settlement within our national borders. In New Orleans, again, a wealth of romantic and picturesque and gayly colored reminders of shifting dynasties and exciting history beats in upon my mind. Finally I came to Mississippi, and at Biloxi stood upon the ground whereon M. d'Iberville planted the flag of his royal master of France in 1699, nearly 200 years ago, but 157 years after De Soto sailed the Father of Waters that fronts that same State. Ah! I can be very happy indeed when I find myself in Carlyle's favorite tobacconist's in Chelsea by the Cheyne Walk, but I can command a more brilliant panorama, and one that moves as directly toward my own proud citizenship, when I pursue the same bent of mind in my own country.

To Biloxi one goes to get sick in order to be happy. That is one of the peculiar charms of the entire Gulf coast of the State of Mississippi. Surely as you go there you will fall ill of the local distemper, and that is one of the main incentives for making the journey. When I was in Chattanooga, not long ago, the cream of the gentry were ill and contented by reason of an enforced command for general vaccination to ward off a threat of small-pox which never materialized. But down at Biloxi and Pass Christian (pronounced chris-*chan*) and Ocean Springs and those other bits of dreamland on the Mississippi coast nobody gets sick in order not to be sicker. No one down there takes the local illness in preference to some other disorder. In that peculiar region every one becomes invalided as badly as possible solely for the love of the malady.

I first heard of it in a barber's shop. A man came along, and the barber hailed him. "When are you going to come and get my hot-water apparatus and mend the leak in it?" he asked. "Can you take it now?"

"No," said the mechanic. "I'll call around very soon. I was going to come and get it a couple of weeks ago; and then, again, I was pretty near coming for it the week before that. I'll get around. Y'ain't in no hurry, are you?"

"Oh, well—er—not a reg'lar hurry," said the barber. "I'd be using the thing every day if it was in order. But I'll get along all right."

I was in a holiday resort, and this was certainly a holiday spirit which both men were displaying, and yet it seemed that both were rather too slow even for a holiday couple.

"How does that fellow make a living?" I asked.

"Oh, he's a creole," said the barber. "He don't require much for a living. A cigarette and a glass of water makes a creole breakfast, you know, and down in this country you give any young fellow a dugout and a cast-net and he's able to marry."

After a pause the barber said, proudly, "Oh, we've all got the Biloxi fever."

"What sort of a fever is that?"

"You'll find out when you have been here awhile. How long have you been here?"

"About two hours," said I.

"Well," said the barber, "you'll have it bad to-morrow—that is, it will seem bad at first, though really it gets worse and worse the longer you stay. Why, the natives have it so that there's dozens of girls here who are becoming old maids because it is too much of an effort for their beaux to propose to 'em."

The fever seized me at eleven o'clock of the next forenoon, as with my friend Mr. Fletcher, of New Orleans, I was pursuing the truly Northern custom of "taking a walk." Before half a mile had been traversed, a store porch appeared before us and impeded our progress. It is true that it was on one side of the thoroughfare, and the way past it was broad and level. But it was a demon porch—a thing with the soul if not the song of a siren. In the sunlight it seemed to smile on us seductively, and it spread its two side-posts like a welcoming lover's arms, while its clean warm floor appeared to advance and insinuate itself under us, so that, without knowing how or why it was, we found ourselves seated there, stricken with the fever and at ease.

One must catch the complaint to appreciate it. It is not fatal any more than Nirvana is, and in my practical Occidental way of thinking it is very like Nirvana, and better, because it has the advantage of leaving you on earth, and with the same enjoyment of food and flowers and wine and song that you had before. It is not laziness. None but a dull hind would call it that. It is the very thing that the Europeans who criticise us for our fever of unrest should recommend as a substitute, for it is a fever for rest. A mere doctor would describe it as a malady peculiar to the Gulf coast from Mobile to New Orleans. He would say that it has been observed that large numbers of men and women, by combining in large cities,

are able to exercise sufficient will power to ward it off, so that it is prevalent in Mobile and New Orleans only among the colored people. Then he would go on to say that its first symptoms are a stiffening of the motor muscles of the legs, followed by a sense of leaden heaviness in the patient's feet. The patient will be observed to talk rationally, and to sustain an ordinary light conversation, but will on no account move from a chair, except it be to drop into the next one he comes to.

In the absence of chairs the patients are observed to sit upon barrels, boxes, store porches, and door-steps in the public streets, even though, before they were stricken, they were in the habit of applying harsh names, such as "loafers," "trash," and "tramps," to those who did the same thing. They sit upon wharves and upturned boats and tree stumps, upon grassy ledges and fallen logs, and, if they are permanent residents of the infected districts, they build seats all about their open grounds. They put benches about on the grass and piazzas, and even on the road-sides. In many cases they order great pavilions like giant nests built around their trees, and having no energy with which to conjure a new and fit name for these airy perches in which they while away precious time, they call them "shoo-flies," a name utterly without significance in that connection. They will hear the news of the day if any one will tell it or read it to them, but they cannot be prevailed upon to take up a newspaper. Northern men, when at home, who take three morning newspapers, an afternoon paper, and a score of weeklies and magazines, show the same aversion for printed news as those who cannot read at all. An instance is related of a Northern editor coming to Biloxi and falling a prey to this strange disorder. Having a New Orleans paper pressed upon him with the hint that it contained a description of the burning of his newspaper building during the previous night, he pushed the sheet away, saying: "Let her burn. I am here for rest, and don't want business mixed up with it." The same leading medical journal which records this case—so a mere doctor would continue—also cites an instance of a Northern broker in stocks who arranged to pay extra for his board on condition that the hotel clerk should tell him if Western Union dropped below 81¾, but should never, under any other circumstances, mention any serious matter to him during his stay in the hotel.

Thus a professional student of the disease would describe the Biloxi fever, missing the very essence of that which any person affected with the complaint would speak of at the outset. That point is its

and chicken-pox, and in such a case I can easily fancy that a man with a good supply of the fever would neglect his wife and babies, and sit on the head of a barrel in the sun for years, without saying who he was to any detectives that might be hired to find him and bring him out of Biloxi.

GROTTO AT BILOXI.

engaging character, its sensuous, dreamy, delicious, soothing nature. No one who has it would be cured of it on any account, until the time came to make a supreme effort of will and catch the train for the North. A poet might liken it to floating on whipped cream in a rose leaf. Or, to put it so that the dullest mind can grasp it, the feeling is what you are sure a great good-natured Newfoundland dog enjoys when he lies blinking at the sun after a hearty dinner. To be sure, it may be carried to extremes, just as some persons go to great lengths with the measles

At all events, we sat down on the store porch in the fever-stricken town, and just then a fire broke out. It was announced by a half-dozen lazy strokes of a bell, which created a great disturbance. There was no yelling or rushing about or surging of crowds. The disturbance was confined to a dozen volunteer firemen. They were resting in their homes and shops and offices, and the alarm was unexpected. Some had to dress, and others had to hunt up their fire-hats. These were things that are not done recklessly in Biloxi, but are well and carefully consid-

ered beforehand. It was therefore some
little time before the firemen began to appear in the streets and to come calmly—
as Matthew Arnold would have had all
us Americans do—up to where my friend
and I were seated, and then next door to
the engine-house. On the way, at nearly
every gate, the women halted them to ask
where the fire was, and in every case the
firemen took time to formulate a well-
digested polite answer, to the effect that
they were sorry not to be able to say at
that time anything of value about the
fire. In time they got the handsome old-
fashioned hand-engine out into the street,
and after a little badinage and a resting-
spell they shrewdly paused to discuss the
route by which they might most easily

er of disturbing and unwelcome information.

After a long time the firemen came
back in the same leisurely, dignified way
as they had departed. We heard a woman ask them if they had saved the building, and we heard a fireman's reply, "No,
ma'am; the building had gone when we
got there; but we saved the ground."

It is to be hoped that before the fever
seizes you the country round about the
town will have tempted you to enjoy its
many delights. They speak down there
of the strange habit the Northern men
and women have of taking long walks, a
thing the Southern mind staggers at newly at each presentation of the phenomenon. In our far South, if one has not a
horse or a sail-boat, and
cannot borrow either,
there is nothing to do
but to stay at home. To
be sure the Northern pe-
destrians take few walks
before they are fever-
stricken and leg-stiffened
and stranded in chairs in
the sunshine. But what
walks! Along the beach
the water flashes before
the town, all aglitter in
the sunlight, and be-
yond lie the long green
islands of the Gulf,
fringed with spreading
trees, now dense and now
mere green lace-work,
with the blue sky and blu-
er Gulf visible through
it. The pedestrians turn

JEFFERSON DAVIS'S MANSION, BEAUVOIR, AT BILOXI.

reach the general locality indicated by
the number rung out by the bell. There
being several discordant opinions to
weigh, this also consumed a few minutes.
Finally, like a well-ordered body, they
and the machine got under headway and
presently disappeared, leaving us to the
full enjoyment of the succeeding quiet,
which was only disturbed by a thought-
less question put by one of us to a street
boy as to what sort of a tree it was that
spread its noble height and width across
our horizon. The boy replied that it was
a pecan (he said "pecawn"), and had he
stopped at that all would have been well,
but he launched out upon a perfect clat-
ter of facts about the nuts the tree bore,
the number of bushels it yielded, the
price they brought, and, in short, a show-

away and explore the land only to come
back enraptured, telling of the templelike
forest of pines that overspreads the land,
of the light and shade, of the vivid green
feathered against the clear blue, of the
white sand underfoot with its soft red
carpeting of dead pine needles, of the stillness and the purity and almost parklike
semblance of order everywhere within the
forest. Alas, that they should soon lose
the energy to renew such pleasure, and
that it should joy them only in their
memories!

The village is picturesque, and but
that this one is the oldest of these Gulf
resorts (and was a summering-place for
New Orleans folk in the long, long ago),
what is said of it will answer for all the
others. It is made up of little cottages

They talk to all who pass their way, and if a stranger like myself refuses to make a free exchange of his business for theirs, they will give up theirs quite as freely, if he will stop and listen.

These are often Western folk, for our Eastern people have not discovered this perpetual summer land, but have allowed men and women from the other end of the Mississippi Valley to steal this march upon them. Therefore we find a small section of the

of pretty and uncommon designs that have sprung from French beginnings. Often the second stories project beyond the parlor floors so as to provide a lower porch; and here and there are seen prettily shaped openings in the upper stories so as to make additional galleries. When vines trail up the house fronts and frame these galleries the effect is very pretty. Vegetation is abundant, the trees are of great size, and flowers grow in luxuriance, though it is whispered that there is sufficient chill in the air of winter nights to make it prudent to pull the potted plants in-doors in cold spells. The green gardens and chromatic cottages lie prettily beside white sand streets, where there are no sidewalks, but borders of grass instead. Natives point out the trees as chinaberries, willows, cypresses, magnolias, oranges, pecans, peaches, plums, and apples. The people love the castor-bean, because it has a tropical look, I suppose, and thrives so well down there. I have seen fifty-three orange-trees in one garden, checkered with golden fruit and greenery, and have found the oranges as delicious as any I ever ate. The buds come upon the trees before the fruit is plucked. The people in the tiny streets and gardens are extremely democratic.

IN THE LIBRARY AT BEAUVOIR.

place spoken of as a Michigan settlement, and in addition there are many regular winter visitors from Wisconsin, Iowa, and Illinois. They discovered the Gulf coast about seven years ago, and make it a habit to come either in November or after the holidays, and to stay till warm weather reaches the North. The greater number go to Pass Christian, a rather new place, prettily spread along the beach, and with a large well-managed hotel maintained by Chicago people. Ocean Springs, Bay St. Louis, and Biloxi are the other resorts. Biloxi, the oldest, is the most quaintly typical,

BACHELORS' QUARTERS, BEAUVOIR.

slightly Frenchified Southern town of them all. Bathing, fishing, driving, and cottage and hotel life are the diversions.

A great many of these visitors buy cottages and modernize them, renting them for a hundred or a hundred and fifty dollars when they go away in the summer, at which time the New Orleans folk come along.

At Mrs. Drysdale's altogether excellent, old-fashioned, but brand-new hotel in Biloxi I could find no fault with anything, but it is said that the Western visitors cannot abide the high seasoning with chile pepper and garlic which the creole taste demands, or the Southern tendency to fry everything, even the fruit, or the coffee that is made "so strong that it stains the cups," or the singular Gulf-coast custom of breaking fast at nine o'clock in the morning and dining at two o'clock in the afternoon. Cottage life, therefore, has the greater number of votaries in that region. They go there to escape the Northern winters, and are told that the Gulf coast has only two cold spells in each winter—one in November and one in February. When these come they are found to bring a temperature like that of boarding-house tea. Bathing can be indulged in all the year—enjoyed all the year by the men, I should say, and indulged in by the women, for the custom down there is for the women to immerse themselves in little pens under the bath-houses, between lattice-work walls.

Interesting Southern peculiarities are

plentiful down there. I never saw a pecan-tree, for instance, that I did not think of the famous "nigger candy" of New Orleans—the irresistible candy of the Crescent City sidewalks. There they take the pecan-nuts, which we eat raw, as if we had no more ingenuity than squirrels, and sprinkling them in great cakes of pure brown sugar, produce a confection to which they give the French name of *praline*, but which is so unlike any other candy in the world as to deserve a new American name of its own. The old "mammies" make the candies in disks big enough to cover the bottom of a silk hat, and even yet keep the trade to themselves and away from the merchants, although the visitors to the gay city buy up whole trays of them, and even ship them to the North and East. Down here in Mississippi the scuppernong grape finds its farthest Southern foothold, I think; at least, I have not found it farther away. Travellers to Asheville and Florida will remember that it is the wine that is served at that celebrated railway restaurant in North Carolina where the proprietor and the waiters vie with one another in forcing "extras" and second portions of the nicest dishes upon the wayfarers. There can scarcely be such another restaurant as that. "Do have another quail," says the proprietor. "Let me give you more of this scuppernong wine. It is made near here, and is perfectly pure." "Won't you take an orange or two into the cars with you?" or "Here's a bunch of fresh flowers to give to your ladies." The scuppernong wine has even more of that peculiar "fruity" flavor than the best California wines—a flavor that I am barbarian enough to prefer to the "pucker" of the imported claret. You may have it with your meals in Biloxi. And if you are a drinking man, which Heaven forefend, you may have "toddy" in the style that obtains from Virginia to farthermost Texas, and that has been imported to Arkansas, Missouri, and the Indian Territory.

It was on the banks of the Arkansas River, in Indian Territory, that I made the acquaintance of this method of—as a friend of mine would say—"spoiling good liquor." The famous Indian champion, Mr. Boudinot, introduced me to a planter whose two cabins, side by side and joined by a single roof, formed the most picturesque home that I saw on that splendid river. I was introduced as plain "mister," but that would not do down there.

"*Colonel* Ralph," said the planter, "enjoy this yer boundless panorama of nature. Feast yo' eyes, sah, on the beautiful river." (Then aside: "Wife, set out the mixin's in the back room.") "Colonel Ralph, you are welcome to share with us this grand feast of scenery and nature's ornaments. But, sah, I think my wife has set out something—just a little something—in the house. I dun'no' what it is, sah, but if you find it good, I shall be delighted, sah."

So we went into the back room with this other Colonel Mulberry Sellers, and there on the dining-table stood a bottle, a bowl of sugar, three glasses and spoons, and a glass pitcher full of spring water.

"Serve yourself to a toddy, colonel," said my host.

"I'll watch you first," said I; "I don't know what a toddy is."

"Don't know what a toddy is?" said the hospitable man. "Why, sah, that does seem strange to me. Back in gran' ole Virginia, sah, we children were all brought up on it, sah. Every morning my revered father and my sainted mother began the day with a toddy, sah, and as we children appeared, my mother prepared for each one an especially tempered drink of the same, sah, putting—I regret to say—a little more water in mine than the others' because I was the youngest of the children."

As he spoke, he dipped some sugar into his glass, poured in a little water, sufficient to make a syrup when the two ingredients were stirred with a spoon, and then emptied in an Arkansas "stiffener" of whiskey—a jorum, as the English would say. That is the drink of the South, where drinking, without being carried to any excess that I ever witnessed, still remains a genteel accomplishment, as it was held to be by the English, Scotch, and Irish who were the progenitors of nearly all our Southern brothers.

Beauvoir, the seat of the family of Jefferson Davis, is close by Biloxi, and as Mississippi reveres his memory as that of her most distinguished citizen, I rode over to visit the old place. I had thought of Mississippi as the last stronghold of the Southern sectional feeling, and so it may be, but I discovered even less signs of it there than anywhere else in the South. Nowhere did I encounter a greater and a closer mingling of the natives with the new immigrant element, which latter is growing strong there in the development of that new relationship which is springing up between the Western people at the head of the Mississippi Valley and the Southern people at the foot of it. That is a new growth of trade and friendship which the student of this country's development will soon need to take into account.

But it is a strong fresh memory, that natives and new-comers share alike, of the ex-President of the Confederacy as he journeyed to his upper plantation or to New Orleans or walked through the white streets of Biloxi, a tall, spare, impassive man of great natural dignity, and always clad in a suit of Confederate gray, under a soft military hat, until he was seen for

SLEEPING-ROOM IN THE LIBRARY, BEAUVOIR.

the last time. Although a Kentuckian by birth, his life is bound up with the history of Mississippi. For that State he served as an elector in 1844, voting for Polk and Dallas. He was a planter there, and went from there to Congress in the next year. As Colonel of the First Mississippi Volunteers he fought bravely in the Mexican war, and later he was one of the Senators of his State in the Federal Congress and Secretary of War under President Pierce. After the collapse of the Confederacy he made Beauvoir his most favored retreat and resting-place, and there, until he died, he received letters from the young college students of the South asking his advice as to their future courses in life, and visits alike from Northern and Southern folk, the one to make his acquaintance, the others to tender their sympathy and respect.

form columns of the forest, the meetings of their limbs overhead, and the closing shallow vistas, as of naves, on every hand. The dwarf palmetto, or Spanish-bayonet, grows in little clumps or singly, as one would distribute it for ornament, and the very tropical long-leaf pines, leaping high in air before they put out a branch, and then spreading their tops like palms, are the chief denizens of these silent depths. Here and there are wet spots, it is true, and then the parklike character of the woods changes to a jungle, but a jungle so thick with gum, bay, magnolia, and other trees that one cannot see the dank water they shut in.

By the wood road the back of Beauvoir is first reached, and is found to be a tract of ten acres, devoted to the cultivation of the scuppernong grape. The vineyard is a scene of disorder and neglect. The rude arbors are rotting and falling upon the vines, and the young persimmon and pecan trees that have been set out there are endangered by the weeds that grow riotously, to exaggerate the suggestion of desolation. The mansion is around a bend of the road, commanding the dark blue Gulf, from behind ample grounds whose fence separates the place but does not hide its beauties from the white beach drive that skirts the water. The greatest storm in many years had torn up the road when I was there, and, worse yet, had played havoc with the splendid trees that beautified the noble estate. There are many giant live-oaks and a

READING-ROOM IN THE LIBRARY, BEAUVOIR.

The way to Beauvoir lies either along the beach or through the woods; but I chose the forest road, that I might as many times as possible enjoy its wonderful order and neatness and beauty. The trees rise, at short distances apart, above the level clean sand, and there is nowhere a suggestion of impurity either upon the ground or in the clear sweet balsamic air. There is a constant suggestion of something cathedral-like in the regular uni-

few hickories and cedars, but, alas, the ground was littered with the débris of their wreckage, and some were prone upon the earth—one of the dead being a splendid big hickory, which it would have been supposed no wind could maltreat. The gate was tied up, and the house was closed, so that had it been pointed out to me as a haunted house, abandoned by its owners, the scene presented there would have been exactly accounted for.

THE POTTERY OF BILOXI.

It has been a noble place, and could be made so again with little trouble and expense. No house that I have seen in the South is more eloquent of the full possibilities of the aristocratic baronial life of the planter before the war. To look upon it even now is to recall a thousand tales and anecdotes of the elegant life, the hospitality, and the comfort of the old régime. The main house is a great, square, low building, with a gallery on three sides, reached by a broad, high flight of steps. A great and beautiful door leads to a wide central hallway, through which one could see, when the house was open, either the blue Gulf and distant islands in front, or the great oaks with their funereal drapery of Spanish moss in the rear. Two other similar but smaller houses stand, like heralds of the old hospitality, a little forward on either side of the mansion. Both are square, red-roofed, one-story miniatures of the manor-house. Each has its roof reaching out to form a broad porch in front. One is the bachelors' quarters, for guests and relatives of that unhappy persuasion, and the other is Mr. Davis's library and retreat. There

everything is as he loved to have it around him when he sat in-doors, and out on the beach is the ruin and wreck of a seat under some live-oaks where he used to sit and look upon the broad water and reflect upon his extraordinary and most active life. Behind these three buildings is the usual array of out-buildings, such as every Southern mansion collected in its shadow—the kitchen, the servants' quarters, the dairy, and the others.

I went into the little library building and saw his books, his pictures, his easy-chair and table, and—behind the main room—his tiny bedroom and anteroom, the bedroom being so small that it could accommodate no larger bed than the mere cot which is shoved against the window. His books would indicate that he was a religious man with a subordinate interest in history. In a closet he kept a remarkable collection of prayer-books, and in an open case were many volumes of novels, which the care-taker of the place called "trash," and accounted for with the explanation that Mr. Davis maintained a sort of circulating library for the use of his ex-Confederate soldier friends. The pictures that still hang upon the walls struck me as a strange collection. One shows some martyrs, dead, in a gladiatorial amphitheatre; one is of a drowned girl floating beneath a halo in a night-darkened stream; one is a portrait of our Saviour beside several madonnas; and only one is a military picture. Thither came constant visitors, for it was "the thing to do" in Biloxi—far too much so for the privacy and comfort of the family, I suspect; but it is recollected that Mr. Davis delighted in showing his library to all who called after twelve o'clock noon. The main house was seen only by those who had a claim upon his affections. I visited it and found it made up of noble rooms and decorated beautifully with fresco-work. But nearly all the furniture and ornaments and pictures were packed up or covered as if ready for removal. The effect upon my mind was sad and almost tragic, and I hastened from the widespread scene of havoc and of neglect, which even threatens the house itself. I learned enough to know that this does not reflect discredit upon the little family that was bereaved by the Southern leader's death, for the maintenance of the place would entail an expense which, if they were able to meet it, would still be an unwise disposition of their means.

It was with less pleasure that, on returning to Biloxi, I conjured up a picture of the old man threading the village streets, where every man who passed him lifted his hat, where all who had grievances stopped him to get his ready sympathy, and where those who had served him pressed his hand as they met him. It may be fitting, in view of everything that has passed, that Beauvoir should become a ruin, but hardly so soon as this.

I said so to the honest old German who is in charge of the place, and whom I found battling hopelessly with the tons of wreckage left by the last great storm. He shook his head, and it seemed to me that his eyes were moist.

"Were you a Confederate soldier?" I asked.

He turned upon me quickly.

"Of course I was," he said; "else I should not be here."

Every prospect from the shore about Biloxi includes at least one of the long low wooded islands in the glittering Gulf, and every look establishes a telegraphic communication by which the islands seem to say, "Come out to us; we will give you joy." On the mainland, too, the people urge you to accept the invitation. "They are different from the shore, and prettier," they say. Lucky are you if you yield to all these solicitations. They are jewels—emeralds studding the turquoise Gulf. They are foreign. You feel, even though you have never been to the Sandwich Islands, that these are like them, and that you are in a new and unfamiliar but beautiful country. The mainland had seemed like a bit of ornament, of lace-work on the edge of our country, but these islands appear to be not of our country at all. They are Polynesian, if they are not Hawaiian. They are all long and narrow, sometimes eighteen miles long and only half a mile wide, and they are said to be crawling in the direction they point to—towards Mexico. It is said that the time was when they were joined to Florida, Alabama, and Mississippi, but the water cut them off, and now it keeps cutting away the landward ends and building out the further points, so that they seem to be lazily moving to the tropics. I do not vouch for the story, but give it as I got it, because it accords with their foreignness to think of them as lazy indolent travellers, seeking a climate more congenial than that with which fate first bound them.

Out on those islands the sand is as white as the whitest sugar, the water is as deep a blue as that of the Adriatic, and the sky is like the side of a lighted lantern of pale blue silk. The snow-white sand is continually shifting, changing its surface forms, travelling constantly, as if the progress of the islands was too slow for it. Thus it happens that you see towering white dunes of it which reach a knifelike edge into the water, and then rise gradually higher and higher in a soft white plane until they are forty feet high, and there they end abruptly, so that from behind they appear like towering smooth white walls. They bury the trees, of many sorts that you do not remember to have seen on shore, and their dead trunk ends and black bodies protrude here and there above or in the faces of the devouring white hills.

The water is apt to be as gentle and calm as it is blue, basking eternally in the brilliant sunlight. But when a breeze ruffles it billions of brilliant gems appear as its upturned points sparkle all over it.

It is a piscatorial Eden, alive with fish. It is so clear that you may see them at their play and work, fishes of ever so many and ever such queer kinds. Great turtles are among them, and sharks and porpoises and gars, darting or hanging, as if they too had the Biloxi fever, above schools of sheep's-head and pompano, and I know not how many other sorts of creatures. You could not see them better if you were looking through the clear at the hotels and in the streets. They put the little loafing-places in touch with a great deal more of the world than the railroads introduce there, for these generally jolly mariners come from Norway and Sweden and France and England, and even from more distant lands. The fact that you do not see their ships lends a little touch of mystery to their presence, but it is a short-lived mystery if you attack it with the first natural question, for then

SHOO-FLY, BILOXI.

glass walls of a vast aquarium. You undress and plunge in to find the water just as you would order it if you could, a mere trifle cooler than the atmosphere, but ever so buoyant. You float and loll and lie about and dream in it, thanking the Creator that you are the veriest bit amphibious, and fancying yourself completely so.

There is little other animal life than what you bring on most of the islands. On some there are people enough to spoil them, but on others there may be only one shanty or a light-house, or no habitation at all, but grazing cattle here and there.

An unexpected feature of life in some of these little Gulf resorts is due to the number of sea-captains one is apt to meet

you learn that their vessels are lying within shelter of the islands off shore, loading with lumber. This lumber they swallow up in prodigious quantities. They do this in such a way as to suggest those people whom Munchausen found on an adjacent planet to this, who used to open a door in their stomachs and pop in food for several days when they were going off on a journey. Just so these lumbermen swallow sections of forests without having them cut up to go into their holds, by opening a door into their stomachs, in the shape of a great hole in each bow, into which the long tree-trunks are slid. We are apt to think of lumber and timber as products peculiar to Maine and Michigan, Minnesota and Washington, but every one of the Southern States is a

COTTON AND ITS CAPITOL, JACKSON, MISSISSIPPI.

grand storehouse of valuable timber, and none is greater than Mississippi.

That part of her territory which is covered by forests is just four times the size of Massachusetts—or more than twenty-one millions of acres. The reader wonders how that can be true of the king of the cotton States, since that royal rank implies a vast farming area. It is because Mississippi is larger than Pennsylvania by a thousand square miles, or nine times larger than Massachusetts. Her great agricultural development has been reached by denuding more than half of her surface of forests.

To understand this, and the State, it is necessary to remember that Mississippi is divided into three longitudinal belts: 1, the Delta strip, along the Mississippi River; 2, the hilly belt down the middle of the State; and 3, the so-called "prairies," on the side next to Alabama. The Delta soil is alluvial and very rich, and is very productive, of cotton mainly. The hillock land, that which was until recently considered the very poorest land outside of the swamps, is now the source of great

wealth, because here are grown the vegetables and small fruits whose introduction is revolutionizing and enriching the State. It is rich also because it is cultivated in small holdings by white labor and by economical methods. We better understand how such an influence affects a people when we reach the prairie belt, now the poorest part of the State, though its soil is black and vegetation planted there becomes luxuriant. It is farmed in large plantations like the Delta land, but it does not flourish because these are rented out and not kept up by their owners. Like the Irish landlords, they spend their money elsewhere instead of on their land, as the small holder does, in fertilizers, improvements, and repairs.

But while this division of the State is actual, the reader must now imagine all three of these belts covered by a vast virgin pine forest from the middle of the State to the Gulf. To be exact, let me say that this forest extends over nearly the whole area between Alabama on the east and the Illinois Central Railroad in the west, and between the Gulf and a line drawn across the State from the city of Meridian to the railroad I have mentioned. This forest region is about 90 miles wide and 180 miles long, and is in the main as beautiful as a park. Pine, gum, oak, and cottonwood are the trees, though on the Delta side cypress, ash, poplar, hickory, and gum are abundant. For fifty years or more this district has been "lumbered" wherever the logs could be floated down the many streams that all flow to the Gulf of Mexico, and yet it is said that but a tiny fraction of the valuable wood has been cut, and not even yet have the lumbermen been obliged to go to a distance from the streams. It is estimated that to-day there remain eighteen millions of feet of long-leaf pine in this region, while in the northern part of the State more than one-third as much short-leaf pine is standing.

In this great Southern district of forest a large amount of Western capital has been invested in lumbering, and of the men engaged in the pursuit fully one-half are from the West and the North. Immense tracts of this woodland are held untouched for the great rise in their value that must certainly follow the destruction of the timber resources of the Northwest. These Mississippi forest lands were public, government land, and the speculative corporations bought enormous tracts at prices that were sometimes as low as a dollar and a half an acre. This unjust and scandalous absorption by the wealthy of that which should have been held for the people and for the enrichment of the State aroused the indignation of those who watched it, and two or three years ago the people obtained Federal legislation, by which what remains of the land is saved for the possession of actual settlers exclusively. Less than half of it—possibly little more than a third—was thus preserved. That which is being cut is not only shipped to Europe, as I have described, but it also goes in great quantities to the West—to Chicago and intermediate points, and to St. Louis as the distributing-point for the farther West.

Down on the Gulf coast I had shown to me the tidy home and thrifty-looking farm of a man who was said to have walked into that section "with nothing in the world but a shirt, trousers, and boots"—the very sort of man that most of my Southern friends say that they don't want as a type of the new blood they aim for in their efforts toward attracting immigrants. But this man picked up a living somehow, as men of the stuff to emigrate are apt to do, and presently he had saved enough to buy a patch of woodland. Then he turned that into a farm, and has become a comfortable citizen, growing vegetables the year around, and demonstrating that a man with the will can establish himself in the South in the same way in which poor men have built up whole Western States, and with as great individual success, if not greater.

Among the places that I visited in Mississippi was Jackson, and there the condition of the old State House suggested the thought that perhaps the rebellious subjects of old King Cotton are more interested in the present day than in any part of their past. Like Beauvoir, it was a pitiful object of neglect. The old clock face on its front had turned into a great plate of rust, the unlooked-for statues of Bacchus and Venus in the once noble lobby beneath the dome now stand ridiculous in a scene of untidiness and slow decay. The Senate-Chamber has its roof upheld by rough trusses of raw wood, and the originally fine hall of the Assem-

GOVERNOR'S MANSION AT JACKSON.

bly is ornamented with the advertisement of an insurance company, the faded banner of a lodge of Confederate veterans, hung awry on one side of the Speaker's chair, and a cheap portrait that dangles threateningly overhead.

The capital itself is a busy and a prosperous place, stirred by men of modern ideas and interests, who proudly show a visitor their rows of fine residences and two bustling business streets, their promising college, founded by a banker in the town who loves his fellow-men. And these leaders are fully alive to the revolution that is pushing the State into prosperity. The Governor's mansion, so strongly recalling the White House at Washington, is one of the sights of the town, but to me nothing was so interesting as the continual movement of baled cotton through the streets, and the habit the people have of piling it up beside the Capitol, so that one sees the palace of the threatened king, neglected and in need of general repairing, rising above the mountain of the bales that typifies his throne.

Cotton-mills are not as numerous in the State as in the Carolinas and Georgia, and yet one—that at Wesson—is one of the finest in America. There is a yarn-mill at Water Valley, and there are mills for the making of unbleached cotton at Enterprise, near Meridian, and at Columbus. The Wesson cotton and woollen mills show so triumphantly what can be done in the South, as well as wherever enterprise determines to make success, that I wish to speak of them at length. They were founded in 1871, and have been so phenomenally successful as to give certain goods that bear their name an almost world-wide celebrity and rank—so successful as to increase the value of the stock ten dollars for one that has been invested in them. By the reinvestment of the dividends they have been brought to their present completeness and excellence. By constantly replacing old machinery with that which is newer and better they have been made as modern as if they were equipped yesterday. They manufacture all classes of cotton goods— cotton rope, rag carpet, twines, hosiery, jean, wool jeans, cassimeres, ladies' dress goods, and flannelette. They consist of three large brick buildings, equipped with electric lights, automatic sprinklers, and water-towers. The annual output of manufactured stuffs has been about a million and a half dollars' worth. The operatives number 1500, are natives of the State, and are all white. The commercial depression

of 1893 caused a partial closing of the mills in August of that year, but the attitude of the owners toward their work-people is such that no misery followed. Winter fuel and house-rent free were given to all the operatives, and the heads of the families were kept employed in order that there should be money for necessaries for all. It did not surprise me in hearing this to learn further that there has never been a labor union nor a day of what is commonly known as "labor trouble" in Wesson. James S. Richardson, of the noted family of cotton-planters, is president of the mills, and the directors are W. W. Gordon, John Oliver, and R. L. Saunders.

But Mississippi has many good tidings of progress and of approaching liberation from the cruel thraldom of that product in which she once led the South. New farming industries and new uses for the land are forcing themselves upon the public as well as the local attention. The Illinois Central Railroad, with its quick and direct service, is fetching sturdy Western people into the State, and sometimes they are leading, sometimes copying the more ambitious natives in the movement away from the exclusive growing of cotton. In Madison, in the county of that name, the pioneer was Dr. H. E. McKay, the President of the State Horticultural Society. A dozen years ago he began experimenting with strawberries, and with such success that his little town of 100 inhabitants now ships as many as five car-loads of luscious berries daily during a season of from four to six weeks. He has 120 acres planted in strawberries, his brother, Dr. John McKay, has between 80 and 100, and their neighbors manage strawberry patches of from 15 to 80 acres each. It was a brand-new business a dozen years ago, and it had to be learned; but to-day all engaged in it are more than satisfied, and declare it to be far better than cotton-planting. I do not know whether the average Northern reader appreciates the importance of experiments and examples like this, but to me these steps toward assured wealth for the South—especially since I know how belated they have been, and how slowly they are taken even yet—are most interesting.

The Madison berries are the second to enter the market. The first are grown around Hammond, in Louisiana, where the farmers — in the same piny-woods soil that Mississippi's new trucking region consists of—began by raising early spring produce for the North. To-day they embrace their full opportunity down there co-operating with the natives in the raising of truck. Tomatoes, pease, cucumbers, and beans are the chief growths, and the town shipped as many as thirty carloads of "table" tomatoes in one day of

SENATE-CHAMBER AT JACKSON.

in Louisiana, and actually ship produce every day, the year around. I will not print the necessary half-page list of what they grow, but it embraces all garden-truck, many small fruits, and much beside; and soon after cabbages are ready for shipment, in December, the next year's full round of incessant crops begins. But to return to Mississippi, where the same processes will eventually bring fortunes to great communities not yet established, let me add that thousands of fruit trees have been planted on the strawberry farms, and some are beginning to yield. The people mean to put their eggs in more than one basket. They are going into trucking also.

At Crystal Springs, south of Jackson, on the Illinois Central Railroad, a few of those Western people whom that iron highway is bringing into Mississippi are

last June. In that month Crystal Springs earned and got $350,000, which came just as the cotton-planters needed money. The manner in which these new agricultural methods bring money into the State at all seasons is one of its advantages that is of more moment than we, who live nearer the financial centres, can easily imagine. Durant and Terry are other towns that are feeling this agricultural revolution.

The entire middle section of the State is becoming a great horse-raising region, and it is said that there are as many horses in Mississippi as in Kentucky. This, too, is the best hay section in the South, except the blue-grass region. Large quantities of hay are being shipped to New Orleans and to the Delta planters, who give up their lands to cotton. Bermuda and other grasses grow naturally there, but the lespedeza, or Japan clover, is the best. It mysteriously appeared after the close of the war. It had undoubtedly been brought there by the Northern soldiers. Its seeds blow everywhere, and it has spread marvellously far and fast. On the poorest hill land it grows tall enough to mow and bale. It is preferred to any other hay by the cattle, and it fetches ten dollars a ton. In the western part of the State, in Clay and Chickasaw counties, a large number of Northern people have gone into the horse business. They are mainly raising working stock, such as used to be brought in from Tennessee. The butter and milk dearth is ended in central Mississippi. A number of dairy farms have been established, and the keeping of cows is becoming general. Even on the poorest land and among the poorest farmers pork and beef are being raised to insure meat for the families, whether cotton fetches paying or losing prices.

It is thus that the South is forced to acknowledge that the original Plymouth plan is better than the Jamestown experiment. The Jamestown or Virginia idea was to grow nothing but tobacco, and then use it to buy everything else that was needed to support life. The Plymouth plan was to grow the necessaries of life and sell the surplus, if there was any. To-day, from the Norfolk (Virginia) truck farms to the truck farms of Louisiana, the South is paying tribute to the Yankee notion. She is prosperous wherever that is the case. She is otherwise wherever the Jamestown method still obtains.

To be thoroughly successful the Plymouth method required personal industry, on the part of the small farmer at least. They are finding this out also in Mississippi; but to a Northern man, who believes that "work elevates and ennobles the soul," it sounds very funny to hear the people apologizing for what they are doing. Mere farm-work is considered plebeian and vulgar, but they find "dairying and horticulture more refined." They say that men of education do not like to do with the plough and the stable, but that "you see gentlemen and their sons at work in the orchards and berry-fields, and around Crystal Springs you may see a hundred young ladies of good families at work packing fruit." That is great progress and a great concession for the South. So long as the people work they will thrive, and if they sugar their lives by calling fruit-farming by the name of "horticulture," it does not matter so long

FORT MASSACHUSETTS, SHIP ISLAND, MISSISSIPPI.

as they acknowledge the truth of Poor Richard's maxim that

"He who by the Soil would Thrive
Must either hold the Plough or Drive."

The rule of the Jamestown plan is broken in Mississippi but not destroyed. The cotton-planters in the bottom lands own between 500 and 1500 or 2000 acres each. They farm out these plantations to the negroes. Each negro gets a cabin, a mule, a plough, and a little garden-patch free, as the tools with which to work. He is to plant and pick fifteen acres of cotton, and is to receive half of what it brings. The cotton yields between half a bale and a bale per acre, and fetches just now $25 a bale. The negro needs the help of his wife and many children to pick it. At an average return of, say, ten bales of cotton to fifteen acres the negro gets $125 for his year's work. The cotton seed brings seven to ten dollars a ton, so that from the sale of that he gets $35 more. Some planters grow corn for market, and others allow the negroes to plant a good deal of corn to live upon. Unfortunately the rule with the negro is to sell his corn before Christmas at 50 cents a bushel, and buy it back in February at $1 25. The negroes deal with the local merchants, who are mainly Hebrews, on the credit plan. They are made to pay two prices, and the Jews limit them to what it is thought their crops will bring. These merchants add about fifty per cent. for the hazard of poor crops, death, losses by storms, and whatever.

The negro is holding the South back in this as in other respects. The small white farmer can adjust himself to circumstances. He can say that if cotton does not pay at this year's price of five cents a pound, he will raise more meat and corn for home consumption. He can also raise enough to feed what tenants he employs. But the negro affects the larger situation. He is not a landlord. He must rent the land he works, and the average planter needs him as much as the negro needs the land. But when the two meet, and the negro asks, "What are you going to pay me for working your land?" the planter can only reply, "Cotton," because corn won't sell in the first place, and in the second place the negro likes cotton, and understands the handling of it better than anything else that grows in the ground. Furthermore, to understand the situation fully, the reader needs to remember that there are a great many more negroes than whites in Mississippi.

The Illinois Central Railroad has come into a lot of rich land through the purchase of a railway nearer the great river than its main line, and it is bringing down a great many Western farmers, who do not go there for their health or for the sake of the scenery, but to make money. They are largely from Wisconsin, Illinois, and Iowa. They are going into horse-raising, dairying, trucking, fruit-growing, and whatever will pay best, and they will exert a tremendous influence for prosperity down there. But on the hilly land of the interior, where the railroad influence is not at the bottom of the immigration, a great many new-comers are seen to try cotton first. They hear that they can get land for from three dollars to ten dollars an acre, and that they can raise a bale on two acres, with a chance of getting $40 for the bale. It does not work. There is too much cotton. It is bringing only five cents a pound, and it has been observed that under eight cents the planters do not pay their way. Contrary to the Carolina experience, the bankers of Mississippi declare that cotton costs seven and a half cents a pound for the raising. And even then "it takes thirteen months in the year to raise it," as they say down there — meaning, of course, that before one year's crop is picked the planter must be preparing for the next. With land cheaper than dirt usually is, with taxes very low indeed, with a combination of soil and climate fitted for the growth of every product of the temperate zone, and many others beside, it is astonishing that the State does not fill with earnest industrious bidders for the fortune that will so surely be theirs when they embrace the opportunity. The reader may say that there must be some important hinderance, but I know of none. The white people are law-abiding and hospitable, the climate is healthful, the heat is by no means unendurable or such as need deter a Northern man from going there, and, indeed, Northern men have told me that the Northern midsummer heat is far more trying. The only problem is what to do with the negro after the white farmers come in, but that will not affect any white man who goes there to work for himself. The negro will have to learn to work as the white man does, or—but that is his concern.

A VISIT TO A COLONIAL ESTATE

AS it was first settled, and has been least disturbed, the section of Virginia between Richmond and the sea affords to-day the best preserved landmarks of the beginnings of the nation.

These South Virginia counties show up in a sadly neglected condition; their principal merit consists in the fact that they are dotted thick with relics from the colonial era—dwelling-houses, churches, monuments, estates. One may fancy that Washington, who was familiar with and lived in the neighborhood, would recognize it at sight if he were to be suddenly brought back to life. To a certain extent things remain pretty much as they were looked upon by that serene countenance. There has been no immigration: the people are of the original stock, handed down from father to son, with the same speech, manners, and ways, and are sparsely settled on large estates and small farms. Two small intersecting railroads scarcely mar the retrospect. In many respects, however, the appearance of this portion of Virginia is vastly different from that presented under its well-to-do owners who were the contemporaries of Washington. Then it flourished under the impulse given by wealthy and intelligent English settlers, who established perforce their homes where they first landed. Gradually, as they died off, their descendants

moved to other more fertile and healthy portions of the State, and ultimately spread out upon the continent. As this gradual abandonment of the first area settled was persevered in, it is not surprising that the counties between Richmond and the sea became, as it were, obsolete, and at last fell into the wrecked and ruined condition in which they are now seen. The attractions elsewhere being so great, the area of the early settlements, even with their fine old buildings and monuments, but also with their swamps and fevers, was given up, and thus it was, according to the Virginian claim, that North Carolina, Tennessee, Kentucky, and several other Indian reservations were peopled and enabled to be admitted as States in the Union. Within the decayed circle there still exist under cultivation several large estates inherited from the old colonial owners; but as a rule the land has a sorry, forlorn aspect.

Upon invitation the writer recently visited the owner of a colonial estate situated on the Pamunkey River, in the counties of King William and New Kent. A truly rural railway passes through this estate on the way from Richmond to the village of West Point, at the head of York River; but as it is a short line (the distance being only forty miles), and little patronized, its accommodations are

WASHINGTON'S BREAKFAST-TABLE; SILVER AND GLASS WARE FROM THE PARKE CUSTIS AND WASHINGTON FAMILIES.

rustic, its trains running at such a moderate rate of speed as to create the impression in the wayfarer's mind that the engine-drivers are opposed to disturbing the sweet repose of the wilderness to which they are accustomed. For verily the line passes through a wilderness of trees and swamps.

When we had reached a distance of thirty-four miles from Richmond, the conductor obligingly stopped the train to put us off at the station called for by our tickets. The name of this station—a roof on four poles—was "Romancoke," and "Romancoke" also was the name of the colonial estate whither we were bound. Emerging from the clump of pines around the station, we soon came in view of refreshingly open fields extending for miles, and saw, about a mile distant, the jaunty cottage inhabited by the owner of "Romancoke," Mr. R. E. Lee, Jun., the youngest son of General R. E. Lee. "Romancoke" and "White House," consisting of a tract of eight thousand acres, constitute what was formerly known as, and is still called, the "Washington estate," from the fact that Washington came into possession of it by his marriage with Mrs. Martha Custis, and lived at the "White

House" a short while after his marriage, before transferring his residence to Mount Vernon. George Washington Parke Custis, the adopted son of Washington, bequeathed the estate to his daughter, who was the wife of General Lee, and from her it was inherited by his son.

The "White House" portion of the estate is about ten miles from Romancoke, and the site of the old building in which Washington and his wife dwelt is now occupied by a small modern structure. As one nears the "White House," *souvenirs* bearing upon the great national hero thicken. Not far off, on the road leading from Richmond to New Kent Court House, there is still pointed out the farm of "P. Chamberlayne, Esq.," at whose country-seat the hero first met the blooming young Martha Custis, then a widow of three years' standing, with two children.

Although G. W. Parke Custis, in his *Recollections*, states that Washington's marriage took place at the "White House," then the residence of Mrs. Martha Custis, and other historians have merely followed his statement, it is still a mooted point whether the marriage took place there or at St. Peter's Church, which is three miles distant. The tradition of the neighborhood is that the ceremony occurred at the church. The Rev. Henry S. Kepler, who was the last rector in charge of it, related to his son an account of the affair, obtained from an aged servant of the Custis family, which asserts the marriage to have taken place at the church. In substance this account was as follows: "I recollect all about it, because I was one of the servants at the 'White House' at the time. The wedding took place at St. Peter's Church. I saw them married, and I saw the wedding party coming back from the church to the 'White House,' where the festivities, dancing, etc., occurred. All the servants on the entire estate were given a holiday for the day, and all, in their holiday attire, joined in the general merrymaking. Washington and Mrs. Custis rode to the church in a gorgeous chariot, and the invited persons followed them in vehicles of various shapes. When they stood up before the minister to be married, Washington tow-

himself smiling upon and chatting with several of the attendants. He looked very youthful and handsome, and tripped around in a very lively manner. When

ROBERT E. LEE.—[FROM THE PORTRAIT BY WEIR AT ROMANCOKE, PAINTED JUST AFTER THE MEXICAN WAR.]
Photographed by G. S. Cook, Richmond, Virginia.

ered beside his betrothed, who looked unusually small and low in stature, and this difference was remarked on by all who had been present. Washington was in uniform, and Mrs. Custis was arrayed in a fine white silk dress. As they came out of the church the newly united couple had a joyful appearance, Washington

the whole party got back to the 'White House,' it rang with laughter, merriment, music, and dancing; a good deal of wine was drunk at the supper, which was of the genuine old-fashioned sort, but there was no intoxication or disorderly proceedings. Washington and his bride took part in the dancing of the minuet, but re-

LANGSTON, CHIEF OF THE PAMUNKEYS.

tired early; the rest of the assembly enjoyed their fun until a very late hour, some staying in the house all night, and others departing for their homes. All the house servants were given a piece of the wedding-cake and a small gratification in money. The next morning Washington, who was an early riser, took breakfast with his bride in their chamber before any of the guests had risen."

That the couple took breakfast "in chambers," as it were, is rendered quite likely from a tradition to that effect, and a piece of furniture handed down in the Custis family, viz., the identical small table upon which the wedding breakfast

was served, and which was transferred from the "White House" to the cottage at Romancoke, where it is now preciously preserved, along with the old warming-pan which was used in airing the sheets on the wedding bed. The table is small, about three feet square, but quite sufficient to hold a *déjeuner à la fourchette*, such as we may fancy that to have been, although all signs or notes of the *menu* are lacking. Of course this little table is dingy and rickety now; a part of the top has been removed, but the bottom slips still hold the four legs firmly together.

St. Peter's Church was erected in 1703, at a cost of 146,000-weight of tobacco—currency of the locality; its steeple was put up twelve years afterward. Both on account of its record and its simple, pleasing old English architecture, it is the most attractive colonial church still standing in Virginia. It is built in the form of a parallelogram, with tower and surmounting steeple connecting at one end with the body of the edifice, all the proportions finely harmonizing. The walls of red brick are three feet thick, the windows are small, with rounded tops; the tower is quite large, with four rising projections capped with spheres, and is surmounted with a low steeple, holding on its extremity the cross-keys of St. Peter as a weather vane.

A short distance below the "White House" we passed through a curious collection of log huts and cabins, situated on the banks of the river, and constituting

FISHING SHORES—INDIAN RESERVATION.

what is styled in the neighborhood "Pamunkey Town." It is a settlement of Indians, the last remnant of King Powhatan's fierce Pamunkeys and Mattaponies, who were the terror of the early English settlers. They number about sixty persons, including men, women, and children, and are the most peacefully inclined part of the State's population to-day.

whole. They still make pottery after the fashion of their ancestors, and it is said that their jars, whether from the peculiar quality of the clay or the making process, have the advantage of keeping milk sweet for a long time. A habit of yearly sending presents of game and fish to the Governor of Virginia is one of the very few

ST. PETER'S CHURCH.

the State's population to-day. They have a government reservation adjoining of fifteen hundred acres of land, which they cultivate, and upon which they hunt and fish, these latter pastimes being the ruling passions strong in their decay. None of these Indians, who have dubbed themselves the "Pocahontas" tribe, are of pure blood, as their progenitors for several generations intermarried with the negroes, whom they resemble in appearance and habits, despite the distinct Indian marks stamped on their faces. The land on which they reside is exempted from taxation by the State government. Hunting and fishing being their chief delights, it need scarcely be remarked that they are poor farmers, and rather thriftless on the

old customs they adhere to. Not a trace of Indian language is to be found in their speech, which consists of corrupt English.

The present owner of Romancoke has in his possession the original deed by which the estate was conveyed to the Custis family. This yellow-stained old parchment bears the signatures of Thomas Jefferson and Carter Braxton ("signers") as witnesses. "Romancoke" is an Indian name, used on Captain John Smith's map, and it has been construed to mean a circling of water, as at that point the Pamunkey River makes a bend of seven miles, which at its neck is only a quarter of a mile across. The land enclosed in this bend is only covered with grass and weeds, and presents a fine open-plain view

HENRY LEE ("LIGHTHORSE HARRY"), 1780.

backed by forest and hill. The Romancoke cottage is located immediately on
the banks of the river, near the narrowest
portion of this little peninsula; the site is
charming, as one can stand in the vine-

covered porch and scan the passing panorama of steamers, tugs, and sail craft of
every description as these dot the distant
horizon. There are no stately trees around
the cottage, and it stands out emphatical-

ly in bold relief on the plain, though there is an orchard with young fruit trees, and shrubs and flower bushes in the garden round about. The owner of the estate is a practical farmer, and all its operations are carried on under his personal supervision and direction. The nearest neighboring dwelling is three miles away. The building is tasteful in external form, and cozy and comfortable within. Its contents, rather than the house itself, are noteworthy, for, with the exception of a few modern implements and contrivances, most of the furniture and other household objects date from the olden days, and have been inherited from the Washington, Custis, and Lee families.

Naturally many of the articles in view have reference to General Lee. A good deal of their acuteness has been bestowed by the genealogists upon R. E. Lee, somewhat in the way that Napoleon Bonaparte was tackled by gentlemen of the same calling after he became famous. Thus there is at Romancoke a curious and quite an elaborate document claiming to connect Lee by an unbroken genealogical chain with no less nor later personage than Duncan, King of Scotland.

The pictures, painted and photographed, hung on the walls of the principal rooms in the cottage are entirely family illustrations. There is a representation of Stratford House, situated in Westmoreland County, on the Potomac River, where General Lee was born, and the residence of his father, "Light-horse Harry." Stratford is yet a very well preserved building, and owing to the solid excellence of its architecture, it is unequalled by any other colonial structure now existing in Virginia. A large oil-painted portrait of General Lee hangs on the wall of the dining-room. It was painted by Professor Weir, of the United States Military Academy at West Point, at the time Lee was its superintendent, and represents him in the uniform of a lieutenant-colonel. Just over the mantel-piece in the same room is the companion portrait of his wife, represented as a young woman, painted by Hansen. Both are well done, and both bear evidence of a remarkably handsome couple. They were married in 1831 at Arlington, where Mrs. Lee was born and raised.

Over the mantel-piece in the parlor are two small portraits of George Washington Parke Custis and Nelly Custis in their old age. The reminiscences of the owner of Romancoke in regard to his maternal grandfather are very vivid, as he was brought up from childhood at Arlington, which was built by this somewhat queer and extremely patriotic old gentleman. Arlington, in all its amplitude of Grecian portico, and fronting the Capitol at Washington, was the favorite residence of the many he owned, but its erection nearly ruined him. He had not sufficient capital to complete the building, and accordingly one of the largest rooms was left only lathed and roughly plastered. This room he occupied as a studio, his greatest delight being to shut himself up in it and paint the livelong day; for he was a painter —decidedly an amateur artist—as well as an author. In both art and literature his only subject, his whole "stock in trade," was the "Father of his Country," whom he spoke of as "THE CHIEF" at all times and to all persons: Washington was a bonanza on which he set his whole heart. His style of painting was a very loud one; his pictures were sensational, not from the love of sensationalism, but because his subject-matter required to be treated in deep colors and big, broad lines. Extensive—ay, colossal—canvases stood on his easels or propped against the walls, aiming to portray the leading events and some of the principal battles of the Revolutionary war, and whether the unities allowed or not, on all of them the foremost figures were "General Washington on a white horse, and the British streaking it." In alluding to his reminiscences of the war of 1812 he was wont to say that he had been present at the battle of Bladensburg, "the only fight" he had ever seen, and "never saw the enemy except running." The British were always "going it" in his eyes: dreaming or awake, he fondly had them on a perpetual run, with Washington and American bayonets driving them into space. In reality he never saw a shot fired.

The silver, porcelain, and glass in ordinary use at Romancoke antedate the republic, many of the articles having seen service in the beginning of the last century. These silver bowls, pots, mugs, cups, candlesticks, graceful and light yet substantial, porcelain plates, cups, and saucers, queerly shaped champagne-glasses, etc., have, in addition to the family associations clinging around them, an intrinsic solidity combined with high artistic merit quite eclipsing the similar ware of modern invention. At the present day Romancoke is well cultivated, the improvements made upon the estate having greatly increased its yield. An abundance of game is to be found roaming through its forests and over its broad fields, and parties of gentlemen from Richmond and Washington frequently visit the mansion in order to indulge their taste for the chase. Fox-hunting is still followed throughout these lower counties, but it is no longer the delight, as it used to be among the "fine country gentlemen" of one hundred years ago, when England was much nearer, so to speak, than she is now. The citizens of to-day find that this is an age in which work passes before pleasure, even the pleasure of keeping a pack of hounds, with horses to match.

AT HOME IN VIRGINIA

ON a May day in 1758, as he spurred upon the way to Williamsburg, under orders from the frontier, Washington rode straight upon an adventure he had not looked for. He was within a few hours' ride of the little capital; old plantations lay close upon the way; neighborly homes began to multiply; and so striking a horseman, riding uniformed and attended, could not thereabouts go far unrecognized. He was waylaid and haled to dinner, despite excuses and protests of public business calling for despatch. There was a charming woman to be seen at the house, his friend told him, if a good dinner was not argument enough—and his business could not spoil for an hour's stay in agreeable company. And so, of a sudden, under constraint of Virginian hospitality, he was hurried into the presence of the gracious young matron who was at once, and as if of right, to make his heart safe against further quest or adventure. Martha Custis was but six-and-twenty. To the charm of youth and beauty were added that touch of quiet sweetness and that winning grace of self-possession which come to a woman wived in her girlhood, and widowed before age or care has checked the first full tide of life. At seventeen she had married Daniel Parke Custis, a man more than twenty years her senior; but eight years of quiet love and duty as wife and mother had only made her youth the more gracious in that rural land of leisure and good neighborhood; and a year's widowhood had been but a suitable preparation for perceiving the charm of this stately young soldier who now came riding her way upon the public business. His age was her own; all the land knew him and loved him for gallantry and brave capacity; he carried himself like a prince—and he forgot his errand to linger in her company. Dinner was soon over, and his horses at the door; there was the drilled and dutiful Bishop, trained servant that he was, leading his restless and impatient charge back and forth within sight of the windows and of the terrace where his young colonel tarried, absorbed and forgetful; man and beast alike had been in the service of the unhappy Braddock, and might seem to walk there lively memorials of duty done and undertaken. But dusk came; the horses were put up; and the next morning was well advanced before the abstracted young officer got at last to his saddle, and spurred on belated to Williamsburg. His business concerned the preparations then afoot for General Forbes's advance upon Duquesne. "I came here at this critical juncture," said Washington to the President of the Council, "by the express order of Sir John St. Clair, to represent in the fullest manner the posture of our affairs at Winchester"—lack of clothes, arms, and equipage, lack of money, lack of wise regulations touching rank and discipline. General Forbes had been in Philadelphia a month already, awaiting the formation of his army in Virginia; Sir John St. Clair, his quartermaster-general, had come into the province to see that proper plans were made and executed; it was necessary that matters should be pressed forward very diligently and at once; and Washington, when once at the seat of government, was not slack to urge and superintend official action. But, the troublesome business once in proper course, he turned back to seek Mrs. Custis again, this time at her own home, ere he went the long distance of the frontier. The onset was made with a soldier's promptness and audacity. He returned to his post, after a delay too slight to deserve any reasonable man's remark, and yet with a pledge given and taken which made him look forward to the end of the campaign with a new longing as to the winning of a real home and an unwonted happiness.

The campaign dragged painfully far into the drear autumn. December had come before the captured post on Ohio could be left to the keeping of Colonel Mercer and a little garrison of provincials. But when at last he was free again there was no reason why Washington should wait longer to be happy, and he was married to Martha Custis on the 6th of January, 1759. The sun shone very bright that day, and there was the fine glitter of gold, the brave show of resplendent uniforms, in the little church where the marriage was solemnized. Officers of his

THE OLD CAPITOL AT WILLIAMSBURG.

Majesty's service crowded there, in their gold lace and scarlet coats, to see their comrade wedded; the new Governor, Francis Fauquier, himself came, clad as befitted his rank; and the bridegroom took the sun not less gallantly than the rest, as he rode, in blue and silver and scarlet, beside the coach and six that bore his bride homeward amidst the thronging friends of the country-side. The young soldier's love of a gallant array and a becoming ceremony was satisfied to the full, and he must have rejoiced to be so brave a horseman on such a day. For three months of deep content he lived with his bride at her own residence, the White House, by York River side, where their troth had been plighted, forgetting the fatigues of the frontier, and learning gratefully the new life of quiet love and homely duty.

These peaceful, healing months gone by, he turned once more to public business. Six months before his marriage he had been chosen a member of the House of Burgesses for Frederick County —the county which had been his scene of adventure in the old days of surveying in the wilderness, and in which ever since Braddock's fatal rout he had maintained his headquarters, striving to keep the border against the savages. Small wonder that he led the poll taken there in Winchester, where through so many seasons men had seen him bear himself like a capable man and a gallant, indomitable soldier. 'Twas no unwelcome duty, either, to take his young wife to Williamsburg in "the season," when all Virginia was in town in the persons of the Burgesses and the country gentry come to enjoy the festivities and join in the business then sure to be afoot. The young soldier was unused to assemblies, however, and suffered a keen embarrassment to find himself for a space too conspicuous amidst the novel Parliamentary scene. He had hardly taken his seat when the gracious and stately Robinson, Speaker of the House and Treasurer of the colony these twenty years, rose, at the bidding of the Burgesses, to thank him for the services of which all were speaking. This sudden praise, spoken with generous warmth there in a public place, was more than Washington knew how to meet. He got to his feet when Mr. Speaker was done, but he could utter not a syllable. He stood there, instead, hot with blushes, stammering, all atremble from head to foot. "Sit down, Mr. Washington," cried the Speaker; "your modesty is equal to your valor, and that surpasses the power of any language that I possess."

Again and again, as the years passed, Washington returned at each session to Williamsburg to take his place in the Assembly; and with custom came familiarity and the ease and firmness he at first had lacked upon the floor. His life broadened about him; all the uses of peace contributed to give him facility and knowledge and a wide comradeship in affairs. Along with quiet days as a citizen, a neighbor, and a country gentleman, came maturity and the wise lessons of a various experience. No man in Virginia lived more or with a greater zest henceforth than Colonel Washington. His marriage brought him great increase of wealth, as well as increase of responsibility. Mr. Custis had left many thousand acres of land, and forty-five thousand pounds sterling in money, a substantial fortune, to the young wife and the two little children who survived him; and Washington had become, by special decree of the Governor and Council in General Court, trustee and manager of the whole. It needed capacity and knowledge and patience of no mean order to get good farming out of slaves, and profitable prices out of London merchants; to find prompt and trustworthy ship-masters by whom to send out cargoes, and induce correspondents over sea to ship the perishable goods sent in return by the right vessels, bound to the nearest river; and the bigger your estate the more difficult its proper conduct and economy, the more disastrous in scale the effects of mismanagement. No doubt the addition of Mrs. Custis's handsome property to his own broad and fertile acres at Mount Vernon made Colonel Washington one of the wealthiest men in Virginia. But Virginian wealth was not to be counted till crops were harvested and got to market. The current price of tobacco might leave you with or without a balance to your credit in London—your only clearing-house, as it chanced. Your principal purchases, too, must be made over sea and through factors. Both what you sold and what you bought must take the hazards of the sea-voyage, the whims of sea-captains, the chances of a foreign market. To be farmer and mer-

THE WHITE HOUSE, ALEXANDRIA, VIRGINIA.

chant at once, manage your own negroes and your own overseers, conduct an international correspondence, to keep the run of prices current, duties, port dues, and commissions, know the fluctuating rates of exchange, to understand and meet all changes, whether in merchants or in markets, three thousand miles away, required an amount of information, an alertness, a steady attention to detail, a sagacity in farming and a shrewdness in trade, such as made a great property a burden to idle or inefficient men. But Washington took pains to succeed. He had a great zest for business. The practical genius which had shone in him almost prematurely as a boy now grew heartily in him as a man of fortune. Messrs. Robert Cary and Company, his factors in London, must soon have learned to recognize his letters in the mere handling, by their bulk. No detail escaped him, when once he had gotten into the swing of the work. They must be as punctilious as he was, they found, in seeing to every part of the trade and accounting with which he intrusted them, or else look to lose his lucrative patronage. He was not many years in learning how to make the best tobacco in Virginia, and to get it recognized as such in England. Barrels of flour marked "George Washington, Mount Vernon," were erelong suffered to pass the inspectors at the ports of the British West Indies without scrutiny. It was worth while to serve so efficient a man to his satisfaction—worth while or not, he would not be served otherwise.

He had emerged, as it were, after a tense and troubled youth, upon a peaceful tract of time, where his powers could stretch and form themselves without strain or hurry. He had robust health, to which he gave leave in unstinted work, athletic strength, and an insatiable relish for being much afoot and in the open, which he satisfied with early rounds of superintendence in the fields where the men were at their tasks, with many a tireless ride after the hounds, or steadfast wait at the haunts of the deer; a planning will that craved some practical achievement every day, which he indulged by finding tasks of betterment about the estate, and keeping his men at them with unflagging discipline; a huge capacity for being useful and for understanding how to be so, which he suffered his neighbors, his parish, his county, the colony itself, to employ when there was need. To a young man, bred these ten years in the forests and in the struggle of warfare upon a far frontier, it had been intolerable to live tamely, without executive tasks big and various enough to keep his energy from rust. The clerical side of business he had learned very thoroughly in camp, as well as the exceeding stir and strain of individual effort—the incessant letter-writing necessary to keep promised performance afoot, the reckoning of men and of stores, the nice calculations of time and ways and means; the scrutiny of individual men, too, which is so critical a part of management, and the slow organization

of effort: he had been in a fine school for these things all his youth, and would have thought shame to himself not to have learned temperance, sagacity, thrift, and patience wherewith to use his energy. His happy marriage did him the service to keep him from restlessness. His love took his allegiance, and held him to his home as to a post of honor and reward. He had never before had leave to be tender with children, or show with what a devotion he could preside over a household all his own. His home got strong hold upon him. His estates gave him scope of command and a life of action. 'Twas no wonder he kept his factors busy, and shipped goods authenticated by the brand.

The soldierly young planter gave those who knew him best, as well as those who met him but to pass, the impression of a singular restraint and self-command, which lent a peculiar dignity and charm to his speech and carriage. They deemed him deeply passionate, and yet could never remember to have seen him in a passion. The impression was often a wholesome check upon strangers, and even upon friends and neighbors, who would have sought to impose upon him. No doubt he had given way to bursts of passion often enough in camp and upon the march, when inefficiency, disobedience, or cowardice angered him hotly and of a sudden. There were stories to be heard of men who had reason to remember how terrible he could be in his wrath. But he had learned, in the very heat and discipline of such scenes, how he must curb and guard himself against surprise, and it was no doubt trials of command made in his youth that had given him the fine self-poise men noted in him now. He had been bred in a strict school of manners at Belvoir and Greenway Court, and here at his own Mount Vernon in the old days, and the place must have seemed to him full of the traditions of whatsoever was just and honest and lovely and of good report as he looked back to the time of his gentle brother. It was still dangerous to cross or thwart him, indeed. Poachers might look to be caught and soundly thrashed by the master himself if he chanced their way. Negligent overseers might expect sharp penalties, and unfaithful contractors a strict accounting, if necessary work went wrong by their fault. He was exacting almost to the

point of harshness in every matter of
just right or authority. But he was open
and wholesome as the day, and reasonable to the point of pity in every affair of
humanity, through it all. Now it was
" my rascally overseer, Hardwick," in his
diary, when certain mares were sent home
" scarce able to highlone, much less to
assist in the business of the plantations ";
but not a month later it was " my worthy
overseer, Hardwick, lying in Winchester
of a broken leg." It was not in his way
to add anything to the penalties of nature.

A quiet simplicity of life and a genuine
love of real sport rid him of morbid humors. All up and down the English
world, while the eighteenth century lasted, gentlemen were commonly to be found
drunk after dinner—outside New England, where the efficient Puritan Church
had fastened so singular a discipline in
manners upon a whole society—and Virginian gentlemen had a reputation for
deep drinking which they had been at
some pains to deserve. A rural society
craves excitement, and can get it very
simply by such practices. There is always leisure to sleep afterwards, even
though your dinner come in the middle
of the day; and there is good reason you
should be thirsty if you have been since
daybreak in the saddle. To ride hard
and to drink hard seemed to go together
in Virginia as inevitably as the rhymes
in a song; and 'twas famous hard riding
after the fox over the rough fields and
through the dense thickets. If Washington drank only small-beer or cider and a
couple of glasses of Madeira at dinner, it
was no doubt because he had found his
quick blood tonic enough, and had set
himself a hard regimen as a soldier. He
did not scruple to supply drink enough
for the thirstiest gathering when he presented himself to the voters of the country-side as a candidate for the House of
Burgesses. " A hogshead and a barrel of
punch, thirty-five gallons of wine, forty-
three gallons of strong cider, and dinner
for his friends," was what he cheerfully
paid for at his first election, and the poll
footed but a few hundred votes all told.
Mount Vernon saw as much company
and as constant merriment and good
cheer as any house in Virginia; and the
master was no martinet to his guests,
even though they came upon professional
errands. " Doctor Laurie came here, I

may add drunk," says his quiet diary,
without comment, though the doctor had
come upon summons to attend Mrs. Washington, and was next morning suffered to
use his lancet for her relief. No doubt
a good fellow when sober, and not to be
lightly chidden when drunk, like many
a gallant horseman and gentleman who
joined the meet of the country-side at the
hospitable place to follow the hounds
when the hunting was good. There was
fox-hunting winter and summer, in season and out, but the sport was best in the
frosty days of January and February,
when the year was young and the gentlemen of the country round gathered at
Belvoir or Gunston Hall or Mount Vernon two or three times a week to warm
their blood in the hale sport, and dine together afterwards—a cordial company of
neighbors, with as many topics of good
talk as foxes to run to cover. The hunt
went fastest and most incessantly when
Lord Fairfax came down from his lodge
in the Valley and joined them for days
together in the field and at the table.

Washington loved horses and dogs
with the heartiest sportsman of them all.
He had a great gust for stalking deer
with George Mason on the broad forested
tracts round Gunston Hall, and liked often to take gun or rod after lesser game
when the days fell dull; but best of all
he loved a horse's back, and the hard
ride for hours together after the dogs and
a crafty quarry—a horse it put a man to
his points to ride, a country where the
running was only for those who dared.
His own mounts could nowhere be bettered in Virginia. There was full blood
of Araby in his noble Magnolia, and as
good hunting blood as was to be found
in the colony in his Blueskin and Ajax,
Valiant and Chinkling. His hounds he
bred "so flew'd, so sanded," so matched in
speed and habit, that they kept always
tune and pace together in the field. "A
cry more tuneable was never holla'd to,
nor cheered with horn," than theirs when
they were let "spend their mouths" till
echo replied "as if another chase were in
the skies." 'Twas first to the stables for
him always in the morning, and then to
the kennels.

It had been hard and anxious work to
get his affairs into prosperous shape again
when the war was over, and those long,
hopeless summers on the stricken frontier. Stock, buildings, fences—everything

had to be renewed, refitted, repaired. For the first two or three years there were even provisions to buy, so slow was the place to support itself once more. Not only all his own ready money, but all he got by his marriage too, and more besides, was swallowed up, and he found himself in debt before matters were finally set to rights and profitable crops made and marketed. But, the thing once done, affairs cleared and became easy as if of their own accord in the business of the estate. The men he had to deal with presently knew their master: the young planter had matured his plans and his discipline. Henceforth his affairs were well in hand, and he could take his wholesome pleasures both handsomely and with a free heart. There was little that was debonair about the disciplined and masterful young soldier. He had taken Pallas' gift: "Self-reverence, self-knowledge, self-control, these three alone lead life to sovereign power. And because right is right, to follow right were wisdom in the scorn of consequence." But he took heed of his life very genially, and was matured by pleasure no less than by duty done. He loved a game of cards in almost any company, and paid his stakes upon the rubber like every other well-conducted man of his century. He did not find Annapolis, or even Philadelphia, too far away to be visited for the pleasure of seeing a good horse-race or enjoying a round of balls and evenings at the theatre, to shake the rustic dulness off of a too constant stay at home. Mrs. Washington enjoyed such outings, such little flings into the simple world of provincial fashion, as much as he did; and they could not sit waiting all the year for the short season at Williamsburg.

A young man at once so handsome, so famous, and so punctilious in point of dress as Colonel Washington could not but make a notable figure in any society. "I want neither lace nor embroidery," was the order he sent to London. "Plain clothes, with a gold or silver button (if worn in genteel dress), are all I desire. My stature is six feet; otherwise rather slender than corpulent." But he was careful the material, the color, and the fit should be of the best and most tasteful, and that very elegant stuffs should be provided from over sea for Mrs. Washington and her children, and very substantial for the servants who were to be in attendance upon the household—a livery of white and scarlet. 'Twas a point of pride with Virginians to know how to dress, both well and in the fashion; and the master of Mount Vernon would have deemed it an impropriety to be less careful than his neighbors, less well dressed than his station and fortune warranted. He watched the tradesmen sharply. "'Tis a custom, I have some reason to believe, with many shopkeepers and tradesmen in London," he wrote bluntly to the Messrs. Cary, "when they know goods are bespoken for exportation, to palm sometimes old, and sometimes very slight and indifferent goods upon us, taking care at the same time to advance the price," and he wished them informed that their distant customers would not be so duped.

He longed once and again to be quit of the narrow life of the colony, and stretch himself for a little upon the broader English stage at home. "But I am tied by the leg," he told his friends there, "and must set inclination aside. My indulging myself in a trip to England depends upon so many contingencies, which, in all probability, may never occur, that I dare not even think of such a gratification." But the disappointment bred no real discontent. There could be no better air or company to come to maturity in than were to be had there in Virginia, if a young man were poised and master of himself. "We have few things here striking to European travellers (except our abundant woods)," he professed, when he wrote to his kinsman Richard Washington in England; "but little variety, a welcome reception among a few friends, and the open and prevalent hospitality of the country;" but it was a land that bred men, and men of affairs, in no common fashion.

Especially now, after the quickening of pulses that had come with the French war, and its sweep of continental, even of international, forces across the colonial stage, hitherto set only for petty and sectional affairs. The colonies had grown self-conscious and restless as the plot thickened and thrust them forward to a rôle of consequence in the empire such as they had never thought to play, and the events which succeeded hurried them to a quick maturity. It was a season a young man was sure to ripen in, and there was good company. The House of Burgesses was very quiet the year Washington first took his place in it, and stood abashed to hear himself praised; but before Mr. Robinson, its already veteran Speaker, was dead, a notable change had set in. Within five years, before the country on the St. Lawrence and the lakes was well out of the hands of the French, the Parliament in England had entered upon measures of government which seemed meant of deliberate purpose to set the colonies agog, and everybody of counsellors in America stood between anger and amazement to see their people in danger to be so put upon.

The threat and pressure of the French power upon the frontiers had made the colonies thoughtful always, so long as it lasted, of their dependence upon England for succor and defence should there come a time of need. Once and again—often enough to keep them sensible how they must stand or fall, succeed or fail, with the power at home—their own raw levies had taken part with the King's troops out of England in some clumsy stroke or other against a French stronghold in the North or a Spanish fortress in the South; and now at last they had gone with English troops into the field in a national cause. Provincials and redcoats had joined for a final grapple with the French, to settle once and for all who should be owners and masters on the coveted continent. The issue had been decisive. By the summer of 1760 Washington could write his kinsman in England that the French were so thoroughly drubbed and humbled that there remained little to do to reduce Canada from end to end to the British power. But the very thoroughness of the success wrought a revolution in the relations of the colonies to the mother-country. It rid them of their sense of dependence. English regiments had mustered their thousands, no doubt, upon the battle-fields of the war in order that the colonies might be free to possess the continent, and it was hard to see how the thing could have been accomplished without them. But it had been accomplished, and would not need to be done again. Moreover, it had shown the colonial militia how strong they were even in the presence of regulars. They had almost everywhere borne an equal part in the fighting, and, rank and file, they had felt with a keen resentment the open contempt for their rude equipment and rustic discipline which too many arrogant offi-

cers and insolent men among the regulars had shown. They knew that they had proved themselves the equals of any man in the King's pay in the fighting, and they had come out of the hot business confident that henceforth, at any rate, they could dispense with English troops and take care of themselves. They had lost both their fear of the French and their awe of the English.

'Twas hardly an opportune time for statesmen in London to make a new and larger place for England's authority in America, and yet that was what they immediately attempted. Save Chatham and Burke and a few discerning men who had neither place nor power, there was no longer any one in England who knew, though it were never so vaguely, the real temper and character of the colonists. 'Twas matter of common knowledge and comment, it is true, that the men of Massachusetts were beyond all reason impatient of command or restraint, affecting an independence which was hardly to be distinguished from contumacy and insubordination ; but what ground was there to suppose that a like haughty and ungovernable spirit lurked in the loyal and quiet South, or among the prudent traders and phlegmatic farmers who were making the middle colonies so rich, and so regardful of themselves in every point of gain or interest? Statesmen of an elder generation had had a sure instinct what must be the feeling of Englishmen in America, and had, with "a wise and salutary neglect," suffered them to take their own way in every matter of self-government. Though ministry after ministry had asserted a rigorous and exacting supremacy for the mother-country in every affair of commerce, and had determined as they pleased what the colonies should be suffered to manufacture, and how they should be allowed to trade—with what merchants, in what commodities, in what bottoms, within what limits—they had nevertheless withheld their hands hitherto from all direct exercise of authority in the handling of the internal affairs of the several settlements, had given them leave always to originate their own legislation and their own measures of finance, until self-government had become with them a thing as if of immemorial privilege. Sir William Keith, sometime Governor of Pennsylvania, had suggested to Sir Robert

Walpole that he should raise revenue from the colonies. "What!" exclaimed that shrewd master of men. "I have Old England set against me, and do you think I will have New England likewise?"

But men had come into authority in England now who lacked this stout sagacity, and every element of sound discretion. English arms and English money, they could say, had swept the French power from America in order that the colonies might no longer suffer menace or rivalry. A great debt had been piled up in the process. Should not the colonies, who had reaped the chief benefit, bear part of the cost? They had themselves incurred burdensome debts, no doubt, in the struggle, and their assemblies would very likely profess themselves willing to vote what they could should his Majesty call upon them and press them. But an adequate and orderly system of taxation could not be wrought out by the separate measures of a dozen petty legislatures; 'twere best the taxation should be direct and by Parliament, whose authority, surely, no man outside turbulent Boston would be mad enough seriously to question or resist. It would, in any event, be wholesome, now the colonies were likely to grow lusty as kingdoms in their roomy continent, to assert a mother's power to use and restrain—a power by no means lost because too long unexercised and neglected. It was with such wisdom the first step was taken. In March, 1764, Parliament voted it "just and necessary that a revenue be raised in America," passed an act meant to secure duties on wines and sugars, and took measures to increase the efficiency of the revenue service in America.

George Grenville was Prime Minister. He lacked neither official capacity nor acquaintance with affairs. He thought it just the colonists should pay their quota into the national treasury, seeing they were so served by the national power; and he declared that in the next session of Parliament he should propose certain direct taxes in addition to the indirect already in force. He saw no sufficient reason to doubt that the colonies would acquiesce, if not without protest, at least without tumult or dangerous resistance. It was a sad blunder. Virginia resented threat and execution alike in such a matter as deeply as did litigious Massachusetts. A long generation ago, in the quiet year 1732, when bluff Sir Robert was Prime Minister, there had been an incident which Governor Keith, maybe, had forgotten. The ministry had demanded of Massachusetts that she should establish a fixed salary for her governors by a standing grant; but she had refused, and the ministers had receded. The affair had not been lost upon the other colonies. That sturdy onetime royal Governor Alexander Spotswood, in Virginia, had noted it very particularly, and spoken of it very bluntly, diligent servant of the crown as he was, to Colonel William Byrd, when he came his way on his "progress to the mines." He declared "that if the Assembly in New England would stand bluff, he did not see how they could be forced to raise money against their will; for if they should direct it to be done by act of Parliament, which they have threatened to do (though it be against the right of Englishmen to be taxed but by their representatives), yet they would find it no easy matter to put such an act in execution." No observing man could so much as travel in Virginia without finding very promptly what it was that gave point and poignancy to such an opinion. That quiet gentleman the Rev. Andrew Burnaby, Vicar of Greenwich, was in Virginia in 1759, and saw plainly enough how matters stood. "The public or political character of the Virginians," he said, "corresponds with their private one; they are haughty and jealous of their liberties, impatient of restraint, and can scarcely bear the thought of being controlled by any superior power. Many of them consider the colonies as independent states, not connected with Great Britain otherwise than by having the same common King and being bound to her with natural affection." Not only so, but "they think it a hardship not to have an unlimited trade to every part of the world." All this, and more, Grenville might have learned by the simple pains of inquiry. One had but to open his eyes and look to see how imperious a race had been bred in the almost feudal South; and, for all they had never heard revolutionary talk thence, ministers ought to have dreaded the leisure men had there to think, the provocation to be proud, the necessity to be masterful and individual, quite as much as they had ever dreaded the stubborn temper and the quick capacity for united action they had once and again seen excited in New England.

It was not necessary to try new laws to see what the colonies would do if provoked. The difficulty already encountered in enforcing the laws of trade was object-lesson enough; and the trouble in that matter had grown acute but yesterday. For long, indeed, no one in the colonies questioned the right of Parliament to regulate their trade; but it was notorious that the laws actually enacted in that matter had gone smoothly off in America only because they were not seriously enforced. "The trade hither is engrossed by the Saints of New England," laughed Colonel Byrd, " who carry off a great deal of tobacco without troubling themselves with paying that impertinent duty of a penny a pound." The Acts of Trade practically forbade direct commerce with foreign countries or their dependencies, especially in foreign bottoms; but ships from France, Spain, and the Canary Isles came and went very freely notwithstanding in colonial ports; for royal officials liked to enjoy a comfortable peace and the esteem of their neighbors, and very genially winked at such transgressions. Cargoes without number were sent to the Dutch and Spanish West Indies every year, and as many brought thence, which were undoubtedly forfeit under the navigation laws Parliament had been at such pains to elaborate and enforce; and privateering as well as smuggling had for long afforded the doughty seamen of Boston, Salem, Charleston, and New York a genteel career of profit. Things had come to such a pass that where business went briskly the people of the colonial ports demanded as of right "a full freedom of illegal trade," and broke sometimes into riot when it was denied them. The Boston *News Letter* had been known very courteously to mourn the death of a worthy collector of his Majesty's customs because, " with much humanity," he had been used to take "pleasure in directing masters of vessels how they ought to avoid the breach of the Acts of Trade." Seacaptains grew accustomed to very confidential relations with owners and consignees, and knew very well, without official counsel, how to take the advice " not to declare at the Custom-house "; and things went very easily and cordially with all parties to the understanding.

In 1761 that understanding was of a sudden rudely broken and the trouble began, which Grenville had the folly to add to. The Board of Trade determined to collect the duties on sugar, molasses, and rum, so long and so systematically evaded in the trade between New England and the West Indies, at whatever cost of suit and scrutiny, and directed their agents in Boston to demand " writs of assistance " from the courts, giving them leave to enter what premises they would in search of smuggled goods. There was instant exasperation and resistance. General search-warrants, opening every man's door to the officers of the law, with or without just and explicit ground of suspicion against him, no English subject anywhere would submit to; and yet these writs authorized nothing less. Issued under a questionable extension to America of an exceptional power of the Court of Exchequer, they violated every precedent of the common law, no less than every principle of prudent administration; and the excitement which they provoked was at once deep and ominous. Sharp resistance was made in the courts, and no officer ever ventured to serve one of the obnoxious writs. Such challenge of the process was uttered by colonial counsel upon trial of the right, moreover, that ministers would be without excuse should they ignore the warning, so explicit and so eloquent of revolutionary purpose. It was James Otis who uttered it. He had but the other day carried the royal commission in his pocket as Advocate-General in his Majesty's Court of Admiralty; but he would not have scrupled, even as his Majesty's servant, he said, to oppose the exercise of a power which had already cost one King his head and another his throne. To oppose in such a case was to defend the very constitution under which the King wore his crown. That constitution secured to Englishmen everywhere the rights of freemen; the colonists had, besides, the plain guarantees of their own charters; if constitution and charter failed, or were gainsaid, the principles of natural reason sufficed for defence against measures so arrogant and so futile. No lawyer could justify these extraordinary writs; no King with an army at his back could ever force them to execution.

Protest not only, but defiance rang very clear in these fearless words; and ministers must avow themselves very ignorant should they pretend they did not know how Mr. Otis had kindled fire from one end of the colonies to the other. But Grenville was resolute to take all risks and push his policy. He did not flinch from the enforcement of the measures of 1764, and in the session of 1765 calmly fulfilled his promise of further taxation. He proposed that the colonists should be required to use revenue stamps upon all their commercial paper, legal documents, pamphlets, and newspapers; and that, at once as a general measure of convenience and a salutary exhibition of authority, his Majesty's troops stationed in the plantations should be billeted on the people. Parliament readily acquiesced. It was thus Grenville purposed "defraying the expenses of defending, protecting, and securing" the colonies; but he came near losing them instead. The act was passed in March; it was not to go into effect until November; but the colonists did not keep him waiting until November for their protests. It was the voice of a veritable tempest that presently came over sea to the ear of the startled minister. And it was not the General Court of turbulent Massachusetts, but the House of Burgesses of loyal Virginia that first spoke the general indignation. Already in the autumn of 1764, upon the mere threat of what was to come, that House had spoken very urgently against the measures proposed, in a memorial to King and Parliament, which, amidst every proper phrase of loyalty and affection, had plainly declared it the opinion of his Majesty's subjects in Virginia that such acts would be in flat violation of their undoubted rights and liberties; and the committee by which that memorial was drawn up had contained almost every man of chief consequence in the counsels of the colony, the King's Attorney-General himself not excepted. But it was one thing to protest against measures to come and quite another to oppose their execution when enacted into laws. The one was constitutional agitation; the other, flat rebellion—little less. It was very ominous to read the words of the extraordinary resolutions passed by the Burgesses on the 30th of May, 1765, after the Stamp Act had become law, and note the tone of restrained passion that ran through them. They declared that from the first the settlers of "his Majesty's colony and dominion" of Virginia had possessed and

enjoyed all the privileges, franchises, and immunities at any time enjoyed by the people of Great Britain itself; and that this, their freedom, had been explicitly secured to them by their charters, " to all intents and purposes as if they had been abiding and born within the realm of England "; "that the taxation of the people by themselves or by persons chosen by themselves to represent them " was " a distinguishing characteristic of British freedom, without which the ancient constitution" of the realm itself could not subsist; "and that his Majesty's liege people of this most ancient colony " had " uninterruptedly enjoyed the right of being thus governed by their assemblies in the article of their taxes and internal police," had never forfeited or relinquished it, and had seen it "constantly recognized by the Kings and people of Great Britain."

Spoken as it was in protest against actual legislation already adopted by Parliament in direct despite of all such privileges and immunities, this declaration of rights seemed to lack its conclusion. The constitutional rights of Virginians had been invaded. What then? Resolved, therefore, "that his Majesty's liege people, the inhabitants of this colony, are not bound to yield obedience to any law or ordinance whatever designed to impose any taxation whatsoever upon them, other than the laws or ordinances of the General Assembly aforesaid," and "that any person who shall, by speaking or writing, assert or maintain " the contrary "shall be deemed an enemy of his Majesty's colony." Such had been the uncompromising conclusion drawn by the mover of the resolutions. What other conclusion could any man draw if he deemed the colonists men, and proud men at that? But the Burgesses would not go so far or be so explicit. They feared to speak treason; they were content to protest of their rights, and let the issue bring conclusions to light. It had been hot fighting to get even that much said. The men hitherto accepted always as leaders in the House had wished to hold it back from rash and heated action, and there had been bitter debates before even those significant premises for a revolutionary conclusion had been forced to adoption. Old leaders and new, young men and old alike, had willingly united in the memorial of 1764; but now that the Stamp Act was law, conservative members shrank from doing what must look so like a flat defiance of Parliament. Only young men would have had the audacity to urge such action; only very extraordinary young men would have had the capacity to induce the House to take it. But such long time in the colony; they lived back from the tide-water counties where the real aristocracy had its strength and supremacy; they were of that middle class of yeomen-gentlemen who love liberty but do not affect rank. "A vigorous aristocracy favors the growth of personal

WILLIAM AND MARY COLLEGE, WILLIAMSBURG, AT THE PRESENT DAY.

young men were at hand, their leader as veritable a democrat as had ever taken the floor in that assembly.

Patrick Henry was not of the aristocracy of the colony. Good Scots blood ran in his veins, quickened by the lively strain of an old Welsh stock. His father came of a race of scholars, and, good Churchman though he was, knew his Livy and his Horace better than his Bible. His mother came of a vivacious line of easy-going wits and talkers, which but a touch more of steadiness and energy might any day have made famous. His father had served his county of Hanover very capably and acceptably as surveyor, colonel, magistrate, and his uncle had been beloved as the faithful pastor of quiet parishes. But they had been no eminence even in those who are not of it, but only near it," and these plain men of the middle counties were the more excellent and individual in the cultivation of their powers by reason of the contact. But there was a touch of rusticity, a neglect of polish, a rough candor of speech, about them which set them apart and distinguished them sharply enough when they came into the presence of the courtly and formal gentlemen who practised the manners of London in the river counties. Patrick Henry, at any rate, must have seemed a very rustic figure to the Burgesses when he first came to take his seat amongst them on a May day in 1765. He was known, indeed, to many. This was the man, they must have known, who had won so strange a verdict from a jury

WILLIAM AND MARY COLLEGE.
From an old print.

two years ago in the celebrated parsons' case at Hanover court-house, against the law and the evidence. But his careless dress and manner, his loose, ungainly figure, his listless, absent bearing, must have set many a courtly member staring. For such men as Washington, indeed, there can have been nothing either strange or unattractive in the rough exterior and unstudied ways of the new member. Punctilious though he was himself in every point of dress and bearing, Washington's life had most of it been spent with men who looked thus, and yet were stuff of true courage and rich capacity within. The manner of a man could count as no test of quality with him. His experience had covered the whole variety of Virginian life. He was an aristocrat by taste, not by principle. And Patrick Henry had, in fact, come to the same growth as he in essential quality and principle, though by another way. Henry's life had been wilful, capricious, a bit haphazard; Washington's all the while subject to discipline; but both men had touched and seen the whole energy of the commonwealth, knew its hope, could divine its destiny. There was but one Virginia, and they were her children. It could not take long to bring them to an understanding and comradeship in affairs.

It was characteristic of the new member that he should step at once and unhesitatingly to a place of leadership when debate of the Stamp Act stirred the House, and that he should instantly sweep the majority into his following with a charm and dash of eloquence that came like a revelation upon the quiet assembly. He was but twenty-nine years old, but he had spent all his life in learning how the world went, and by what manner of speech it was moved and governed. He had roamed the woods with no thought but for sport, or a quiet hour with a book or his fancy in the shade of the trees. He had kept a country store, and let gossip and talk of affairs of colony and country-side take precedence of business. Finally he had turned with a permanent relish to the law, and had set himself to plead causes for his neighbors in a way that made judges stare and juries surrender at discretion. In everything he had seemed to read the passions of men. Books no less than men, the chance company of an old author no less than the constant talk of the neighborly land he lived in, seemed to fill him with the quick principles of the people and polity to which he belonged, and to lend him as inevitably every living phrase in which to utter them. The universal sympathy and insight which made his pleasantry so engaging to men of every stamp rendered his power no less than terrible when he turned to play upon their passions. He was not conscious of any audacity when he sprang to his feet upon the instant he saw the House resolved into committee to consider the Stamp Act. It was of the ardor of his nature to speak when conviction moved him strongly, without thought of propriety or precedence; and it was like him to stand there absorbed, reading his resolutions from a fly-leaf torn from an old law-book.

It seemed no doubt a precious piece of audacity in the eyes of the prescriptive leaders of the House to hear this almost unknown man propose his high recital of Virginia's liberties and his express defiance of Parliament—in tones which rang no less clear and confident upon the clause which declared "his Majesty's liege people" of the colony in no way bound to yield obedience, than in the utterance of the accepted matter of his premises. Debate flamed up at once, hot, even passionate. The astounding, moving eloquence of the young advocate, his instant hold upon the House, the directness with which he purposed and executed action in so grave a matter, stirred the pulses of his opponents and his followers with an equal power, and roused those who would have checked him to a vehemence as great as his own. The old leaders of the House, with whom he now stood face to face in this critical business, were the more formidable because of the strong reason of their position. No one could justly doubt that they wished to see the Old Dominion keep and vindicate her liberty, but they deemed it folly to be thus intemperately beforehand with the issue. Almost to a man they were sprung of families who had come to Virginia with the great migration that had brought the Washingtons, in the evil day when so many were fleeing England to be quit of the Puritan tyranny—royalists all, and touched to the quick with the sentiment of loyalty. 'Twas now a long time since Cromwell's day, indeed; generations had passed, and a deep passion for Virginia had been added to that old reverence for the wearer of the crown in England. But these men prided themselves still upon their loyalty; made it a point of honor to show themselves no agitators, but

constitutional statesmen. It made them grave and deeply anxious to see the privileges that were most dear to them thus violated and denied, but it did not make them hasty to quarrel with the Parliament of the realm. They had intended opposition, but they feared to throw their cause away by defiance. 'Twas as little wise as dignified to flout thus at the sovereign power before all means had been exhausted to win it to forbearance.

It was not the least part of the difficulty to face the veteran Speaker, John Robinson, so old in affairs, so stately in his age, so gravely courteous, and yet with such a threat of good manners against those who should make breach of the decorous traditions of the place. But the men chiefly to be feared were on the floor. There was Richard Bland, "wary, old, experienced," with "something of the look," a Virginian wit said, " of old musty parchments, which he handleth and studieth much," author of a "treatise against the Quakers on water-baptism"; with none of the gifts of an orator, but a veritable antiquarian in law and the precedents of public business, a very formidable man in counsel. Quiet men trusted him, and thought his prudence very wise. George Wythe was no less learned, and no less

HANOVER COURT-HOUSE.

influential. Men knew him a man of letters, bringing the knowledge of many wise books to the practice of affairs, and set great store by his sincerity, as artless as it was human, and sweetened with good feeling. It made Randolph and Pendleton and Nicholas, the elder orators of the House, seem the more redoubtable that they should have such men as these at their elbows to prompt and steady them. And yet they would have been formidable enough of themselves. Edmund Pendleton had not, indeed, the blood or the breeding that gave his colleagues prestige. He had won his way to leadership by his own steady genius for affairs. He read nothing but law-books, knew nothing but business, cared for nothing but to make practical test of his powers. But he took all his life and purpose with such a zest, made every stroke with so serene a self-possession, was so quick to see and act upon every advantage in his business of debate, and was withal so transparent, bore himself with such a grace and charm of manner, was so obviously right-minded and upright, that it meant a great deal to the House to hear him intervene in its discussions with his melodious voice, his cool, distinct, effective elocution. Robert Carter Nicholas added to like talents for business and debate a reverent piety, a title to be loved and trusted without question, which no man ever thought to gainsay. And Peyton Randolph, with his "knowledge, temper, experience, judgment, integrity" as of a true Roman spirit, was a sort of prince among the rest. No man could doubt he wished Virginia to have her liberties. He had gone over sea to speak for her in Dinwiddie's day, though he was the King's attorney, and had lost his office for his boldness. But there were traditions of loyalty and service in his breeding which no man might rightly ignore. His father before him had won knighthood and the royal favor by long and honorable service as his Majesty's attorney in the colony. Pride and loyalty had gone hand in hand in the annals of a proud race, and had won for the Randolphs a prestige which made it impossible Sir John's son should very long be kept from the office he had so honorably inherited. And so Peyton Randolph was now once again the King's attorney. It was not as the King's officer, however, but as an experienced Parliamentary tactician, a trained debater, a sound man of affairs, that he had set himself to check Henry in his revolutionary courses.

Henry found himself, in truth, passionately set upon. Even threats were uttered, and abuse such as proud men find ill to bear. They cried "Treason! treason!" upon him when he dared declare the King would do well to look to the fate of Cæsar and Charles the First for profitable examples. But he was not daunted a whit. "If this be treason, make the most of it," was his defiance to them. One ally who might have stood with him, had he known, was absent. Richard Henry Lee would have brought to his support a name as ancient and as honorable as any in the colony, and an eloquence scarcely less than his own. But, as it was, he was left almost

TAZEWELL HALL, THE HOME OF THE RANDOLPHS.
After a print in *Omitted Chapters of History disclosed in the Life and Papers of Edmund Randolph.* By courtesy of G. P. Putnam's Sons.

PEYTON RANDOLPH.

alone, and won his battle with no other aid than very plain men could lend by vote and homely utterance. The vote was very close, but enough. Randolph flung out of the House, muttering in his heat that he " would have given five hundred guineas for a single vote." Henry, taking the triumph very simply, as was his wont, and knowing his work for the session done, quietly made his way homeward that very day, striding unconcernedly down Duke of Gloucester Street, chatting with a friend, his legs clad in buckskin as if for the frontier, his saddle-bags and the reins of his lean nag slung carelessly over his arm.

The Assembly had adopted Henry's declaration of rights, not his resolution of disobedience, and had softened a little the language he would have used; but its action seemed seditious enough to Fauquier, the Governor, and he promptly dissolved them. It did little good to send Virginians home, however, if the object was to check agitation. The whole manner of their life bred thought and concert of action. Where men have leave to be individual, live separately and with a proud self-respect, and yet are much at each other's tables, often in vestry council together, constantly coming and going, talking and planning throughout all the country-side, accustomed to form their opinions in league, and yet express each man his own with a dash and flavor of independence; where there is the leisure to reflect, the habit of joint efforts in business, the spirit to be social, and abundant

GUNSTON HALL, THE HOME OF GEORGE MASON.
From a photograph showing in the foreground the northwest corner room in which the Virginia Declaration of Rights is supposed to have been drafted.

opportunity to be frank withal — if you will, you may look to see public views form themselves very confidently, and as easily without assemblies as with them. Washington had taken no part in the stormy scenes of the House, but had sat calmly apart rather, concerned and thoughtful. He was not easily caught by the excitement of a sudden agitation. He had the soldier's steady habit of self-possession in the presence of a crisis, and his own way of holding things at arm's-length for scrutiny—"like a bishop at his prayers," a wag said. He had a soldier's loyalty, too, and slowness at rebellion. His thought, no doubt, was with the con-servatives, whatever may have been the light that sprang into his quiet eye when Henry's voice rang out so like a clarion, calling Virginia to her standard; and he went home, upon the dissolution, to join and aid his neighbors in the slow discus-sion which must shape affairs to an issue.

"The Virginia Resolutions" had run like a flame through the colonies—not as the Burgesses had adopted them, but as Henry had drawn them, with their ex-press threat of disobedience. Nor was that all. October, 1765, saw delegates from nine colonies come together in New York, at the call of Massachusetts, to take counsel what should be done. Every one knew that Virginia, North Carolina, and Georgia, the only colonies absent from the "congress," would have sent delegates too had their Governors not prevented them by the dissolution of their Assemblies before they could act on the call. A deep excitement and concern had spread everywhere throughout the settlements. Not only did the impending enforcement of the act engross "the con-versation of the speculative part of the colonists," as Washington wrote to Fran-cis Dandridge in London; it promised to engross also the energies of very active, and it might be very violent, men in many quarters, and it began to grow ev-ident that some part of government itself would be brought to a standstill by its processes. "Our courts of judicature," declared Washington, "must inevitably be shut up; for it is impossible (or next of kin to it), under our present circum-stances, that the act of Parliament can be complied with . . .; and if a stop be put to our judicial proceedings, I fancy the merchants of Great Britain trading to the colonies will not be among the last to wish for a repeal of it." The congress at New York drew up nothing less than a bill of rights and immunities, and sent resolutions over sea which arrested the attention of the world. The Virginian Assembly despatched like papers for itself; and Richard Henry Lee, when he per unshaken, was slowly coming to a clear vision of affairs in all their significance. Fox-hunting did not cease. He was much in the saddle and at table with the Fairfaxes, whom nothing could shake from their allegiance, and who looked

GEORGE MASON.

had assisted to draw its memorials, hastened home to form in his own Cavalier county a "Westmoreland Association," whose members (four Washingtons among the rest) bound themselves by a solemn covenant to "exert every faculty to prevent the execution of the said Stamp Act in any instance whatsoever within this colony." The ministry could not stand the pressure. They gave way to Lord Rockingham, and the act was repealed.

Meanwhile Washington, his calm temper the colony was in. It was proper they should speak so if they deemed it just, and Washington had no intolerance for what they urged. But George Mason, the neighbor whom he most trusted, was of a very different mind, and strengthened and confirmed him in other counsels. Mason was six years his senior; a man, too, cast by nature to understand men and events, how they must go and how be guided. They conferred constantly, at every turn of their intimate life, in the field or in the library, mounted or afoot in the forests, and came very deliberately and soberly to their statesman's view. Randolph and Pendleton and Wythe and Bland had themselves turned, after the first hesitation, to act with ardent men like Lee in framing the memorials to King, Lords, and Commons which were to go from the Burgesses along with the resolutions of the Stamp Act Congress in New York; and Washington, who had never hesitated, but had only gone slowly and with his eyes open, with that self-poise men had found so striking in him from the first, came steadily with the rest to the at last common purpose of resolute opposition. The repeal of the act came to all like a great deliverance.

Governor Fauquier had deemed it his duty to dissolve the Assembly upon the passage of Henry's resolutions, but he had acted without passion in the matter, and had kept the respect of the men he dealt with. He was not a man, indeed, to take public business very seriously, having been bred a man of fashion and a courtier rather than a master of affairs. He loved gay company and the deep excitement of the gaming-table, not the round of official routine. Affable, generous, elegant, a scholar and real lover of letters, he vastly preferred the talk of vivacious women and accomplished men to the business of the General Court, and was a man to be liked rather than consulted. Washington, always admitted to the intimacy of official circles at Williamsburg, very likely relished the gallant Fauquier better than the too officious Dinwiddie. It was, unhappily, no portent to see a man still devoted to dissipation at sixty-two, even though he were Governor of one of his Majesty's colonies and a trusted servant of the crown; and Fauquier's gifts as a man of wit and of instructed tastes made his companionship no less acceptable to Washington than to the other men of discernment who frequented the ballrooms and receptions, ate formal dinners, and played quiet games of cards during the brief season at the little capital. It did not seriously disturb life there that the Governor upheld the power of Parliament to tax, while the Burgesses strenuously opposed it. Washington, for one, did not hesitate on that account to be seen often in friendly talk with the Governor, or to accept frequent invitations to the "palace." He was of the temper which has so distinguished the nobler sort of Englishmen in politics: he might regard opposition as a public duty, but he never made it a ground of personal feeling or private spite. In a sense, indeed, he had long been regarded as belonging to official circles in the colony more intimately than any other man who did not hold office. He had been put forward by the Fairfaxes in his youth; men in the Council and at the head of affairs had been his sponsors and friends from the first; he had been always, like his brother before him, a member of one of the chief groups in the colony for influence and a confidential connection with the public business. It was even understood that he was himself destined for the Council, when it should be possible to put him in it without seeming to give too great a preponderance to the Fairfax Interest, already so much regarded in its make-up.

The first flurry of differing views and conflicting purposes among the Virginian leaders had passed off. The judgment of high-spirited men everywhere sustained Henry — gave him unmistakable authentication as a leader; put all public men in the way of understanding their constituents. Some were bold and some were timid, but all were animated by the same hope and purpose, and few were yet intemperate. "Sensible of the importance of unanimity among our constituents," said Jefferson afterwards, looking back to that time when he was young and in the first flush of his radical sentiments, "although we often wished to have gone faster, we slackened our pace, that our less ardent colleagues might keep up with us; and they, on their part, differing nothing from us in principle, quickened their gait somewhat beyond that which their prudence might of itself have advised." Patrick Henry was received to the place he had earned; and although the older leaders resumed that sway in counsel to which their tried skill and varied experience in affairs fairly entitled them, there was no longer any jealous exclusion of new men. Henry's fame crept through the colonies as the man who had first spoken the mind not of Virginians only, but of all just men, with regard to the liberties of Englishmen in America. Before a year was out Richard Bland himself, parchment man and conservative that he was, had written and published a pamphlet entitled "An Inquiry into the Rights of the British Colonies," which said nothing less than that in all that concerned her internal affairs Virginia was "a distinct, independent state," though "united with the parent state by the closest league and amity, and under the same allegiance." A colony "treated with injury and violence," he exclaimed, "is become an alien." When antiquarians and lawyers, fresh from poring upon old documents, spoke thus, there were surely signs of the times.

The government at home kept colonial sentiment very busy. Even Lord Rockingham's government, with Burke to admonish it, coupled its repeal of the stamp duties with a "declaratory act" which sought to quiet controversy by giving the lie direct to every argument urged against its authority in the colonies. "Parliament has power to bind the colonies in all cases whatsoever," was its round assertion: "a resolution for England's right to do what the Treasury pleased with three millions of freemen," cried Chatham. Though Rockingham's government would not act on that right, its successors, without scruple, would; and they were soon about it, for Rockingham's ministry retained office scarcely a twelvemonth. Grenville was, indeed, discredited; but Grafton and Townshend were as bad, as stubborn in temper, as reckless in policy. The year 1767 saw taxes proposed and enacted on glass, paper, painters' colors, and tea imported into the colonies, with a purpose to pay fixed salaries to the crown's officers in the colonies out of the proceeds, and the contested ground was all to go over again. To show their temper, the new ministers suspended the legislative powers of the Colonial Assembly in New York for refusing to make provision for troops quartered upon the colony. To complete their fiscal arrangements they presently created a custom-house and board of revenue commissioners for America. It was an ominous year, and set opinion forward not a little in the colonies.

The House of Burgesses broke, at its next session (1768), into fresh protests and remonstrances, and there was no one to restrain or rebuke it. Fauquier was dead, and gone to his reckoning; the reins of government were in the hands of gentle John Blair, President of the Council, a Virginian every inch, and with never a thought of checking his fellow-colonists in the expression of their just opinions. The autumn brought Lord Botetourt, the new Governor-General, who came in showy state, and with genial display of courtly manners and good feeling; but his arrival made little difference. The Burgesses smiled to see him come to open their session of 1769 with pageant of coach and six, brave display of royal insignia, and the manner of a sovereign meeting Parliament, and turned from him almost in contempt to denounce once more the course of the ministers, argue again the rights of America, declare they would draw the colonies together in concerted opposition, and call upon the other colonies to concur with them alike in their principles and in their purpose. Botetourt came hot foot to dissolve them; but they only shifted their place of meeting, gathered again at the private house of Mr. Anthony Hay, and there resolved no longer to import the things which Parliament had taxed in despite of them. George Mason had drawn the resolutions, at Washington's request, and Washington himself presented them.

Mason's thought had hastened very far along the path of opposition under the whip of England's policy, and Washington's quite as far. The government had not only sent troops to Boston and dissolved every Assembly that protested, but had advised the King to press prosecutions for treason in the colonies, and, should there be deemed sufficient ground, transport the accused to England to be tried by special commission. It was this last measure that had provoked the Burgesses to their hottest outburst. "At a time when our lordly masters in Great Britain will be satisfied with nothing less than the deprivation of American freedom," wrote Washington to Mason, with a sudden burst of passion, "it seems highly necessary that something should be done to avert the stroke, and maintain the liberty which we have derived from our ancestors. . . . That no man should scruple, or hesitate a moment, to use a-ms in defence of so valuable a blessing, on which all the good and evil of life depends, is clearly my opinion. Yet a-ms, I would beg leave to add, should be the last resource." Addresses to the throne and remonstrances to Parliament had failed: it remained to try "starving their trades and manufactures," to see if that at last would arrest their attention. No doubt even that would prove of little avail; but it was at least peaceable and worth the trial. The next month, accordingly, he got unhesitatingly to his feet in the private meeting of the Burgesses at Mr. Hay's and moved George Mason's resolutions; nor did he forget to subscribe his quota to the fund which was to defray the expenses of the "association" there formed.

The next evening he attended the "Queen's Birth-Night" at the palace with the same naturalness of demeanor and frankness of dealing towards the Governor as before. Botetourt was not all show and gallantry, but was a genuine man at bottom. He had come to Virginia thinking the colonists a pleasure-loving people who could be taken by display and cajoled by hospitality: he had been told they were such in London. But he knew his mistake almost as soon as he had made it; and was prompt, even while he upheld prerogative, to do what he could to deal with them in a liberal and manly spirit. He had acquiesced very heartily at the outset of his administration in a decision of the Council that writs of assistance could not legally be issued in Virginia; for the process had been tried there too. He made such representations with regard to the state of the colony to the ministers at home as were both just and wise; was assured in reply that the ministers were willing to make every necessary concession; pledged his word in Virginia that there should be a substantial change of policy; and died the sooner (October 15, 1770) because the government would not, after all, redeem his promises. "Your Governor is becoming very popular, as we are told here," wrote Arthur Lee to his brother, from London, "and I have the worst proof of it in the increased orders for fineries from the ladies." Virginians did not find it easy to break an immemorial habit in order to starve the English trades and manufactures; and it was more than once necessary to urge and renew the non-importation agreements alike among the Burgesses and merchants at Williamsburg and by means of local associations throughout the colony. But Washington was punctilious to observe to the letter the agreements he had himself proposed. Again and again he bade his mercantile agents in London assist him to guard against any inadvertent breach of them: not to send him the articles Parliament had picked out for taxation in the colonies.

Life still continued to go, it is true, with something of the old sumptuousness at Mount Vernon. It was in June, 1768, that Colonel Washington ordered a new chariot, "made in the newest taste, handsome, genteel, and light, to be made of the best seasoned wood, and by a celebrated workman," which was to cost him, fittings and all, one hundred and thirty-three pounds. For all he grew uneasy lest the colonies' disagreement with England should come at last to a conflict of arms, he pushed his private interests with no abatement of thoroughness or self-possession, as if there were no fear but that things would long enough stand as they were. He had not run surveyor's lines for Lord Fairfax or assisted to drive the French from the Ohio without seeing what fair lands lay upon the western rivers awaiting an owner; and, though there was still doubt how titles were to be established in that wilderness, he took care, through the good offices of an old comrade in arms, at least to be quietly beforehand with other claimants in setting up such titles as might be where the land lay richest and most accessible. "A silent management" was what he advised, "snugly carried on under the guise of hunting other game," lest there should be a premature rush thither that would set rival interests a-clashing. A strange mixture of the shrewdness of the speculator and the honesty of the gentleman — claims pushed with privacy, but without trickery or chicane—ran through his letters to Captain Crawford, and drew as canny replies from the frontiered soldier. Business gave way often to sport and pleasure, too, as of old, when politics fell dull between sessions. Now it was the hunt; then a gunning party in the woods; and again a day or two aboard his schooner, dropping down the river, and drawing the seine for sheep's-heads upon the bar at Cedar Point. Even politics was mixed with diversion. He must needs give a ball at Alexandria on the evening of his election to the House which was to meet Lord Botetourt, no less than on other like occasions, of whatever kind the business of the Assembly was likely to be. He did not lose his passion for fine horseflesh, either, at the thickest of the plot. In 1770 he was with Governor Eden, of North Carolina, at the Jockey Club races in Philadelphia, no doubt relieved by the news that all but the tea tax had been repealed. The next year it was the races in Annapolis that claimed him; and in 1773 Jacky Custis held him again at Philadelphia on the same errand. It was wholesome to be thus calmly in pursuit of diversion in the intervals of trying business. It bespoke a hearty life and a fine balance in the man.

There was one matter to which Washington felt it his bounden duty as a soldier and a man of honor to devote his time and energies, whether politics pressed or not. A grant of two hundred thousand acres of the western lands had been promised by the government of the colony to those who enlisted for the war against the French and Indians in 1754; but nothing had ever been done to fulfil the promise, and Washington undertook to act as agent for his comrades in the business. In the autumn of 1770, accordingly, he turned away for a space from the deepening trouble in the east to plunge once more into the western ways and search out proper tracts for the grant along the reaches of the Ohio. 'Twas a two months' journey, for he did not stop till he had gone close upon three hundred miles beyond Fort Pitt. And when he was home again no one in the government who could lend a hand in the matter got any peace from the stirring, thorough man until the business was put finally into shape. There was a tidy profit in the grant for himself: for his own share was large, and he providently bought, besides, the shares of others who were unwilling to spend or co-operate in the matter. But there were months upon months of weary, unrequited service for his comrades, too, given with hearty diligence and without grudging. Their portions were as well placed as his own, they were to find, when it came to the survey. He came off from the business very rich in western lands—buying the Great Meadows, among the rest, for memory's sake—but richer still in the gratitude and admiration of the men for whom he had labored.

Meanwhile events darkened ominously. A new administration had been formed in England under Lord North, and had begun its government by repealing all the taxes of 1769 except that on tea. But it was Parliament's right to tax them that the colonists were fighting, not the taxes themselves, and one tax was as hateful as a hundred. The year had been marked in sinister fashion, moreover, by a broil between townsmen and troops in the streets of Boston, in which arms had been used and men slain, and in the heated imaginations of the colonists the affair had taken on the ugly aspect of a massacre. The year 1771 went quietly enough for Virginians. Botetourt was dead, and that good merchant of York, William Nelson, President of the Council, sat in the place of authority throughout the year. Although the whole country refused the taxed tea, the attention of the ministers, as it happened, was fixed chiefly upon Massachusetts, where trade centred at a growing port and opposition had a local habitation. In Virginia there was no place to send troops to, unless the whole country were occupied, and so long as Mr. Nelson was acting Governor, Colonel Washington could go without preoccupation to the races, and gentlemen everywhere follow their own devices in the quiet counties. There was rioting—rebellion even—in North Carolina, so uneasily did affairs go there; but Governor Tryon was a soldier as well as a despot, and did not need to trouble his neighbors about that. It was not until the first months of 1772 that Virginians began to read plain signs of change in the face of their new Governor, John Murray, Earl Dunmore—a dark and distant man, who seemed to the Virginians to come like a satrap to his province, who brought a soldier with him for secretary and confidential adviser, set up a fixed etiquette to be observed by all who would approach him, spoke abruptly and without courtesy, displayed in all things an arbitrary temper, and took more interest, it presently appeared, in acquiring tracts of western land than in conducting the government of the colony. The year of his coming was marked by the secret destruction of the revenue-schooner *Gaspé* in Rhode Island, and by many significant flaws of temper here and there throughout the colonies; and 1773 saw affairs at last come to a crisis.

Dunmore had summoned the Burgesses to meet him upon his first coming, but had liked their proud temper as little as they liked his, and was careful not to call them together again till March, 1773, though he had promised to convene them earlier. There was instant trouble. In view of the affair of the *Gaspé*, Parliament had again resolved upon the trial of malcontents in England, and the Burgesses were hot at seeing the sentiments of the colonies so flouted. Conservative men would still have waited to try events, but their fellow-members of quicker pulse were diligent to disappoint them. Leadership fell to those who were bold enough to take it; and Patrick Henry, Richard Henry Lee, Dabney Carr, and Thomas Jefferson, radicals all, drew together, a self-constituted committee of guidance. Evening after evening they met in a private room at the Raleigh, with now and again one or two other like spirits called into counsel, to consult what should be done. Richard Henry Lee proposed that the colonies should be invited to join Virginia in appointing committees of correspondence, through which to devise steady concert of action, and that Virginia's committee, to be appointed at once, should be instructed to look into the character of the new court of trial lately established in Rhode Island. Dabney Carr was directed to move the resolutions, and the eloquence of Lee and Henry won for them an instant and hearty acceptance. Dunmore promptly dissolved the Assembly, and Washington was free to set out for New York to place Jacky Custis at King's College, lingering on the way in Philadelphia to see the races, and pick up the talk of the hour during half a dozen evenings at the rooms of the Jockey Club, at the balls and assemblies of the gay town, and at the hospitable tables of his friends.

The opening of the year had found Washington in a very genial humor, his letters touched with pleasantry and gossip. "Our celebrated fortune, Miss French, whom half the world was in pursuit of," he wrote, in February, to Colonel Bassett, "bestowed her hand on Wednesday last, being her birthday (you perceive, I think myself under a necessity of accounting for the choice) on Mr. Ben Dulany, who is to take her to Maryland. .... Mentioning of one wedding puts me in mind of another"—and so through the news of Miss More, "remarkable for a very frizzled head and good singing," and

the rest of the neighborhood talk. But the year turned out a very sad one for him. He had been scarcely ten days back from New York when Patsy Custis, whom he loved as his own daughter, died. It called forth all the latent Christian faith of the thoughtful, steadfast man to withstand the shock. And Master Jack Custis, the girl's wayward brother, gave him little but anxiety. He would not study, for all Washington was so solicitous he should have the liberalizing outlook of books, and be made "fit for more useful purposes than horse-racer," and though he was but twenty, could hardly be induced to see the year out at college before getting married.

It was no doubt very well that public affairs of the first consequence called Washington's mind imperatively off from these private anxieties, which could not but be dwarfed in the presence of transactions which threatened to shake the continent. As the year drew on, the government in England undertook to force cargoes of the East India Company's tea into the ports. When all resisted, and Boston, more forward even than the rest, threw three hundred and forty odd chests of tea into the harbor, acts passed Parliament giving dangerous increase of power to the Governor of Massachusetts, and directing that Boston port be closed to all commerce on and after the first day of June, and it became evident that vigorous action must be taken in response. The Burgesses in Virginia (May, 1774) resolved that June 1st should be set apart as a day of fasting and prayer—prayer that civil war might be averted and the people of America united in a common cause. Again Dunmore dissolved them; but they gathered in the long room of the Raleigh tavern, and there resolved to urge a congress of all the colonies, and to call a convention for Virginia to meet at that place on the first day of August to take action for the colony. They showed no spleen towards the Governor. Washington dined with him the very day of the dissolution, spent the evening at the palace, even rode out with him to his farm on the following morning and breakfasted there; and the Burgesses did not fail to give the ball they had planned in honor of Lady Dunmore and her daughters on the evening of the day they had held their meeting in the "Appolo room" at the Raleigh. But there were fasting and prayer on the 1st of June ; the convention met on the first day of August; very outspoken resolutions were adopted; and Peyton Randolph, Richard Henry Lee, Patrick Henry, Richard Bland, EdmundPendleton,George Washington,and Benjamin Harrison were directed to attend the congress of the colonies appointed to meet in Philadelphia on the fifth day of September. When the time came for the journey, Henry and Pendleton joined Washington at Mount Vernon. It must have been with many grave thoughts that the three companions got to horse and turned to ride through the long August day towards the north.

CHARLESTON AND THE CAROLINAS

AFTER one good look around Charleston, South Carolina, the thing which most amazed me was that no one had ever happened to prepare me for finding a city so unlike our others that it actually may be said to be "built sidewise," as if all its houses were at odds with the streets. Strange also it seemed that no one had warned me that I should find it a water-color city of reds and pinks and soft yellows and white set against abundant greenery, and with horse-cars of still stronger colors flaming through the streets in the sunshine. Its own lovers, down there, like to speak of it as "old and mellow," but that expresses only a little bit of what it is.

First, it is very beautiful; next, it is dignified and proud; third, it is the cleanest city (or was when I was there) that I have yet seen in America; and, last of all, it is a creation by itself—a city unlike any other that I know of. It is built on a spit of land with water on three sides, like New York, and this gives its people that constant and enduring delight which continual views of moving water never fail to provide. . Part of its early history is that of a planters' summer resort, and something of that forgotten holiday air still clings to it. If it suggests any city that I have ever seen, it is New Orleans—perhaps because of an indefinable Latin trace that is seen in the stuccoed houses and walled gardens, and again, because of the important part the gardens play there, and the profusion of flowers that results from them.

The most peculiar feature of Charleston is the arrangement of its houses, which, as a rule, are built sidewise on the streets, with the end of each dwelling toward the pavement. This has been done to provide for either a southern or western prospect from the galleries, or "piazzas," as they call them, with which each house is prettily and invitingly adorned. Because of this method of building, the entrances, which, without knowing better, we would take to be the front doors, in reality admit the members of each household either to the end of the lower porch or into the garden, the true main doorway being on the side of the house. Full enjoyment of the gardens is thus combined with privacy; and though one may get only glimpses of these little preserves from the streets, strong hints of their prettinesses are often carried up to the lofty balconies in the forms of vines and potted plants, like extensions of the gardens, the which whoever runs may enjoy. How very pretty and how very peculiar Charleston has thus become only a visit can disclose. Wherever one sees a fine garden, the palmetto, which gave the State its popular nickname, is chief among its treasures; but the trees have all been transplanted, for they do not naturally grow there, but on the islands and low shores of the coast. In the public grounds about the Capitol at Columbia, in the interior of the State, there is a majestic palmetto, but it is made of iron, the triumph of an ingenious metal-worker.

I quite boldly referred to the French appearance of the city during my visit, and though there were those who upheld me in my opinion, one very prominent gentleman, himself of Huguenot descent, insisted that I was mistaken. He thought it more than likely—almost positive—that the courtly manners and formal politeness that distinguished the leaders of Charleston's best society in the city's palmiest days, and that have by no means yet departed, were a direct inheritance from the French. But for the rest he insisted that, such was the strength of the English domination, Charleston was always and is to-day pure English at all important points. In 1793 nearly five hundred French refugees from San Domingo made Charleston their refuge, and one thoughtful citizen argued, without insistence, that possibly that mere essence which made the place seem French to me was due to the San Domingans. However, the discussion was and will be futile, and for myself I can only say that much in the style of many of the houses suggests the same adaptation from the French that we see in and around New

Orleans, and in the decorations and ornaments that continually confront a visitor the French style is pure and indubitable.

Mr. Yates Snowden has gathered in a published paper some notes of the various immigrations of the French to Charleston, and if they were not influential in the life and accessories of the people, it will at least be admitted that they were numerous and important. He shows that after the various large immigrations of the Huguenots there came to South Carolina fully twelve hundred Acadian refugees in 1755-57, and thirty-six years later the five hundred French came from San Domingo and settled in Charleston. The contrast between the results of these immigrations and those which have caused New Orleans to be still a partially French city is so great as to make the points of comparison few and weak. The San Domingans made a very small impression upon Charleston. Whether they had been weakened by an indolent life in the

THE IRON PALMETTO-TREE AT COLUMBIA.

tropics, they certainly were not a forceful people. They clung to their French customs and language, it is said, and yet they were swallowed up to such an extent that traces of them were few even fifty years ago. The Huguenots, on the other hand, coming as humble folk, disowning France and warmly adopting our country as their own, made a very great impression even upon the aristocracy and the history of the State. To return to Mr. Snowden's paper, he mentions the fact that one of the active philanthropic societies of Charleston is of French origin. "The South Carolina Society," he says, "founded in 1736 as the French Club, afterward known as the Two Bit Club, and called the Carolina Society when the Huguenots more thoroughly identified themselves with their new home, is probably, with one exception, the oldest organization in active operation in the South."

But from whatever its peculiar foreignness may be derived, Charleston is old and finished and complete—a small, inviting, pretty—a dignified, almost splendid little city.

While I was in Charleston preparations were making for the celebration of the coming of age of a notable fashionable dancing circle in New York. Twenty-one years is indeed a long time for a coterie of purely fashionable pleasure-seekers to hold together, and that age, perhaps, represents with some fairness the period during which the great fortunes made since the war have both aided and incited our own wealthy people to display their good fortune with more ostentation and in circles more conspicuous by numbers than used to be either the rule or the possibility in earlier times. And yet at that very time I read the following notice in a fresh copy of the *News and Courier*, the great and dignified daily journal of Charleston:

MEETINGS.

St. Cecilia Society.—The One Hundred and Thirty-first Anniversary Meeting will be held at the South Carolina Hall on Wednesday, Nov. 22, at 8 p.m.

Wilmot D. Porcher,
Secretary and Treasurer.

That notice concerned the members of what I suppose must be the oldest social fashionable organization in America. If it is no longer wealthy, it will nevertheless be conceded that no such circle is

AN OLD RESIDENCE, CHARLESTON.

more exclusive than it is, or than it has been for a longer time than our government has existed. Its name indicates its original purpose. That name, which is said to have been adopted by more musical societies than bear any other title, all over Christendom, was chosen in Charleston to distinguish a musical coterie formed from among the leading people. Next, the St. Cecilias, as they are called, added dancing to music, and finally their sole purpose became that of giving three grand balls every winter. Two hundred men form the membership, but they issue about four hundred invitations to ladies, the number of persons who are thus entitled to attend the dance being between five hundred and six hundred. The invitation list is the élite directory of the town, so to speak. Once the name of a lady is entered upon it, that name is never taken off, unless the lady dies or marries out of the membership.

A BIT OF CHARLESTON FROM ST. MICHAEL'S CHURCH.

The eligibles are declared to be "any person in whose family there has been a member, as well as all men in Charleston who are credited with possessing the manners and instincts of gentlemen, without regard to birth or worldly condition." A great many men of wealth in Charleston could not be admitted if they desired to, and for some who have made the attempt there have been heart-burnings, as must always be the case where a society attempts to keep its membership wholly and thoroughly congenial. On the other hand, young men who boast neither wealth nor pedigree are admitted annually when their course of life and traits of character have won them the support of the others. As a rule, whoever has the entrée of the houses of the members has little or nothing to fear if he applies for membership; then he needs only the support of four-fifths of those who attend the meeting at which his application is considered. The society is managed by a president, vice-president, secretary, and treasurer, and twelve managers, chosen annually.

Intensely proud among themselves, the members eschew display and notoriety so far as the society is concerned, and the rule that nothing concerning its annual dances shall be printed or given out for publication is believed never to have been broken. The only publications concerning the society that are ever made are the notices of its annual meetings and of the days on which the balls are given. Josiah Quincy, in his memoirs, mentions having attended a meeting of the society prior to the war of the Revolution, and speaks of the care then taken to make it private. Amid all the old things in

ST. PHILIP'S CHURCH.

Charleston (and it is a veritable museum, with its ancient churches, its pre-revolutionary post-office building, its library of colonial origin, and its old Chamber of Commerce), the fashionable society is itself largely composed of men and women rather younger than those of similar societies in other cities. The beautiful Battery —situated like that in New York—is so dependent upon nature that it is forever young and gay, and is the promenade for the St. Cecilias and the rest. It faces the beautiful harbor, with the sea and Fort Sumter (looking very small for anything with so big a history) in the distance across the broad blue bay. Facing the Battery, in turn, is a curving row of residences, almost as fine and as beautiful as any in America. The especial beauty of the show they make is due to the fact that they, also, keep up a process of rejuvenation, by the addition of new houses of the latest fashion. The result is a number of noble old-time mansions lording it over ample semi-tropical gardens, with their shady, breeze-inviting piazzas commanding the water and the promenade, side by side with dainty modern dwellings of what we would call suburban villa types, that give Charleston's old Battery a distinct air of youth and vigor. The men who enjoy these luxuries of the promenade and the fine houses of the showy parts of town are mainly those who maintain the Charleston Club, in which so many New-Yorkers have been so well entertained, and the Carolina Yacht Club, with its notable fleet and its fine sailing courses, both in the harbor and at sea.

Somewhat more popular in its scope is the Queen City Club, also a fine organization. Society, it is explained, is in the hands of the young because their elders have not the means to entertain as they would prefer to do; but however that may be, it seems to me an admirable society, in which mere money cuts as slight a figure as it is possible to conceive. But it is wonderful—and doubtless sad from the former point of view—to note how the wealthy class has changed since the days when the planter was king. On the Battery, once a row of planters' mansions, only one house is that of a planter. Now the homes there are those of retired factors, prosperous lawyers, bankers, real-estate operators, and men who have accumulated their means elsewhere and returned to the charming old city.

The custom these people maintain of eating dinner at three or four o'clock in the afternoon will strike a stranger from the North as peculiar. In some degree it obtains all through the South—at least, after one leaves North Carolina. Another thing—a trifle, but equally odd—is the habit the shopkeepers have of hanging cards in their doors to show the legend "Shut" or "Open." To a fevered

New-Yorker it is lovely to think that perhaps this indicates that when trade is slow or the shopkeeper desires to attend a wedding, he can close his shop, and that the customers who come will exclaim, "Bother! It's shut. I must come again to-morrow," as they used to do under the same circumstances in New York not so very long ago.

A very notable charity, distinguished further by being the only one of its kind in the South, is the "Home for the Mothers, Widows, and Daughters of Confederate Soldiers." It was founded by women and is managed by women, solely for women and girls. The chief spirit among the founders was Mrs. M. E. Snowden, who has seen the noble work flourish for a quarter of a century, who has mourned the loss of many who were associated with her at the outset, and yet who remains active and at the head of the foundation. The undertaking has been completely successful. The women own the home building, and have a handsome bank account besides. They have given relief to as many as 2000 persons, and an education to hundreds who could not otherwise have obtained it. The home now shelters about thirty women and something like fifty girls, who must have been under fourteen years of age when entered there. The schoolgirls spend ten months in each year in the building. They are the offspring of the families of the upper grade, as a rule, though the only requirement is that they shall be white. The women are not all of the same social standing.

The Home is in a historic building. Where now is the school-room the sessions of the United States court were held, and at one sensational session in 1860 one of the Federal judges threw off

his robe, saying, "The time for action has come." Tossing his robe on the floor, he left the room, and thus summarily ended the Federal jurisdiction in South Carolina. However, it is a dove-cote now, and breathes an atmosphere of grace, mercy, and peace, whose genius is felt amid such surroundings that the glimpse I got of the garden, with its cool piazzas, its banana-trees, and its happy tenants, seemed altogether idyllic.

In nothing is Charleston more admirable and interesting than in its church buildings. Better yet, the people know this—which is not always the case in such matters—and are as proud of them as they should be. The two old English churches of St. Michael's and St. Philip's are to the city what superb statues are to a park. They are beautiful ornaments —monuments to a wealth of pride and

CHARLESTON CLUB HOUSE.

taste which may exist there, but will not be easily excelled in any modern memorials. But the Huguenot Church, the only one in America, is equally beautiful in its history. Its pastor, the Rev. Dr. Charles S. Vedder, has written this concise statement of its claims upon those who venerate the cause of religion, and especially that of these liberty-loving exiles of old. These are his words:

"Established by French Protestants, Refugees from France on account of Religious persecution. Their Descendants, venerating that steadfastness to principle so conspicuous in their Ancestors, continue to worship To-Day with the same liturgy (translated) published at Neufchatel in 1737 and 1772, in this, the ONLY Huguenot Church in America."

In a paper which Dr. Vedder read before the Huguenot Society of America a few years ago he declared that the first Protestant settlement on this continent was made in South Carolina by Huguenots. Admiral de Coligny, seeking a place of refuge for the unhappy French Protestants, fitted out an unlucky expedition, which made an abortive effort to form a settlement in Brazil. Then he despatched another expedition, under Jean Ribaut, which formed a settlement at or near the site of Port Royal, South Carolina, in 1562, which, as the Doctor says, was forty-five years earlier than the English colonization of Virginia, fifty-two years before the Dutch settlement of New York, and fifty-eight years before the foundation of the Plymouth colony. And yet more than a hundred years were to pass before the Huguenots became important factors in the making of South Carolina. Fire destroyed this first fort of the Protestants; distress fell upon them; and while Ribaut was away attempting to bring them reenforcements, they built a ship, and after fearful hardships and losses of life a few survivors reached England. In 1680 the second Charles of England sent over fifty families to raise wine, oil, and silk, the English colony being then ten years old, and after the revocation of the edict of Nantes in 1685 there was "a constant stream of Huguenot immigration to South Carolina." Four settlements were founded, and one historian, who saw the French there in 1700, says that, being temperate and industrious, they "have outstripped our English who brought with them large fortunes." But the colonial government was English, and the Huguenots were made to suffer great discomfort on account of their religion, even the right to vote being denied to them. At last the three rural congregations merged their churches into the Established (Episcopal) Church, translating the English liturgy into the French tongue for their own use. This was not done in Charleston, but after 1728 the services were held in English. The church itself was established there in 1681–2, and in the interval between that time and this the Marions, the Laurenses, the Manigaults, and many, many others have distinguished the Huguenot race, and their own State as well.

The two Episcopal churches of St. Philip's and St. Michael's are, as I have intimated, the most beautiful church edifices in the Carolinas. They ennoble almost every view of Charleston that one gets. St. Philip's has the third building in which the congregation has worshipped, but it copies the second one, destroyed in 1835, of which Edmund Burke said that it was "executed in a very handsome taste, exceeding everything of that kind which we have in America." The dramatic poem, still recited wherever English is spoken, which tells of the daring of a slave-boy who climbed a steeple to put out the fire that threatened its destruc-

THE CUSTOM-HOUSE, CHARLESTON.

tion, wherefore his master set him free, tells the true story of an incident in the history of St. Philip's. The poem credits the incident to St. Michael's, but that is a mistake. Both these churches are of the general style of our old St. Paul's in New York, but both are very much handsomer. St. Michael's is said to be very like St. Martin's-in-the-Fields in London, so familiar to most Americans who have visited that city. The steeple is made up of a series of graduated chambers, so well proportioned that each new study of them is a fresh delight. It is no wonder that the Charlestonians like to mention that it has always been a tradition that Sir Christopher Wren was the designer of the building, though there is better reason to believe that it was Gibbs, the architect of the London church which it so greatly resembles. In the steeple hang the bells which are Charleston's most beloved possession. Not only were they imported from England in 1764, but when the British retired from the city at the close of the Revolution they were seized as a military perquisite and sent to London. There a Mr. Ryhiner, who had been a merchant in Charleston, bought them and sent them back to Charleston. In 1861 they were sent to Columbia for safety, and when that city was burned by the Federal troops they were ruined by the flames. In 1866 they were sent back to England to be recast by the descendants of the original founders, and in another twelve months they were back again, practically the same eight bells, but held by the government for the payment of $2200 duty. That was paid, and the money has since been refunded by especial act of Congress.

Two old institutions carry a strong suggestion of Yankee influence, or, at least, of Yankee kinship. One is the Charleston New England Society, a century old, which observes Forefathers' day with regularity; another is an influential old Congregational church, now worshipping in a fourth and very fine modern edifice; and—I had almost forgotten it—there is actually a Unitarian church, which one day split off from the Congregational

ST. MICHAEL'S CHURCH, CHARLESTON.

church quite as it might have done in Boston.

Nothing in Charleston seemed more peculiar to me than the colony of buzzards which the citizens have developed by taming and protection, and which spends a part of each day around the market in the very heart of the city. There one may almost stumble over these huge black birds, which are elsewhere scarcely seen, except at great heights, circling and sailing like creatures of another world. I one day counted thirty-eight buzzards on the cobble-stones of the street upon only one side of the market. They are quite as large as eagles, and as black and lustrous as crows, but have white legs, and bare wrinkled brown necks that make them look like caricatures of old-fashioned parsons in high "chokers." They are extremely ungainly, stiff-legged, and awkward when they walk, and when they begin that flight which they are able to master so that they appear even more at ease in the air than are fishes in the sea, they start out with a supremely ridiculous upward movement, during which their long legs hang down straight, and their heads and tails flap almost together on either side of their feet. They then look as if they were being lifted by a string around each one's middle, and were struggling to get free. I do not think they are

OLD IRON GATE, CHARLESTON.

the common buzzards, without which no view in the Southern country is complete, but I could not find in book or acquaintance any enlightenment on the subject further than the jocular statement that they are called "the Charleston canaries."

They are splendid scavengers. They roost on the low gutters around the market, and wait until the butchers begin business. Then, as customers come and the men of the cleaver and knife begin to cut off and discard the fag ends and worthless bits of the meat and toss them into the street, the great birds drop down, one by one, and begin eating the waste. I said I almost stumbled over them; I certainly could have walked upon and over them for all the heed they gave me.

"Well," said I to a negro man who was priding himself on having found the sunniest loafing-place in the neighborhood, "these are mighty independent buzzards."

"Yaas," said he, "dey is in'pendent, an' dey is proud. Dey's gittin' so tame,

now, dey hangs round de city all de while. When de butchers done leave, de buzzards done leave. Then de buzzards light out to de pen where de meat am slaughtered. Oh, dey knows what's goin' on; doan't need no one to tell 'em.

"Dese yer buzzards use ter sleep 'crost de ribber in de woods. Over dat away dey isn't king, like dey is here. Over dere de raid-haid raven is king, an' dese yer big birds ain't nuffin like so in'pendent an' proud like you see 'em here, 'cause dey ain't king. De raid-haid raven is a bigger bird, an' he bosses de whole roos'. If carrion lay .daid a day or two days, dese yer buzzards dassent tech it; no 'deed dey dassent. Dey doan't meddle wid nuffin tell de raid-haid raven comes. Pretty soon, when he just gits ready, he comes 'long, more proud an' in'pendent dan de king lion hisself, an' he picks out de eye ob de carrion. After dat dese yer birds is 'lowed to pitch in an' eat all dey want to. Dese yer buzzards doan't know dat carrion is sure enough daid till de raid-haid raven comes an' teks de eye."

Queer people are the darkies, and a queer thing about them is that they believe there is always a king over every bird and beast and creeping thing around them.

It is a statutory offence to molest these "Charleston canaries," and as the law is enforced, they revel there as if they owned the market.

Long ago Charleston grew tired of "fighting the war over again," and left it to the Northern politicians to do. Business and activity is what they talk of now, not as of things they possess in sufficiency, but as of essentials which they cry for. The city has been left in an eddy. Its local railways are but links of a great line which makes Charleston an incident and at times a side issue. The hope and prayer of the people is that their city may become the terminus of some great system—the Louisville and Nashville, perhaps. The relation of the city to the North, the West, and the Southwest, and to Europe, could easily become very important, for her position would seem to guarantee it as an eventual certainty. The deepening of the entrance to the harbor is a necessary preliminary, and this is being accomplished by the Federal government. The harbor itself is sufficiently deep, but there were only sixteen feet over the bar. This is being increased to a depth sufficient to admit modern ocean vessels.

BUZZARDS NEAR THE MARKET.

In the old days the cotton of South Carolina and northern Georgia was all handled and shipped at Charleston. A very great number of persons shared the profits. The factors who bought and shipped the cotton made their profits; the men who mended the bales, those who pressed them, the stevedores — all lived upon the business. Now the cotton is shipped directly from every point where a thousand bales are collected, and it is even sent to Europe from mere railroad stations which may not have importance from any other cause. If it had not been for the phosphate industry, Charleston could not have supported 25,000 souls.

The phosphates are found to the northward of Charleston, mainly on the Ashley and Stono rivers, and in less extent and of inferior quality between the Ash-

INTERIOR OF ST. MICHAEL'S.

ley and Cooper rivers. The best phosphates, and those that are "most workable," are along the west bank of the Ashley. Then, again, in Colleton County, between the Edisto and Ashepoo rivers, there are deposits, but they are more expensive to handle because they are not as handy to navigable water as those which lie near the Ashley River. These are all land phosphates, and the title to them lies in the land. The river phosphates are in the Stono and the Edisto rivers, though the greatest and best deposits are in the waters around Beaufort and Port Royal, the best being in the Coosaw River, on the bottom beneath the water. The phos-

lotte, Columbia, and many interior towns in the neighboring States. The greater part of the water phosphates has been shipped direct to Europe, though some has been used at home when the price has been lower than that of the land rock. The State owns the water phosphate, and charges the companies that work it one dollar a ton royalty. Last year this tax netted $234,000 to the State. As I write, this enormous business is stagnant, owing to the demands made upon it by the State. Florida phosphates of equal grade are being marketed quite as cheaply, and the South Carolina trade is menaced. The remedy must be a reduction of the State

A NEGRO FUNERAL.

phates have to be washed and ground, and then treated with sulphuric acid, which frees the phosphoric acid from the lime, and gives free phosphoric acid of the kind generally used in the manufacture of fertilizers. Charleston has fifteen factories, situated along both the rivers that flow past the city, and making 200,000 tons a year. There are two factories near Beaufort, and there are others elsewhere in the State. That phosphate which is treated in these factories is used for what may be called home consumption in both Carolinas, Alabama, Georgia, and, to less extent, in Mississippi. A great deal of land phosphate, washed, but not ground, is shipped to Baltimore, Atlanta, Char-

tax. That this relief will have been granted before this paper is published I have very little doubt.

Taking South Carolina as a whole, we find it singularly attractive to immigration, and yet singularly avoided by it. It is one of the richest of our States in the possibilities of its soil, which are very varied indeed. Yet it has only about one-third of its acreage under cultivation by a population more largely black than white, and so little infused with the foreign elements which have literally populated and enriched great parts of our domain that its Governor truly says of it: "The people of South Carolina are homogeneous. Most of the whites have com-

PLANTING RICE ON A CAROLINA PLANTATION.

mon origin." But the majority of the people are negroes, who, being under little stimulus toward social improvement, or any ambition except that of being able to live from day to day, deprive the State of that reservoir of latent strength and potential wealth which an industrious and ambitious multitude of the not-at-all-to-be-despised foreign immigrants would bring to it.

We find stern competition in Florida threatening the revenue from the phosphates, and still more injurious competition in Louisiana injuring the returns from the Carolina rice, and yet the prospect for the State is not gloomy. The diversification of its farm industries and the remarkable growth of the cotton-milling business make it otherwise. Within the last six months (this is written at the opening of 1894) no less than three millions of dollars have been expended in the building of new mills in the Carolinas, and the people of those States and of Georgia are not unreasonable in insisting, as they do, that in time the mills generally must come to the cotton, and that the bulk of the manufacture of cotton must be done in the South. Governor Tillman did well in calling attention (in his paper prepared for the Convention of Southern Governors in Richmond last

April) to the abundance and cheapness of the water-power in his State. He says: "Mr. Swaim, the special agent of the census of 1880, made a careful estimate of the water-power of our streams as reaching a million horse-power. If developed, these would give employment to six millions of operatives in cotton-mills," and allow for a corresponding increase of population. He says that "owing to want of capital in the State, these powers can be bought cheaply now, and they would prove capital investments. The winters are so mild that there is comparatively no trouble from freezing. The benignity of the climate makes living cheaper, and this adds to the advantages offered to manufacturers by our water-powers."

The use of fertilizers has pushed the cultivation of cotton to the very feet of the mountains in the western part of the State, and though it has been overdone, as it has everywhere else in the South, there has been no need to caution the planters, for with the consequent decline of the price of their staple they have learned wisdom—bitterly as it so often comes—and are beginning to diversify their crops, at least sufficiently to provide themselves with meat and bread, as well as, in some parts of the State, to raise fruits and vegetables for market. In the mean time the starting of cotton-mills has gone on, until from a possession of twelve mills in 1870 the State had forty-four in 1892, representing a capital of $12,000,000, and employing thousands of operatives—nearly all white.

Turning to North Carolina, we find this particular industry much more extensive. The latest statistics I have been able to procure—the truly excellent hand-book prepared for the Columbian Exposition by the North Carolina Board of Agriculture—include the facts and figures concerning one hundred and forty cotton-mills, and a statement that six other mills were then under construction. To these should be added thirteen woollen mills, one of which manufactures both cotton and wool. The strangest thing about this woollen industry is that though the State is admirably calculated to rank high as a wool-producing one, and though the industry would be highly profitable, the fact remains that many of the principal mills buy their wool elsewhere, because the ravages of the dogs make sheep-raising profitless, and because the people of the State will not enforce or permit the enforcement of the laws for the protection of the sheep.

But the manufacture of tobacco has brought more prosperity to this truly enterprising State than any other industry.

It has not only awakened, enriched, and increased many towns, but it has built up several new ones, like Durham and Winston and others. The business is enormous. The State contains no less than one hundred and ten factories where plug tobacco is made, nine smoking-tobacco factories, and three cigarette-factories. Several of these are world-famous and truly enormous. The plug-tobacco-making town of Winston sold eleven millions of pounds of manufactured tobacco and paid more than $660,000 revenue tax in 1891. Durham paid $616,000.

It has been said that the activity in cotton-manufacturing has stimulated the many other manufacturing activities that we find keeping the Old North State astir. To my mind the fact is that the character of her people, her most admirable climate, and the opportunities afforded by her extraordinarily varied resources are at the bottom of it all, the cotton manufacture as well as the rest; at all events we certainly find the activity reaching out in many new industries, notably the manufacture of buggies and wagons; of furniture; of paper, in several mills; of cotton hosiery and other knitted goods, in ten places; of canning, in twenty-eight establishments, exclusive of several oyster-canneries; of cotton-seed-oil manufacture, by nine mills; of fertilizers, extensively, in very many places. And, finally, among something like two dozen establishments for the making and working of iron, there has been newly founded a million-dollar steel and iron plant at Greensboro.

The Capitol of North Carolina, at Raleigh, is a materialized echo of the past, in and about which there is no note of the transformation of the State and its

COURT-HOUSE AND CITY HALL, RALEIGH.

A TOBACCO MARKET IN NORTH CAROLINA.

people. Built sixty years ago by a slave-holding people, it has remained unchanged through the calamities of war and the brilliant evolution of the new spirit of enlightened industry. There it stands, classic, dignified, aged, but well preserved, as if it typified all that was good and enduring in the courtly, generous, but feudal masters whose rule has passed away forever in the Old North State. The beautifully proportioned old palace stands embowered among trees at least as old and majestic as itself in a rather modern-looking little park. The building is of granite quarried near by. The last glimpse and the first, like all the views one gets of its interior, suggest just such a strange blending of age and careful keeping as one notes in the ancient trinkets which now and then some wrinkled old spinster brings out to exhibit as the choicest, tenderest relics of a distant generation of her people.

The walls and floor are clean and fresh, for instance, but on the doorway to the Assembly Chamber is the strange legend, "Hall of Commons." An aged but diligent servitor who guides you wastes no time over the great portrait of Washington on one wall, but dwells feelingly upon the fact that in the cruel, tyrannical days of "carpet-bag rule" the negroes, who were then the legislators, broke two of the precious old hard-wood chairs which were the especial treasures in that chamber. He takes you across the hall—carrying with his spare, bent form a strong suggestion of a past as extensive as that of the capital itself—and there you are stirred by the sight of the prim but noble mahogany provided for the statesmen of the luxurious past to rest and to write upon. The old man stirs you in quite another way by the remark that a Northern firm has offered to exchange modern furniture for all that is in the old room. A bust of John C. Calhoun is the chief ornament in the Senate Chamber, though the neatness and reverential order that rule there strike you as better than any ornament could be.

You carry with you to the executive offices downstairs a mind wholly given up to reflections upon the past, and, lo! the officials in those ancient rooms all but stun you with the zeal and zest with which they press you to consider the present needs of the State, its bustling progress, and its wealth of unworked resources. You'd hardly find a quicker spirit in Ohio or Rhode Island. Moreover, there is little buncombe about it. If they tell you, as they will, that no State in all our Union has such varied capabil-

PREPARING TUBEROSE BULBS FOR THE NORTHERN MARKET.

largely grown in North Carolina. The way in which the Yankee-like old State came to be robbed of the credit for its peanuts was this: For years the farmers of eastern North Carolina have been raising the nuts and shipping them in crude condition to Norfolk. There they have been cleaned and bagged and sold as Virginia produce. This is yet the case, although the eastern North Carolina nuts are unexcelled by any others that are grown in the world. But the wedge of justice has been inserted in this case. The work of separating and cleaning the nuts has been begun in a small way by the North Carolina farmers, and the world at large will soon learn that though Virginia and Tennessee grow good peanuts, they never produce finer ones than are grown in North Carolina. As for the "goobers" that gave Georgia its nickname of "the Goober State," they are small and poor by comparison.

ities, or that its climate embraces nearly the full extremes that are represented in our minds by Maine and Florida, they make their words good by showing you photographs of the snow-silvered spruce forests of the western mountains, and palm-littered, all but tropical views taken along the sunny coast.

They boast a little, as good Americans always do, and if some of the things they say show a trifle of jealousy, or if some of the topics they choose seem somewhat unsentimental, you must remind yourself that the jealousy springs from a pride that has been wounded, and that the best elements of wealth are not apt to be of a poetic nature. Thus they tell you that the excellent peanuts which North Carolina raises in abundance have failed to bring her the credit she deserves, and that the golden, beautiful tobacco which for generations has been known as "bright Virginia leaf," so much admired for use in pipes and cigarettes, was and is

It is different with the splendid tobacco of the State. At last North Carolina is establishing a reputation for its own excellent "weed that cheers." Buyers now come to the North Carolina market-towns, and the best bright leaf is coming to be classed under its true name. The town of Durham, so famous among men who smoke, is the capital of the golden-tobacco belt, which embraces ten or twelve counties in the middle of the State. The "mahogany," or plug-tobacco leaf, is grown in the western part, and Winston, which maintains forty plug factories, is its industrial capital.

From the Northern evergreen to the perennial Southern palm is the measure of the State's fertility, and her people do not hesitate to say that all that should bridge the two extremes is also theirs. That they can and do grow whatever is grown elsewhere in the United States is true, with a few marked exceptions that distinguish the extreme South. It is the boast of the people that at Chicago's great exposition no State displayed such a great variety of the products of the soil.

Under such circumstances the most practical student of the commonwealth cannot be altogether prosaic in listing its products. If I have the good fortune to possess the eye of that friend whom the novelist always addresses as "fair reader," let me also turn directly to her and ask what she thinks of whole farms given up to tuberoses. Such, it seems, are among the triumphs of North Carolinian husbandry. Some farms devote as many as twenty-five acres, "in a patch," to the cultivation of tuberoses. During the first year the tuberose bulb multiplies, and does not flower. It is during its second year that it spreads its delicate, waxen,

THE CAPITOL AT RALEIGH.

and aromatic blossoms, and a great industry in this State is the development of the bulbs in the earth for the first year, and then the shipment of them to the North in barrels, to be sold by the florists, and set out to blossom. North Carolina is chosen for this graceful branch of farming because of the properties of the soil, and because the bulbs can be kept out in it all winter. It is true that in fancy I see the pink and white nose of my fair reader lift a little at the disclosure that the suggested fields of aromatic flowers prove only to be furrows of raw earth hiding bulbs, but only think how many of the flowers are not sent away, but mingle their beauty and sweetness with the vast bouquet that blossoms all over such a region. And only think, when next you see a tuberose in bloom, that it was in the Old North State that it started on its fragrant, and, alas! too often pathetic, mission.

It will be equally interesting to all my readers—for I fear I have not been alto-

Thus does North Carolina so cheapen the flowers with which we deck ourselves and our homes, and which we have so long mistaken for Northerners, like ourselves. She may be said almost to hand them to us—in the profusion in which we have them, at least—as a charming sister brightens the chamber of a gallant knight.

With the flowers go the fruits, as they naturally should. The growing of berries and of garden-truck is an industry that has developed truly magnificent proportions in North Carolina. It is mainly confined to the sea-coast section, but it

RAILWAY STATION AT RALEIGH.

gether successful with my special address to the fair ones alone—to know that in Raleigh thousands and tens of thousands of rose-cuttings are planted in the gardens and fields for the Northern market. The Northern florists send the cuttings down to be planted and kept a year in order that they may grow roots, and that each may become a plant, a baby rose-bush. Then they are shipped back in the spring to be sold as young plants. It is too expensive to do this under glass, as it would have to be done in the North, but it costs a mere trifle, by comparison, to assist nature at the task down there in Raleigh; for in that clement city the people actually keep tulips, hyacinths, and such plants out in their door-yards all winter.

is rapidly covering the whole of the front of the State. This particular phase of the industrial revolution in the South, which we shall have to mention again and again as different sections are treated, may not be as revolutionary as the appearance of the cotton-manufacturers in such great force in three of the States, but it is, nevertheless, very remarkable. Along the Atlantic edge of Virginia, the Carolinas, Georgia, and Florida the planters in the ante-bellum time grew little else than cotton, and depended wholly on the money it brought for the purchase of everything else, even to the goods that were made of the cotton. If vegetables and small fruits were seen to grow on this land in those days the fact made no

AGRICULTURAL SCHOOL AND DORMITORIES, RALEIGH.

easy access to the Northern market was afforded all the coast-line between Florida and Norfolk, the first market-town of the new trade in garden-truck. As each State grasped the new opportunity the arrival of spring and summer produce was hastened in the North, and Georgia came to be first with her treasures, then South Carolina, next North Carolina, and then Virginia, last where she had been first, but still in demand to lengthen the link between summer and summer, and to shorten the period of winter deprivation in the North. As early as 1884 Charleston alone was shipping half a million quarts of strawberries, a tenth as many barrels of potatoes, and 62,333 packages of vegetables in a season.

impression, and the insignificant produce got only contempt. But cotton fell in value; it proved itself a monarch in which too many persons had trusted blindly. There ensued an era of distress and gloom. It was in southeastern Virginia, close to the borders of North Carolina, that the warm climate, the humid atmosphere, and the rich soil were found to offer the essentials for maturing small fruits and vegetables in advance of those for which the Northern people waited yearly with impatience. Here truck-farming grew from an experiment to a successful industry. Then came the travel to Florida as a winter resort, and then the almost wild scramble for land in that State for or-ange orchards—a scramble in which, as I have shown, the land that grew no oranges and that which grew poor oranges went with the rest. The nat-ural shortening of the journey be-tween Florida and the North was rap-idly brought about by railroad combi-nations and enter-prise, and by the perfection and in-crease of steamship facilities. Thus

To-day the Commissioner of Agriculture announces truck-farming to be "among the foremost occupations in North Carolina as a money resource." The best district is around New-Berne, where there are 8000 acres planted in

GOVERNOR'S MANSION, RALEIGH.

STATE PRISON, RALEIGH.

strawberries, asparagus, green pease, cabbages, beans, kale, beets, turnips, Irish potatoes, tomatoes, cucumbers, egg-plants, radishes, etc. During the shipping season

STOCKADE AT THE STATE PRISON, RALEIGH.

the railroad has run from one to three trains a day from this district, and two steamers have made five trips a week laden with the produce. It is said, as a result of careful calculation, that this New-Berne section realized $750,000 from its produce in the season of 1891, and the farmers netted half a million of dollars. Wilmington, Elizabeth City, Goldsboro, are other large shipping-points for other districts, but there are many others that are marked by mere railway side-tracks, where many cars are loaded daily in the season. There is a good deal of very enlightened farming down there, and, in consequence, there are farmers whose profits at the end of a single year are what the mass of men would call fortunes. On one—the farm most wisely managed, perhaps—we find 170 head of cattle, 66 horses, 139 hogs, a dairy, a saw-mill for the needs of the box-factory, and a fertilizer-making plant. On this farm 600 acres were put into truck last year, and 300 were sown with oats and grass. When one considers how short a time it is since the farmers there were exclusively planters of cotton, and what a precarious living their methods brought, this seems indeed a long stride ahead.

And this is not true merely of the truck region of the coast. "The low price of cotton and the high price of everything else," as one State official put it, "have led the farmers, in great numbers, to diversify their industry and to raise what they consume at home." More meat was killed in North Carolina last year than ever before. Hogs, cattle, horses, milk, butter, fruit, vegetables, and corn are products that are increasing very rapidly. Sheep also are multiplying, though sheep-raising calls for so much outlay in guarding the stock against dogs that only men with capital make a business of it. Raleigh is now supplied with all the milk and butter it uses, though not sufficient dairying is yet done to make the products articles of export. The result of all this, as might have been expected, has been a remarkable removal of mortgages all over the State within the past few years. And this prosperity reflects upon the State itself, so that her debt is trifling, and at least one issue of bonds by the commonwealth rates almost as high as the bonds of the Federal government.

The revolution is also reflected in the cities. Wilmington is a bustling, wide-awake town, with a solid and very active business quarter, and all the superficial signs of a prosperous and ambitious population. Charlotte, the richest city in the State, has invested so heavily in cotton-mills and other ventures in various other towns and sections that it is said she would have a population of 60,000 were her industries all at home. It is doubtful whether the place would then be as inviting as it is now, for though it is busy, it is also beautiful. Raleigh, the capital, which is so well shaded that a bird's-eye view of it discloses little else than trees, is at once neat and substantial, and rather more Northern than Southern looking, except for the (typically Southern) great width of its main streets. And yet these are paved and well cared for, besides being busy. The city is credited with 17,000 inhabitants, and maintains three cotton-mills, several machine-shops, two fertilizer-factories, an oil-mill, a car-works, and several candy-factories, one of which is celebrated far beyond Raleigh. It is also a trading centre, and has large commercial

establishments. All these businesses are supplied with local capital, and it is important to add that this is generally the case in both the Carolinas.

Raleigh has several fine educational foundations, but one that interested me very much indeed was the College of Agricultural and Mechanic Arts. The other Southern States possess more or less similar institutions, maintained with Federal aid, and if they are in any great degree as well and even proudly managed as this of North Carolina, it is a grand thing, particularly where men have been

PHOSPHATE MINES NEAR WILMINGTON.

too prone to think it undignified to work for themselves. Here we find an expensively housed and well-equipped institution, which, although only four years old, has already graduated one class, two-thirds of whose members obtained situations at once. Both teachers and pupils were alike enthusiastic when I went through the buildings. I found there a fine smithy, a forge-room, a machine-shop (in which stood a steam-engine made by the graduates); a wood-turning department and joiner-work class-room; a very fine chemical laboratory presided over by an ambitious Cornell man; a model barn, a dairy building, a large experimental farm, and an agricultural experiment and State weather station. The young men are here fitted to become intelligent, educated, and practical farmers, horticulturists, cattle and stock raisers, dairymen, as well as machinists, carpenters, architects, draughtsmen, manufacturers, and contractors. I do not mean to claim too much in saying this; what I do mean is that they learn the rudiments of these occupations, as well as to use their brains

NEGRO CEMETERY AT WILMINGTON.

and their hands. A full mathematical course is part of the curriculum, and a much more important source of strength to each pupil is the association with the ambitious young fellows of the State, and the daily intercourse with the able and accomplished members of the faculty. Here were some boys from very humble homes, and yet so intent upon becoming masters, instead of dependents, as to be found waiting on the others at the dining-table in order to earn their living while they studied. A certain number of pupils are admitted free, subject to an examination in rudimentary studies. They pay $8 a month for board and extras. The others pay $20 a year for tuition in addition to the same charge for board and extras.

But the good work of the institution does not stop there. The officers reply to all requests for information by the farmers of the State, and hold farmers' meetings wherever requested for the discussion of subjects connected with practical farming. Dr. H. B. Battle, as head of the experiment station, also issues frequent and very valuable bulletins, sent free to thousands of farmers, telling them how to guard against insect pests, warning them against inferior or fraudulent fertilizers, discussing methods of farming, explaining how waste can be prevented, how they can determine the best things to grow, and, in a sentence, scattering the most practical and most needed advice, in thick pamphlets as well as mere fly-sheets, among the agriculturists of the State. Farther yet, the station is pushing an almost unique plan of spreading information by sending out stereotyped-plate matter free to the newspapers of the State. Alexander Q. Halladay, Esq., is the president of the college and its allied farm and stations.

Leaving agriculture out of further consideration, we will observe that, for variety, the resources of the State do not depend upon that industry, though it is, of course, mainly and primarily a farming State. But its turpentine stills are a source of revenue, its forests are of great extent and value, its fisheries employ about 6000 persons, gold-mining is carried on in several counties, and the quarrying of marble, granite, sandstone, and of Belgian blocks for the paving of city streets is done in many parts of the State. The story of the traveller who, on being shown a beautiful piece of mahogany furniture, replied, "Yes, where I live they make fence rails of mahogany," could be paralleled by many citizens of western North Carolina if any were called upon to admire a granite building, for they might truly say that in their parts of the State there are towns where all the fence posts are made of granite. Coal-mining is a new industry in North Carolina, but it is carried on with all the rest. There are two coal belts there. A company of Northern capitalists is working a rich field of good bituminous coal at Egypt, and another Northern company owns some mines of what is called semi-anthracite a little southwest of that place. At Kings Mountain a company has been formed to develop a tin-bearing

A CAROLINA MANSION.

region, which it is thought they can mine profitably.

The exporting of grapes and even the manufacture of wine have been a source of revenue to North Carolina during a quarter of a century. A new and quickened interest in these businesses is shown in the gradual multiplication of vine-

A WILMINGTON RESIDENCE.

FERRY AND NAVAL STORES, WILMINGTON.

yards, and in the profits and growth of certain of the older ones, and, since wild grapes are said to have grown naturally all over the State, these may yet become important industries. Mineral springs of more or less celebrity are numerous; and of popular resorts for tourists and invalids, led by the thriving and beautiful town of Asheville, there are many, as well as sites for ten times as many more, in the healthful and picturesque mountain districts. The population of the State is no greater than that of New York city, but, unlike South Carolina, the whites are nearly twice as numerous as the negroes, the difference (according to the last census) being that there were 1,055,382 whites and 562,565 colored persons. One would argue from this fact that North Carolina would attract immigrants in greater number than almost any of the more southerly States, and yet in 1890 there were only 3742 foreign-born persons in the State. John Robinson, Esq., the Commissioner of Agriculture, says, upon this subject: "The immigration into North Carolina is largely from the New England, Middle, and some of the Northwest-ern States, and gives many and much-desired and much-valued accessions to sources of material development."

It seems, then, to whatever small extent this increase comes, the Old North State is enjoying what the most influential men in all the Southern States desire and demand. The South wants men with capital, and not men with mere hands and energy and willingness to work. It wants men who will buy and cultivate plantations, who will establish mills, and who will organize corporations for the development of its resources.

The Charleston *News and Courier* of November 22, 1893, says, "Those who would not make desirable citizens *should not be encouraged* to seek homes in the South." After arguing that those farmers in New England and parts of the West whose farms are poor would do well to leave them and go South, it generously asserts that there is room for such new-comers "as the Germans, Scandinavians, Swiss, Scotch, and Yankees"—an intentional compliment, for he adds, "*none but the best are good enough for South Carolina.*"

INDUSTRIAL EDUCATION IN THE SOUTH

SOME aspects of cotton-mill life in the Southern States are depressing enough, but the picture as a whole is by no means so dismal as it is often painted. Its unfavorable features had their origin partly in conditions long antecedent to the development of cotton manufacture in these States, and in some part they are due to the extraordinary rapidity of that development. Naturally the promoters of the industry were at first mainly concerned with its financial success; but for some years not a few of them have with equal seriousness been grappling with the moral issues involved.

Thirty years ago the capital invested in all the mills from Virginia to Texas would not have aggregated three million dollars; to-day it approaches 150 million. The increase has been greatest in the last half of the period, and the immense labor supply has been drawn, not from foreign immigrants nor the large number of negroes at hand, thousands of them without occupation, but from a particular element of the native white population, the most backward, the most unfortunate, of the white citizenship of the South. In part they have been up-country people, venturing forth uncertainly from the poverty, ignorance, and isolation of their mountain cabins; in part the tenant farmers of the cotton belt or the wire-grass, men who each year made the land they rented poorer and themselves no richer, willing to exchange their hap-

hazard labor of the field and a measure of independence for the steady work and steady wages of the factory. The transference of so large a body of people, largely illiterate, from the most primitive of rural surroundings to the peculiar environment of the cotton-mill could not but bring to them perils, physical and moral, and to their employers difficulties, and doubtless temptations, not always justly appreciated by observers from the outside. In any suddenly effected social or economic change it is inevitably the weakest who must suffer from its disadvantages, and in this particular case the weight of injury has fallen upon childhood. It is difficult, when once the eye is arrested by this fact, to extend the view beyond it, and to perceive that in reality mill life is a step in the slow ascent of a backward class towards civilization and culture.

The newer mill plants, as a rule, have the best attainable equipment, reducing the operative's labor to a minimum, abundant light and air, good sanitary conditions, and fairly comfortable houses for their employees. Many of them maintain schools of considerable efficiency at the expense of the corporation, some amusements are provided, and the general welfare of the operatives is carefully looked after. Usually there is an admirable spirit of good-will and confidence existing between management and people. So much commendation cannot always be

THE LITTLE ARMY KNOWN AS "DINNER-TOTERS"

given. At some of the older plants the housing is poor, the sanitation bad, the moral conditions deplorable. Everywhere wages are reasonably good, at least when compared with those paid in some other employments, and the work affords training not only in a special industry, but in the habit of occupation,—both of value to laborers unskilled in the one and largely undisciplined to the other. The hours of labor in some States are limited to sixty-six a week; in some they have reached as high as seventy-two. Recent laws have fixed the age at which children may be employed at twelve years, except in Georgia and Mississippi, where the matter is still left to the discretion of the parents and the humanity of the mill-owner. So far as educational advantages are concerned, all these States have free county schools, running, as a rule, four or five months in the year; the public schools of the larger towns and cities have of course a term of nine months, but in mill communities located either in town or country it is generally the case that most of the chil-

dren who should be in school are at work in the mills, taking care of younger children at home, or running the streets in idleness. In some localities women's clubs, church societies, or private charity forestalls in a measure the evils of later years by giving to the little ones the saving influences of the kindergarten; and the city of Augusta has set a shining example by making the kindergarten in her mill district a part of the public-school system, paying the expenses of one of her ablest teachers also while studying manual training and social-settlement work in the North with reference to the peculiar needs of this same district.

When it comes to the consideration of the mill operative's part in this matter of progress, the study becomes more complex. Factory people are by no means homogeneous, but differ as widely as do those in other walks of life. In general, however, they fall into three grades. Lowest of these is that shiftless, immoral class who seem to be a survival from the nomadic age of the race. They rove from

State to State, from mill to mill, from one street of the mill village to another, serving no useful purpose beyond the day's labor under the eye of the factory boss,—often a positive moral evil, and employed at all only because of the scarcity of better labor. Much removed from these is that body of thrifty, self-respecting, and intelligent, if sometimes uneducated, workers who in the course of time buy homes outside the mill grounds, make possible the work of the local churches, and educating their children, see them enter employments higher than their own in the social estimate. Between these two extremes lies the great middle class, which constitutes both the opportunity and the responsibility of the enlightened mill-owner and the unselfish settlement worker. Few if any of this class will ever rise superior to their personal disabilities without the direct aid of men and women higher than themselves in the social scale. It is not merely that many of them are illiterate; to this must be added an ignorance of the simplest domestic arts, of the ordinary laws of health, and of the world at large that is almost beyond belief. Often a woman of this class cannot cut a garment or sweep a floor; her husband has never conceived of any other social organism than that of which his factory boss is the head; and they and their children are diseased in body and stunted in mind even less from their labor in the mill than because of wretchedly cooked food, uncleanliness, and the unlimited use of snuff and tobacco almost from infancy. As an offset to all this one often finds among them a shrewd humor, willingness to learn, loyalty to employers, and unimpeachable honesty. Often, too, there are mechanical aptitudes, which one may almost regard as an inheritance from the time when the manufactured products of Virginia, the Carolinas, and Georgia exceeded in value and variety those of all New England, before the spread of slavery had stifled manufacturing enterprise and bound up the fortunes of the South with those of a single institution.

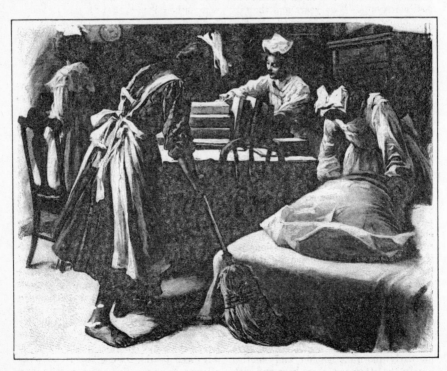

NEATNESS AND CLEANLINESS ARE TAUGHT

The mechanical aptitudes just noted, together with the general indifference to education among these people, suggest one direction which the forces intended for their help might profitably take. Since their homes are so comfortless, why not instruct them in the ordinary domestic arts which lie at the foundation of all wholesome and peaceful living? Since their children are so little attracted by the routine of book study, why not awaken their intelligence first by the training of hand and eye, and give the knowledge obtained from books some useful connection with the interests of daily life? These questions have been occasionally asked, but the practical response to them has been rare and inadequate. The child of the Southern cotton-mill—as well as the poor child outside it, whether white or black—remains untaught in that which he needs most and to which, if rightly presented, he would give readiest response. The one effort, therefore, to supply this lack, which has taken fully organized form, is worthy of particular attention both in its methods and in its present and possible results. Two years ago the city of Columbus, Georgia, opened its Primary Industrial School for the factory children, the only one of its kind in the South, and the first in the United States to be organized as a part of a public-school system independent of the uses of a training-school for teachers.

The school had its inception partly in the public sentiment for the betterment of the factory children created by the excellent work of the Free Kindergarten Association maintained by a number of ladies in the town, partly in the enterprising spirit of Mr. Carleton B. Gibson, superintendent of the public schools. The immediate aim of the institution was to reach by means of a night school mill operatives of any age who would be willing to attend, and in its day sessions the little army of children known as "dinner-toters," to whom the public schools were unavailing because for several hours in the day—from about ten till two o'clock —these children had to help prepare and carry to the mills the midday meal for the other members of the family. By establishing a school which should have an early morning session and another late in the afternoon, these boys and girls

could be provided for. Also, in a school like this the experiment of industrial education could be tested to a better advantage than in the ordinary schools. The means for housing the school and for its equipment for three years were furnished by Mr. George Foster Peabody. The principal was called to his present position from the summer school of the Chicago University, where he was aiding with the manual training. He brought with him two assistants, one a trained kindergartner, the other a public-school teacher of experience. It may be said here that of the 105 pupils registering the first three months for the day school, and ranging in age from six to sixteen years, not one could read even in the simplest primer; and the members of the night school, the oldest being sixty-five years of age, were in but little better case.

The only house available in the mill district for the new enterprise was a two-story wooden building, which long before had degenerated into a factory tenement-house, when this ceased to be a residence portion of the town. The 84 pupils who gathered there that September morning were at least not embarrassed by any unfamiliar grandeur of cleanliness and order, but had found at last an institution which met them on their domestic level of discomfort and uncomeliness.

The two hours of ordinary school-room work arranged for the forenoon were soon established, and for some months opportunity for the industrial work of the afternoon sessions was found in the necessary repairs and furnishing of the different parts of the house. The equipment for the manual-training room had come, and, with the aid of some pupils of the night school, floors were relaid or calked, roofs mended, and windows set with glass. Besides the plain shelving immediately necessary, the pupils have since constructed mouldings, the fittings of cabinets, artistic racks for the dining-room, bookcases, etc., until each room is a model of convenience as well as of simple beauty. When it was nearly time for the Christmas party, the boys measured, cut, and put down the matting for the one room in the house whose floor was to be covered, and the older girls had so far advanced in the sewing lessons as to be allowed to make the white muslin cur-

We raised these
radishes in Same
garden.
The leaves are gree
The roots are

FREDERIC COLBURN CLARKE

Half-tone plate engraved by F. A. Pettit

A CLASS IN DRAWING

tains which, inexpensive as they were, were to give such an unimagined daintiness to the spotless windows. Long before this the pupils had been allowed to unpack the trunks and boxes which arrived from time to time, and to dispose of their contents as their teacher, Mrs. Neligh, suggested. Nothing could have been more charming than the children's wonder at the books—whose number, not very striking, seemed to them beyond all computation—and their delight in the pictures, the ornaments, the delicate china, and the few choice bits of pottery. Again and again a little girl would hug some article ecstatically to her breast, and it is safe to say that the marble Psyche and the sofa pillow with the pretty young lady's head on it are still kissed and fondled just as they were on the day of their first appearance. Thus from the beginning the children were led to feel a sense of possession in the house and all it contained. Nothing has been put under lock and key, nothing forbidden them. For their little feasts the choicest things in the china-closet have been freely used, and after two years not one piece has been so much as chipped, nor the most insignificant article in all the equipment of the house, to these starved little natures so marvellous and so beautiful, been carried away. Nothing could better illustrate their honesty. If one feels compelled to add that pilfering from the dinner-baskets piled in the back yard on the return from the mills sometimes occurs, the offence seems no real discount on their good principles, and almost venial when one learns that each child has to secure his own dinner from the fragments left after the hunger of the toilers in the mill has been satisfied.

A most interesting result of the children's share in the furnishing and arrangement of the different parts of the house has been their perception of the fact — grasped very slowly — that in a properly appointed dwelling certain rooms are to be used for certain purposes, and not in any haphazard fashion that indolence or indifference might suggest. To every newcomer it is at first inexplicable that Mr. and Mrs. Neligh should have a special room in which to receive their visitors, another to sleep in, and a kitchen that is not a place to eat in as well. Similarly, the discovery of the appropriate furnishing for different rooms, the proper fittings for bed, bureau, sideboard, etc., has never lost its charm. Following this perception has come, almost with no formal instruction, the idea that a difference in apartments suggests a difference in one's personal appearance when engaged in each. When people gather in the pretty room that has in it the books and piano and the beautiful marble lady, they must themselves look as well as they can. When one helps to cook, one must have clean hands and nails as the teacher has, must cover one's head with a white cap, and protect one's dress with a large apron. Since a bed is something to be so carefully supplied with two sheets and a white spread, since its pil-

FREER J. MULHAUPT

EXERCISES IN THE SCHOOL YARD

A LESSON IN PRACTICAL HOUSEKEEPING

lows must be so spotless and so exactly placed, then one should not sleep in the soiled garments worn through the day, but in a night-dress made and kept clean for the purpose.

It need not be inferred from this that the path of the teachers has been altogether an easy one. To the difficulties which might naturally have been anticipated have been added others which the suspicion and prejudice of an inferior social level are prone to create. When the first cooking lesson was announced there was an unexpected mutiny,—"We didn't come here to do you-all's cookin'!" The violence of the refusal grew out of the idea that certain forms of labor done for another are dishonoring. It was all right to hire one's self in a cotton-mill, but for one white person to cook or to wash clothes for another was to sink to the level of an inferior race. So the first laundry lessons waited the time when the children's own white caps and aprons

should become soiled, and only the teacher's tact and good humor conducted the earliest demonstrations in cooking safely through from the mixing of ingredients to the serving of the finished product by Mrs. Neligh herself to the pupils seated around the dining-room table. Since then, lessons in these two branches have grown in popularity, and no privilege is more prized by the children than taking home with them some dish of their own composition, or serving the refreshments prepared by themselves when their parents come to the social evenings which have become such an important feature of the school.

Pottery and basket-making are also very popular. Clay for the former was obtained by the children during one of their field lessons from a neighboring hillside, was precipitated under Mr. Neligh's direction, and the articles made from it baked in the kitchen kiln. The rows of knobby little jars used by the

A POPULAR LECTURE FOR THE PARENTS

pupils for washing their brushes during the painting lessons may not be very artistic, but they have served in addition to other good ends the very excellent one of sending these boys and girls back to the habits of their ancestors in making use of materials close at hand instead of thinking everything needed must be purchased ready-made at a store. The work in basketry has resulted in some really beautiful productions, and has been directly serviceable in strengthening weak muscles and in helping to correct the stooping postures almost universal. For, of all the pupils enrolled since the opening of the school—and owing to the peculiar habits of mill people the number has been double what it would have been in any other school—not one physically normal child has been found, and the correction of physical defects has been matter for constant care. Better habits of cleanliness, free-hand gymnastics, given every fine day in the shaded front yard have done much to improve the general health and spirits of the pupils.

A valuable adjunct to the school equipment have been the two gardens, both overrun with weeds and nutgrass when first acquired, but being gradually put into good shape, and already yielding a fine supply of vegetables. These the children take away with them,—a much-needed incentive to their parents to cultivate the garden - plots around their homes. Window-gardening is also taught; and the long piazzas of the building are bordered with the boxes which the boys constructed from some rough timber given by one of the mills, filled with properly prepared soil, and planted with vines and annuals. The children are to see these grow and blossom, for the school, like the mill, takes no summer vacation. Throughout the hot months the two-hour morning session is held, partly because there are always some pupils who want to come, but largely because the management is unwilling to lose any of the hold upon the community acquired at such pains.

Does one wonder that the school dare

risk no loss of influence? One must remember its constituency is made up of men and women to whom the mill is the one all-inclusive fact of life—its authority the one law; its signals of toil and release, and not the rising or setting of the sun, that which marks the coming and passing of the days; its wages the price of existence; its narrow aisles, vibrating ever with the roar and crash of machinery, the final destiny of every child born within their homes. Is it to be wondered at that to these toilers the mild authority of the school should seem of little consequence, its natural life of simple industry and innocent relaxation a trivial or far-off thing, its lovely appeal to eye and ear and heart almost meaningless? At least by a few that appeal has been heard, its meaning in a measure grasped and recognized as gracious. Touching have been the proofs that this is so. Families moving away to other mills, when the breaking of two dams sent them elsewhere for employment, return at the first opportunity because the children are "pinin' after" the school. A feeble old man comes from the other end of the town when his long day of toil is over and brings some small gift in token of his gratitude for what the teachers have done for his grandchildren. An old woman who in the first month of the school brings about the withdrawal of twenty-two pupils because, as she convinces their parents, "they've been thar better'n two weeks an' ain't learnt to read an' write," is induced at last to attend one of the evening meetings for parents, to inspect the rooms, and to see for herself the real work of the pupils. Shrewd and honest, she sees her mistake and confesses it, and coming again and again, the hungry cry of her heart bursts into utterance: "Oh, Mis' Neligh, I ain't never been inside a rich person's house, an' never seen no finery of no kind 'tel I seen it here. If the good Lord was able to do such a thing for a po' old woman like me that ain't never knowed nothin' but hard work all my life, I'd ask Him please to let me be born agin, an' git the chance of goin' to this here school an' growin' up diff'unt. An' if such a thing could happen, Mis' Neligh," —tears flowing down her yellow cheeks,—

"I'd do my best to grow up as nigh like you as I could."

The next step, slow in its coming, but sure, will be the appearance in these people's homes of something of the order and grace of the school, which represents to them not a school at all as they think of schools, but the beautiful home which all their lives they have regarded as the peculiar prerogative of the rich. Some reproduction of its features one may even now see in a few of the lowly homes around it. White muslin curtains patterned after those at the school windows have here and there displaced those of coarse lace, tawdry and dust-begrimed; geranium slips brought home by the children are blossoming scarlet. Books are here also, not indeed by right of ownership, but borrowed from the school library,— little books with colored pictures and easy words in them, and over the pages the head of a grandfather, grizzled and unkempt, and a little child's are bent together, and by the light of the winter fire she is teaching him to read.

The school that has been described is not some extraordinary venture alien to the needs of the situation and impossible of imitation. At every other mill school, public or private, some of its features might be reproduced. The schools of all the more progressive mill plants are already better housed, several have more books in their libraries, and many are better situated for conserving their influence and making every effort count to the utmost. It is first the home life of this school, the exhibition of right domestic ideals, and second the awakening of intellectual energy and its application to the real needs of the pupils, which constitute the unique value of this Columbus school. In every mill community, whether of five hundred people or five thousand, the great need is a home which will be both an exemplification of wise and wholesome living and a centre of gracious helpfulness. It is the terribly centralizing power of the mill which needs to be counteracted; counteracted by magnifying the pleasures of family life, social intercourse, recreation, and a diversity of occupation. The time left for these things is not much, but the utilizing of what there is is correspondingly more important.

GENERAL LEE AS I KNEW HIM

EVER since the end of the war, I have intended to write a sketch of General Lee. Many times I have sat myself down with pen in hand to do this, but now, after forty-four years, the sketch has not been written, has not even -been begun. It simply would not get itself written, and I have often wondered why.

I had known General Lee from my boyhood. I was at school with Custis, his son, at Clarens, a school near Alexandria, and knew the General as a boy knows a man. I was present when he stormed the engine-house at Harper's Ferry in 1859 with a detachment of marines under Lieutenant Green, and during the war had seen a great deal of him, having been twice assigned to duty at his headquarters, and having served as assistant chief ordnance officer from August, 1862, to December, 1862, and from October, 1863, to the end of the war in 1865 in that capacity. I had seen him during my service at his headquarters daily and sometimes many times a day, and as a man I had known him and the members of his family in a social way. Of course, during the time I served at his headquarters the social side was eliminated as far as my intercourse with the General was concerned, but my relations with his family did not change.

General Lee has been the only great man with whom I have been thrown who has not dwindled upon a near approach. And I have seen some of the great men of my time, of this and foreign countries, and have had opportunities of knowing something about them.

The element of success looms large to the world in making up her verdict upon her sons. To Napoleon the world grants greatness, but not goodness, whereas, if he had succeeded, the goodness might have been added. If Washington had failed, he would have been accounted a good man, but never a great one, and of Lincoln the same may assuredly be said. To Robert Edward Lee has been accorded in defeat that highest niche in the Temple of Fame which the world reserves for her greatest and her best.

While I have abandoned the idea of a character sketch of General Lee, I have determined to write an account of some of my experiences and interviews with him, confining myself to a simple relation of facts of my own knowledge, leaving those who may read to make up the character sketch, each one for himself.

And first I may say that General Lee in a drawing-room was a very different man from General Lee in the field. In the drawing-room he was just a dignified and quiet gentleman, very kindly and gentle, especially with women and children. In the field he was the general, the commander in all essential points, and somehow without the least exhibition of haughtiness and without perceptible change of manner. A soldier will understand how this might be, but citizens will hardly comprehend it. He was just as grave and courteous in the field as in social life, but no one in his social acquaintance ever thought of fearing him; yet I believe all his officers feared him. They loved him as men are seldom loved, but they feared him, too. In social life he liked to talk to women or children. I have seen him with a child on his knee, and he never seemed to tire of its prattle, while the talk of an ordinary man would have bored him almost to extinction. And I never heard General Lee laugh. He would have his joke and was very fond of having it, and his face would light up with a smile, but I never heard the sound of his laughter.

It was during the winter of 1863-4 at Orange Court House that I found out that the officers of the army had a wholesome fear of General Lee. For myself, I had no fear of him, and laughed at my messmates when I found out their fear. They said: "You wait and see. You have known the General socially. You have now to make his acquaintance as your commanding officer." And I found they were right. Before that winter and spring were over I feared General Lee as much as any one.

Not long after we went into winter quarters at Orange Court House in December, 1863, General Lee invited his staff to luncheon. O'Brien, his orderly (a United States soldier who followed the General's fortunes when he resigned and came South), delivered the invitation verbally. I did not know whether or not I was privileged to consider myself a member of his staff, and therefore did not go. After my messmates had gone, O'Brien came to my tent and said, "The General is waiting for you, and desires you to come at once." I hurriedly dressed, and in ten minutes joined them. When I entered the General's mess-tent, he and his staff were standing around, evidently waiting. The General, looking as grave and imposing as usual, said, "Captain Ranson, do you think it right to keep us all waiting in this way?" I made my apologies in rather a lame fashion, and felt for the first time an awe of General Lee.

The luncheon consisted of the contents of a large box, a present received that morning. It was filled with turkeys, hams, pickles, plum cake, mince pies, etc., and several bottles of Madeira, older than the century. There was little conversation, the good things, so rare to us, were devoured almost in silence, and after that the Madeira was decanted into a tin pitcher, and we drank it out of the ordinary tin cups which came in nests in every camp-chest equipment.

The silence was rather oppressive, and wishing, I suppose, to show that I was not afraid of General Lee, I attempted some wretched joke about drinking old Madeira wine out of tin cups. It was a fearful mistake. As the youngest man present, I should have held my tongue, but I saw my mistake when it was too late to mend matters. My poor joke was received in silence. General Lee said gravely but kindly that the wine was a gift from an old lady friend in Petersburg, and he was afraid she would not relish my joke. Of course I was ignorant of the personal side of the present, but nevertheless I should have remained silent. I felt as if I would be glad if the earth would open and swallow me up. My awe of General Lee had greatly increased, and I began to understand why it was his staff were all afraid of him. I had tried to play when there was no one to play with, and I had to play with my foolish self.

The latter part of the winter my wife came to Orange Court House to visit me. I engaged board for her at a house in the village, where many officers' wives were quartered.

One Sunday—it was communion Sunday—I went to church with my wife. General Lee was also there, and while we were standing in the aisle awaiting our turn at the altar rail, and General Lee was just in front of us, I noticed that my wife pressed forward and stood very close behind him and took hold of one of the buttons on his coat. It was a singular move, and I asked the meaning of it as we walked home after church. She said: "I did not think you or any one saw it. I only wished to be able to say when I went home that I had touched the hem of his garment." I write this here because it was an illustration of the reverence and love with which General Lee was regarded by the women of the South. At that time my wife knew the General by sight only.

With the opening of spring, the usual order of "Women to the rear" was issued. There was as yet no sign of the opening of the campaign, and many of the officers' wives lingered on in disregard of it, and my wife followed the example of the others. Finally, however, she started for home, and I went with her as far as Staunton. Soon after the train left Orange Court House, General Lee entered the car in which we were seated and came slowly down the aisle. He looked larger and more imposing than ever to us who had disregarded his order. When he came to where we were sitting, he stopped and said, "Captain Ranson, I wish you to introduce me to Mrs. Ranson." My wife rose instantly (I was already standing) and said: "Oh, General Lee, I disregarded your order. It was my doing, not my husband's, and I beg you to forgive both of us." The General said: "Pray do not disturb yourself. My order was not intended for you at all. It was intended only for your husband. I intend to get a great deal of work out of him this summer, and he cannot do his work unless his horses are in condition. Every evening for some weeks, about nightfall, I have observed that he mounted his horse behind his camp and galloped off toward Orange Court House, three miles away, and every morning he came galloping back about sunrise. Now you know this is not good for the horses. By the time I should need his services they [the horses] would be worn out, and I was obliged to put a stop to it." He then took my seat by her and talked to her so pleasantly that her fears were relieved and her love and veneration were greatly increased. But there was in General Lee's little joke a reproof and warning to me, and although my wife's fears were relieved, he had let me know that he had had his eye on me and that he knew more of my movements than had been supposed. A wholesome fear of him came upon me then and there.

I do not wish to make the impression that I had neglected my duties, for I had performed them all before leaving camp for the night, and I was not disobeying orders. An officer had the privilege of leaving camp when his duties had been performed, provided he was within call in case of an emergency, and a courier would have been sent for me whenever I might have been needed at any hour of the night; but I was wearing out my horses in a measure, and I knew it, but I did not know that the General knew it.

One night during the campaign from the Wilderness to Richmond we halted and went into bivouac on the roadside. We had been marching and fighting all day. It had rained hard, and the road was muddy. The wagons had not come up, and there was every prospect of a hungry and comfortless night. However, in a few moments the camp-fires were blazing for miles in front and behind us, and that was cheering and comforting. I was about to turn in for the night, when a courier rode up and said that General Lee wished to see me. When I got to his fire (there were no tents), he asked me if I knew the way to Ashland. Ashland was on the road to Richmond and about half-way, seventeen miles from our camp and eighteen miles from Richmond.

I said I did not, but was sure I could find the way. He then gave an order that a cavalryman, one who had lived in that part of the country and who knew the way to Ashland, should be ordered to report to me at once. He explained to me that at Ashland there were several trains of freight-cars loaded with supplies, that Grant's movements threatened that point, and that I must ride there as rapidly as possible and order all the trains back to Richmond.

When I got to my camp, the cavalryman was there in waiting, and we mounted and rode off.

The first part of the way for a mile or so was along the road lighted by the fires of the troops and was bright and cheerful, but the courier said ten miles of the road were through a thick forest. When we came to the woods, we had left all the troops some distance behind, and the darkness was in strong contrast to the bright light of the camp-fires. I could not see my hand before me. I put the trooper in front and told him to ride at a quick trot and I would follow. But soon I found this was no easy task. The branches of the trees, heavy with rain, hung low and caught me in the face, delaying my progress, while the trooper, knowing the road and having the confidence of that knowledge, outfooted me, and I had to halt him until I could come alongside. I told the trooper to ride more slowly. He agreed, but soon he was far ahead again, and once more I halted him. I think both the trooper and his horse not only knew the road, but also knew that they were going home, and this gave them a speed I could not rival. I could not see him, and only knew by the sound of the splashing of his horse's feet on the wet road how far he was ahead of me. After halting him and repeating my instructions a number of times, there came a time when I received no answer to my call, although I could hear his horse's tread far ahead of me. I put my mare at full speed, regardless of the branches which slapped me in the face every moment. I stopped and listened. There was no sound. The forest was as still as death and silent as the grave. The rascal had deserted me.

There was but one thing to do. I pressed on in the darkness at the best speed I could make, but finally the branches had increased in number, and now and then my knees came in contact with the body of a stout tree. Moreover, the sound of the splashing of my mare's feet in the water had ceased, and, dismounting and feeling the ground, I found I was out of the road, and on rough ground covered with pine tags.

What to do was now the question. I remembered that all the way the picket-firing had been on my left, and just then there was a shot on my right. Concluding that my mare had turned about and was making for our late camp in the rear, I turned her around and waited for the next shot. It was on my left. I knew then that I was headed in the direction of Ashland and that the army was behind me. Again I pressed on through the thick woods, keeping the picket-firing on my left. It was slow going. Every moment brought me in contact with branches which tore my face and trees which bruised my legs. Still I pressed on, it seemed to me for hours, always keeping the firing on my left and turning the mare's head sharply when it came from in front.

At last there came a sound from in front as of an approaching storm. There was no lightning or thunder, but the sound increased every moment. I stopped to listen, and there was the familiar sound of rattling sabres. I knew then that it was the approach of a body of cavalry coming on at great speed. Whether they were friends or enemies I did not know. Taking no chances, I dismounted, and selecting a good-sized tree by feeling for it, got behind it, holding my mare by the bridle. The cavalry swept by me in the darkness, not one word being spoken. When they had all passed, I mounted and rode on in the darkness, increasing my speed in desperation, always keeping the picket-firing on my left.

How long this lasted I knew not, but I feared that my ride would be a failure, and my heart was sad indeed. Presently, without any intimation of approaching day, it became lighter, and riding about a little, I found I was out of the woods. But where was I? I pressed on, and soon came to a fence. Listening for the picket-shots, I found they were immediately in front. Then I turned sharply to the right and followed this fence. I knew if I followed the fence far enough I would get into the road I had left, as by the picket-shots it (the fence) was at right angles with the direction of the road; and I was right. Riding rapidly now along the fence, I presently came to a road, at right angles to the direction of the fence. Turning to the left and putting my mare at full speed down it for several miles, I came to a light in a field on my right hand. Riding to this light, I found a house, and in answer to my call, a girl came out on the porch with a lamp. I asked her how far it was to Ashland. She answered, "You are just coming to Ashland," and in answer to my question as to the time, she said it was just twelve o'clock. She explained, "Keep the road you have just left for a mile and you are there."

Ashland is a long, straggling village with one street running through it, and the railroad is on that street. I saw a light in an upper window, and, hailing, found the quartermaster's office was there. Leaving my mare in the street, I bounded up the stairway, and soon had him awake and gave him General Lee's orders. He seemed doubtful, and finally declined to move the trains without written orders from General Lee's Headquarters. Then I wrote out the order and signed it:

" By command of General Lee.

A. R. H. Ranson,

Capt. Asst. Chief Ord. Officer A. N. Va."

It was the first time I had signed such an order, as Colonel Baldwin had always signed them, and when I saw General Lee and asked him about it, he said, " In such an emergency you must always use my name," and I always did.

The quartermaster awoke the firemen and engine-drivers, and there soon was the sound of hissing steam from one end of the street to the other. Presently there was the creaking and grinding of wheels, and all the trains slowly backed out of the town.

I followed them down the street until they were all gone, and then, seeing a nice front yard covered with grass, rode in the gate, and taking saddle and bridle off my mare, shut the gate and left her to enjoy herself. I lay down on the porch and was soon fast asleep.

When I awoke in the morning, the sun was shining in my face and a man was standing over me, looking curiously at me. He did not recognize me, but I knew him instantly. He was a cousin of mine, named Page. We had not met during the war. He was surgeon of the post, and invited me to breakfast. I accepted very gladly, first going to the quartermaster for some corn for my mare. And such a breakfast! Hot rolls, beefsteak, butter, and coffee. I can taste it now.

After breakfast I rode down the street and saw General Lee sitting on a porch, a little girl of two or three years on his knee. He said: " Well, you got the trains out. After all, there was no need of sending you, as I got here myself before Grant. Soon after you left I became uneasy, and put the army in motion, and the head of the column is very near here now. I have telegraphed the trains to come back." I never told General Lee about the trooper. He was much concerned about my scratched and bruised face. I said nothing about my bruised knees, but I had Doctor Page and his good wife to look after me. After all, I had succeeded, and that was the best salve for my scratches and bruises.

I told the General of the cavalry I had met in the forest, and he replied that a new regiment had joined us the day before and had been sent out on picket duty. It was their first experience in war. Their outposts had been attacked in the night and had been driven in. They came in yelling, " The Yankees are upon us," and the half-awakened regiment was instantly stampeded, leaving everything but their horses behind them. This accounted for their speed through the forest, for nothing but the frantic fear which prevails in a stampede of men and horses could have occasioned it.

When we reached James River, some miles below Richmond, I supposed we would have a rest and get up our wagons and tents, but General Lee crossed the river the next morning and took the road to Petersburg. We had not ridden far when a courier met us and handed a despatch to the General. Glancing over it, he put his horse Traveller out on a long, sweeping gallop, and the staff followed. We did not draw rein until we entered the town. On the road we passed the advance of the army marching in close order and quick time. Their left flank was protected by a line of skirmishers, who (from the firing and whistling of bullets over and around us) were actively engaged. The line of march was protected by an advance-guard, also in close order and marching rapidly toward Petersburg. General Lee evidently feared the town would be occupied by the enemy before he could get there, but we found it safe, and the early arrival of our men ended all anxiety.

The General's headquarters for the moment were in some public building, and the ladiés sent in breakfast. Loaves of hot bread, butter, and coffee. During breakfast the General astonished me by saying, " Capain Ranson, I fear you have not had a good mother." I was indignant, and rather hotly replied: " You are mistaken, General. I have the best mother in the world." The General replied: " Well, I may be wrong, but there is one thing she did not teach you—how to cut bread and butter. I will show you how." He then took the loaf of bread in his hand, and spreading the butter on the end, cut off a slice and handed it to me, saying: " Now that is the way to cut bread and butter. Look what a mess you have made by cutting off your slice first and then trying to butter it afterward." Now if this had happened the year before, I would probably have been angry, and might have made a fool of myself, but now I was beginning to understand General Lee and that this was his little joke, and that I should not deprive him of the pleasure of it. I knew he was a grave and serious man and had few moments of fun. He was carrying the weight of the whole Southern cause on his own shoulders, almost unassisted, and sometimes very seriously handicapped. Moreover, I became aware that he was treating me like a son when he scolded me, and I tried to remember this in later days, when his scoldings were hard to bear. On this occasion I took the slice of bread and thanked him gravely for teaching me something.

About two months after we arrived at Petersburg, General Lee sent for me and said that he wished me to move a heavy gun, 22,000 pounds, from our line in front of Petersburg and send it down the line toward James River. I went down and found the gun in a pit, a little in the rear of our line of works, and the pit was on a knoll which enabled us to fire over our lines. It would be necessary to move the gun to Petersburg, to load it on a flat car, and send it down the railroad to its new position. It was down grade all the way, and the car would run down itself by gravity, but it had to be done at night, as the railroad was in sight of the enemy's lines and in easy range of their guns. Also there was a marsh in the rear of the pit, with a sluggish stream of water flowing through it, and so a bridge must be built over the stream and a plank road laid on the marsh. I reported all this to the General with many other necessary details, and he gave me authority to make all the arrangements. I wanted a heavy tripod and men to work the falls, railroad jacks to raise the gun, and blocks to block it up under the carry-log, and mules to pull the big carry-log with the gun swung under it. I got the carry-log and the blocks with great difficulty from a lumber-yard at Blanford, in plain view of the enemy, and the work had to be done under a heavy fire from their big guns. I gave the orders for the bridge and the plank road to the engineers, and made all the other preparations. Of course all the work had to be done at night, as the pit was in plain view of the enemy, and was within range of both musketry and artillery, about three hundred yards distant.

When all was ready I went down one night, taking with me twenty-eight pairs of mules hitched to a ship's cable, sailors to work the falls, and twenty-five other men for lifting, etc. We set the tripod over the gun and were raising it, when a storm came up. The lightning revealed to the enemy that something was being done, and they opened on us with musketry and artillery. We were obliged to lie still behind the pit until the storm was over. When the storm had ceased, we raised the gun, swung it over the crest of the pit, and rolled it down to where the carry-log was waiting. We then jacked it up, blocking it as it was raised, and secured it with heavy chains to the carry-log. The mules were put to and stretched out in a straight line, each pair having a rider.

I had noticed by daylight that a wide sweep had to be made so that we could strike the bridge at a right angle to the stream. When all was ready I rode to the leading mule, and taking it by the bridle rein, swung around on a wide curve. It was dark, but we hit the bridge squarely in the centre, the mules going down-hill at a gallop, and the lead mules were nearly over the plank road on the farther side, when suddenly something happened in the rear. There was a quick stop, and the mules were jerked back on their haunches with great force. I rode back and found the high wheels of the carry-log had cut through the bridge like a knife through a cheese and into the mud underneath, the gun resting on the bridge. We jacked it up and tried another start, but there was no more pull in the mules that night; a dozen pairs would pull forward, but a dozen more would pull back, and after seesawing for a while, I sent the mules back to Petersburg. The day was now breaking, so we cut green bushes and twined them about the high wheels of the carry-log to deceive the enemy, and then returned to camp, arriving about sunrise.

I had been sleeping in my tent for an hour or two, when I heard General Lee asking for me. I went out and found him sitting on his horse. He asked me if I had gotten the gun out, and I explained. " Then you failed," he said. I went on to say that if he would give me two hundred men who would pull together when ordered, I could get the gun out that night, the bridge having been strengthened. He turned away, saying: " No, sir; you have failed. I will send Captain W. to report to you."

Captain W. came in the course of a day, and I rode down and showed him over the ground. He made rather light of it. He had moved the heavy guns from Fort Sumter, and therefore had experience. I cautioned him that moving guns over the paved streets of Charleston was a different proposition from this. He tried it that night, but did not move the gun six feet. The next night another officer tried it and failed. On the third morning General Lee rode up to my tent and said, " What was it you said to me about moving that gun with men?" I said that with two hundred men who would act with intelligence and pull together at the word of command I could bring the gun out. He was turning away, when I said, " Am I to try it to-night, General?" " No; you failed; I will not give you another chance. I will send an officer to you."

During the day another officer called, and I went down with him and his two hundred men that night, and by two o'clock the gun was in Petersburg and loaded on the car. It was started and went safely down in an hour, two men, one at each end of the car, working the brakes. I have always thought this was hard lines, but at the same time I know that General Lee was teaching me a lesson, and that I should be thankful for the trouble he was taking.

In the latter part of December a barrel was delivered at our camp, marked " General Lee and Staff." We opened it, and found it was packed full of turkeys. We sent word to General Lee, and he rode over to our camp. There was snow on the ground, and we had laid the turkeys out on a board on the snow, the biggest in the middle and the others tapering off to the smallest at each end. There were about a dozen of them.

General Lee dismounted and joined the group gathered around the present, carrying his unslung and undrawn sword in his hand. He was told that the big turkey in the middle was his. He stood looking down at the turkeys for a moment and then said, touching the big turkey with the scabbard of his sword: " This, then, is my turkey? I don't know, gentlemen, what you are going to do with your turkeys, but I wish mine sent to the hospital in Petersburg, so that some of the convalescents may have a good Christmas dinner." He then turned on his heel, and walking to his horse, mounted and rode away. We looked at one another for a moment, and then without a word replaced the turkeys in the barrel and sent them to the hospital.

In September I was ill in the Officers' Hospital in Richmond with malarial typhoid fever, contracted in my night work on our line of works.

One day General Lee visited the hospital. After he had gone over it, a half-dozen juleps were handed round to him and his staff. General Lee took one, and after the others were helped, put it back on the waiter and told the man to carry it to some convalescent officer who needed it more than he. I think I got that julep.

But I must now return to the Petersburg campaign. It was then, and now is, evident to me that General Lee intended to fall back to Lynchburg before the spring opened, and that his plan was overruled. I was sent in January to Lynchburg to store large quantities of ordnance stores, shipped there from Petersburg, and I caused to be filled several of the tobacco warehouses and some churches. In February I was sent again to Lynchburg, with orders to ship back these stores to Petersburg. This showed certainly a change of plan, and I do not think the change was made by General Lee. Petersburg was a trap, and General Lee was avoiding that trap. Our right flank was our weak point, and I believe General Lee selected his headquarters on the south side of the river so he would be near his right flank, the inevitable point of attack. When the blow came, our cause was lost.

One Sunday morning, early in April,

news came of Grant's attack on our right, and the disaster to Hill's corps. Grant was marching up the south side of the river, and we must now retreat up the north side. I rode into Petersburg and met General Lee in the street. He told me the place would be evacuated during the day, and I must save what ordnance stores I could. As there were no engines to haul the trains or wagons either, my efforts were in vain. I spent the day, however, in trying, and did not cross the bridge until about midnight. When I looked back, the bridge was burning and also the long trains of ordnance stores. I spent the remainder of the night trying to extricate the long trains of wagons and artillery stuck in the marshy road of our retreat, and failed there also. In the morning I came to a farmhouse immediately on the road. The farmer had his wood-pile in the public road in front of his house. A log had fallen off the wood-pile and was lying on the ground, and sitting on the log, with his back resting against the wood-pile, was General Lee, asleep, with the rising sun shining on his face. I was sitting on my horse looking at him, when he opened his eyes and said, "I think I have been asleep." I made my report, to which he listened, but said nothing concerning it. He told me to go to the barn and feed my mare, and come back and get my breakfast. "They are cooking something in the house for me, and you must have some of it."

One day during the retreat, General Lee sent me to a point about six miles in front and on the river. He said the stragglers from Hill's corps were retreating by a bridge over the river at that point, and that I must stop them, arm them, and try to defend the bridge. I started, taking with me two wagons loaded with arms and ammunition, and some picks and shovels and two couriers. When I arrived I found the river was overflowing its banks, and that the retreating men, coming in squads of from two to ten, had to wade in the water on the south side to reach the bridge, and then wade from the bridge to the north bank. They came out wet and wretched-looking, generally without arms. I began to form them into squads, placing an officer over each squad, and put them to work. I

piled the rails of an old fence along the bank and threw up dirt, forming a very good protection against musketry. But the men soon got tired and many of them sat down, saying they were hungry and could not work. I told them I would get some food for them, and sent back the two couriers I had with me and the empty wagons with written orders, " By command of General Lee," for rations. This seemed to encourage them, and the work went on until dark. By that time I had 600 men and divided them into companies, the whole in charge of a colonel. I had built quite a good bridge head for musketry, extending about three hundred yards along the river, and had manned it. Then I left them, in order to report to General Lee and hurry up the rations; but, alas! no rations were to be had.

When I arrived at headquarters, General Lee was in a tent, sitting with General Longstreet on some bundles of rye straw (the ground being wet from the rain), at the upper side of the tent, with one candle for a light. I made my report, and the General told me to wait, as he wished to see me. He asked me if I had had anything to eat, and I told him no. He said he was sorry he had nothing to offer me. He gave me a bundle of straw and told me to sit near the door. It had been raining all afternoon, and I was quite wet. I was also very tired, so I put my foot through the bridle rein of my mare standing outside, and lying down on the bundle of straw, was soon asleep.

I was awakened by voices, and looking up, saw the colonel I had left in charge of the troops at the bridge standing in the tent. He reported that the rations had not arrived, and the starving and discouraged troops had all deserted in the darkness, leaving their arms in the trenches. General Lee heard him to the end of his account, and then with a wave of his hand dismissed him. Turning to General Longstreet, he said: "This is very bad. That man is whipped. It is the first time I have seen one of my officers who had been whipped. It is very bad." The conversation between the generals was then resumed in low tones, and I again fell asleep. I must have slept for some length of time, when I was awakened by General Lee's voice, speaking in loud tones, louder than I had ever heard from him. He was saying, "General Longstreet, I will strike that man a blow in the morning." General Lee sometimes spoke of General Grant as "that man," and of the Federal army as "those people."

General Longstreet replied in low tones, giving the strength and condition of his command, and the strength and position of the enemy, and concluded by saying, "But you have only to give me the order, and the attack will be made in the morning." Again the conversation was resumed in low tones, and I fell asleep. I must have slept for an hour at least, when again I was awakened by the loud, almost fierce tones of General Lee, saying, "I tell you, General Longstreet, I will strike that man a blow in the morning." General Longstreet again recounted the difficulties, ending as before, "General, you know you have only to give the order and the attack will be made, but I must tell you I think it will be a useless waste of brave lives."

Thinking I had been present long enough at such an interview, I coughed and got up from the straw, and drawing back the flaps of the tent, looked out into the darkness. General Lee said: "Captain Ranson, I beg your pardon. I had forgotten you. Go now and get something to eat and some rest. I will see you in the morning."

I found my poor mare lying flat on her side in the rain and fast asleep. It was past midnight and very dark, but I reached our camp, though neither I nor my mare got anything to eat that night.

The morning came, and I listened for the sound of our attack, but all was still. There *was* no attack; our fighting days were over.

When General Lee rode out of our lines to meet General Grant, the stillness in our camp was awe-inspiring. We all knew what his going meant, although no word had been spoken.

When he rode back into our lines, erect and grand—grander than ever—his army broke up into a loving mob and followed him, holding on to his hands, his feet, his coat, the bridle of his horse, and its mane, weeping and sobbing as if their hearts were breaking. I saw one of his generals of the Second Army Corps

sitting on a stump, crying loudly and bitterly, as a child will cry. General Lee's head was not bowed, he held it high as usual, but there was a look of sorrow and pain in his face which I had never before seen there. He tried to speak to his men, but the words stuck in his throat (I was within twenty yards, and if he spoke I did not hear him), and then I saw the tears were coursing down his face. He had halted for a moment, but now rode on to his camp. His men followed, but I did not. I knew there were no more orders for me, and as I could be of no use to him, I did not wish to intrude upon him in his hour of agony. When I saw the men returning to their camp, I went to headquarters, and there learned of his surrender and the terms. He had recovered his composure and was as calm and dignified as usual. His officers had gathered around him.

When I knew that the surrender was a fact, I mentioned to Colonel Baldwin, my chief, that the secret-service money of the army was in our wagon, and asked for instructions. The secret-service money of the army was used in paying spies and informers who ran the blockade and entered the enemy's lines in search of information, and to obtain such supplies as were not obtainable in the South. Up to the time when Overton Price, clerk at the ordnance office of the chief of ordnance, left, the box containing the money was in his keeping, and he paid out all moneys. No books or records were kept. When an order was presented, the money was paid to bearer and the order was instantly destroyed. Nothing was kept that could incriminate any one, and the reason must be apparent when it is remembered that a spy met death as a certainty when detected.

Colonel Baldwin asked General Lee about the money, and he replied, "I know nothing about it." Colonel Baldwin said, "But, General, I am asking for instructions." General Lee replied, "Colonel Baldwin, I know nothing at all about the matter, and will not discuss it."

Colonel Baldwin then asked General Longstreet, who said: "Divide it up among the officers present. The government owes me a month's pay and I should like to have it."

I brought the iron box containing the money, and Colonel Baldwin counted it. I have forgotten how much there was— only a few thousands, however. I had had charge of the box ever since Overton Price had been ordered back to his company in March, and had opened it but once, and that was at Amelia Springs. Colonel Baldwin did not join us on the retreat until we reached Amelia Springs. He asked for the box, and gave Generals Fitz Lee and Rosser $2,500 each, they intending to cut their way out and join General Joe Johnston. The money was in fifty and one hundred dollar bills, United States currency, and some gold. Colonel Baldwin gave me one hundred dollars, put one hundred dollars in his own pocket, and then gave each of the officers present one hundred dollars, beginning with General Longstreet. The money soon gave out, and Captain Duffy, chief gunsmith of the Reserve Ordnance train, coming up and complaining of having been left out, Colonel Baldwin gave him fifty dollars, the half of his own one hundred dollars. I heard at the time that Colonel Baldwin offered General Lee some of the money and that he refused it. I was not present when this occurred, but I am perfectly sure it is true.

The morning after the surrender I went to General Lee's tent to see if I could be of any use. He told me he was busy, and asked me to see that he was not disturbed. I was ill, suffering from a malady which had sent me to the hospital several times, and which had been aggravated by the hard life during the retreat. I had had little rest, and Doctor Gild gave me some morphia tablets. I took them all night, but lay awake until morning upon the bare ground, looking up at the stars and wondering they could shine so brightly on our dark and sorrowful world. Tired and suffering, I lay in front of the General's tent. Looking up, I saw three Federal generals, mounted and looking down at me. Their sleek horses and bright uniforms and trappings were in strong contrast to what we were accustomed. They asked me if they could see General Lee, and I said no, he was engaged. They then asked why I lay on the damp ground, and I said I was ill. They said I looked ill and dejected, and they could not understand why I should

be dejected. One of them said: "If I were you, I would be the proudest man in the world. When I rode into your lines this morning and saw the poor remnant of the army which had baffled us so long, I was ashamed of myself." He then asked me if I had had any breakfast, and I said no. As he turned away he said, "I will send you something." He took my name and gave me his card. I lost the card and have forgotten his name. I think, however, he said it was General Humphries.

In a short while a wagon drove up containing a barrel of hams, a barrel of hardtack, and a barrel of whiskey. I sent the wagon to my camp, and it was distributed among the hungry men. Every man and officer who came along was given a canteenful of whiskey and a good meal of bread and ham. The barrels were soon empty.

While I was guarding General Lee's tent, a man named White, a clerk in the Adjutant-General's office, came out and handed me an envelope. He said, "The General says this is all he has to give you in return for your services on his staff, especially during the retreat." I opened the envelope, and it was the farewell address of General Lee to his army, generally known as General Order No. 9, addressed to me as Captain A. R. H. Ranson, Assistant Chief Ordnance Officer, Army of Northern Virginia, and signed by himself. I have it now, and consider it the most valuable of my possessions.

Now that everything was over I began my preparations for my journey home, about two hundred miles distant. I formed a mess with Colonels Latrobe and Fairfax of Longstreet's staff. General Grant allowed us a wagon and team of mules, as the journey had to be made across country. We kept our horses and side arms by the terms of surrender. When my preparations were completed I went to General Lee's tent. He knew I was going, he could see the preparations, and the wagon now stood in front of his tent ready to start. When I entered, he arose from his seat, extended his hand, and looked straight into my face. When his grasp relaxed I withdrew my hand and turned away. Not a word had been spoken, and this was my parting with General Lee. I never saw him again.

HERE AND THERE IN THE SOUTH

BY REBECCA HARDING DAVIS.

I.—OLD AND NEW.

THE train that rushed out of the wide winding suburbs of Washington down into Virginia, in the dawn of a cold February morning, was filled with Northerners going to New Orleans. They had, oddly enough, the alert, expectant air of explorers into an unknown country. The men looked out on the sleepy streets of Alexandria with as critical eyes as if it had been its namesake in Egypt, and the women buttoned their tight ulsters more closely, and slung their alligator satchels to their sides in readiness for any emergency.

They were intelligent people of the class who have leisure; they were familiar with the upper range of States; many of them ran over to Europe or to California every summer. But this three-cornered segment of their country, which had a climate, history, and character of its own, was foreign to them as Arabia Felix.

"I was in the South thirty years ago," said one fidgety old gentleman. "Visited a college found in eastern Virginia. Queer life! Great scrambling house in a large plantation, crowded with guests; leaky roof, magnificent old family plate, patched carpets, negroes swarming everywhere. Saddled horses hitched always by the door in case you wanted to cross a field. Old families, each with its coat of arms and pride of birth. The most generous, unmethodical, kindly people in the world."

The old gentleman in his enthusiasm took off his silk travelling cap, letting the cold wind blow over his bald head with its fringe of gray hair. His wife—a pudgy, prim little woman—replaced it with, " You forget, my dear!"

"Yes, yes. I forget I'm a broken-down old invalid when I think of those days. It makes me a lad again to get into the South," turning to his listening neighbors. " I've been pastor of a church in western New York for forty years, you see. Never took a holiday. Some chronic trouble set in last fall, and the doctors said—Europe. My people raised the money at once. But I said, I'll go South and rest. No Europe for me. Why, gentlemen, in all the drive and struggle of those forty years the remembrance of the leisure and quiet, the laziness if you like, of the South, has come before me like a glimpse of the Isles of the Blest! Life there is not all money-getting. They take it as they go."

His companions listened to the eager talk of the garrulous old fellow with assenting nods and smiles, he being one of those people to whom the world in all of its humors says yes and smiles. But they did not at all agree with him. Having the usual large careless good-humor of the American, they had no lingering grudge or bitterness against the South because of the war. But it was alien to them, as it had always been; they were men whose occupations and thoughts ran in fixed and narrow ruts, and like the great mass of average Northerners they knew the South only through long-ago recollections or hearsay traditions. It was in their minds a vague tropical stretch of sugar and cotton and rice fields, peopled by indolent, arrogant men and haughty, languid women, their feet still firmly set on the necks of the negro race.

The names of the stations, too, began to recall the fact that they were in a once hostile country, and among a people who had been their foe. As the conductor shouted "Fairfax," "Manassas," "Culpepper," they looked out eagerly at the snow-covered fields and the unpainted wooden station-houses which replaced the brick Queen Anne villas affected by Northern railways, expecting to find something novel and foreign. A few lean, nervous-looking white men were at work on the platforms, and a crowd of negroes shouldered each other away from the car windows.

" Fried chicken, sah ?"

" Col' boil tongue ? Nice snack !"

" Hyah's yoh wine-saps! Albemarle apples!"

Mr. Ely, the old clergyman, bought apples and tongue from half a dozen, looking out laughing from the window as the train rolled on, leaving them squabbling and joking over the money.

A pursy young man from Chicago was superciliously calling attention to the worm-fences, the lean fields, the forlorn houses, as—

" Wretchedly poor, sir ! Now there is really no excuse for such poverty. Even grant that the State was laid waste by the war. All that was twenty years ago. Twenty years is enough for any man to get upon his legs again."

"It is all due to lack of energy !" decisively said a close-shaven, trig little ironmaster from Pennsylvania. "We all know the South. Some of the best books in American literature are descriptions of these people. Did you ever read *Uncle Tom's Cabin*, or *A Fool's Errand* ? They show you that a more indolent, incapable, pig-headed race never breathed. The men spend their time in idling, duelling, and drinking. The women are merely lovely, helpless babies."

Mr. Ely, with an indignant snort, girded himself to make battle; but at that moment the train stopped in the suburbs of Charlotteville. Steep streets ran up into the picturesque town, back of whose peaked roofs rose the snowy hills. A crowd of students from the University filled the platform. An elderly man, after much hand-shaking with them, entered the car.

"Hello!" said Mr. Ely; "surely I know that face, Sarah ? Except for the bald head—" He bristled up. "I beg pardon. It is a long time ago. But are you not Wollaston Pogue ? I am James Ely. Don't you remember ? I visited the Medills in Accomac in '55, and you—"

"Bless my soul! Of course I remember. Why, my dear sir, I *am* glad to see you back in Virginia. And how has the world used you in all these years ?"

"Well, well! roughly enough," said

Drawn by W. H. Gibson.   Engraved by J. Tinkey.

A GLIMPSE FROM THE CAR WINDOW.

Ely, with a sigh. He had, in fact, a comfortable home, and until lately sound health, yet, as the two men sat side by side, it was the anxious, lean' Northerner who most looked like the victim of a destructive war. The Virginian was a stout, ruddy, overgrown boy. Prosperity apparently oozed out of every pore, from the red fringe of hair about his shining pate to his beaming spectacled eyes, and the gurgling laugh of pure enjoyment that bubbled out every minute.

"Changes?" he said, rubbing his knees meditatively, as Ely plied him with questions. "Oh, great changes! Necessarily. The houses in which you visited have all passed from the old families. Except the Grange. That is a place of summer resort, kept by Mrs. Leigh."

"Not that lovely Anna Page who married Joe Leigh?"

"The very same. Beautiful as a dream, wasn't she? But she is making money fast, keeping boarders. The house was torn out by the Yan—by one of the armies. After the surrender that woman put up partitions, hung doors, glazed windows, papered, painted—with her own hands. She's equal to a whole troop of mechanics."

"And John Medill?"

"Killed at Manassas. His son lost a leg, and was invalided for life. His daughters carry on the plantation. Virginia is in the saddle every morning before dawn. She herself ploughed and dug until she was able to hire hands. She had the banner crop of tobacco in that county last year."

Mr. Ely made a clucking sound of amazement and dismay. "And what became of the Allaires?"

"They lost everything. The boys as they grew up went to work. Fred in an iron-mill in Richmond, and St. Clair as brakesman on this road. They have both risen steadily."

"No lack of energy there!" said the old clergyman, with a sharp glance toward the scoffing iron man. But he fell into a depressed silence as his friend continued his history. Brakesmen and boarding-house keepers! He had cherished for so many years his picture of the stately Southern homes and their indolent landlords, and now it was crumbling to pieces. If he had found a decayed, mouldering aristocracy, passively wasting away in their ruined homes, it would have been in mournful keeping with his recollection. But this busy, commonplace stir, this sudden plunge of the defeated South into the world's market-place, bewildered and annoyed him.

"I hope the troubles did not injure you, Mr. Pogue?" he said at last.

"Major Pogue," quietly amended the Virginian. "I had that rank in our army. Yes"—nodding good-humoredly— "I was left without a dollar. Fortune of war, eh? But I was young, and could accept the situation. It went harder with the old men. Our Southern women, I will say, were the first to stagger to their feet. In every household it was invariably the woman who first faced the inevitable and tried to make the best of it. The old men never have quite recovered from the blow. Some of them even yet fancy that the old issues are still alive. But it is the men who were children in '65 that have their hands on the lever now; they make no mistake about issues. Where their fathers dreamed of reopening the slave-trade and of conquering Mexico and annexing Cuba, to form a great empire, they talk of new cotton-gins, and Bessemer steel-works, and coal-mines, and a thousand other ways of developing our resources. It is the young men who are the New South. I fancy you Northern people know little about the New South."

"Very little indeed," replied Mr. Ely, smiling uneasily. "In fact, I did not know until five months ago that there was such a nation."

"You will see"—laughing significantly.

"But what did you do after the surrender? Start afresh, like your New South?"

"Precisely. Got a position as clerk in Atlanta. I have an interest in two or three concerns there now, and have my home near the town. I have just been up to see my boy at the University. You'll stop and make us a visit?" he added, anxiously. "Oh, I'll take no denial! Mrs. Ely will plead for me. I intend to take my daughter down to New Orleans to the Exposition, and we can form a pleasant party. Come, now, old friend; it is all arranged."

Mr. Ely fidgeted and protested. He would have fallen again easily into those lax, hospitable ways. But his wife settled the matter in her slightly nasal, decisive tones.

"Of course we shall stop and wait for you and Miss Pogue, Major. But you must allow us to stay at a hotel. We really should prefer it." Mrs. Ely, away from home, usually was only a dumb, smiling adjunct to her enthusiastic husband. But there were times when she felt it necessary to put down the brakes. Yet she was secretly excited at the thought of studying one of the dark-eyed, languid Georgian women in her own home. During the afternoon, as they passed down through the close, shouldering hills and lonely villages of central Virginia, she tried to picture to herself the indolent grace and flower-like beauty of these Southern women, as she had read of them in their songs and novels. For herself, she was quite willing to be taken in the South as a fair specimen of the cultured Northern women, though, after all, the culture amounted only to a nice taste in Kensington art work, and a mania about drainage. But she pleased herself by thinking that she would open new worlds of thought to the Major's daughter, who doubtless knew nothing of society, or literature, or plumbing, or any of those great social questions which Mrs. Ely, like a brown sparrow in big grain fields, had picked at in turn. "The mind of any woman," she said to her husband, "in these lifeless villages must be limited, and their talk *kleinstädtisch* beyond bearing."

They stopped for a day in Lynchburg, which recalled Pittsburgh to Mr. Ely. "It is almost as busy and as black," he said, as they sauntered past the towering factories, "and the business men look as if, like ours, they were challenging life at the point of the bayonet. We wear out brain and body in our haste to be rich, at the North, and you are following us, I'm afraid."

The Major laughed good-humoredly. "We were forced into the race. The Southerner, when he goes into business, throws the same ardor into it that forty years ago he did into his fun, or courting, or fighting. A steam-engine will pull, you know, Mr. Ely, no matter what kind of load you put behind it." He pointed out the solid blocks of business houses and tasteful dwellings, "built since the war."

The next day, in Charlotte, the same story was told and retold. Instead of descanting, as he would have done ten years ago, on the ancient glories of the old South lost in the struggle, the Major was eager to show every sight of the solid foundation which the New South was laying for an enduring, stable prosperity. Spartanburg, Greenville, and other pretty towns followed, each with its wide shaded streets, its new mills in the suburbs, its "cheap stores," its imposing new hotel, its stir of freshly awakened life.

"But who has done all this?" asked Mr. Ely, half annoyed. "Northern men?"

"At first, yes. They were the first to see that money was to be made here. They usually met a cold welcome, as you know. Our old men wanted to run the South in the old tracks—cotton, politics, fighting. But our own young men, as I told you, are getting the reins now in their own hands. Our leading manufacturers, brokers, newspaper men, and even city officials, everywhere, are as a rule Southerners, and under fifty."

"Atlanta!" shouted the conductor.

"But this is a Northern city!" exclaimed Mr. Ely, as they stepped out into a large station, grimy with bituminous smoke, and walled in by blocks of huge warehouses that opened into crowded streets of conventional banks, hotels, and shops, solidly built, and offering an odd contrast to the irregular, straggling, green-bowered thoroughfares of Richmond, Charleston, and Savannah.

"Atlanta is the capital of our new nation," said the Major, as he handed Mrs. Ely from the car. "It is the head-quarters for shrewd, pushing men from all the Gulf States. Outsiders call us Georgian Yankees."

Two motherly negro women, turbaned and white-aproned, boarded the train instead of porters, took Mrs. Ely's wraps, and led her to the waiting-room. A lady, very little and very young, was standing in the centre of the dingy room, watching the door. The alert, intent figure caught Mrs. Ely's eye.

"A teacher from Boston," she decided, as she scanned the thin, eager features, the vigilant eyes, the mass of yellow hair. "I wonder if she ever takes time to sit down or draw a long breath?"

But the Major hurried to meet the little lady, kissed her, and presented her as "my daughter Lola." In her dismay the clergyman's wife was awkward, and posed self-consciously. But the Major's daughter welcomed her with a quiet simplicity to which Mrs. Ely paid instant homage.

"*She* has never had any doubt of her breeding or social position," she thought. "She would be just as sure of it in rags as in that velvet." The little girl stood waiting for her guests, polite but utterly incurious. "She does not even observe how I am dressed," thought Mrs. Ely. "These Southerners all act as if they 'had that within which passeth show'— of money or clothes."

In many ways their old ideas were demolished that day.

"When I was young," said Mr. Ely to his wife at night, "the South sent North for even its pins. It made nothing for itself. But here in Atlanta, Pogue tells me, they manufacture everything, from a house to a match. All since the war. Take out the money value of the slaves, and Georgia never was so wealthy as she is to-day. The same is true of the Carolinas. Once let these hot-blooded, eager Southerners get a firm footing as manufacturers and producers, and they'll run the North hard in the business world. So Pogue says."

Their acquaintance with the Pogue family brought them countless invitations during their stay in Atlanta. The new stately dwellings and their æsthetic interiors became familiar objects to them.

"Here are the very same etchings, the same bric-à-brac and Daghestan rugs, that I left behind in New York and Philadelphia," Mrs. Ely complained to Miss Pogue as they drove out together one afternoon. "The same hats on the women, the same dishes at dinner, and the same talk too, only that it runs in a more leisurely current."

"You would see more distinctive life in the country," Lola said, turning her

ponies into a broad grass-edged highway.

In an hour they were in the pine woods.
At long intervals there were openings
in which was a wide, low, many-galleried
house, with its appendage of dilapidated
negro quarters and neglected farm lands
—a gray, hoary wreck of prosperous days.
The snow, which still lay in drifts in the
woods, had melted here from the saffron
stubble fields. The houses usually appeared to be over-full; all of the windows
shone redly in the closing dusk; the rooms
were alive with children, with gay young
people; matrons with delicate, fastidious
faces bent over their work; portly, handsomely dressed men loitered in the galleries or rode down the long avenues.

"You would find the old habits of hospitality kept up in these houses," said
Lola. "Family connections are large in
the South. A Georgian of the higher class
has cousins all through the Carolinas and
the Gulf States, just as the Virginians and
Kentuckians are really all of one blood.
From five to ten guests may drop in unin-
vited for any meal, or come to stay a week.
They are always sure of a welcome. The
old class of Southerners would rather
give up their chance of heaven than the
pleasure of keeping open house for their
friends on earth."

Mr. Ely's face flushed. "It is a gracious, beautiful custom!" he exclaimed.
"We lost much that was worth keeping
with the old feudal systems."

"Yes," said Miss Pogue, dryly. "I
have known a dinner prepared in our
house for four persons, and before it was
served twenty guests arrived unexpectedly. So it goes on all the year round."

"That is delightful," hesitated Mrs.
Ely. "It takes one quite back to patriarchal life. But it would not suit Northern house-keepers nor Northern cooks and
chamber-maids."

"It does not suit here," said Lola,
promptly. "Our mothers were used to
it when they had plenty of money and of
servants. But now that we have not
enough of either, the custom keeps many
a family poor, and makes life a tread-mill
for most women. The generation I belong to, Mrs. Ely," she said, after a pause,
her thin, decisive features heating, "have
learned to practise small economies in poverty, and they are forced to see that there
is a great leakage in their incomes through
these old customs which seem to you so

beautiful and grand. Yet," she added,
with sudden pride, "I doubt if the Southerner will ever give up *that* custom."

Mrs. Ely, talking matters over that
night as usual, declared that "the Georgian girl talked and thought precisely
like a New-Englander. And, as far as I
can see, she is not an uncommon type now
in this New South. I have met women,
since we came here, capable, shrewd, and
alive with energy. They manage plantations and shops; they raise stock, hold offices, publish newspapers. Indeed, while
Northern women have been clamoring for
their rights, Southern women have found
their way into more careers than they.
They keep up with all the questions of the
day. Miss Lola actually gave me some
new hints on drainage. I suppose we
Americans have but one blood, after all,
and a hard struggle with poverty will produce the same woman in Georgia as in
Connecticut."

The next day our travellers, with the
Major and Miss Pogue, left Atlanta for
Montgomery. They soon left behind the
leafless, deciduous woods and the snow,
and entered interminable pine forests rising out of the rich red earth, pale green
in the spring air. Occasionally the endless phalanx of pines crowded back in dis-
gust to make way for a flat plateau of yellow clay, out of which rose "a clarin," a
forlorn huddle of gray, unpainted cabins.
Not a tree, nor flower, nor blade of grass,
appeared in the wide swamp of mud. Negroes in rags lounged against the worm-
fence, too lazy to look up at the train;
lean woolly cows, their sides daubed with
mud, lazily got out of the way of the cars:
leaner hogs wallowed in the lower deeps
of mud, looking up to wink sleepily at the
puffing engine. The men of the hamlet
lounged about the station-house, yellow-
skinned and heavy-eyed from long diet of
pork and whiskey.

Mr. Ely, catching his wife's look of
consternation, hastily explained. "You
must remember, my dear, that up to the
beginning of this century this part of Alabama was an absolute wilderness, broken
only by a few settlements of half-breeds
and Spaniards, with neither law nor religion. Pennsylvania and New York
were then open to the great tide of immigration. It never has set in here. What
progress has been made is due to the people themselves, not to European influence,
as is the case with us."

Drawn by W. H. Gibson.

"A CLARIN."

"Alabama turns her poorest side to the railways," said Major Pogue. "But we will soon skirt the 'Black Belt,' which is full of rich plantations under scientific cultivation. As good soil as you have in Pennsylvania."

Mr. Ely smiled anxiously. The flat gray sky, and the monotonous pillared pines which held it like a roof, oppressed him; he had not drawn a full breath all day. To live always walled by these changeless trees into solitude and poverty, away from the life and motion of the world—how soon it would make a man narrow and prejudiced and virulent! No wonder these people fight with the obstinacy and courage of tigers!

The train halted that moment at a little lonely station at the foot of a hill. At its top stood a picturesque old mansion, which seemed to him to embody all the tragedy of the departed South. The sunset flamed redly up behind its gray walls and steep roof, the black shingles of which were mossed with age. A thin wisp of smoke drifted from its great outside chimney across the cold sky; the wind swept through the empty galleries, no light shone from its windows. A little apart from it three ancient cedars stood on guard; they flung their distorted arms toward the east, bent by the winds that in winter swept the hill-top.

"They are pleading against the disaster that has fallen on the house," thought the old clergyman, smiling on his own gloomy fancy.

A tall man, dressed in the coarse homespun and wide-rimmed hat of the farm hands, came down the hill, and entering the car, sat down in front of him. Undoubtedly a laborer: face, hands, and neck tanned one saffron hue; the high boots patched and muddy. But Mr. Ely detected a haughty reserve in the high-featured face, better befitting a cavalier than a ploughman.

"The typical Southerner at last!" he thought. "With that face, he might have ruled a thousand slaves, or led a regiment into the jaws of death."

Two passengers, Western men, sitting near, loudly discussed the lean pigs, the bony cattle, the poor buildings on the farm; but the owner's face remained calm as though dogs barked at his heel. Mr. Ely rushed to the rescue. "You forget, gentlemen," he said, "that the South for nearly a century had but one occupation—agriculture. The loss of her slaves

Drawn by W. H. Gibson.   Engraved by J. Hellawell.

THE BLOSSOMING RUIN.

crippled her in that. She is turning now with all the strength she has to other industries. She asks us Northerners in a friendly, brotherly way to come down to see in this New Orleans Exposition what she has done; if we go at all, it should be in the same friendly spirit—not to insult her."

The men laughed, but were silent, and Mr. Ely presently fell into talk with the Alabamian, questioning him on the resources of his State.

"You should go to the northern part of Alabama," he said, in a grave, measured tone, "if you wish to get a clear idea of her enormous undeveloped wealth. Near

Selma, cotton raising is carried on now with so much skill and certainty that the sons of the great planters in Mexico are sent there as pupils, staying for years. You have been in Birmingham ?"

"No. Is it a typical Southern city ?"

The planter smiled. "I hope so; but not of the old South. Twelve years ago it was a cotton plantation. Now they are working coal-mines with an output of over 4000 tons a day, and iron-mines that yield metal which they tell me is as good as the best Swedish. With both, they can put pig-iron in the Northern market six dollars a ton cheaper than it is done in Pennsylvania."

"It is a fact," struck in Major Pogue, after greeting the farmer as an old friend. "The enormous mineral wealth of Alabama is but just opened. She has rich virgin soil, and though you may not believe it, Mr. Ely, a law-abiding, God-fearing population, anxious to work. She has good waterways, and one of the best harbors on the whole coast at Mobile. What she wants is capital and skilled labor."

Meanwhile Miss Pogue was talking of the planter with Mrs. Ely at the back of the car.

"It is Dupré Mocquard," she said. "I have heard he was considered the handsomest man in New Orleans before the war. A brave fellow too; he fought half a dozen duels. He belonged to a wealthy creole family; they equipped a regiment for the war, which he commanded."

"And after—"

"After—" with a shrug. "He is overseer now, where he was master, on one of his own plantations. He is as eager, I have heard my father say, about raising cotton as he was in duelling or flirting. His four children must live, you see."

They reached Montgomery that night, and remained there for several days. Colonel Mocquard drove out with them almost every day. He did not lose any of his picturesqueness, at least in Mrs. Ely's eyes, when he had laid aside his working clothes for ordinary dress.

"His old-fashioned, high-shouldered courtesy," she told her husband, "would become a deposed monarch."

The weather on the day after their arrival was cold. High winds drove light purplish clouds over a clear sky. The streets of the first Confederate capital stretched before them wide and muddy, the sidewalks of clay or boards sheltered by fine old trees. Back among trim gardens and groves of green magnolias or leafless China-trees, brown with feathery clusters of last year's flowers, were set quaint, low, many-galleried dwellings, which the Northern visitors admired enthusiastically.

"They are picturesque, and they belong to the climate and scenery," said Mr. Ely. "But I am sorry to see here and there a towered brick house, or one of those pretentious villas with which we in the North abuse the memory of poor Queen Anne."

"Those houses are built, for the most part," said Lola, "by wealthy Hebrews, brokers or dollar-store men. The Jews 'entered in and occupied the land' as soon as the war was over. You will find them in every village and town in the Gulf States, living usually in the best houses, which old Southern families could no longer hold."

"That's all right, my dear," interrupted her father. "They loaned us all, blacks and whites, money when we had none. Fair business transaction."

Lola's delicate features flushed hotly. "At fifty per cent.—yes. The day will come, perhaps, when 'the king shall enjoy his own,'" she replied, sharply. Then, hastily controlling herself and changing her tone: "Montgomery, as you may imagine, Mr. Ely, is a beautiful city in summer. This large building on the hill is the Capitol. The first Confederate Congress met here, you remember."

They alighted and passed through the empty lofty halls, coming out again on to a high flight of steps which commanded a view of the quiet city and its superb rampart of rolling hills and rich plantations.

"Just here, on these steps," said Lola, "Jefferson Davis stood when he was inaugurated President."

Neither she nor the other Southerners betrayed any further remembrance of the great tragedy which had opened on this little grassy hill-top. The story was too familiar to them, and their own stinted lives too much a sequence and part of the tragedy, for them to see it merely as a great historic drama. But the old clergyman's heated fancy instantly peopled the hill with the men whose hour's work that day had had such limitless results. A cold sunny day like this, perhaps, and each had come up from his own home, sincere, eager, ready to risk his property, life, and sacred honor for the cause he believed to be true.   And now—

The old man was loyal to the Union; his brothers had died fighting for it.   But for the moment he looked through the eyes of this other unknown brother, believed as he believed, felt the wrench of his defeat.   His heart beat thick, and a hot film darkened his eyes.

They drove through the plantations in the suburbs of the city, passing stately old dwellings in disrepair and ruins, their parks overgrown with weeds and brambles.   Before one a great stone lion, splendid in its day, lay broken and overthrown.

The next moment they passed through the "new town"—streets of cheerful rose-covered cottages belonging to the colored people.   Nowhere in the South have the freedmen made more steady and swift progress to thrift and intelligence than here.   Swayne College, their principal school, was just dismissed, and a long procession of colored girls and lads marched down the street in tidy, bright-colored clothes, turning to the strangers clear, watchful faces.

They drove to the hotel through streets of new warehouses and shops, while the Major and Colonel Mocquard discussed eagerly some new mining company just forming among the capitalists of the city.

"I think," said the clergyman, quietly, "you have shown us to-day the significance of both the Old South and the New."

HERE AND THERE IN THE SOUTH.

BY REBECCA HARDING DAVIS.

II.—IN MOBILE.

WHILE they were in Alabama our tourists visited some of the large cotton plantations, and found them equipped with the most modern and costly machinery.

"But the dwelling-houses of the planters," said Colonel Mocquard, as they were returning from one of these excursions, "must strike you as bare and comfortless. Yes; pardon me. I know that it is so. I have been in the North recently, and I saw how the love of art and house decoration was growing among you with each year. Compare our plantation dwellings with the house and lawns of a wealthy Pennsylvania or New York farmer! But we—we are too busy trying to live. If the South had the money and leisure she once had," he continued, with a lofty complacency, "she would, I suppose, have long been the foremost in the modern dilettante race."

Mrs. Ely controlled a smile of amused superiority. Her husband said, hastily, "The South is learning a higher lesson than any which bric-à-brac or pictures could teach her."

"We will hope so," replied Mocquard, dryly. "It is certain that there is now a very small number of men among us who are wealthy enough to indulge luxurious tastes. The great mass of our people have been forced to go to work."

"Yes, and it is better for them, Mocquard," said Major Pogue, who was in the carriage. "But the great error they make is in giving their whole efforts and thought to one kind of work—that of raising cotton. It is the road to a competency with which we are most familiar, and we are apt to think it the only one; so we neglect a thousand other industries which in the North are common and lucrative. Now this plantation, for instance, which we are passing. A little time and care would give the planter the finer fruits and vegetables for his table and for the market, would surround his house with flower-gardens and well-kept lawns, and fill it with comforts if not elegance. But he turns his back on everything but cotton. That one crop disposed of, his duty for the year is over."

Colonel Mocquard frequently went with them on these exploring journeys. Mr. Ely was impressed with the business qualifications of the ex-soldier and fire-eater.

"Shrewd and economical he will never be," he said to his wife. "It isn't in the blood. But he has energy and a tremendous · capacity for work. The North does not suspect what stuff is in these men. I

Drawn by W. H. Gibson.

GOVERNMENT STREET, MOBILE.

have been looking over some industrial statistics to-day, and I find that over three and a half millions have been invested already in this year right here in Alabama in new enterprises, principally in coal-mining and lumbering. I heard you and Mocquard bemoaning the lack of pictures and bric-à-brac. Stuff and nonsense! They are laying solid foundations of prosperity now; they will put on the gilding by-and-by."

Colonel Mocquard drove them one morning through the business streets of the city, showing them the manufactories of ice and soaps, and the ginneries where cotton-seed oil was made.

"Ready," laughed Lola Pogue, "to be exported to Italy, and returned to the North as *L'huile de Lucca.*"

They came home through the "new town"—a suburb filled with pretty cottages (not cabins) belonging to the negroes. It was a warm evening, and they were out sunning themselves on the galleries, the women and children in gay print gowns. Many of them, who had been his slaves, ran down to speak to "de Boss" as Mocquard passed. There was evidently hearty good-will on both sides.

Down the narrow street, as the sun was setting, came a procession of blacks and mulattoes reverently following a hearse. They marched with linked fingers, and were dressed in black, both men and women wearing a bright purple cape edged with gold braid.

"It is a beneficiary society," explained Major Pogue. "The freedmen have formed them everywhere throughout the South. They very seldom are political or religious in their aim, but are based solely on the idea of mutual help in time of sickness or death. Each has its secret device or password, however, and they gratify their dramatic sense by some bit of color in the dress or badge."

"To me," said Mocquard, "the tendency of the negroes to co-operate is one of the most significant signs of their progress."

The party were to have separated the next day, Colonel Mocquard going back to the plantation, while his friends went on to Mobile. He insisted, however, on accompanying them for at least a few days longer. Mrs. Ely nodded significantly when she heard this offer.

"Depend on it," she said to her husband, "Miss Pogue is the cause of his

courtesy to us. And a very good thing that match would be. He is poor, a widower, with a houseful of children, and she would make an economical, managing Yankee wife."

"No doubt when you die, my dear, you will be sent out as a match-making angel," was his only reply.

Although the spring was the latest known in the South for forty years, the change in latitude was abruptly marked as they neared the Gulf. They left all traces of snow behind; the grass was rank. They passed through close forests of scrub pines springing out of white sand, as on the New Jersey coast. Below the pines came heavy thickets of live-oaks, sycamores, hickories, pecans, and the bur trees, bare but for their brown knobs, while near the lagoons rose impenetrable jungles of undergrowth, knit together by thick trunks of wild grape. The road everywhere was walled in by ramparts of vegetation, to which the dwarf palmetto, sharp-bladed and defiant, and masses of bristling cacti, gave a tropical aspect.

A heavy thunder-storm darkened the last part of their journey, but as they entered Mobile the clouds rolled back, heaping themselves in vast folds upon the horizon, while a soft tender sunset glimmered through, throwing into the foreground the shaded streets of the quaint old town, the dripping, glistening magnolias and camellias in the gardens, the airy church spires, while far in the back the masts at the levee drew sharp black lines against the red sky.

They found the Battle House crowded with people returning from the Carnival at New Orleans. Mobile, French and Catholic, also had kept Mardi-Gras, and the house fronts were still gay with flags and wreaths of flowers. Half a dozen old-fashioned carriages were ranged before the hotel. The horses nodded, and the negro drivers dozed in the warm light.

"Father," said Miss Pogue, "there is 'Mosheer,' who drove us and instructed us so mightily last Mardi-Gras. Let him take us out the Bay Road. Call him. There will be time before dark."

The beautiful little Georgian had by this time insensibly assumed control of the party, managing shrewdly to save all odd ends of time, to drive good bargains with shopkeepers, and to keep hotel bills down, to the cordial approval of Mrs. Ely, who, like most women, was penny-wise.

The Major beckoned to a greasy mustached old Frenchman with a wooden leg, wearing a coat and high hat a world too big for him. "What is your name, my good fellow?"

"Mosheer Dechiré. I drive all ze strangers who come to Mobile. Carr'ge, zare," waving his whip toward a shabby open barouche. "Ver sheap."

Lola nodded approval, and they all crowded into it. No sooner had they started than "Mosheer" turned sideways, abandoning his horses to Providence, the most eager of ciceroni.

"I know Mobile, zare. Mobile knows Dechiré. I trow in my lot here tirty year ago. V'là Government Street, madame. Ze most grand boulevard in ze Souf, zey tell me. Ve zall not drive zere now. Tonight you zall see ze Shell Road. Ah-h! Eef you could zee dat Shell Road in de old times! On zis side de beautiful houses on ze pleasure-grounds; on zat, ze bay; and going to an' fro, to an' fro, ze fine carriages fill' viv lovely ladies an' les messieurs on horseback. And ah! ze horses! Mobile have horses zen zat all ze vorld know by name."

He stopped for them to see a famous grove of huge live-oaks draped with the trailing Spanish moss. They saw here, too, for the first time, the great green knobs of mistletoe, white with waxen berries, high on the yet leafless tree.

The sun was warm, the salt wind bracing; on their left hand the waters of the bay stretched, rippling and glittering, until they were lost in low silvery mists; on the right lay plantations and dwellings, many of which bore traces of old magnificence. Mosheer scrambled zealously up and down, bringing the ladies bunches of moss, of scarlet berries, of the brown seed-vessels of the bur tree. He overheard Mrs. Ely's remark that a little care would make comfortable dwellings of some neglected houses.

"Ah, madame," he cried, "you zall see no such grand mansions in ze Norf! Mobile vas a gay, rich, happy city, but ze var took her by ze troat. She begins but to breathe again. She have many rich men who push her on an' on. Ze young men zey vill make great harbor, great railroads; zey vant to hear no more of ze var"—shrugging his shoulders.

"Did you take any part in the war?" asked Mrs. Ely.

"Oui, madame. A little. Yonder" —pointing with his whip—"jus' under zat speck of cloud, I vork forty days at ze eartvorks at Fort Powell. I leave my shop. Madame Dechiré, and ze leetle chil-

BY THE ROAD-SIDE.

Drawn by W. H. Gibson.　　　　　　　　　　Engraved by F. Levin.

THE SHELL ROAD, MOBILE.

dren zey have small portion to eat zose days. I vas shoemaker by trade. Mais que voulez-vous? I vas *man*, aussi. Ah! every day ve vork, vork, and ve say, 'Notting can take zis fort!'" He had stopped the horses by this time, and was gesticulating toward the bay from his high seat, his flabby face distorted with excitement. "You see, zare? you see, madame? zat black line in ze mist is ze island, Dauphin. Jus' vhere I point my finger is Fort Morgan, von great fort, many guns. At zat side is Fort Gaines. Up ze bay—ah, it vas von day in August, ver' hot—up ze bay come ze Yankee fleet, two by two, lashed togezzer like von pack of hounds. Close to ze shore vas ze great Monitors, ze *Tecumseh* in front."

A WAY-SIDE GROUP.

"The *Tecumseh!*" exclaimed Mr. Ely. "My dear, was not George on the *Tecumseh?* A lad of whom we were very fond," he explained to the Major—"an orphan, the son of a dear friend. But go on, my good man; go on."

"Here," continued Mosheer, "vas Admiral Buchanan and our fleet. Under ze vater jus' in ze path of ze Monitors vas ze torpedoes."

"Just in the path of the Monitors," whispered the old clergyman, nervously, turning his face away quickly from them toward the bay, reddening now in the low, peaceful light.

"Yes, zare," eagerly rejoined Mosheer. "Ah-h, it is very clean vater now, you tink? Notting in it but ze fish? Look, zare; look, madame. Jus' vhere I point, your *Tecumseh* struck a torpedo an' vent down—down! I see ze water boil an' choke; zat is all. Presently it rush over an' lie smooth again. Ze great Monitor gone, like a leetle pebble sunk!"

The old clergyman did not answer; his eyes were fixed on the rippling, smiling water. His wife, who was less excitable, slid her hand under her shawl, unseen, into his, and pressed it.

"And that," she whispered, "is poor George's grave."

The Major raised his hat. "There were brave men buried there that day," he said, gently.

Mosheer broke the silence. "Yonder our Admiral attacked Farragut. Ze bay vas black viz ze smoke an' ze roar of ze cannon. An' in ze middle of it ze Yankees creep in—in on Dauphin Island. Vell"—with a shrug, gathering up his reins—"ze end had come! In four days Fort Powell vas blown away. An' our eartvorks—all gone. Mon Dieu! how my back did ache building zose eartvorks! All gone!"

"Then, I suppose," said Lola, indignantly, "you gave up the cause, and went back to your shoemaking?"

"No," with a sheepish grin. "I vas in hospital. I lose my life for dem eartvorks. Madame Dechiré et les petites zey vor hungry many days. Mais que voulez-vous? Every man had his trouble. I no vorse zan ze oders."

Mr. Ely turned his distressed face to the man, full of pity and sympathy. "The war never seemed so real to me before," he said; "that is, your side of it."

"But, my good man," interrupted Mrs. Ely, severely, "why did you go into the war at all? You were a foreigner: had you no respect for the flag or the constitution of your adopted country?"

"Perhaps he believed in State rights?" suggested Miss Pogue, slyly.

"State rights an' ze constitooshun? I know notting about dem. But here vas my home—here in Mobile. I trow in my lot here tirty year ago. Mine leetle house vas here, an' mine vife. So I fight. Eef I had live in New York, viv my leetle house, an' ze Souf come to fight, I—I can-

not tell. It may be I zall be Yankee—moi!"

The men laughed, but both the ladies were indignant.

"Northern men went into the war with a principle!" cried the older woman.

"And Southern men," exclaimed Lola, "gave their lives for a great cause! But this man talks as if patriotism was a matter of geography."

"Hush-h! I am afraid, my dear, that Mosheer speaks for a large party on both sides," said her father.

After the first day, the travellers had no more occasion for Mosheer's services. Major Pogue and Colonel Mocquard had a few friends in the city, and as soon as it was known that they were at the hotel,

THE OLD BONE MAN.

Drawn by W. H. Gibson.

RED-SNAPPER FISHING.

they, with the clergyman and his wife, were welcomed as though they were visiting princes, and overwhelmed with invitations to dine, to drive, to spend evenings, days, weeks, with their new friends.

Good Mr. Ely was in raptures with this cordiality. "It renews one's faith in human nature," he said to his wife as they were dressing for dinner, brushing his thin gray locks up to cover his bald pate. "I told you how it was in Virginia, my dear. And to think how we have fought them since and ruined them, and that they are the first to hold out their hands in friendship! I wish all Northerners could come down and see these people as they are. Great heavens! what injustice we do them!"

"My dear!" said his wife, reprovingly. She had not quite made up her mind in this matter. She was very silent when with her new acquaintances, and could not enter, as her husband did, with fervor into their pride in the "stately buildings," the "magnificent streets," etc., of Mobile, described in guides to the Exposition. Secretly she thought the Southerners a good deal like children, as vain, and as thin-skinned to criticism, and suspected that the war had probably been useful as dis-

cipline in lowering their self-conceit. Like many other Northern visitors to the Exposition last winter, she was always startled to find among "our enemies" the same good sense, feeling, or knowledge that she expected as a matter of course from her own people. Her husband, on the contrary, criticised nothing. "Why should I?" he said. "Because we had the most money and the most men twenty years ago, does that give me the right to come down here and sneer at their cows, their horses, their manners; or even to pat them approvingly on the head?"

He urged all of his new friends to visit him in Pennsylvania. He preached on Sunday in one of the city churches on "human brotherhood" out of so full a heart that the tears rose to the eyes of many a prejudiced hearer. Everybody accepted and trusted the old man. "I shall think better of the world because he was born in it," said Colonel Mocquard.

But even Mrs. Ely at last confessed that Mobile was a beautiful city, unlike any other. She is charming, rather than stately. Like Savannah, Charleston, and the French quarter of New Orleans, she still remains characteristically Southern. Her avenues are broad and well shaded; the dwellings large and airy, and half hidden in exquisite gardens and sloping lawns. Even in the poorer streets roses, magnolias, camellias, and jasmine fill the air with fragrance. The pretentious brick houses with Mansard-roofs and colored glass, so common in Eastern cities, which the Northern and Jewish new-comers are beginning to erect in some of the Southern towns (quite unconscious, apparently, that they are not only ugly, but totally unsuited to a warm, damp climate), have not as yet vulgarized Mobile's old-time grace. She turns to the stranger a quiet, home-like, friendly face, with that undefinable gracious air of good-breeding in it which only generations of ease and hospitality can give even to houses. No money or architect can impart it to blocks of magnificent mansions built for display.

Among their new friends was a Madame de Parras, a bent, white-haired old lady of eighty, who was lodging in a cheap house in St. Joseph Street.

"Over a bakery, my dear," explained Mr. Ely to his wife, who had not then seen her. "But she might have been a duchess, in the days of the Bourbons, from her manners. With her brilliant black eyes and white hair, leaning on her ebony cane with its floating ribbons, you could not imagine a more picturesque figure. She is a descendant of a Marquis de Parras, who came to this country with the French refugees in 1816, and settled in Marengo County."

"You find so many black swans!" complained Mrs. Ely. "Why does this princess lodge over a bakery?"

"Because she is a dethroned princess, I suppose," said Mr. Ely. "An old friend of Mocquard's. She reigned in New Orleans in her days of power, and she is on her way there now from a poor plantation on the Tombigbee. She has a little granddaughter with her. I don't think," he added, hesitating, "that the war or poverty has inoculated them with any Northern energy, as they have your friend Miss Pogue."

"Lola might have been a New-Englander," said Mrs. Ely for the twentieth time. "She is just the woman to help on Colonel Mocquard's fortunes. Pushing, close—"

"Men don't usually look first for those qualities in a wife," said Mr. Ely, impatiently. "And I suspect that Southern women will gain such virtues out of their poverty much sooner than Southern men

will learn to admire them in their wives and sweethearts."

"Probably. I don't pretend to understand men," said Mrs. Ely, with calm superiority.

The next day they went on an exploring expedition to Point Clear, with the Major and his daughter, Colonel Mocquard and some friends from Mobile, among them Madame de Parras.

"Is that her granddaughter in the brown flannel dress?" asked Mrs. Ely, when they were on the little steamer *Annie*.

"Yes; and a lovely little creature she is," replied the clergyman.

"I do not agree with you," she answered, quickly. "I should call her positively homely. She is nothing but a child. I must say I like some style in a girl. You would not find a Northern young lady cling to her grandmother's side and blush when she is spoken to in that way. Yet she sent Major Pogue on an errand just now as calmly as I should a servant."

"Southern women are taught to believe that they are born with a sceptre in their hands. I suspect, my dear," he added, slyly, "that Mocquard agrees with me in my opinion of this little girl."

"Absurd! I give him credit for too much hard common-sense. He wants a capable manager as a wife, with his children and straitened means. What could a chit like that, made up of eyes and a smile, do for him?"

Mr. Ely shrugged his shoulders, and strolled to the end of the boat to listen to Major Pogue, who was descanting on the merits of Point Clear as a winter resort for Northerners. The Major, with many other shrewd capitalists in the South, had foreseen the large profits to be made by the growing habit of migration among invalids, and had invested a little money and much thought and time in building up different resorts in Florida, Georgia, and the North Carolina mountains.

"The time for drugs is over," he was saying now, while a group of sallow, coughing travellers wrapped in furs gathered close, listening eagerly. "A famous physician in the North once said to me, 'Give me the air I want for my patients, and I will not give them a dose of medicine.' Well, sir, now he can have every kind and quality of air he wants, from the warm damp breezes off the Gulf, in Florida or Louisiana, to the bracing dry winds in the piny woods in Georgia or northern Alabama or the Carolinas. Our people understand now what is wanted. You will find well-kept hotels at all these places. Point Clear is a little jut of land running out into Mobile Bay, about halfway between the city and the Gulf, and it is claimed that the climate is equal to that of Florida. Any of the resorts on the Gulf frequented by Southerners in summer ought to be suitable for invalids from the North in winter."

Lola, who was sitting by Mrs. Ely, laughed. "I suppose the South may count your invalids among her new 'industries,' just as your farmers, they tell me, reckon summer boarders a more profitable crop than potatoes. Of course one is sorry for the poor creatures, but these migrating invalids papa talks of are becoming quite too marked a feature of Southern travel, it seems to me."

Little Betty de Parras turned with quick assent, her brown eyes wide with pity. "Oh, we have met them everywhere! So pale and weak, some of them just ready to die. And one can do nothing—not even speak."

"Dear me! I don't want to speak," answered Lola. "They mass themselves together in cars and hotel parlors, and discuss their pills and symptoms. 'Did you try Aiken?' and 'How did Pensacola suit you?' It is horrible: the poor spectres racing from point to point catching at every hope. The Dance of Death is cheerful to it."

"If one could do anything!" said Betty, under her breath, the tears coming to her eyes.

"It sounded very heartless in Lola, I confess," said Mrs. Ely to her husband afterward, when the girls walked away; "yet no doubt she would be the most efficient nurse of the two, if put to the test. She has a remarkable skill in giving drugs, her mother told me—doses all the negroes on the plantation."

"Perhaps so. But that little girl's pitying eyes and soft pat of the hand would go farther than drugs to cure me," he persisted, obstinately.

There is a large hotel at Point Clear, the porches of which overlook the bay. The men of the party went out fishing, bringing in drum, red-fish, and a red-snapper caught by the old clergyman, to his great delight.

They came back to the city in high spirits the next morning, a brisk west wind feathering the waters of the bay, and driving bright flakes of cloud across the sky with sudden jubilant gusts.

During the fortnight that followed, Mr. Ely and Colonel Mocquard explored every quarter of the quaint old city. A singular *camaraderie* had sprung up between the old clergyman and the Confederate soldier. They spent whole days fishing together at the Snapper Banks in the Gulf, or hunting among the lagoons which empty into the bay, sitting sometimes for hours on some sunken log in the wild tangle of vines and bushes, with blazing colors in every weed about them, in eager talk, their guns idle at their feet; or they loitered along the wharves or through the cotton-mills. The older man had keen perceptions and sympathies, and at every step he was moved and excited by some dramatic revelation in the lives of these people who were struggling to their feet after savage disaster. They often drove out through the groves of magnolias and live-oaks which hedge in Mobile. The environs are full of quiet beauty; pleasant country-seats are set on the crests and in the valleys of the wooded hills which rise in low ranges behind it. Spring Hill contains the prettiest of these homes, and is to Mobile what Bryn Mawr is to Philadelphia, or the shores of the Hudson to New York.

Here lives the most famous woman, probably, of the South — Mrs. Augusta Evans Wilson, the author of *Beulah*, *Macaria*, etc. She is held in as proud regard by the mass of Southern people as was George Eliot by the English. Her beautiful home on Spring Hill is a kind of Mecca to which her admirers make pilgrimages.

"All American authors," said Mr. Ely, "should be born in Boston or the far South."

"The South never neglects her gifted children," replied Colonel Mocquard, gravely, "when they are true to her."

The Colonel never tired of hunting out with Mr. Ely traces of the first settlers on the coast. The old clergyman took a keen interest in the romantic story of the three noble brothers who discovered and colonized the coast for France. He insisted on going down to Dauphin Island. "Just here, I fancy," he said, after long consideration, "the lad Bienville first leaped on shore, and here was the heap of human bones which made him call it the Isle of Massacre."

Colonel Mocquard showed him the point on the island on which tradition states young Bienville, coming back from Biloxi two years later, with his younger brother and La Salle, built a warehouse for their stores, and the location of the fort, St. Louis de la Mobile, at the mouth of Dog River.

"The Quaker botanist, old William Bartram," he said, "found the ruins of the fort here in 1777. But it was at the mouth of Mobile River that the two brothers built their principal forts and huts of unbarked trunks of trees covered with earth and palmetto leaves. Close by their fort was the temple of the tribe of the Mobilians, in which a light burned that never was suffered to go out. All the Southern tribes of Indians came here for their holy fire. It was in one of these huts that De Sanvolle, the younger of the lads, died, and when D'Iberville, the eldest of the brothers, sailed up the bay a week afterward, he found Bienville standing alone on the shore to welcome him. The tradition is that he took the boy in his arms and they wept aloud. D'Iberville died soon afterward, and Bienville was left alone."

"The whole story of that man is tragic to me," said Mr. Ely, enthusiastically. "I always believed him to be a true knight by nature as by birth. Conceive the horrible solitude of life here for such a man, chivalric, sensitive, in a miserable little colony on the edge of a wilderness that covered the continent, peopled by wild beasts and savages, and the colony made up of men who for forty years hated and maligned him! Yes, sir, Bienville was one of those gentle, heroic souls that grew and flourished in the hardships of the early history of the Southern colonies. We do not pay them honor enough. Look what New England has done for her grim, bigoted forefathers!"

The Colonel laughed. "No doubt Bienville was a courageous and tough fellow. He certainly persisted in founding trading sites throughout the wilds and jungles of lower Louisiana at the risk of his office and his life. But the proofs of his gentleness are not so clear to me. It was owing to his obstinate whim, you remember, that the capital of the State was placed in the mud flats where New Or-

leans now stands, below the level of the river, rather than on the dry sandy height of Biloxi. And he had a habit of chopping off the heads of men who displeased him, which was eccentric even in that day. Eighteen at once, here in Mobile, if I remember rightly."

Mr. Ely laughed feebly, and hastily turned his inquiries to the truth of the legend that the wife of Alexis, the son of Peter the Great, had escaped from her brutal husband and fled to the French settlements on the Gulf, becoming one of the pioneers in the little hamlet of Mobile.

"It may be true," said Mocquard. "The history of the early French and Spanish colonies along this coast is full of romance. Love and jealousy and a mad passion for adventure had more to do with bringing Bienville, De Cadillac, and even De la Salle half round the world into these bayoux and jungles than any hope of gain."

"Those ancient traditions, with the background of this tropical scenery, are a fine untrodden field for some American novelist," said Mr. Ely, and hinted that a cousin of his own, a promising young journalist in Massachusetts, was just the man to use this "material."

But Colonel Mocquard dryly observed that probably only a Southern hand could do justice to it, and suggested that it was not too late for an afternoon's fishing.

Mrs. Ely became impatient with this idle loitering. She had gone through Mobile with the energy of the intelligent American sight-seer, had visited the Medical College, the ice factory, the markets, the Marine Hospital, had astonished the Sisters with extraordinary questions in the Academy of Visitation, and was familiar with all the handsome houses on Government Street. She was urgent now that they should go on and see something else, and told Mr. Ely so when he came in from one of his long expeditions.

"I wish we could stay," he sighed. "I am in love with this quaint old town. If I could breathe this balmy, warm air for a year or two I should be as indolent and ready to let the world wag its own way as the old-time Southerner ever was. I don't blame him. If Sumner or Garrison had been born on one of these sleepy plantations, with a thousand darkies to earn his living and wait on him, breathing the bay air loaded with the scent of magnolias all his life, he would have been as conservative as Mocquard. Character is much more a matter of the thermometer than you think, my dear."

Mrs. Ely, who was knitting at some soft woollen stuff, listened with the patience that she felt was always due to a man's whims.

"I think we had better go on," she said, quietly. "You will probably be quite as enthusiastic about New Orleans."

"We shall never see Mobile again as it is now, I am convinced," he persisted. "The charm of its quiet and calm will soon be gone. The whole South is fast losing its repose and identity. It used to be delightful to drop out of the hurry and struggle of the North into this sunny, drowsy calm, where nobody was in a hurry. But they are beginning to drive and push here everywhere just as we do."

"Time for them!" ejaculated his wife.

"As for Mobile," he continued, earnestly, "it must be the chief sea-port of the Gulf States. That is inevitable. And when these new industries are developed, here is their outlet. Consider the enormous advance made by this State in the last ten years—the opening up of her coal and iron regions, the lumbering trade, the capital invested in manufactories! Why, the State is as rich as Pennsylvania in her natural resources. Here in Mobile must be the centre of her foreign trade. A very few years will make it the New York of the South. But its charm will be gone then for me."

"I am sure I hope you are right," she said. "But I think we had better go on. You and Colonel Mocquard would poke about hunting up historical points for months. Major Pogue proposes that we shall stop at one or two quiet little villages between here and New Orleans that he is interested in as winter resorts. We have seen everything here but the cemeteries, and we will go to them this morning. Lola says we had better take the noon train to-morrow."

"Oh! if you and Miss Pogue have decided it, there is no more to be said. But I don't want to see your cemeteries."

"I never feel that I have done a town properly until I see where they put their dead," said his wife, placidly snapping off a thread.

Late that evening, accordingly, a stout lady in black, accompanied by two slight girlish figures, strolled down the grassy avenues of a large burying-ground in the outskirts of the city. She stopped to read the inscriptions on all the more costly monuments, while the girls glanced impatiently toward the carriage waiting at the gate. The wind from the bay blew sharp and damp; the sky had sunk down overhead flat and lead-colored; the sun hung like a fiery ball ready to drop out of sight.

"Yes, yes; I'm coming. It is late. I feel quite ready for tea. But look at this shaft. It must belong to a family of importance. Have you no idea of the cost, my dear? Dear me, there is a carriage coming along the road. Who can it be?"

"It is Mosheer bringing Mr. Ely and Colonel Mocquard," said Betty, with a gurgle of delight. "Thank goodness! I thought they would come to take us home safely."

"Safely? What on earth could happen to you, child?"

"Oh, it is nearly dark. We ought to have a gentleman to take care of us," lisped Betty, in her soft cooing voice, as she ran forward and caught the old clergyman by the arm.

Mrs. Ely glanced significantly from the Colonel's approaching figure to Lola. "I don't know how much devotion girls expect nowadays, but when I was young such watchful care of me would have touched me very much."

Lola gave an astonished glance at Mrs. Ely and the Colonel. "I don't know what you mean," she stammered.

"Do you not? then you are duller than I thought you," said the old lady, calmly, going forward to meet her husband.

Lola stood motionless, staring at the lichen on a head-stone, a red heat rising slowly to her face underneath the chalk and touch of rouge, with which, like too many Southern girls, she usually covered her pretty skin.

Care of her?

Could this be true? Miss Pogue was not the kind of woman who in any circumstances would give all for love and count the world well lost. But the circumstances of her life had kept the idea of love and marriage further in the background than with ordinary women. She had shared in her father's struggles for the necessities and at last the luxuries of life. These were the sharp realities which kept her shrewd, practical brain busy. But Lola was not a mercenary woman.

The idea that Dupré Mocquard, after all his hard fight in the world, loved her, and wished to make her his wife, touched her. A deep wave of feeling seemed to surge up in her brain and heart. It startled herself. Was it possible that she was in love, and with this man? She looked at him keenly as he came toward her between the cypress-trees and white shafts. He was not a young man, but he had the face and figure to which a Southern woman, however practical, would pay homage. One of Arthur's knights might have looked like this overseer.

"He need no longer be overseer—if—papa could take him into partnership in the mills. He lives in the Mocquard house, and I could keep it up in its old state for one-half the money he wastes with a house-keeper and lazy negroes. As for the children — are there four or five?" Her eyes kindled as these thoughts flashed through her mind. The untidy house, the children, the lazy servants, quickened and warmed her blood as the sight of a disorderly regiment would kindle the wits of an energetic drill-sergeant.

Colonel Mocquard, when he came up, fancied that Miss Pogue, for whose blond beauty he had a fervent appreciation, appeared embarrassed and irritated.

"Do let us go home," she said, turning shortly away. "I want to get among living things again. I have no sympathy with dead people. Come, Betty."

She walked quickly toward the carriage; but Betty, all of whose motions were slow and gentle, looked at the graves,

her brown eyes full of pity. "Suppose they could hear her?" she murmured, with a scared, nervous laugh. "Not sorry for them! To think of them alone here, and that we cannot reach them or do anything for them never again!"

"There are the living still for you to help, Cousin Betty," said Colonel Mocquard, offering her his arm, and bending over her with a wistful face as they went down the avenue.

"That child's heart is full of longing to comfort and work for others—even the dead," said the clergyman, as he followed with his wife.

"Ah," she snapped, sharply, "I would rather see a little work with the hands than all these heart-longings. She cannot button her own shoes. Why, poor as that girl and her grandmother are, she must have a negro maid to dress her like a baby. Help others, indeed!"

"Madame de Parras clings to the old usages," stammered Mr. Ely.

"A pretty wife for the Colonel!" grumbled Mrs. Ely. "But it's no affair of mine."

"No, my dear," said her husband, plucking up courage. "It is not, happily. And, after all, a man does not want the work of her hands from his wife so much as sympathy and companionship. You," he added, earnestly, "gave both, Jane."

Her old face was warm and smiling as she entered the carriage, and she beamed graciously even on little Betty as they drove back to the city.

HERE AND THERE IN THE SOUTH.

BY REBECCA HARDING DAVIS

III.—ALONG THE GULF.

"WE have all agreed, I believe, to make our first halt at Biloxi, in Mississippi," said Mr. Ely, as the train with our tourists on board rolled out of Mobile.

"And why Biloxi?" asked his wife.

"Ah, madame," said Madame de Parras, "do you not know it is the town nearest to the Beauvoir plantations? I am sure we shall all wish to pay our respects to President Davis."

"Biloxi," said Major Pogue, "is a place which ought to be a winter resort for Northern invalids. I am interested in bringing it into notice. I want you to see it."

"Biloxi," exclaimed Mr. Ely, eagerly, "is the point where Iberville with Bienville and the Franciscan Père Athanase landed and built the first fort. It must be full of traces of those old adventurers. Mocquard and I intend to search them out."

"*I* want to stop at the town," said Lola, "to lay in a supply of preserved figs and of shrimps for the family. There are large canning houses there, and I expect to save ten per cent. by buying wholesale."

"Mr. Ely is going to take me fishing," lisped Betty, with an ecstatic gurgle. "Some people that my grand'mère knows in New Orleans have a summer cottage in Biloxi. They told me that they bathe and fish, and picnic in the pine woods. Only think how delicious!" shutting her eyes and shaking her curly head in a way which made Major Pogue and the old clergyman exchange looks of delight, while Mrs. Ely groaned inwardly at the hopeless imbecility of men. She began instantly to question Lola as to the prices of canned vegetables in New Orleans, hoping that Colonel Mocquard would hear how well posted the young lady was in the state of the market.

Biloxi is a long scrambling village, built on a ledge of sand-hills between the bay and quiet stretches of pine woods that roll back over Harrison County.

"The very place for invalids with incipient throat troubles!" Major Pogue declared, enthusiastically. "The south wind blows to them straight from off the Gulf of Mexico, and the north wind sifts all the healing for them out of these pine forests."

Biloxi is but little known as yet as a winter health resort. Our travellers found an old-fashioned inn among the few houses that were open; a pile of galleries in tiers about a court into which cozy little chambers opened, each with its cheery fire and canopied French bed. A creole family had it in charge. What they lacked in English they made up in gestures and good-humor. The house was full of consumptive and asthmatic patients from the Southern States, with a few from Chicago and other points in the Northwest. The average American meets even death with good-humored *sang-froid*. These pale doomed folk made up fishing parties every morning, and sailed away, coughing and singing, to the islands which lay like blots of shadow in the rolling fogs of billowy silver that filled the bay; they came back, coughing, chattering, and joyous, in the evening, up out of the red sunset, with enormous loads of fish, which they displayed in the court-yard of the inn, under the lamps which hung in the huge live-oaks, while their wives and children and the negroes gathered about them as excited as if these were the first fish ever haled out of that water.

There was a delightful disorder and spontaneity in the whole place. At uncertain hours a gray old negro went through the galleries shouting "Breakfast," or "Dinner," or "Supper," as if it had just occurred to him that somebody might be hungry, and everybody set out in search of a remote dining-room, to find a plentiful meal, peppery and high-flavored, after the creole fashion. After supper everybody, again headed by the invalids, crowded into the cheery little parlor, and danced as merrily as if they had just drawn out new title-deeds to life and youth.

The greasy court-yard with its clumps of live-oaks stretched down to the bay, thrusting long fingers of piers in to clutch the water. On both of the curving shores on either side rows of large hotels or restaurants faced the bay. They were closed now, and tenanted only by melancholy cats, which prowled about their empty galleries.

"Biloxi is a resort in summer for monstrous excursion or fishing parties from New Orleans," explained Major Pogue, as they sauntered through the deserted wharves and silent hotels.

"And they drink beer occasionally," suggested Mr. Ely, nodding to the vast heaps of empty bottles in the courts. Back in the village, too, which straggled through green lanes into the edge of the woods, they found millions of these stone and glass bottles, stuck inverted in the ground to make borders for flower beds in the gardens, or as curb-stones for the sidewalks. Mrs. Ely was so appalled at the seas of beer which these endless gray and black lines indicated that she began to drop temperance tracts into the pretty flower-gardens and to thrust them under the front doors.

"I always take a supply with me to carry on the good work," she explained, nervously, to Miss Pogue, who watched her with polite astonishment. "And really the amount of liquor consumed in the South must be enormous! The incessant treating that even I have seen dismays me."

Mr. Ely, noticing the angry color on Lola's cheek, hastily interposed. "Yes, yes, my dear; we hear a great deal at home about the amount of drinking in the South, but we forget the cause. The uneventful, solitary life on farms or plantations always drives men to some kind of devil's work. In the cattle-herding ranches of the Northwest, I've been told, tacks the Southerner. He grows morbid; he becomes disgusted with his wife, and takes another. 'Bills' of divorce have made the domestic relations of some of

preachers of temperance. Our young men, as they are brought into friction with the world, will find out the folly and vulgarity of this perpetual tippling."

A TYPICAL HOUSE.

our communities almost as unsettled as those of Utah. He grows disgusted next with orthodox forms of religion; he begins to taste all kinds of heterodoxy, spiritualism, Buddhism, and the rest. Better tipple in whiskey than in free-thinking, in my judgment. The Southerner is better fed in body, and has a healthier mind. He may drink, but he worships sincerely in the faith his mother taught him, and he is, as a rule, a faithful and fond husband and father. The moral shortcomings of both sections arise, as I said, from precisely the same cause. The pot need not sneer at the kettle."

"You're right there, Mr. Ely!" exclaimed the Major. "For generations our men had little to do; they were idle, friendly, hospitable. The rest goes without saying. There is much less brandy drunk now than before our people went to work —much less. You're right. Occupation, work, prosperity—these are the best

Now and then a party of enthusiastic Georgians or Mississippians, or curious Northerners, visitors to the New Orleans Exposition, would run up to Biloxi and drive out through the pines to the Beauvoir plantations to call on the ex-President of the Confederacy, from whom they all received a courteous welcome. Mrs. Ely sternly repulsed any meek hints of a desire to go with them from her husband as disloyal.

"I have a natural curiosity, my dear," he reasoned, "to meet and judge for myself a historical character."

"Have you no respect for the flag?" she demanded. "I never expected to find you, at this late day, aiding and abetting rebellion!"

Mr. Ely, as usual, did not argue with his wife. The next day, however, when Madame de Parras and her granddaughter went out for a drive, the clergyman and Colonel Mocquard accompanied them.

BAY SAINT LOUIS.

The whole party came home, excited and pleased, late in the evening, wearing bunches of white pinks on their breasts, which the ladies hastened to put away as sacred relics. They observed a significant silence while they ate their suppers, and Mrs. Ely thought it wise to ask no questions.

When they left Biloxi, however, taking the railway which follows the coast closely to New Orleans, she was the most eager of the party to catch sight of the plain wooden farm-house at Beauvoir, dimly seen through groves of pine.

The coast-line nearing New Orleans is set with picturesque little villages—Ocean Springs, Moss Point, Mississippi City, Bay St. Louis, and Pass Christian, some of them the summer resorts of Louisianians since the last century. They are all alike in feature—airy, hospitable cottages set in the midst of groves of enormous live-oaks,

STREET IN PASS CHRISTIAN.

DOMESTIC DEFENCES.

draped with gray moss, which the wind incessantly sways to and fro: quiet lanes winding through thickets of cypress, magnolia, and palmetto trees; everywhere roses, thrusting themselves up to perfume the air, covering the houses, the trunks of the trees, the ground, with sudden flames of crimson and gold; in the background a rampart, dark and gloomy, of pine forests; and in front the Gulf, stretching to the horizon, a vast shifting plane which in this peculiar shadeless sunlight incessantly glows with opalescent tints strange to Northern eyes.

The march of improvement is at work, however, on these beautiful little nooks, building a line of canning factories and huge hotels from Mobile to the Mississippi.

Mrs. Ely besought her friends to push on to New Orleans. "There will soon be nothing left distinctively Southern here but the weather and the foliage," she complained. "This hotel might have been transplanted from New York: gas, electric bells, cookery; and all this ash furniture is from Grand Rapids; the clerk and the landlord are Connecticut men, and most of the guests are Chicagoans. I went to-day out of that grove of magnolias directly into a Sixth Avenue auction store, with its piles of ready-made clothes, gilt jewelry, cheap soap, and vases. There was the Jewish sales-lady with her black bang, bracelets, and hooked nose. 'Did this store come entire from New York?' I asked. 'Just as you see it, ma'am. And me too,' she said, with a smirk."

NOTES FROM THE CREOLE QUARTER.

"You could repeat your experience in every town in the South," said the Major. "But when we reach New Orleans I promise to find you some corners which belonged to the France of a hundred years ago."

It was to this French quarter of New Orleans that Mr. Ely, when they reached that city, gave himself up wholly. His wife and Miss Pogue "did" the Exposi-tion thoroughly; they repaired early every morning to Canal Street to secure seats in the Prytania Street cars; they priced every exhibit; they knew just where to find the cheapest sandwiches in the cafés.

"Nobody," Mrs. Ely (still bent on match-making) told Colonel Mocquard, "had viewed the Exposition more intelligently and economically than Miss

Pogue." But the Colonel, while he had the most vivid admiration for Lola's golden hair and blue eyes, had no appreciation of economy or intelligence in any woman.

"He is a very narrow-minded man; he very seldom finds his way to the Exposition," Mrs. Ely complained in her nightly gossip to her husband; "and when he does come, is quite taken up with cotton-gins and steam-ploughs. And he's a creole, too! Lola speaks of him as a typical Southerner—a fire-eater and duellist, and full of chivalry. But he goes about like the rest of them in a narrow-rimmed hat, poking into cotton-gins and ploughs. I must say I'm disappointed."

Mrs. Ely, like the majority of Northerners at the Exposition, was perpetually in search of something "typically Southern." She went to the French Market on Sunday morning with the mob of tourists, and fell a victim to the Jew peddlers who had orange-wood canes for sale manufactured of pine in New York. She promenaded the Boulevard Esplanade, looking out for Mr. Cable's creoles, and regarding every old man with white hair and black eyes with awe as a possible Grandissime. She made vain pretences of asking her way from people whom she fancied were Legrees, or Madame Delphines, or Texan cow-boys; but they all turned out to be from Duluth or Chicago. She had heard all her life of the wickedness of New Orleans, and she took a fearful joy in venturing into quarters which were said to be its worst haunts; but they now turned gay, decent faces to the passing stranger.

The splendor of the private hospitality in New Orleans overpowered the good woman. She wrote home to the Ladies' Sewing Circle of magnificent banquets to which she was bidden, and of the simple, unpretending people who gave them. She described minutely some of the immense private houses, set in sloping lawns, with fountains, and groves of palm, and orange-trees heavy with golden fruit. The long galleries at the back, as in Eastern houses, closed around an open green court. "Forty chambers I counted in one," she wrote, "and all filled with guests during Mardi Gras. And the mistress of it, who once counted her slaves by the thousand, a meek, quiet little Presbyterian body, who insisted on making a plaster herself for my rheumatic shoulder. Indeed, I wish

you knew these people better in the North. The closer you come to them, the more you find they are very much like ourselves at heart."

The Exposition bewildered and stunned her husband. After a day or two he forsook it, and set out to study historic New Orleans, Colonel Mocquard willingly neglecting his business to go with him. When Major Pogue escorted the rest of the party down the river to inspect the jetties, the two cronies refused to go, being impatient to hunt out the precise spot on the miles of levees, now crowded with shipping from all the world, where Bienville first sprang to the shore of the untrodden wilderness from his little barkentine.

"I look upon this great city," the clergyman said to Colonel Mocquard, "as the outgrowth of the dogged obstinacy of that one man. Was there ever so mad a thing done as to found the capital of a great territory a hundred miles from a harbor, on a swamp lower than the water on either side, with a perpetual fight for life before it against tides, wind, and fever?—and in spite of the constant opposition of the French government. I am convinced, too, that Bienville foresaw the future importance of these possessions, or he would not have persisted in founding colonies among the jungles as high as Natchez."

The two enthusiasts traced from point to point the strange drama played by the old town, in which French and Spaniards of good blood, Irish refugees, negroes and Indians, were actors. Down in the lower part of the French quarter stood the first orange and fig groves planted by Governor Perrier. In the Faubourg de Ste. Marie the Jesuit fathers planted the slips of sugar-cane, a gift sent them by their brethren in San Domingo, together with a few slaves skilled in its culture.

On the levee below the French Market landed the first slaves, the thousand Children of the Sun imported by Bienville into the miserable little hamlet. A few feet from this spot Governor Du Perrier burned six Natchez braves at the stake. Here, too, guarded by priests and *Sœurs de la Charité*, were brought ashore the pious maidens, each with her box of linen, sent from France by the Church to be wives to Bienville's followers. Several of the old families of New Orleans still sacredly treasure relics of a revered ancestress who was one of these *filles de la cassette.* The Colonel recalled to Mr. Ely an old tradition, that with each importation these pious maidens grew uglier, until General Duclos was forced to hint that his men would prefer more beauty, even with less solid virtue.

In the old Place d'Armes, fronting the Cathedral of St. Louis, Bienville gave to his colony a name; here the citizens met to revolt against their cession to Spain; and here they welcomed victorious Jackson after the battle of Chalmette.

They followed up the traces of Spanish occupation with great difficulty. But two decayed old buildings remained to tell of that stormy period.

"Philadelphia and New Orleans have a more dramatic history than any towns on the continent," grumbled Mr. Ely, "yet they are the most indifferent to their ancient landmarks."

Wandering through the Exposition buildings he found hints of every phase of Southern life. There was, most prominent of all, the portly, florid business man, the railway magnate, iron manufacturer, banker, merchant, usually heavily bearded, full-voiced, keen-eyed, a trifle more masculine, more aggressive, more genial and grandiloquent in ideas and words, than his congener of New York or Philadelphia. There was the rawboned, grizzled planter from upper Mississippi, with his flock of eager boys and girls about him. "Enohmously expensive trip, suh, to bring them all," he told Mr. Ely, anxiously; "but it's a chance foh education I cahn't afford to throw away foh them, suh." There were crowds of country girls with thick ivory skins and black eyes, more carefully chaperoned, more beplumed, beflounced, and powdered, than their Northern sisters, but for the rest members of the same giggling, flirting, innocent flock. There was now and then a French overseer or an American workman from some inland parish, speaking a *patois* quite unintelligible to Mr. Ely. But he found in the manner of many men of this class a deference to their employers, a tacit acknowledgment of inferior social station, quite impossible to the mechanic of Pennsylvania or the West. He did not, oddly enough, find this survival of the habits of the old *régime* among the negroes, except in an occasional gray-haired freedman not yet quite sure that he was free.

Occasionally he met one of the gentle-women of that same old *régime*, well guarded by the men of her family, graceful, white-handed, with that sweet, pathetic treble in her voice also peculiar to Virginian women (quite different from the unctuous Georgian drawl). There was always about her, too, an air of perpetual appeal for protection, and yet something beneath it which told you that she was an absolute monarch in her own sphere. The clergyman found a charm in this imperious helplessness, which touched him more nearly than the self-reliance of Mrs. Ely's friends at home. When one of these women had gone by he felt as if he had heard a verse of a song, sweet and familiar, but of which he had lost the beginning and the end.

In the evenings the negroes arrived in crowds, gayly dressed, chattering a bastard French.

There were ranchmen from Texas, German, Irish, and English; cow-boys; hosts of the wives of small planters, curious, intelligent, and voluble ; judges from South Carolina, colonels from Georgia, orange-growers from Florida—all unlike, yet alike in the uneasy air of having come up out of some remote place where they ruled into a crowd where they were insignificant. In no city in this country could such an exhibition have called together an audience as foreign or as vivid in its contrasts.

The singular dual life of the Crescent City took vehement hold of the imagination of the old clergyman.

On one side of its great artery, Canal Street, is a powerful American city, firmly established, fully abreast of the trade and industry of the time, and clutching eagerly for its share of the commerce of the world. It is vitalized now with an energy which, if not pure Yankee in character, is very closely akin to it.

Here are miles of wharves heaped with cotton and sugar; thoroughfares massively built, through which the endless tides of human life ebb and flow all day; magnificent avenues stretching away out to the country, lined with modern hotels, club-houses, and huge dwellings, each flanked by one or two picturesque towers, which, on inspection, turn out to be only cisterns.

There is the necessary complement of black shadow below these vivid high lights. Poverty and Vice live more out-of-doors in New Orleans than in Northern cities. There they are, barefaced, leering, always on the familiar pave, to be seen and known of all men. Back of all signs of wealth and gayety, too, is the mud, a material, clammy horror. The water, a deadly enemy here, perpetually fought and forced back, rushes in, whenever a day's rain gives it vantage, at every crevice; floods the streets and clogs the drains. It oozes out of the ground wherever you step on it, drips down the walls of your drawing-room, stains your books a coffee-color, clings to you, chilly and damp, in your clothes and in your bed, turns the air you breathe into a cold steam, and washes your dead out of their graves.

"This Queen of the South has soiled and muddy robes," said Mr. Ely; "but she is still a queen."

He delighted to stroll in the afternoon with the Colonel across Canal Street, to find this lusty American city vanish suddenly, and to enter a quiet French provincial town of the days of Louis XIV. Here was no stir, no clamor.

"Voilà la vraie Nouvelle Orléans!" lisped little Betty, as she guided him for the first time into the labyrinth of narrow streets branching off of La Rue Royale. It was her old home, and very beautiful and dear to her. Madame de Parras was confined to the house with rheumatism, and was willing to trust her to the escort of her reverend friend. So the old man and the girl, being about the same age ("as old as the Babes in the Wood," quoth Mrs. Ely), fell into the habit of strolling in the early morning or gathering twilight through the net-work of oddly silent streets, so narrow that the overhanging eaves nearly met over the cobble-stone pavements. Steep roofs, scaled with earthen tiles and green with moss, hooded dormer-windows peeping out of them like half-shut eyes, rose abruptly from the one-storied houses. Here and there a cobbler sat on his bench in the street plying his awl and singing to himself, or a group of swarthy, half-naked boys knelt on the banquette, flinging their arms about in a gambling game for pennies, and shrieking in some wild dialect, half negro and half French.

Their walks usually ended on the Boulevard Esplanade. Even that wide thoroughfare fell into quiet in the afternoon as the long shadows of the trees lay heavily across it. Within the close walls they could catch a glimpse of the courts about which the houses are built, the glitter of fountains shaded by orange-trees and broad-leaved tropical plants. Sometimes a jalousied window would be left open, and they would catch the tinkle of a guitar or the sound of a woman's voice singing.

Mr. Ely, like most Northerners, knowing New Orleans only through Mr. Cable's marvellous pictures, spoke of them once or twice to Betty. But she shook her head impatiently. She would not hear of these photographs of herself and her creole kinsfolk.

"Why put us in a magazine story to amuse the world?" she demanded. "You should read Gayarré's books on Louisiana, or Picket on Alabama. They are books of dignity, monsieur. We have had our historians!" pluming herself like a little pigeon.

Betty had her friends everywhere: in the stately old creole houses, and among the cobblers, and the market women, and the shrieking boys who played morra. The quaint old city was as familiar to her as the far-distant brisk New York town in which she lived to Mr. Ely. He began to see where the strength of the little girl's character lay, and why the soft, foolish creature had so powerful an attraction for men and women of all kinds.

"She is the most human being I ever knew," he told Colonel Mocquard. "I suppose she knows nothing of books or of business, like Miss Pogue. But she knows men and women. She goes straight to the innermost nature of each with her wonderful instinct. These people in her old home she sees but once a year, yet she keeps every thread of their lives in her hands, and comes back eager to be of use. You should see her with some of their old slaves. There are some women who are not at all intellectual, or even capable; they are just well-springs of love and comfort in the world."

Colonel Mocquard bowed with a gravity which showed how sacred the subject was to him, and Mr. Ely, recollecting his former suspicions, hesitated, stammered, and was silent.

That very afternoon Betty claimed his help on an exploring expedition. "I wish to find a negro, a woman who have belong to my grand-père—oh, a very old woman," was all the explanation that she vouchsafed, except to state presently that "Mère Deché" was sometimes to be found in the French Market.

"Where does she live?" asked Mr. Ely.

Betty glanced uneasily about her, and then, with a nervous laugh, answered: "If you would believe the negroes, nowhere. They insist that nobody for years has been able to find where she eats or sleeps. She just appears sometimes. But that is their superstition. I am not so foolish."

"No, of course not. I infer that this agreeable friend of yours is a Voodoo witch, then?"

Betty held his arm more tightly. "Hush-h! these negroes are so absurd with their horrible superstition. It is Pierre who worries me now. Our old coachman. He comes to tell me to-day that Mère Deché had bewitched him—you call it. His food shall no longer nourish him. He goes to die. Oh, it is quite true, monsieur. His skin is gray; he is lean. I tell him I will go find Mère Deché, and compel her—com-pel her, I say—to take off the spell. She is a murderess!" with a vindictive nod.

"But you don't really believe—"

"No. But Pierre does, and the effect is the same on him as if it were true. It is a mystery, monsieur. Now attend. Three years ago the negroes still went out to the shores of Lake Pontchartrain on certain nights. There is a flat marsh there, and the water oozes up in ponds, black, dreary. Mère Deché would be there, a great fire kindled beside her. The poor black people dance around her. They believe she comes from the evil one, and if they do not obey her they will be accursed. Now they do not go to the lake any more, and—" she shrugged her shoulders significantly.

"Poor Pierre is accursed? Well, here is the market. Upon my word, a witch would not be out of place in it."

It was late in the afternoon. The traffic for the day was over, and the crowd of buyers, visitors, and Jew peddlers had left the long market, which runs for a mile and a half through the French quarter. It was filled now only with the French and Spanish fish-mongers and butchers, and the negresses and Indian women.

They had dropped heavy curtains of canvas over the sides of the market, shutting out the already fading daylight. Floods of muddy water poured over the brick pavements. Mr. Ely and his companion climbed on some planks to escape the deluge, and forgetting the dying Pierre,

watched the odd scene before them, laughing and curious.

It was like looking into an immense narrow tent filled with a yellow-tinted darkness. Here were groups of old fish-women, the size of cotton bales and the color of coffee, knitting and chattering in a shrill treble; there a dozen swarthy, black-browed Italians gesticulated as though they had discovered a murder over a case of green figs; on the ground squatted some Indian women, dumb and motionless, beside bags of gumbo filé. Suddenly a shrill cry piped out, and the whole fraternity broke into wild confusion. In the far distance red flames flashed up from a long furnace, lighting the dark faces and hurrying figures. Men in white paper caps and women with red and yellow turbans rushed to and from the furnace, each carrying a shining pewter vessel, coming up suddenly out of the darkness into the red light, and disappearing into it again. Two hideous old negro women at the furnace filled the vessels from the caldron.

"What does it mean?" asked Mr. Ely. "It might be a meeting of witches."

"It is only hot gumbo," laughed Betty. "They take now their afternoon goûter."

"These Latin American people are incomprehensible!" exclaimed Mr. Ely. "They cannot eat a meal without as much fervor and excitement as if it were a political conspiracy, falling, too, into pictures that Rembrandt might have painted. Look at that hag with the red light streaming across her. What an eye for effect she must have! She has no color about her like the others. Don't you see? She is wrapped in dust-color; her skin is wrinkled like an elephant's hide, only her wool is white. How old she is! She is age itself. She is one of the cave-women who lived here before the mound-builders came, and she has crept out of her den with the earth still about her."

Betty, laughing, and peering eagerly into the shifting crowd of faces in the darkness to find the woman, started, and held her breath. "That is Mère Deché," she whispered. "I go to speak to her."

"Pardon me, no," said a voice behind her, and Colonel Mocquard joined them. "I heard of your errand, and followed you. You are pale, mademoiselle. Come out into the fresh air."

"But Pierre?"

"I will talk to Mère Deché. A dollar or two will make her lift the spell from

Pierre; or, better still, the sight of a policeman."

"Have these Voudoo women a strong hold on the negroes?" asked Mr. Ely, as they walked away.

"Not so much as formerly, but the dread of them extends even yet into classes where you would think it impossible they should be noticed at all. This Mère Deché, for example, is a Guinea negro really of great age—she claims to be a hundred and forty. One can imagine that a mass of paganism and ignorance in the world for that time could gather any amount of magic and murderous spells about it," he said, jokingly, glancing aside at Betty's white face. "The principal victims of the Voudoo women now are the field hands. The house servants begin to see that the old witches have designs on their wages, or on their mistresses' spoons. Even our witchcraft in the South," he added, laughing, "has taken on a commercial quality. You will find your old cave-woman yonder will succumb to a five-dollar bill as quickly as if she had been born white of American parents. Eh, mademoiselle?"

But Betty shook her head without a smile.

HERE AND THERE IN THE SOUTH.

BY REBECCA HARDING DAVIS.

IV.—AMONG THE BAYOUX.

OUR old clergyman and his wife soon felt at home in
New Orleans. They were both warmly welcomed by
their new friends, but—with a difference. There was always
a difference in the way in which the world accepted these
two. Mrs. Ely was honest, keen, observant, and civil enough
(usually) to keep her prejudices out of sight. Madame de
Parras and her
friends were ready
to talk pleasantly
to her, to discuss
the Exposition, or
the mud, or the last
new fashion or
book. But there

the intercourse stopped. She came no nearer to their real selves than if they had been built up each in a cell like the ancient anchorites, with only their eyes looking out at her through the wall.

But the single-minded old man, with his gentle voice, and fiery zeal in your affairs, and gay little jokes, was everybody's kinsman. Men intrusted their business ventures to him, young girls confided to him their innocent plans, and mothers, sitting by the fire at night, told him of the children who had played on the hearth (ah! such a little while ago!), but who were gone, never to come again. There are still men in the world who, like the ancient prophets, have a gift of healing, and all hurt and wounded creatures, knowing it, come near them.

Every day Mr. Ely felt the difference between the Latin American race who surrounded him and the more logical, thinner-blooded people with whom he was more familiar. "And every day," he told Colonel Mocquard, "I am more convinced that I should have been born here."

The color and fire which these men and women put into life, their gayety, their melancholy, their inconsequence, all seemed natural to him. *He* should have entertained his friends by the score, or shouted for King Rex on Mardi-Gras.

One day he and his wife lost their way in the French quarter, and Louis, who was a merchant of candles, undertook to set them right, and Jacques, the cobbler, left his bench on the banquette to dispute as to the cars they should take, and his

GLIMPSE THROUGH A GATEWAY.

OLD ROOKERY, NEW ORLEANS.

wife, baby in arms, with a red kerchief on her head, came to help him, and Baptiste and his wife, and all the boys playing *morra*, followed, and the whole troop escorted them to the corner, anxious, chattering, watching them out of sight, and waving them good luck.

"What a noisy rabble!" said Mrs. Ely, with a groan of relief, as they escaped.

But her husband looked back, laughing. It flashed on him that in some state of being he had been Baptiste or the cobbler, and had chattered and sat singing in the sun, and had só thrown himself vehemently into trifles with tears and laughter.

They paused a minute, waiting, until a funeral should pass, to cross the street.

"Entrez! entrez!" cried a shrill voice behind them, and a woman, very lean and ragged, threw open the door of her cellar. Like herself, it needed water badly. But the bed had a canopy of Turkey red muslin looped up with bunches of old paper flowers, and on the wall hung gay prints of the Virgin and of St. Agnes, decorated with scraps of lace and tinsel rosettes. The woman herself, with all her lean poverty, had brilliant eyes and a pleasant smile, and welcomed them with a sort of airy grace.

"They decorate their misery, and even their religion!" cried Mrs. Ely, with a vindictive horror, as she hurried away.

But her husband said that he had

caught sight of the photograph of a baby framed in a rag of black *crêpe*, and fastened to the breast of the Virgin. "The poor woman gave her dead child to that other mother in heaven. I can't find fault with her, Sarah, nor with her poor little symbol."

"Rank superstition!" muttered Mrs. Ely.

The old clergyman perceived soon after this that his little friend Betty and her grandmother had fallen into some trouble or perplexity. Even Mrs. Ely discovered it.

"Money difficulties, no doubt," she said. "Trouble of that kind is common enough in the South. But it loses the sting here it has with us, for these people do not feel it a disgrace to be poor. They are incomprehensible to me."

"I do not think any anxiety of that kind would distress our friends so deeply as they are now," said Mr. Ely, gently. "Madame de Parras has a certain stoical philosophy underneath her French vivacity which would not let her succumb to petty annoyances."

"So you call a bill that can't be paid a petty annoyance!" retorted Mrs. Ely, severely.

"It is no trouble of that kind with our friend," said Major Pogue. "It is no secret; but it dates back a long way. Olave de Parras, Betty's father, inherited all his father's estates. He was an affectionate, weak, light-hearted fellow, just the man to be the prey of a sharper who knew how to win his friendship. A Colonel Jean Vaudry, from Point Coupée, soon took him in hand, made a drunkard of him, and then a gambler, and when he had sucked him dry, threw him off. De Parras had spent every dollar he had, and died at thirty, when Betty was a baby in her cradle. Old Vaudry came back to New Orleans about a year ago, a mere wreck in mind and body. He has been lying ill in one of the hospitals for months."

"Serves him right!" exclaimed Mrs. Ely. "Oh, I tell you, Major, there is justice in this world, as well as in the next!"

"He suffers terribly from some incurable disease," said the Major. "Madame de Parras hears of him from the good Sisters every day, and fears he will die before he has made his peace with God. She has offered to go to him, to be friends with him before he dies, but he will not see her."

Mrs. Ely drew a long breath. "Certainly she is acting like a good Christian. I don't believe I could do that."

Colonel Mocquard had entered while the Major was speaking. "De Parras should have shot the scoundrel like a dog!" he said, hastily. "But, as he is alive, it is Madame de Parras's part to forgive him, assuredly. So our Church teaches."

"Oh, any Christian Church would teach the same," rejoined Mrs. Ely, quickly. "But—"

"If he was her friend, kindness to him would be easy enough," said Mocquard, gravely; "but being her enemy, it is her duty, she being a woman."

A week later Madame de Parras sent for Mr. Ely. She was seated in her easy-chair, disabled by rheumatism. Betty, in her street dress, stood beside her. Both were laboring under strong excitement.

"My little girl wishes your escort for her and her maid," said the old lady, trying to smile. "You are so kind to her, and you are a man of God. She is going to the hospital. There is there a poor miserable, who goes soon to die. He will better rest in his grave if he is forgiven by—by those whom he has wronged. Go, my child. Tell him that Olave de Parras's mother and child forgive him; tell him that we will have masses said for the repose of his soul."

When they left the room, Colonel Mocquard followed them, walking, as Mr. Ely noticed, on the other side of Betty, as if he had the right to protect her. They passed in silence through the French quarter. It was a dark, gusty day; the quaint foreign-looking streets were in deep shadow, and the wind sobbed through them fitfully. Betty's face, usually smiling and full of arch coquetry, was set and colorless, and her soft eyes were dull. She had hardly strength enough for her high purpose. The two men kept guard over her, alike awed and silent.

Suddenly she stopped. "Ah, *mon Dieu!* we are too late!" she cried, pointing to a square of black-bordered paper hanging to a lamp-post. On it was the picture of a tomb and weeping-willows, and below, in the old French fashion of a hundred years ago, the passer-by was "prié d'assister au convoi et à l'enterrement de feu *Jean Vaudry*, natif de France, décédé ce matin, âgé de soixante-neuf ans. Le corps est exposé rue Ste. Anne, à l'Asile. De la part de sa famille."

They stood a moment uncertain; then turned and quietly retraced their steps. Betty drew her veil over her face, crying silently.

"You are too late, my child," whispered Mr. Ely. "But God knows."

When they came to the Cathédrale de St. Louis, she went quietly into the little passage at the left, and entering the old church, fell on her knees. The negress who accompanied her retreated into a corner and took out her beads. The old Protestant minister remained in the background, his head reverently bared. He had always been used once a year to preach in a perfunctory way upon the "errors of Rome," but he had never been in a Roman church before. He did not see the gilt and decorated shrines or the burning lamps; nothing but the simple faith of the child, which made it a matter of course for her, being in trouble, to kneel and pray for help. An old woman, evidently the mother of a family—poor, shabby, and hungry-looking—kneeled beside him, muttering her prayers in Spanish; some men, negroes, Irish, and Italians, from the market, baskets or wooden pails on their arms, came in from time to

A GLIMPSE OF JACKSON SQUARE.

time, and dropped down silently in the dark corners. As each rose, crossing himself, and went noiselessly out, the heart of the good old man went up to God, hoping that 'he' might have left some of his trouble behind.

"I too pray for help," he thought, "but I am ashamed to do it so openly. Why?"

His eyes that moment rested on Colonel Mocquard, who stood, with bowed head, near him, watching Betty, with all the hunger of a solitary soul in his face. At last he went toward her slowly, as if drawn by a power outside of himself, and fell upon his knees beside her. The old clergyman went hastily out of the church. It seemed to him that he was an intruder. They were alone together before God. He found a quiet seat under the trees before the cathedral, and waited for them. When they came out they walked side by side, and there was a happy shining in both of their faces.

That evening Mrs. Ely told her husband that Major Pogue and his daughter intended to return to Atlanta next week. "And it is my belief that Colonel Mocquard will let the chance slip by of winning Lola. Very well: he never will find a better manager or more economical house-keeper. She has given me some of the most admirable recipes for cheap desserts, and her soups are simply perfect; but he is infatuated with the baby face of that little De Parras girl."

"It is more than that, Sarah. When a man and woman can kneel together with their love before God, they can make life happy even without good soups and cheap recipes."

"I am not so sure of that," said Mrs. Ely, shaking her head.

The party which had clung together so long broke up the next week. Colonel Mocquard escorted Madame de Parras and her granddaughter back to their plantation, and Mrs. Ely accepted the invitation of her friend Miss Pogue to make her a visit in Atlanta, while Mr. Ely carried out a scheme which he had formed of exploring the bayoux and prairies of western Louisiana.

"It is the first time that he ever proposed to make a journey without me," Mrs. Ely said to her friend, "and I give him just twenty-four hours to take cold and have his pocket picked; then he will come post after us to Atlanta."

Mr. Ely was a fond husband; yet when he found himself alone at early dawn the next day on the ferry-boat to Algiers, he thought of his favorite hero, Eichendorff's Good-for-Nothing, when he turned his back on work and wages, and set off, fiddle in hand, to explore the lazy, sunny, happy world. The old gentleman took a vicious delight in jerking off his hat from his bald head and standing in a draught, and when a whining beggar came up he emptied his pockets of all his loose cash with a snap of his fingers to far-off Mrs. Ely and the Organized Charity clubs.

Algiers for nearly a century has been the workshop of New Orleans—at times a disorderly and rebellious shop enough. It looked peaceful, in the chilly morning light, as Mr. Ely sauntered about the dry-docks, waiting for the starting of the train on the Morgan and Southern Pacific Railway. He was just making friendly advances to a couple of villanous-looking Lascars who were sunning themselves on a hogshead, when a young man behind him caught his arm and hustled him into the train, adding a good-humored punch in the ribs.

"Hillo, granddad! you really oughtn't to be gittin' into sech cutthroat company when you're out from home."

His protector was a natty youth in a new suit of ready-made clothes, with a high beaver hat, blue satin cravat, seal ring, and shining patent-leather shoes as decorations. His hair was cut close to his scalp, and hair, scalp, and face to the eyelids were burned to a dull terra-cotta hue. "Set right down thah," plumping him into a seat in the car. "I'm goin' to smoke. I saw you buy your ticket. Sez I, he's been to Orleans to see the sights, same's me. But he'll be picked up. I'll look after him. Lord! don't mention it. Lots uv rank strangers a-runnin' round Orleans now lookin' fur sights. Cow-boys, frinstens. They talk uv cow-boys 's if they woz roarin' bulls or rep-tiles. Why"—beaming redly down on Mr. Ely—"I'm a cow-boy. Not much uv the rep-tile about me, I reckon"— stroking down his new lavender trousers. He strutted away complacently to the smoking-car, while a ponderous old gentleman, who consisted principally of a furry coat, an aquiline nose, whiskers, and a huge windy voice, dumped himself heavily into the seat beside Mr. Ely.

"Been to Exposition, suh?"

"Yes, I have, I have," responded Mr.

Ely, rubbing his thin hands eagerly. "A vast enterprise, sir."

"Vast? E normous! An answer, suh, to the great economic problem of the American future. It hints that the industrial centeh of the republic will at no distant day be the South, and her best market the South American continent. Did you see no significance in the display of our mineral resources, our agricultural wealth, our rapidly increasing manufactures, and in close juxtaposition the friendly greetings from Mexico, Brazil, the West Indies, and the smaller South American states? Are you aware that those Latin American peoples import nearly seven hundred millions' worth of goods in a year, cottons, clocks, shoes, hats, tools—everything—and that not two millions' worth comes from the South, suh? Why should we not supply it all —*all*? And when we do, we shall take our proper place among nations; then, and not till then, suh."

Mr. Ely assented gently, but soon crept away into another seat. He saw that he had encountered the man with one idea, the pioneer with his axe, who always goes before the army of progress, and he was in no mood to-day for wielding any axe or for welcoming any new ideas, however practical or vast. He wanted to sit in the hot sunshine that streamed into the car, and be borne into some unknown world where he should meet with strange adventures, and where neither wife nor deacons could raise their eyebrows with dismay at his queer tastes or his company. He wanted to slip aside out of these vast currents of trade into which his neighbor panted to plunge, into some obscure corner where there never had been talk of money-making. Turning to look out of the window, his conscience gnawing him with the folly of his own fantastic whims, he beheld his wish accomplished. He had surely found a world unknown before.

From Alabama to Canada this country wears very much the same features—the same golden wheat or green corn fields color all the slopes, and the same pines, maples, oaks, and nut trees give them shadow. The same familiar ferns feather the streams from Maine to Oregon, and the busy five-fingered ivy (which, by-the-way, ought to be our national symbol) trails its soft drapery over the rocks and ugly places of the whole continent.

But here Mr. Ely lost all these life-long familiar companions. The track ran through interminable swamps of giant cypresses, magnolias, and fig-trees. Their myriads of gray trunks stood knee-high in water, opening in silent vistas on either side as the train passed through. Overhead huge vicious coils of vines knotted these bare columns together. It was March, but there was no coy, tender approach of spring here. Nature was a savage — fierce, prolific. The very leaves which in the North would have put forth a timid green burst open here like clots of blood or an angry glare of white; even the thickets of saplings were hoary as with age. Strange red and orange birds flashed through the sombre recesses; now and then a huge alligator rose out of the plane of slimy water, stared at the train with dead eyes, and plunged into it again.

They were on the border of that coast country of Louisiana which fronts the Mexican Gulf between Barataria and Calcasieu bays, a remarkable region, unlike any other in North America in its peculiar features, and in the sombre splendor of its scenery. The cause of its peculiarity is easily explained.

The Mississippi in Louisiana makes a huge bend westward in the shape of a bow or a crescent, the upper point being at Vicksburg, the lower at New Orleans, the middle of the arc running nearly parallel with the distant coast. To the northwest of this arc a stretch of pine-barrens, intersected by ranges of low rolling hills, and broken by numberless lakes and ponds, extends into Texas. Through these the heavy blood-colored flood of the Red River urges its way, carrying with it all lesser watercourses, and emptying itself into the Mississippi near the highest point of this bow or detour. Its red stain tinges the water and the banks of all the outlets of the great river thereafter to the Gulf.

With this last great influx (holding all the streams in the Texan llanos and the mountains of Mexico), the Mississippi now receives the whole drainage of the continent between the Rocky and Appalachian ranges. Every spring and rainfall in that vast territory helps to swell its tremendous tide below Bayou Sara. Hence the flood of water there pushes its way directly to the sea with resistless power, not only on its acknowledged highway, the Mississippi, but through the whole southern half of Louisiana. It literally enters in and occupies the land, forcing itself seaward, not only by more than three hundred bayoux, many of which are mighty rivers, but by sluggish, scarce-moving streams, by a perpetual soaking, creeping, oozing, through all the earth, showing itself on the surface in countless lakes, ponds, and enormous dismal swamps, and above it in incessant heavy rolling fogs and mists. You cannot dig three feet down in all this district without reaching water.

We must remember, too, that this spongy soil has been soaking in for ages the fat washings of all the rich alluvial river-bottoms on half of the continent. No such conditions enter into the formation of any other soil in the world. If Louisiana can ever be drained and rescued from the sea and the river, her fecundity under the hot tropical suns would be unparalleled.

As it is, the parishes in this region include the richest cotton, sugar, and orange-bearing ground in the States. The forests grow to the size of the woods before the flood; even the ghastly impenetrable swamps choke with rank life.

Mr. Ely during the next month wandered aimlessly through this territory. Leaving the railway, he explored one bayou after another, in a bateau, or in the little steamers which make leisurely voyages up the larger ones, stopping wherever the captain thinks it safe.

Bayou La Fourche was the first of these bright slow-moving rivers which he entered. As early as 1810, Breckinridge and Schultz, making journeys from Canada to the Gulf, noticed and wrote of the beauty of this bayou and its shores, although, as the land was then owned by French and Spanish *paysans*, it was not guarded by proper levees, and inundations occurred almost yearly. Opulent creole planters, however, soon bought up the grounds of the *petits habitants*, and the result is the immense estates which now line the shores of the upper La Fourche like a beautiful panorama. Not even a small New England farm can surpass in order and method a great sugar plantation. The levees run along either side of the bayou—green ramparts covered with fern, smilax, wild roses, and purple flags. Back of them, and lower than the stream

RETURNING FROM MARKET.

at high tide, lies the ground, absolutely flat, hundreds of acres often enclosed in a single field, the whole seamed by the plough with mathematical precision, and covered in the spring with delicate lines of feathery green. At one end of the plantation stands the engine-house and works, of substantial brick; at the other, the dwelling of the planter, usually an airy verandaed structure, more or less in need of paint, but covered with such splendor of crimson and golden roses, and so hedged in by orange groves and sloping lawns, and gigantic oaks hung with curtains of moss and wealth of brilliant flowers, that each gay wooden house might put forth its claims to be the fabled dwelling of Selim in the valley of Cashmere.

The old clergyman found his lazy voyages up these bayoux full of picturesque surprises. When the boat stopped at the landing of a plantation, whether early in the morning, or at noon, or in the clear yellow sunset, there was a horde of half-naked black boys half in and half out of the water, or a gray-haired old negro waiting for packages for "de house," or the planter, high-featured and swarthy, surrounded by children and dogs, watching, as eager as they, for the good fortune of an unexpected guest; or perhaps he would catch a glimpse in the grove near the levees of a group of olive-skinned vivacious creole women, or of American girls, shyer of glance and slower of tongue than their Northern sisters.

Thibodeaux, the capital of La Fourche Parish, is a typical Louisianian town, with the usual excess of beauty in the gardens, mud and pitfalls in the streets, and abounding hospitality of soul in the people. There is much solid wealth in this parish, which is the centre of the large sugar plantations of the State.

The shores of Bayou Plaquemine resemble those of La Fourche. The soil is exceptionally rich. The estates have been for the most part in the same families for generations. When the Mississippi is gorged, its waters rush through this outlet with a force equal to that of the St. Lawrence below Niagara. It overflows into the Atchafalaya, or the Old River, as it is sometimes called, because of an Indian tradition that it was ages ago the Mississippi itself.

The Teche is a gentle, good-humored stream, which rises in the uplands of St. Landry's Parish, and follows a zigzag

HOEING SUGAR-CANE.

EVENING AT THE QUARTERS.

course through some of the highest and pleasantest farm-lands of Louisiana, until it too is lost in the Atchafalaya. It has a better character than any other bayou, never having been known to overflow its banks. The live-oaks grow, in the region through which this river lazily flows, to such enormous size that a Louisiana Senator, fifty years ago, offered in Congress to "float enough ship timber down the Teche into the Gulf to build navies for the whole world." Fifty years is a mere moment in the lives of these ancient patriarchs; they have only wrapped themselves in a heavier cloak of moss since then, and are as ready now as they were when De Soto first saw them to help some ship-builder to fortune.

The rich cotton districts lie in the valley of the Red River and its affluents, but Mr. Ely did not travel so far northward. An accident turned him in another direction.

Coming back from a drowsy voyage up one of the bayoux, he struck the railway again one evening near Morgan City. He found that metropolis of the future, as it calls itself, lost for the nonce in fog and rain. A gray drizzle filled the sky, clammy drops trickled down the faces of the discouraged-looking houses, the backs of the tired mules plodding through the mud gave off steam, while white deathly mists crept in from the Atchafalaya, which swept past in the darkness like an angry sea.

The few glimmering lights of the town stared bewildered through the night.

"'Into the hell of waters,' as Byron would have called it," our good clergyman thought, as he too stared out of the window of the hotel into the limitless dark and wet. The damp crept into his marrow, his teeth chattered, though the night was warm. He turned for comfort to the glowing stove, and to a fellow-traveller who was puffing his cigar with his legs stretched out and his hands clasped behind his head.

"This is a wonderful region," ventured Mr. Ely. "Marvellous scenery. But the universal wetness is appalling. I feel to-night," he added, with a nervous laugh, "as the Egyptians must have done when the walls of water rushed in on them from every side."

"Not a Southerner, I infer?" said the other, dryly.

"No. But I appreciate the splendor of your scenery to the full," eagerly. "And yet, do you know, I really have great respect for the Germans," lowering his voice confidentially.

"As how?"

"For their choice of a home in this country. The Puritans were satisfied with the bare New England rocks, and the French with this low-lying delta; but the Germans chose the rich high grounds and temperate air of Pennsylvania, the garden spot of the States, sir."

"*I* am a Louisianian," was the curt reply. It drove Puritans, Germans, the inhabitants of all other quarters of the world, into the background.

Mr. Ely, rebuffed, glanced at him deprecatingly; then came nearer, startled, curious. "Why—is it possible? A Louisianian? Weren't you—surely you are Nettley Pym, of Connecticut? Don't you remember the Senior Class and little Jem Ely?"

His old classmate suddenly sloughed off his swelling importance, and shook hands heartily again and again.

"Jem Ely? I should think I did remember! Always tail of the class, and writing verses to some pretty girl. Minister, eh? Of course you'd choose some starving business! You never were one to lay dollar to dollar," giving a swift glance over the old clergyman's well-kept clothes and cheap shoes.

"You, I suppose, have been more fortunate?" said Mr. Ely, drawing back a little.

"Oh, so so! I came down to this country thirty years ago—tutor—married a rich girl, and have been running a cotton plantation ever since. Naturally I have identified myself with my adopted State. There are not many men who understand what Louisiana can do, and is likely to do, as clearly as Nett Pym."

"You think there is a great future before her, then?" said Mr. Ely, settling himself into a warm corner by the stove.

"That depends," said Nett Pym, who, by-the-way, had gained the title of Judge in his adopted State, besides nearly three

ON BAYOU TECHE.

OPELOUSAS PRAIRIE.

hundred pounds of flesh, and an accent half French and half negro—"that depends wholly on the action of our leaders iu this crisis of our history. The majority of our public men are eager to throw open our ports to immigrants, Irish, Dutch, Scandinavians, to compel them to make New Orleans their port of entry, even if they only remain a month or two on their way to the West. *I,* sir, am opposed to this policy." The Judge fell into an oracular singsong, pulling through his fingers the black beard which fringed his broad pasty face. "We of the South, sir, should control our own interests. We are urging Northern capitalists to come and develop our resources, and foreign workmen to fill our mines and mills. What will be the result? In ten years Northerners and foreigners will run the South. They will edit our papers, own the mines, manufactories, and railroads; take the lead in our business, our politics, and our society, while we Southerners will be pushed to the wall. I—it is true I am not a Louisianian by birth," he stammered, recollecting himself, "but I sympathize with them wholly."

"What would you have them do?"

"Train the mulatto into a skilled laborer, keep out the foreign workmen, put their own capital and energy into other pursuits than agriculture, develop their own resources, and reap the profit themselves."

Mr. Ely drew a long breath of resignation. He could not, it seemed, escape the man of ideas. The Judge had now diverged into facts. "You must study the resources of this State, sir; you must carry home an accurate account of them— the enormous lumber interests, for example. Look at our cypress forests—absolutely illimitable! There is no more durable or beautiful wood. It is as rich a mine of wealth to us as its pine woods are to Maine. Are we to wait until some sharp-eyed Northerner comes here to gather in that crop? As for iron, come with me north of Red River and I will show you iron ore in Ouachita, or south of it, in Natchitoches, Sabine, or Rapides. Four of our parishes produce ore containing nearly fifty per cent. of pure metal. The same parishes have large deposits of coal. Talk of Pennsylvania, indeed! We have petroleum and natural gas as well as Pennsylvania; sulphur and gypsum too; and rock-salt, which your Quaker State has not. You must go to Calcasieu to examine these resources. I'll go with you; I've business in that direction."

"You are most kind," stammered Mr. Ely. "I will consider the matter."

"You must come to Opelousas. There is a country for you! It contains eight thousand square miles. Fine prairie-land, cotton and sugar plantations, sheep and cattle ranches, and the soil black, oily, sir! Stick in your cane, and it roots and leaves! You must assuredly visit Opelousas. I will myself take you to the principal points of interest."

"Does Opelousas extend to the Gulf?"

"No. Below it is Attakapas. Five thousand square miles. Running from the Atchafalaya to the Gulf. Vast prairies, and on the coast marshes — endless marshes. Peopled by the Acadians, who came here when they were banished from Nova Scotia."

Mr. Ely kindled into eager interest.

"They have altered greatly, no doubt? Become modern—American?"

"Not a whit. They are as ignorant and guileless as their own sheep. No progress among *them*. You need not waste your time in that direction."

They parted for the night soon after this. Mr. Ely could not sleep. If he waited until morning he knew he would be swept away to investigate iron, hematites, indigo, or sulphur.

He packed his valise and fairly ran away, leaving a note of courteous regret, stating that he had a deep interest in the Acadians, and had gone on an exploring journey into Attakapas.

The Judge stared at the words in dumb amazement. "The same useless, feather-headed Jem Ely!" he muttered; and lighting his cigar with Ely's note, went on his way.

DATE DUE
